Thanks to Life

Thanks to Life

A Biography of Violeta Parra

ERICKA VERBA

The University of North Carolina Press
Chapel Hill

Set in Minion Pro Regular by Westchester Publishing Services
Manufactured in the United States of America

Library of Congress Cataloging-in-Publication Data
Names: Verba, Ericka Kim, author.
Title: Thanks to life : a biography of Violeta Parra / Ericka Verba.
Description: Chapel Hill : The University of North Carolina Press, [2025] |
   Includes bibliographical references and index.
Identifiers: LCCN 2024035429 | ISBN 9781469682945 (cloth) |
   ISBN 9781469682952 (paperback) | ISBN 9781469679631 (epub) |
   ISBN 9781469682969 (pdf)
Subjects: LCSH: Parra, Violeta, 1917–1967. | Singers—Chile—Biography. |
   Composers—Chile—Biography. | Artists—Chile—Biography. |
   Folklorists—Chile—Biography. | BISAC: BIOGRAPHY & AUTOBIOGRAPHY /
   Music | SOCIAL SCIENCE / Ethnic Studies / Caribbean & Latin American
   Studies | LCGFT: Biographies.
Classification: LCC ML420.P26 V47 2025 | DDC 782.42164092 [B]—
   dc23/eng/20240806
LC record available at https://lccn.loc.gov/2024035429

Cover art: Photograph by Javier Peréz Castelblanco, 1966.

To my familia

Contents

Illustrations

Note to the Reader

If you are familiar with Violeta Parra, then you already know how extraordinary she was as a musician and an artist. For those readers who are not yet familiar with her, I urge you to stop reading and take some time to get to know her work. Listen to her perform Chilean folk songs and her own compositions on a music streaming service or YouTube (I recommend, for starters, "Gracias a la vida" and "Cueca de los poetas" from her album *Las últimas composiciones de Violeta Parra*). Look at the images of her paintings and embroidered tapestries made available by the Violeta Parra Foundation. View the photographs of her, also made available by the foundation. Watch the documentary, produced for Swiss television in 1965, where she demonstrates her artistic techniques, sings, and dances the cueca (Chile's national dance) dressed in a patchwork dress made by her mother. Explore. And please note that I will also be citing the full titles of songs, albums, paintings, tapestries, and other music and visuals throughout the book for you to listen to and view. Violeta Parra fought hard, often against insurmountable odds, to be seen and heard during her lifetime. It seems only fitting that we honor her wishes.

Thanks to Life

Figure 0.1 Map of Chile. Library of Congress, Geography and Map Division.

Introduction

In 1964, Chilean musician and artist Violeta Parra (1917–67) became the first Latin American to have a solo show at the Musée des Arts Décoratifs (Museum of Decorative Arts), housed in the Louvre Palace in Paris. The exhibit featured her paintings, sculptures, and embroidered tapestries. It was visited by dignitaries and a "who's who" of the Parisian and expatriate Latin American artistic community. Parra sold several of her tapestries, including one to the Baroness Rothschild. In 2022, three pieces from Parra's 1964 show were included in one of the most prestigious art events worldwide, the Venice Biennial.[1]

Parra's artistic achievements, past and present, are all the more remarkable given that she was and is more well known as a songwriter than as a visual artist. Her songs inspired a generation of musicians in the Chilean *nueva canción* or New Song movement, a genre of protest music that emerged in the late 1960s and flourished under the Popular Unity government of President Salvador Allende (1970–73) before being brutally repressed under the dictatorship of Augusto Pinochet (1973–90). During the long years of military rule, Parra's music became synonymous with resistance in Chile and worldwide. More recently, her songs have become an essential part of the repertoires of student and feminist movements throughout Latin America.

Parra is also celebrated for having written the song that gives this book its title: "Gracias a la vida," "Thanks to Life." The song has been translated into more than twenty languages and performed and recorded by an ever-expanding roster of musicians, including country music star Kasey Musgraves, cellist Yo-Yo Ma (instrumental version), Latin pop singer Shakira, K-pop duo Davichi, folk singers Joan Baez and Mercedes Sosa, and Cuban singer Omara Portuondo of the Buena Vista Social Club.

Parra's success as a musician and an artist would not have been predicted by her background. She was born in 1917 in the small town of San Fabián de Alico in the south of Chile, some 7,400 miles from the Louvre Palace. Her childhood was marked by hardship. She almost died of smallpox as a young girl, a disease that left her face permanently scarred. Her family, like many families struggling through the post–World War I economic crisis in Chile, was seminomadic in the early years of her life before settling in the southern city of Chillán for a time. Her schoolteacher father died when she was ten, leaving her mother to fend for their large family with the meager income she earned as a seamstress. Parra and her siblings sang on the street and performed in traveling circuses to help make ends meet.

At age fifteen, Parra moved to Santiago, where she attended a teacher-training program that was the equivalent of high school for two years before dropping out. From age seventeen into her thirties, she made her living as a barroom singer, eventually building a respectable career performing a pan–Latin American repertoire with the duo that she formed with her sister Hilda, Las Hermanas Parra (The Parra Sisters).

In her mid-thirties, Parra abruptly and definitively left this commercially oriented music behind and turned to the authentic, first in her work as a folklorist, and then as a musician, poet, and visual artist. As a folklorist, she collected some 3,000 songs, folktales, proverbs, riddles, and medicinal cures from all over Chile. She also hosted her own radio show, *Así canta Violeta Parra* (Violeta Parra Sings). As a musician, she wrote more than 200 songs. Some are on the themes of love and loss, and others denounce the social injustices she experienced and witnessed across her lifetime. Parra also composed experimental music for guitar, documentary soundtracks, and a folk ballet. In the realm of the visual arts, she was a painter, sculptor, ceramicist, and tapestry-maker. In all of her creative activities, she drew inspiration from tradition, experimented with materials, and invented new techniques.

Parra spent her most productive years in various cities on two continents: Santiago, Concepción, Buenos Aires, Paris, and Geneva. A communist supporter, she traveled twice to Europe to participate in the Soviet-sponsored World Festival of Youth and Students, the first time to Warsaw (1955) and the second to Helsinki (1962). Each time, she toured the Soviet Bloc, then made her way to Paris, a mecca for Latin American expatriate artists, where she resided for prolonged periods. In the many places where she lived and worked, she participated in interconnected networks of musicians and artists who became her friends, creative collaborators, and sometimes her perceived enemies.

Her personal life was unconventional. She was twice married and divorced, and she had several other romantic relationships. She had four children, one of whom died in infancy. Parra suffered from mental illness and would likely be diagnosed with bipolar disorder were she alive today. Her frequent battles with depression culminated in her suicide on February 5, 1967.

Parra's success as an artist was neither guaranteed nor cemented during her lifetime. Her full embrace as an international figure occurred only after her death. As a case in point, the Museum of Decorative Arts selection committee at first rejected her proposal for a solo show; though they found her work to have artistic merit, they considered Parra herself too much of an "unknown." The project went forward only after a sympathetic museum official intervened. Filled with self-doubt upon learning of the committee's initial rejection, Parra wrote a letter to a friend in which she asked, "How could I have an exhibit at the Louvre, I, who am the ugliest woman on the planet, who come from a tiny country, from Chillán, at the end of the earth?"[2] This biography endeavors to answer Parra's rhetorical question.

How does an "ugly" woman of undistinguished origins from the south of Chile travel the social and cultural distance to the Louvre Palace in Paris? I posit that the answer lies in the ways that Violeta Parra's work and identity as an artist interacted with mid-twentieth-century notions of authenticity. "Authenticity" is the term most frequently and consistently associated with Parra, during her lifetime, through her impressive afterlife. Parra is an authentic *campesina* (used in this context to mean a person of rural extraction), an authentic artist, an authentic woman, the authentic representative of the Chilean people, or just authentic.

This biography is a study of how Parra came to embody authenticity, in the eyes of her public and in her own sense of self. It is premised on the idea that authenticity "is not inherent in the object or event that is designated authentic but is a socially agreed-upon construct."[3] Though it has no fixed meaning, authenticity is always claimed in reference to modern society; it represents "a peculiar longing, at once modern and antimodern."[4] It is a quest on the part of seekers of the authentic to experience the "real," the "pure," the "timeless" as an antidote to the superficiality and impermanence of modern society, a quest that relies on the attributes of modern society in its pursuit.

I use the "wake for the little angel," the Chilean traditional funeral ceremony for an infant who died before the age of baptism, as illustration. This heartbreaking ceremony originated in the *campesino* (peasants, agricultural workers) communities in Chile's extensive agricultural region known as the Central Valley. In it, the infant's corpse was dressed like an angel and placed on an altar decorated to look like heaven. A circle of traditional singers, customarily all men, sang traditional songs that had been passed down across the generations for the comfort of the mourners through the night. The ritual was still practiced in parts of the Chilean countryside during Parra's youth, which she would later affirm is when she first gained knowledge of it. It subsequently became an important aspect of her work as a folklorist as well as a source of inspiration for her music and artwork after the loss of her youngest daughter.[5]

At a basic level, the wake for the little angel may be understood as a cultural response to the grief produced by Chile's high infant mortality rate, which lasted well into the twentieth century, among those most likely to suffer its losses: the poor.[6] The ritual itself carried no intrinsic cultural value, only that which was assigned to it in a given historical moment. From the late nineteenth to the mid-twentieth century, Chile's modernizing elite derided the ceremony as a barbarous custom of backward peasants, an excuse for drunken debauchery. By the 1950s, the ritual was believed to be on the verge of extinction due to the forces of urbanization and modernization. This is when a generation of Chilean folklorists, with Parra at their forefront, revalued the wake for the little angel, elevating it to an "authentic" expression of Chilean folk culture. Parra re-created the nightlong ritual on her weekly radio show, for example, albeit in a condensed, thirty-minute version. She did so for the purpose of revealing Chile's timeless traditions to her modern public. In short, she made the ritual authentic. The same ceremony, practiced in the Chilean countryside with no one beyond the grieving family, friends, and traditional singers present, was neither authentic nor inauthentic. It was simply the saddest of rites.

Parra herself most certainly would have rejected any claim that authenticity is a social construct (though she likely would have appreciated my underscoring her role in its construction). She was so determined to faithfully re-create the wake for the little angel on her radio show that she insisted on going to the shops outside Santiago's central train station—the ones frequented by rural migrants to the capital—to purchase the customary attire for the "little angel." In this case, the "little angel" was a baby doll that Parra brought to the radio station and, once dressed in its proper attire, placed on the altar she had assembled there—to the great bewilderment of her radio colleagues. For Parra, authenticity was so "inherent in the object or event" that she felt the need to build an altar even though her listening audience could not see it.

Parra firmly believed that she was the authentic representative of the Chilean *pueblo*, used here and throughout the book according to the Spanish term's class-based meaning as "the folk," "the working class," or the "working poor." Her authenticity, likewise, would be a matter of faith for many of her admirers, in Chile and throughout the world, during her lifetime and into the present. The tension and even disjuncture between the premise that authenticity is a social construct and its experience as a social fact run through this book and, I would venture, through much recent scholarship on Parra.[7] I would offer, further, that this challenge enhances our work.

———

My approach to this biography is historical and transnational: I examine how Parra helped to define the meaning(s) of authenticity in her era, in Santiago, Warsaw, Paris, and the multiple other sites where she performed, within the broader context of the cultural Cold War. My analysis is informed by the field of transnational studies. In particular, I adopt ethnomusicologist Thomas Turino's conceptualization of cosmopolitan cultural formations through which "ideas, practices, and technologies . . . travel through communication loops independently binding people culturally who are not, otherwise, related by location or heritage."[8] As Turino has established, the advantage of this framework is that it allows the researcher to move beyond the obfuscating dyads of traditional/modern, underdeveloped/developed, or more recently, local/global that would situate Parra as somehow outside or "other to" the cosmopolitan milieu that she operated in and whose values she shared. To use Parra's 1964 exhibit at the Museum of Decorative Arts as illustration, its French and expatriate Latin American visitors and Parra herself were all members of the same cosmopolitan cultural formation. As such, they shared a set of aesthetic sensibilities and social values, including their understanding of the value of Parra's artwork.

Precisely because Parra was a transnational figure, her biography sheds light on significant cultural trends to emerge over the course of her lifetime. The concurrent folk revivals taking place in the 1950s in Chile, Great Britain, the United States, and elsewhere are one example. The protest song movements of the 1960s and 1970s are another, and Parra is often referred to as the "mother" of the politically engaged song movement that would eventually become known as Chilean New Song.[9] Parra's biography also illuminates the larger social, cultural, and political transformations of her times: the urbanization and modernization of Chilean society; the expansion of mass media and consumer culture; the worldwide "invasion" of the US entertainment industry and local attempts to counteract it; the intensification of the Cold War and political divisions; the emergence of youth culture; and the global 1960s, to name the most salient.

Turning from this wider vista to a more intimate one, Parra was part of an extensive clan of musicians, poets, and artists, now generations deep. Her biography is thus inescapably a family history. Her brother Nicanor Parra (1914–2018) is the sibling who most closely rivals Violeta in celebrity; a world-renowned poet, his work has been translated into multiple languages and has earned him countless accolades, including the highest distinction awarded to writers in the Spanish language, the Miguel de Cervantes Prize (2011). The personal and professional lives of Violeta Parra and her nine siblings and three children were so intermeshed that it is at times difficult to write about her in the singular. As Julio Fernando San Martín, biographer of Violeta Parra's brother Eduardo "Lalo" Parra, notes, "when writing about or conversing with one member [of the family], it's impossible not to have a glass of wine with all of them."[10] As this is the case, and as the members of Violeta's clan share her last name, I refer to her and her relatives by their first names in the numerous sections of this book where their lives overlap.[11]

This biography contributes to a collective effort to comprehend Violeta Parra in all her dimensions. Parra left us ample sources to work with toward that end.[12] In the late 1950s, when she was in her early forties, she wrote an autobiography in the ten-line traditional verse form of the *décima*.[13] She wrote an ethnographic manuscript, published posthumously as *Cantos folklóricos chilenos* (Chilean Folk Songs), containing first-person accounts of her encounters with her folk informants.[14] She wrote a copious amount of letters, many of which are published in her daughter Isabel Parra's collage-like book about her mother, *El libro mayor de Violeta Parra*.[15] Violeta also granted numerous interviews to the press, in Chile and abroad, many of which are collected and published by author and popular music critic Marisol García in *Violeta Parra en sus palabras: Entrevistas (1954–1967)*.[16] A few of Parra's radio shows are also preserved, as either recordings or transcriptions.[17] Parra was additionally the subject of the 1965 Swiss documentary *Violeta Parra: Brodeuse chilienne* (Violeta Parra: Chilean Embroiderer).[18] Finally, there are the abundant products of her creative efforts, including her music, artwork, and poetry.[19]

This book draws on the experiences of those who knew Parra. Many of their recollections are assembled in two key works. The first, *Violeta Parra: Canto de todos* by Patricia Štambuk and Patricia Bravo (originally published as *Gracias a la vida: Violeta Parra, testimonio* in 1976), contains excerpts of interviews with Parra's family members, colleagues, and friends that the authors conducted in the early 1970s.[20] The second is the aforementioned *El libro mayor de Violeta Parra* by Isabel Parra. Several family members have also written books about Violeta: her son Ángel Parra, *Violeta se fue a los cielos*, which Andrés Wood's 2011 feature film of the same title is based upon; and her brothers Eduardo and Roberto Parra, both of whom, in true Parra fashion, composed their accounts in traditional verse.[21]

Many of Violeta's friends and acquaintances in the artistic circles that she was a part of wrote memoirs or private diaries, since published, that touch on her life. They include Swiss musician and Parra's lover, Gilbert Favre, in detail, and Leonard Bernstein and Allen Ginsberg, in passing.[22] Lastly, there are the many interviews, conducted over the decades since her death, with everyone from Parra's closest relatives and colleagues to the woman, then well into her nineties, who once shared a desk with Parra in elementary school.[23]

This biography benefits from past biographies of Violeta Parra, especially those by Víctor Herrero, Fernando Sáez, and Carmen Oviedo.[24] I am grateful as well to be part of an interdisciplinary network of scholars whose research on Parra's creative activities has enriched every aspect of my own. The breadth of our varied approaches to her work is testimony to Parra's equally varied talents.

My research is aided by the efforts of an international community of Parra's ardent admirers. Sometimes referred to as "Violetalogists" or—perhaps more accurately—"Violetamaniacs," we are generous when it comes to exchanging information and resources. Hannes Salo deserves special acknowledgment and may therefore serve as an example: a Swedish musician and medical doctor, he has amassed the most complete collection of Parra's recordings, including a 1956 single produced in Leningrad that was previously unknown, as it mistranslated her name from the Cyrillic script as "Violeta Barra." Salo is responsible for Parra's discography, including detailed notes on album contents and photos of their covers, on the website dedicated to songwriters in the Spanish language, www.cancioneros.com.[25] This biography is bolstered by his efforts and those of countless other people who share a commitment to make Violeta Parra's work known.

Two sister Violetamaniacs require recognition for their unsurpassed contribution to this biography. They are Nancy Morris and Patricia Vilches, who, working as a team, are responsible for all of the translations of the verses culled from Violeta's autobiography in décimas and excerpted song lyrics. Here is their explanation of their process: "Translating parts of Violeta Parra's *Décimas* and songs constituted both a cherished and monumental task for us. We worked through successive draft translations, parsing and refining line by line and at times word by word. We sought to maintain the vibrancy of Parra's poetry and songs while staying faithful to her meaning, and to convey the meter, pacing, rhythm, tone, and, where achievable, rhyme of the original texts."[26]

My own Violetamania dates back to my early teens when I first became friends with a Chilean family of musicians and artists that includes composer and film producer Miguel Picker and painter Sebastián Picker.[27] The family taught me my first Violeta Parra songs and guided my political awakening to the brutality of the Pinochet dictatorship and the role of the US government in installing and supporting it. As a musician and member of the US-based New Song groups Sabiá and Desborde, I have been performing Parra's music since the late 1970s. I wrote my undergraduate senior thesis on Parra's autobiography in verse in 1980, and gave my first academic presentation on Parra at the Second International Conference on Women in Music in 1982.[28] In 1996, I was musical director and arranger for a tribute concert to Violeta Parra, held in Los Angeles with the participation of LA-based musicians from four continents.[29] As a professor of Latin American history since 2004, I have welded my research on the history of women in Chile with my interest in Parra to acquire a deeper understanding of the social context and gender dynamics that shaped her life.[30] Suffice it to say that this book is the culmination of my decades-long curiosity about Violeta Parra and engagement with her work.

Writing the biography of someone who inspires such interest raises its own set of challenges. The ongoing dispute over the exact site of Parra's birth is a prime example. The Fundación Violeta Parra (Violeta Parra Foundation), an organization established by her children to safeguard and promote their mother's legacy, lists Parra's birthplace as the town of San Fabián de Alico on its website.[31] The municipality of San Carlos de Itihue, twenty-seven miles northwest of San Fabián de Alico, proudly declares itself the "Cradle of Violeta Parra" on its official website and offers a digital copy of her birth certificate as proof.[32] Violeta's brother Oscar explains the San Carlos birth certificate by the fact that San Fabián did not have its own independent civil registry at the time of his sister's birth—a claim the town of San Carlos vehemently contests.[33]

The unresolved debate over Parra's birthplace underscores the biographer's dilemma that even the most simple facts of a person's life are not always that simple. In Parra's case, the murkiness of the past is compounded by her propensity to exaggerate and invent, and by similar tendencies displayed by many of her admirers. In the end, this telling of Violeta Parra's life story results from my sifting, weighing, and selecting from available and sometimes contradictory sources. It goes without saying that any errors that derive from the process are my responsibility.

———

This book is organized into ten chapters. The first two cover the years from Parra's birth in 1917 to her mid-thirties. Chapter 1 chronicles her childhood and early adolescence, spent for the most part in the south of Chile. It explores how Parra's upbringing, far from the nation's capital and close to the campesino communities of Chile's Central Valley, furnished her with the cultural materials and social awareness that would shape her creative activities as an adult. Chapter 2 covers the two decades from her move to Santiago in 1933 at age fifteen to her emergence as a folklorist in the early 1950s. It addresses the period in her life when she made a living performing the more commercial styles of music that she would later reject as inauthentic or "anti-material" when she became a folklorist. It documents her first and second marriages and the birth of her first three children and examines how Parra eschewed gender conventions to follow a musical vocation.

Chapter 3 focuses on Parra's work as a *folklorista*, used here and throughout the book in the Spanish term's dual meaning as someone who both collects and disseminates folklore. It traces Parra's transformation into a leader of the 1950s folk revival in Chile and discusses her contribution to the larger debate on *chilenidad* or Chilean identity of the era. The chapter focuses on her initial activity as a folklorista, from 1952 to her departure to Europe in mid-1955, though many of the topics extend into the period between her two European sojourns, covered in chapters 5 and 6.

Chapter 4 is an account of Parra's first prolonged stay in Paris, from July 1955 to the close of 1956. It explores Parra's insertion into the vibrant Latin American music scene in Paris and probes how her performance in Europe intersected with complex and often competing notions of authenticity in circulation at the time on both sides of the Iron Curtain.

Parra's return from Europe marked the beginning of an intense period of artistic exploration that would continue through the remainder of her life. Chapters 5 and 6 examine the new pathways Parra pursued in music, poetry, and the visual arts during the "volcanic" period of the five and a half years between her return to Chile at the close of 1956 and her departure for Europe in mid-1962. Chapter 5 encompasses her six-month residency in the southern city of Concepción over 1957 and 1958, and chapter 6 her stay in Argentina over the first part of 1962.

Chapters 7 and 8 chronicle Parra's second European sojourn, from June 1962 to August 1965, which she spent dividing her time between Paris and Geneva, with a brief interval in Chile in mid-1964. Chapter 7 considers Parra's reinsertion into the evolving Parisian–Latin American folk music scene, now more Andean-inspired and revolutionary. Chapter 8 investigates the process and success of her Museum of Decorative Arts exhibit.

Chapters 9 and 10 cover the last eighteen months of Parra's life, following her final return to Chile. Chapter 9 looks at her complicated relationship with the young generation of musicians in the emerging Chilean New Song movement, her children Isabel and Ángel Parra prominent among them. It discusses Parra's Carpa de La Reina: the part performance space, part art gallery, and part residence that she created under a large circus tent (*carpa*) in a remote part of the Santiago neighborhood of La Reina. Chapter 10 recounts Parra's final months. It discusses her last LP (long-play record), *Las últimas composiciones de Violeta Parra* (Violeta Parra's Latest Compositions, though *últimas* can also mean "last" in Spanish), that includes her song "Thanks to Life." It chronicles her deteriorating mental health and increasing isolation that ended with her suicide in early 1967.

————

There was no clearly demarcated route from the small town in southern Chile where Violeta Parra was born to the Louvre Palace. She had no formal training in music or the fine arts. She lacked the social connections and economic security that could have eased her trajectory. She faced substantial obstacles for being a woman in a patriarchal society. Many Chileans deemed her unattractive due to her pockmarked face, while many Europeans exoticized her as "Indian" due to her darker skin tone and slighter stature. Parra's biography is at once a study of the exclusions of class, gender, race, and nationality and a record of her efforts to overcome them. Viewed from the standpoint of her intersecting marginalities, the audacity of the dare-to-self embedded in her rhetorical question that guides this biography is nothing less than stunning. Finally, then, this book is a tribute to Violeta Parra.

Chapter 1

Materials

In June 1954, Violeta Parra landed her first feature interview in Chile's premier entertainment weekly, *Ecran*.[1] Then thirty-six, she was a rising star in Santiago's flourishing folk music scene and the host of her own radio show, *Así canta Violeta Parra* (Violeta Parra Sings). *Ecran* reporter Marina de Navasal opened the interview with a summary of Parra's personal data (married, three children and one on the way) and the days and times of her radio program. The reporter then asked, "When did you start to learn our folklore?" Parra answered, "From the moment I was born."[2]

In this and subsequent interviews, Parra unfailingly traced her artistic and professional achievements back to her roots in the south of Chile. She had ample reasons to do so: her childhood years furnished her with the cultural tools, creative inspiration, and social awareness that would inform and shape her life's work as a folklorista, musician, and visual artist. To borrow from the lyrics of her most well-known song, "Gracias a la vida" (Thanks to Life), her childhood provided her with the "materials that make up my song."

What follows is an account of Parra's childhood years, from her birth in 1917 until she moved to Santiago at age fifteen, with an eye toward discerning the materials she gathered during this formative period.

Familia

Violeta del Carmen Parra Sandoval was born on October 4, 1917, in San Fabián de Alico, a hamlet at the foot of the Andes mountain range in the southern province of Ñuble. At the time, San Fabián was so small (pop. circ. 900) that her parents had to travel the twenty-five miles to San Carlos (pop. circ. 7,500), the closest town with a civil registry, in order to record her birth.[3] Violeta was the third of what would eventually be ten children born to the union of Nicanor Parra Parra and Clarisa Sandoval Navarrete.[4] Violeta (nickname "Viola") was preceded by Nicanor and Hilda, and followed by Eduardo ("Lalo"), Roberto, Lautaro, Caupolicán ("Polito"), Elba Brunilda, Eliana del Carmen, and Oscar René ("Nene"). The early deaths of Caupolicán and Eliana would reduce the number of children to eight.[5] Their mother, who had been a young widow when she married their father, brought her two daughters Marta and Olga from her first marriage to the blended family.

Music must figure foremost among the materials Violeta gathered as a child. Her father, Nicanor senior, was a schoolteacher and talented musician, with some classical training and considerable joie de vivre. He performed works by Schubert and Mozart on the violin and habaneras and other popular song styles on the guitar, piano, and harp, and he was known to quickly master whatever other instruments he came across. He was a great lover of opera and taught his children to sing his favorite arias. He was reluctant for them to learn how to play the guitar, however, and kept his in its case under lock and key when not in use.[6] The range of music he enjoyed may help explain the breadth of Violeta's musical tastes later in life, which her daughter Isabel reports included "Chopin, Beethoven, tangos by Carlos Gardel, [Mexican] corridos, and paso dobles and [other] Spanish songs."[7]

In contrast to her more worldly husband, Violeta's mother Clarisa came from a rural background. She had received little formal education as a child, musical or otherwise, and had grown up immersed in the oral and musical traditions of the region. She knew many traditional songs that she passed on to her children. Clarisa and Nicanor senior often sang together as a duo. Their combined musical gifts would have a profound and enduring impact on Violeta as well as on her siblings.

Although by the 1920s the Victrola or gramophone was becoming commonplace in more affluent homes, Violeta's family could not afford one on their father's schoolteacher salary. Without this most modern purveyor of mass culture, the Parras relied on their own resources for entertainment. "We had to make the party happen on our own," is how Violeta's mother put it.[8] Under their father's playful direction, the children staged elaborate skits, complete with makeshift costumes and pretend entry tickets. They competed in singing contests lasting well into the night. Gifted among the gifted, Violeta thrived in this environment. She was the frequent victor of the children's singing marathons—though apparently this was as much due to her stamina at outlasting her sleepier siblings as it was to what one of them recalled as her "cleverness and . . . enormous memory."[9] She was especially adept at performing the arias that her opera buff father so enjoyed. She was also reputedly the first among her siblings to learn to play the guitar—though most of the others would soon follow suit.[10] The story goes that she found the key to her father's guitar case and taught herself how to play the instrument by re-creating the guitar chords' fingerings from memory. She was so small in comparison to the guitar that it did not fit in her lap and she had to lean it on the floor to play it.[11]

Not all was harmonious in the Parra household. By all accounts, Violeta's parents fought often and hard. Though he may have been the life of the party, Nicanor Parra senior suffered from alcoholism, a disease that caused him to be an unreliable and often absent figure in his children's lives. Clarisa became the bedrock of the family in his absence. According to Violeta's brother Nicanor junior, their mother was the opposite pole from their father: "like a rock, immovable, . . . the lives of all of her children revolved around her. And [our father] could be there or not."[12] Clarisa's fortitude was matched only by the violence of her temper, which her husband routinely provoked when he stumbled home after one of his all-night parties with his drinking buddies. That said, Clarisa enjoyed a good party as much as any of the other members of her family. Her playfulness and keen sense of humor served as counterweights to her determination to hold the family together and the rage she accumulated in striving to do so.

Violeta traced her roots on both sides of the family to the Ñuble province, located toward the southern end of Chile's fertile Central Valley. Her father's side hailed from the province's capital city of Chillán. They were people of means and education, the class of family that both valued and could afford to have their children study classical music—hence Nicanor senior's ability to read sheet music along with his virtuosity on the violin.[13] Violeta's paternal grandfather was an educated man, versed in the law, who owned several properties within the city and agricultural lands on its outskirts.

Violeta's family on her mother's side were campesinos or people who lived from agriculture, as did more than half the population of Chile in the first decades of the twentieth century. Reflective of the preponderance of small landowners in Ñuble, they owned a decent-sized parcel, including a small vineyard, in a rural community ten miles west of Chillán known as Malloa, where they cultivated the land and raised livestock.[14] Violeta's maternal grandfather was also employed as an overseer and a horse trainer on the nearby estate of a local landowner.

As a socially conscious artist later in life, Violeta would exaggerate the exploitation and poverty of her maternal grandfather's circumstances in a symbolic effort to graft the injustices of Chile's agricultural system to her family history. In fact, his status as a semi-independent small farmer meant that he and his family were better off than the large majority of inhabitants of the Central Valley, who worked either as impoverished tenant farmers (*inquilinos*) or as even more impoverished day laborers (*peones*) on the estates of Chile's landed elite.[15] Obvious contrasts notwithstanding, both sets of grandparents enjoyed a certain level of economic well-being and social standing within their respective communities and lived at comparably impassible distance from the economic and social stratosphere inhabited by Chile's minute upper class.[16]

In terms of her ethnic-racial background, it is likely that Violeta had both European and Indigenous ancestry. This was the case with many Chileans, given the history of race relations in Chile. Violeta would not have been viewed as Indigenous by her fellow Chileans during her lifetime, however, for complex reasons related to cultural boundaries and racism. In contrast with racial systems in place in societies where, historically, blood quantum or one's degree of "Indian blood" made one Indigenous, culture and land were the determining factors in the classification of a person as Indigenous in twentieth-century Chile, as in much of Latin America.[17] People who spoke an Indigenous language, dressed in traditional Indigenous clothing, and resided in Indigenous communities were considered Indigenous. People who did not were considered Chileans, with Violeta's family on both sides falling squarely into the latter category.[18] Deep-seated prejudices against Indigenous peoples that permeated twentieth-century Chilean society were an added disincentive to acknowledging an Indigenous background.[19]

Violeta would eventually lay claim to an Indigenous identity. This would not occur until the early 1960s, however, when she was in her mid-forties, no doubt influenced by the broad fascination of the era with all things Indigenous. Even then, she would only claim it while traveling abroad in Argentina and Europe—both sites where she was often racialized as Indigenous a priori due to a combination of her physical appearance and Eurocentric conceptions of the other.

In early twentieth-century Chile, as in many parts of Latin America to this day, the *familia* (family) consisted not just of grandparents, parents, and children but of a multigenerational and extensive network of people. Violeta's family fit this more rotund definition. It included relatives by blood or marriage, and fictive kinship relations forged over decades of shared histories and reciprocal assistance. Its members drew scant distinctions to degrees of genealogical proximity; they were simply "uncles," "aunts," and "cousins."

Violeta's familia was as elastic as it was extensive, taking on various constellations depending on the circumstances. Sometimes the immediate family shared living quarters with other branches of their extended clan. Other times Violeta's parents left one or more of their children in the care of relatives. Nicanor junior, for instance, recalls how he, Hilda, and Violeta found themselves at one point living in the home of their paternal grandparents in Chillán along with two of their cousins—though he could not recall why they had been left with their grandparents or the whereabouts of either set of absentee parents. On a grimmer note, he remembers the day his maternal grandmother came to take away his half sister, Olga, who had gotten herself into "very sensitive matters . . . having to do with love."[20] His recollections and numerous other instances from the Parra family history demonstrate how the household could expand or contract in response to any number of factors—an abundance or scarcity of resources, job transfers, new babies, scandals, health crises, and so on.

Violeta learned the value of being part of a familia as a child. She would rely on relatives, be they her mother, siblings, or "aunts," "uncles," and "cousins," in countless ways throughout her life, as they would rely on her. Violeta and her siblings were especially close, to the point that they often would live in compound-like settings once they had families of their own. "We formed a real tribe" was how Nicanor put it.[21] Violeta would also live with or near the respective extended families of her first and second husbands at times, though those situations did not tend to last very long as they were not to her liking. She would continue the tradition of entrusting her children to assorted members of her familia, especially when her work as a folklorista or performer involved extensive travel. So would her brother Nicanor and, presumably, the rest of the Parra siblings. Their parental decision to leave their children in the care of others would not have been viewed as particularly unusual or irresponsible, given the challenges, economic or otherwise, that families often faced, along with the customs of the day.

Violeta's family was Catholic in the same way that the vast majority of Chilean families were Catholic in the era. They attended church and, for the most part, kept up with the important sacraments—baptisms, communions, confirmations, last rites and funerals, and holy matrimony in the case of first spouses.

Evidence suggests that Violeta would continue some aspects of her family's religious traditions once she became a mother. It is almost certain that all four of her children were baptized, for example, and likely that they also had their first communion.[22] Beyond these basic rites, Violeta would maintain her distance from the church and even become its vocal critic in her last years. Hers was a nonofficial, hybrid sort of Christianity that was and is practiced widely in Chile and throughout Latin America. Often referred to as *popular* religion in the class-based sense of the term as emanating from the people, as opposed to top-down or official religion, it allowed and encouraged her to maintain a direct and deeply personal relationship with God throughout her lifetime, as evident in her letters, poetry, songs, and visual art.

Pat'e Perro (Wanderer)

The Parra family's economic circumstances while Violeta was growing up were often precarious, like those of the majority of Chileans in the early twentieth century. The relative financial stability that both sets of Violeta's grandparents enjoyed was not passed down to her parents. Her maternal grandfather's agricultural prosperity as a small landowner would erode, presumably by the 1930s.[23] Violeta's paternal grandfather, for his part, proved either unable or unwilling to ensure the financial security of Nicanor senior and his growing family. Nicanor senior's bohemian lifestyle also played a significant role in the family's economic instability.[24]

Not unusual for residents of the Central Valley who found themselves in financial straits, the Parra family became itinerant, moving from one place to the next in hopes of improving their lot. The Chilean expression for those who wander is *pat'e perro* or "dog's paw." Economic necessity, combined with the ease that the extensive train system permitted, made many Chileans pat'e perro in the first part of the twentieth century, Violeta's family included. By the time Violeta was ten years old, they had moved five times: from the rural hamlet of San Fabián to the nearby town of San Carlos shortly after her birth; then north to Santiago for two years or so; then south to the town of Lautaro for several more years; and finally to Chillán in 1927. Violeta, who did not have her own fixed address until she was forty-two, would claim to have inherited her parents' nomadic ways in her autobiography in verse: "As I was born a restless wanderer / Not even the devil could catch me" (*Como nací pat'e perro / ni el diablo m'echaba el guante*).[25]

Little is known about Violeta's earliest years spent in the small towns of San Fabián and San Carlos in the Ñuble province. The contours of her time in Santiago, roughly from ages two to four, are somewhat more filled in. The family's living and economic situation was tenuous at best. They stayed with relatives at first, as was common among newly arrived migrants to the capital. They next moved to a poor neighborhood near the Central Market that was rapidly expanding thanks primarily to the arrival of migrant families such as their own. Nicanor senior picked up odd jobs—tramway inspector, prison guard—while Clarisa, who was a gifted seamstress, found work at a department store.

In 1921, the family's fortunes improved considerably after Violeta's father was offered a teaching position with a military regiment stationed in the town of Lautaro, some 400 miles south of Santiago. The journey to Lautaro would be an entirely different matter, however. It became the setting of a childhood trauma that literally scarred Violeta for life.

The family left by train from Santiago at the height of a smallpox epidemic, one of several to strike the Chilean population in the early twentieth century.[26] Violeta contracted the disease, her symptoms first appearing en route. The ravages of smallpox brought her close to death and left her face permanently pockmarked. In her autobiography in verse, Violeta ruefully declares,

Here my sorrows begin
I say this sad and aggrieved,

They mock me by calling me "weed"
Because my appearance is frightening.

Aquí principian mis penas
lo digo con gran tristeza,
me sobrenombran "maleza"
porque parezco un espanto.[27]

Within the context of a larger society that shunned deformity, Violeta was transformed at a tender age, from someone who was pretty to someone whose appearance drew stares from strangers and taunts from classmates. Her "ugliness" did not fade with time, try as she did to get rid of the pockmarks with creams and other skin treatments. With the same casualness that in some parts of Latin America a chubby person is nicknamed *garda/o* (fatso), a skinny one *flaca/o*, or someone with a limp *coja/o* (gimp), family, friends, acquaintances, reporters, and public figures commented openly and often on Violeta's physical appearance.[28] Her brother Roberto explained in an interview how he had affectionately nicknamed Violeta "la 'Carcocha' [junk heap] because her face was all pitted from pestilence."[29] Socialist Party representative Carmen Lazo in her eulogy to Violeta, delivered to the House of Representatives just days after Violeta's death in 1967, first praised her talents, then noted that she "was not a beautiful woman; one could even say she was ugly."[30] Ricardo García, popular radio announcer and Violeta's collaborator and loyal promoter, was kinder in his delivery, if not his assessment: Violeta was "beautifully ugly."[31] Violeta shared the consensus; she consistently referred to herself as "ugly" or, in the extreme, as "the ugliest woman on the planet." Her childhood disfiguration would limit her options as a musician later in life in an industry that increasingly valued physical "beauty," especially when it came to women performers.

Violeta eventually recovered from smallpox. With the threat of disease lifted, her family found reprieve in Lautaro from the hardships they had endured in Santiago. Located in southern Chile in what was then the Cautín province (today Wallmapu), Lautaro was a small town in the 1920s, with a population of around 8,300 inhabitants.[32] Nicanor senior's teaching position came with a large house on the banks of a river that had more than enough room for his growing family, along with a garden, orchards, and one or two servants.[33] The young Parra siblings would later associate their five-or-so years in Lautaro with swimming in rivers, climbing trees, and eating ripe fruit straight from the branch. In a 1966 interview granted months before her death, Violeta would recall her family's stay there as "the best days of my life."[34]

Lautaro had a substantial Mapuche population, the largest Indigenous group within the territory claimed by Chile. Nicanor, who became an advocate for native rights, affirmed that he "got to know the Mapuche people from close up" growing up there and even learned how to count in their native language of Mapudungun.[35] Living in the region also made a strong impression on Nicanor and Violeta's parents, if the fact that they named their fourth and fifth sons after Mapuche warriors Lautaro and Caupolicán is any indicator. For her part, Violeta's early experiences in Lautaro may have inspired her interest and concern for native people. As a folklorista in the late 1950s, she would return to Wallmapu to collect material among the Mapuche.[36] In the early 1960s, she would draw attention to the situation of the Mapuche in songs and artwork that depicted their rituals or denounced their historical oppression.[37]

In 1927, the family's happy times in Lautaro came to an abrupt end after General Carlos Ibáñez del Campo assumed the presidency in July of that year. Ibáñez was an authoritarian leader. He immediately enacted a series of measures as part of his modernizing agenda, among them a decree banning civilians from working for the military. Nicanor senior lost his position as teacher of the regiment from one day to the next.[38] With nothing to hold them in Lautaro, Violeta's parents decided to return to their family roots in Ñuble. Violeta was ten years old when the family moved back to Chillán. She would form her most lasting childhood memories in and around this provincial capital which, though not exactly the "end of the earth," was still a far cry from Chile's political, economic, and cultural capital of Santiago 250 miles to the north. Of the many places she lived in her first fifteen years, Chillán would become the one Violeta most strongly identified with, and she would proudly proclaim herself a *chillaneja* (person from Chillán) in poetry and in song.[39]

Chillaneja

Chillán was a lively market town of some thirty thousand inhabitants when Parra moved there with her family in the late 1920s. Linked by railroad to all points north and south, it was the trading hub for the Ñuble province and beyond. The Parras moved into a house in Chillán's working-class neighborhood of Villa Alegre or "Happy Town." Conveniently located near the city's train station and marketplaces, Villa Alegre was home to a variety of establishments that catered to the needs of both local residents and rural customers in transit; small shops, homestyle restaurants, bars, and more than a few brothels that gave the neighborhood its name. Its principal thoroughfare was paved with cobblestones; the rest of its streets were dirt roads.

Villa Alegre functioned as the geographic, social, and cultural meeting point between urban Chillán and its rural outskirts. On market days, campesinos from agricultural communities in the surrounding area steered oxcarts laden with produce down its main street to the marketplace. Ranchers drove their cattle along the same route on days when the livestock market was held. As the herds passed directly in front of the Parras' home, a stray cow would wander in on occasion.[40] Salesmen from Villa Alegre traveled the inverse direction to the outlying rural areas to sell manufactured goods. A constant rural–urban exchange was thereby woven into the fabric of the neighborhood's daily life. The municipal cemetery was just down the road, and the Parra children became equally familiar with the slow, sad processionals that carried the deceased to their final resting place as they were with the daily hustle and bustle of commerce and the boisterous socializing that marked the completion of successful transactions.

Once installed in their new home, the children enrolled in elementary school, one for the girls and another for the boys.[41] Parra excelled in school. Close to a century later, an elderly woman who had shared a desk with Parra as a child would recall Parra as an eager and gifted classmate, who curried the teacher's favor, and who contributed her precocious literary and musical talents to school events.[42] Parra's siblings remembered her similarly as something of a star pupil.[43] In contradiction, Parra would profess to have loathed everything about school in her autobiography in verse:

> I won't even mention school;
> I hated it with heart and soul,
> From the textbook to the bell,
> From the blackboard to the pencil,
> From the teacher to the desk.
> And I begin to love the guitar and
> Where I hear the sounds of a party
> It's there I learn a song.

> *Mejor ni hablar de la escuela;*
> *la odié con todas mis ganas,*
> *del libro hasta la campana,*
> *del lápiz al pizarrón,*
> *del banco hast' el professor.*
> *Y empiezo 'amar la guitarra*
> *y adonde siento una farra*
> *allí aprendo una cancion.*[44]

When not in school, Parra engaged in the typical pastimes of children from her neighborhood. She played with her siblings and other children, made mischief in the cemetery, combed the countryside for specimens for Nicanor's insect collection, and drank stolen *chicha* (a drink made from fermented maize) from the barrels stored in a neighbor's shed.[45] She recited children's rhymes, most of which involved wordplay and humorous subversions.[46] She learned how to sew from her seamstress mother, and stitched together miniature outfits for the ragdolls that her mother made for her and her sisters.[47]

Chillán would prove a propitious environment for Parra to gather the "materials that make up my song." Her informal education in the region's cultural practices would have far greater influence on her professional and artistic pursuits later in life than whatever formal education was imparted to her in school. The inhabitants of greater Chillán, and especially those who resided in the rural communities on the city's outskirts, maintained a full calendar of rituals and festivals associated with both Catholicism and the agricultural cycle. As a young chillaneja, Parra participated in religious holidays such as the Crosses of May and celebrations of the Saints' days. She joined in the many secular practices and fiestas that were linked to life and work in the countryside such as the wheat threshing celebration (trilla) or the mutual aid ritual known as mingaco, a term adopted from Mapudungun. She saw the black, anthropomorphic ceramics of the women potters from the nearby town of Quinchamalí, who sold their wares at the market in Chillán. Parra would revisit these childhood experiences as a folklorista in the mid-1950s and as an artist in the 1960s. She would draw on the celebrations and rituals of rural life for the thematic content of her weekly folk music radio show. She would reference the imagery of the Quinchamalí ceramics in her work as a visual artist.

Parra imbibed the musical traditions of the region as well. These were interwoven into every aspect of life in Chillán. As Parra explained in an interview, people sang a lot where she was from; "they were always singing, for births, for weddings, for deaths, for harvests."[48]

The Aguilera family, who lived in the same rural community where Parra's mother was born, figure prominently in Parra's early musical education. On weekends and holidays, Violeta and her siblings would hike along dirt roads and footpaths for three hours to visit the family in Malloa. They called the Aguilera children their "cousins" because the relations that existed between their mother's family and the Aguileras were "truly ones of kinship."[49]

Violeta was particularly drawn to the Aguileras and spent entire summers living at their homestead. The family's five daughters were all gifted musicians. Together they exemplified the musical practices of rural women singers of early twentieth-century Chile: they were from the same family; they sang tonadas, cuecas, and other traditional song styles that had been passed down to them across the generations; they accompanied themselves on guitar and harp; and they performed not as professionals but for the enjoyment of their families and community.[50] In her autobiography in verse,

Parra extols them and identifies several of the traditional song styles that they played:

An orchestra made of five sisters
Carefree and nonchalant
With "rondas" and "chapecaos,"
With "pericones" and "cuecas."

las cinco son una orquesta
con todo su desenfado
en "rondas" y "chapecaos,"
en "pericones" y "cuecas."[51]

Parra would consistently credit the Aguilera sisters with initiating her into the rich traditions of the region once it became her life's purpose as a folklorista to preserve and disseminate those traditions. She would name the Aguileras, along with her mother, as her earliest folkloric sources and refer to the songs they had taught her as "folk songs." The fact that Parra as a young girl had learned an entire repertoire of traditional songs from her campesina mother and "cousins" provided the basis for her claim in her 1954 *Ecran* interview that she began learning the folklore of Chile "from the moment I was born."[52]

The daily life of the inhabitants of Malloa was steeped in tradition. Parra would later claim that it was there that she first attended a wake for the little angel, the funeral rite for a baby who died before baptism discussed in this book's introduction.[53] It was also most likely in Malloa that she first encountered the form of traditional poetry original to Chile's Central Valley known as *canto a lo poeta* or "songs in the style of the poet," referred to hereafter as "poet-songs." The impact that this traditional song style would have on Parra's eventual career as a folklorista, songwriter, and poet cannot be overstated.

The poet-songs were the direct descendants of the décimas or ten-line verses, cultivated by bards of the Spanish royal court during the sixteenth and seventeenth centuries, and brought to Latin America during the colonial period.[54] In Chile's Central Valley, the bards' songs evolved over the centuries into a unique style of sung poetry that accompanied rural celebrations and religious rituals, including the wake for the little angel. The poet-songs preserved the décima form of their courtly ancestor but adopted the language and worldview of Chilean campesinos. Some of them covered religious subjects such as the legends of the saints and various Bible episodes. Others glossed more earthbound topics—birds, animals, and, of course, humans and their varied activities. A few of the themes of the poet-songs trace back to medieval times. "Verso por el mundo al revés" (Verses for a World Upside Down), for instance, continue the carnivalesque tradition, dating back to at least the Middle Ages, of satirizing those in power through a symbolic inversion of the social order, as the following verse from a song that Parra collected demonstrates:

The servants are crowned as rulers,
While kings are scrubbing the floor,
The devil is up in heaven
And soldiers are going to jail.

Los pajes son corona'os,
los reyes friegan el piso,
el diablo en el paraíso
y presos van los solda'os.[55]

The poet-songs were sung by singers from the community, all men customarily, who sat in a circle and took turns versifying on specified *fundamentos* or themes. Their singing often lasted from night until dawn, and did so perforce when the purpose of the gathering was a funeral wake. The traditional singers accompanied themselves on the *guitarrón*, a large guitar with twenty-five strings, which is also unique to the Chilean Central Valley.[56]

In the traditional musical practices of the Central Valley, the poet-songs were considered the province of male singers, so Parra was not taught them as a child. They nonetheless would have an enduring impact on her life's work. As a folklorista in her mid-thirties, Parra would become one of the exceptional women to join the traditional circle of singers and, even more exceptionally, to take up the guitarrón. As a songwriter and poet, Parra would incorporate elements of the poet-songs into her own literary arsenal. With her brother Nicanor's encouragement, she would pen her autobiography in décimas in the late 1950s. Violeta's brothers Nicanor, Eduardo, Roberto, Lautaro, and Oscar would display commensurate facility in the décima and other poetic styles of the region as poets and performers later in life.[57] The Parra siblings' shared fluency in the poetic language of the Chilean countryside is a testament to the influence that their childhood would have on their respective artistic trajectories.

Popular Music

Though profoundly marked by rural traditions, Violeta and her siblings were by and large townspeople. As denizens of Chillán, they were exposed to the latest trends in the music industry to reach the provincial capital. These amounted to a mixed bag of national and international musical genres that fit under the broad rubric of "popular music," defined by scholars as music that is "mediated, massified, and modernizing": it is mediated by the entertainment industry and technology, massified in its potential to reach millions of people simultaneously, and modernizing in its "symbiotic relationship with the cultural industry, technology, media and urban sensibilities."[58]

The popular music that the Parra children listened to encompassed many genres and styles. It included parlor music like the instrumental dance pieces that their classically trained father performed at social events, which he most likely learned from sheet music purchased at the city's music store. It comprised contemporary popular songs, the lyrics of which appeared in the chapbooks that were printed in small runs at local print shops and peddled in market stalls and at the train station. It included live performances by second- or even third-tier touring artists who included Chillán on their itineraries, and by the local musicians who provided the accompaniment for the silent movies of the era.[59]

In the early 1920s, the possibilities of listening enjoyment for the inhabitants of Chillán expanded swiftly and exponentially when a new purveyor of popular music was introduced to their city: the Victrola or gramophone.[60] The Victrola quickly became a required fixture in the parlors of upper- and middle-class chillaneja families. Within a few years, some families in the Parras' more modest neighborhood of Villa Alegre could also boast of owning the device. According to Nicanor junior, the Victrola even made its way onto one or two of the homesteads in rural Malloa, though not that of the Aguilera sisters.[61]

The first generation of Victrola owners in and around Chillán could purchase imported discs covering a broad spectrum of cosmopolitan tastes, from the arias of Italian tenor and international sensation Enrico Caruso to Spanish cabaret songs to foxtrots performed by the finest New York orchestras. Or they could buy recordings of these international styles performed by Chilean musicians such as the Chilean big bands that played foxtrots and other dance music styles that were the latest rage in Chillán, Santiago, and the world over during the roaring 1920s. They could also enjoy recorded versions of a pan–Latin American repertoire of popularized song styles. Often referred to as *música criolla* (music that is native or "from here"), in Chile the category included a standardized fare of Cuban guarachas and habaneras, Mexican *corridos*, Peruvian *vals*, and the two Chilean-identified song styles of tonadas and cuecas.

A few of the recordings circulating in Chillán in the late 1920s featured a genre of folk-derived music, still in its early formation, that would eventually be labeled *música típica chilena* (Chilean "typical" or "folkloric" music) or simply *música típica*.[62] Música típica drew on the traditional songs of rural communities in the Central Valley, but modernized them to meet both the musical expectations of urban society and the technological requirements of the Victrola's discs, which could hold only three and a half minutes of content per side.[63] Two traditional song styles predominated in this process of musical renovation: the lyrical tonada and the cueca, which is both a song and a courtship dance (see figure 5.4). The near exclusive purview of rural women singers like the Aguilera sisters until the 1920s, these two song styles were now refashioned and urbanized by professional singers, both male and female, into the hallmarks of música típica.[64] The bands Los Huasos de Chincolco and Los Cuatro Huasos—with *huaso* a Chilean term for a skilled horseman, similar to the Mexican charro or the Argentine gaucho—were among the first Chilean recording artists to help birth this new musical category, which would only grow in popularity over the ensuing decades.[65] By the time Parra took up the vocation of folklorista in the early 1950s, música típica and the huaso bands that performed it had become consummate symbols of *chilenidad* or "Chilean-ness."

The traditional cantos a lo poeta or poet-songs would not undergo comparable metamorphosis. Whereas the more malleable lyrical tonada and upbeat cueca met the modernizing demands of the rapidly expanding Chilean music industry, the poet-songs did not. This was no doubt due to the poet-songs' frequently obscure themes, slow tempo, monotonous accompaniment, and lengthy narrative structure, which, when the songs were performed in their entirety, could reach a grand total of fifty-four phrases sung over approximately six minutes.[66] These qualities, in combination, made the poet-songs unwieldly to popularize and literally impossible to record for commercial release, given the existing technologies. They therefore persisted in their traditional state, awaiting discovery by successive generations of folklorists, including Parra in the 1950s.[67]

Regardless of the absence of the poet-songs, there were more than enough varieties of popular music for the residents of Chillán to choose from in the expanding catalog of sound recordings available in the 1920s. With no need for electricity, the Victrola introduced the recorded voices and sounds of a national and international roster of artists into the intimacy of homes across Chile, while more portable models, conveniently built into "orthophonic suitcases," allowed for the machines' easy transport to picnics and outings.[68]

The fact that people could now listen to popular music whenever and wherever they wanted altered the way they listened to and made music, and the change would only accelerate and deepen with the spread of commercial radio in the 1930s. The technological innovations that allowed for the massive audible reproduction of music would free it from its temporal and geographic confines. Entire libraries have been written on the worldwide impact of mass media on twentieth-century society and culture. To summarize just a few salient points as regards popular music: it would turn music from an experiential practice into a consumer product; democratize its consumption; lead to the professionalization and specialization of musicians; create distance between performers and their public; and erode the boundaries between regional, national, and international musical styles. As the century progressed, these same global processes, in combination and interrelated with modernization, industrialization, and rural-urban migration, would radically transform cultural life in rural areas, threatening the oral traditions of Chile and the world over with extinction.

Parra's early musical education reflected the cusp-like quality of this moment in the evolution of oral traditions and popular music in Chile. She could hike for three hours to her cousins' homestead in rural Malloa, where the Victrola had yet to make its full appearance, and be taught traditional cuecas and tonadas by her cousins. At the same time, diverse forms of stylized folk music from Chile and across Latin America were becoming the audible staples of her daily life in Chillán. The talented Parra learned songs from this modern, commercial, and mass-delivered repertoire as effortlessly as she did the traditional songs from her campesina mother and the Aguilera sisters.

Later in life, Parra would draw a distinction between traditional songs, both the ones she learned as a child and those she collected as an adult, and all forms of commercial music, homegrown or imported. As a folklorista, she would devote her passion and energy to the conservation and dissemination of the former, now defined as "folklore," and reject the latter as "trivial" or worse. As a young chillaneja in the late 1920s and early 1930s, Parra made no such distinction; the songs that she learned from the campesina side of her family and the ones that she learned from the recordings that her Villa Alegre neighbors played on their Victrolas were all welcome in her ever-expanding repertoire.

Hard Times

Parra gathered many materials, musical and otherwise, during her childhood years. This period of her life was hardly idyllic, however. It included a long stretch of abject poverty. Her family's hard times resulted from an unfortunate collision of personal and global factors. After being laid off from his post in Lautaro, Nicanor senior fell into a downward spiral of drinking and depression. He would never hold down a steady job again, and he squandered what inheritance he received with the death of his father on speculation and barroom deals gone bad. He died on October 6, 1930, after a prolonged illness, leaving Clarisa alone to fend for their ten children.[69] Violeta had just turned thirteen.

Nicanor senior's death occurred one year after the US stock market crash, the effects of which swiftly radiated southward to the export-driven nations of Latin America. In the case of Chile, the League of Nations would later declare it the country most devastated by the ensuing global crisis. Copper, Chile's most important export, may serve as an example: copper sales to the United States plummeted from 87,000 to 5,000 pounds between 1931 and 1933, while its price per pound fell from 17.47 to 5.6 cents over roughly the same period.[70] The consequences of economic depression for the Chilean people included rampant unemployment, social dislocation, and hunger.[71] A local witness to the crisis in Chillán recalled hundreds of unemployed workers, many of them refugees from the shuttered northern mines, roaming the streets with their wives and children, begging door to door.[72]

The loss of their father, first to alcohol and disease and ultimately to his death in the midst of what was arguably the worst economic crisis to grip the nation, left the Parra family on the brink of indigence. Clarisa struggled to keep the children fed and clothed as best she could by taking on work as a seamstress. As a child, Violeta assisted her mother in her labors. As an adult, she would devote several poems of her autobiography to Clarisa's efforts. One provides a fanciful list of finished items waiting to be picked up—shirts and undershirts, a dressing gown, a gypsy outfit, a soldier's dress coat, circus costumes, drapes, tea towels for a convent, a funeral shroud, a communion dress, hospital bandages, and the mended robe of a statue of Saint Sebastian.[73] Another poem praises Clarisa for her seemingly miraculous ability to clothe her children out of the scraps left over from her commissions.[74] Still another depicts Clarisa sewing late into the night as an exhausted Violeta holds an oil lamp above her head to light her work.[75] Decades later as an expatriate artist in Europe, Violeta would symbolically wear her childhood to her art openings and other events, greeting her public in a patchwork dress that her mother had sewn for her by request and that Violeta explicitly linked in interviews to the poverty she had known as a child.

As hard as Clarisa worked, she was unable to make ends meet. The Parras were soon evicted from their home on Villa Alegre's thoroughfare. From there they moved into a far smaller abode that had somehow escaped the creditors' notice. Violeta's brother Eduardo repeated the word "dire" over and over again when speaking of this somber period for the Parra family.[76] He remembered how their mother would put them to sleep early on Christmas Eve so that they would not overhear the festive sounds of their neighbors partaking in the traditional holiday feast following midnight mass.[77] Violeta's brother Roberto recalled the siblings suffering through painful winters, their feet cracked and frozen for lack of shoes. In his customary jocular vein, he pronounced that the Parra children were so poor that they had to borrow clothing just to dress up as ragamuffins.[78]

In response to their situation, the Parra children did what poor children did then and do now the world over: they learned to fend for themselves. Nicanor, the oldest, was the first of the siblings to figure out how. Long a star pupil, he found work as a live-in tutor for the children of a well-off local butcher. The butcher's family thus offered the young, gifted scholar a lifeline that allowed him to remain in school. Shortly after, Nicanor moved to Santiago, where he completed his secondary education on scholarship at the prestigious public boarding school, the Barros Arana National Academy (Internado Nacional Barros Arana or INBA).

Nicanor junior was the only Parra sibling to take the academic route out of poverty. The others remained at home and worked at odd jobs to help their mother and fill their bellies. They cleaned the crypts in the nearby cemetery for spare change. They helped with Sunday barbecues at the outdoor restaurant that the butcher's family that had taken Nicanor in owned. Eduardo and Roberto shined shoes in the city's plaza. Violeta worked for a time as a live-in nanny caring for a young disabled child, until "God took him away."[79] Roberto became the traveling assistant to a blind itinerant singer.[80]

According to her siblings, Violeta was the one who came up with the idea that they go out and sing for their supper. She left their home one morning with a large basket and a borrowed guitar and returned in the afternoon, the basket laden with food. She would later recall her mother's mix of emotions upon viewing the cornucopia that her young daughter brought home to feed their hungry family: Clarisa's grateful tears, and her angry scolding and extraction of the promise that Violeta would never do it again. If Violeta failed to keep her word, it was not for lack of respect but out of necessity. As she wrote in her autobiography in verse,

There is no job or trade in existence
That I have not attempted
After my cherished papa's
Life of sacrifice ended.
Though *mamita* denied me permission
That did not deter me,
As a young girl I knew clearly
That every single morning

Ten hungry mouths were yearning
For their blessed daily bread.

No existe empleo ni oficio
que yo no lo haiga ensaya'o,
después que mi taita ama'o
termina su sacrificio.
No me detiene el permiso
que mi mamita negara,
de niña supe a las claras
qu'el pan bendito del día
diez bocas lo requerían
hambrientas cada mañana.[81]

Hilda, Eduardo, and Roberto, who were closest to Violeta in age, soon joined her. The musical siblings culled their repertoire from the potpourri of Spanish-language songs known loosely as música criolla that they learned in their Villa Alegre neighborhood. As Eduardo described it, they played "tonadas, cuecas, Mexican corridos that are so popular among the people in the countryside, and a few waltzes."[82] The children sang in the street and at train stations and marketplaces. They received coins from passing strangers and gifts of food from the market women in return. They sang and passed the hat in neighborhood bars and even ended up unintentionally performing at one or two of the brothels that earned Villa Alegre its name. They would realize this only in hindsight, however, as at the time they were "truly innocent kids" with "no knowledge of the ways of the world."[83]

The children gradually expanded their performance radius to include small towns in Chillán's vicinity, which they traveled to by train. Most times they made it back home by bedtime. Other times they spent the night wherever it found them and returned the next day, to their mother's great consternation. The children brought Clarisa what little earnings they made, which she then used to buy shoes for them, one pair at a time.

The Circo Pobre ("Poor Circus")

By necessity and by will, the Parra siblings embarked on their careers as performers before fully entering adolescence. They soon joined up with a series of small family circuses. All of the circuses that the Parra siblings traveled with in their youth fit under the rubric of *circo pobre* (poor circus), a term that affectionately captures the circuses' reduced size and resources along with the overall quality of their acts.

By custom, the circo pobre was a family enterprise representing several generations of performers who had been born and would live and die "under the tent." A handful of additional artists completed the troupe. Operating in the interstices between itinerant theater traditions and modern mass media, the circo pobre served a key function as an agent of change in the Chilean countryside during the first decades of the twentieth century, introducing modern concepts and cultural practices to a relatively isolated rural audience. The expanding reach of modern mass media over the course of the twentieth century would lead to the circo pobre's eventual decline, parallel to that of oral traditions in the same regions.[84]

The first circo pobre that Violeta and her siblings joined was the Tolín Circus, a circus so poor that it still used ox-drawn carts for transport. Next came the circus owned by the husband of the Parra siblings' half sister, Marta. It was named the Argentine Circus in honor of the circus performers' stint in an Argentine jail due to an unfortunate illegal border crossing. It had a rental truck and large tent with a capacity for 400 spectators. Next came the even more impressive Millas Brothers' Circus.[85]

The circuses promoted themselves by promising their audiences an entertainment extravaganza, with a lineup of thirty or more "world famous" artists, all with exotic, foreign-sounding names. In actuality, their rosters were so small that the performers had to fulfill multiple tasks in order to cover the varied roles of ringmaster, clown, acrobat, mime, contortionist, musician, singer, fortune teller, ticket taker, and crew. One clown coined the term "everything-ists" to describe himself and his colleagues, as they inevitably had to do everything in the circo pobre.[86]

An everything-ist if ever there was one, Violeta performed a variety of functions in the circus. She sang and danced on street corners as part of the circus parade, a long-standing tradition where the circus artists paraded raucously through town to announce their upcoming shows (that was eventually replaced by trucks with mounted loudspeakers). She sewed costumes and undertook numerous other tasks both in and outside of the circus ring. Her siblings kept themselves equally occupied.

The Parra children toured with the circo pobre throughout the provinces of Ñuble and neighboring Maule in the Central Valley's southern region. Sometimes a wealthy landowner would hire the circus to perform for the campesinos on his estate at a cost of 200 or 300 pesos—which according to Roberto was good money in those days.[87] When these more lucrative opportunities failed to pan out, the circus traveled to remote small towns in the region where it often found its best audiences. The circus artists would set up their tent and send out the parade party to drum up spectators. If attendance was good, the circus would put on multiple performances over several days. If attendance was poor, it would offer the bargain admission price of two-for-one or even three-for-one. When the audience waned or became nonexistent, the circus would pack up and move on to the next town. The circus traveled during the summer months, and returned to Chillán for the off-season, during which time its artists put on shows for the locals and worked out new material for the next summer's tour.

The Parra siblings would later recall their time spent as young roving musicians and circus artists as both difficult and rewarding. They earned only loose change and some food for their impromptu street concerts and barely more for their versatile and seemingly interminable circus duties. Life on the road was demanding and took time away from their schooling. Although Violeta and Eduardo reportedly did well regardless, Hilda and Roberto had to struggle to catch up.[88] At the same time, Violeta and her siblings' musical travels were never dull and often fulfilling. As Roberto would later note, "[the circus] is great fun when you are young, the artistic life it offers is grand and full of adventures."[89]

The Parra siblings would maintain a lifelong association with the circus. Chilean circus artists forged a large and close-knit network based on the intimacy and intensity of their shared livelihood. Though they had not been "born under the tent," Hilda, Violeta, Eduardo, and Roberto Parra, along with their younger brothers Lautaro and Oscar, were adopted into this extended circus family. Eduardo, Lautaro, and Oscar would go on to establish full-fledged careers in the circus.[90] Hilda and Eduardo would both marry circus artists: Hilda, the Argentine Circus's owners' son; and Eduardo, its tightrope walker's daughter.[91]

For her part, Violeta was purported to have lamented that the Argentine Circus owner did not have more sons, as she too would have happily married into the circus.[92] She would continue to occasionally perform with the circus after her move to Santiago at the age of fifteen. As a working musician mother later in life, she would run her family very much like the circus families she had known as a child; her expectation would be that her children adapt to and, ideally, incorporate themselves into her work-life as a performer.

The circus would become a recurrent theme of Violeta's creative activities as well.[93] In the mid-1950s, she and Hilda would record the song "La cueca del payaso" (The Clown's Cueca) as the duo Las Hermanas Parra, accompanied by a full circus band, and Violeta would reprise the song as a circus band instrumental on her 1959 LP *La cueca presentada por Violeta Parra* (The Cueca, as Presented by Violeta Parra).[94] As a visual artist, Violeta would depict the circus in one of her more well-known tapestries, appropriately titled *The Circus*. She would devote the last year of her life to the creation of a cultural center, the Carpa de La Reina. It was housed in a circus tent or carpa that she installed in the outlying Santiago neighborhood of La Reina, hence its name. The project would ultimately fail. The Carpa de La Reina would become the site of her suicide in 1967.

A Social Education

Parra learned the unwritten norms of the workings of Chilean society as a child, which I refer to here as her social education. The hierarchical nature of class relations—and the fact that one could move up or down in that hierarchy, depending on one's family's circumstances—would be one of its enduring lessons. Poverty was her first teacher. The destitution that she and her siblings endured after the premature death of their father would lead her to identify with the poor of Chile no matter her economic circumstances (which were never that auspicious, in any case).

Parra's education in classism was furthered by her schoolmates who came from more affluent households than her own fallen middle-class family. As she describes in her autobiography in verse,

> What's even worse, dozens
> Were showing off their silver,
> Viola, a little bug in the corner
> Child of a small-time teacher,
> With small-time wages so meager
> Worth barely a bit of tin.

> Pa' más desgracia, docenas
> lucían su buena plata,
> la Viola, una garapata
> menor d'un profesorcito,
> de sueldo casi justito
> se nos volvía hojalata.[95]

Parra's social education continued through her travels with the circo pobre. On the landed estates where the poor circuses performed, the class distance between the landlord and the inquilinos (tenant farmers) who labored for him was marked not only by an inestimable difference in wealth but by ritualized social interactions meant to underscore and safeguard that distance. The landowner and his wife were supposed to comport themselves in a lordly manner by playing the role of generous benefactors; they became "godparents" to their inquilinos' children, for example, or treated them to a show by a traveling circus. The inquilinos, in turn, were to demonstrate their unquestioned submission by assuming the classic stance of hat in hand and eyes lowered on those rare occasions when they were called to address the landowner, whom they addressed as "your Grace" (*su merced*).[96] The great disparity between landowner and inquilino was thus ceremonially enacted for all to see—visiting young circus artists included.

Parra's political sympathies were shaped by her childhood experiences, both the hard lessons that she learned from her own family's diminished fortunes and the social inequalities that she witnessed. Her father's political views, perhaps in keeping with his more privileged upbringing, had aligned with the middle-class and upwardly mobile orientation of the reform-minded Radical Party. Parra, in contrast and from an early age, became a staunch supporter of the Communist Party, the political party that unambiguously proclaimed itself on the side of working people (the pueblo) and the class enemy of the rich. According to her brother Eduardo, Violeta attended rallies organized by the Communist Party with him and Roberto while they were teenagers in Chillán.[97] Though never a card-carrying member, Violeta would retain her sympathies for the Communist Party over the rest of her life, as would many of her siblings. In a society divided at its most basic level between a tiny and immensely wealthy upper class, a small and struggling middle class, and the poor masses, Parra would proclaim herself a *mujer del pueblo* (woman of the people, everywoman) and identify with the masses.

Parra learned the nuances of Chilean racial hierarchy in tandem with her education in class relations. Chilean society in her time—and to this day—had a notable racial-class overlay where both skin tone and, to a lesser degree, height were often linked to social class. As regards physical appearances, upper-class Chileans tended to have traits associated with people of European background (lighter skin, taller), and working-class Chileans traits associated with people of mestizo or mixed Indigenous and African and European backgrounds (darker skin and, in some cases, shorter).[98] As regards social perceptions, taller people with lighter skin tone tended to be seen as upper class, while shorter people with darker skin tone tended to be seen as working class. This nexus of class and race was fluid, so that markers of social class (a fancy car, a maid's apron) could influence how a person's physical appearance was perceived. The inverse, however, was not likely to occur. A day laborer who happened to be on the lighter and taller side of the racial-class spectrum would not be seen as wealthy, for example. Similarly, a rich woman who was on the shorter and darker side of the spectrum would not be seen as poor—though she might affectionately be called *la morena* (the darker one) in family circles.

Parra landed in the shorter and more morena/o (darker) region of this racial-class spectrum, alongside the majority of Chileans. Her mestizo-like features would prove multivalent and malleable over the course of her lifetime. Given the racial-class prejudices of Chilean society, they could factor into her marginalization from Chilean academic and cultural institutions and elite social circles. Yet they could also bolster her self-construction as a mujer del pueblo or everywoman. In short, Parra's physical appearance would not so much determine how she was perceived as it would allow for a certain range of interpretations, depending on the social context.

The social education Parra received was also an education in gender rules and restrictions. The customary gendering of life's practices established that Violeta and her siblings attend two different schools, one for boys and one for girls; that, after the death of their father, her brothers work as shoe shiners and she as a nanny; and untold other details of the Parra siblings' childhood years. Violeta would not experience the full weight of the patriarchal order, however, until she moved to Santiago as an adolescent and faced head on the reduced list of career paths open to women along with the sexual double standards that ruled women's lives, working or not.

As a young girl, Parra thus acquired a basic education in the hierarchies of class, race, and gender that structured Chilean society along with a budding sense of her position within it based on intersecting—and often shifting— coordinates. At the same time, her childhood contained elements of freedom and invention that were arguably lacking in the more socially regimented lives of the privileged, and particularly of privileged women: the freedom of childish pleasures and mischief. The freedom of movement, of her pat'e perro or nomadic family in her earliest years, and of her later itinerancies with the circo pobre. The freedom from having to keep up with social appearances, which became not just a luxury but an impossibility once her family descended into poverty. There was a certain freedom of mindset as well, one that allowed her to envision how scraps of cloth could become a ragdoll's dress, or how one could feed an entire family with an empty basket and a borrowed guitar.

Parra would carry that sense of possibility, born of necessity, into her adult life. It helps explain how she could transform empty burlap sacks and remnants of yarn into vast tapestries and then picture them hanging on the walls of the Louvre Palace in Paris. It factored into countless of her other accomplishments as well. Though perhaps less tangible than some of the other materials that she gathered in her youth, her early practice in self-determination and imagination must still figure among the materials that make up her song.

———

In 1933, at age fifteen, Violeta received a letter from her brother Nicanor urging her to join him in Santiago to continue her education. Soon after, she left southern Chile to go to the capital.[99] According to Hilda, the two girls were at the train station in the town of Linares, Maule, on their way home from a singing jaunt when Violeta decided to take off for Santiago. Violeta made her exit without saying goodbye to their mother and without asking for Clarisa's permission. She carried with her the materials she had gathered in her childhood. She brought the performance skills that she developed first as a participant in family skits and singing contests, then on the more demanding "stages" of street corners and circus rings. She took her guitar and a substantial repertoire of songs: traditional ones passed on to her by her campesina mother and cousins, and corridos, waltzes, and urbanized cuecas and tonadas learned in her childhood neighborhood of Villa Alegre.

She embarked on her journey with a strong sense of identity and place. It was shaped by her parents and extended family. It was solidified in the provincial capital of Chillán and in the many other towns, landed estates, and rural communities she had traveled to in her short life. It was fortified by her family's experience of poverty and by the ways the Parras had risen to its challenges. At age fifteen, Violeta may not have known exactly where she was going, but she knew where she came from. As she states in the song that is arguably her manifesto, "Yo canto la diferencia" (I Sing the Difference):

> I sing à la chillaneja
> If I have something to say,
> And I don't pick up the guitar
> To get a round of applause.
> I sing the difference
> Between what is true and what's false.
> Otherwise, I do not sing.

> *Yo canto a la chillaneja*
> *si tengo que decir algo,*
> *y no tomo la guitarra*
> *por conseguir un aplauso.*
> *Yo canto la diferencia*
> *que hay de lo cierto a lo falso.*
> *De lo contrario no canto.*[100]

Chapter 2

Anti-Materials

The period between Parra's arrival in Santiago in 1933 and her emergence as a "new talent" in the Chilean folk music scene of the early 1950s was eventful and productive. Parra spent the first two years enrolled in a teacher training program, which would end up being the extent of her post–primary school education. She married and separated from her first husband, had her marriage annulled (as divorce was illegal at the time in Chile), and married her second husband. She gave birth to three of her four children, two with her first husband and one with her second. On the artistic front, she spent many of the twenty-some years in question performing música criolla in working-class bars and taverns. She pursued a successful if short-lived career as a flamenco artist as well. Toward the end of the period, she and her sister Hilda began playing some of Santiago's more upscale venues as Las Hermanas Parra (The Parra Sisters). The duo also made their entrée into the mass entertainment industry via radio and several recordings for RCA Victor.

Despite its comparative longevity and significant achievements, Parra typically glossed over or simply left out this chapter of her life in interviews regarding her trajectory as an artist. One compelling explanation for her reticence is that the commercialized musical activities that she was involved in across this period ran counter to the more idealistic values she would later espouse as a folklorista and an artist. Her childhood years had provided her not only with the materials that she would later incorporate into her music, poetry, and visual art but also with those biographical elements that she would use to explain how and why she became a folklorista and an artist. In contrast, the two decades over which she sustained herself and her family by performing popular musical genres from across Latin America and Spain did not lend themselves to the narrative.

This is not to suggest that Parra was somehow inauthentic before she became authentic; the concept that something or someone could be the opposite of authentic—as in "fake"—is as much a social construct as authenticity itself. Parra's career as a singer, composer, and eventual recording artist of various styles of Chilean and pan–Latin American popular song styles as well as her sideline as a flamenco artist were neither authentic nor inauthentic. They were how she earned her living.

This chapter chronicles those musical practices that Parra engaged in during her twenties and early thirties that she would mostly abandon and even reject when she turned to the authentic. Borrowing from Nicanor Parra's wordplay in the title of his 1954 book of poetry that brought him his first national and international recognition, *Poemas y antipoemas* (Poems and Antipoems), it is about her "anti-materials."[1]

If Parra was able to devote time and energy to performing more commercial genres of music that she would later discard, it was only because of her steadfast refusal to conform to the gender expectations of her era. To continue with the wordplay, she was anti-conventional. In addition to examining her life, then, the following account tracks Parra's movement away from conventional pathways for women and toward her chosen artistic pursuits.

Santiago

Parra arrived in Santiago in 1933, fifteen years old and alone.[2] She traveled there summoned by her older brother Nicanor, who had become his younger siblings' "father-brother" after the premature death of their father.[3] Then in his twenties, Nicanor was pursuing simultaneous tracks in the sciences and humanities that would eventually lead to his dual careers as a respected physicist and celebrated poet. Though a university student, he continued to reside at the Barros Arana National Academy (Internado Nacional Barros Arana or INBA), the boarding school where he had completed his secondary education and where he now worked as a resident supervisor in exchange for room and board.

Nicanor's plan was to gradually bring each of his siblings to Santiago so that they too could further their studies. He had only one condition: that they leave their guitars behind. Nicanor reached out to Violeta first because she seemed to be the most promising pupil of the lot.[4] She left for the capital on the spur of the moment, without sending advance notice of her impending arrival and without complying with Nicanor's one proviso. He would long remember the day when the doorman informed him that someone was asking for him at the boarding school's entrance and went there to find Violeta, guitar in hand, but no suitcase.[5]

Viewed in reverse perspective, Violeta awaited her brother in front of a monumental building, the grandeur of which equaled or surpassed that of any edifice in the siblings' hometown of Chillán. Designed at the start of the twentieth century by French architect Victor Henry de Villeneuve, INBA occupied almost an entire city block on the edge of Santiago's spacious park, the Quinta Normal. The public high school was established by government decree in 1902 for the purpose of recruiting gifted male students from the nation's provinces and providing them with the rigorous training in the humanities and sciences that would prepare them for entrance to the university. During its "Golden Age" in the 1930s, the boarding school housed around 1,000 pupils a year and featured lecture halls, athletic fields, ateliers, laboratories equipped with the latest scientific instruments, and its own cinema, heated pool, bookstore, post office, and tailor.[6] INBA's extensive roster of illustrious alumni, Nicanor Parra among them, attests to the success of its mission, as their collective accomplishments include national and international honors in the sciences, arts, and humanities and service at the highest echelons of government and commerce, including one president of the republic.[7]

Nicanor attended INBA on a full scholarship. He would later attest to the magnitude of the education, both formal and informal, that he received there; it had opened him to "the spirit of modern culture."[8] He and several of his fellow pupils formed a close-knit band of young writers and artists so impressive it would later be dubbed the "mythical ones" of the Barros Arana National Academy.[9] The budding scholar-artists absorbed the teachings of European philosophers and devoured the works of Spanish and French poets as well as Chilean poets Vicente Huidobro, Pablo de Rokha, and Pablo Neruda. At night, they would sneak out to the bars in the "city's underworld" (bajos fondos) of the working-class barrio of Matucana—the same neighborhood where, a few years later, Nicanor's musician siblings could be found hustling between barroom gigs.[10]

The image of Violeta Parra standing outside of a cultural institution that barred her entry could serve as a leitmotif of her biography. In this instance, her exclusion was insurmountable: Violeta could not attend the Barros Arana National Academy because it was (and remains, at the time of writing) a school for boys.[11] There existed no female equivalent to the prestigious national institute because there was no analogous expectation that talented provincial girls would someday attend university and therefore require the academic preparation that INBA provided.

As Violeta could not room with Nicanor, he took her to live with the family of one of their uncles.[12] Nicanor then enrolled Violeta in the public Normal School for Girls No. 1, a teacher-training school located just blocks from the INBA.

In Chile as elsewhere, "normal schools for girls" were the female counterpart to teacher-training schools for men, which were simply called "normal schools." Though many of the young women who passed through the normal schools for girls went on to accomplish great things, this was by no means the schools' purpose.[13] Their far more modest charge was to prepare their female pupils to become primary school teachers, one of the few occupations of the era that was considered appropriate to their sex. Accordingly, the normal schools for girls imparted an education calibrated to the low academic expectations and high moral standards that society set for young women.[14] Violeta attended the normal school for girls for roughly two years. She boarded there during the school week and spent weekends at her uncle's.

Impoverished and confining as her own studies may have been, Violeta was the indirect beneficiary of Nicanor's far more expansive academic and experiential opportunities. Nicanor visited her regularly on weekends, often in the company of one or more of his INBA cohort. When this happened, Violeta and her host family were temporarily integrated into the young men's world of creative explorations. They read poems, sang songs, and mounted theatrical productions, complete with makeshift sets, reminiscent of the ones the Parra siblings had staged under their father's direction as children.[15] These weekend gatherings were an early example of what would amount to a lifetime of brotherly tutelage where Nicanor would introduce Violeta into intellectual and artistic circles like the one he and his fellow "mythical ones" of the INBA formed that she would never have had access to otherwise.

Within the span of a few years in the 1930s, the rest of the Parra family joined Nicanor and Violeta in Santiago. The Parras thus participated in the massive migrations of the first decades of the twentieth century that dramatically transformed Chilean society from a predominantly rural one to one where a majority of the population lived in urban centers of 200,000 or more by the late 1930s.[16] This migratory process was advancing at a steady flow in the 1910s when Violeta's mother migrated from the rural hamlet of Malloa to the provincial capital of Chillán. It turned into a flood when an economic crisis struck the nation—and world—in the late 1920s and 1930s.

Santiago was the preferred destination of the migrants. Its population burgeoned from 270,000 to 700,000 between 1900 and 1930, with much of the increase due to internal migration.[17] The Parra family's migration pattern of the oldest son "pulling" one sibling, then another, and eventually the entire family was also a standard practice. Eduardo was the next sibling after Violeta to move to the capital, arriving in 1934. Nicanor arranged for him to stay with an aunt and enrolled him in INBA. Clarisa and most of the rest of the family soon followed. They moved into a house that Nicanor rented for them in the working-class barrio of Matucana.

It was around this time that Violeta made the anticonventional decision to drop out of teacher-training school and resume her musical career. Her actions responded at least in part to economic exigencies. With the Chilean economy still reeling from the effects of global crisis, her family's financial situation in Santiago remained precarious at best despite Nicanor's valiant efforts, and Violeta surely felt the obligation to help out. No doubt she was also fleeing the cloistered life at the normal school for girls.[18] This was dull and regimented compared with the intensity and independence of the perform-ing lifestyle she had inducted herself into at an early age. It is also entirely possible that Violeta had never wanted to become a primary school teacher in the first place.

Nicanor was surprised and initially disappointed by his sister's decision to drop out of school. His feelings were soon compounded when Eduardo, who disliked boarding school life as much as or more than Violeta, deliberately flunked out of INBA on her advice at the end of his second year.[19] The for-mer pupils moved in with their mother, and the musical foursome of Hilda, Violeta, Roberto, and Eduardo were reunited at last. The siblings soon landed their first gig at the working-class bar La Popular. They performed as much out of necessity as by inclination. As Hilda put it, "We needed to earn our living one way or another, and in those days things weren't very easy, espe-cially since the only thing we knew how to do was sing."[20]

The Music Scene

The Parra siblings resumed their musical pursuits during the heyday of Santiago's live music scene, lasting roughly from the 1930s through the 1940s. The varied roster of acts in vogue included Cuban *rumberas*, Spanish and Brazilian dancers, French songsters, singers of Argentine tangos, tropical boleros, and Mexican rancheras, along with every kind of orchestra and band—Viennese, folk, jazz, tropical, and huaso. A musician active in the era reminisced that there were some 300 Santiago venues where musicians could work seven nights a week, many of which featured rotating sets of jazz bands and folkloric ensembles. Musicians could work from two in the afternoon until early the next morning. Most performed for multiple establishments on any given day.[21]

The Parra musicians swiftly inserted themselves into this vibrant scene, where they found plenty of work. Eduardo attributed their good fortune to the large number of rural migrants in the capital: "We performed in cantinas that would fill up with *huasos*, people from the countryside, and they asked for this music."[22] The musical siblings' prospects were also enhanced by the nationalist cultural policies enacted by the Center-Left reformist governments in power in the 1940s, especially the law mandating that all live music venues include Chilean acts in their lineup.[23]

At first, the Parra siblings performed close to home in the bars and tav-erns of their Matucana barrio—*boliches* (dives) like El Tordo Azul, El Túnel, and the appropriately named La Popular. These venues were *popular* in the Latin American sense of the term as pertaining to the "popular sectors" or the working class; they were frequented by blue-collar workers along with that rare delegation of escaped INBA pupils or more mature writers and artists in search of a bohemian thrill. On weekends, the siblings performed at various *quintas de recreo*, rustic open-air restaurants on the city's outskirts that attracted Chilean families from across the class spectrum. Or they toured the small towns and landed estates that surrounded the capital with their half sister and brother-in-law's Argentine Circus. They found abundant seasonal work performing the cuecas and tonadas of música típica during the month of September, when popular consumption of this musical genre expands dramatically due to the festivities marking Chilean Independence Day of September 18. When Violeta and Hilda began making a name for themselves as Las Hermanas Parra in the late 1940s, they were able to pick up additional work at some of the ritzier venues in downtown Santiago that were frequented by affluent society.

On the opposite end of the social scale from the downtown nightclubs in terms of propriety, though not necessarily clientele, brothels were yet another type of establishment where at least some of the Parra musicians found gainful employment. Sexual commerce was legal, though morally condemned, in Chile during the first half of the twentieth century. Numerous brothels—or "houses of tolerance," as government officials and social reformers alike euphemistically called them—functioned in Santiago and other parts of the country at the time. Many if not most of the brothels offered live music as part of their fare.[24] Roberto Parra is known to have worked as a brothel musician for years. Eduardo, for sure, did so as well as did likely others of their musical brothers at one point or another in their respective careers.[25] For their part, Violeta and Hilda had performed—albeit unwittingly—at one or two of such establishments as "truly innocent kids" in Chillán, and some of the clubs where Violeta performed as an adult, if not brothels per se, provided much the same services.

The Parra siblings performed together in various configurations from the mid-1930s through the 1940s and in many instances beyond. Sometimes Hilda, Violeta, Roberto, and Eduardo performed as a quartet, other times as duos or trios, and on rare occasions as soloists. Most often, Violeta paired up with Hilda, and Eduardo with Roberto. The siblings thus continued two Chilean performance traditions: that of family members performing together as duos or larger ensembles; and that of musical acts consisting of performers of the same sex, a practice that both reflected and reinforced the gender distinctions that permeated their profession.

Brothers and sisters alike alternated their stage dress depending on the nature of their performance. When they were hired to perform for the celebrations commemorating Chile's independence from Spain or other patriotic events, they wore the *típica* (typical, folkloric) costume assigned to their gender: the huaso outfit of ponchos and spurs for the brothers, and the *huasa* (female counterpart of the huaso) outfit of flowery dresses with white laced aprons for the sisters (see figure 2.1). For their regular gigs in barrooms and clubs, Eduardo and Roberto donned the standard attire for male musicians of the era of jackets and ties—equally appropriate for bar or brothel—and Violeta and Hilda wore everyday clothing.[26] After the sisters' duo became more successful, they performed in fashionable dresses that they purchased secondhand. Their attire was elegant yet demure. It coded the sisters as "respectable women" and thereby differentiated them from other categories of women performers—cabaret singers, burlesque dancers—for whom sexual display was a defining feature of their act.[27]

For their repertoire, the Parra siblings revived the música criolla that had been their mainstay on the streets of Chillán, updated and expanded to include the latest "hits." The Spanish-language popular songbook of the 1930s and 1940s was largely the product of a booming record industry, reinforced and amplified by two new forms of mass media: radio and a no-longer-silent cinema.

Radio's expansion during these decades was "simply spectacular" in Chile and across the globe. The first radio station had gone on air in Santiago in 1923. By the 1930s, hundreds of stations were broadcasting news programs, popular music, and radio-theater the length of the country.

Sound cinema's contemporaneous global expansion was equally staggering. Many of the first sound movies produced anywhere in the world were musicals. Chile imported musicals from Mexico and Argentina throughout the 1930s and 1940s. The nascent Chilean film industry soon developed its own version of the genre; modeled after its Mexican and Argentine counterparts, it replaced the Mexican rancheras and Argentine tangos with Chilean cuecas and tonadas performed by the likes of Chilean música típica diva Ester Soré or the huaso band Los Cuatro Huasos. Although Chilean musicals never achieved the pan–Latin American distribution of the more robust Mexican and Argentine film industries, they were immensely popular within Chile itself. It goes without saying that the viewership of Hollywood exports vastly outnumbered the combined viewership of all Spanish-language cinema, musicals and dramas, national and imported.[28]

Together, the record industry, radio, and cinema shaped popular tastes in music and, by extension, the Parras' repertoire. The siblings performed tropical boleros, Mexican corridos, Argentine tangos, and Chilean tonadas and cuecas. "Whatever the public asked for" is how Hilda described it.[29] They learned many of the songs they performed through the same mass media channels as their public. The young and talented Violeta, who was already on her way to becoming a prolific songwriter, enhanced their sets with original numbers composed within these popular song styles. She wrote to-nadas and cuecas, the defining song styles of Chilean música típica, and songs in styles associated with other Latin American countries or regions such as corridos (Mexico), valses (Peru), and boleros (the Caribbean).[30] Her most popular number was a Cuban-inspired guaracha called "Funicular."[31]

The fate of this guaracha and many of the other songs that Violeta composed during this period serves to illustrate the concept of anti-materials. A dozen or so of the songs appear on a series of singles that Violeta and Hilda recorded as Las Hermanas Parra in the late 1940s and early 1950s and are thus preserved. The lyrics of a few others have been recovered from Violeta's note-books.[32] The majority of Violeta's original songs from this stage in her artis-tic trajectory have apparently been lost to posterity. The guaracha "Funicular," for instance, is nowhere to be found.

Though this state of affairs stems in part from the throwaway nature of the early Chilean recording industry, it was also much of Parra's own making. When Parra reinvented herself as a folklorista in the early 1950s, she drew a line between those of her compositions that were "serious," and that she there-fore retained in her repertoire, and those that were "trivial" and that she therefore discarded.[33] While in her twenties and early thirties, Parra did not base her repertoire on the idealized criteria that she would later adhere to as a folklorista, of "serious" versus "trivial," "traditional" versus "fashionable," "Chilean" versus "foreign." She assessed the value of the songs she composed and performed by their potential to earn her a living. She and her siblings played "whatever the public asked for."

Music and Sexual Politics

The musical career that the Parra siblings chose—or perhaps that chose them—was by no means an easy one. The work was poorly paid and its pace grueling, as they had to perform at several venues on any given night in order to earn the semblance of a living wage. When the sisters began performing as a duo at more fashionable clubs, their pay scale and work conditions improved somewhat, but their workload remained just as hectic, if not more so.

Additionally, some of the establishments where the Parras performed were seedier than others. In contrast to the more heterosocial downtown clubs or family-oriented quintas de recreo, the bars and taverns where they played most nights catered to a predominantly male and oftentimes down-and-out clientele. In these locales, the effects of alcohol could combine with the pres-sures of economic hard times to make for sleazy and at times menacing work environments. In his biography in verse, *Mi hermana Violeta Parra—Su vida y obra en décimas* (My Sister Violeta Parra—Her Life and Work in Décimas),

Eduardo Parra recounts in poetic detail the altercations and straight-out brawling that he, Violeta, and Hilda got caught up in while working as barroom musicians.[34]

The potential dangers of the profession were multiplied for women. Beyond routinely low wages and whirlwind work schedules, women singers faced the added challenge of sexual harassment, especially in those instances when they performed without a male relative present to "protect" their honor. Sexual harassment was a constant hazard for all working women in Chilean patriarchal society, no matter their occupation. In the case of women performers, its risk was heightened by two interrelated circumstances: first, that both women singers and prostitutes earned their living in entertainment; and, second, that the two professions were historically associated to some degree.[35]

Parra illustrates how sexual harassment or the threat of far worse factored into her line of work in a series of graphic poems from her autobiography in verse. They are set in one particularly questionable establishment, which she refers to alternatively as a "cantina," "bar," "restaurant," and "convent," where she worked "unwillingly (*sin ganas*)" for a measly forty pesos a week. The "convent," though perhaps not officially a brothel, was frequented by pimps, prostitutes, and the prostitutes' clientele. Parra felt unsafe performing there, especially "In the early morning hours / When the meanest and most vicious / Gang was on the prowl" (*a l'hora 'e la madrugá' / cuando estaba la gallá' / más peligrosa y malina*). She would sing extra loudly in order to drown out their "cheeky remarks" regarding matters "from the waist down." In the harshest poem of the sequence, she decries the rape and murder of a woman named Teresa, a crime that Parra claims took place only a few blocks from the bar.[36]

The "convent" represented the dregs of the varied places where Parra performed. Others of the bars and restaurants were veritable hubs for a buoyant working-class sociability, thanks in no small part to the festive ambience that the Parra musicians helped create through their music. By all accounts, Violeta thrived in these settings, on and off stage. The owner of the bar La Popular recalled Violeta as a lively and energetic young woman of good character who was also "good for a fight" if need be. She confirmed that men at her bar liked to flatter Violeta with compliments, and she claimed that Parra was somewhat of a flirt herself, though the bar owner was quick to add that Parra would not put up with any nonsense.[37] In short, the bar owner saw Parra as a vivacious performer who took pleasure in her work, was well liked by her public, and knew how to stand up for herself when needed.

Alongside its considerable challenges, then, Parra's musical career allowed her satisfaction and freedom that she would have had difficulty attaining had she devoted herself to more conventional women's work. There is perhaps no more vivid example of this than Parra's attendance at the after-parties held at Santiago's well-known brothel, La Carlina. In a 2004 interview with the newspaper *El Mercurio*, Eduardo Parra reminisced about the times when he, Violeta, Hilda, and Roberto would round off their long nights of gigging at La Carlina—where he could get the house discount if he wanted to "be with one of the girls."

Eduardo's comments appear as part of a longer article looking back on the Golden Age of the brothel. Named after its owner and matron, La Carlina was a favored haunt of politicians, intellectuals, writers, and musicians in mid-twentieth-century Santiago. The "house of tolerance" by definition tolerated and encouraged the licentious behavior of its male clients, no matter their creed. The reporter recounts an anecdote about one brothel regular, "an honorable senator from the most conservative party in the nation" who, when confronted by an old friend about his questionable hobby, shamelessly responded, "Well, I'm pious by day, and a tomcat by night."[38] La Carlina, together with its sister establishments, was probably the only enterprise in the era to offer steady and even preferential employment to men who were openly homosexual or to transgender people, as brothel proprietors deemed them less likely than cisgender male employees to become embroiled in dramas with the "girls."[39]

The brothel thus recalled the "world upside down" theme of the traditional poet-songs: it was a place where a woman governed, the pious were lewd, men dressed like women, the day began after midnight, and professional musicians played for the fun of it. Parra's exposure to the brothel's disinhibiting atmosphere may well have contributed to her own willingness and ability to break with social norms. Her casual witness to the moral hypocrisies of some and the drag performances of others might have made it easier for her to flaunt the rules that would govern women's proper behavior, or to act "like a man" when she so desired. Her recurrent exposure, in turn, to both the sexual commerce that was the institution's raison d'être and the sexual banter that accompanied it might account for the degree of her sexual assertiveness, unusual for women of her generation.

As a working musician, Parra regularly entered sites that functioned at the fringes or beyond the pale of respectability. Sometimes she did so unwillingly, as when she worked at the sordid "convent," other times willingly, as when she met up with her musician colleagues to "finish the fiesta" at La Carlina. Either way, Parra took whatever liberties her musical profession afforded her at far greater risk to her reputation than her brothers would ever have to face for comparable or greater transgressions. This was because in the reigning double standards of the era, a woman's honor was indivisibly linked to her sexual virtue. A man's was not. Eduardo's discounted purchase of sexual services, for instance, was considered morally inconsequential both in the moment of transaction and in that of his early twenty-first-century nostalgic disclosure to the reporter from *El Mercurio*, in accordance with the license implicit in the adage "Boys will be boys."[40] No comparable moral pass was issued to women.

First Marriage

Parra met the man who would become her first husband while performing at El Tordo Azul, one of several bars in the Matucana barrio that the Parra siblings regularly graced with their musical talents. Located across the street from the railroad yard, El Tordo Azul was a popular watering hole for railroad workers, Luis Cereceda among them. Parra was nineteen and Cereceda seventeen when the pair met and fell in love in 1937.[41] "Clang, clang, the bell is ringing / Rumbling in my heart / For the young railroad machinist / Who makes funny faces at me" (*Talán, talán, la campana / retumba en mi corazón / por el joven conductor / que me hace mil musarañas*), Parra would later write in her autobiographical décimas.[42] Cereceda, for his part, would later recount that Parra's singing had reminded him of the French chanteuse Edith Piaf.[43]

The couple married the following year. Their daughter Violeta Isabel Cereceda Parra was born the year after that on September 29, 1939. The young family moved frequently due to Cereceda's work, so the chronology of their marriage remains imprecise. They likely spent their first two years in Santiago. They resided in the Valparaíso region for the next few years, first in the port city of Valparaíso, where their son Luis Ángel Cereceda Parra was born in 1943, and then in the small town of Llay Llay, some fifty miles inland. The family returned to Santiago sometime in 1944. Jaime Cereceda, Luis Cereceda's son from a previous relationship, lived with them for several years over the duration of Parra and Cereceda's marriage.[44]

Luis Cereceda entered the state of matrimony with firm and traditional expectations about the gendered division of labor within it. He was therefore unhappy when Parra continued working as a musician for a stretch after they first got married. He put up with it, though, since the way he saw it, "when you're newlyweds, you get along better." Once the honeymoon phase was over, Cereceda asked that Parra stop performing; "I earned a good salary and there was no need [for her to work] so we decided that she would stay home" is how he explained it.[45]

Parra did in fact put her singing career on hold during the initial years of their marriage, though it is unclear whether this hiatus resulted from their mutual decision (Cereceda's "we"), her less mutual (and out of character) acquiescence to her husband's demand, or other factors, including unfamiliar cities and towns with no musician siblings in sight, and two pregnancies and then two young children in need of care and supervision. Most likely it was some combination of all the above. Regardless, Isabel's birth certificate lists her father's occupation as "worker" and her mother's as "none."[46]

Parra continued to sing and play her guitar around the house and at parties or community events in the various places where the family resided. She channeled her creative energies into writing poetry and even won honorable mention in a literary contest sponsored by the town of Quillota, outside of Valparaíso. For the most part, however, Parra recused herself from her musical career in the early years of her marriage to Cereceda and dedicated her time to more domestic tasks. "We lived a family life" is how Cereceda summarized it.[47]

Violeta de Mayo

Parra did not last long playing the role of traditional housewife. Her foray into Spanish music is a case in point. Spanish music, which had long been enjoyed in Chile, became even more popular and pervasive in the late 1930s with the influx of thousands of refugees from the Spanish Civil War. This was when Parra first became enamored with it.[48] By the mid-1940s, she had fashioned a decent career for herself singing and playing flamenco.

Violeta credited her brother Nicanor with encouraging her to pursue her interest in Spanish music beyond singing along to it on the radio.[49] She quickly mastered a repertoire of songs and dance styles—paso dobles, zambras, fandangos, sevillanas, farrucas—most of which fit under the generic label of "flamenco music." She learned songs from radio shows and recordings and even taught herself how to play the castanets—to the great irritation of those exposed to her incessant practicing.[50] Flamenco was also a musical area in which Violeta received some degree of formal instruction, as Isabel remembers attending classes with her mother at a dance academy run by the Spaniard Jesús López.[51]

The results of Parra's efforts were notable and swift. In 1944, she took first place in a singing contest at a gala organized by the Spanish community at Santiago's landmark Baqueadano Theater—a distinction all the more impressive as the twenty-some other competing artists were all from Spain.[52] The triumphant flamenco artist put her promising career on hold when her family moved to Valparaíso for Cereceda's work, then recommenced where she had left off upon their return to Santiago in 1946. In 1947, Parra made a guest appearance singing Spanish songs on Radio del Pacífico in what may have been her first radio performance. A positive notice in Ecran described Parra's voice as "exceptionally harmonic and strong" and wondered why she did not have her own program.[53]

In the custom of multigenerational performing families, Parra incorporated her children Isabel and Ángel into her flamenco act. The two generations of Parras appeared with the theater company of the Spanish actor and radio soap opera star Doroteo Martí, best known for his over-the-top dramatic productions. Violeta acted, sang, and played the guitar; Isabel sang and danced to her mother's accompaniment; and Ángel, who was four or five at the time, joined his mother and sister on stage to sing and dance in the show's grand finale. The family trio also landed a gig performing at teatime at the Casanova, a tearoom by day and nightclub by night in downtown Santiago.[54]

Violeta was a strict stage mother. Nicanor claimed she did not let Isabel and Ángel play like other children because they had to practice their Spanish songs and dances.[55] The children performed the material they rehearsed multiple times a week in shows that often lasted late into the night. Perhaps not surprisingly, both Isabel and Ángel would later speak of their experience as child performers in terms of "work."[56]

Parra performed as a flamenco artist for a little short of a decade. She chose the stage name Violeta de Mayo (Violet of the Month of May) for her act.[57] She is also purported to have adopted a Castilian accent to sing her Spanish repertoire.[58] A studio photo taken during this period shows Violeta and a young Isabel striking dramatic poses in matching flamenco costumes.[59] A promotional poster for a variety show that included "Violeta de Mayo" announced her as the "faithful interpreter of Spanish folklore."[60]

The irony that Parra's "faithful" interpretation of Spanish folklore involved her performing songs under a stage name, in full costume, and with an affected accent points to the reasons she would abandon her Spanish repertoire upon embarking on her career as a folklorista. Ángel claims that his mother's "rupture" with Spanish music occurred after she attended a performance by the flamenco dancer and international sensation Carmen Amaya, the "Queen of the Gypsies."[61] In a review of her 1950 show at Santiago's Municipal Theater, Spanish writer-in-exile Ramón Suárez Picallo praised Carmen Amaya for the purity of her flamenco interpretation, which he attributed to the fact that she was an authentic "artist by blood."[62] Even without having read Suárez's review, Parra would have surely grasped that authenticity was best acquired by birthright.[63] Following the same nativist logic with which she would later lay claim to the folklore of Chile "from the moment I was born," she would dismiss her almost decade-long performance of flamenco music as "so much nonsense."[64] She thereby relegated flamenco to her anti-materials, alongside her abandoned songbook of less-than-authentic originals such as her Cuban-inspired guaracha, "Funicular."

Political Unity, Marital Strife

In 1945, Parra, Cereceda, and their children returned to Santiago from Valparaíso in what would turn out to be their last move as a family. At first they stayed in a small apartment in the same complex where Cereceda's mother and extended family resided in the Quinta Normal neighborhood. After several unhappy months living in close proximity to her in-laws, Violeta moved her immediate family into a large *casa quinta* or "country house" that her brother Nicanor had rented in the barrio of Los Guindos (today La Reina). Parra siblings Nicanor, Violeta, and Eduardo and their respective spouses and children all lived together at the country house, which quickly became the preferred site for the entire Parra clan to convene.

The country house also became a gathering spot for Chilean artists and intellectuals along with the occasional international visitor. Cuban poet Nicolás Guillén came by to pay his regards.[65] So did Chilean poet, communist, and eventual Nobel Prize laureate (1971) Pablo Neruda, whose own residence was a few blocks away. Other Chilean writers, poets, and scholars who were frequent visitors included Tomás Lago, Enrique Lihn, Gonzalo Rojas, Pablo de Rokha, and Héctor Fuenzalida. Fuenzalida would later recall the Parra compound: it was like a "great circus tent that moves, with nothing fixed in place, with no specific style, with an ever abundance of Parras . . . coming and going . . . [all] innate strategists of cookouts, wine, and song." According to Fuenzalida, "the entire circus came to life under the loving care of the tremendous Violeta Parra."[66]

Violeta's residence in the country house, roughly from 1946 to 1948, represented another occasion when her brother and mentor ushered her into his cultural sphere. Many of the poets, writers, and artists who came calling for Nicanor would become Violeta's allies and, in some cases, lifelong friends. Pablo Neruda would host her debut recital as a folklorista in his home in the early 1950s; Tomás Lago would invite her to give a concert at the Museo de Arte Popular Americano (Museum of Folk Art of the Americas), of which he was founder and director; poet Enrique Lihn would collaborate with her on the scripts for her radio show, *Violeta Parra Sings*; professor and poet Gonzalo Rojas would hire her to teach classes on folk music at the University of Concepción; poet Pablo de Rokha would offer her expatriate companionship over a long Parisian winter.

Violeta's presence in her brother's predominantly male artistic circles sometimes produced gender unease among the other participants. Such was the case of country house visitor Héctor Fuenzalida. By his account, the "tremendous Violeta Parra," in addition to being caring, was nervous, loud, and domineering. She "drank like a man," ran the house like a "primitive chiefdom," and had risen to power by "exercising a man's authority."[67] Fuenzalida's charge that Parra was somehow "manlike" in her assertive behavior would be echoed by others across her lifetime. It reveals the entrenched prejudices that anticonventional women faced in the era (and beyond).

Parra's years as a young wife and mother in her twenties were full ones, with children, poetry, song, dance, and, for those years spent in Santiago, an extended network of family and friends to keep her occupied and inspired. They also represent the phase in her life when Parra engaged most intensely with the Chilean Communist Party, which was one of the strongest in the Western Hemisphere.

Parra's rank-and-file activism during her marriage to Cereceda was no doubt influenced by her husband's staunch militancy. Cereceda was active in the Communist Party (CP) itself, the railway workers union (a CP stronghold), and the CP-led Workers Federation of Chile (Federación Obrera de Chile or FOCH). According to Ángel, the three entities were for Cereceda what the holy trinity was for a Catholic, offering as proof the fact that his father installed a plaster relief of Stalin in their backyard "in the same way that others installed one of the Virgin of Lourdes."[68]

Parra supported the CP's political campaigns as a rank-and-file activist alongside her card-carrying husband during the years the couple were married. Cereceda's communist loyalties may have been one of the things that attracted Parra to him in the first place; her own sympathies for the party dated back to her youth in Chillán and would outlast their marriage.[69]

Parra and Cereceda had wed in 1938, the same year that Pedro Aguirre Cerda assumed the presidency of Chile at the head of the Popular Front, a coalition of centrist and leftist political parties, including the CP, akin to contemporaneous popular fronts in France and Spain. During Aguirre Cerda's time in office, the CP organized working-class neighborhood committees aimed at alleviating the widespread hunger produced by economic crisis. Parra pitched in by running a food distribution center out of the newlyweds' home. The party supplied her with basic staples, which she then sold at cost to neighborhood families.[70]

At the other end of their decade-long marriage, the activist couple worked on the 1946 presidential campaign of Gabriel González Videla, the chosen candidate of another broad-based political coalition that included the CP. (Once elected, González Videla would betray the CP by declaring it illegal under pressure from the United States.)[71] Parra and Cereceda turned their home into a quasi-official campaign headquarters for the neighborhood. Parra organized a committee of housewives in support of González Videla's bid for the presidency.[72] The "housewives" were barred from actually voting for their preferred candidate, however, since Chilean women would only win the right to participate in presidential elections in 1949.[73] It is worth noting—though hardly noteworthy—that Cereceda and Parra's core activities in support of the party, which in Parra's case were distributing food and organizing housewives, were considered suitable undertakings for communists of their respective genders.

Parra also showed her support for the party through poetry and song during this period, as she would continue to do over the remainder of her life. Her poem "Eulogía" (Eulogy) was published in the Communist Party daily, *El Siglo*, in February 1946. It pays homage to fallen young activist Ramona Parra (no relation), who was killed by police at a protest in support of miners earlier that year. In a published letter to the newspaper, Ramona Parra's parents gave thanks to various organizations for supporting them in their hour of grief, and also to "Miss Violeta Parra, poet of the workers, who honored [their daughter's] memory with such skill."[74] In 1947, Parra recited her poem dedicated to labor leader and founder of the Chilean Communist Party Luis Emilio Recabarren (1876–1924) at a May 1st rally commemorating International Workers' Day in Santiago.[75] A photo from around this time shows Parra singing and playing guitar on stage in front of a large crowd at an event organized by *El Siglo*.[76]

Parra and Cereceda were thus united in their shared—albeit differently weighted and gendered—activism in the Communist Party. Where the couple diverged was over how their marriage should work. With Violeta's reincorporation into the daily life of the Parra clan at their country house in Los Guindos, she had recommended performing with various combinations of her musician siblings. Her insistence on pursing an artistic career—or any career, for that matter—clashed with Cereceda's more traditional views on marriage. These were the same as those of his beloved party. Cereceda linked the dignity and rights of the worker—read male—to his ability to provide for his family. On the flip side, Cereceda firmly believed that Parra belonged at home, where she could find all of the sense of accomplishment she would ever need by fulfilling her duties as a loving housewife and mother. To his great disappointment and frustration, his wife detested the monotony of domestic life and proved unwilling to give up her musical profession.

Parra and Cereceda had other marital conflicts as well. Cereceda's drinking and infidelities and Parra's corresponding rage and recriminations were foremost among them. The couple's arguments became more and more frequent over the course of their marriage. A few turned violent. Isabel recounted how she returned home toward the end of her parents' marriage to find her mother sobbing at the kitchen table with a gash on her head and her father nowhere to be found.[77] Ángel attested that his mother was often the instigator of the spouses' physical altercations, where she gave as good as she got: "She was like a lioness," Ángel claimed in an interview. "If she was in a big fight with her husband, she would give him a few well-aimed slaps on the face. And if she encountered resistance, she would grab whatever was at hand." "This is what happened with my father," Ángel stated, noting further that it also happened with Violeta's second husband.[78]

Under the circumstances, it should come as no surprise that Cereceda's "we"—as in "We decided that [Violeta] would stay home" and "We lived a family life"—lasted only a decade, and a rocky one at that. Cereceda later recounted the demise of their marriage as follows: he would return home, exhausted after a long day's work, only to find Parra out performing at some bar or another, until one night he finally had had enough and told her, "Very well, go on with your art. I'm out of here." And he packed up his things and left.[79]

On her end, Parra blamed their marriage's failure on Cereceda's complete lack of appreciation for her artistry. She further accused him of wanting not a *compañera* (comrade), but a maid.[80] She would devote one décima out of the ninety-six that make up her autobiography in verse to her marriage with him. She dismisses it as "ten years of hell." She ends the poem in defiant third person:

After ten years had passed
And I was skin and bones
The cinch wrapped three times round,
The reins were cut at last
And so to regain my path
Again I took up the guitar;
Forcefully Violeta Parra
Two kids on her back, the trio
Departed for Maitencillo[81]
To cut the ties that bound her.

A los diez años cumplí'os
por fin se corta la güincha,
tres vueltas daba la cincha
al pobre esqueleto mío,
y pa' salvar el sentí'o
volví a tomar la guitarra;
con fuerza Violeta Parra
y al hombro con dos chiquillos,
se fue para Maitencillo
a cortarse las amarras.[82]

Second Marriage

Parra's marriage to Cereceda all but over, she and the children moved back in with her mother. Remaining in the country house in La Reina was no longer an option, as Nicanor had left to study cosmology for two years at Oxford University and Eduardo and Violeta could not afford the rent. According to Hilda, Violeta was "deadly sad" over her separation from Cereceda. Her siblings tried to console her by telling her that everything was going to be fine, that she should just leave him for good, and that together they would form a band and find work.[83]

Bolstered by their reassurances, and with the added incentive of two children to support, Violeta began gigging in earnest again. She performed her flamenco act at the bar El Túnel, where she was followed by her brother Oscar and his comedy routine.[84] She sang with Hilda accompanied by their younger brother Lautaro at the No Me Olvides restaurant. The sisters performed at the popular quinta de recreo Las Brisas, whose owner was kind enough to provide them with a cot backstage so they could rest between sets.[85] They performed at the succession of restaurants that their mother opened in Barrancas, a poor neighborhood on the outskirts of Santiago—including the restaurant El Sauce, the site of Violeta's interview with her first folkloric "source" Rosa Lorca in the early 1950s.[86]

In the meantime, Cereceda made his way back to the small town of Llay Llay from where he would send Parra their children's monthly allowance, though the legally required amount he provided proved woefully insufficient.[87] The two exes would maintain contact and, as wounds healed, a friendship that endured over the years.

As all those who knew her would confirm—and at the risk of sounding trite—Parra was a passionate woman. She rarely found herself uninvolved in some sort of romantic relationship over the course of her adult life. Within a year of her separation from Cereceda, she had moved in with the man who would become her second husband: another Luis, last name Arce.

Arce was the son of a neighborhood woman who sold high-end second-hand clothing out of her home. Arce and Parra's paths crossed when she visited his mother in search of a "new" used outfit to perform in. He was seventeen at the time and therefore fourteen years younger than Parra, who was then thirty-one. It was an age gap that was notable chiefly, if not solely, because the woman constituted the older party in their relationship, contrary to customary patriarchal arrangements.

Neither Parra nor Arce appeared overly concerned with the age gap. They courted briefly, then moved in together in 1949. The couple were legally married in 1953 after the annulment of Parra's first marriage finally went through.[88]

They would have two daughters together, Carmen Luisa (born August 26, 1950) and Rosa Clara (born September 22, 1954).[89] Their marriage would not survive the tragic death of Rosa Clara within a year of her birth, while Parra was away on her first trip to Europe.

Parra's second marriage, first de facto and then de jure, proved very different from her first. Arce supported Parra's artistic activities wholeheartedly and had few, if any, ambitions of his own. According to Ángel, his stepfather approached work with "disciplined irregularity," and spent a significant portion of his free time in the pool hall.[90] The family first lived in the apartment above the Arce family's upholstery business, which they shared with Arce's widowed mother and sisters. They then moved to a nearby apartment and, later, to the outlying community of La Cisterna in Santiago's southern sector.

For income, Parra continued to perform with various combinations of siblings, while Arce worked as an upholsterer. Parra attempted diverse strategies to supplement what little the couple brought in from their respective occupations. She rose before dawn to make and sell *sopaipillas* (a traditional fried pastry) in front of their home to passing workers. She acquired a corner store with the financial backing of her mother-in-law, then delegated its day-to-day operations to the young Isabel and Ángel, resulting in it closing soon after it opened, as might be expected.[91] Despite all of Parra's efforts, some more well thought out than others, the family's economic situation at the time was "stretched thin," in Isabel's words.[92]

Violeta's troubles went beyond whatever financial woes her family was facing. She showed an initial warning sign around this time of what would become a lifelong battle with depression. The incident occurred in the late 1940s or early 1950s, when Parra was in her early thirties. Amparo Claro, who was only a teenager at the time, was a young witness to Parra's struggles. Parra was friends with Claro's mother, who in addition to being a client of Arce's upholstery business admired and supported Parra's musical talents. Claro would later recall the time that her mother took Parra in and cared for her for several days after Parra had cut her wrists. According to Claro, who would herself become Parra's friend in the 1960s, that was when she and her mother realized that "[Parra] had a tendency toward suicide. It was dreadful."[93]

Las Hermanas Parra (The Parra Sisters)

In 1952, Parra put together a traveling revue, in part to generate some much-needed income and in part to better incorporate Arce into her creative life. She named the revue *Estampas de América* (Postcards of the Americas). Parra was its artistic director and Arce, who was lacking in stage talents, its manager. The rest of the troupe consisted of Hilda, Hilda's circus artist husband, a comedian, a singer, a magician, and several dancers, for a grand total of twelve adults and an unknown number of children. The company's first and only tour was partly subsidized by the Center-Left reformist government in power at the time, which covered half of the expenses in exchange for the artists' willingness to carry chilenidad (Chilean-ness, Chilean identity) into the remote mining region of northern Chile—though given the show's name and eclectic content, the chilenidad of its fare appears to have been somewhat dubious.

The troupe lost two thirds of its members halfway through the tour to arguments over pay. With the cast stripped down to the Parra sisters and their husbands and children, its artistic director resorted to her "everything-ist" training in the circo pobre (poor circus) to come up with enough new material to stretch the show out to its requisite two hours. Parra is even purported to have danced the mambo—an apparent first and last in a long and diverse performing career.[94]

The failed *Postcards of the Americas* traveling revue was really just a sideline to Violeta and Hilda's increasingly popular duo, Las Hermanas Parra (see figure 2.1).[95] By the time Las Hermanas Parra began to take off in the late 1940s, duos and trios of sisters performing folk music together were an established feature of Chile's music scene, akin to if not as ubiquitous as the huaso bands. Like the huaso bands, the folkloric sister acts drew on the traditional singing and instrumentation (harp and guitars) of the rural women singers of Chile's Central Valley but modernized them to appeal to an urban audience.[96] To complicate matters (and because musical categories are famously porous), the folkloric sister acts' performance style overlapped with and was at times indistinguishable from that of other women singers who fronted huaso bands and who were labeled música típica artists.

Las Hermanas Parra quickly became one of the more in-demand folkloric sister acts of the late 1940s and early 1950s. In addition to their regular gigs in working-class dives and weekend performances at the quintas de recreo on the city's outskirts, they moved up into some of the more fashionable downtown establishments that catered to a predominantly well-to-do clientele.[97] They played the Casanova, the same venue where Violeta de Mayo performed flamenco with her children at teatime, whose prestigious evening shows were headlined by some of Chile's most well-known performers and on occasion international touring artists such as a Mexican or Venezuelan bolero star or the US African American dancer and "exotic" sensation Josephine Baker.[98] Las Hermanas Parra also performed regularly at the trending *music hall*, the Patio Andaluz.[99]

Hilda would later retrace a typical workday-night for the sisters during the duo's stint of success: "We sang in the usual boliches in Matucana; from there

Figure 2.1
Las Hermanas Parra.
Originally published in
Vea, February 9, 1967.

we went to [the neighborhood of] Franklin, to an establishment called El
Banco, where all the slaughterhouse workers hang out. . . . Afterward we went
to the Rancho Grande. . . . From there to La Nave . . . and the Casanova. . . .
And we still had the energy to go to another venue . . . called El Ensayo. And
from El Ensayo to the Patio Andaluz, which was the biggest and grandest
[club] in those years. . . . In short, we played everywhere."[100]

Hand in hand with their entrance into some of Santiago's classier entertainment venues, Las Hermanas Parra made headway into the expanding
world of mass media. The duo appeared regularly on Radio Agricultura's
popular program, *Rapsodía Panamericana* (Pan-American Rhapsody).
Promoted under the slogan "Greetings from the Land of Mexico," the show
is credited with helping to popularize Mexican music in Chile. Its format
alternated Las Hermanas Parra's live performance with recorded numbers by

Mexican song luminaries such as Agustín Lara, Pedro Vargas, and Jorge Negrete.[101] The duo performed on several other radio programs as well, including *Fiesta Linda* (Beautiful Fiesta) on Radio Corporación, which in 1950 proudly proclaimed itself the most powerful broadcasting system in all Latin America and the first to reach the entire length of Chile.[102]

In addition to their radio appearances, Las Hermanas Parra recorded several singles for the Chilean subsidiary of RCA Victor in the early 1950s, only three of which survive today.[103] In both their form and content, the Parra sisters' recordings resembled those of other folkloric sister acts (and música típica women artists) of the era. They feature Violeta and Hilda on vocals accompanied by unidentified studio musicians on a variety of instruments—guitars, harp, accordion, piano, bass, and tambourine. Half of the songs from the three surviving singles are cuecas. As such, they incorporate the *sketch* and *animación* (literally, "animation") that are requisite performative elements of recorded cuecas: the first consisting of a short audio skit in order to help fill the track, as the cueca format is very short in duration; and the second, shouted phrases that are intended to "animate" the singers.[104] The remaining songs are romantic numbers in the popular musical genres of vals, corrido, and tonada.

Las Hermanas Parra did stand out from other folkloric sister acts (and música típica women artists) in two aspects. First, all but one of the songs they recorded are Violeta originals.[105] Second, their voices, and particularly Violeta's, had a less trained, rougher quality than those of most of their colleagues. Violeta would stand out from her cohort of traditionalist folk singers in the mid-1950s and 1960s for precisely the same reason.

Las Hermanas Parra's radio appearances and recordings granted them access to a national audience that would have seemed inconceivable when they first began making the rounds of the working-class bars of Matucana in the mid-1930s. Even as the mass entertainment industry opened up new possibilities, it was hardly a panacea. The duo's rising popularity did not necessarily translate into monetary gain, as most of their club gigs and radio work continued to pay poorly, and as they received only a pittance in royalties for the albums they sold.[106]

The industry also placed substantial barriers to the duo's continued ascension. This was because "beauty," long a factor in show business, would play an ever more influential role in the prospective careers of women performers over the course of the twentieth century, in accordance with the increasing visuality of the entertainment industry. In an interview with Chile's most important entertainment magazine, *Ecran*, the glamorous film star and música típica singer Ester Soré, whose nickname was La Negra Linda (Darling Beauty), offered precise quotients for the formula for a successful musical career: "I believe that an artist's appeal breaks down as follows: 50% of her performance . . . depends on her physique; 25% . . . on her voice, and the other 25% . . . on the charm that she radiates out to her audience."[107]

The same formula that lifted up "Darling Beauty" would thwart the careers of an unknown number of talented women performers whose physical appearance did not satisfy the beauty equation of the era—Hilda and Violeta among them. Neither sister embodied the Europeanized beauty standards of the Hollywood film idols who graced *Ecran*'s covers, nor did the sisters possess what was widely regarded as the homegrown beauty of Ester Soré.[108] In the case of Violeta in particular, the consensus was that she was at best not attractive, at worst just plain ugly. To further compound matters, Violeta often failed to put the thought or care into her appearance that was expected of a woman in her profession—perhaps in defeat, perhaps in defiance, or perhaps because she was simply uninterested.[109] Bottom line, Parra possessed neither the conventional beauty nor the suitable disposition to be star material in the music industry, regardless of the breadth of her talents.

Not one to be easily defeated, Parra proposed her own anti-conventional beauty equation for success in her autobiography in verse. Inverting the negative value of "ugly" to a positive, she celebrates her good fortune of having been spared the humiliations or worse that "beautiful" women are forced to endure in their pursuit of a musical career:

I give thanks to God that I'm ugly
And have well-established habits,
If not what strange distractions
Might enter into the struggle . . .
Singing is beautifully wondrous,
And better still with a guitar, . . .
Without cosmetics or pretense
The songstress can undertake
To sing to the dawning day
Like the little sparrow does.

Gracias a Dios que soy fea
y de costumbres bien claras,
de no, qué cosas más raras
entraran en la pelea. . . .
Cantar es lindo deleite,
mucho mejor con guitarra, . . .
sin mañas y sin afeites
puede llegar la cantora,
cantarle a la blanca aurora
como lo hace el chincolito.[110]

The many challenges of their profession notwithstanding, Las Hermanas Parra were gaining in popularity by the early 1950s. They even landed a contract with Odeon Chilena, rival recording label of RCA Victor. Violeta was nonetheless being called in a different direction. Even as she kept pace with the duo's full calendar of club gigs, radio shows, and recording sessions, she had commenced her parallel labors of collecting and performing the songs that would catapult her to the forefront of the 1950s Chilean folk revival.

Violeta tried to meld her simultaneous musical projects by convincing Hilda to include a few of the songs she collected into the sisters' repertoire of more commercialized tonadas, cuecas, and valses, but Hilda would have none of it. As Hilda explained, "We couldn't promote or sing [folklore] in the popular bars where we worked. We just couldn't. We had to sing whatever the public asked for. If they asked for a Mexican song, then we had to sing a Mexican song, to keep our audience and employers happy. People just didn't get folklore."[111]

Then in 1953, Las Hermanas Parra's promising career careened to a halt when Violeta broke up the duo in anger after Hilda accepted a gig without her. What happened was this: The popular band Las Torcazas needed someone who could sing harmony for their upcoming performance at an international fair. Hilda informed Violeta of Las Torcazas' invitation, and Violeta warned Hilda that either the band hire both sisters or the duo was over. Hilda, who needed the money, ignored her sister's threat and took the job anyway, and the furious Violeta made good on her promise.[112] Her rage was so great that she refused to work with Hilda to fulfill the duo's contractual obligation to Odeon Chilena and substituted her daughter Isabel, then thirteen, in her place.

Violeta would eventually forgive Hilda and the two sisters would remain lifelong friends. They often sang together informally over the years and would reunite to make another recording as Las Hermanas Parra in 1958. As Ángel noted, "they got along marvelously; they liked to sing as a duo; and why not admit it, they felt the economic necessity to do so."[113]

The dissolution of Las Hermanas Parra marked a definitive turning point in Violeta's artistic trajectory, away from commercially oriented, pan–Latin American genres of music and toward traditional music and the authentic. Though the consensus of all those who were close to her at the time is that she broke up the duo for personal reasons, Violeta herself would not acknowledge as much, at least not publicly. At first, she simply avoided the question. As her reputation as a folklorista grew, she attributed the sisters' parting of ways to ideologically driven creative differences; she had tried to incorporate the traditional songs that she had learned as a child in Malloa into the duo's

repertoire, but Hilda had vetoed the idea. This, in turn, had led Violeta to conclude that "musically speaking . . . we were no longer on the same path."[114] In
the ensuing years, Violeta's formidable production as a folklorista, songwriter,
and visual artist would eclipse whatever passing triumphs she had had with
the more commercially oriented Las Hermanas Parra. When this occurred,
she would downplay or omit her prolonged career performing "whatever the
public asked for" in accounts of her life and work. At last in full possession of
her authentic self, it had become immaterial or, better put, anti-material.

It is easy to draw a direct line between Parra's childhood years in the south of
Chile and her overlapping future careers as a folklorista, songwriter, composer, and visual artist that would eventually bring her international fame.
Parra would effectively do just that in every biographical interview she granted.
It is more problematic to connect the musical activities that consumed much
of her time from her 1933 arrival in Santiago at age fifteen to the breakup of
the Parra sisters' duo in 1953 with her accomplishments later in life. From her
standpoint as a leader of the Chilean traditionalist folk revival of the 1950s,
she would reject the pan–Latin American songbook of música criolla—with
its corridos, valses, tangos, and guarachas, covers or original—that had helped
sustain her from her preadolescence in Chillán through the following two
decades. She would also dismiss her more recently acquired flamenco repertoire. More damning than their "foreign" origins, the popularity and immense
reach of these imported musical styles were widely perceived as threatening
Chilean oral traditions with extinction.

Yet these were precisely the types of songs that Parra performed for years—
in the bars of Matucana, in the quintas de recreo on Santiago's outskirts, at
teatime at the Casanova and other upscale downtown clubs, on tour with
the *Postcards of the Americas* revue, and on the radio and recordings of Las
Hermanas Parra. Parra devoted her creative energies to these varied activities because she was good at them and needed the money and, simply and
undeniably, because she wanted to.

If there is a thread that ties this earlier chapter in Parra's creative life back
to her childhood and forward to the folklorista and multifaceted artist that
she would become, it is Parra's determination to make her own way. As a child,
Parra had learned courage and resourcefulness from having to fend for herself and her family and from the everything-ist improvisations of her time
in the family circus. In her twenties and thirties, she built up her endurance
through the routine practice that her work as a musician afforded her at com-
manding an audience and standing up for herself in the male-dominated

and often rowdy bars of Santiago. She drew strength from her extended family and network of fellow musicians. She was encouraged by her brother Nicanor Parra and inspired by the circle of artists and intellectuals that she was invited to enter in as his sister. She was softened by love and hardened by her experiences of surviving a failed marriage and the perceived betrayal of her sister. She would approach the next stages of her life as an artist with equal passion and resolve.

Chapter 3

Folklorista

In early 1957, Chilean writer Jorge Edwards penned a feature article on Violeta Parra for the Chilean women's magazine *Eva*. Then thirty-nine, the folklorista was recently returned from a lengthy European sojourn where she had introduced her European public to Chilean folklore. Of far weightier import than her success abroad, Parra had "revealed our own folklore to ourselves," a feat that was only made possible thanks to her "untiring investigation and absolutely accurate instinct for what is authentically of and by the people." Edwards went on to summarize what were fast becoming the indispensable elements of Parra's biography as a folklorista—her musician father, campesina mother, and time spent with the Aguilera sisters in the rural hamlet of Malloa. After passing mention of the duo she had formed with her sister and the artistic differences that led to its demise, Edwards writes, "It was from that moment forward that Violeta Parra's true career began: she not only performs the songs from her childhood along with new ones that she has composed in the folk style, but she labors tirelessly at collecting our folklore. By herself, in a short space of time and with no official assistance of any kind, she has been able to accomplish more in regard to the actual dissemination of Chilean folklore than many of the institutions that specialize in that area have been able to do in combination."[1]

As Edwards attests, Parra's rise as a folklorista was precipitous. In the slightly over three-year period between the breakup of Las Hermanas Parra in late 1953 and his 1957 article, Parra coproduced and cohosted the radio show *Violeta Parra Sings*; was interviewed in Chile's premier entertainment magazine *Ecran*; recorded her first solo album as a folklorista on the record label Odeon Chilena; and won the Caupolicán Award for best folklorista of 1954 (awarded June 1955). On the wings of her laurels, she traveled to Europe, where she participated in the 1955 World Festival of Youth and Students in Warsaw, Poland; toured Czechoslovakia; and performed on radio and television and made several recordings over an extended period in Paris and a brief stay in London. She continued to work at breakneck pace upon her return to Chile in late 1956 through the remainder of the decade, recording four more albums of folk music for Odeon; founding a museum of folk art in the southern city of Concepción; and performing in countless concerts, radio appearances, and other events.

The scope of her activities and the recognition they earned her lend weight to Edwards's contention that Violeta Parra had finally found her "true" career when she became a folklorista. Other admirers, in his time and since, have voiced similar sentiments. Some take Edwards's assertion even further: for them, Parra's emergence as a folklorista marks the moment when Violeta Parra became Violeta Parra.[2] This sweeping judgment would not appear to be based on the intensity of Parra's efforts or the depth of her talents, which had been and would remain consistent over the course of her rich and varied life as a performer. Rather, the magnitude of this claim reflects the radical nature of the change in course of her professional and artistic trajectory.

Parra was hardly alone in her interest in folklore. She was part of a small but influential cohort of Chilean folkloristas active across the 1950s into the 1960s and in many cases beyond. The folkloristas undertook their project of folk revival propelled by cultural nationalism and a sense of impending peril; they firmly believed that there existed a "true" and untouched folklore in Chile awaiting their discovery and that this folklore was under attack on all fronts.[3] They considered themselves the last line of resistance in what Parra declared a "battle in defense of our authentic music."[4] In their interlocking practice of definition and defense of tradition, they contributed to the ideological struggle over chilenidad or what it meant to be Chilean in their era.

Folk Revival

Chile has a long tradition of folklore studies, dating back to the beginning of the twentieth century and maintained ever since at varying degrees of intensity.[5] It was home to the first folklore society in Latin America, the Chilean Folklore Society, established in 1909. The organization's distinguished members collected and categorized folkloric artifacts such as songs, folktales, and broadsides of traditional poetry (lira popular), held conferences, and published their findings in scholarly journals and monographs. After this initial burst of activity, the field remained somewhat stagnant until 1943, when it took on renewed vigor with the founding of the Institute for Folk Music Research at the University of Chile (Instituto de Investigaciones del Folklore Musical). The institute supported fieldwork, archiving, courses, publications, concerts, radio shows, and the first commercial recordings devoted to folk music.

The efforts of the institute and other like-minded academic organizations and individuals were complemented by the educational and cultural policies of the Center-Left reformist governments in power at the time aimed at fostering a civic sense of national cultural identity among the citizenry.[6] These policies included the use of folklore in schools and other official settings and the passage of laws requiring that Chilean artists be featured on radio programs and at entertainment venues. A decree passed in 1945, for example, mandated that 30 percent of radio programming must consist of "live acts and of Chilean music," and that 80 percent of the artists performing must be Chilean.[7] The Department of Information and Culture (Dirección de Informaciones y Cultura or DIC) also organized concerts and other cultural events and subsidized touring companies that were willing to carry chilenidad into more remote areas of the country—like Parra's failed traveling revue *Postcards of the Americas.*[8]

By the time Parra became a folklorista in the early 1950s, the Chilean folk revival was in full swing. Parra's cohort of folkloristas had much in common with their predecessors. Like prior generations, they conceived of Chile as the sum of its varied regions, and the folklore of these regions as the nation's patrimony. Their common charge was to rescue the folklore of the Chilean people from its state of oblivion for the good of the entire nation. Because the practice of "collecting" was simultaneously a process of selection and definition, the 1950s folkloristas played a key role in determining what constituted "folklore" in their era.

The folk revivalists of the 1950s viewed their task as urgent, as Chilean folklore was widely perceived as being on the verge of extinction due to rapidly expanding processes of modernization and urbanization. To give just one striking example of the momentous changes that were occurring in Chile, the population of Santiago grew from roughly 500,000 in 1920 to over 2 million by the early 1960s, with much of the increase attributable to rural migration to the capital.[9] As rural migrants poured into Santiago and other cities and towns, they shed their traditional ways and adopted the more cosmopolitan cultural practices of urban life. Moving in a contrary direction, mass popular culture, produced as nearby as Santiago and as far off as Hollywood, had been spreading throughout the Chilean countryside via the modern media of records, radio, and cinema from the 1920s onward. By the 1950s, the dominance of popular music was near complete, and one was far more likely to hear someone belting out a Mexican *ranchera* or crooning a tropical bolero in a rural community like the one where Parra spent her childhood summers than one was to hear a traditional singer intoning the verses of a poet-song.

As oral traditions were quickly becoming relics of the past, a new generation of Chilean folkloristas made it their mission to seek out the traditional singers, "collect" the songs that had been passed down across the centuries before they died out completely, and restore them to the Chilean people.

The 1950s folkloristas thus practiced their profession according to the dual meaning of the Spanish-language term: as someone who collects folk songs (folklorist), and as someone who performs them (folk singer). Many of the 1950s folkloristas were soloists. Toward the end of the decade, they were joined by a number of younger musicians who performed in folkloric ensembles, the most famous of which were Conjunto Cuncumén and Millaray. The performative aspect of their work is what fundamentally differentiated this cohort of folkloristas from preceding ones. Whereas folkloristas in earlier decades had been content to keep their findings within academe, their mid-twentieth-century counterparts were committed to disseminating the folklore they collected to the widest audience possible via all the modern means at their disposal. These included concerts, radio shows, sound recordings, documentary films, and eventually television. The fact that the folkloristas sought to preserve and restore Chilean traditions by availing themselves of the very same media that threatened these traditions with extinction reflects the Sisyphean nature of their quest. Parra was well aware of this paradox. As she commented to a French reporter in a 1964 interview, "radio has, at the same time, killed folklore and popularized it."[10]

As performers, the folkloristas transformed and resignified the traditional material they and their colleagues collected to appeal to the expectations and sensibilities of their modern urban audience.[11] Musicologists and other scholars have coined the term "folkloricization" to refer to this process, so as to differentiate it from the interrelated process whereby certain songs (and not others) are constituted as "folklore."[12] A short notice in *Ecran* may serve as illustration. It announces the 1956 radio debut of "new folklorista" Gabriela Pizarro and features a posed photograph of her playing a ribbon-adorned guitar. Her hair is in braids, and she is dressed in the requisite huasa costume of women folk singers of a flowery dress and white laced apron (see figure 2.1). The notice promises that Pizarro will be performing "authentic songs from our folklore" in a style somewhere between Violeta Parra's and that of fellow folklorista Margot Loyola, then cites Pizarro's own explanation of her act: "Margot Loyola taught me how to sing folklore just the way it is, but musically; in other words, omitting only its defects."[13]

As the combined presence of Violeta Parra, Margot Loyola, and debuting folklorista Gabriela Pizarro confirms, women played a leading role in the 1950s folk movement in Chile.[14] At one level, this was a product of women's increasing incorporation into all aspects of public life over the course of the first half of the twentieth century, in tandem with the modernization of Chilean society.[15] It also stemmed from the folkloristas' rigorous categorization of folk traditions as either male or female, a practice that perforce required both women's and men's participation in folkloric shows. On a deeper level, women's noteworthy activity in the folk revival reflected and reinforced contemporary gender notions that essentialized women as the timeless conservers of tradition. This made it comparatively easy for women to participate and even assume leadership positions in the folk movement during a period when their entry into other academic and artistic careers was far more restricted.

In terms of their social biographies, the majority of the 1950s folkloristas came from middle- or even upper-class households. Most were university educated, and many could read and write musical notation and had at least some academic training in the field of folkloric studies. Few could claim to have campesino roots (though several maintained that they had been initiated in their love of folklore through the singing of their campesina "nannies" (nanas).[16] They approached folklore from an outsider perspective, out of modern curiosity or academic interest or a combination of the two. With her campesina background on her mother's side and lack of formal training in music or folklore studies, Parra stood apart from her colleagues in this regard. Her distinctiveness would become an integral part of her identity as a folklorista.

In terms of their political orientation, many of the musicians who participated in the Chilean folk movement were on the left of the political spectrum, most of them Communist Party supporters, Parra included. The Communist Party was generally supportive of the leftist folklorists in return, as it saw their work as furthering its political agenda.[17] The folk revival was not a project exclusive to the Chilean Left, however. In contrast to the protest songs associated with the Chilean New Song of the late 1960s and early 1970s, the songs that the 1950s folkloristas collected and performed were traditional and therefore not overtly political. They were the expression of an idealized pueblo (translated as folk), rural, timeless, and past, rather than the militant pueblo (translated as the poor and working class) of class struggle in the here and now. As a result, the folk revival constituted one of the few cultural spheres during the politically charged decade to allow for some degree of nonpartisan collaboration.

The Chilean folk revival transpired across a decade marked by government repression of the Left and particularly of the Communist Party, which was banned from 1948 to 1958 under the Law for the Permanent Defense of Democracy.[18] Though the law was in some respects more draconian than US anti-communist legislation, the careers of communist-identified Chilean folkloristas do not seem to have been imperiled due to their political affiliations to the same extent that the careers of blacklisted US folk singers were derailed under McCarthyism.[19] As a case in point, the fact that Margot Loyola and Violeta Parra were named in conservative politician Sergio Fernández Larraín's 1954 anti-communist screed Informe sobre el comunismo (Report on Communism) did not prevent either folklorista from at some point being employed by the right-wing station Radio Agricultura.[20]

The comparison of the fate of Chilean folk singers who were communist supporters with that of their US counterparts sheds light on a crucial aspect of the Chilean folk revival: though nationalist in spirit, it was part of a transnational wave of folk revivals occurring in the 1950s and 1960s, from neighboring Argentina to the United States to the countries of Western Europe.[21] The adherents of these parallel folk movements were motivated by a shared critique of the social and cultural consequences of the rise of consumer capitalism in the post–World War II era and a longing to recover and restore that which they believed was being lost through modernity.[22] They were aware of each others' movements and supportive of each others' activities, to varying degrees, through their travels and through organizations like the International Folk Music Council (headquartered in London), international folk festivals, and newsletters. They proposed a counteroffensive to the ever-expanding reach of modern mass media, especially that of the world-dominating US entertainment industry. At this global scale, extending down to the local level, folk music represented an active if somewhat murky battlefield in the cultural Cold War.

Even at the peak of the Chilean folk revival, traditional folk music never appealed to more than a niche audience. It was vastly overshadowed by more popular musical genres. There was the pop music imported from the United States that dominated the Chilean musicscape of the 1950s and 1960s (and before and since)—or, as Parra referred to it, that "dreadful invasion of foreign music . . . from North America (no offense to Paul Anka)."[23] There were the Chilean imitation bands that US pop music inspired.[24] There was the pan–Latin American songbook of imported musical styles: Caribbean guarachas, Argentine tangos, Peruvian vals, and the oh-so-popular Mexican rancheras and corridos. In her 1954 *Ecran* interview, newly minted folklorista Violeta Parra labeled it a "crime" that talented Chilean artists would choose to sing and record foreign song styles and not "our own authentic folklore," the strength of her musical nativism all the more conspicuous given how recently she had been performing a pan–Latin American repertoire and appearing regularly on the popular Mexican-themed radio show *Pan-American Rhapsody* with Las Hermanas Parra.[25]

In addition to imported musics and their imitators, the 1950s traditionalist folkloristas had to contend with the highly stylized, folk-derived music known as música típica chilena and its most popular purveyor, the huaso band. Huaso bands first appeared on the music scene in the 1920s when they became some of the earliest Chilean recording artists to produce gramophone disks. They received a boost from the Center-Left reformist governments of the 1930s and 1940s, which, as an integral part of their broader cultural agenda to strengthen nationalist sentiment among the general population, worked in symbiotic relationship with the music industry to elevate the huaso bands' status to full-fledged national icon. The combined government and industry efforts proved wildly successful, and by the 1950s the huaso band was widely perceived to be a fundamental element of chilenidad.[26]

The bands were typically made up of all male musicians, though a few had female lead singers like "Darling Beauty" Ester Soré y sus Huasos (Ester Soré and Her Huasos). Their musical arrangements featured multilayered vocal harmonies interspersed with slick guitar solos reminiscent of Mexican trio music. Their lyrics conveyed the joys and simplicity of rural life on an idealized Chilean hacienda. For their stage dress, the men wore the típica huaso getup of elegant ponchos and spurs that more closely resembled the outfit that a landowner might wear when surveying his estate on horseback than anything one of his ranch-hands wore. The women dressed in the standard huasa costume of a flowery dress and laced apron that established a symbolic association with rural culture but that in no way resembled the actual dress of a Chilean campesina.[27]

From the purist standpoint of the traditionalist folkloristas, Parra among them, the huaso bands and other música típica artists did more to distort Chilean folk music than they did to preserve it. In her 1954 Ecran interview, Parra declared it a shame that so many "quality artists"—all of them musica típica artists whom she called out by name—lacked a clear orientation regarding the "true folklore" of Chile, and she offered to teach it to them free of charge.[28] In a later interview, she derided the "[manufactured] folkloric bands . . . born in the city," with their "over-stylized arrangements, pretentious outfits, crooning singing styles, and fake smiles."[29] She reserved particular disdain for Chile's most commercially successful huaso band, the Huasos Quincheros, whom she accused of being a bunch of "impostors . . . country club, postcard huasitos [little huasos]."[30] Leftists like Parra and her folklorista comrades condemned the Huasos Quincheros and other huaso bands two times over: first, for promoting a distorted version of Chilean folk music and second, for painting a bucolic picture of rural society that masked the exploitative class relations of the hacienda system.

The huaso bands would prove intractable adversaries of the traditionalists in the arena of Chilean musical nationalism. This was because the notion that the huaso bands were the standard bearers of Chilean "traditions" was so thoroughly entrenched in the national psyche by the 1950s that it was difficult if not impossible for the traditionalist folkloristas to convince the public otherwise. The traditionalists' challenge was compounded by the fact that the government's nationalist cultural campaigns treated the two schools of folk music as equally valid or even as one and the same. The entertainment industry similarly failed to draw distinctions between what it considered to be at most variations among the branches of one expansive (and ideally lucrative) folk music tree. A 1954 piece in Ecran, for example, noted that there were different ways to sing "our folklore": the "more commercial" way of radio actress and singer Marta Pizarro, the "stylized" way of Ester Soré, and the "distinctly folkloric" way of Violeta Parra, then affirmed that all three ways were "pleasant and correct."[31] The traditionalist folkloristas' campaign to convince the Chilean public that there was a clear divide between themselves and the huaso bands was further undermined by the fact that the vast majority of traditionalists, Parra included, performed in "traditional" (típica) huasa and huaso costumes identical to those worn by their musical rivals.

The 1950s Chilean folk revival never grew to the level of a "folk boom," as in neighboring Argentina or the United States. It lasted a little over a decade, arguably waning by the early 1960s, when it was overshadowed by new genres of folk-derived music more in tune with the fast-paced, youth-oriented culture that defined the decade. Like other folk revivals, it may best be understood as the product of a particular historic moment, when oral traditions were fast disappearing, and when it still seemed within the traditionalists' grasp that they could stop the process before it was too late. Though the revival proved short-lived, the 1950s folkloristas' efforts at preservation and dissemination produced an invaluable legacy that would inspire generations of Chilean folkloristas over the decades and into the present.

Parra's Turn to the Authentic

Violeta began to shift her attentions to Chilean folklore sometime in the early 1950s, while she was still performing with Las Hermanas Parra. As was so often the case, her brother and mentor Nicanor was a major influence on her decision to do so. While the siblings could agree on this point, they diverged in their explanations as to when and why Violeta's transformation occurred. Although precise answers remain elusive, it is clear that both Nicanor and Violeta were swept up in the era's cultural current of folk revivalism, each in their own way.

In a lengthy interview conducted over two sessions in 1979 and 1980, Nicanor offered a plausible, if unverifiable, account of Violeta's "moment of illumination."[32] As Nicanor tells it, he had long been trying to convince her to leave all that commercial crap behind, to no avail. Then one afternoon in the early 1950s everything changed. Nicanor, recently returned to Chile from a two-year academic residence at Oxford, had become absorbed in the study of broadsides of poetry known as *lira popular*. The broadsides continued the décima tradition of the canto a lo poeta or poet-songs that accompanied the rituals and celebrations of rural communities in Chile's Central Valley, but with modernized content akin to that of the sensationalist press.[33] They were produced in small print shops and peddled in Chilean marketplaces and train stations from the late nineteenth through the early twentieth century. In essence, they constituted a transitional genre of street literature marking the juncture between oral traditions and twentieth-century mass media. Members of the newly founded Chilean Folklore Society had collected and published samples of the street poetry in the early 1900s, which is likely how Nicanor came across them. Nicanor's interest in the lira popular may have been inspired by the attention it was receiving from the Chilean Communist Party, which published a write-in column of popular poetry on topical themes—appropriately titled "Lira Popular"—in its newspaper from 1950 through 1955.[34] He may have also been influenced by the British folk revival, which he was almost certain to have encountered while at Oxford.

Whatever the case, Violeta dropped by his apartment on that eventful day and found him engrossed in their study. She inquired what he was reading, and he shared a few verses with her. Perplexed, she asked, "And you study those things?" According to Nicanor, it was in formulating this question that Violeta "saw the light." She told Nicanor to wait there, that she would be right back, and hurried off, only to return a few hours later with a stack of pages full of folkloric-sounding verses that she had composed "on the fly." She handed them to Nicanor and triumphantly commanded, "Study these."

"My God, Violeta!" Nicanor exclaimed, "Who wrote these?" "Well, who do you think?" she responded. Nicanor explained that what she had written were quartets but that the ten-line verse or décima is what "really matters." He read her a few sample décimas, and Violeta recognized them immediately. "But those are the songs that the drunkards sing." "Which drunkards?" Nicanor asked. Violeta answered, "Why, the drunkards of Chillán, of course." As her brother was apparently unaware that the printed verses he had been studying so intently could also be sung, Violeta sang him a few bars of the poet-songs she recalled from hearing them as a child. She returned to Nicanor's apartment by mutual agreement a few days later, guitar in hand, and the two siblings spent the day reviewing varied aspects of the poet-songs. Nicanor explained what he had learned from books, Violeta sang him the poet-songs she remembered from their childhood, and the two were joined in "an indissoluble alliance" from that day forward.[35]

Assuming that there is some veracity to Nicanor's account of a "moment of illumination," it is in itself illuminating. On the one hand, it is indicative of how valuable the materials that Violeta had gathered in her youth would prove to her career as a folklorista; she embarked on it already endowed with a rich collection of traditional songs that she had learned as a child, and with a fluency in their language and meter that would facilitate her own songwriting in a "folk style" for years to come. On the other hand, Violeta's initial incredulity at her brother's interest in "those things," coupled with her subsequent remark equating the poet-songs with the songs of drunken *chillanejos*, suggest that her early education in the oral traditions of the Chilean countryside, though essential, was insufficient preparation for her new profession. Contrary to Edwards's assertion, in his 1957 feature article, that Violeta possessed an "absolutely accurate instinct" for folk culture, it appeared that she would need to acquire a certain cosmopolitan sensibility in order to grasp its true value. According to Nicanor, this is where his mentorship became indispensable, as he possessed the "necessary criteria" thanks to his university education, intellectual colleagues, and more worldly experiences that she lacked at that point.[36]

On a more theoretical level, the anecdote serves as a reminder that cultural artifacts carry no intrinsic value, only that which is assigned to them in a historic moment. Hawked in the marketplaces of Chillán and Santiago, the broadsides of décimas were worth the pennies they sold for. Collected and published by a first generation of Chilean folklorists, they transformed into the "national customs and the literature of the people" that so piqued Nicanor's interest decades later.[37] Similarly, the songs of drunken chillanejos became fitting examples of the "musical beauty of our past . . . that serve to accentuate our spirit of respect for our nation" when Violeta recorded them on her first solo folk album, self-titled *Violeta Parra*, in the mid-1950s.[38] In other words, the songs became authentic.

Violeta's own explanation of how she came to be a folklorista did not include a moment of illumination, either in Nicanor's apartment or elsewhere—though this does not necessarily mean that it did not occur. In her foundational narrative, there had never been a time when she had not grasped the true value of Chilean folk traditions. They had been at the core of her being "from the moment I was born." Violeta traced the roots of her authenticity back to her earliest years, to her semirural origins, and to the long summer days she spent with the Aguilera sisters learning the old songs the same way that her folkloric "sources" learned them: through oral transmission. In Violeta's telling, her artistic pursuits prior to her emergence as a folklorista were of little consequence, all "trivia" barely worth mentioning. She sang and danced flamenco and had even won first place in a competition, but then she decided to give up "all that nonsense." She composed popular songs, including the Cuban-inspired hit "Funicular," but she herself had never thought much of them.[39] She performed for a time with Las Hermanas Parra, but she broke up the duo when her sister Hilda did not share Violeta's yearning to incorporate traditional songs into their repertoire. Only then had she turned to Nicanor, as he was the brother who had always known how to guide her.[40]

Perhaps Violeta first "saw the light" that afternoon in Nicanor's apartment. Perhaps she had somehow always sensed the value of folklore. More likely, both accounts hold some element of truth. Both Parras were masters at self-invention, and Violeta would have had just as much reason to downplay Nicanor's role as Nicanor would have to exaggerate it. Over time, Violeta would prove consistent and convincing in framing her foundational narrative, as would her supporters in the media, in what became a mutually reinforcing representational loop. As the less-than-authentic activities that she had devoted her creative energies to in her twenties and thirties faded from public memory, reporters stopped asking her about them and she stopped mentioning them, until all that was left was a seamless narration stripped down to its essentials: a childhood spent imbibing the folklore of Chile, and a lifetime dedicated to its rescue and dissemination. As this occurred, Nicanor's version of events became the outlier, as there could be no aha moment in Violeta's biographical continuum of authenticity.

"Unearthing Folklore"

After the breakup of Las Hermanas Parra in 1953, Parra began her "battle in defense of our authentic music" in earnest. She swiftly made her way to the forefront of the Chilean folk revival, her stature perhaps second only to that of folklorista Margot Loyola (1918–2015), with whom she established a close friendship and rivalry (see figure 3.1).[41] The intensity with which Parra pursued her newfound vocation of folklorista led several of her contemporaries to resort to religious imagery to capture it, referring to her work as a "folkloric crusade" that she pursued with "the mystical zeal of a convert."[42] Indeed, Parra's fervent embrace of Chilean folklore and her simultaneous disavowal of her earlier activities as a popular singer lend a quality of conversion or rebirth to her transformation. She would never return to performing the mélange of pan–Latin American and Chilean popularized song styles that had been her mainstay from preadolescence into her thirties. She would devote a large portion of her unmatched energies over the remainder of the decade to collecting Chilean folklore and performing it for audiences throughout Chile, and in Argentina and Europe.

Parra collected with passion and determination, eventually filling countless notebooks and reel-to-reel tapes with the material that her folkloric sources shared with her.[43] It is estimated that she collected thousands of folk songs over the course of her career—everything from the lengthy poet-songs to more lyrical tonadas, cuecas, Christmas carols, and *parabienes* or congratulatory songs. She also collected dances, sayings, medicinal herbs, and musical instruments. Her most intense and prolific years as a collector spanned from 1953 until her departure for Europe in July 1955, and again after her return to Chile in December 1956 through 1960.

Figure 3.1 Violeta Parra (right) with folklorista Margot Loyola. Photograph by Julio Bustamante. Archivo CENFOTO-UDP, Fondo Julio Bustamante, N000014, Violeta Parra y Margot Loyola, 1965.

Parra began collecting folklore close to home in Barrancas, a burgeoning shantytown on the outskirts of Santiago that was home to thousands of rural migrants to the capital.[44] Doña Rosa Lorca, a resident of Barrancas, holds the distinction of being Parra's first folkloric source. I use the Spanish honorific title of *doña* (for women) here and, later, *don* (for men) when referring to Parra's folk informants because Parra used these markers of respect when addressing them, as was customary. Doña Rosa was a traditional singer, healer, neighborhood midwife, and a "dresser of little angels," the woman who adorned the small corpse with cut-out wings and arranged the altar to look as if the "little angel" were ascending to heaven in the "wake for the little angel."[45]

Doña Rosa was in her mid-sixties when Parra made her acquaintance. At the time, she was living in a rented room at Parra's mother's restaurant compound, El Sauce, in Barrancas. Parra overheard her singing there one day and asked if she would teach her the songs that she knew. Doña Rosa assented, and so commenced the regular sessions between the novice folklorista and her first folk informant. In recorded commentary, Parra pays enduring homage to doña Rosa: "How could I possibly imagine when I went out to collect my first song one day in 1953 . . . that I would learn that Chile is the best book of folklore that has ever been written. When I went to Barrancas and conversed with doña Rosa Lorca, that book seemed to open up for me."[46]

Don Isaías Angulo—aka "the Prophet"—also played an early and impactful role in Parra's work as a collector. He was a traditional singer, poet, and instrument maker who, alongside Nicanor, reintroduced Violeta to the traditional poet-songs. In the early 1950s, upon hearing of his prowess, Parra sought out don Isaías at his home in Puente Alto, a semirural area to the south of Santiago. According to don Isaías's daughter, Violeta showed up one morning at their door, took out her guitar, and sang to don Isaías as her means of introduction. He answered in kind, and the two spent the rest of the day swapping songs. Parra returned the next morning, suitcase in hand, and informed don Isaías of her plans to remain in his home until she learned how to play the guitarrón—the large, twenty-five-string guitar that is used to accompany the poet-songs and that, like the songs, was then on the verge of extinction.[47]

Don Isaías helped Parra establish a collecting relationship with a loose-knit group of elderly traditional singers, most of whom worked as tenant farmers on various landed estates in the area.[48] At her urging, they re-created the traditional circle of singers, which she now joined. Parra's participation as a woman in the circle of singers was highly unusual, and her intent to master the guitarrón even more so.[49]

Parra also collected a significant number of songs from her familia, defined in its expansive meaning as both her immediate and extended family. She cites both of her parents as sources on her folk recordings, and gives her mother her own chapter—along with doña Rosa Lorca and don Isaías Angulo—in her manuscript that would be published posthumously as *Cantos folklóricos chilenos* (Chilean Folk Songs).[50] Parra also renewed contact with Lucrecia Aguilera, her campesina "cousin" from Malloa who initiated Parra into the oral traditions of the Central Valley when she was a young girl and who now transformed into one of Parra's folkloric sources. Also within the familia, Parra learned songs from her second husband Luis Arce's great aunt and from his grandmother, doña Flora, whom Ángel hailed as one of Violeta's "most abundant and crystalline sources" in his book about his mother.[51]

Parra thus initiated her career as a folklorista remembering old songs and learning new ones from her relatives and from doña Rosa, don Isaías, and other rural migrants to the capital and its surrounding areas. She would eventually extend her collecting efforts to cover nearly all the geographically and culturally varied regions of Chile. As she writes in her autobiography in décimas, she was ". . . Travelin' to and fro / Unearthing folklore" (. . . *ando de arriba p'abajo / desenterrando folklore*).[52] The harsh living and working conditions that she encountered on her collecting excursions would furnish the material for some of her most well-known protest songs in the 1960s.

Parra traveled throughout Ñuble, which was familiar territory thanks to her early years touring with the circo pobre, and the other provinces of Chile's Central Valley. She ventured farther south to Lautaro, where she had lived as a child, and to more remote towns in Wallmapu, where she made recordings of several Mapuche singers. She lived for several months in 1957 and 1958 in the southern city of Concepción, where she collected folk songs and founded a museum of folk art under the auspices of the University of Concepción. She spent several weeks on the southern island of Chiloé collecting the songs of the fishermen. She visited Chile's northernmost region, where the Indigenous cultures of the Aymara and Quechua peoples prevail. She made it her purpose to explore the folklore of cultural areas other than Chile's relatively well-studied Central Valley and to include Indigenous traditions within her conception of Chile's patrimony.

Parra journeyed by car, bus, train, horse, mule, or foot depending on the remoteness of her destination and the resources available to her. She worked with pen and paper, and even invented her own system of musical notation to make up for her lack of knowledge of formal musical transcription (see figure 3.2). Once she was finally able to get her hands on one, she lugged around a "portable" tape recorder that weighed over fifty pounds—often to no avail, as many of the more secluded communities that she visited had no electricity (see figure 3.3). She ventured out alone or accompanied by family and colleagues. Sometimes she would spend two or three hours collecting; other times she would remain as a guest in the humble home of one of her folk informants for several days or even weeks. Occasionally she worked under far more luxurious conditions. She visited the landed estate of her friend Alfonso Letelier, dean of the College of Musical Arts and Sciences at the University of Chile, for example, where the estate inquilinos (tenant farmers) came to the manor house to share their folk material with her.[53] Or she traveled in style, chauffeured by photographer and upper-class scion Sergio Larraín in his Land Rover or latest-model convertible. Ángel would later recall riding in the convertible's backseat "happy as fleas on a dog."[54]

Violeta is likely to have collected folk songs from over one hundred informants over the course of her career as a folklorista. She would arrive in a hamlet or town, ask around for the old people who knew the old songs, seek them out, and convince them to share their material with her. "I find folklore

Figure 3.2 Violeta Parra with traditional singer Antonio Suárez, Fundo Tocornal, n.d. Photograph by Sergio Larraín. Fotografías Colección Violeta Parra, Museo Pedro del Río Zañartu, Concepción, Chile.

everywhere," she happily informed Edwards for his 1957 *Eva* article. Most of Parra's sources were elderly people or *viejitos* (old folks), as she affectionately referred to them. Many of them suffered the frailties of memory corresponding to their advanced years, and Parra would often have to piece together a complete song from the remembered fragments that she learned from one or another source along the way. Almost all of Parra's informants were poor, some extremely so. Accordingly, she would come bearing gifts of used clothing, or sugar and tea if they were in short supply, or a bottle of liquor to help break the ice. Once she became something of a radio celebrity, she would give away autographed photographs of herself as well. As her renown grew, she was frequently greeted with warm recognition: "Violetita has come to visit! Come in, what can we offer you to drink or eat?"[55] One source led to another until she had made the rounds of the traditional singers in the area.

Parra approached collecting in the spirit of *convivencia* (conviviality), translated to mean a sharing of life's experiences. Often staying in the homes of her folk informants, she would toil alongside them at their daily tasks. Rare and strikingly similar commentary from her sources indicates the success of her efforts to gain their trust. Rosa Viveros, a folk informant from a rural

Figure 3.3 Violeta Parra tape-recording traditional singers Emilio Lobos and Isaías Angulo (with possibly Gabriela Pizarro and Nicanor Parra present as well), n.d. Photograph by Sergio Larraín. Fotografías Colección Violeta Parra, Museo Pedro del Río Zañartu, Concepción, Chile.

community outside the city of Concepción, recalled Parra fondly: "[Mrs. Parra] was very humble, very ordinary. When she would visit it was just like having one more person [in the home;] she would peel potatoes, fetch the water."[56] Folklorista Patricia Chavarría interviewed several campesinos, also near Concepción, with whom Parra had interacted. According to Chavarría, they spoke very highly of Parra; they liked that "she did not come down from the stratosphere to collect 'things' that were lost, she was an equal, she helped with the food, she went to fetch the water, she peeled the potatoes."[57] Though not of her doing, Parra's physical appearance might have made it easier for her sources to identify with her as well. Viveros, for example, described the folklorista as morena (dark-skinned), "skinny," and—revealingly—"about the same height as me."[58]

Parra collected songs in urban settings as well. Her embrace of urban popular culture as a legitimate expression of the people, alongside rural traditions, made her one of the more innovative folkloristas of her generation. Photographer Sergio Larraín recalled the time he accompanied her to what was for her the familiar setting of a Santiago working-class boliche (bar, dive) that was "so down-and-out" that he had been concerned for their safety. But Parra had reassured him, then began singing and drumming on the table with her hands. Little by little the men in the bar joined in. "They sang beautiful songs," Larraín recounted. "They were guys who seemed very dejected, but that's where the music was! When I saw her like that, I would think to myself that Violeta was capable of anything, I believe that is why she was able to research all sorts of aspects of folklore that most of us were unfamiliar with."[59]

Parra quickly earned a reputation for being able to coax even the most recalcitrant sources to share their material with her. Many of her colleagues attributed her singular talent at collecting to her down-to-earth style. Music journalist Magdalena Vicuña, for example, affirmed that Parra's "secret" was that she approached the traditional singers "[not] in the spirit of a scholar searching for things of interest, but like a big sister." Vicuña's use of the term "big sister" underscored the simultaneously familial-like and hierarchical relationship established between folkloristas and their informants.[60]

Parra proposed her own explanation as to why she was so effective at collecting material from her sources: it was because she was just like them; she too had campesina roots; she too had been learning folklore "since the moment I was born." Parra thereby cast herself not as her folk informants' "big sister," as music critic Vicuña would have it, but as their equal. In an oft-cited quote, she asserted, "The Chilean pueblo identified with me immediately, because I am a common woman. I am a daughter of the pueblo. To become known by them was easy because I live like them."[61]

Parra's assertion that she was pueblo or folk just like her sources became an integral part of her identity as a folklorista (and, later, with some variations, as a songwriter and visual artist). Parra affirmed it by emphasizing those elements of her biography that made her most resemble her folk informants—her campesina mother and cousins, most prominently—or that most distinguished her from the other folkloristas in her cohort—her lack of formal training in music or folkloric studies. Parra also dressed the part; a skilled seamstress like her mother, she made herself a simple peasant blouse and rustic skirt to wear when she was out collecting. A set of Larraín's photographs from the period captures her interacting with intimate ease with several of her folk informants, dressed purposefully in her campesina-like outfit (see, for example, figure 3.2).[62]

What no one disputed was that Parra was an exceptional collector of folklore. She was denied agency in this regard, however. Instead, her considerable skills, though recognized, were widely deemed to be innate. Edwards, as noted, credited Parra's capacity to accomplish all that she did to her "absolutely accurate instinct." Similarly, Vicuña opened her 1958 piece on Parra: "Attracted by an unerring intuition and guided by her instinct . . . Violeta

Parra has been able to grasp the genius of our pueblo and discover their most precious treasures, which she now shares with all of Chile."[63] Here, Edwards and Vicuña expressed the consensus view. It was based in part on Parra's success despite her lack of academic training. But it further reflected deeply held beliefs that associated women with being "instinctive," "intuitive," "natural," and other passive attributes. Parra's admirers would make these same gendered assumptions about her work as a composer and visual artist when she began her explorations in those areas. On her end, Parra would embrace the consensus view, in part as an expression of her own belief in her intuitive powers and in part as a means to advancing herself and her work—with the line between the two options so blurred as to be indiscernible.

"With No Official Assistance"

Parra's accomplishments as a collector did not translate into support for her work. As Edwards points out in his *Eva* article, she received little to no assistance from Chilean academic or cultural institutions for her efforts prior to her first European sojourn. She would be offered only slightly more support upon her return—with the six months spanning 1957 and 1958 that she spent in Concepción under the auspices of the university there the notable exception.

Despite her proven skills and commensurate results, the differences between Parra and her scholarly colleagues were simply too vast for them to grant her serious consideration. First, she lacked the basic credentials required by institutions of higher learning and related establishments. Second, and somewhat ironically, the very same down-to-earth style that made her so successful as a collector barred her entry to the halls of academia. Her methods were too unorthodox, her work product too unrelated to that of university-trained folklorists in both form and content.[64] The latter produced "rigorous," "scientific" reports focused on "human subjects" and "artefacts"—and written in academic speak—that rendered the investigator-author invisible in the name of a presumed "objectivity." In contrast, Parra's sole ethnographically oriented manuscript, published posthumously as *Cantos folklóricos chilenos* (Chilean Folk Songs), is essentially a first-person narration of her interactions with her folk informants, interspersed with humorous commentary. The fact that Parra's relationship to her informants is front and center lends a performative quality to her work, one in which Parra plays a leading role. Parra's stated and markedly personal goal: "to make the traditional singers' souls, their thoughts known in the same way that I have known them, in the same way that I have heard them speak."[65]

It is worth underlining here that Parra did not necessarily look upon her colleagues in academia with any higher regard than that with which they viewed her. Academically trained folklorista Margot Loyola recalls, "[Parra] didn't like the academy too much, she made fun of academics."[66] Musicologist Gastón Soublette, who received his training at the Paris Conservatory, claims in turn that Parra "vehemently attacked the professional distortion of scholars who viewed things from a distance, according to a purely technical criteria," admitting further that "in a certain way . . . that is the problem that she had with me."[67]

With scant support from institutional channels, Parra financed her collecting efforts on her own as best she could, often at great sacrifice to her and her family's comfort. Ángel remembers one particularly long winter when the family ate from what seemed to be a bottomless sack of beans and covered themselves with Violeta's guitar case for warmth at night. Violeta nonetheless managed to somehow make ends meet. As a friend once observed, she was "very skilled at being poor."[68]

Parra had never been much of a traditional housewife and mother. Her nomadic pursuits as a folklorista made her all the more unconventional. Sometimes she brought her family along on her collecting trips, especially on day trips to nearby Barrancas or Puente Alto. Other times she would simply declare, "I am going to see my old folks," and take off. She could be gone for a day or two, or for weeks on end. Her family had no idea where she was, until she finally reappeared bearing gifts. "She would wake us up at four in the morning," Ángel recalled. "She always brought us something: 'Okay, little ones, time to eat!'"[69]

With no one fulfilling the traditional roles assigned to women, the family's homelife became somewhat chaotic; "messy" is how Ángel described it.[70] Nor did Parra's second husband pick up the slack; although Arce supported his wife's professional aspirations, he was neither inclined nor equipped to see to the children's daily care. Unwilling to give up her calling, Violeta sought other solutions. She relied on a woman from the neighborhood to care for the children while she was away.[71] She taught Ángel how to cook so he could prepare dinner.[72] She sent him to live for extended periods with don Isaías Angulo—the option he chose when she presented him with the alternative of either that or boarding school.[73]

As her negotiations with Ángel suggest, Violeta appears to have been as unconcerned with ensuring that her children receive a formal education as she was with maintaining an orderly household. Isabel professed to attending school "late, poorly, or not at all," barely making it past elementary school.[74] Ángel claimed that he learned the "basics" at home from his mother: "how to read, write, add, subtract, multiply, sing, [and] dance the cueca."[75] The first actual school he attended was high school, where he was admitted after successfully passing its placement exam. He also studied oboe at the conservatory for a stint, though he never made it past a beginner's level (and the sound he produced led Violeta to tease that he was more of a worm charmer than a snake charmer).[76] Information on Carmen Luisa, though scant, suggests she may have attended school more regularly than her older siblings (perhaps because she spent less time under her mother's care than they had).[77]

In contrast with her disregard for their conventional schooling, Violeta cultivated her children's musical aptitudes and activities from an early age. This explains Ángel's inclusion of singing and dancing the cueca on his list of basics. Isabel described her and her siblings' musical education: "It happened very naturally, at home, because that was our school, our apprenticeship. . . . We already knew the songs, the notes, we learned just by listening to [Violeta]."[78]

Not surprisingly, all of Violeta's children became musicians. In Isabel and Ángel's case, it would be the only profession either of them would ever know.[79] One could argue that this was the logical and perhaps inevitable outcome of having Violeta as their mother: "We were disciples, whether we liked it or not," Isabel would later affirm.[80]

If Violeta's children at times wished for a more typical upbringing, I can find no record of their saying so. In a 1973 piece about her mother, Isabel explained: "I think that my brother and I got used to having a life that was absolutely disorganized: but at the same time we knew intuitively what kind of person our mother was, and we understood her and went all over the place with her on her adventures."[81] Ángel claimed to have grasped the importance of his mother's work even as a young child: "She would say to us that she was doing this for Chile, for the folklore, for the workers and their music, and well, we understood her!"[82] Although not a statement of opinion regarding her mother's frequent travels per se, Carmen Luisa proudly remembered the time she accompanied Violeta and the photographer Sergio Larraín on a collecting trip to the Chilean north in his Land Rover and all the people in the places they traveled to, no matter how remote, knew of Violeta Parra. "It was fantastic."[83]

Folk Singer

As talented as she was as a collector, Parra was equally or even more impressive as a folk singer, the performative facet of her dual career as folklorista. She gave her debut recital in late 1953 at the home of world-renowned Chilean poet and communist Pablo Neruda and his second wife, the Argentine artist Delia del Carril. The couple's home was a grand, old colonial-style house replete with grounds and a small outdoor amphitheater built for such occasions. Fellow poet Nicanor Parra had asked Neruda to host Violeta's recital there in order to usher the budding folklorista into Santiago's artistic and intellectual circles. Nicanor even wrote the libretto for her performance.[84]

That night, Violeta wore her long hair pulled back in a braid and an exotic, "gypsy"-style outfit of hoop earrings, a white peasant blouse, and a long, dark skirt that signaled to her audience that something out of the ordinary was about to take place. She sang the poet-songs that she had collected from don Isaías Angulo and his Puente Alto associates for a select audience of poets, writers, artists, university professors, and important figures in the Communist Party. Her impact was immediate and profound. To cite author José Miguel Varas, "She left us astonished and bedazzled by her singing."[85]

Parra's repertoire of poet-songs was a revelation for many of those in attendance. Chilean intellectuals had long experienced a certain sense of inferiority based on the belief that Chilean folklore was somehow impoverished in comparison to the folklores of other Latin American nations. It was felt to lack the vitality of those with a marked African influence, or the mysticism of those rooted in Indigenous cultures.[86] Or else it was perceived as having been permanently contaminated by the overly sentimental, highly stylized singing of the ubiquitous huaso bands. And now Parra had come along to show that as nearby as Puente Alto a rich vein of Chilean folklore persisted with roots that could be traced all the way back to sixteenth-century Spain. Musicologist Gastón Soublette expressed it well: "Violeta's singing . . . allowed me to discover that . . . Chilean folklore had aspects to it that were far worthier than what I had initially assumed. It's just that we were so used to that cardboard, criolla tackiness that we thought that's all Chilean folklore was about, and we never suspected that the traditional singers even existed."[87]

But it was arguably Parra's voice that most impressed the attendees at this and similar soirées. It had an untrained—some might even say harsh—quality that contrasted with the more polished singing style of other folkloristas. Varas described hearing her voice for the first time: "[It] was raw and so country-like, unadorned yet musical at the same time, it felt like the real thing, and not just an artistic interpretation."[88] Others would express similar appreciation for what they perceived as Parra's authenticity in interpreting the folk songs she collected. Edwards celebrated her "purity of style" that distinguished her from her folklorista colleagues, wherein the folkloric remained "uncontaminated."[89] A concert reviewer lauded Parra for the way she performed each song "as if channeling its original living source."[90] Some of her followers carried the process even further: Violeta Parra was "like her music, modest, campesina."[91]

Varas's and Parra's other admirers' conflation of someone who was a seasoned performer with a campesina or authentic "other" represents the beginning of a process of authentication that would continue throughout Parra's folk singing career and spill over into her soon-to-be concurrent creative activities and identities as a songwriter, composer, and visual artist. For her part, and irrefutably, Parra would assist in the process of her own authentication.

Parra's "real" and "uncontaminated" singing style was not to everyone's liking. Some people, perhaps many, found her voice unpleasant or even grating. Nor was Parra's repertoire of rediscovered poet-songs universally acclaimed. The songs' sheer length, coupled with their melodic repetition and often obscure themes, could be off-putting. Take, for example, the time música típica star Ester Soré heard Parra sing the poet-songs at an event and, surprised and irritated, was overheard to ask who that woman was and whether the songs that she was singing were some kind of joke.[92]

Regardless of Parra's detractors, her debut recital at Neruda's house opened new opportunities for the up-and-coming folklorista. In December 1953, Tomás Lago—scholar, family friend, and frequent visitor to the Parras' "country house" in the 1940s—organized a concert at the Museum of Folk Art of the Americas, where he served as founding director.[93] Other concerts followed soon after.

Parra's singing style would remain the constant and defining feature of her folkloric performance. Beyond this, her stage presentations did not deviate substantially from the standard didactic folkloric show of the era. She relied on a libretto, although perhaps more as a guide for her improvisations than as an actual script. She introduced each piece with a detailed explanation of its origins. She wore the obligatory huasa costume that traditionalist folklorista women shared with their música típica counterparts. Her stage presence was at times solemn, as when she intoned a particular poet-song in its entirety—which, at fifty-plus lines of verse, could last over six minutes. Most of the time, she was spontaneous and playful. A concert reviewer captured the spirit of her performance: "She spoke, recited poetry, sang, played the guitar, and danced, all as if among family. The family was her audience, a public that, sophisticated or not . . . identified with the multitude of ingeniously marvelous things that came out of her mind and mouth."[94]

Folklorista Margot Loyola also helped to launch Parra's folk career. Loyola was already well established in the field when she "discovered" Parra at one of Parra's first solo shows, which took place around the same time as Parra's debut recital at Neruda's residence. Loyola was immediately impressed with Parra's obvious talent. A classically trained musician, she proposed to transcribe several of Parra's original songs so that Parra could register them with the Chilean Society of Authors and Composers. This was something Parra had been unable to do on her own, as the copyright process required a musical transcription and she could neither read nor write music. Loyola also took Parra around to those few radio stations that aired folk music as well as to the offices of the entertainment weekly *Ecran*. The noncommittal title of the resultant short magazine piece from November 3, 1953, asks the question, "Is a New Folkloric Talent Emerging?"[95] Its answer would prove to be an unequivocal "yes."

Violeta Parra Sings (*Así Canta Violeta Parra*)

Before the year was out, Parra was hosting her own radio show on the innovative radio station Radio Chilena. Small but influential, the station functioned under the auspices of the Catholic Church, then led by the progressive Cardinal José María Caro. Its mission was to serve as a counterweight to the host of commercial radio stations whose programming was dominated by radio soap operas, news shows, and popular music (mainly imported). The station's artistic director Raúl Aicardi assembled some of the most important cultural commentators and promoters of the era to work with him toward this goal. Aicardi's vision for the station included a new kind of folk music show, one that rejected the commercialized folk-derived songs of the huaso bands and instead broadcast the authentic folk songs of the Chilean people. Of utmost import, it would showcase the matchless talents of the recently discovered folk singer who gave the program its name, *Violeta Parra Sings*.[96]

Aicardi recruited rising radio personality Ricardo García to serve as the show's announcer. Years later, García would relate his first encounter with the soon-to-be folkloric star:

> One day a woman showed up at the radio station who was like a creature from another world for the radio scene in those days. She was wearing a very humble, very simple, dark dress, with her hair loose, and with her face scarred by smallpox. . . . [She] began to play [her guitar], and the people in the control room gathered around, aghast and seemingly dumbfounded. . . . Some laughed, others wondered, "How is it possible that a person so completely lacking in vocal technique is allowed to perform?" etc. All sorts of negative commentaries on the part of some people, and on the part of others, a great admiration and interest. It was truly something different.[97]

The recollections of station manager Jaime Celedón and radio novice Patricio Bañados, who also attended Parra's audition, were more earthbound and class-based. Celedón, like García, had no idea who Parra was at the time. He remembers listening to the singing of a "small woman with long hair who

Figure 3.4
Photo that accompanies Violeta Parra's
1954 interview in *Ecran*. Marina de
Navasal, "Conozca a Violeta Parra,"
Ecran, June 8, 1954.

looked like a campesina" and not liking it, though he would later admit that he had been mistaken not to.[98] Bañados, for his part, recalls his resistant colleagues wondering something along the lines of "Who is this washerwoman?"[99]

As these accounts make clear, Parra performed her authenticity off stage as well as on. In her daily life, she dressed modestly, wore no makeup, and ignored the latest fashions in hair styles. She thus marked herself as different— from "another world" or social class—than the other women in the cosmopolitan circles in which she traveled.

Parra's appearance reflected her challenging economic circumstances. But it was also deliberate. Fashion is a critical aspect of the modern lifestyle, and Parra was very much a modern woman. Photos from this period show her dressed in a variety of fashions depending on what the occasion warranted: a homemade skirt and peasant blouse for when she was out collecting; a stylish turtleneck and lipstick for her first feature interview with *Ecran* (figure 3.4); a tailored suit-dress for a radio station cocktail party; an evening gown for a performance at an award ceremony (figure 3.5).[100] Parra's decision to dress most often as a *mujer del pueblo* (woman of the people, everywoman) was therefore an intentional and assertive representational act that identified her with the pueblo and differentiated her from other, more privileged classes of people. On a more personal level, Parra's frequent lack of concern for appearances seems to have been a consistent personality trait, as those who knew her made note of it both before and after her midlife turn to the authentic.[101]

Perhaps more significant than any interrogations as to why Parra dressed the way she did were the repercussions of her presentation as a woman of the people. On the positive side, it allowed her admirers to experience not just her performance but the artist herself as the "real thing," to borrow author José Miguel Varas's words. This worked to Parra's advantage, and one can un-

Figure 3.5
Violeta Parra (right)
performing with her
daughter Isabel Parra at
an award ceremony. Photo
accompanies Isidoro
Bassis Lawner's article
"'Caupolicanes' entregaron
periodistas especializados,"
Ecran, July 2, 1957.

derstand if she encouraged it. At the same time, Parra's humble demeanor, in combination with her physical appearance as a relatively short and morena (dark-skinned) woman, could just as easily lead to her marginalization, given the rampant classism-racism in Chilean society. The initial reactions of incredulity, discomfort, and even disdain on the part of many of those present at her Radio Chilena audition exemplify the social exclusion that Parra would confront again and again as she strove to advance a professional and artistic agenda that increasingly depended on her interactions with members of Chile's cultural elite.

Fortunately for Parra, her admirers at Radio Chilena held sway over her critics. *Violeta Parra Sings* aired on the station Thursday nights (repeated Sunday mornings) for the better part of 1954. Ricardo García served as its announcer and principal writer, while Parra supplied him with the show's thematic material. A promotional piece in *Ecran* promised an "authentically folkloric series" in which "every thirty-minute program will present a traditional celebration in its entirety."[102] Effectively, *Violeta Parra Sings* featured audio re-creations of traditional festivals and rituals, recorded in part in studio and in part on location in one of the semirural neighborhoods on Santiago's outskirts, with Parra's mother's restaurant El Sauce a favored site. The same persuasive talents that made Parra so effective as a collector were often key to the success of these more elaborate productions, as she was known to knock on the door of complete strangers and convince everyone inside the home, young and old alike, to come out and participate in a radio reenactment of the particular folk practice that was that week's theme.

Parra concerned herself with every aspect of the program down to its tiniest detail. Her resolve to remain true to tradition is what led to the incident, first discussed in this book's introduction, when she insisted on buying the dress for the doll that she planned to use in a radio version of a wake for the little angel at the stalls outside of the central train station because that was where such dresses were sold. In the same spirit of fealty, Parra would invite actual traditional singers to perform on her radio show in its later iterations.

Violeta Parra Sings was an unexpected hit. It drew its fan base in part from the same mix of urban intellectuals as the select group that had been present at Parra's coming-out recital as a folklorista—artists, writers, classical music lovers, anti-imperialists, and communists—expanded exponentially to thousands of followers. Many of Parra's radio listeners shared a sense of revelation similar to that experienced by the attendees at her debut recital, as they "discovered" the traditional songs and folk rituals for the first time thanks to her program. As one recent convert wrote in a fan letter, "I, who believed myself definitively anti-folklorista, have since realized, thanks to the voice of Violeta Parra, that I did not know my own music."[103]

Photographer Sergio Larraín would later liken Parra's role to that of a "translator so that we could know ourselves, so that we would not constantly be looking outside Chile" to Europe or the United States. He expanded on her impact:

> We were really into everything from Europe and the US, we listened to—and imitated—their music, bought their novels, saw their movies. Everything Latin American was worthless. . . . There was nothing here! . . . But then we started to feel alienated from all that foreign stuff, we couldn't identify with it anymore. . . . And that is when Violeta became a sort of bridge, a connection with Chile. There was nothing in Chile! But, yes, there was. There was all of this life among the pueblo and Violeta had the ability to enter into it and to love it and restore it through her songs.[104]

Violeta Parra Sings also developed a substantial following among recent rural migrants to Santiago as well as in those rural communities that the broadcast reached, where avid fans would congregate around what few radios were available to listen to the show on Sunday mornings.[105] For this more extensive group of listeners, the radio show represented a process of recovery more than discovery. Letters poured into the station from all over Chile thanking Parra for reconnecting her listeners to their "real music" that many of them had not heard since childhood, and embracing her as one of their own.[106] Perhaps the program's most crucial impact was on the traditional singers themselves, who gained renewed pride when they heard the poet-songs being performed on the radio. They began to sing in their circles again and to have new guitarrones built with which to accompany themselves. Now, they were sometimes joined by a younger generation of singers eager to learn the old songs, their interest piqued by the attention the poet-songs were receiving thanks to Parra's radio show.[107]

Parra thus captured the hearts and minds of her listeners, both urban and rural. Working with her was a different story. In all probability, it would have been challenging to work with Parra at any point in her variegated musical career.[108] Once imbued with a quasi-religious sense of purpose as a folklorista, Parra became as capable of alienating colleagues with her impatience and combativeness as she was adept at winning over folk informants with her patience and solicitousness. According to radio producer José María Palacios, who worked alongside Parra on several folk music shows, "she would get into fights every day and for the slightest reason, because she was a pushy woman, she was like a wild demon trying to get people to take her seriously."[109] Musicologist Gastón Soublette, who collaborated with Parra on various projects over the years, came to both expect and accept her recurring outbursts. As he explained it, he "finally understood that, along with her creativity, her bravery, and the strength of her personality, there was a hidden side to her, a bitter and irascible essence that periodically emerged. . . . It was the price she had to pay for being an exceptional person, a hyper-gifted woman."[110]

Together, Palacios's and Soublette's comments suggest that Parra's combative work relationships and her status as a nonconventional, talented woman in a patriarchal society were linked. Parra understood this all too well. As she once informed a dear friend and fellow gender rebel, Adela Gallo: "If I were not the way I am, no one would pay any attention to me."[111]

A New Life, a First Folk Recording, and an Award

For reasons that are unclear, *Violeta Parra Sings* ended up airing for less than a year, roughly from January to October 1954.[112] The radio show's influence on Parra's career as a folklorista would prove entirely disproportionate to its brief on-air existence. This was because it catapulted its star into the national limelight. Nicanor recalled leaving the city to teach an extension course at a southern university for a few weeks and returning to find that "the only thing everyone was talking about in Santiago was Violeta Parra!"[113] Folklorista Raquel Barros confessed to a similar experience; she had no idea who Violeta Parra was or that she even existed, and within a few months "one would have to be living in a world completely divorced from reality" to not know of her.[114]

Opportunities came, along with the limelight. By June 1954, Parra landed her first feature interview in *Ecran*. In July, she performed alongside Margot Loyola at both the opening banquet and closing gala of the weeklong celebrations surrounding the fiftieth birthday of Chile's most well-known communist, Pablo Neruda, each of which was attended by a lengthy roster of national and international writers and artists.[115] According to fellow biographer Víctor Herrero, Parra's participation in the festivities marked her official entry into "the cultural nomenklatura of the Communist Party, which was rapidly gaining favor with the country's intellectuals and artists."[116] What this entailed in practice was that Parra now might be invited to Neruda's subsequent birthday celebrations, which were always extravagant affairs, and that she for sure would be asked to participate in countless CP-sponsored events, major and minor. Her status as a friend of the Communist Party—or "fellow traveler," as communist supporters who were not card-carrying party members were called—made it more likely for her to be selected to join the Chilean delegation to the biennial World Festival of Youth and Students, which she attended in 1955 in Warsaw and again in 1962 in Helsinki. It would also supply Parra with invaluable contacts while traveling and living abroad.

Sometime also during of the short lifespan of Violeta's show on Radio Chilena, she successfully concluded Las Hermanas Parra's contract obligation with Odeon Chilena. She did so by recording and releasing a single with her daughter Isabel singing Hilda's parts.[117] The album featured the tonada "La jardinera" (The Gardener), a Violeta original that became something of a hit. Violeta used the royalties from the song to purchase a small plot of land in a formerly semirural area of Santiago at the foot of the Andes that was quickly becoming a residential neighborhood for middle-class professionals and that would eventually be incorporated into the neighborhood of La Reina. Under the skilled guidance of her brother-in-law from her first marriage Juan Cereceda, who was a construction worker, along with additional help from a crew of relatives, Violeta built a rustic wooden house with a tin roof, but no running water or electricity, on her land.[118]

The nine or so months that *Violeta Parra Sings* aired coincided with her fourth and last pregnancy. Parra gave birth to her daughter on September 22,

1954. Doña Rosa Lorca, who in addition to being Parra's first folkloric informant was also the neighborhood midwife, assisted in the delivery. Parra named her daughter Rosa Clara after doña Rosa and Parra's mother Clara (also known as Clarisa).

The evidence suggests that Parra continued her professional pursuits throughout her pregnancy and Rosa Clara's infancy, with minimal interruption. A notice published in *Ecran* in mid-October, or three weeks after Rosa Clara's birth, announced that "Violeta Parra—who has just had her fourth child Rosa Clara, born September 22—is planning to return to the airways ... to host a new series of folkloric programs. Starting in mid-November, she will also offer guitar and folk dancing lessons at Radio Chilena's auditorium and at another location in Las Barrancas."[119] A subsequent notice published on November 2, six weeks after Rosa Clara's birth, reported that Parra had replaced Margot Loyola on a weekly folkloric show broadcast on the National Agricultural Society's radio station.[120] And Radio Chilena's then-managing director Raúl Velasco remembered Parra breastfeeding her infant at the station.[121]

In December 1954, Parra went into the studios of Odeon Chilena to record an EP (an "extended-play" recording with four to five tracks) at the behest of the label's artistic director Rubén Nouzeilles, one of the most influential figures in the Chilean music industry. Self-titled *Violeta Parra*, it was her first record to include liner notes and artwork (albeit the latter generic).[122] The liner notes, which Nouzeilles is believed to have written, are indicative of how quickly Parra's foundational narrative of authenticity was catching hold. Pronouncing her "the voice of the Chilean countryside," they report that Violeta Parra was born in a region particularly rich in folkloric traditions and that she had "dedicated her life to the discovery and study of traditional songs and rhythms."[123] The album's generic artwork, designed for the Odeon series "Songs of Chile," consists of a picturesque drawing of a conventionally beautiful huasa, tall and svelte, sitting on a wagon as she plays her guitar, with an interchangeable small black-and-white photo of the EP's featured recording artist—in this case Violeta Parra—in the upper-right corner.

The EP captures the transitional moment in Parra's musical trajectory. Significantly, it includes two of the poet-songs that Parra had collected, making it among the first (and few) commercial recordings of this particular folk genre to be released in Chile—or anywhere.[124] The poet-songs are performed by studio musicians with intricate arrangements featuring musical introductions, instrumental interludes, layered guitar parts, and varied tempos, all of which are signature musical conventions of Chilean huaso bands but do not correspond to the musical practices of traditional singers of poet-songs. The somewhat schmaltzy end product sounds out of character with the values of the more purist folklorista that Parra was becoming. In that sense, the album represents both an attempt to build a bridge between Parra's more commercially driven musical past and her more ideals-driven folklorista present and confirmation that the two were not easily bridged.[125]

The release of *Violeta Parra* in March 1955 marked the beginning of Parra's career as a solo recording artist with Odeon that would last over a decade. The EP was well received and helped to consolidate Parra's reputation as a folk singer and songwriter. It also proved to be an anomaly. Parra would never again record traditional songs arranged so ornately. She would perform the material on her subsequent albums, with few exceptions, in what became her signature style as a folk singer: Violeta Parra, on voice and guitar.[126]

Violeta Parra would lead to what was arguably Parra's most extensive international exposure in her lifetime. This was gained thanks not to the poet-songs but to the other two songs on the EP: the popular waltz "Qué pena siente el alma" (How Sad Is My Soul) and Parra's original composition based on a folkloric quatrain (four-line stanza), "Casamiento de negros" (The Black Wedding).[127] Capitol Records reissued "Qué pena siente el alma" on its double LP *Special Disc Jockey Package* for May and June 1956, where it appeared alongside such hits from the international pop music scene as Jackie Gleason and his orchestra's "When You're Away" and Yvette Giraud's "I Love Paris."[128] "Casamiento de negros" was picked up by US band leader and composer Les Baxter. Baxter was a pioneer of the musical genre known as exotica that was popular in the 1950s and early 1960s. He renamed the song "Melodia [*sic*] Loca," arranged it as an instrumental for orchestra, and included it on his 1957 Capitol Records album, *'Round the World with Les Baxter.*[129] In typical First World fashion, he failed to credit Parra as the song's composer. In 1959 she would mount a successful lawsuit against him for copyright infringement. She would use the royalties to build a sturdier home than her first on her plot in La Reina.[130]

A few months after the EP's release, Parra was invited to join the Chilean delegation to the Soviet-sponsored Fifth World Festival of Youth and Students, to be held in Warsaw, Poland, later that year. Soon after in late June, Parra reached an early milestone in her career when she was awarded the prestigious Caupolicán prize for best folklorista of 1954 by the Chilean Association of Entertainment Journalists in recognition of her efforts at both collecting and popularizing Chilean folklore.[131]

The award ceremony took place in Santiago's Municipal Theater. Ever the outsider, Parra had not planned to attend the gala event—somewhat akin to the Oscars award ceremony in the United States—whose awardees received a bronze statuette of the Araucanian warrior Caupolicán. Parra's husband Luis

Arce, who had a hunch that she might win the award, convinced her to accompany him to the show. The couple were sitting in cheap balcony seats when Parra's award for "Best Singer of Chilean Music, Exclusively" was announced.[132] Parra hastily made her way down to the stage where she accepted the Caupolicán statuette, overcome by emotion.[133] It was the first and last recognition she would receive from a national organization for her work as a folklorista—or for anything else—during her lifetime.[134]

Parra set out on her journey to participate in the 1955 World Festival of Youth and Students in Warsaw within a week of winning her Caupolicán award. She would lug the bronze statuette along on her visits to Chilean embassies and cultural centers across Europe. In an interview published in the daily *Clarín*, Parra declared that "her Caupolicán statue would be her greatest incentive, pillar of hope and enthusiasm to bring honor to Chile."[135]

———

With a biographer's hindsight, one can easily confirm that Parra's mid-thirties embrace of the authentic was the definitive turning point in her life trajectory that Edwards presciently declared it to be in his 1957 *Eva* article. Her transformation was multifaceted. On the one hand, it represented a return to the rich oral traditions of the campesino communities of her childhood and thus a process of self-discovery. On the other, it required a dramatic and irreversible process of reinvention or, perhaps more precisely, revaluing. When Parra left the popular Las Hermanas Parra duo behind to pursue her solo career as a folklorista, she exchanged not only the genres of music she performed but also how her performance would be appraised. Las Hermanas Parra made no promises to their audience beyond that of entertaining; they sang "whatever the public asked for." Transfigured into a folklorista, Parra's sense of self-worth as well as the way others valued her were now assessed according to entirely different and less tangible criteria that were inextricably linked to modern notions of the authentic. Her impassioned allegiance to what, for her, was a new set of values would soon win her entrance into preeminent global cultural spaces—the Musée de l'Homme in Paris, for example, and the BBC in London—whose access would have been unimaginable had she remained part of a local sisters' act specializing in urbanized tonadas and cuecas.

In her newfound vocation as folklorista, Parra assumed the role of intermediary between the pueblo or folk and her cosmopolitan audience. As Edwards put it in his piece, she "revealed our own folklore to ourselves." Over time, many of her followers would increasingly come to see her not as an interpreter but as one and the same as the folk whose lore she collected and disseminated. A number of factors—some unintentional, others deliberate—contributed to this blurring of lines between folklorista and folk informant: Parra's claim to authenticity as a birthright ("from the moment I was born") and use of members of her familia as sources, especially her campesina mother and Aguilera cousins; her down-to-earth collecting style and the familial-like relationships she forged with her informants; her lack of formal training in music or folkloric studies; her untrained singing voice, unassuming stage presence, and repertoire of ancient poet-songs that allowed her public to experience her not as a performer but as the "real thing"; her offstage appearance as everywoman, including her dress and petite physique and brownish skin color that, in a society where classism and racism were overlaid, associated her with the pueblo or working poor; and finally, and encompassing all the other factors, her steadfast identification with the pueblo. Within this context, Parra's turn to folklore in the early 1950s may be considered the first step in a process of authentication that would span the rest of her life. Her revaluation as the authentic "other" would take on new nuance and dimension over the course of her first prolonged European sojourn.

Chapter 4

Europe I

Parra set off for the World Festival of Youth and Students (WFYS) in Warsaw in early July 1955. The initial plan was that she would spend several weeks in Europe. She ended up remaining there for a full year and a half, returning to Chile only in December 1956. She spent almost all of the eighteen months in Paris, where she performed regularly at L'Escale, a boîte (nightclub) on the city's bohemian Left Bank that featured Latin American folk music. She also recorded for the Musée de l'Homme, UNESCO, and the French record label Le Chant du Monde in Paris, and the BBC in London. She performed on radio and television and for various cultural venues in both Eastern and Western Europe.[1]

At some point during her prolonged European sojourn, she wrote the homesick song "Violeta ausente" (Faraway Violeta). In its lyrics, she laments having ever left Chile and lists all the things that she misses doing in her homeland—dancing the cueca, drinking chicha, going to the marketplace, strolling in the Santa Lucía park in Santiago. The song includes the following verse:

Before I had ever left Chile
I could not comprehend
The value of being Chilean
Oh my, now I do understand!

Antes de salir de Chile
yo no supe comprender
lo que vale ser chilena
¡ay, ahora sí que lo sé![2]

Though not necessarily her intent in writing them, Parra's lyrics encapsulate important aspects of her experience in Europe. First, she would discover "the value of being Chilean" there. The generalized European longing to experience the authentic acquired new vigor in the post–World War II years of mourning, reckoning, recovery, and forgetting. This meant that Parra's performance of Chilean folklore would find appreciative audiences on both sides of the Iron Curtain. Additionally, her European successes would lead to a positive reappraisal of her performance once she returned to Chile, where her ability to claim world renown would enhance her reputation and open up new possibilities. Second, Parra's experience living and working in Europe would allow her to redefine and refine her identity as a Chilean with a clarity and depth of perspective that are often only possible when one is away from one's native land: "Oh my, now I do understand!"

World Festival of Youth and Students

Parra traveled to Europe as a delegate to the 1955 WFYS in Warsaw. The WFYS was a two-week internationalist extravaganza held biennially from 1947 onward for the broad purpose of demonstrating the superiority of Soviet-style socialism over capitalism.[3] Organized Olympics-style along national lines, the WFYS brought together card-carrying Communist Party members, supporters of communism or "fellow travelers," and the curious from scores of countries to compete and participate in every sort of athletic and cultural event: sports, classical music and ballet competitions, film and theater festivals, fine arts and photography exhibitions, folk dance, puppetry, student clubs, leisure activities, tourism, political education, and mass demonstrations.[4]

Folkloric performance was one of the festival's consistent and key components. It fit well with both the Soviet Union's conservative aesthetics and its broad foreign policy objectives of advocating for peace between nations. At the same time, it reinforced a cultural hierarchy that reserved the practice and perfection of the "high arts" of classical music and ballet for Russia and Russians, while assigning folklore as the most appropriate form of expression for all other nations and ethnic groups.[5]

Substantial numbers of Latin American folk musicians traveled to Europe as delegates to the WFYS across the 1950s and 1960s (and beyond), including Parra in 1955, and again in 1962 to attend that year's festival in Helsinki. For Parra and her comrades who were sympathetic to communism, an invitation to the festival was more than simply a ticket to Europe. It represented the fulfillment of their political and emotional commitment to Soviet-style socialism and Soviet-led campaigns for international understanding and solidarity. That so many Latin American folk musicians followed this route to Europe attests to the festival's importance in introducing and promoting Latin American folk music to the nations that made up the Soviet Bloc and, once the festival moved outside the bloc in 1957, to those European nations that were considered neutral: Austria (Vienna, 1959) and Finland (Helsinki, 1962).[6] The festival played a similar role, perhaps unintentionally, in the Western Bloc, as Western Europeans crossed the Iron Curtain to attend it, and as many Latin American folk musicians who originally traveled to Europe to participate in the festival took advantage of their transatlantic journey to perform in Paris and other Western European cultural centers.

The Chilean delegation to the 1955 WFYS in Warsaw was made up of musicians, actors, athletes, and students from across a political spectrum ranging from Center Left to Left, with communists or communist supporters making up the largest group. At 174 people strong, the delegation was by far the largest from any Latin American country.[7] Parra was at first hesitant to accept her invitation to perform at the festival, as her youngest child Rosa Clara was only nine months old and still nursing, but she quickly became convinced (or convinced herself) that the opportunity to disseminate Chilean folklore to an international audience was too worthwhile to pass up. She and Arce agreed that Arce would care for Ángel and little Rosa Clara in the family's new home in La Reina while she was away with the help of a married couple who also lived on the property (most likely in exchange for caring for the house and garden). Arce's mother promised to look in regularly on the children as well. Violeta arranged for Carmen Luisa, who was then almost five, to live in the home of the daughter of Museum of Folk Art director Tomás Lago.[8] The sources do not specify where Isabel, then fifteen, stayed while her mother was in Europe.

Violeta's extended family cobbled together $183 for the trip while she scrambled to get her travel papers in order. She participated in various fundraisers, including the Chilean delegation's farewell gala, held on June 29, featuring diverse musical and theatrical acts and a beauty contest.[9] Parra flew to Buenos Aires, Argentina, a few days later with other members of the Chilean delegation on the first leg of what would be a four-week journey to Warsaw. She was thirty-eight years old, and it was the first time she traveled outside Chile, the first time she flew on an airplane, and the first time she visited Europe. To put things in their social context, hers was a voyage that most upper-class and many middle-class Chileans likely would have already made by the time they were her age, as to travel abroad to Europe or the United States was something of a rite of passage for people of their social and economic status. At the same time, it was a trip that the vast majority of Chileans could not even contemplate.[10]

Parra participated in more fiestas and recitals once she arrived in Buenos Aires. She also made a side trip to a hospital, where she was given a baby to nurse in order to ease the pain caused from having ceased to breastfeed Rosa Clara so abruptly. She would seek out similar relief when the ship that was carrying the Chilean delegation to Europe made a stopover in Rio de Janeiro. As she recounted in her autobiographical décimas, "My swollen breasts are painful / With this sacred nourishment" (*los pechos se me lastiman / con el sagrado alimento*).[11]

The Chilean delegates, together with those from Argentina and Uruguay, set off for Genoa, Italy, on the ocean liner *El Salta* on July 7, 1955. Parra's first transatlantic journey lasted just over two weeks. It was rough in more ways than one. She was seasick for the first portion of it and her breasts remained sore and engorged. The pair of sisters who were her cabin mates turned openly hostile to her over the course of the ship's ocean crossing. Parra's combative personality assuredly had something to do with this, as did her incessant singing and playing of the guitar—a practice that, though consoling to her, made her increasingly unpopular among her fellow passengers. But the animosity of Parra's cabin mates toward her derived at least in part from class prejudice, which was not uncommon among Chilean leftists from privileged backgrounds. The sisters were *señoritas* (upper-class young women) and Parra was not. As her fellow shipmate and friend Fernán Meza would comment decades later, Parra "was not famous yet, and the women treated her like a *rota* because she wasn't beautiful or classy, she didn't have any money"—with *rota/o* used in this context as a classist insult for a socially inferior or poor person.[12]

Parra, who was not easygoing under the best of circumstances, ostensibly became unbearable within the ship's close quarters. She had the annoying habit of referring to herself in the third person, as in "Violeta Parra has arrived!" While those of her shipmates who were also her friends and admirers dismissed her imperious airs as the "egocentrism of an artist," others were less forgiving. According to Meza, most of the delegates considered Parra "an oddball" (*bicho raro*).[13] For her part, Parra dedicates an entire autobiographical décima to "This journey so full of suffering" (*d'este viaje tan sufrí'o*), where "With so much coming and going / Camaraderie gets lost" (*con tanta ida y venida / se pierd' el compañerismo*), and where "Those with the heaviest pockets / Vomit their arrogant outlook" (*los de bolsillo más rico / vomitan su atrevimiento*).[14] Her verses confirm Chilean delegation leader Miguel Lawner's understated observation that "Violeta had a class consciousness that was very marked. . . . For her, the rich were on the other side."[15]

Happily, and as Parra would remind her readers in her following décima, "Nothing lasts forever" (*No hay mal que dure cien años*).[16] When the Chilean delegates finally reached Genoa, their spirits lifted. After being given picnic sacks emblazoned with the festival's official logo, a dove designed especially for the event by Pablo Picasso, they boarded the train that would carry them across Austria to Warsaw, Poland. The delegates arrived just in time for the festival's opening on July 31, 1955. They quickly changed into their tricolored uniforms inspired by the Chilean flag and lined up with the other delegates—30,000 in all, representing 115 countries—to march in the opening ceremony, which began with a parade and ended with the release of thousands of doves into the Warsaw sky.[17]

What followed were fifteen days of cultural activities and sporting competitions with approximately 80,000 people in attendance.[18] Many of the events took place in the newly constructed Joseph Stalin Palace of Culture and Science, a monumental edifice that the Soviet Union had built especially for the occasion as a gift to Poland. Other events took place in the stadium, in smaller theaters, in union halls, and on the numerous outdoor stages constructed in Warsaw's plazas, marketplaces, and parks.[19] The festivities continued in the evenings at embassy receptions, in the streets, and with fireworks displays along the banks of the Vistula River.[20]

Parra performed multiple times and in diverse settings at the festival, to mixed reviews. Her performance at the Chilean gala that was held in the Stalin Palace with over a thousand people in attendance purportedly did not go over that well—perhaps because she appeared solo in a show that mostly featured acts by large ensembles.[21] Parra sang on several other occasions at smaller theaters and outdoor venues over the course of the festival. Fellow delegate Fernán Meza recounts that the public responded "not quite with enthusiasm, but with great interest" when she gave what ended up being a two-and-a-half-hour recital of the traditional poet-songs, a form that was noticeably long and slow.[22] Parra contributed two songs to a live festival album released by the Polish record label Muza (1955), and recorded songs over a two-day session for Polish radio, for which she got paid a tidy sum in Polish currency that she generously dispersed among her friends and acquaintances.[23] She also had the honor of serving as a judge for the festival's folk instrument contest. She would later recount, "I was the only female member [on the panel]. I looked like a little mouse next to the famous European folklorists."[24]

It would appear that this petite solo artist with an unadorned singing style and a stubborn determination to introduce the folklore of her far-off country to the world eventually won the hearts of many festival attendees. Meza recalls strolling through the city with Parra one evening and people coming out onto their balconies to throw flowers at her as she passed by. "It was their way of expressing their sentiments for this woman's singing."[25] On her end, Parra devotes several joyous décimas from her autobiography to celebrating the festival and her accomplishments there.[26]

Parra's success at the festival was a testimony to her ability to reach across language and other cultural barriers through her performance. Viewed from a wider angle, it was simultaneously reflective and constitutive of the immense popularity of Latin American folk music in the Soviet Bloc during the period of cultural opening that followed the death of Joseph Stalin in 1953.[27] In this new internationalist era, the Soviet state promoted cultural interchanges with Latin America as ideationally consistent with and integral to its project of expanding socialism worldwide.

The Soviet public's enthusiasm for Latin American folk music cannot be attributed solely to the effectiveness of top-down government policies, however. It was also fueled by a generalized longing to escape to simpler times and faraway places in their imaginations in the aftermath of World War II. In contrast with the musics of other distant lands, Latin American folk music had the added bonus of hewing closely to European listening tastes; it was "exotic, but not too much so."[28] As Parra would soon discover, audiences in Western Europe shared this appreciation for Latin American folk music, and for many of the same reasons.

The World Festival concluded in mid-August and the Chilean delegates scattered. Parra ended up joining a smaller group of some forty people who toured Czechoslovakia for roughly two weeks. The party visited factories, schools, and cultural centers. They went on a tour of the Pilson brewery that ended with a feast and a public scene where Parra berated delegation leader Miguel Lawner for refusing to dance a cueca with her because he was too inebriated. In an interview granted decades later, an apparently still traumatized Lawner would declare that he had never met anyone in his entire life who could curse someone out (*putear*) quite like Parra. "And the next day, it was as if nothing had happened."[29] In addition to haranguing her fellow delegates, Parra recorded several songs for a Czech radio station during the visit, for which she was purportedly paid 150 korunas.[30]

The USSR Ministry of Culture released a single of Parra's music around this time, most likely culled from the recordings she had made at the Warsaw radio station.[31] It featured Parra performing in what was quickly becoming her signature style of a soloist who sang over her own guitar accompaniment. Side A featured the folk song "Meriana" from the Chilean dependency then known as Easter Island (Rapa Nui today)—one of the rare songs in Parra's folk repertoire that she did not collect herself—and Side B her crowd-pleasing original composition "La jardinera" (The Gardener).[32] Within the space of a year, Parra would rerecord the same two songs for the French label Le Chant du Monde. The inclusion of "Meriana" on both her Soviet single and French album demonstrates that curiosity and perhaps even a preference for places even more exotic and remote than mainland Chile were strong on both sides of the Iron Curtain.

Like all visiting artists to the Soviet Bloc, Parra performed there by invitation of the state, which organized her activities. This meant that she had no reason or incentive to stay on at the conclusion of her official visit, as she would have no way to earn a living. Accordingly, after two weeks in Warsaw and another two weeks touring Czechoslovakia, she traveled back across the Iron Curtain to Vienna. There, Caupolicán statuette in hand, she unsuccessfully lobbied the Chilean ambassador to Austria to support her artistic endeavors.

At his suggestion, and like countless Latin American artists before and since, Parra next made her way to Paris. She arrived at the train station late at night and alone, with all of thirty-four dollars in her pocket, and began to sob inconsolably. A taxi driver took pity on her and delivered her to the Saint Michel Hotel, a known refuge for Latin American expatriates in the heart of Paris's bohemian neighborhood of the Latin Quarter. Parra immediately ran into several compatriots from the Chilean festival delegation, who agreed to put her up in their room for the night. She began looking for work the next day.[33]

"Rosita Has Gone to Heaven"

Parra received the news of the death of her youngest daughter shortly after arriving in Paris. Not yet a year old, Rosa Clara died of pneumonia in the arms of her twelve-year-old brother Ángel as he and Luis Arce raced to the hospital by taxi.[34] Parra's grief was immense and unabated. As she stated in a 1957 interview, "I have a thorn in my chest that stabs at my heart incessantly."[35]

Parra blamed Arce for the death of their daughter and wrote him countless missives accusing him of as much over the ensuing months. That she also blamed herself is made agonizingly clear in her autobiography in verse:

I don't have a pardon from heaven
Nor do the winds forgive . . .
Let the one who left her dear angel
Stranded during the winter
Be hurled into hell's inferno
Unto the ages of ages.

No tengo perdón del cielo
ni tampoco de los vientos . . .
p'aquella que su angelorun
deja botá' en el invierno,
arrójenla en los infiernos
pa' sécula seculorum.[36]

Parra also wrote eulogies to Rosa Clara in décimas, the literary form of the poet-songs that were traditionally sung at that most sorrowful of rituals, the wake for the little angel, which she now understood in all its profundity.[37]

Rosa Clara's death led to a change in Parra's plans: instead of the two months that she had originally promised, she would remain in Europe for a year and a half. Her marriage to Arce crumbled under the weight of their shared grief and Parra's rage and prolonged absence. As Arce explained, "when a child dies, so too do countless other things."[38] As to how Parra's children felt regarding her extended stay in Europe, Isabel remained characteristically reticent on the topic, Ángel wrote that he was used to her absences and knew that she would return, and Carmen Luisa claimed that her first memory of her mother was at age six, when Violeta came to fetch her at her father's house upon returning from Europe in late 1956.[39]

Parra gave no public explanation for her extended absence from Chile, as far as I can ascertain. She left few clues besides her poetry to assist a biographer in deciphering her motives. An avid letter-writer and self-promoter, she did send the Chilean press updates as to her whereabouts and activities in the early weeks of her European sojourn. The first, published in the weekly *Zig-Zag* on September 17, 1955, recounts her triumphs in Warsaw and promises that she will return home soon.[40] The second, published in *Ecran* on October 25, offers a wholly exaggerated list of her Parisian successes—a soon-to-be recorded seven-album series on a major French label, contracted television appearances—and nary a mention of an impending homecoming.[41] Whether her change in plans was due to her inability or unwillingness to face returning home after Rosa Clara's tragic death, the possibilities that Paris opened up to an itinerant Chilean musician, or a combination of these and other factors remains undetermined.

Some of Parra's contemporaries would judge her harshly for staying away from her three other children for as long as she did, interpreting it as proof that she was an "unnatural" mother.[42] Their attitude was both unsurprising and gendered, as to the best of my knowledge no comparable judgment was meted out to Nicanor Parra for leaving his three small children in the care of their mother during his extended studies at Oxford University (from where he came home with a new romantic partner, a younger Swedish woman). As if responding to her critics, in her defensive and ultimately contradictory décima, "Verso por confesión" (Poem of Confession), Violeta asserts,

> It was not my fault,
> I declare myself innocent,
> Everyone comprehends
> That I'm not a bad momma

> *no ha sido por culpa mía,*
> *yo me declaro inocente,*
> *lo sabe toda la gente*
> *de que no soy mala maire.*[43]

The 1950s Parisian–Latin American Folk Music Scene

Parra lived in Paris from September 1955 to December 1956, and again for most of the three-year span from August 1962 to August 1965. Both extended stays fell within the years of accelerated demographic and economic growth in France that are often referred to as the "glorious thirty" in French historiography, lasting roughly from 1945 to 1975. The period was likewise one when the French public sought out the authentic and *le lointain* (far-off places) with exuberance and resolve.

The roots of French and, more generally, European fascination with "exotic" peoples and places reach back to the onset of European expansionism. That established, many factors coincided to produce the "continued potency" of cultural exoticism in post–World War II France during "the period of its most intense and wide-ranging embrace of the modern."[44] There was the widespread desire among Europeans to put war's devastations behind them by escaping in their imaginations to distant and idyllic places. Narrowing the focus to France, many French people felt alienated by the rapid expansion of capitalist consumer culture that was one of the salient features of the "glorious thirty." At the same time, France was undergoing an intensified process of Americanization in the postwar era that appeared to threaten the very existence of French culture.[45] The period was additionally demarcated by the decolonization struggles of France's defeat in Indochina (1954), and of the "Algerian War" of independence (1954–62). Rapid social transformations combined with the brutality of war and ongoing cruelties of colonialism to engender a collective soul-searching about France's place in the world and, more broadly, about the pros and cons of modernity itself. For those French people who found modernity to have more cons than pros, authenticity seemed a promising antidote to its challenges and disappointments.

Latin American folk music assumed a privileged place within the French search for the authentic in the years spanning the "glorious thirty," much as it did within the post-Stalin Soviet Bloc. This was for many reasons, some the same as in the Soviet Bloc, and some specific to France. Musically, Latin American folk music was experienced as exotic in a pleasant but not-too-challenging sort of way. Spanish-language songs had the added advantage of sharing Latin roots with the French language, which meant that their general themes were more or less understandable to their francophone audience. Somewhat ironically given that Latin American culture was "foreign" in France, Latin American folk music was perceived as a nonthreatening and authentic counterweight to the successive "foreign invasions" of Anglophone rock and roll—Elvis in the mid-1950s and the Beatles in the 1960s—the same invasions that folk revivalists were battling against in Chile and elsewhere.[46] Finally, Latin American folk music faced little competition from French folk music. In contrast with most of Western Europe and Latin America, France did not experience a folk revival in the 1950s and 1960s. This was most likely because the Vichy regime's abuse of folklore as propaganda, in ideological sync with Nazi folklorism, made its revival less attractive in France than in other countries in the postwar era.[47]

It was within this context that Parra took up residence in Paris in the early autumn of 1955. She joined a small but vibrant community of Latin American artists, writers, musicians, and students congregated in the Latin Quarter on Paris's Left Bank. Paris had long been the cultural mecca for Latin American expatriates and exiles, and the 1950s and 1960s were no exception. The most renowned Latin American resident in Paris at the time was probably Colombian novelist and Nobel Prize winner Gabriel García Márquez (1982), though back then he was just another unknown writer. While there is no evidence that Parra ever met him, she did share a one-room flat with one of his girlfriends for a while, the Spanish actress María Concepción "Tachia" Quintana. In addition to García Márquez, the (all-male) roster of Latin American novelists, poets, artists, and filmmakers living in Paris in the 1950s who would eventually become internationally acclaimed included Fernando Botero, Carlos Cáceres-Sobrea, Alejo Carpentier, Julio Cortázar, Narciso Debourg, Nicolás Guillén, Alejandro Jodorowsky, Jesús Rafael Soto, and Mario Vargas Llosa.[48] Romano Zanotti, Italian artist, musician, and founding member of the Parisian–Latin American folk music group Los Machucambos, describes the scene: "Paris, in that moment, was not only the capital of South American music, but also the center of the world, and everything that had to do with the visual arts happened right here, within the perimeter of the Latin Quarter. All over the world people were talking about Saint-Germain-des-Prés. . . . We had survived the war, we had suffered immensely, and there was a 'joie de vivre' unlike anything that has been seen since."[49]

To state the obvious, there were plenty of Latin American musicians in "the capital of South American music." The Parisian–Latin American folk music scene of the 1950s represented the latest of successive waves of Latin American musical fads to hit Paris, New York, Santiago, and countless other sites in an increasingly interconnected world over the course of the twentieth century: tango in the 1920s, rumba and samba in the 1930s, mambo and cha-cha-cha in the 1950s.[50] The large community of Spanish exiles living in Paris at the time, many talented musicians among them, helped open the path for Latin American musicians there as well.

Argentine master guitarist and songwriter Atahualpa Yupanqui (né Héctor Roberto Chavero Aramburu) was a trailblazer of the 1950s Parisian–Latin

American folk music scene. Then a member of the Argentine Communist Party, he spent part of 1950 in political exile in Paris, where he won critical acclaim for his music with the support of prominent figures in the French cultural Left. Highlights of his stay included sharing the stage with Edith Piaf, and recordings for the Musée de l'Homme, UNESCO, and the French record labels BAM (Boite à Musique) and Le Chant du Monde.[51] Yupanqui paved the way for other Paris-based Latin American folk musicians. His adoption of an Indigenous-sounding name, reflecting and reinforcing the predilection for all things Indigenous and Indigenous-like of the time, would be echoed by a number of Parisian–Latin American folk ensembles in the 1950s and beyond.

Where Atahualpa Yupanqui was not a trendsetter was in the political content of his repertoire. His songs of social protest presaged the politically radical Latin American folk music scene of the 1960s, but they were unusual for the Latin American folk music scene of 1950s Paris. In that sense, Yupanqui was closer to the French protest songwriter George Brassens than he was to most of his fellow Latin American folk musicians. Those included Parra, who had yet to discover the power of songs to denounce social injustice.

Indeed, the 1950s Parisian–Latin American folk music scene had a decidedly apolitical, escapist bent to it. What mattered was Latin American folk music's capacity to carry enthusiasts to far-off and exotic lands in their imaginations. The duo formed by Argentine folk singers Leda Valladares and María Elena Walsh personified this trend. Two of only a handful of women who made their living performing Latin American folk music in Paris at the time, Léda et Maria (Leda and María) performed dressed as Argentine "Indians" in outlandish matching costumes of ponchos and decorative headbands. This may explain why they were sometimes introduced by equally outlandish geocultural combinations such as the "Incas from Rio de Janeiro" or the "Mexican girls from la Pampa."[52] The duo performed regularly at upscale cabarets, concert cafés, and music halls, where they shared the stage with rising French luminaries such as singers Jacques Brel, Barbará, and Charles Aznavour and mime Marcel Marceau. They also appeared on French radio and television and recorded albums on the Le Chant du Monde label in France and the London International label in England.

By the time Parra arrived in Paris in September 1955, the Latin American folk music scene that Atahualpa Yupanqui and the duo Léda et Maria helped forge was thriving. Parra wasted no time integrating herself. Her friends at the Saint Michel Hotel put her in touch with Chilean musician Renato Otero, a philosophy student who attended university by day and sang at the Latin American–themed boîte L'Escale to finance his studies by night. When Otero first learned of Parra's arrival in Paris, he had expressed interest in forming a duo with her and arranged to meet her. He changed his mind when he saw her in person, however. Parra recounts the encounter in a 1957 interview: "I waved my hand at him. Otero's eyes found my hand, traveled up my arm, and when they reached my face betrayed their obvious disappointment." She responded, "And what were you expecting? A pretty girl? Because I assure you that I can sing."[53]

As Otero was apparently only interested in partnering with a conventionally attractive woman, the idea of the duo was scratched—though the two musicians would sometimes perform together in the months ahead. To his credit, Otero convinced the owner of L'Escale to grant Parra an audition. The owner liked what she heard and offered Parra steady work at the club. This, in turn, earned Otero a place among the six named "archangels" that Parra praises in her autobiography in verse because "They shelter me with their friendship, / And offer me their support / In this land so far away" (*me abrigan con su amistad, / me brindan conformidad / en ese mundo lejano*).[54]

L'Escale

L'Escale was a smoke-filled hole-in-the-wall located in the Latin Quarter. It was a favored haunt for Latin Americans residing in Paris, French fans of Latin American folk music, and the chance international tourist in search of a different flavor of *la vie bohême* (bohemian life). The club was decorated in a maritime theme, with fishing nets draped from the ceilings, and a large map of Latin America hung as a backdrop to its stage. A pair of resident peacocks rounded off the club's exotic vibe.

The musicians who performed at L'Escale on any given night were diverse in terms of both their countries of origin and degrees of talent. Then–starving writers and artists Gabriel García Márquez, Jesús Rafael Soto, Carlos Cáceres-Sobrea, and Narciso Debourg all performed at the club at one time or another in order to fund their other creative pursuits. The club was perhaps best known for its party-like atmosphere and late-night jam sessions. These began after midnight and often lasted until dawn. The boîte's audience was usually made up of students and Left Bank intellectuals, though actress and future supermodel Brigitte Bardot and other French celebrities made the occasional late-night appearance. The club was quite small, and lines of people fifty to one hundred deep would often form outside it, waiting to get in.[55]

L'Escale's importance to the transnational history of Latin American folk music was momentous. It was the birthplace of a genre of pan–Latin American folk-derived music that arguably could only have been birthed in Paris. Encouraged by the club's improvisational, anything-goes atmosphere, musicians from all over Latin America and their imitators-in-admiration from

France, Spain, Italy, and Switzerland came together to invent a new kind of "Latin American" folk music out of elements belonging to "distinct musical universes which would never have met within a Latin American context."[56] Looking back on the era, Spanish Republican exile and L'Escale musician Paco Ibáñez would declare it "the temple of the Latin American music scene in Paris of the 1950s and 1960s."[57]

The Andean-inspired musical group Los Incas had its beginnings at the club. It was formed by two Argentines and two Venezuelans, none of whom had ever lived in the Andes and all of whom learned how to play Andean instruments in Paris. Over the course of a long and successful musical career, the band recorded multiple albums, toured extensively throughout Europe, performed at Grace Kelly's wedding in Monaco, appeared with Brigitte Bardot, and provided the background track for the hit "If I Could" by the popular US duo Simon and Garfunkel.[58] The Costa Rican–Spanish-Italian ensemble Los Machucambos also traced its origins to L'Escale. Its 1959 recording *La Bamba* earned highest honors from the French Academy of Recording Arts, and its cha-cha-cha "Pepito" remained number one on the 1961 French music charts for nine months straight, selling over 7 million copies.[59] The musical trajectories of these and any number of lesser-known bands and solo artists who made up Paris's Latin American folk music scene of the 1950s and 1960s all began at L'Escale.

Parra performed regularly at the club in the mid-1950s and again when she returned to Paris in the early 1960s (see figure 4.1). Over time, she built a receptive, if niche, audience, a mélange of intellectuals, artists, and leftists that in many ways resembled her fan base in Chile, minus the latter's semirural and rural strata. Parra was never one of L'Escale's most popular acts, however. Her professed belief in both the integrity of the Chilean folklore she had collected and the need for its proper rendition in performance made her something of a mismatch with the club's party atmosphere. At the same time, Parra's avid—and, some might say, rigid and dogmatic—Chilean nationalism meant she did not fit very well with the other L'Escale musicians who were actively creating a new kind of "folkloric" music that, with expansive spirit and scant ethnographic precision, would be labeled "Latin American." Nor did her chilenidad (Chilean identity) jibe with the pan–Latin American perspective of her French public, who were far less concerned with a song's national origins than with being transported to a festive, distant, and generic Latin America. As one of the members of Los Machucambos explained, "[Parra] was only interested in Chilean folklore and her own songs. When she sang four or five cuecas in a row, it got a little monotonous . . . and people tired of it pretty quickly."[60]

Parra also had to contend with the challenges of being one of the few women musicians on the scene. In contrast with the Chilean folk revival where

Figure 4.1 Violeta Parra performing with Romano Zanotti at L'Escale, Paris, n.d.
Courtesy of the Zanotti family.

women participated at all levels, including its leadership, the musicians who performed Latin American folk music in Paris in the 1950s and 1960s were overwhelmingly men. To make matters worse, and as her initial encounter with fellow musician René Otero confirmed, Parra lacked those "feminine" assets that likely would have eased her entry into this male-dominated performance arena.

Parra's comparison with Julia "Julita" Cortés, lead singer of Los Machucambos, is telling in this regard.[61] Julita was in her early twenties when Los Machucambos outgrew the bohemian club to become an international sensation. Revealingly, the band's success was widely attributed to Julita's youth, beauty, and graceful stage presence.[62] Parra, in contrast, was almost forty by the time she began performing at L'Escale. Her appearance was considered unappealing by some, and few would have described her stage presence as charming.[63] Lacking those attributes that could ease a talented woman artist's entry into an almost all-male performance space, Parra had to break through the barriers of gender with the force of her talent and will.

In lieu of a ticket to fame, then, L'Escale provided Parra with the more modest return of steady, if demanding, work. The hours were exhausting, as she rotated with two or three other acts over an evening that often spanned from

9:00 P.M. to 4:00 or even 5:00 A.M. The small club lacked proper ventilation. It would become so filled with cigarette smoke that the musicians had to take breaks outside just to catch their breath. People in the audience were rowdy and had no qualms about carrying on loud conversations while the musicians played. Anecdotes abound of Parra throwing a shoe or maraca at members of the public who failed to obey her demand for complete silence during her performance. Even the unruly pair of resident peacocks could not escape her wrath if they dared call out while she was on stage. She lost the battle to be heard more often than she won it.

Small wonder that fellow folklorista Margot Loyola characterized Parra's work at the club as "dramatic and heroic," an appraisal she reached based on her own brief experience performing there.[64] The two folkloristas overlapped in Paris for several months in 1956 and would often seek out each other's company and support.[65] Loyola agreed to fill in for Parra at L'Escale while Parra recovered from a botched skin treatment that had promised to reduce the effect of pockmarks but instead left her face red and swollen. Loyola, who unlike Parra had not been schooled in the hard knocks environment of Santiago's working-class dives, recalled the whole experience as "dreadful."[66] She ended up lasting two nights at the club compared with the months-turned-to-years of her more resilient colleague.

Parra was not paid well for her "heroic" work at L'Escale. Artists and musicians from Latin America and other exoticized regions of the world rarely are, their wages paralleling the low wages paid to "ethnic" workers in other industries. Although Parra would boast upon her return to Chile about how much money she made at the club, the truth was that she could barely cover the rent for a run-down hotel room up the street from it with the little she earned.[67] At closing time in the early morning, she would drag herself the short distance from the club to her tiny, windowless room where she cooked her meals on a hot plate and shared the bathroom down the hallway with other boarders. Ever gifted at being poor, she concocted tasty soups from bones that she got for free from the neighborhood butcher under pretext that they were for her dog.[68]

"Archangels" and Opportunities

Parra sought out other performance opportunities beyond L'Escale, in keeping with her intent to disseminate her homeland's folklore far and wide. As she had done in Vienna, she approached the Chilean embassy in Paris for assistance, to only slightly less dismal results. In addition to the Caupolicán statuette that she hauled across the continent as proof of her accomplishment, she had crafted her own letter of introduction to the Chilean ambassador to

France, Juan Bautista Rosetti. According to fellow festival delegate Fernán Meza, it was an odd document; it stated something to the effect that "Chilean folklorist Violeta Parra advises that she will be arriving in Paris on such-and-such a date and expects to be received by the ambassador," yet it was addressed to someone who likely had no idea who Violeta Parra was given that her recognition as a folklorista was only recently acquired.[69]

Unfortunately for Parra, Ambassador Rosetti was away from Paris when she showed up at the embassy. His staff proved reluctant to assist her. Apparently, they could not imagine how this small woman in nondescript attire could possibly represent their nation in its best light. They maintained Parra at arm's length through the September festivities commemorating Chile's independence from Spain—the one time in the year that Chilean folk musicians were normally guaranteed ample opportunities to perform. Or at least they tried to. In an interview, Parra recounts how she had to fight her way into the embassy's September 18th Independence Day party in order to offer her free and patriotic services as an award-winning folk singer. She described her preparations for the party: "I fixed myself up a little bit (more I could not do, since the result is always the same)." She went on: "I was not a diplomat, but I was Chilean. And wasn't Chile what we were commemorating? Or was it that what really mattered was what gown a woman wore to the reception?" In the end, Parra was allowed to perform but to an all-but-empty room somewhere in the embassy. Ever the class rebel, she turned her outsider status inside out and accused the crème de la crème of Chilean diplomacy of living "in another world, one that was false and vain."[70]

Parra's concerted and, for the most part, ineffectual attempts to gain support within Chilean diplomatic circles did lead to one notable breakthrough: her friendship with former Chilean diplomat Ángel Custodio "Cuto" Oyarzún, his wife Ana Urrutia, and the sculptor María Teresa Pinto. She met them at an embassy function, most likely the very Independence Day celebration that she crashed.[71] According to Parra, "Cuto," who like Parra was a chillanejo or person from Chillán, became so overwhelmed by emotion when he heard her singing the folk songs of his childhood that "he needed to steady himself on a piece of furniture so as not to fall over."[72] The trio of wealthy and well-connected Chilean expatriates would become invaluable allies during Parra's first Parisian sojourn. In her autobiography in verse, she lists all three among the six "archangels" who offered their help "To this wandering singer / In arrogant Paris" (por esta cantora errante / en el París arrogante).[73]

Parra's compatriots put her in contact with Paul Rivet, director of the Musée de l'Homme, who arranged to have her record material for the museum's permanent collection.[74] Rivet also introduced Parra to the staff of Radiodiffusion-Télévision Française (RTF), who scheduled an audition for her in October 1956. Parra's initial attempt to break into French mass media proved unsuccessful, however. As the RTF artistic director of broadcasting explained in his rejection letter, the panel greatly appreciated the quality of Parra's voice but would have preferred "a livelier interpretation."[75]

It is unlikely that Parra received compensation for her Musée de l'Homme recordings. Fellow Chilean expatriate, artist, and family friend Alejandro Jodorowsky chided Parra that the museum had swindled her by not paying her for her work.[76] His admonition makes evident that Parra's position could be reversed within a European context, from a professional folklorista, collector, and interpreter of the authentic to an authentic source herself. Parra did apparently get paid for material that she recorded for UNESCO in 1956, perhaps because the songs were used to produce a half-hour radio show, and not merely collected for preservation.[77]

Parra's well-connected "archangels" also put her in touch with León Moussinac, founder of the communist-affiliated record company Le Chant du Monde. Started in 1937, the company was banned under Nazi occupation and resurfaced after liberation. Its ideological and cultural mission was to provide a musical alternative to the "vulgar, corrupt, and standardized melodic formulas" of the mass-produced music of decadent capitalism, much of which emanated from the United States.[78] In practice, this meant the label both re-released albums of classical music from the Soviet Union, for which it possessed the exclusive rights, and produced its own recordings of folk music from around the world—hence the label's name, which translates as "Song of the World." Le Chant du Monde thus maintained and reinforced the Soviet-drawn division between Russian "high culture" and the folk cultures of the rest of the world's peoples.

By the time Parra was picked up by the label in March 1956, its growing catalog of international folk music contained a fair amount from Latin America, including several albums by Argentine folk singer Atahualpa Yupanqui and one by his compatriots, the duo Léda et Maria.[79] Parra would release two albums on the label: *Violeta Parra, Chants et danses du Chili* (Songs and Dances of Chile), volumes 1 and 2.[80] She recorded the material for both volumes in one sitting on March 26, 1956.[81] On a personal note, Parra's first grandchild, Christina "Tita" Parra, had been born the week before on March 21, 1956.

Parra's French albums consisted primarily of songs that she had collected in and around Santiago, arranged to better suit the musical tastes and expectations of a European audience. Volume 1's canto a lo poeta or poet-song, for instance, is in fact a medley of first verses from three different poet-songs that Parra had learned from doña Rosa Lorca. As such, it is considerably shorter and far more varied than any of the poet-songs would have been had Parra recorded them in their entirety. Another notable concession to European tastes was the inclusion of two songs, one on each volume, from Easter Island (Rapa Nui).[82] This turned out to be a smart marketing decision, as European reviewers rated the songs to be among the recordings' best tracks.[83]

The albums' packaging encapsulates the tension between Le Chant du Monde's ideal of presenting the folk music of the world in its purest form and the dictates of consumer capitalism that would ultimately decide the record company's viability. On the one hand, the biographical insert that accompanied both albums launches an all-out attack on the escapist Latin American music scene in Paris: "What spectator, what listener of good faith would not want to weep at the multiplying of those Latin American ensembles where, all too often, an indigent amateurism competes with a primitive cabaret exoticism?!" On the other hand, the albums' artwork draws on visual clichés that are unambiguous examples of that same "primitive cabaret exoticism" the insert so rotundly condemns.

Volume 1's cover artwork is an expressionistic drawing of a woman—presumably Violeta Parra—playing her guitar (see figure 4.2). The woman's facial features are exaggerated and her hair is plaited into two braids, which when interpreted through a colonial lens would indicate that she was "Indigenous." The artwork's exoticization of Parra was so obvious that an otherwise positive review called it out, accusing its depiction of an "old Indian woman with a guitar" as being "a little bit like 'false advertising.'"[84] (Not surprisingly, ethnic-racial perceptions were as malleable in Europe as they were in Chile, as Parra would be seen as someone with recognizable Indigenous features on her return trip to Europe in the early 1960s.)

Parra's exoticization is carried even further by the cover of volume 2. It shows a still life of artifacts, presumably meant to be from Chile, that amount to a veritable anthropological pastiche—a primitive-looking mask, a colorfully painted ceramic vessel, and a Caribbean-style conga drum adorned with zigzag patterns, all arranged decoratively on a traditional blanket (see figure 4.3). This, for a recording that does not feature percussion of any kind, just, as its cover advertises, "Violeta Parra, song and guitar." Apparently, the record label's denunciation of the exoticism that dominated the Parisian Latin music scene in the era did not prevent it from taking pragmatic advantage of that same exoticism to promote the latest Latin American artist signed to its label.

Parra's well-connected "archangels" were part of the small but caring group of friends who helped sustain her while she was in Paris. So was Alejandro Jodorowsky. In her autobiography in verse, Parra declares her "friend Alejandro" yet another of her "archangels" for "Lifting my spirits in Paris / With a beautiful flower / And a friendly smile" (*que me alentara en París / con una flor de alhelí / y una amistosa sonrisa*).[85]

Figure 4.2 Cover of LP *Chants et danses du Chili*, Volume 1. Le Chant du Monde
LDY-4060, 1956.

On her end, Parra was known to be a generous friend with the little she
had. Tachia Quintana, the Spanish actress who shared a room with Parra before moving in with her lover, Gabriel García Márquez, relates that "[Parra]
was capable of giving away all the money she had just earned in a week or
month of work . . . to a friend who was having problems."[86] Parra was especially kind to those younger and even poorer than herself. She lent struggling
students the key to her room so that they could rest there while she performed.
She offered to wash Jodorowsky's clothing so that the young artist would not
have to spend money at the laundromat.[87] Proud of the nurturing role that
she played in the lives of her fellow expatriates, she boasted in an interview,
"I was like a mother to all of the Chileans [in Paris]."[88]

Figure 4.3 Cover of LP *Chants et danses du Chili*, Volume 2. Le Chant du Monde
LDY-4071, 1956.

In addition to her circle of friends, Parra is purported to always have been
in love with one man or another.[89] She for sure had at least one love affair
during her first Parisian stay. It was with Paco Rus, a Spaniard and the last of
the six archangels she names in her autobiography—though she is careful to
clarify that, in his case "the last is first."[90] Margot Loyola, who met Rus when
she was in Paris, described him as a "very handsome and attentive young
man." As Loyola tells it, Rus was absolutely smitten with Parra, but Parra did
not reciprocate the depth of his feelings and eventually broke up with him.
"That's the way she was," Loyola explained. "She did not like commitments,
her relationships lasted as long as she wanted them to last." Loyola clarified
further that Parra had confided in her that "she got bored with being with
the same man, that she needed to always be meeting new ones."[91] Though

Parra is alleged to have left Rus brokenhearted, she nonetheless remembers him fondly in her autobiography in verse:

My love for him is so sweet,
He surrenders his heart to me,
Beautiful like a cherub,
And therefore I was able
To face up to my destiny.

Mi amor por él es muy fino,
bello como un querubino,
m'entrega su corazón,
así pudo mi razón
hacerle frente al destino.[92]

As even her closest friends freely acknowledged, Parra was difficult to get along with. Many of her social interactions in Paris, as elsewhere, were neither loving nor harmonious. Quite the opposite. Take, for example, Parra's first and only encounter with Argentine folk singers Leda Valladares and María Elena Walsh, aka Léda et Maria. Parra had heard good things about the Argentine duo and took it upon herself to pay them a visit at their hotel. Though by no means luxurious, their room, with its windows, balcony, and ensuite bathroom, contrasted with the windowless, bathroom-less room in the fleabag hotel where Parra resided. The duo could afford the room because they performed regularly on the Parisian café concert circuit as well as at some of the city's chic Right Bank clubs—venues that paid their entertainers considerably more than a bohemian Left Bank boîte like L'Escale. According to Walsh's biographer, Parra sang Valladares and Walsh a few songs, then cursed them out for being a couple of bourgeois usurpers.[93] The anecdote lends credence to Tachia Quintana's assessment, based on firsthand experience, that Parra had both a violent temper and "a sense of self-importance that was absolutely insufferable."[94]

London

In May 1956, ten months into her stay in Europe, Parra made a whirlwind trip to London. In a letter published later that year in *Ecran*, she bragged that she was able to accomplish in ten days there what had taken her ten months to do in France.[95] Despite Parra's documented penchant to exaggerate, she does not appear to have done so in this instance. In the space of less than two weeks, she was interviewed by both the BBC's European music supervisor Norman Fraser and its Latin American Service, the latter on its radio program *Latin*

Americans in London. She performed live on the "mainly for women" BBC television show *Your Own Time,* sandwiched between a segment on fashion and another on table decorations.[96] She recorded twenty songs for the broadcasting system's permanent collection, for which she was generously compensated.[97] She taped material for an LP on the EMI record label, a subsidiary of the same conglomerate as Odeon Chilena (that for reasons unknown was never produced).[98] She gave several concerts and recitals, including one at the Canning House, an aristocratic cultural institution aimed at promoting understanding between Britain and Latin America. She met with and was recorded by renowned US folklorist and folk singer Alan Lomax.

Parra's triumphant visit to London resulted at least in part from propitious circumstances. First, she received the full support of Chile's civil attaché in London, Arístides Aguilera, who was a great admirer of Parra's work.[99] Second, and by sheer coincidence, then–BBC European music supervisor Norman Fraser had been born and spent part of his childhood in Chile. He spoke a fluent Spanish that was peppered with *chilenismos* (Chilean expressions), and he took an immediate interest in Parra.

On a broader level, Parra's accomplishments in London reflected the way her work as a *folklorista* paralleled that of BBC staff members and other cultural promoters with whom she came in contact. Parra's visit to London occurred when the 1950s British folk revival was in full swing, propelled by many of the same forces as the Chilean folk revival.[100] As the home of the International Folk Music Council, London was also an important hub for promoting communication and exchanges between contemporaneous folk revivals on an international scale.[101] In combination, these factors explain why Parra was so well received during her short stay in London; the same nationally specific and solemn performance that provoked grumbling on the part of her public at L'Escale received accolades from the London-based revivalists. Though many of them were even more purist in their approach to folkloric performance than Parra herself, their overall appraisal of her work was favorable.

Parra' s host while she was in London was the folk singer Victoria Kingsley. Kingsley did not share the traditionalist rigidity of others on the British folk music scene. She was an Oxford-educated woman of means who performed songs in sixteen languages, played flamenco guitar as well as other styles, and traveled the world learning folk songs that she then performed in other countries so that no one would say, "Oh, that's not the way it's supposed to be!"[102] Though widely divergent in their backgrounds, Parra and Kingsley shared a certain kindred spirit in the eccentricity and willfulness of their approaches. Indeed, Kingsley's musical eclecticism may well have been one of the sources of inspiration for Parra's own short-lived experimentation with incorporating international folk songs into her concert repertoire upon her return to Chile from Europe at the close of 1956.

Most of Parra's folk revivalist colleagues in London were conscious that Parra, too, was a folk revivalist like themselves—up to a point. They also exhibited a colonialist tendency to confuse her with an actual folkloric source, a bona fide Chilean campesina who had somehow made her way to the BBC studios. BBC archivist Marie Slocombe, for example, described Parra as "a country girl" and noted that she was not "very polished"—a dearth that was considered an asset in traditionalist folk circles.[103] Norman Fraser praised her as a "remarkable peasant folk singer." There was also Alan Lomax, a US folk revivalist who was working for the BBC at the time, having moved to London in order to escape McCarthyism in the United States. Lomax treated Parra as he would any other of his folkloric informants: he recorded her performing five songs and labeled the tape box "Authentic Chile."[104]

The estimations of Lomax and his British peers of Parra suggest that she moved somewhat seamlessly between her on- and offstage performance of the authentic when in Europe. This was most likely tied to Parra's appearance. How else can one explain the disparate way that Lomax responded to Parra versus the Argentine folk duo (and Parra's class enemies) Léda et Maria? The duo traveled to London around the same time as Parra for the express purpose of convincing Lomax to record them for the international folk series he was producing for the US label Folkways, but he politely declined. According to one of Walsh's biographers, Lomax appreciated the duo's talents but was unwilling to include them in his collection for obvious reasons: "How could he convince the people who bought his recordings that these two girls who were so white, so well-adapted to Saint Germain [the Parisian neighborhood known for its nightlife], so knowledgeable of various languages, and so well read, had been born in the mountains of the [Argentine] Northeast, among the goats and droughts?"[105]

Lomax and his revivalist British colleagues found it difficult to mistake the two Argentine folk singers for folkloric subjects. Parra, in contrast, fit her European peers' image of how an authentic "Latin American" should look, which made it easier, in turn, for them to perceive her as an actual folkloric source.

Last Hurrahs

Parra rushed back to Paris from London in time to record the program *Rhythmes du Chili* (Rhythms of Chile) on May 15 for the French Radio station Paris Inter.[106] She resumed singing at L'Escale and landed a few additional performance opportunities before her departure for Chile in late November

1956. She sang at an upscale restaurant where she met a fashion boutique owner who was so impressed by Parra that she made her the gift of a new "huasa" dress sewn from only the finest materials.[107] Parra played the Left Bank cabaret, Port du Salud, whose programming for that year also included Léda et Maria and French chanteuse Barbara.[108] She was one of the few solo acts among a pageant of folk ensembles to perform at the international folk festival held in June at the University of the Sorbonne.[109]

Le Chant du Monde released the first volume of *Violeta Parra, Songs and Dances of Chile* in September 1956.[110] Shortly after its release, Parra attended a reception in celebration of Margot Loyola's birthday. As the gala was hosted by none other than the Chilean ambassador and his wife, Parra took advantage of the occasion to exact a revenge of sorts for the disregard with which the Chilean diplomatic community had treated her over the previous year. Breaking with the social conventions of the Chilean upper-crust, she arrived with a stack of her newly minted albums and proceeded to peddle them to the assembled dignitaries under the astonished gaze of her hostess. As Parra explained, "You can't expect me to just give my work away to rich men like these guys."[111]

The September release of Parra's Le Chant du Monde album together with her expanding network of contacts furnished her with one last milestone at the tail end of her first European residence: in late November 1956, she appeared on the radio arts review *Le masque et la plume* (The Mask and the Feather). The weekly show followed what was for the times an innovative format of a panel discussion of literary works interspersed with musical interludes, all recorded live in front of a studio audience.[112] Luminaries from Paris's literary and musical scene graced the program with their presence from its onset. French author and soon-to-be Nobel Prize winner Albert Camus was the announced guest (though a no-show) on the day that Parra was scheduled to perform. The chart-topping chanteuse Catherine Sauvage (who did show up) was the program's other musical act besides Parra. The show's announcer introduced Parra as "the only person in France who performs authentic folk songs from Chile." He informed the listeners of the recent release of her Le Chant du Monde album. Parra then performed two songs from the recording. That Parra was able to introduce the songs in passable French is an example of the enduring impact of her prolonged residence in Paris.[113]

Soon after she appeared on *Le masque et la plume*, Parra departed for Genoa, Italy. From there, she took a ship back to Chile. She left her guitar with her lover Paco Rus for safekeeping in Paris, as she planned to return there within six months. In her 1957 interview with Jorge Edwards for the Chilean women's magazine *Eva*, she explained how she passed by a music store in Genoa and, unable to contain herself, bought a new guitar for the journey home. As was often the case, her account to the Chilean press of her brief stopover in Italy and subsequent ocean-crossing to Chile—twenty songs recorded for Italian radio and television stations, and an onboard recital with 1,500 of her shipmates and crew members in attendance—was likely embellished.[114]

A Letter to Home

Parra sent out a battery of letters to her contacts in the Chilean press and music industry in preparation for her return home in late November 1956. Published excerpts from one such letter appear in the December issue of *Ecran*. In them, Parra copiously (and no doubt exaggeratedly) enumerated her many exploits over her fourteen months in Paris and ten-day blitz in London. She went on to explain what she believed to be the reason behind her positive reception in Europe: "My sincerity in interpretation is natural and comes from strong and undeniable roots: the folkloric roots of our Chilean countryside. My European public . . . tired of superficial performers and keenly desirous of the real has understood this. Paris has not changed me. I love this capital with boundless affection because it is here that I have found the solution to my artistic curiosity and because it has accepted me as I am."[115]

As her letter suggests, Parra's performance of Chilean folklore appealed to her Parisian audience's modern longing to come into contact with the authentic or "real," and that longing and enjoyment could readily be extended to her public in Warsaw or London as well. In that sense, Parra's European audiences shared much with their Chilean counterpart, excepting its rural component.

At the same time, Parra's letter implies that it may have been simpler for her to find and project her authentic self in the cultural centers of Europe than in Chile. This was in part due to her European public's enhanced appreciation for the authentic in response to the dramatic social transformations of the post–World War II era. But it was also because Europeans "read" Parra's representation of Chilean folklore differently than her fans at home. As a folklorista in Chile, Parra was understood to be primarily an interpreter of the authentic "other" for her Chilean public. She was not, for the most part, conflated with being that "other" (at least not yet, though things were fast moving in that direction). When Parra donned her highly stylized huasa costume in a Santiago theater, for instance, it marked her not as a campesina but as a professional folk singer. Her Chilean audience knew from experience that folkloristas dressed in that fashion, and campesinas did not. In contrast, when Parra dressed up as a huasa and sang in her unrefined and, some would say, harsh voice, she could easily become exoticized as an actual Latin American "country girl" in the European imaginary.

It may have been easier for practical reasons for Parra to be a folklorista in Paris than in Santiago as well. L'Escale offered her steady work performing folk music, a situation that was difficult to replicate in Santiago at the time. Additionally, Parra's pay scale in Paris was almost certainly higher in absolute terms (if not in purchasing power) than in Santiago. In Europe, she had the added advantage of not having to compete with other Chilean folkloristas or, if so, only rarely. In contrast, Parra's being Chilean was not a marketable advantage in Chile. Finally, Parra received more support from European cultural institutions than she had from their Chilean equivalents. Granted, this was an exceedingly low bar, given that Parra had received "no official assistance of any kind" for her work as a folklorista in Chile until then, as Edwards pointedly noted in his 1957 *Eva* piece.[116]

Returning to her published letter, upon declaring her love for Paris and all that it had to offer, Parra avowed that "Paris has not changed me." Acknowledging that I contradict her, I maintain that Parra was profoundly transformed by her first European sojourn. The experience made her even more determined to rescue and disseminate the folklore of Chile. She had left for Europe already an impassioned folklorista. Her encounters with ethnographers and folklorists in Paris and especially in London only served to deepen her convictions. Additionally, she returned home with a heightened understanding of what it meant to be both Chilean and authentic, an understanding that arguably is only attained when far from one's homeland. To revisit her lyrics that open this chapter,

> Before I had ever left Chile
> I could not comprehend
> The value of being Chilean
> Oh my, now I do understand!"

It bears repeating that prior to her 1955 transatlantic journey, Parra had never ventured outside Chile. And now she, a woman from "a tiny country, from Chillán, at the end of the earth," could boast of her European achievements. Her appreciation for the authentic was no longer limited to Chilean folklore, as she had learned to value multiple forms of authenticity in Paris. In his 1957 *Eva* piece, published within months of her return to Chile, Edwards attributed her success abroad to that "special fascination with all that was primitive" that characterized the times, and that was felt particularly intensely in Europe. "It is not strange therefore," he continued, "that Violeta Parra is a great admirer of African art, Egyptian sculpture, and of Picasso, who has been described as the primitive of a future art."[117]

In sum, Parra returned from her first trip to Europe a true cosmopolitan: she had triumphed on the world stage in Warsaw, toured Czechoslovakia, successfully navigated the cultural capitals of Paris and London, become somewhat fluent in French, acquired an appreciation for the authentic cultures of other countries along with modern art, and, according to Edwards, was already planning her return trip to Europe with the intention this time of continuing on to Japan.

But perhaps the most transcendental impact of her prolonged stay in Paris resulted in the ways in which, as Parra herself put it, she found the solution to her artistic curiosity. It was on the ocean liner on her return voyage to Chile that she began the improvisations that would eventually become her "anticuecas," a set of atonal instrumental pieces for guitar that marked the onset of an exploration into new creative territories that would only intensify over the rest of her lifetime. It is difficult to imagine that Parra's post-Europe musical inventiveness was not in some way influenced by her experience working at L'Escale, a club that was legendary for its improvised jam sessions.

Paris opened Parra not only to musical possibilities but to visual ones as well. It was where she became an admirer of both African art and Pablo Picasso. As painter and fellow L'Escale musician Romano Zanotti celebrated (and is worth repeating here), Paris was "not only the capital of South American music, but also the center of the world" where "everything that had to do with the visual arts happened."[118] If his assertation holds true, the seeds for Parra's artistic endeavors that would eventually lead to her solo show at the Museum of Decorative Arts, housed in the Louvre Palace, were likely planted during the year and a half that she lived and performed in what for many of those who experienced it at the time was the center of the art world.

Given all of the above, it would be difficult, if not impossible, to take Parra's claim that Paris had not changed her at face value. Instead, her assertion is best understood within the context of Parra's foundational narrative of authenticity. As her letter makes clear, Parra traced her authenticity to her "strong and undeniable roots" in the Chilean countryside. Within this framework, she could no more be transformed by her Parisian sojourn than she could have had a moment of revelation in her brother's apartment. Hers was an unbreachable continuum of authenticity since birth.

Parra's implausible claim to not have been influenced by her prolonged residency in Paris exposes one of the many pitfalls of building one's artistic career on authenticity's promise. Authenticity, by definition, precludes change and innovation as the authentic must remain pure and timeless in the face of modernity in order to serve as its antidote. This was the case even when that modernity happened to be Paris during the heyday of postwar euphoria that made it one of the most exciting cities, if not the most exciting city, of the era. That Parra felt the need to reassure her Chilean readers that Paris had not changed her in the least points to the very real limitations of cloaking oneself in the mantle of authenticity: precisely because it denies the possibility of transformation and invention, authenticity can become something of an identity straitjacket. Parra would face this very challenge when she ventured beyond the confines of folklore in pursuit of other, more imaginative artistic pathways.

Chapter 5

Violeta Volcánica I

In early December 1959, Chilean musician and composer Miguel Letelier was strolling through the Arts Fair along the banks of the Mapocho River in downtown Santiago when he came across Parra's stall with her recent paintings and ceramic works on display. He found a crowd gathered round her as she played another recent creation: her musical composition "El Gavilán" (The Sparrowhawk). Parra performed the piece that day on guitar and voice, but she fully intended to stage it one day as a ballet accompanied by folk instruments and a symphony orchestra.

Letelier found the piece extraordinary. He immediately offered to record and transcribe it so that Parra could copyright it. Forty years later, he would compare "The Sparrowhawk" to Igor Stravinsky's *The Rite of Spring*. He would affirm that although Parra did not know how to write music, she had nonetheless been "able to take the cueca-tonada pairing, which is the most common folkloric expression of [Chile's] central zone, to an unprecedented level of stylization and development that has not been surpassed to this day."[1]

Letelier's encounter with Parra occurred toward the end of the five-year interval between her return to Chile from Europe in December 1956 and her departure for Argentina at the close of 1961, from where she continued on to Europe six months later. Since returning to Chile, she had resumed and intensified her work as a folklorista in the dual meaning of the term as both a collector and disseminator of folklore. But Parra had also vastly expanded the range of her professional and creative activities. The scene at her booth at the 1959 Arts Fair offers a partial inventory of her diverse undertakings at this stage in her artistic trajectory. To those roles of ceramicist, painter, and composer that it illustrates, one can add songwriter, ethnographer, film music scorer, photographer, museum curator, teacher, poet, and tapestry-maker. A woman of "all occupations" is how her brother Nicanor put it in his 1960 poem "Defensa de Violeta Parra" (Defense of Violeta Parra).[2] Nicanor captures the explosive nature of both Violeta's creative output and temperament during these critical years when, referring to her by her family nickname, he dubs her "Viola volcánica" (volcanic Viola).

Violeta did not create in a vacuum. She was part of an inventive movement of leftist artists and intellectuals intent on eschewing European and US cultural models in order to create Chilean ones. The Chilean folk revival was an early manifestation of this larger undertaking to create and promote an alternative chilenidad or Chilean identity in simultaneous defiance of both conservative strains of patriotism and the US cultural invasion that advanced with increasing force after World War II. Over the course of the 1950s, the cultural Left extended its agenda beyond folklore, with its rural connotations and national boundaries, to embrace the *popular* in the broader sense of its Spanish meaning as related to the working poor, both rural and urban.

The leftists' cultural movement took root and flourished during a crucial moment in Chilean history, one that encompassed the hope and belief that real social change was possible. With the repeal of the anti-communist Law in Defense of Democracy in 1958, previously shuttered avenues of political participation opened up even as the state continued to meet mass protests by students and workers with violent repression. The triumph of the 1959 Cuban Revolution a year later inspired leftists in Chile and the world over, and led both the United States and the USSR to intensify their focus on and intervention in Latin America. In an era of rising social tensions and political polarization that would only increase across the 1960s, a tight-knit community of Chilean artists and intellectuals claimed the power to define themselves.

Parra was an eager participant in this movement. Unlike her transition from popular singer to folklorista, this new phase in her creative life did not entail any break with the past, nor did it follow a specific sequence from folklorista to artist. Instead, Parra continued her work as a folklorista even as she began to experiment with different media and invent new idioms. More importantly, and as Letelier's reference to the traditional cueca-tonada in his commentary on "The Sparrowhawk" demonstrates, Parra welded the folklore that she collected to her own artistic endeavors. "Tradition and invention: that's the pact that made her unique" is how her friend, the writer Gonzalo Rojas, described it.[3]

This chapter and the following one chronicle Parra's artistic activities and achievements between her return from Europe at the close of 1956 and her departure for Europe in June 1962. Parra spent much of this time in Santiago, though she also worked as a kind of folklorista-in-residence in the southern city of Concepción for several months. She traveled frequently on collecting expeditions to other regions as well. She spent the first half of 1962 in Argentina, mostly in Buenos Aires. Whether in Santiago, Concepción, or Buenos Aires, her life as artist was indistinguishable from her personal life. As this is the case, this chapter and the next explore the social networks, artistic collaborations, and friendships she made, maintained, or lost during this interval.

Parra's efforts over her five-and-a-half-year "volcanic period" did not necessarily translate into success or even stability. On the contrary, in many instances both she herself and much of her artistic output were located so far outside contemporary norms and official avenues for artistic recognition as to remain underappreciated or even unremarked. What follows is thus simultaneously and unavoidably a study of Parra's social exclusions.

Return to Santiago

Like the words from her song "Thanks to Life," Violeta's reentry to Chile was marked by both "joy" (*dicha*) and "sorrow" (*quebranto*). After a long ocean journey, she was met at the port of Valparaíso in mid-December 1956 by several of her siblings and her children Isabel (16), Ángel (13), and Carmen Luisa (6). Ángel would later recall how his mother brought him a wristwatch and his older sister Isabel dresses in the latest Parisian styles as gifts.[4] Violeta was also finally able to meet her granddaughter by Isabel: Cristina Isabel Parra Cereceda, born on March 21, 1956. Known as Tita Parra, she would grow up to become a professional musician just like her mother, grandmother, and other Parras.[5]

Violeta's marriage to Luis Arce had ended in her absence thanks to an acrid combination of grief and her recriminations over the loss of their daughter. She returned to find the rustic family home she had built in La Reina all but abandoned. In an autobiographical décima, she laments,

Returning to my country,
A mountain's worth of rubble
Falls down upon the shoulders
Of this forlorn singer;
I can't find even the roots
Of a tree I left behind.

Cuando regreso al país,
el alto montón d'escombros
que cae sobre los hombros
d'esta cantora infeliz;
No encuentro ni la raíz
de un árbol que yo dejara.

Parra grieves: "My dove has taken flight / Never to be seen again" (*paloma emprendió su vuelo, / pa' mí nunca más presente*). And she affirms her plans to move forward:

And so, healthy and calm
I'm facing life head-on . . .

Once again with my songs
I'll gather a few pennies,
And plant another little tree
To shade me and bring love.

Total, con calma y salud
voy enfrentando la vida . . .
de nuevo con mis canciones
voy a juntar centavitos,
y plantaré otro arbolito
que me dé sombra y amores.[6]

Parra spent her first years back in Chile moving from one living arrange-
ment to another in varied familial configurations, in keeping with her bohemian lifestyle as an artist and a single mother. At first, she, Ángel, and Carmen
Luisa lived in a small, two-story house in the middle-class neighborhood of
Las Condes that was the home of José "Pepe" de Rokha, the son of Violeta's
dear friend and fellow poet Pablo de Rokha, while Pepe was away in Europe.
Later, during Violeta's residency at the University of Concepción, the Parras
occupied two rooms off the patio of the large colonial-style house that served
as the School of Fine Arts. Her duties in Concepción concluded, Parra stayed
in the Santiago apartment of a friend while she battled a bout of debilitating
depression.[7] Finally, in 1959, Parra and her family moved into the new home
that she had built on her plot of land in La Reina with the royalties she received from her successful lawsuit against US musician Les Baxter over his
unauthorized use of her song "Casamiento de negros" (The Black Wedding).
Though a marked improvement over the dilapidated *choza* or hut that she and
her family had lived in prior to her departure for Europe, it was hardly the
lap of luxury with its crude wooden floors, outhouse, and electricity siphoned
from a nearby power cable.[8] Parra nicknamed it the "house of sticks." It remains inhabited by her descendants at the time of this writing (though now
with electricity and indoor plumbing).[9]

As regards her professional reentry, Parra returned to Chile with a certain
cachet, one that she had helped originate and fostered through the frequent
and embellished missives that she sent to the Chilean press from Europe. As
scholars in the field of transnational studies have noted, cultural value within
modern capitalism follows a similar course where "the local [must] attain
value, first in the 'World' economy and later in the form of heightened local
appreciation."[10] Parra's case confirms this. Her European triumph greatly enhanced her stature at home, and virtually every Chilean who wrote about
her from 1956 onward proclaimed it.[11] The liner notes, for instance, of Parra's

first LP of Chilean folk music, produced by Odeon Chilena in 1957, boast that she went to Europe with a "criolla [native] guitar under her arm" as her only calling card and ended up ensuring that "the authentic music of Chile would be held in high esteem in the cultural centers of Paris and London and in the central offices of UNESCO."[12] (Appreciation for Parra's European successes only went so far, however. A recap in *Ecran* of the Chilean music industry's highlights for 1956 revealed Parra's place in its transnational hierarchy. It covered, presumably in order of importance: Elvis Presley, Argentine tango artist Héctor Varela and his orchestra, updates on various international record companies, obituaries for several US musicians, expatriate Chilean bolero singer Lucho Gatica, and, finally, "the triumph of Violeta Parra and Chilean folklore in Europe."[13])

Parra wasted no time reincorporating herself into Santiago's cultural scene. The pace of her activities over her first year back from Europe was energetic bordering on frenetic. Within weeks, if not days, of her arrival she was back on the air at Radio Chilena, having lined up work as part of its Christmas programming while still in Paris.[14] She would host her own show at the station three days a week from December 1956 until her departure for Concepción in November 1957, and again upon her return to Santiago in May 1958, interrupted only by the occasional extended collecting expedition further afield.

In what was a first for Chilean folk music radio programming, she brought her folk informants into the studio to sing on her show. The lineup for September 1957 included don Isaías Angulo and four other traditional singers from Puente Alto along with her brother Roberto—who apparently was reinvented (as Parras often were) from a professional (and sometime brothel) musician to a traditional singer for the occasion.[15] Parra's insistence that the traditional singers be paid just like any other professional musician was also a first for folk programming in Chile.

By January 22, 1957, Parra had made her first recording of the year: a single on the Odeon label featuring two original songs in eulogy to the Chilean poet and Nobel Prize winner Gabriela Mistral (1945), "Verso por despedida a Gabriela Mistral" (Poem of Farewell to Gabriela Mistral) and "Verso por el padecimiento de Gabriela" (Poem for Gabriela's Suffering).[16] Parra composed both songs within days of the laureate's passing on January 10th in the style of the traditional canto a lo poeta or poet-song. The recording also shows her experimenting with different guitars (nylon- and steel-stringed) and alternative tunings culled from campesino traditions.[17] The single received favorable reviews but sold poorly, as would be the case with all of Parra's subsequent recordings.[18]

Guitar Instrumentals (and International Folk Songs)

Parra found a new creative outlet during this period as a composer of instrumental music for guitar. It all started in December 1956 when she began improvising on the guitar to pass the time aboard the ship carrying her home to Chile. Here is how she explains the sorrowful origins of this new artistic endeavor: "I discovered this music in the color of the ocean one day when I was already close to Chile: a grayish, opaque color . . . and in the death of my daughter Rosa Clara."[19]

Parra's guitar instrumentals mark the beginning of an entirely different, more inward path of creative inquiry. Until then, her compositions had adhered to the musical and lyrical conventions of the clearly defined musical genres in which they were composed. This was as true for the guarachas, boleros, corridos, vals, and cuecas that she wrote during her years as a performer of música criolla as it was for the folkloric-sounding songs that she wrote as a folklorista, with the eulogies that she composed to Gabriela Mistral in the style of the traditional poet-song her most recent examples.

Parra's guitar instrumentals, in contrast, broke with the conventions of both música criolla and folklore. Her five anticuecas may serve as illustration. She named the compositions "anticuecas" because, as she explained, they incorporated "all the musical elements and all 'the spirit deep inside' of the cueca, but they were not cuecas at all."[20] Their name was undoubtedly also a nod to her brother Nicanor and his prizewinning 1954 book of poetry, *Poemas y antipoemas* (Poems and Antipoems). In her anticuecas, Violeta disfigures and reconfigures traditional rhythms and creates harmonic dissonances by transporting particular chord patterns up and down the neck of the guitar, all the while demonstrating her autodidactic virtuosity on the instrument.[21] Many consider the end result to be among the finest pieces for guitar ever written by a Chilean composer—or, for that matter, any composer, regardless of nationality.[22]

Parra incorporated her guitar instrumentals into her concert repertoire and recorded several of them on her 1957 Odeon EP *Violeta Parra—Composiciones para guitarra* (Compositions for Guitar).[23] The pieces were a surprise to virtually everyone who heard them.[24] In the space of a few years, much of that time spent abroad, Parra had cemented her reputation as one of the most well-known folkloristas in Chile (her decades-long career in more commercially oriented genres of music all but forgotten). And now she was writing and performing works for guitar that could easily be deemed modern or avantgarde. In his liner notes for her instrumental album, musicologist and Parra's sometime collaborator Gastón Soublette alerts the listener that the compositions found on the album were "not folkloric music" but rather "classical music like one hears at any chamber music concert." They were a "new form of musical art," a "beautiful and strange music unlike any other." Parra's accomplishment was the more impressive because she lacked formal training in music; she had learned music "with the same naturalness that one bird learns to sing from another, with neither the need nor desire to know theory, harmony, counterpoint, or musical forms," discovering "her own language, forms of expression, and technique by instinct."[25] Along similar lines, in his review of the EP music producer and *Ecran* columnist Camilo Hernández praised Parra for her "great musical intuition" and talent that had led her to produce "a strange and wonderful music" that was nothing like the melodies found in folk music.[26]

These early commentaries on Parra's guitar instrumentals could serve as a template for how her creative work would be received over the remainder of her life, be they her modern compositions or her embroidered tapestries hanging in the Louvre Palace. Almost unfailingly, Parra's reviewers would recognize her inordinate talent and originality, then proceed to link these merits to her "naturalness," "instinct," and "intuition." In 1950s and 1960s Chile (and before and since), these latter qualities were associated above all with women and social, ethnic, and racialized groups that were perceived as being on the margins or outside of the modern. As such, they contrasted with those more authorial qualities of intention and invention that were almost always the domain of modern men of class and race privilege.[27]

Parra, for her part, proclaimed in a March 1958 interview that she favored her "modern compositions for guitar" over all her many artistic achievements. Although she thereby identified herself as a modern composer, she took care to distinguish herself from the vast majority of composers who were classically trained. In her case, she explained, "it would not be advisable for me to attend conservatory as what I have is pure."[28]

Parra's performance repertoire now included the folk songs she collected, her folkloric-sounding original songs, and her more inventive instrumentals for guitar. In the first year or so after returning from Europe, Parra experimented with incorporating international folk songs into her repertoire as well. She sang Israeli, Italian, and French songs that she had most likely learned from folk recordings that were popular in Paris in the mid-1950s. She also sang two Andean songs, one in Quechua ("Ricur Canqui Yurapa") and the other, "Viva JuiJui" (an alternative spelling for Jujuy, an Argentine place name), popularized by the 1950s Parisian–Latin American folk music bands Les Guaranis and Los Incas.[29] Ironically, Parra was more likely to have learned the songs in Paris than in Santiago despite—or because of—their Andean origins.

The expansion of her repertoire to include songs borrowed from the 1950s folk revivals in countries other than Chile is evidence of the musical cross-pollination of these movements. Viewed through this transnational lens, Parra's expanded repertoire would not be unusual. Many of her contemporaries in the world of folk music made folk songs from other countries a core component of their performance repertoires. This was especially true for those folk singers who were from what was then referred to as the First World—Victoria Kingsley, Parra's host in London, England, for example; or US folk singer Pete Seeger.

In Parra's case, her incursion into the world of international folk music was paradoxical on two grounds: first, Parra built her reputation on the premise of her authentic performance of traditional songs from her native land; second, she was known to berate other musicians for straying from a strictly Chilean repertoire—including her own son Ángel, who was an early and ardent fan of the Argentine songwriter Atahualpa Yupanqui. Perhaps for these reasons, Violeta's inclusion of what the Chilean press referred to as "foreign songs" in her concert repertoire appears to have been only a passing experiment (though she would reprise both Andean songs during her second stay in Europe in response to the increasing popularity of all that was Andean in the 1960s).

Collecting among the Mapuche

Parra resumed her work as a collector with renewed fervor during this period, now with the additional, if cumbersome, assistance of a made-in-Poland tape recorder she brought back from Europe.[30] These days she was often accompanied by musicologist Gastón Soublette, who helped Parra above all with musical transcriptions. Sergio Larraín, Chile's most important photographer of the twentieth century, then at the beginning of his career, was another frequent companion (and, according to one source, a romantic partner as well).[31] Parra traveled north with her colleagues to the town of Salamanca in April 1957 to document the town's Easter celebration, and farther north to the town of Iquique in mid-July to record the traditional Fiesta de la Tirana. She would continue to work with both Soublette and Larraín in the years ahead, most notably on the book project that would be published posthumously as *Cantos folklóricos chilenos* (Chilean Folk Songs).[32]

Somewhat ironically, Parra's work collecting the folklore of Chile's pueblo thus brought her into close association with members of Chile's upper class. This was the case with Soublette and Larraín, both of whom came from wealthy and established Chilean families. Parra consistently referred to them as *pitucos* or "rich snobs"—and in Soublette's case, during a particularly violent argument in what was an often conflictive work relationship, as a *pituco de mierda* (rich asshole).[33] Despite giving them a hard time, she composed and recorded guitar instrumentals dedicated to both colleagues: her "Anticueca N° 1 (o Fray Gastón baila cueca con el diablo)" (Anticueca N° 1 [or Brother Gastón Dances the Cueca with the Devil]) for Soublette, and the polka "El joven Sergio" (Young Sergio) for Larraín.[34]

Parra announced her plans to collect material among the Mapuche even before she had left Europe at the close of 1956: in a letter from France, excerpted and published in *Ecran*, she wrote, "I am coming back to my homeland to study. I will travel to the south in order to learn Araucanian music, that I will bring back to Europe with me, God willing, within the space of six months."[35]

Parra was by no means the first Chilean *folklorista* to show an interest in the Mapuche. Members of Chile's first cohort of *folkloristas* began collecting Mapuche material as early as 1907.[36] Several of Parra's *folklorista* contemporaries continued this line of work. A few incorporated Mapuche songs into their concert repertoires as well, most notably Margot Loyola, who performed the material dressed in full costume as a *machi* or Mapuche spiritual leader and healer.[37] Loyola had additionally recorded a few Mapuche songs for the Musée de l'Homme in Paris. In the spirit of ongoing competition that undergirded the two *folkloristas*' professional and personal relationship, Loyola made sure to share with Parra her accomplishment and the great interest it had elicited.[38] Indeed, Parra's desire to collect material among the Mapuche may well have been inspired by Loyola's reported success at the museum, though contemporary Parisian audiences' fascination with exoticizing musical groups like Les Guaranis and Los Incas likely factored into her decision as well. Whatever her reasons, Parra returned to Chile determined to collect songs from the Mapuche.

Accordingly, she set off alone in May 1957 for Wallmapu.[39] She first traveled to Temuco, a city of about 50,000 residents, where she enlisted members of its teachers' choir to help her in locating Mapuche *machis* and singers.[40] A choir member invited her to Millelche, a nearby town with a large Mapuche population where he worked and lived with his Mapuche wife and their children. Parra stayed with them for several weeks. The family introduced her to the *machi* María Painen Cotaro. Parra would visit her daily at her *ruka* (traditional Mapuche hut) to interview her about the fundamentals of Mapuche culture, from cooking to the medicinal qualities of certain songs, to how to play the ceremonial drum called the *kultrun*.[41]

Parra returned to Wallmapu to collect Mapuche folklore at least once and most likely several times over the next few years, including a trip to the southern town of Lautaro in the heart of Chile's Indigenous region where she had lived as a child. In keeping with traditional practices of reciprocity, she offered her Mapuche informants a small cash payment or item of clothing in symbolic exchange for the material she collected.[42] She also purchased a kultrun and a *pifilka* (Mapuche flute), both of which she would later donate to the museum of folk art in Concepción that she founded.

In all, Parra is known to have worked with seven Mapuche sources: six women and one man.[43] She aired some of her field recordings on the radio and may also have performed "Araucanian music" in concert herself on at least one occasion.[44] She does not appear, however, to have incorporated the material into her own repertoire in any significant way. Parra's reluctance to perform the songs she collected from the Mapuche may be considered an indication of her respect for the autonomy and integrity of their culture.[45] It also likely had something to do with the chantlike quality of the songs themselves. By the time that Parra learned the more melodious songs from Rapa Nui that she recorded in Europe and the song in Quechua that she brought back with her to Chile, they had all been adapted to the esthetic sensibilities of a Western audience. The Mapuche songs from her field recordings, in contrast, were likely too raw and repetitive to appeal to the Western musical palate. Parra's comments in a 1964 interview for the French journal *Partisans* would seem to support this. When asked by the reporter whether Chilean folklore had other influences beyond Spanish ones, she answered, "There are the songs, the poems of the Indians. But I don't know them well. I think that they have not evolved. [The singer] repeats three or four verses."[46]

Instead of performing the songs she collected, Parra proposed to promote the Mapuche singers themselves. As was often the case, her plans did not progress beyond the pipedream stage. She urged a husband-and-wife duo of Mapuche singers to come and perform with her in Santiago to no avail, as the couple could not leave their crops and animals unattended. She extended invitations to machi María Painen Cotaro and traditional Mapuche singer Juan Lemuñir to perform alongside her on respective tours of the United States and Uruguay. Neither tour materialized.[47] In what would prove far more enduring, Parra later incorporated elements from the musical and visual practices of the Mapuche into her own musical and visual creations.[48]

Albums and Soundtracks

At some point among all the comings and goings of her first year back from Europe, Parra went into the Odeon studios to record her LP *Violeta Parra—El Folklore de Chile*.[49] The album inaugurated the label's landmark Folklore of Chile series, which was created by acclaimed record producer Rubén Nouzeilles. Nouzeilles had also been responsible for Parra's 1955 debut EP as a solo folk singer—the one with the ornate arrangements, since abandoned. Violeta Parra would be the featured artist for the series' first four volumes, recorded between 1957 and 1959.[50]

Figure 5.1 Cover of LP *Violeta Parra—Folklore de Chile*, Volume 1. Odeon LDC-36019, 1957.

With slight variation, volume 1 provided a model for volumes 2 and 4 in the series (with volume 3 the exception). The LP constructs and reinforces Parra's reputation as a consummate professional even as it affirms her proximity, bordering on fusion, with her folkloric sources. It features Parra on voice and guitar performing songs that she collected from her folk informants, including members of her immediate and extended family, along with three folkloric-sounding original songs. The cover photo shows Parra dressed in fashionable attire, seated in front of a microphone in the recording studio as she strums her guitar; she is the embodied conduit between the recording industry's modern technologies and the album's traditional content (see figure 5.1). Penned by media man Raúl Aicardi, the liner notes praise Parra for her unique talent and tenacious effort at collecting and disseminating folklore and provide all of the customary data found on traditionalist folk recordings of the period—musical genre, age, and place of origin of its source for each song. Aicardi emphasizes the relationship between folklorist and folk informant through the frequent use of phrases like "collected from the lips of." He compares Parra's original songs to actual folk songs in their simplicity and beauty and claims this confirmed Parra's status as an "authentic folk singer." Notably, "authentic folk singers" is how he refers to Parra's informants elsewhere in the notes.[51]

Odeon released the LP in September to coincide with the prolonged festivities surrounding Chile's Independence Day of September 18th in hopes that the month's patriotic zeal would help boost sales. The label would do the same for most of Parra's subsequent recordings. The album received sparse but positive reviews. *Ecran* columnist and music producer Camilo Hernández referred to it as a "priceless" recording made up of "seventeen little jewels of our folk music."[52] The columnist who wrote under the pseudonym Hablador (The Gossiper) was even more effusive. Noting that it was the first long play (LP) of Chilean folk music ever made, he declared its release "one of the most important events in the history of the search for and dissemination of Chilean folk music . . . the justified pride of its label and a genuine triumph for Violeta Parra and her passion for the authentic music of our people."[53]

Parra returned to the studio in October 1957 to record her EP, *Violeta Parra—Compositions for Guitar* (released in December), featuring six of her novel guitar instrumentals. The cover photo, a close-up of her head and torso, portrays Parra with her hair pulled back, her expression pensive, dressed in black (à la French chanteuse Edith Piaf), without superficialities or distractions (see figure 5.2). That is, it portrays Parra in her newest persona as an original and soulful artist.

With the exception of Camilo Hernández's review, the album remained largely overlooked during Parra's lifetime. Apparently, her original compositions for guitar were found to be even more niche than her repertoire of folk songs. They gained serious consideration only upon her death and, more recently, with the celebrations of the centennial of her birth in 2017.

Parra took on one more major project before embarking on her residency in Concepción: she composed the soundtrack for Chilean cineaste Sergio Bravo's landmark short documentary, *Mimbre* (Wicker). Bravo was one of the founders of what became known in the 1960s as the *nuevo cine chileno* or Chilean New Cinema. He and the other New Cinema filmmakers produced films that linked their political militancy with their aesthetic ambitions, paralleling the New Song musicians of the 1960s with whom they often collaborated.[54] *Mimbre* tracks the handiwork of master artisan Alfredo Manzano, aka "Manzanito," as he weaves rattan into baskets and fanciful animals

Figure 5.2 Cover of EP *Violeta Parra—Composiciones para guitarra.*
Odeon MSOD/E-51020, 1957.

in his atelier-home. Bravo shot the nine-minute film as a silent movie, then invited Parra to create its soundtrack. As she watched its footage, Parra improvised modern-sounding, atonal music on the guitar to the movements of the basket weaver to produce what Bravo described as the film's musical "narration," as it has no spoken one.[55] The film that resulted from the collaboration between Bravo and Parra is an indisputable milestone in twentieth-century Chilean cultural history.[56]

Parra would collaborate with Sergio Bravo on the soundtracks of two additional short films over the next few years: *Trilla* (1959), about the traditional celebration that accompanies the *trilla* (wheat-thrashing); and *Casamiento de negros* (The Black Wedding, 1959), about the distinctive ceramics from the town of Quinchamalí, near Chillán, featuring Parra's song by the same title.

Parra would also contribute music to two documentaries by the husband-and-wife cineaste team Jorge di Lauro and Nieves Yankovic: *Andacollo* (1958), about the popular religious festival venerating the Virgin Mary in the northern town of that name, and *Los artistas plásticos de Chile* (Visual Artists of Chile, 1960). With the exception of *Visual Artists of Chile*, the documentaries that Parra collaborated on cover subjects related to the pueblo in some way, in keeping with the political-artistic ethos of the times, which corresponded to her own artistic proclivities.

Amid all the activity of her first-year home, Violeta managed to find time to initiate her daughter Isabel, then seventeen, in her own career as a folk singer—though one could argue that Violeta had been grooming Isabel for a musical career since Isabel was a little girl. Violeta invited Isabel to sing on her radio show and provided the guitar accompaniment when Isabel performed at the gala ceremony for that year's Caupolicán awards.[57] She guided Isabel's recording of her first single, which featured a Violeta original on one side and the waltz "La celosa" (The Jealous Woman) on the other. Both songs are arranged in the more commercialized style of sister folk acts and música típica women artists.[58] Released in time for the September 1957 Independence Day celebrations, the single made fifth place on the list of most played songs that month on Chilean radio.[59]

In her book about her mother, Isabel makes clear that this debut single and the two solo EPs that followed it in 1958 were entirely the product of Violeta's initiative and direction: "In those days, truth be told, I had no idea . . . whether I would continue singing or not, or what I would sing. I was very young and inexperienced. . . . My mom encouraged and channeled the continuity of her efforts, and that way made sure that we [her children] were well suited to become musicians."[60] As Isabel's wording suggests, Violeta tended to view her children's musical careers somewhat narcissistically as "the continuity of her efforts" or an extension of herself. Her attitude would engender a fair amount of friction when her children chose to branch out on their own as musicians.

To recap Parra's "volcanic" activity, in the short space of her first eleven months back in Chile: she returned to hosting her own radio show; recorded a tribute single to Gabriela Mistral, an LP of folk and original songs, and an EP of original compositions for guitar; collected folklore in and around Santiago and in northern and southern Chile, including for the first time among the Mapuche; collaborated with musicologist Gastón Soublette and photographer Sergio Larraín; improvised music for the soundtrack of Sergio Bravo's documentary *Mimbre*; and helped launch her daughter Isabel's career as a folk singer. She also found time to celebrate her fortieth birthday on October 4, 1957.

Concepción

In November 1957, Violeta moved with Ángel and Carmen Luisa to Concepción, then Chile's third largest city (population circ. 130,000), located 270 miles south of Santiago.[61] Concepción had long been known for both its leftist-leaning politics and bohemian nightlife.[62] The Parras went there at a time when the city was experiencing a cultural renewal spearheaded by reform-minded administrators and faculty from the University of Concepción, which was itself undergoing a process of modernization that earned it international recognition.[63] Parra was hired to establish a museum of Chilean folk art as her contribution to this larger effort. Truth be told, she was not the university rector David Stitchkin's first choice for the task. But when Stitchkin's more grandiose attempt to recruit a European expert to organize the museum according to the standards set by the Landesmuseum in Vienna proved unsuccessful, Parra's name was floated as an alternative.[64] After all, she was a world-renowned folklorista, recently returned from Europe, where she had worked with both the Musée de l'Homme and the BBC.

And that is how Parra arrived at the train station in Concepción on November 10, 1957, with two children, multiple guitars, and at least one guitarrón. Eschewing the more conventional and presumably more comfortable hotel where the university usually lodged its guests, she moved her family into two rooms off the back courtyard of the sprawling colonial-style building that housed the university's School of Fine Arts. Its larger rooms had been converted into classrooms where students could study painting, printmaking, murals, sculpture, drawing, and soon, folk song and dance with Parra as their instructor. Other rooms served as art studios for faculty and students. The building was also home to the university's theater arts program, whose professional troupe rehearsed in one of its many patios during the summer months.[65]

Parra slept with her children in one room equipped with a brazier and enamel basin that also served as their kitchen and washroom (and, in the case of the basin, sometimes musical instrument). She reserved the adjacent room for practicing. Parra was not the only artist in residence at the time. Santos Chávez, a young Mapuche art student on scholarship, lived there as well. Parra and Santos were soon joined by the poet Pablo de Rokha, who was visiting Concepción on a writing fellowship.

Remarkably, the six-months-or-so period when Parra lived and worked in Concepción under the auspices of the university was the only time in her life when she earned a steady income. She maintained a packed work schedule and an impressive and interconnected social life across its duration. She devoted much of her first two months to collecting, often traveling considerable distances over harsh terrain to do so. She boasted to the local press that she had covered over 500 miles since her arrival and had learned how to ride horseback so that she could reach the more remote hamlets and towns of the region.[66] She also taught herself photography so that she could take pictures of her informants with an expensive imported camera that had somehow landed in her possession.[67]

Parra collected more than one hundred cuecas in the region, which she would later declare "the most beautiful [cuecas] in all of Chile."[68] By now her reputation as a folklorista often preceded her. This made collecting easier, as most people were eager to assist. They sought her out at the School of Fine Arts to share their material with her or mailed her song lyrics accompanied by affectionate letters. They sent her the names of traditional singers and instrument owners in their area in response to an ad she placed in a local newspaper soliciting information from the public.[69] Parra also learned several songs from a maid she hired, which apparently was a common collecting practice among her cohort of folkloristas.[70] Parra collected folkloric artifacts such as traditional instruments and clothes from the region as well. She convinced the institution to hire Gastón Soublette to transcribe the songs she collected. Her requests to the university for the use of a van and guide went unanswered, however.

A Museum of Folk Art

Parra's primary purpose in Concepción was to found a museum dedicated to the folk arts. She envisioned it as having four rooms: one to exhibit instruments and other folk objects; the second for photographs of traditional singers; the third, an auditorium where documentaries could be screened; and the fourth, an administrative office.[71] The National Museum of Folk Art was inaugurated on January 4, 1958. Its official designation vastly overstated its size and holdings; as one person observed, "It was pretty dismal. I think it filled two small rooms, and that was the museum."[72] Its collection consisted of three harps, two guitars, one guitarrón, one kultrun (Mapuche drum), one pifilka (Mapuche flute), one tambourine, one *matraca* (noise maker), a *charrango* (zither-like instrument made out of a plank of wood and wires pulled taut over two bottles), a pair of wooden shoes, two old songbooks, a gramophone, and an empty oil can that local truckers had repurposed into a percussion instrument.[73] Of the musical instruments on exhibit, Parra had likely collected only the charrango and empty oil can since arriving in the region.

Parra's inclusion of the oil can in the museum's collection exemplifies her more expansive definition of folklore as encompassing not just those practices associated with a supposed premodern campesino culture but also those that emerged from a modern urban lifestyle, including instruments made out of common industrially produced household items. In displaying the oil can, Parra challenged the romanticism of her more traditionalist peers who upheld a division between a "pure" folklore of the countryside, and the modern and, as a result, tainted culture of people living in urban settings. She was therefore met with some criticism.[74] In a similar vein, Parra also included a gramophone—that once-modern invention that had irreversibly altered how the residents of her childhood barrio in Chillán and people the world over enjoyed music in the early twentieth century—in the museum's collection.

Parra completed the exhibit with a display of the photos that she had taken of her folk informants, along with explanatory notes. The museum also housed the lyrics of fifty cuecas Parra had collected in the area along with their musical transcriptions, courtesy of Soublette. Little else is known about the folk museum, except that it never really got off the ground.

Teaching and Performing

In addition to collecting and establishing the museum, Parra taught a course on Chilean folk music and dance at the university's summer school, one of a growing number of "seasonal schools" that were held over the summer and winter breaks in the academic year (which in Chile correspond to the months of January and July). First established under the Center-Left reformist governments of the late 1930s and 1940s, the seasonal schools represented an effort by Chilean institutions of higher learning to reach beyond their ivory towers to the general public. The study of folklore was an integral component of the seasonal schools' curriculum.[75] All of the significant folkloristas of the 1950s and 1960s participated in them, some as teachers like Margot Loyola and Violeta Parra, and some as students like the future members of the folk music ensembles Cuncumén and Millaray.[76]

Parra was hired by the director of the university's extension program, Gonzalo Rojas, who had also encouraged the university to bring her to Concepción in the first place. A poet and longtime friend of the Parra family, Rojas had been a regular visitor to the Parra siblings' "country house" in La Reina in the mid-1940s. A decade later, he was overseeing the transformation of the University of Concepción's extension program, and especially its summer school, into a "social, cultural, and political happening."[77] By the time Rojas hired Parra as an instructor in January 1958, the summer school offered dozens of classes and workshops that enrolled nearly 3,000 people, over 150 of them international students. Course topics ranged from recent advances in endocrinology, to an acrylic painting class taught by visiting artist and Parra's new friend Nemesio Antúnez, to Parra's own class on how to sing and dance

Figure 5.3 Violeta Parra teaching a class at the University of Concepción, 1958. Courtesy of Fondo Archivo Fotográfico Pinacoteca Universidad de Concepción.

the cueca. With seventy pupils, Parra's class exceeded all expectations as the highest-enrolled course in the entire program (see figure 5.3).[78]

The summer course was Parra's first experience teaching. Based on the recollections of her pupils in this and future classes, Parra was an exacting and somewhat imperious instructor. One anecdote has Parra kicking a student out of class for falsely claiming to have no knowledge of the cueca when in fact she was quite skilled at the dance.[79] Another has Parra yanking the ears of those unlucky pupils who were too slow at mastering the basic moves.[80] All reports concur that after drilling her students on the cueca's traditional steps and forms, Parra insisted that they "dance it as they felt it."[81] One former pupil elaborates: "Most of the time she taught us in a more structured way, but then she would undermine her own teachings on purpose and tell us all to 'let yourself dance however it comes out, because that's how you'll get the hang of it'" (see figure 5.4).[82]

Parra did not fit the mold of a typical folkloric instructor. Ever the boundary pusher, she appeared eager to test the limits of women's propriety with the material she selected. This testing of boundaries was something that the folk songs themselves accomplished, arguably, given their frequent use of sexual innuendo, flirtatious humor, and sarcasm. The lyrics of the three cuecas that Parra chose to teach her students that summer in Concepción illustrate this. In "La mariposa" (The Butterfly), which happens to be a euphemism for

Figure 5.4 Violeta Parra dancing the cueca. Courtesy of Fondo Archivo Fotográfico Pinacoteca, Universidad de Concepción.

"prostitute" in Chile, the song's lyrical subject or "I" declares that "Like the butterfly / That takes to the air, / Once in a while / I have sweet love affairs" (*Como la mariposa / que va volando, / tengo mis amorcillos / de vez en cuando*). In "La niña que está bailando" (The Girl Who Is Dancing), the girl is dancing accompanied by a young man whose mouth is watering because the girl's slip is showing. The cueca "Yo soy la recién casada" (I Am a Newlywed) is both a denunciation of domestic abuse and a declaration of independence. Its lyrical (and sardonic) subject has a husband who treats her "Like a queen: / I don't have one rib / That he's left unbroken" (*como una reina: / no me deja costilla / que no me quebra*). He soon abandons her, and the lyrical subject declares, "I take my freedom / To seek my destiny" (*para buscar mi camino / yo tomo mi libertad*).[83]

Parra also taught her pupils the polka "El sacristán" (The Sexton), a bawdy song about a sexton whose love is "as sweet as honey," with verses like the following:

> The holier-than-thou woman
> Who has not known a sexton's love
> Has never tasted cinnamon
> Nor chocolate with flan.

> *La beata que no ha tení'o*
> *amores con sacristán,*
> *no sabe lo que es canela*
> *ni chocolate con flan.*

The chorus proclaims,

> Oh, how I love
> The sexton.
> The bell is ringing
> Ding ding dong, ding ding dong.

> *Porque me gusta*
> *el sacristán.*
> *Toca la campanilla,*
> *tilín-tintín, tilín-tintán.*[84]

Some of the dances Parra taught her students were even more risqué than the songs. According to one former pupil, Parra showed them not only the "refined cueca of the aristocracy" but also the "cueca diabla" or "devilish cueca" as it was danced in brothels, with the dancers' skirts held high.[85] Parra surely would have witnessed this raunchier cueca style back in the 1940s at Santiago's most illustrious brothel, La Carlina, where she and her musician siblings would go to "finish the fiesta" after a long night of gigging. She was likely reminded of it when, as part of her collecting efforts in Concepción, she is said to have convinced some of her companions in the social circles that she traveled in to take her on a late-night tour of its bordellos so that she could see how the cueca was danced there.[86] Clearly invested in the shock value of this dance demonstration, Parra warned her students, most of whom were women, "You will not be able to dance it, as you need to be whores to be able to dance it and that is not very likely."[87]

In January 1958, the First Conference of Chilean Writers was held at the University of Concepción. Conceived and organized by Gonzalo Rojas to coincide with the university's summer school, the undertaking brought twenty-six of the nation's leading novelists, essayists, scholars, and poets (including Nicanor Parra) to Concepción for ten days of lectures and discussion. It was a tremendous success. Rojas next organized a Second Conference of Chilean Writers, which convened in July 1958 in Parra's hometown of Chillán. He followed the two national conferences with a far more ambitious hemisphere-wide First Conference of American Writers, held in Concepción in January 1960, an extraordinary assembly of authors that, according to one literary critic, helped to "unleash the so-called *boom* in the Latin American novel."[88]

Parra performed at all three conferences. Playwright José Ricardo Morales recalls her performance at the First Conference of Chilean Writers of January 1958 in front of "an impassioned crowd that joyfully sang along to her songs." At one point, Parra turned an ordinary oil can into "a prodigious percussion instrument that provided an unusual rhythmic intensity to her audience's participation, who found themselves in turn transformed, from passive spectators, to an active chorus." Morales, who had to deliver a lecture on seventeenth-century theater directly after Parra's presentation, professed, "Never have I been in such a tough situation."[89]

Two years later, Parra played the washbasin, instrumental cousin of the oil can, as part of her performance at the First Conference of American Writers. In his memoir, communist leader and author Volodia Teitelboim captures the intentional irreverence of her performance: "She arrived with a washbasin in her hands. In the middle of the conference, she sat down on the ground with her legs open, placed the washbasin face down between them, and began to drum on it. Then she began to sing in her unique voice. . . . It sounded like a symphony orchestra of the poor."[90]

The writers conferences that Parra performed at were overwhelmingly male affairs, the first one exclusively so in terms of its invited authors. Parra's memorable recitals thus made her yet again the exceptional woman to participate, albeit from the periphery, in what were clearly and consistently male-identified creative spheres. When asked in a 2004 interview about women's participation (or lack thereof) in the historic conferences, Rojas insisted that his intention had always been to be inclusive, then defensively rattled off the names of the less than a handful of women who participated in them, cumulatively. As if an afterthought, he clarified that Parra was different. Employing the family nickname by which he had long known her, he explained, "Viola was a special case: she was embedded among us, she was part of all of us who were rethinking our cultural work."[91]

Collaborating and Socializing

Parra's daily life in Concepción was one of intense artistic activity and collaborations. She set a poem by Gonzalo Rojas to music, "Sátira a la rima" (Rhyming Satire), a scathing critique of the bourgeoisie in verse and one of Parra's earliest political songs.[92] She became fast and true friends with fellow visiting artist Nemesio Antúnez, who was experimenting with referencing folkloric and popular elements in his artwork at the time (as Parra would soon do in her own). In reciprocal admiration, Parra composed an experimental piece, without lyrics, for voice and guitar in his honor, while Antúnez painted the block-style portrait of Parra that adorns the cover of her 1959 LP, *La tonada presentada por Violeta Parra* (The Tonada, as Presented by Violeta Parra).[93] Parra accompanied visiting cineaste Sergio Bravo, with whom she had previously collaborated on the documentary *Mimbre*, to film the threshing festivities in the nearby town of Calquinhue for his documentary *La Trilla*, and she would later contribute to its soundtrack.[94] She composed the soundtrack music for the two-minute culminating project by Bolivian film student and soon-to-be internationally known film director Jorge Sanjinés.[95] Parra also continued to compose guitar instrumentals and may well have written significant portions of her autobiography in décimas during her residency in Concepción.

Parra's creative energies were no doubt nurtured by the artistic ebullience of Concepción's social scene. The School of Fine Arts building where she both taught and lived during her residency was its unofficial headquarters, the chosen gathering place for artists, actors, writers, poets, and other creative types. Parra was a welcome, albeit demanding, addition to the scene.[96] Perhaps inspired by the presence of visiting poet Pablo de Rokha, a known gourmand and author of the poem "Epopeya de las bebidas y comidas de Chile" (Epopee of Chilean Food and Drink), accounts of the memorable soirees that were held in the school tend to provide a full menu of the "appetizers, sweet wines, barbecues, stews, and other regional delicacies" that were consumed.[97] Parra almost always had a hand in the food preparation.

Sometimes the revelers convened on the green expanse of Ecuador Park in front of the school. Other times the party would move to one of the two homes that novelist Daniel Balmar maintained, apparently with no shame or public disapproval: one for his wife, and the other for his mistress.[98] On other occasions, Parra would go on all-day excursions with her children and friends, old and new, to a nearby lagoon where they would picnic on roasted lamb and Chilean flat bread cooked over a campfire. No matter where the party was located, there was always plenty of wine and lively discussion about "politics, poetry, earthquakes, passions, and wrecked relationships."[99]

Not everything about Parra's social life in Concepción was ideal. There, as elsewhere, her forceful character and lack of concern for the preferences of others engendered tensions. Partygoers grew tired of her stubborn demand for complete and utter silence whenever she sang, as if they were attending a formal concert and not a social gathering. Frustrations rose to the point that some more determined revelers resorted to organizing social events behind Parra's back, much to her ire and their collective chagrin when they were discovered.[100]

There was also a shared sense that Parra was slowly taking over the whole building that housed the School of Fine Arts, first with her living quarters and then with the museum. Apparently, the expression "It's spreading out just like Violeta Parra in the School of Fine Arts" was coined to describe the phenomenon of an individual's encroachment on other people's space, "like when you give someone a tiny corner of your house and then they go on to occupy the entire house."[101] There was also the more subtle discomfort produced from having those chores that women normally did in the privacy of their own homes—or in the case of domestic servants, in their employers' homes—on full display, as when Parra quite literally washed her dirty laundry in public.[102]

Finally, and related to the last point, there was the question of Parra's personal hygiene. The summer heat and long days in the countryside collecting folklore led at least one person to complain that Parra smelled of perspiration.[103] In an interview conducted years later, art student Consuelo Saavedra defended Parra posthumously: "She was totally clean, like any normal person."[104] Saavedra's defense only confirms that Parra's cleanliness was considered an issue. Her critics' discernment would have been both based on modern values of hygiene and inherently classist. This would not be the last time that Parra would be accused of not living up to bourgeois standards of cleanliness.

Parra had one of her more noteworthy love affairs while in Concepción. It was with the artist Julio Escámez (1925–2015). She met him at the School of Fine Arts, where he was teaching mural painting after returning from studying mural techniques in Italy. Parra's romance with Escámez once again reversed the customary gender-age formula, as she was eight years his senior.

She is purported to have "won" him away, romantically speaking, from a woman much younger than he. Her victory over her rival was such that she convinced Escámez to paint over the young woman's image on the mural he was working on at the time and portray Parra in her place. Perhaps not coincidentally, Parra supplied him with a photograph of herself as a young woman to use as his model.

By all accounts, the affair did not end well. Most sources relate that Escámez literally fled from Parra's wrath, though how her wrath manifested itself varied from one anecdote to another. She created a public scandal at a university event.[105] Or else she slashed several of his paintings with a kitchen knife.[106] Or she burned the mattress where they had made love.[107] Or she chased him into the woods in the dark of night.[108] Or she broke a guitar over his head—with this last anecdote something of a cliché, given the number of guitars she is purported to have broken over people's heads (forty-eight, according to Nicanor's tally).[109]

Though fleeting, the affair produced enduring works by both artists. In addition to painting Parra in his mural, Escámez designed the record covers for volumes 2 (1958) and 3 (1959) of her albums for Odeon's "Folklore of Chile" series. On her end, Parra composed the instrumental "Las manos de Escámez" (Escámez's Hands) during a more tender phase in their relationship, which later made its way onto the soundtrack of Bravo's documentary, *La Trilla*. She poured out her sorrow over the downturn in their affair in three autobiographical décimas and set one of them to music. The resulting song, titled "La muerte con anteojos" (Death with Glasses On), appears on volume 2 of her folk music LPs with Odeon, which she recorded during a brief stint back in Santiago in March or April 1958.[110]

Parra's work was her stated priority during her residency in Concepción. As she anti-conventionally affirmed in a 1957 interview with the local press, "My life revolves around my work. The challenges all we women face are secondary to me."[111] One of women's challenges that Parra was no doubt referring to was childcare. Secondary to her or not, Parra was still likely the only visiting artist at the University of Concepción that summer to have brought children along with her. Parra took care of them there the way she always had: through a mixture of integrating them into her work-life, placing them with familia, and leaving them to their own devices.

Each child had a different story. Ángel kept very busy. Then fourteen, he was a part-time assistant to his mother and part-time caregiver to his seven-year-old sister, Carmen Luisa.[112] Sometimes, he accompanied his mother on her collecting expeditions. Other times, he stayed with their newly reacquainted cousins, "Aunt" Blanca and "Aunt" Olga.[113] He also attended boarding school for a few months. The school was located directly in front of the School of Fine

Arts, which Ángel surmised was how his mother came up with the idea to send him there. It would be the first and only time that he remembered going to school.[114] Carmen Luisa spent hours hanging out at the rehearsals of University of Concepción's theater company, held in the School of Fine Arts, until one day she astonished her mother and brother by reciting the entire play that the troupe was rehearsing word for word while imitating the voice of each actor.[115] Isabel visited often with her young daughter Tita in tow.

Back in Santiago

Parra's residency in Concepción ended in mid-1958, and she returned to Santiago. She stayed for a spell in the downtown apartment of her friend, the writer and editor of the art review *ProArte* Enrique Bello. Back in Santiago, Parra fell into what was almost certainly not the first and definitively not the last immobilizing depression that she would suffer over her lifetime. She had left Concepción in a bad way. She had gotten into a terrible fight with the director of the School of Fine Arts, Oscar "Tole" Peralta. It was over money. She argued that she deserved to be paid more for all that she had done for the university, he disagreed, and the two were no longer on speaking terms. Then in mid-June the university rejected her petition that it sponsor a proposed tour of Europe by covering the relatively modest sum of her third-class ocean passage there.[116] Finally, she was emotionally devastated by the end of her relationship with Julio Escámez which, as she wrote in her autobiography in verse, left her heart "a thousand degrees below zero" (*a mil grados bajo cero*).[117]

Parra shut herself into a spare room in Bello's flat and refused to eat or drink. Her friend Adela Gallo, one of the few people Parra would allow to visit, brought her lunch every day, then stayed until she could cajole her into eating something. This went on for several weeks, until Parra's depression finally lifted and she could get on with her life.

"El Gavilán" (The Sparrowhawk)

Parra is purported to have composed "El gavilán" (The Sparrowhawk) while she was shut away in Bello's apartment.[118] This was the piece that stopped music professor and composer Miguel Letelier in his tracks at the 1959 Arts Fair. In a January 1960 radio interview, Parra performed a fragment of it and spoke at length about her larger project.[119] She envisioned the final work as a ballet in three acts on the theme of the epic battle between Good and Evil. It would feature traditional folk instruments, backed by a full choir and symphonic orchestra. The ballet's male protagonist was the sparrowhawk, and its female protagonist a hen. Parra would sing the part of the hen because "suffering cannot be sung by a trained voice, a conservatory voice. It has to be the voice of someone who has suffered, someone like me." Leading Chilean choreographers and dancers would help with the dances, which would draw inspiration from the folk dances Parra had collected up and down Chile. In a not-too-subtle critique of the Eurocentrism of traditional Chilean ballet companies, Parra clarified that the ballet could not be danced by those who had been "working for years on things that are practically anti-Chilean." It would need to be performed by young dancers with energy and creative curiosity, and "with a more Chilean sentiment and a longing to create something that is truly national."[120]

At some point Parra's friend and succorer Adela Gallo designed costumes for the ballet and even a miniature set out of wire and paper.[121] Parra's plans to see "The Sparrowhawk" staged as a full-scale production never progressed beyond Gallo's diorama during her lifetime.[122] She did leave us three recorded versions of the composition for guitar and voice that the ballet was to be built around beyond the fragment she played in the January 1960 radio interview. All three are home recordings: one made by Miguel Letelier at Parra's "house of sticks" in 1960, another at Margot Loyola's home the following year, and a third at the apartment of Argentine musician Héctor Miranda in Paris in 1964.[123]

The consensus of musicians, composers, and scholars was and continues to be that "The Sparrowhawk" is extraordinary, in concordance with Letelier's initial reaction. Letelier considered it to be "the sublimation of Chilean folklore" that "marks a before and after" in Chilean composition.[124] Loyola called it "a masterpiece that was ahead of its time."[125] Cuban musician and songwriter Silvio Rodríguez describes it as "the most conclusive thesis of continuity and rupture . . . ever heard from a Latin American singer."[126]

Recently scholars have drawn connections between the piece and the songs of the Mapuche, both in the rhythms it employs and in the emotional textures of Parra's vocal performance.[127] One scholar has written an entire tome about the piece (which in its longest version is twelve minutes in duration) based on Jungian analysis. She concludes that the piece is both "unclassifiable and unfathomable."[128]

Given this last assessment, it would appear futile to try to describe "The Sparrowhawk." Author and New Song artist Patricio Manns nonetheless merits citation in his valiant attempt to do so: "By means of isochrony, syncopation, syllabic division, playing with parts of words, accelerated breaks, dislocation, and the unexpected fusion of words, together with the use of surprising glissandos, tonal changes, and excellent dissonant resources in her guitar work, Parra has created one of the most original works in both textual and musical terms that we have ever heard in Chilean folk art."[129]

A Range of Recordings

Parra's next musical project puts to rest any notion that her artistic activities can be plotted as progressing along a single axis. It was a complete throwback to her folkloric sister act days. In mid-1958, Parra temporarily reconstituted Las Hermanas Parra, albeit solely for recording purposes. She did so in two different configurations, one with her daughter Isabel and the other with her sister Hilda, recording an EP of popular cuecas with each. The most likely impetus for this reprise of Las Hermanas Parra was Odeon's release in 1957 of an EP featuring previously unreleased tracks by the duo dating back to before its dissolution in the early 1950s.[130] The commercial success of Isabel's 1957 chart-topping single recorded in the style of música típica was likely another motivating factor.

Shifting the topic briefly to Parra's love life—the subject of much innuendo both during her lifetime and since—Parra is rumored to have had an affair, most likely around this time, with Odeon studio musician and master guitarist Humberto Campos.[131] Campos was almost certainly among the unnamed studio musicians who accompanied Las Hermanas Parra on their RCA Victor singles in the early 1950s, and he is known to have participated in the 1958 recordings of the temporarily (and diversely configured) duo with Odeon.[132] According to one of Campos's musician colleagues, they were on their way together to perform with música típica star Ester Soré in the city of Talca when they ran into Parra at the Santiago train station, suitcase in hand. Campos inquired where she was going. She responded, "I'm going with you," and then joined the party of traveling musicians for the duration of their trip to Talca. Although the incident is unverifiable, both Campos's biographer Mauricio Valdebenito and I think it entirely plausible.[133]

Parra would record two more LPs for the "Folklore of Chile" series during this period, one of cuecas and the other tonadas. Recorded in October 1958 and released in January 1959, *La cueca presentada por Violeta Parra* (The Cueca, as Presented by Violeta Parra) demonstrates Parra's more inclusive definition of folklore. The album breaks with the voice-and-guitar model of what a traditionalist folk music recording should sound like, a model that Parra herself helped establish with her previous two volumes in the series. Instead, the LP's twenty-four cuecas cover a range of rural and urban styles. Parra sings one a cappella while drumming on a large can like the one displayed at the museum of folk art in Concepción. She sings two in duet with Isabel, one in the unison style of the rural women singers of the Central Valley, and another in the urban folk style of Las Hermanas Parra. Three of the cuecas are instrumentals performed, respectively, by a harmonica player, an organ grinder, and a full circus band. The LP also includes "La cueca larga de Meneses" (Meneses's

Long Cueca), Violeta's musical setting of verses extracted from Nicanor's 1958 book-length poem, *La cueca larga* (The Long Cueca).[134] In sum, the album showcases the cueca in all its glory as the shared legacy of urban and rural singers, folkloric sister acts, street musicians, circus performers, and a prize-winning poet.

Violeta's broadminded take on the cueca did not please everyone. According to Isabel, when Violeta invited the organ grinder and circus band to perform at the LP's release concert, held in the Hall of Honor of the University of Chile in January 1959, "some officials lamented this 'outrage.'" "The general public, which was at overflow capacity," on the other hand, "happily gave them a standing ovation."[135]

Parra's next LP was *La tonada presentada por Violeta Parra* (The Tonada, as Presented by Violeta Parra), released in September 1959. The album featured fifteen tonadas, all of them collected by Parra. It would be her last recording to showcase her work as a folklorista, as the vast majority of songs on her subsequent solo albums would be Parra originals.

In the years surrounding the LP's release, Parra repeatedly expressed her frustration that the folk songs she so lovingly "unearthed" failed to appeal to a larger audience. In a 1958 radio interview, for example, she lamented that she remained only slightly less alone than before and called on everyone—fellow performers, radio station artistic directors, local businesses—to aid her in her "battle in defense of our authentic music."[136] The sense of defeat captured in a January 1960 radio interview suggests that her pleas remained unanswered: "I have to fight with half the world just to make some headway, because to this day not even one tenth of the Chilean population appreciates our folklore, so it's almost as if I have to wage a house-to-house battle. . . . It's still incredibly difficult."[137]

Seasonal Work

The folk song and dance course that Parra taught in January 1958 at the University of Concepción initiated her into what could be considered her "side gig" as a teacher. Teaching was perhaps not Parra's calling. According to Margot Loyola (whose commentary, given the two folkloristas' friendship-rivalry, should always be taken with a grain of salt), "[Parra] did not appear to have been born to teach, she didn't like it very much."[138] Whether Loyola's assessment was true, false, or somewhere in between, it did not impede Parra from accepting seasonal work as a teacher when and where it was offered, if not for love of the craft, then for the much-needed income. Starting with that first summer in Concepción, she found periodic employment teaching at various seasonal schools nearly every summer or winter until her departure for

Argentina in December 1961. The work took her almost the entire length of Chile, from the northern border town of Arica to the southern town of Castro on the Island of Chiloé.[139] Parra would take advantage of each out-of-town teaching position to pursue her passion for collecting songs and other folklore, at times extending her stay past the weeks that the seasonal school lasted to a few months.

September brought a different kind of seasonal occupation: it was and remains the one month in the year when traditionalist folkloristas and música típica artists alike could look forward to a full slate of activities thanks to the festivities commemorating Chile's independence. In September 1958 and most likely every September that followed until her departure for Argentina, Parra added a new project to her already packed agenda: she built and ran her own *fonda*.[140] In Chile and elsewhere, a fonda is a temporary, rustic structure traditionally built out of wooden posts and eucalyptus leaves and devoted to providing food and entertainment.[141] Patriotic entrepreneurs put up their fondas in designated parks and other public spaces every September so that Chileans of all social classes can gather to dance the cueca and imbibe traditional fare as part of the monthlong independence celebrations.

Parra's fonda, like all fondas, was a genuine organizational feat. She had to rent a plot of land, order supplies of wine, chicha, and empanadas (meat-filled pastries) and make sure there was "lots of wood and nails for the tables, costumes, a dance floor, a stage, a frame for the roof and branches to cover it with."[142] Her friends and family worked alongside her from setup to strikedown four days later. They helped decorate the fonda with the requisite strings of miniature Chilean flags. They took turns performing, waiting on tables, plying customers with empanadas and *ponche* (punch), and seeing to all the other fonda-related chores. It was exhausting work and left the singers hoarse by day two, but Parra "loved all the hustle and bustle."[143] It was also potentially a good business venture, as a well-run fonda could generate several months' worth of income.[144]

Parra's fonda stood out from other fondas due to its clientele. It was frequented by a mix of leftist intellectuals and artists—the one where "all the poets were" was how one visitor poet described it.[145] What drew these select patrons to Parra's fonda was that it offered them an alternative and, from their perspective, more authentic way to celebrate their chilenidad. Neighboring fondas relied on the standard fare of canned patriotism propagated by the huaso bands and other música típica artists, either live or via recordings. Parra's fonda, in contrast, presented nonstop performances by both established and emerging folkloristas who strived to convey not a postcard version of Chile but the very soul of its people through their music. The lineup on any given night drew from a lengthy roster of Parra's family, friends, mentees, and folk informants. It included Parra's musician siblings and children; members of the up-and-coming traditionalist folk ensembles Conjunto Cuncumén and Millaray; and, on occasion, the traditional singers from Puente Alto.

After dark, Parra would turn the fonda into a makeshift outdoor movie theater where she projected Sergio Bravo's documentaries featuring her soundtracks onto an improvised screen made of sheets. Once she expanded her creative activities into the realm of the visual arts, her fonda doubled as a pop-up gallery that displayed her paintings and tapestries. (Inversely, she would transform her booth at the annual Arts Fair held in Santiago beginning in 1959 into a fonda-like space. Reviews and photos of her European performances from 1962 to 1965 confirm that she carried the concept overseas as well.)

An Autobiography in Décimas and Other Unpublished Works

Three book projects are included on the long list of creative activities that Parra undertook during this period. Two were of the folk songs she collected, and the third was her autobiography in décimas. None would be published during her lifetime.

The first and most elaborate project was the ethnographic manuscript that would eventually be published as *Cantos folklóricos chilenos* (Chilean Folk Songs). It was a collaborative effort consisting of first-person vignettes of Parra's encounters with fifteen folk informants, including doña Rosa, don Isaías Angulo, and Parra's mother Clarisa; the lyrics of fifty-eight folk songs; accompanying musical transcriptions by Gastón Soublette; and photos by both Sergio Larraín and Sergio Bravo. Despite Parra's repeated pronouncements in the press that the book was already at the printer and that it would be out any day now, it would not be published until 1979.[146]

Parra made similarly optimistic claims about a forthcoming collection of fifty cuecas from the Concepción region that has yet to be published.[147] According to the friend who accompanied her, Parra brought just the lyric sheets to the offices of Nascimiento, the same press that published her brother Nicanor Parra's poetry. An employee of the press leafed through the pages and, noting that there were no musical transcriptions, asked Violeta if she had studied music, to which she answered, "No, but if I had, I would be the Bach of Chilean music."[148]

Parra's third book project was her autobiography in décimas. Perhaps more than any other of her creative endeavors, this collection of ninety-six poems welded her work with that of the traditional singers whose folk poetry she dedicated years of her life to collecting and disseminating. Parra read excerpts of it on a January 1960 radio interview. She explained that her brother Nicanor was the one who had suggested that she write her autobiography in verse. At first, she had refused, as she had "other more important things to do, like taking care of my home and battling for folklore."[149] Quoting from her décimas, she continued:

> But heeding my brother's counsel,
> I thought about the matter,
> And then I took pen in hand
> And began to fill the pages.

> *Pero, pensándolo bien,*
> *y haciendo juicio a mi hermano,*
> *tomé la pluma en la mano*
> *y fui llenando el papel.*[150]

Parra would eventually fill entire notebooks and sheaves of paper with her verses. At least one page included a shopping list on its margins—"1 liter of milk, 2 kg of meat, buttons."[151]

A poetic exercise in self-discovery and self-construction, Parra's autobiography covers the period from her childhood through her return from her first European stay. The verses encompass a reckoning with her past: her father's alcoholism and other prolonged illness, the family's destitution after he squandered his inheritance, his premature death, long evenings spent helping her mother as she sewed, the failure of Parra's first marriage, the sordid atmosphere of the "convent" or bar where she worked, and her feelings of sorrow and guilt over the loss of her infant child. A few of the décimas chronicle Parra's adventures in Europe. Several address less personal topics. Some are philosophical. Others critique society's injustices and hypocrisies, presaging Parra's 1960s protest songs. Loose poems at the end of the manuscript include her homage to Gabriela Mistral, and musings on love's disillusions inspired by the end of her affair with Julio Escámez.

Parra's autobiography signaled a shift in emphasis in her foundational narrative of authenticity, from her affinity with the humble, rural pueblo or folk that sustained her work as a folklorista, to her identification with the oppressed pueblo of class struggle that would underpin much of her politically engaged songwriting and visual artwork in the 1960s. Parra established her identity as a mujer del pueblo or "woman of the people"—with "people" now understood in its more politicized meaning as the working poor—in two principal ways. First, she highlighted her own experience of poverty as a child, with her mother working late into the night to feed her children its most salient illustration. Second, she provided an exaggerated account of her maternal grandfather's exploitation.

Parra presented both of her grandfathers in a sequence of poems devoted to her family lineage. Her poetic portrayal of her paternal grandfather was accurate, on the whole. She wrote that he was an "esteemed" and "educated" man, who wore a pink tie, resided in a "grand old house," and was visited by "The ladies, fans aflutter / The gentlemen in suits / Perfumed and snooty / As the rich always are" (*las damas con abanico, / de fraque los caballeros, / perfumosos y altaneros, / como son siempre los ricos*).[152] In effect, although Violeta's paternal grandfather would not have been considered rich in Santiago where the Chilean upper-class was centralized, he was "rich" by the standards of Chillán. "An elegant man" with a "certain provincial prestige" was how Nicanor characterized him.[153]

Violeta's depiction of her maternal grandfather was far more inventive. She wrote that "the rich man, in all of his grace," held her grandfather as a "bonded laborer" (*obliga'o*).[154] In her 1960 radio interview, she clarified that this meant he was an inquilino (tenant farmer) and *explotado* (someone who is exploited)." In fact, her maternal grandfather was a small landowner, of which there were many in the Ñuble province, who also worked as the administrator of a nearby landed estate. Nicanor described him as "pretty well off," from the "campesino middle class."[155]

Violeta's representation of her maternal grandfather as a poor and oppressed agricultural worker was an early example of the practice that would lead Nicanor to jokingly label her a "social descender" (*abajista*), his play on words for a person who exaggerated their social status downward as opposed to a social climber or *arribista*.[156] And the downward slant Violeta gave to the Parra family history would only grow steeper with time. Moving forward, she would shed references to her paternal grandfather's provincial-scale privilege and double down on casting her maternal grandfather as poor and exploited. Her accentuation of her and her family's experience of poverty would bring her narratively closer to the pueblo or working poor with whom she identified and whom she now proposed to give voice to through her songs and artwork.

It is not clear precisely when and where Parra began to work on her autobiography in verse. She must have considered it complete or near completion when she premiered it on the radio in January 1960. She presented it later that year to members of the Communist Party's cultural commission in hopes that they would publish it.[157] The encounter took place in Pablo Neruda's newest home, La Chascona, a rambling house in the bohemian Santiago neighborhood of Bella Vista that he shared with his third wife, Matilde Urrutia, and that, like his other houses, served as an unofficial headquarters of the cultural Left. Upon hearing Parra's work, the literary critic of the communist daily *El Siglo* pronounced it extraordinary and compared it to the well-known epic poem "Martin Fierro" by the late nineteenth-century Argentine author José Hernández.[158] Their praise notwithstanding, party officials were unable to reach a consensus in support of the manuscript's publication.[159]

In the end, Parra's sole publication in Chile within her lifetime was a one-page article on the folk ritual of the wake for the little angel, appearing in the December 1958 issue of the art review *Pomaire*.[160] That Parra was unable to get her work published in Chile was a great source of aggravation to her. In what seems to have become the pattern of her life, she would find better success publishing her work abroad, first in Argentina and later in France.

No matter the challenges Parra faced, they could not dampen her creative spirit and drive. On the contrary, her powers of invention appear to have been boundless during this period. There is perhaps no better example of this, unrivaled for its sheer exaggeration, than her invention of the *centésima*. Parra introduced the centésima during the January 1960 radio interview in which she premiered her autobiography in décimas. After reading a few examples of the traditional ten-line verse, Parra went on to explain that she had since moved on from the décima to the centésima, a new form of folk poetry that she had invented with verses of one hundred lines. She proceeded to read her centésima in its entirety on the air. In an animated voice, she then informed her listeners that she was working on a *milésima* that would go all the way up to 1,000. The radio program host and Parra jokingly agreed that from there she would have to go up to 10,000, then on to 1 million. As Parra affirmed, "[the possibilities] are infinite."[161]

Chapter 6

Volcanic Violeta II

In the early 1950s, when Parra was in her mid-thirties, she reinvented herself as a folklorista. Now in her early forties at the close of the decade, she continued to demonstrate exceptional skill in that area while simultaneously pursuing new creative pathways. The visual arts would figure prominently among them. It was during these "volcanic" years that Parra began her explorations in ceramics, painting, and the *arpilleras* or embroidered tapestries that would eventually lead to what was beyond question the pinnacle of her varied career as an artist: her 1964 solo show at the Museum of Decorative Arts (MAD) in the Louvre Palace.

Although Parra's sources of inspiration for taking on these new activities were surely multiple, two stand out. One was the significant presence of visual artists in the Latin American expatriate community that Parra was part of during her prolonged stay in Paris. The second was her six-month residency at the School of Fine Arts in Concepción, spanning 1957 to 1958, where she witnessed artistic activities every day and where she forged close and, in the case of Escámez, intimate relationships with several local and visiting artists. An overlapping source of inspiration was the sheer number of Parra's friends, at home and abroad, who were themselves visual artists.

Parra's first known foray into the visual arts came about thanks to the University of Chile's Musical Education Extension program, and specifically its shoestring budget. When Parra was hired to perform in a concert series organized by the program in the late 1950s, the funds available for the event were so meager that its director Carmen Orrego suggested that, in lieu of printing posters for the event, Parra make her own hand-painted signs. Orrego even supplied Parra with paints and brushes. According to Orrego, the signs were a great success and may have launched Parra's subsequent pursuits in the art of painting.[1]

The artist Teresa Vicuña is credited with encouraging Parra's first incursion into sculpture. Parra first met Vicuña at the Café Sao Paulo, a popular gathering place for artists and intellectuals in Santiago, and the two women became instant friends.[2] Parra often visited Vicuña at her art studio, where she would freely opine on the sculptor's works in progress until one day, fed up with her incessant suggestions, Vicuña handed Parra some clay and told her to make her own piece just the way she wanted it. And that is how Parra began sculpting with clay.[3]

When Parra contracted hepatitis sometime in 1959, her prolonged illness became an unexpected impetus for her to expand her artistic endeavors.[4] Her doctor confined her to bed rest until she was fully recovered. As Parra was incapable of remaining idle, she began experimenting with different creative outlets. At first she painted. Folk singer and mentee Silvia Urbina recalls visiting Parra while she was convalescing and finding her in bed surrounded by paintings, her pillowcase and sheets covered with paint, as she had been using them to clean her brushes.[5]

Parra next tried embroidery. In a 1965 Swiss documentary, she described her first attempts: "One day I saw some yarn and a piece of cloth and I began to embroider something, anything, but that first time nothing worked. . . . The second time . . . I wanted to copy a flower, but I couldn't. When I finished the embroidery, it wasn't a flower at all, but a bottle. Then I wanted to put a cork on the bottle, and the cork came out looking like a head. . . . I added eyes, nose, and a mouth. The flower was not a bottle, then the bottle was not a bottle, but a woman."[6] The quote captures a basic claim about Parra's creative process, one that she herself helped establish, and that was echoed and amplified by her many admirers: that her creative process was completely spontaneous. "Magical" is how multiple fans would characterize it over the years. For her part, Parra would describe it as working "according to the needle's whims."[7]

As with all of her performances of self, it is difficult to gauge to what extent Parra's claim to instinctiveness and spontaneity reflected her actual creative process and to what extent it was a performance for the benefit of her (presumed) more sophisticated audience, what art historian Serda Yalkin describes as a "strategy of the authentic."[8] Whatever its measure, it would become core to her identity as a visual artist. Although this would lead most people in the art world to consign Parra to the categories of folk or naïve art, she would insist that she was an artist without limits.

Parra employed diverse materials and techniques for her artwork. This was as much out of necessity as her desire to experiment. As Violeta's granddaughter Tita Parra explained, "Sometimes Violeta did not have any materials to work with, but then she would gather paper, wire, wood, jars of paint, etc. that were lying around the house and with this she was able to create grand and wonderful pieces."[9] Isabel recounts how her mother went through an intense phase when she was so bent on producing her tapestries that "it was not unusual to arrive at her home and find a window without curtains or a bed without sheets. And all because Violeta was embroidering."[10] Hilda's husband, who worked in a paper factory, supplied Violeta with cardboard for her large paintings, so no domestic sacrifice was required in their case. Yvonne Brunhammer, the French museum official who oversaw Parra's MAD exhibit, summed it up: "[Parra] had an extraordinary capacity for invention, and for transforming any poor material into a significant and symbolic work."[11]

Not one to doubt her own abilities, when the call went out for exhibitors to display their work at the Arts Fair (*Feria de Artes Plásticas*), held in December 1959, Parra arranged to get her own booth. The fair was a major cultural event, the first of its kind in Chile. Its organizers hoped to create a space where Chilean artists, art students, and artisans alike could exhibit their work. The Arts Fair of 1959 was an overwhelming success and went on to become an annual event held, with few exceptions, through the 1960s.[12]

In its early years, the Arts Fair took place in the Forestal Park, a shady expanse that follows the banks of the Mapocho River in downtown Santiago and that transformed into a bustling midway for the week of the fair, with hundreds of stalls and thousands of visitors daily. Chilean artists who had received their training in fine art academies at home or in the cultural capitals of Europe exhibited their paintings, prints, and sculptures. Master artisans—including basket weaver Luis Manzano, aka "Manzanito," the subject of Sergio Bravo's documentary *Mimbre*—demonstrated their techniques and showed off their finished handiwork to curious onlookers gathered around their stalls. Printers from the graphic artists' collective Taller 99—the brainchild of Nemesio Antúnez, Parra's friend from her residency in Concepción—operated a printmaking press. Celebrated poets and novelists—including Nicanor Parra—signed copies of their most recent works at the writers' booth. A large stage set up at one end of the park offered free entertainment in the afternoons and evenings. Ice cream and cotton candy vendors and the occasional mime weaved their way through the crowds.

Parra participated in the Arts Fair in 1959, 1960, and 1961 and again upon her return from Europe in 1965.[13] At the 1959 fair, she displayed her ceramic creations, including creches for the holidays, singers, odd-shaped ducks and birds that were reminiscent of the pottery of the town of Quinchamalí, and vases with the likeness of Pablo Neruda's face on both sides that the communist daily *El Siglo* dubbed "Pablo pitchers."[14] In subsequent years, Parra exhibited her tapestries and paintings as well. At all of the annual arts fairs, she offered demonstrations of her craft, whether molding figures out of clay or embroidering her vast tapestries (see figures 6.1 and 6.2).

Not surprisingly, music was an important element of Parra's participation in the fair. She performed on stage as "Violeta Parra and Her Ensemble" at the 1960 Arts Fair—with the ensemble most likely Isabel and Ángel.[15] She also sang and played her guitar at her stall, which is how Miguel Letelier discovered her piece "The Sparrowhawk." She blasted out her folk recordings on a

Figure 6.1 Violeta Parra modeling clay at the 1960 Arts Fair. Photograph by Antonio Quintana Contreras. Colección Archivo Fotográfico, Archivo Central Andrés Bello, Universidad de Chile.

sound system she set up for that purpose. This was not to everyone's liking. As a reporter noted, Parra's loud and incessant playing of music "brought complications." The artists from neighboring stands complained so vociferously that the fair's organizers cut off Parra's source of electricity until they were able to reach an accord: she could play her music as long as she set the volume so that the sound would not carry beyond her booth.[16] Parra set up a cot and slept at her stand in order to safeguard her work and to be there first thing in the morning, ready for another full day.

Parra received some attention from the local press in her new role as a visual artist—and not just because she was bothering people with all the "noise" she made. One reporter commenting on her work on display at the 1959 Arts Fair appeared underwhelmed by it, observing that "Violeta continues to have more

Figure 6.2 Violeta Parra embroidering a tapestry at the 1960 Arts Fair. Photograph by Mario Guillard Pérez-Villamil. Colección Archivo Fotográfico, Archivo Central Andrés Bello, Universidad de Chile.

success as a folklorista than as a novice ceramicist. People visit her stand to hear her sing more than to see her ceramics."[17] In their review of the 1961 Arts Fair, another and far harsher critic panned Parra's work outright: "The third Fair has dreadful things in it. . . . For example the pieces of cardboard smeared with paint by Violeta Parra."[18]

Other reporters were more sympathetic. Borrowing from the same gendered template that critics had used to describe her modern guitar instrumentals, they associated Parra's work not with the modern artist's quest for self-expression but with an intuitive and naïve creative process that was at the same time linked to Chilean folk art practices. Journalist José María Palacios, for instance, noted in his article on the 1960 Arts Fair that the renowned folklorista Violeta Parra was now also a painter and a "weaver [tapestry-maker]," then opined that "the line she draws, weak like that of a child, offers in exchange that imponderable elementality . . . that approaches the transcendent, not with reason, but with intuition." He found her ceramics, in turn, to be similar to the works of rural potters in their "graphic functionality."[19] Another reporter located Parra's clay figures, just like her songs, in Chile's idyllic past; they represented Chile "the way it was and the way it should be: so very innocent, unassuming, and expressive, without banalities or affectation."[20]

The 1960 Arts Fair organizers' award to Parra of "honorable mention" in the category "folk art" confirms that they viewed her work in a similar light, not as individual, but as an expression of the collective traditions of the Chilean people (the prize went to the woman potters of Quinchamalí).[21] Parra's use of embroidery as one of her media, widely seen as a women's craft, only solidified her association with the folk arts.

In characterizing her work as folk or artisanal, both Parra's reviewers and the fair organizers situated it as "lesser" or inferior to the fine arts. Intentionally or not, the 1960 documentary *Los Artistas Plásticos de Chile* (Visual Artists of Chile), by di Lauro and Yankovic—the husband-and-wife film-making team with whom Parra had worked on their 1958 documentary *Andacollo*— simultaneously reinforced this hierarchy between high and folk art and positioned Parra squarely in the second camp. The film's narration grants individual identity to a select group of elite artists, who are portrayed at work in their studios over a soundtrack of music by Benjamin Britten and other classical composers. In contrast, Parra and master artisan Manzanito are shown at their stalls in the outdoor Arts Fair in a fleeting segment that has no identifying commentary, just Parra's voice singing a folk song in the background, as anonymous as the folk songs she collected.[22]

With a few notable exceptions, art critics and documentary makers in Chile, Argentina, and the nations of Europe would continue to categorize Parra's artwork as naïve and folk—and, in the case of Europe, Indigenous— throughout the remainder of her life. One such exception occurred early in Parra's career as a visual artist: in October 1961, her tapestries and paintings were exhibited alongside the works of some twenty other Chilean artists at the Museum of Modern Art in Rio de Janeiro, Brazil. The man responsible for her inclusion in the exhibit was Brazilian poet Thiago de Mello, who was serving as Brazil's cultural attaché to Chile at the time and who was both Parra's friend and an admirer of her work. According to the group show's press release, it assembled the "most representative artists" in order to provide "a clear view of modern trends in the visual arts" in Chile.[23]

Parra's inclusion in the group show in Rio de Janeiro constituted yet another instance when international recognition of her talents, in this instance in the realm of the visual arts, preceded any acknowledgment in her native

Chile. Parra would gain the latter only in death. As painter Eduardo Martínez Bonatti acknowledged at a 1968 roundtable organized in her memory, "When Violeta Parra's tapestries hung at the first Arts Fair several years ago, we passed them by and were unable to grasp their meaning. . . . Now perhaps all of us want to own a tapestry by Violeta Parra."[24]

Cultural Emissary or Maid

Nicanor continued to be something of a "cultural guru" to Violeta throughout this period, and she is purported to have declared on more than one occasion that "without Nicanor there would be no Violeta."[25] The siblings' relationship now expanded to encompass not only Nicanor's mentorship but their creative collaboration. Violeta set several of her brother's poems to music, including excerpts of his 1958 book-length poem, *La cueca larga*, which drew its inspiration from Chilean folk poetry—and which serves as a reminder that Violeta was hardly the only Parra sibling fluent in its idioms.[26] She provided the musical background to Chilean actor Roberto Parada's reading of sections of *La cueca larga* for the EP that accompanied a new and enhanced 1960 edition of the book that also featured illustrations by Nemesio Antúnez.[27] Nicanor penned his prescient poem "Defense of Violeta Parra" that same year, which he would later read and record over her musical accompaniment on her 1965 LP, *Recordando a Chile* (Chile on My Mind).[28]

Nicanor, whose reputation was growing at home and abroad, continued to welcome Violeta into his social circles. Thanks to him, Violeta met international figures such as Salvadoran poet Claribel Alegría and US beat generation poet Allen Ginsberg.[29] Ginsberg, who traveled to Chile in January 1960 to attend the historic First Conference of American Writers in Concepción, then stayed on as Nicanor's houseguest in Santiago, even mentions Violeta in his journal.[30] Violeta was a frequent guest at the artistic soirées hosted by Pablo Neruda as well.

Violeta also became something of a cultural emissary herself, the go-to person for introducing Chilean folk culture to prominent visiting artists. *Ecran* reporter Marina de Navasal, tongue-in-cheek, credited Parra with assigning herself this role of folk ambassador: "Violeta Parra not only researches Chilean music . . . she also insists on performing it for those in the know." Navasal proceeded to list the experts in question: world famous pianist and Chilean expatriate Claudio Arrau, Mexican symphony conductor Luis Herrera de la Fuente, Chilean composer Acario Cotapos, and "each and every musical eminence who chances within her reach."[31]

In May 1958, Parra met yet another international luminary: US composer and conductor Leonard Bernstein. Bernstein was on a seven-week tour of

South America with the New York Philharmonic that included four sold-out concerts in Santiago.[32] He heard Parra perform at a reception in his honor at a private home and was so impressed that he ended up praising her at length in his opening address to the two-month cultural event, "Image of Chile," sponsored by the US State Department. Bernstein delivered his speech in Washington, D.C., in September 1963: "Apart from anything else, I long to sit again in a little room on the outskirts of Santiago and listen to the magical folk-singing of Violeta Parra. I have always been a folk-music fan, ever since I can remember . . . [but] I have never felt so close to a newly discovered folk music as I did to those heartbreaking *Saludas* [*sic, saludos* or songs of greeting] and *Parabienes* [songs of congratulations] that poured out of Parra's mouth and soul."[33] Bernstein would later base a section of his "Mass: A Theater Piece for Singers, Players, and Dancers," commissioned by Jacqueline Kennedy for the 1971 inauguration of the Kennedy Center, on a folk song that he all but admitted in an unpublished interview was a "direct steal" from one of Parra's recordings.[34]

Parra had been invited to perform at Leonard Bernstein's reception as a representative of "the real thing" or the authentic other. Along with its benefits, there could be negative aspects to this positioning. In classist-racist Chilean society, Parra's otherness, which at times earned her entry to select cultural settings, could sometimes result in her being marginalized or excluded from the very cultural institutions and media outlets upon which her livelihood increasingly depended.

The following incident, occurring shortly after Parra's return from Europe at the close of 1956, is illustrative of this. It was humorously recounted by an anonymous chronicler of the history of the Santiago radio station Radio Cooperativa. The station broadcast a show geared toward housewives that included a segment where unemployed domestic servants could introduce themselves on air to prospective employers in the listening audience. Radio announcer Miguel Ángel Yañez was walking through the station when he noticed a woman sitting on a couch. Not realizing that she was Violeta Parra, recently returned from Paris and waiting to meet with the station director, he informed her, somewhat impatiently, that the domestic servants lined up outside.[35] The anecdote makes clear that an alternative reading to Parra as "the real thing" was as a poor person.

Given their class-racial prejudices, members of Chile's middle and upper classes were generally most at ease when poor people like the domestic servants lined up outside the radio station remained either "in their place" or invisible. It goes without saying that Parra neither knew her place nor made herself invisible. This is illustrated by another anecdote when she was again mistakenly treated as a servant. At some point, most likely in 1958, Parra was hired by a family of her acquaintance to sing at their daughter's birthday party. It was held at the Union Club, the principal gathering spot for politicians and government officials from Chile's conservative elite, housed in a mansion a few blocks from the presidential La Moneda Palace in Santiago.[36] Wives and children were admitted only on special occasions such as the young woman's birthday party where Parra performed. When Parra's presentation concluded, she was invited to go to the kitchen to have something to eat. This was when all hell broke loose. According to Ángel, "When my mom got mad, it was serious. . . . She told each and every one of them where they could go. When she got home, she proudly told us the whole story between laughs: 'I taught those stuck-up bastards a lesson that they were not expecting. They thought I was a resigned and obedient *huasita* [country girl].'"[37]

The 1960 Earthquake

In May 1960, Violeta, Isabel, Ángel, the folk music ensemble Cuncumén, and a classical string quartet embarked on a tour of southern Chile sponsored by the University of Chile's cultural extension program. It was on this tour that Parra and her fellow musicians experienced one of the most dramatic events of their lifetimes: the strongest earthquake in recorded world history. It occurred on May 22, 1960, at 3:00 P.M. in the vicinity of the southern town of Puerto Montt. The earthquake measured 9.5 on the Richter scale, lasted for approximately ten minutes, and was followed by a tsunami. The natural disaster left thousands of people dead and as many or more homes damaged or destroyed. It would be an unforgettable experience for all those who survived it.

The earthquake was preceded by two days of smaller tremors in the region. This, in turn, gave rise to what may be the strangest anecdote in a life full of anecdotes. The incident, as recounted in a radio interview by Cuncumén musician Silvia Urbina, occurred just hours before the big earthquake. Most of the touring musicians were away on a midday excursion to a nearby island. Urbina and Parra had stayed behind in Puerto Montt, in Parra's case because she wanted to ask the local fishermen about their songs and celebrations.[38]

Noontime found them strolling through the city's center when, fed up with the earth's jolts and the frayed nerves these were producing, Parra marched into the telegraph office and proceeded to dictate a telegram. This was not unusual in itself, as telegrams were how people communicated over long distances in those days. What was unusual was Parra's intended recipient: none other than God themself. Specifically, she asked God to send an earthquake once and for all because, as she explained, "the world needs fixing." When the young clerk at the counter informed Parra that she was unable to send the missive, Parra asked to speak to the manager. He came out and immediately recognized Parra. After a warm greeting, he informed her that he planned to attend her performance that evening. He read her message, laughed heartily, and assured her that he would send the telegram off right away and that she need not worry about payment, as he would collect all charges at the receiving end. A few hours later, the earthquake struck.[39]

My point in recounting this anecdote is not to imply that Parra was somehow able to summon earthquakes. Rather, it is to highlight an aspect of Parra's personality that is often overlooked or eclipsed: her sense of humor.[40]

The ensuing earthquake was anything but funny for those who survived it. This included Parra and her fellow musicians, several of whom were left traumatized to the point that they sought psychiatric therapy in its aftermath.[41] Perhaps unsurprisingly, Parra's response was to write the song "Puerto Montt está temblando" (Puerto Montt Is Trembling). In it, she recounts experiencing the earthquake in all of its terrifying details:

Puerto Montt is trembling
with furious resentment
and I am witness to
a world that is ending . . .

I was in my hotel room
up on the second floor
when a hailstorm erupted
from that fierce purgatory;
washbasins and mirrors
sliding down the walls.

Puerto Montt está temblando
con un encono profundo:
es un acabo de mundo
lo que yo estoy presenciando . . .

Estaba en el dormitorio
de un alto segundo piso
cuando principia el granizo
de aquel feroz purgatorio;
espejos y lavatorios
descienden por las paredes.

Living through an earthquake of unfathomable magnitude is probably as good a reason as any to interrogate God. Parra does precisely this:

"Lord could you perhaps
calm down for just a bit?"

And he responds, irate:
"As you sow, you shall reap."

Ladies and gents, thus I've described
the sad exchange of views
that while the earth was moving
I had with the Almighty.

*"Señor, ¿acaso no puedes
calmarte por un segundo?"
Y me responde iracundo:
"Pa'l tiburón son las redes."*

*Así fue, señores míos,
la triste conversación
que en medio de aquel temblor
sostuve con el Divino.*[42]

In combination, Parra's telegram addressed to the Almighty and her song "Puerto Montt Is Trembling" open a window onto her relationship with God. Here, I do not consider her views on institutional religion. These ranged from ambiguous (she likely baptized all four of her children, yet did not attend Sunday mass), to critical (she wrote songs that denounced the Church's complacency in the face of social injustice), to sarcastic bordering on blasphemous (she enjoyed leading her audiences in rousing sing-a-longs of the chorus of the bawdy song "The Sexton," whose love was "as sweet as honey"). Rather, I refer to her direct and intimate relationship with God that is exemplified by both the telegram and the song, each in its own way. To borrow from the song's lyrics, they formed part of her ongoing "exchange of views . . . with the Almighty."

Parra conveys that same personal relationship with God in her décimas, lyrics, and other writings, often broadening her range to include the Virgin Mary and the saints. Her familiarity with God and their divine entourage was deeply rooted, not in official Catholic doctrine but in popular religion. It was enacted in the religious festivals that she participated in as a child and documented as an adult. It found its expression in the traditional songs that she collected as a folklorista and drew inspiration from as an artist. They included the poet-songs of loving devotion that welcome an infant into heaven, and songs in a more jocular vein that report on the antics of *santos* (male saints) and *santas* (female saints) who flirt, drink, and compete in rodeos.[43] This popular branch of Catholicism, which her friend and fellow poet Pablo de Rokha aptly characterized as "more pagan than Christian," was the only religion Parra practiced with any consistency.[44]

"Work Trenches"

Parra's possibilities may have felt infinite to her, as she enthusiastically affirmed after reciting all one hundred verses of her newly invented centésima to her radio audience. Her financial resources were sorely finite, however. Parra's artistic energy and versatility did not guarantee her a steady source of income, let alone prosperity. Instead, she cobbled together a living through performances and other activities in a constant battle to provide for herself and her family. Parra liked to refer to these seemingly endless undertakings as her "work trenches."[45]

It bears reiterating here that except for her six-month residency in Concepción, Parra received almost no support for her work as a folk collector. This was not for a lack of trying. In a typed two-page letter dated December 16, 1960, she begged and cajoled Alvaro Bunster, then provost of the University of Chile, to sponsor her.

Parra opens her letter dramatically: "It has been ten years now that I have been researching the music of the Chilean people. With no support from anyone. Without a salary. Without health care or other assistance. Alone like a bird." She goes on to provide a full inventory of the fruits of her labor: her soon-to-be-published ethnographic manuscript (that would in fact only be published posthumously); forty magnetic tapes containing some five hundred songs sung by folk informants; recordings of herself singing approximately 120 songs; a dozen notebooks of folk poetry. She proceeds to lay out her objective: to collect the approximately 300,000 songs that she estimates still needed to be collected throughout Chile. She submits a wish list of items needed in order to achieve her goal: a "Land Robert [sic, Land Rover]," a movie camera able to capture sound, a generator, a portable typewriter, and a notebook. She concludes with the rhetorical question, "Don't the ten years that I have been working on the sidelines, without any assistance at all, earn me the right to solicit the university's backing?"[46]

Parra reveals in her letter that this was her third appeal to this particular university official. As was the case with her previous two letters, the support she requested never materialized. The most she was able to obtain was a loose affiliation with the university's Institute for Folkloric Research, and this was largely due to her friendship with Alfonso Letelier, the dean of the College of Musical Arts and Sciences (and father of composer Miguel Letelier). Parra was a prolific letter writer. I cannot help but wonder how many of her appeals for institutional backing went unheeded over her lifetime.

Whatever sense of rejection Parra felt was accompanied by a fair amount of resentment. She is reported, for instance, to have chased away a journalist from the University of Chile's Public Relations office, after agreeing to be interviewed by them, because they requested to be allowed to record her singing, but did not intend to pay her for it.[47] Parra's protests that she was not being treated with the respect that she deserved would grow louder in the last years of her life, when she failed to receive the recognition for her artwork that she had earned during her second stay in Europe in her homeland of Chile, and when she was increasingly overshadowed by a younger generation of folk singers who would eventually found the Chilean New Song. Her ailing mental health no doubt factored into the rising volume of her grievance.

Parra brought in some income from concerts she gave in Santiago and other cities and towns that she visited. These were often formal, ticketed events in theaters and university halls, with printed programs and notices in the local press. They were usually produced by an academic or cultural institution on a shoestring budget, however, and therefore tended to pay poorly. They were also few and far between; one every two or three months, if that.

If Parra's concert opportunities were scarce, her chances of landing a regular gig at a nightclub or other commercial entertainment venue were all but nonexistent. The situation stood in sharp contrast to the numerous locales where the popular duo Las Hermanas Parra had performed in the late 1940s and early 1950s. In part, this disparity signaled the passing of the heyday of Santiago's nightlife. But it also resulted from what Hilda had succinctly conveyed as the reason for her reluctance to incorporate traditional songs into Las Hermanas Parra's repertoire: "People just didn't get folklore."[48]

Hilda's caution was not unfounded. Even at the height of the folk revival, Parra found the doors of most entertainment establishments in Santiago and elsewhere in Chile all but closed to a folk singer like herself. She had had better luck in this regard in Paris, where she could at least count on her work at L'Escale. There was no equivalent to the Left Bank boîte in Santiago in the late 1950s and early 1960s. That would have to wait a few more years until 1965, when Isabel and Ángel Parra opened their Peña de los Parra, the *peña* or folk club they modeled after the bohemian clubs where they worked during their own lengthy stay in Paris, but with a leftist political slant.

Along with the occasional paid concert, Parra's "work trenches" included her more regular radio performances. In the early 1960s, Parra made her first appearances on television as well. These were all on Channel 9—one of the three university-based stations founded in 1959 and 1960 that constituted Chile's nascent and, at the time, non–commercial television industry.[49] The newly founded station offers a prime example of how close-knit Santiago's cultural scene was, how rapidly it was developing, and how thoroughly Parra was integrated into it. The station operated out of the University of Chile's only slightly less newly founded Film Department, whose first director was Sergio Bravo, the documentary filmmaker who had worked with Parra on past projects. Its first station director was Raúl Aicardi, former artistic director at Radio Chilena who had given Parra her first radio show at the close of 1953. And Isabel and Ángel both worked for the TV station, where they were part of a ten-person team that covered all the tasks necessary to run it.

For all of these reasons, Channel 9 was the obvious choice for Parra's television debut: a special on Chilean folk music. Broadcast in December 1960, it was the first program of its kind to air in Chile.[50] This initial appearance along with Parra's subsequent ones would prove more groundbreaking than financially rewarding. As Isabel would later explain, in the early years of Chilean television "there was no budget and we worked for practically no pay."[51]

It is probable that Violeta did not earn much from the soundtracks she contributed to either, given the limited resources of the documentary filmmakers with whom she worked. She certainly did not make what she thought she deserved. In an interview granted in 1980, filmmaker Nieves Yankovic insisted that she and her creative partner Jorge di Lauro had gone out of their way to pay Parra generously for her work on their 1958 documentary *Andacollo*, as Parra had been broke at the time and they had wanted to support her. But Parra had had grand illusions: first, that the documentary was somehow going to be a blockbuster and second, that she would somehow receive a percentage of the proceeds. When neither of these proved to be the case, this created some temporary friction between the filmmakers and Parra, but it eventually blew over.[52]

Ever resourceful, Parra found myriad ways to bring in a little extra income. In addition to teaching folk music courses at seasonal schools, running her fonda during the month of September, and selling her artwork at the annual Arts Fair, she taught private folk music lessons to Miguel Letelier's sister, Carmen Luisa Letelier, and ran a makeshift folk dance academy in the spacious apartment of her *pituca* (wealthy) friend, the poet Ester Matte.[53] Then there was the time when Violeta and Isabel made a side trip to the duty-free port of Iquique after co-teaching a course in the northern city of Antofagasta. They purchased suitcases full of imported goods: "nylon polo shirts, knitted English ensembles, cashmere vests, corduroy shirts, soaps, exfoliants, spices from the US . . . and great quantities of Camay soap, thermoses, lipsticks, and magical anti-wrinkle creams."[54] After a small markup in price, Violeta sold the wares to friends and acquaintances back in Santiago.[55]

Despite all her exertions—and to her great aggravation—Parra continued to struggle to make ends meet. In an interview, Isabel described a typical day spent with her mother:

After scolding me about my hair or my skirt, we would go off first to visit Carmen Luisa where she [Violeta] would argue with her mother-in-law

[Luis Arce's mother]. Next: to the office of Mr. Apple [*sic*], business manager for Odeon records. Usually I would hear my mother loudly accusing Apple of a thousand and one slights toward her on the part of the record company. She would almost always leave these meetings crying and shouting about how she was going to break her contract. I never saw her leave happy. If she was not crying, then she was trembling with fury. Third: grab a bite to eat downtown. Fourth: go to the composers' association to fight for an advance on her royalties. After that we would go to the Café Sao Paulo or Palmeiras. . . . She followed the same itinerary throughout this period. Where she suffered the most was at the radio stations and the record company. She hated bureaucrats with all her heart, to her they were "lazy shits."[56]

Given her low regard for bureaucrats, Violeta considered accusing someone of being an *oficinista* or office worker—used in this instance in the derogatory sense as "paper-pusher" or "bean-counter"—one of the more demeaning slurs in her arsenal.[57] She hurled the insult often and freely. This may explain why, according to Roberto Parra, the office workers at the Bureau of Copyrights would hide under their desks when they saw Violeta arriving.[58]

Violeta's precarious economic situation could not be blamed, as she would have it, entirely on office bureaucrats. In all fairness, they were usually just enforcing the terms of her contract. Parra had received what was for her a substantial sum in royalties from her international lawsuit against US band leader Les Baxter for his use of one of her songs without her permission. Parra's exclusive contract with Odeon Chilena was a different story. The royalties she earned from the record company were paltry at best. This was in large part because the contract that she signed with Odeon in 1955 included a fixed and non-renegotiable flat rate of 1.5 percent that was highly unfavorable to the artist (though not unusually so for the place and time).[59] It is doubtful that Parra received much compensation as well from her recordings with the reconstituted Parra Sisters duo in 1958.[60]

But the problem was not just one of exploitative contracts. Parra earned little from her record sales because her records sold poorly. She was well known, but not popular. Artists who build their careers on the claim to authenticity rarely are, as by definition the authentic represents an alternative or counterweight to market forces.

Parra's lack of mass appeal is confirmed by a mid-1960 mail-in-ballot contest sponsored by *Ecran*, Chile's premier entertainment magazine, asking readers to vote for their "favorite national artist." Lucho Gatica, a Chilean bolero singer who found fame in Mexico, won first place, hands down. Other celebrities in the top ten included disc jockey Ricardo García (Parra's former radio collaborator), Chilean rock star Peter Rock (né Peter Mociulski von Remenyk), música típica artists Ester Soré (aka "Darling Beauty") and the huaso band Los Quincheros, along with an assortment of other singers. Parra, the only folklorista in the running, received less than twenty votes.[61] (The contest cannot be used as a measure of Parra's popularity among the Chilean pueblo, as voters were required to send in three original coupons from the magazine, and the working poor could ill afford to participate.)

Parra's limited and poorly paid performance opportunities and low return on royalties and record sales duly noted, her economic insecurity was also, at least in part, of her own doing. Instead of prudently saving for a rainy day, Parra was what her friend and future biographer Alfonso Alcalde affectionately referred to as a "spendthrift." Alcalde clarified that he used the term according to its "best connotation" to refer to the way Parra squandered whatever money came her way by redistributing it as needed among her extended family and friends.[62] In addition to helping others, Parra would use the money to buy art supplies or, in one rare instance when she was particularly flush, a high-end imported camera. As this last purchase suggests, Parra was also prone to splurge, funds permitting. Isabel recalled her and Violeta's particularly extravagant shopping-spree visit to Iquique, the one where they brought back duty-free goods to sell in Santiago: "We had a great time. We stayed in the finest hotel in Iquique, where Violeta's motto, which I enthusiastically embraced, was: 'I'll take one of these and one of those.'"[63] Flat broke or soon to be so, Parra always figured out how to get by. As she liked to brag, "Nobody beats me at being poor."[64]

Friend, Mentor, Fellow Traveler, Party Host

Whatever Parra may have lacked in material wealth she made up for in the richness of her social life. She was part of an extended family of poets, musicians, and circus artists. She was friends with painters, sculptors, musicians, filmmakers, actors, poets, novelists, journalists, musicologists, historians— in sum, the cultural innovators and chroniclers of her time. Parra built her relationships with friends and familia alike on loyalty and reciprocity. She wrote songs and guitar instrumentals dedicated to them (Gastón Soublette, Sergio Larraín, Nemesio Antúnez, Julio Escámez, Enrique Bello); embroidered tapestries in their honor (Thiago de Mello); and set their poetry to music (Gonzalo Rojas, Nicanor Parra, Pablo Neruda).

Parra's friends and relations, on their end, supported her work with their diverse resources and talents. They transcribed the folk songs she collected along with her original compositions (Margot Loyola, Gastón Soublette,

Miguel Letelier). They contributed to her albums and other projects with their singing (Isabel Parra, Hilda Parra), circus cheers (Oscar Parra), artwork (Julio Escámez, Nemesio Antúnez), liner notes (Raúl Aicardi, Gastón Soublette), and photography (Sergio Larraín, Sergio Bravo). They lent her the use of their apartments (Enrique Bello, Ester Matte), supported her creative activities in the visual arts (Teresa Vicuña, Thiago de Mello), and wrote verses in her honor (Nicanor Parra, Pablo Neruda).

Parra's unofficial headquarters for creative conversations and collaborations was the Café Sao Paulo, Santiago's "cultural epicenter" of poets, journalists, musicians, actors, dancers, Spanish exiles, booksellers, and other artists and intellectuals.[65] In an era when a large majority of Chileans—Parra included—lacked private telephone service, the downtown café functioned for all intents and purposes as Parra's office. It was the place where she received and left messages and where she could be found most days when she was not traveling.

Journalist Virginia Vidal captured the scene: "At noon, in the middle of the happy disorder, people went from table to table, shouting at one another, bumming cigarettes." Vidal goes on to describe Parra's presence there: "A hoarse voice asks insistently, 'Buy me a coffee!' Violeta Parra, precursor of the hippies, with her flowery blouses and long skirts that she made herself, her hair loose, and her face without makeup."[66] Ángel, who often accompanied his mother to the café, recalled her dressed in a different yet equally nonconformist ensemble of her favorite white leather jacket and mismatched colored stockings, an outfit that amused the women and scared the men because "small-town people have no appreciation for originality."[67]

These days, Violeta was no longer the little sister of the poet Nicanor Parra. She was a cultural figure in her own right, someone who, as Vidal points out, "sparked interest and could not be ignored."[68] Based on Parra's highly original fashion statements, if nothing else, she clearly welcomed and even courted the attention.

Parra became a friend and mentor around this time to a new generation of folkloristas who would eventually give birth the Chilean New Song movement. It included Rolando Alarcón, Silvia Urbina, and Víctor Jara, who would be brutally murdered in the first days of the 1973 military coup. The young folkoristas would seek Parra out at the Café Sao Paolo. From there, they would go to the nearby studio of one of her artist friends. Parra would prepare an enormous pot of beans, and "there would be wine and lots of discussion, sharing of songs, guitar-playing, storytelling, until it was time to go back to work."[69]

Parra ended up mentoring two of the most successful folk ensembles of the era: Conjunto Cuncumén and Millaray. Cuncumén was founded by a group of students who took a folk music class taught by Parra's colleague and rival,

Margot Loyola, at the University of Chile's 1955 summer program (though a few of them had initially met as delegates to the 1953 World Festival of Youth and Students in Bucharest, Romania). Víctor Jara, who had a background in theater, soon joined the ensemble as its artistic director. Under his leadership, Cuncumén rose to the undisputed rank of most popular and polished folk group of its time. Millaray was started by emerging folklorista Gabriela Pizarro in 1958 after she failed an audition with Cuncumén. In an interview, she gave her explanation as to why: "Since in those days it was a model band, well, you needed to have certain measurements to get into Cuncumén . . . [and I] was skinny, ugly, with thick glasses, shy and timid. . . . Forget it!" Faced with rejection, Pizarro decided to form her own folk ensemble with musicians who could be "fat, pot-bellied or tall or skinny or old, whatever" as long as they were good people with "an esthetic taste for rural folklore."[70] In keeping with the idealization of Indigenous cultures of the era, both folk ensembles adopted Indigenous names: *cuncumén* means "babbling water" and *millaray* "golden flower" in Mapudungun, the language of the Mapuche.[71]

Parra taught both folk ensembles traditional songs and drilled them on how to perform them correctly. She lobbied record producer Rubén Nouzeilles to include both groups in Odeon's Folklore of Chile series. The label signed Conjunto Cuncumén without hesitation but was at first not interested in Millaray. According to Pizarro, "Violeta [then] appeared and cursed them out . . . and well, in the end we recorded five long-plays [with the label]."[72] Parra forged an especially strong bond with Víctor Jara, who was then at the beginning of his songwriting career. She is credited with encouraging his move away from theater to full-time musician.

Most of the people in Parra's growing circle of friends, relatives, creative collaborators, and mentees were associated with the Chilean Communist Party (CP) in one way or another. Some were card-carrying members. Others were active in the party's youth branch, including Isabel, Ángel, and Víctor Jara. Still others were communist supporters or "fellow travelers," as they were known.

Parra was in the latter category. She showed her support for the party by performing at political rallies and other events, including at the opening of the CP-sponsored First Congress of Latin American Women, held in Santiago in November 1959.[73] She also participated in artists' meetings called by the Communist-affiliated antinuclear organization, the Committee for Peace, and other CP-related activities.

Alongside her contributions, Parra benefited from her ties with the Communist Party. In Chile, her communist affiliation meant that she was part of a large and vital network of intellectuals and artists. Abroad, it had allowed her to make contact with like-minded comrades during her first visit to Europe, and it would soon serve the same purpose in Argentina, then Europe again. Indeed, both of Parra's European sojourns began with invitations to join the Chilean delegation to the communist-sponsored World Festival of Youth and Students.

Parra was not guaranteed a place on the party's A-list of performers, however. The head of the organizing committee for the 1960 Congress of the Communist Youth of Chile, for example, had to convince his fellow committee members that Parra was the right musician to headline the folk festival that opened the congress, as "at the time ... [she] was not appreciated."[74] Parra's relationship to the Chilean Communist Party from the standpoint of party officials is perhaps best summarized by party leader Eduardo Contreras: "We cannot maintain that she was an exemplary militant from the point of view of discipline or regular party life, but we can affirm that her commitment was steadfast and that she acted accordingly."[75] Secretary general of the party Luis Corvalán assessed Parra along similar lines: acknowledging the many political events and campaigns that Parra had contributed her music to, he concluded that "without being a member, she had a great admiration and affection for the communists and was very conscious of the people's struggles."[76]

As Corvalán noted, Parra never officially joined the Chilean Communist Party. Her artistic temperament made her ill-suited for party membership, with the ideological rigidity and practical demands that it entailed. It is also not certain whether the party would have had her, had Parra wanted to join. Communist youth leader Gladys Marín recalled that Parra was "well liked, but at the same time, very criticized," while Víctor Jara acknowledged that "we had our doubts" about her.[77] Neither CP militant proffered reasons for their reservations. Given the moral authority that the party asserted over its membership, and borrowing Contreras's terminology, I submit that Parra's less than "exemplary" comportment when it came to "discipline" (i.e., toeing the party line) and "regular party life" (i.e., fulfilling the duties of a traditional housewife) almost certainly played a role.[78]

Parra also had a reputation for being somewhat of a prima donna. This led some party members to dismiss her as too individualistic and self-promoting to make a good comrade.[79] Parra was not the only artist associated with the Chilean CP in her day to have this reputation; Pablo Neruda was notorious for being self-centered. Nicanor alleges, for instance, that Neruda feigned a cold at one of his legendary soirées so as to retire early due to his displeasure at being upstaged by Violeta Parra, who was giving a particularly compelling performance that evening.[80] Neruda's aversion to sharing the limelight with Parra or anyone else would seem the very definition of a "prima donna." The fact that there is no masculine equivalent for the term strongly suggests that it was easier for Parra to be perceived as having crossed the line between taking herself seriously and taking herself too seriously as a woman than it would have been had she been a man.

Though it could not compare to any of Neruda's residences, Parra's house of sticks nonetheless became a favored spot for people to congregate during this period. Cuncumén member Silvia Urbina fondly recalled the time the band threw Parra a housewarming when Parra first moved into the house in late 1959. As the house was still unfurnished, Urbina and her bandmates arrived with table settings and plates full of food. They left empty handed at the end of the evening when Parra, ever thoughtful, kept all the tableware for herself. That way, she explained, they would not have to lug everything back with them. And besides, now there would be dishes for the next party.[81]

Parra eventually acquired furniture and even a piano. She installed shelves to display the clay figurines made by women artisans in Pomaire and Quinchamalí that she had collected and she built a clay oven outside for making empanadas. A *jardinera* or gardener just like the title of her popular song, she planted flowers around the house and tended a vegetable garden.

Parra's house of sticks would remain a party house over the years. Actress Verónica Oddó recalled how the gatherings "happened just like that, for no reason other than our eagerness to sing. People played and sang for hours."[82] Isabel claimed that "the get-togethers with [Violeta's] friends took place non-stop." Not one to draw lines between her socializing and her work, Violeta once handed out yarn to her guests in the middle of a party so they could help her roll it into balls; "We rolled some thirty skeins to the rhythm of the music," Isabel recounted.[83] In the ensuing years, Violeta would create several paintings depicting the gatherings she hosted at her house of sticks.

In what was one of Violeta's more notable (and noted) idiosyncrasies, she used her bed as a sort of office or workspace. Unconventional and unguarded, she was known to additionally receive visitors while in bed, where she made clear they were welcome to sit down and join her. Sometimes they even ended up joining her under the covers.[84] Her children, for their part, remembered partaking in all-day parties in their mother's bed, complete with food and music, in celebration of the family's reunion upon her return from a collecting expedition or some other occasion.[85]

Parra's unusual practice may have been linked to her recurrent ailments, particularly after she had hepatitis. Her bedroom hospitality may have also corresponded to what one acquaintance described as "a certain intimacy and sentiment . . . that was characteristic of the way of life in the Chilean countryside."[86] Both Nicanor and Ángel recalled that, even as a grown woman, Violeta would climb into her own mother's bed with her whenever she visited her, a conduct that would seem to support the argument that Violeta's unconventional relationship to beds was a cultural vestige of rural Chile.[87]

Parra maintained her propensity to work and socialize while in bed across the diverse living spaces she inhabited in Chile, Argentina, and Europe. Many people dismissed the practice as just another of her eccentricities. Others shared that they found the whole situation more than a little uncomfortable. Those who knew and loved Parra would claim that they were so used to it that they did not notice.[88]

"Musician from a Foreign Land"

Parra met Gilbert Favre, the great love of her life, at one of the many parties she hosted at her house of sticks. A wandering Swiss musician, just shy of twenty-four, Favre had traveled to Chile in the mid-1960s to take part in a Swiss archeological expedition to Chile's northern Atacama desert. He was a classically trained clarinet player and a bon vivant who loved wine, jazz, and the songs of French protest singer George Brassens. Parra nicknamed him the "Musician from a Foreign Land" and convinced him to take up the Andean flute known as the quena. Favre would eventually master it to become a world-class *quenista* (quena player).[89]

The couple met on October 4, 1960, at Parra's forty-third birthday party. A folk music enthusiast, Favre had gone to the University of Chile to inquire as to who the best Chilean folk singers were when he ran into Parra's friend Adela Gallo and asked her opinion. She informed him that Violeta Parra was the best, that by chance it was Parra's birthday tomorrow, and that he should accompany her to the celebration at Parra's home. Gallo and Favre took the bus to Parra's house the next day, where they were among the last of the partygoers to arrive. This was problematic, as Gallo had promised Parra she would take charge of the barbeque. When she finally got there, Gallo went to find Parra; "she was in her bedroom, in bed, dressed but in bed, as usual." Parra started to give Gallo a piece of her mind. Gallo recalls, "I told her, 'Don't scold me, Violeta, I've brought you a gringo as a present. . . .' And that's how it happened. The party was great and lasted until four in the morning. Then I left and the gringo stayed."[90]

Parra and Favre felt an immediate connection. In his autobiography, Favre recalls how he had stayed awake talking until dawn with Parra that first night.[91] "They were two souls who had been looking for each other" is how Ángel put it.[92]

Favre left on his archeological expedition to the Atacama desert within days of the party. He returned to Santiago a few months later and went to the university in the hopes of finding someone who could give him Parra's address. By chance, he ran into Ángel, who gladly escorted Favre to his mother's home. Violeta was happy to see Favre again. She gave him a tour of the garden, showed him her paintings and the 200-or-so loose pages that were her autobiography in décimas. She took out her guitar and played him some folk songs and her own songs. She told him about how she had survived the massive earthquake in the south of Chile. She shared stories about her family: that they had been poor, that one of her siblings was a mathematician but that all of the others were musicians and circus people, and that she used to perform flamenco dressed like a gypsy before turning to folklore. Reflecting on all he had learned that one afternoon, Favre recounts, "It was truly fascinating. I realized that I was in the presence of someone who was truly exceptional."[93]

Favre moved in with Parra that same day. In his autobiography, he claims that Parra did not want him to find work even though they were broke, for fear that he would meet another woman and go off with her. Money got tight, so they sold the piano. Then, as Parra was loath to part with her original artwork, they agreed that Favre would devote his time and energy to fabricating some decent forgeries of her paintings on cardboard (presumably for her to sell at the December 1960 Arts Fair). As her only customers were "shitty bourgeois" and as none of them ever complained about their purchases, neither Parra nor Favre felt any real qualms about running their scam.[94] Favre also picked up temporary work building sets for Chile's nascent television station, Channel 9.[95]

Parra and Favre's relationship would last over five years. It would be passionate and conflictive and involve frequent and sometimes prolonged separations. It is documented in all its intensity in the countless letters that Parra wrote to Favre over the years and in Favre's autobiography, penned shortly before his passing in the late 1990s based on his diaries, and published online posthumously.[96]

Toda Violeta Parra (All of Violeta Parra)

In October 1961, a year after Parra and Favre met, Parra went into the studio to record her fifth LP for Odeon. The album was released the following month. Though ostensibly part of the label's Folklore of Chile series, it consisted entirely of original compositions. Appropriately titled Toda Violeta Parra (All of Violeta Parra), it marks and celebrates Parra's coming into her own as a songwriter and artist.[97]

The album cover reinforces the promise, implicit in its title, that the listener will know "all of Violeta Parra." The text is handwritten in cursive, lowercase letters that evoke a personal note or letter, and that those familiar with Parra's handwriting will immediately recognize as hers. Fernando Krahn, yet another of Parra's artist friends who was destined to become world renowned, shot the album's photographs in Parra's house of sticks.[98] The front cover

Figure 6.3 Cover of LP *Toda Violeta Parra*. Odeon LDC-36344, 1961.

photos capture Parra lost in thought as she plays her guitar, dressed in a bulky sweater, her hair falling loosely around her face, one of her tapestries hanging on the wall behind her (see figure 6.3). The back cover photo shows her eating a simple meal at a wooden table. Together, the photos convey the impression of having entered the artist's inner sanctum to view her at work and at rest.

The liner notes, written by Gastón Soublette, depict Parra in equally intimate terms: "With this composer, there is no difference or separation between her art and her everyday life: they are one and the same. To visit Violeta Parra in her house . . . and converse with her under its wooden roof, to see her surrounded by her paintings and tapestries, children, dogs and cats, and an incorrigible and beautiful disorder of papers, flowers, tapes, guitars, *guitarrones*, and harps; to listen to her speak [of the *canto a lo poeta* (poet-songs)] is to know the very substance of her music."

The notes explain that the album's material, which ranged from the first tonada that Parra ever wrote to her most recent compositions, was purposefully selected to "reveal the overall evolution of [Parra's] style on its path to achieving its authentic and full expression."[99] The LP's songs included two numbers that were originally recorded by Las Hermanas Parra in the early 1950s along with Parra's early hit "Casamiento de Negros" (The Black Wedding), all three songs now reprised in the sparer folk style of solo voice and guitar. The remaining eleven songs were all new releases. They included "Puerto Montt está temblando" (Puerto Montt is Trembling), about Parra's experience of the 1960 earthquake; "Veintiuno son los dolores" (Twenty-one Sorrows), whose lyrics comprise the first forty lines of her wonderfully exaggerated centésima or one-hundred-line poem; and "El día de tu cumpleaños" (On Your Birthday), composed at the behest of her friend Enrique Bello so that he could be celebrated with a "typically Chilean" song, and not that "overused and horrible 'Happy Birthday.'"[100] The album also featured three musical settings of poems. One is an excerpt of Pablo Neruda's epic "Canto general," set to one of Parra's experimental guitar pieces, which she titled "El Pueblo" (The People).[101] The other two are by Nicanor.[102]

The LP encompassed a momentous addition to Parra's repertoire, one that signaled yet another innovative pathway for her as both an artist and an activist: three of its songs are protest songs.[103] In her impetus to write them, Parra was almost certainly influenced by the developing transnational trends in politically engaged songwriting of the era. She would have been familiar with the protest songs of Atahualpa Yupanqui through Ángel, given his early and enduring admiration for the Argentine singer-songwriter, and she was sure to have been introduced to the music of French protest singer-songwriter George Brassens either during her first European stay in the mid-1950s or through Favre, who was an ardent fan.[104] But Parra's politically engaged songs also expressed her political convictions, born of her lived experience and witness of the injustices of Chilean society.

Parra's aforementioned setting of Neruda's verses to music that she titled "The Pueblo" is one of the LP's three protest songs. Parra's song in homage to Chilean independence hero Manuel Rodríguez, "Hace falta un guerrillero" (We Need a Guerrilla Fighter), is a second. In it, she affirms that she would like to give birth to a son who was like Manuel Rodríguez so that she could instruct him "On what steps need to be taken / When they sell our homeland / As if it were a trinket. / I want a guerilla fighter son / Who will know how to defend it" (lo que se tiene que hacer /cuando nos venden la Patria / como si fuera alfiler. / Quiero un hijo guerrillero / que la sepa defender).[105] Parra had originally composed the song with a related project by cineaste Sergio Bravo in mind. Given its timing, title, and content, however, the song may have also been an expression of Parra's support for the Cuban Revolution.[106]

The third song is one of Parra's most powerful songs of social protest: "Yo canto la diferencia" (I Sing the Difference). It was inspired by a dramatic instance, recounted by Favre in his autobiography, when Parra was called to assume the unexpected role of midwife to her neighbor Luisa, a Mapuche woman who cleaned house for Parra a few days a week and who lived and farmed with her husband on one of the few agricultural plots that remained in La Reina.[107] In her song, Parra sets the baby's delivery in the midst of Chile's Independence Day festivities, thereby creating a stark contrast between the conditions of squalor in which Luisa gave birth and the pageantry of the official government celebration. The song opens with the following verse:

I sing à la chillaneja
if I have something to say,
and I don't pick up the guitar
to get a round of applause.
I sing the difference
between what is true and what's false.
Otherwise, I do not sing.

Yo canto a la chillaneja
si tengo que decir algo,
y no tomo la guitarra
por conseguir un aplauso.
Yo canto la diferencia
que hay de lo cierto a lo falso.
De lo contrario no canto.[108]

"I Sing the Difference" may be considered Parra's manifesto. It declares both who she is—a chillaneja or person from Chillán—and her purpose as a songwriter: to expose the truth. The LP's liner notes quote Parra explaining why she wrote the song: "It is the obligation of every artist to offer their creative powers to the service of mankind." In a thinly veiled barb aimed at the huaso bands, with their cliché-laden repertoire of paeans to rural idyll, she admonishes, "These days, it is outdated to sing to the lovely brooks and flowers. These days, life is harder and artists can no longer remain indifferent to the people's suffering."[109]

Parra's declaration did not represent a newfound commitment to the poor on her part. Rather, it announced a new and forceful way for Parra to give voice to that commitment through her songs. In the coming years she would write many more songs denouncing the social injustices of Chilean society and expressing her solidarity with the struggles of poor and oppressed peoples the world over. Although she may not have known it at the time, Parra had reached another turning point in her artistic trajectory. No longer content to collect and disseminate traditional songs and compose songs in their style, her repertoire from this point onward would rely heavily, if not entirely, on her own compositions, with a significant number of these political in content. The themes expressed in her songs would carry over into her other artistic endeavors to the point that her creative activities, as multiple and diverse as they were, may best be understood as one cohesive body of work.

Two Photo Shoots

Parra participated in two photo shoots around this time. One was with the photographer Fernando Krahn for her 1961 LP *All of Violeta Parra*, shot at her house of sticks (see figure 6.3). The other was with Javier Pérez Castelblanco at his portrait studio in downtown Santiago (see figure 6.4).[110] Juxtaposed, the resulting images reveal the range and fluidity of Parra's self-presentation as an artist.

Krahn recalls his photo shoot with Parra in the 1994 documentary *Violeta Parra, flor de Chile* (Violeta Parra, Chile's Flower). He notes that Parra was very good at posing and happy to follow his suggestions. He continues, "The impression that I got as well as my intention in photographing her was to achieve something that in my mind was like the figure of the Virgin made out of wood, something pure, spontaneous." The intimate photos that Krahn took for the LP *All of Violeta Parra* reflect his vision of Parra, whom he sums up as "a visceral woman; she was like the earth itself."[111]

Little is known about Parra's late-1961 photo shoot with Javier Pérez other than its studio setting and approximate timing.[112] Perhaps it had been scheduled in advance. Perhaps Parra made the decision to have the pictures taken on the spur of the moment. What is clear is that the resulting images could not be further from Krahn's earthy depictions. Instead of a bulky sweater, Parra is wearing a tailored suit with a ruffled blouse. Instead of her hair hanging loose and unkempt, it is pulled back in a bun. Instead of the rustic intimacy of her home, Parra appears in front of the portrait studio's blank background—with the exception of two photos that break the mood by revealing the studio's lighting equipment.

What are we to make of these two sets of images, both shot around the same time? They confirm that, much in the same way that Parra gave free rein to her creative explorations, she tried on different public personas during this volcanic period. Together with the many musical styles she performed (the folk songs she collected, and her own folkloric-sounding songs, temporary

Figure 6.4 Violeta Parra at photographer Javier Pérez Castelblanco's Rays Studios. Photo by Javier Pérez Castelblanco. Courtesy of the family of Javier Pérez Castelblanco.

repertoire of international folk songs, modern compositions for guitar, experimental music for film and ballet, commercial-sounding songs with Las Hermanas Parra, and recent songs of social protest), other media she explored (ethnographic writing, poetry, painting, ceramics, sculpture, embroidery), and outfits she donned (a homemade peasant blouse and skirt, a favorite white leather jacket, a huasa costume, bohemian black, professional attire, an evening gown, the simple clothes of everywoman), they signal Parra's refusal to limit her choices both as an artist and as a public figure. Her total disregard for consistency, in turn, helps to explain why her biography so often feels like a study in contrasts and contradictions.

A Small Town in the Argentine Pampa

The close of 1961 found Parra living a full life of intertwined artistic, social, and political activity. Her house of sticks was a hub of creative interchange and frequent celebration; she was in a loving, if challenging, relationship with Gilbert Favre; and her LP, *All of Violeta Parra*, that marked her shift from folklorista to songwriter had just been released. She would not have the chance to promote it. On December 31, 1961, she up and left all this behind when what she initially had intended to be a short visit to Argentina on a family emergency turned into three and a half years abroad, first in Argentina and then in Europe.

Here is what happened: a few days after Christmas, the Parra clan received a telegram informing them that Violeta's brother Lalo (Eduardo) had been hospitalized in the town of General Pico, Argentina. What had occurred was horrific. After his wife's tragic death from cancer in 1957, Lalo had moved with his two young children to Argentina, where they eventually made their way to General Pico (pop. circ. 18,000), some 370 miles from Buenos Aires in the fertile province of La Pampa. There, Lalo and his daughter Clarita earned their living performing as a duo both in town and on the road with a family circus. When Clarita, who was ten at the time, declared that she wanted to quit touring and work as a live-in maid with a family in town, Lalo fell apart. First he hit the bottle. Then, in a moment of desperation, he tried to kill himself and his four-year-old son Francisco with an overdose of tranquilizers. A neighbor found them in time and both father and son survived.

The Parra family made an urgent collection and sent Clarisa and Violeta to his rescue. When they arrived in General Pico three travel days later, Lalo was being held in prison on suspicion of attempted murder of his son. Francisco had been placed in an orphanage in a town three hours away, and Clarita was in the home of her new employers.[113]

Violeta began knocking on doors and was quickly able to enlist the assistance of a local government official named Joaquín Blaya. An exceptionally kindhearted man, Blaya arranged for Lalo to be released from prison and reunited with his children under the promise that he would return to Chile immediately. Blaya even covered the train fares to Buenos Aires for the three generations of Parras. Clarita would later recall how her still-convalescing father and Violeta broke into a full-throttle and cathartic rendition of the tango "Mi Buenos Aires querido" (My Beloved Buenos Aires) as they stepped onto the station platform.[114]

Lalo, his children, and Clarisa then flew to Santiago. Violeta, who had left Chile with only her guitar and clothes for a few days, did not return with them as expected. Instead, she made her way back to the home of the Blaya family in General Pico. She stayed in the town as their houseguest for over a month, during which time she performed regularly at the town's peña or folk club El Alero.[115] She also led workshops for women on arts and crafts at the town's community center and worked on her paintings and tapestries.[116]

What motivated Parra to remain in this provincial town, hours from any major city, in a country not her own? Perhaps the answer lies in what Parra seems to have found there: a moment of respite from the breakneck pace of her work-life in Santiago and the intensity and drama of her relationship with Favre. According to accounts from those who knew her there, Parra was genuinely content during the weeks that she resided in General Pico. As a "famous" folk singer, the houseguest of a local government official, she likely felt like a big fish in a small pond. In an interview, Joaquín Blaya's son Cristian, who was a boy at the time, posited that Parra's stay allowed her to recover her strength "because she rested, she could unwind." He recalled Parra working on her paintings, tapestries, and ceramics in the dining room, which she had turned into a makeshift art studio, and performing in front of an attentive and enthusiastic audience. As he saw it, she felt appreciated.[117]

Not everyone in General Pico was as accepting of Parra as the Blaya family and those involved in the local folk scene. According to the daughter of the peña El Alero founder Rafael Eiras, the more conservative element of General Pico was up in arms about Parra's presence in their town. After all, Parra's brother had been in prison. As if that were not enough, she was a woman who was both traveling solo and raising money to move on to her next destination through her own efforts in an era when independent women were automatically viewed with suspicion.[118]

Parra's memory of her stay in General Pico was not tarnished by the disapproval of some of its townspeople. She would maintain a loyal and affectionate correspondence with Joaquín Blaya over the years, writing to him from Buenos Aires, Helsinki, Baku (Azerbaijan), Geneva, and Paris. One such letter opens, "I greet you with the same affection as always, for the immense gratitude that ties my heart to a small town in the Argentine pampa."[119]

Buenos Aires

In February 1962, Parra packed up the paintings and tapestries that she had made in General Pico and left for Buenos Aires. The area known as Greater Buenos Aires, comprising the city and its surrounding communities, was a bustling metropolis of nearly 4 million. To put it in perspective, its population was almost twice that of its trans-Andean equivalent, Greater Santiago, and over 200 times that of the town General Pico.[120]

Parra would end up spending the next four months in Buenos Aires, with Favre joining her there for the last one. Her stay coincided with a turbulent moment in Argentine politics. Within two months of her arrival, then-president Arturo Frondizi was deposed in a military coup that unleashed troops and tanks into the streets of the capital and led to increasing political repression and censorship. In correspondence, Parra described the situation as a "colossal mess" and railed against the Argentine government, military, and clergy.[121]

Political turmoil aside, things were working out for Parra. As she related in a letter home, "I am getting by respectably and without major problems."[122] Buenos Aires had long been an important destination for Chilean and other South American musicians, no matter their musical genre.[123] In Parra's case, it helped that Argentina was in the midst of a folk "boom." Lasting roughly from the late 1950s into the 1970s, the Argentine folk music movement had clear Andean inspiration in both its instrumentation and song genres. Buenos Aires was its epicenter, but it extended into the provinces as well—which explains how a small group of folk music fans in General Pico could sustain a vibrant folk club like the peña El Alero.[124]

This was not Parra's first visit to the Argentine capital. She had passed through in July 1955 on her way to the World Festival of Youth and Students in Warsaw, when she and the other Chilean delegates had been feted by their Argentine comrades. Now, almost seven years later, she would have to make her own way in a city she described in one of her bleaker moments as "cold, difficult, and indifferent."[125]

The first thing she did was to rent a small room in the somewhat decrepit Hotel Fenix in downtown Buenos Aires. In a letter to Blaya confirming her safe arrival to the capital, she explained that she was giving herself the weekend to rest up so that, come Monday, she would be ready to devote all of her energies to "moving nuts and bolts in order to set the folkloric machinery in motion."[126] What this meant in practice was reaching out to contacts in the overlapping Argentine Left and folk music movement furnished to her by both her comrades in Chile and her new friends in General Pico.

Several of Parra's contacts in Buenos Aires were affiliated with the Argentine Communist Party, which though wielding only a fraction of the political clout of its Chilean counterpart nonetheless counted many of the nation's most important artists, musicians, writers, actors, and folkloristas among its ranks. Practiced as she was at self-promotion, Parra made calling cards that included the quatrain dedicated to her by Chile's most recognized and revered communist, Pablo Neruda:

The great Violeta Parra came in
Violetting the guitar,
guitaring the guitarrón,
Violeta Parra came in

entró Violeta Parrón
Violeteando la guitarra,
guitarreando el guitarrón,
entró Violeta Parra[127]

Things were touch and go at first, but Parra's exertions eventually paid off. Over the space of a few months, she performed at small clubs and a large theater, appeared on radio and television, and recorded an LP. She also continued to work on her paintings and tapestries. In his memoir, publisher and music producer Jorge Álvarez—one of several of Parra's Argentine admirers who generously provided her with art supplies—described her as "having a Picasso attack, she was painting day and night."[128] Parra sold her artwork out of her hotel room and, later, at her first gallery show. As she triumphantly announced in a letter to a colleague back home (utilizing the third person, as was her style), "I see and feel that a great door is opening onto the destiny of the Chilean Violeta Parra."[129]

The highlight of Parra's stay in Buenos Aires, beyond question, were the two sold-out shows she gave at the Idisher Folks Teater (Yiddish People's Theater) at the end of April 1962. The IFT, as it was known, had a capacity of 650 and was loosely affiliated with the Argentine Communist Party. It had been built by left-leaning members of Buenos Aires' extensive Jewish community in 1952 primarily to stage plays in Yiddish. By the time Parra performed there, the IFT had become an important cultural venue.[130] A group of Argentine law students who were both communists and avid fans of Parra's music helped organize and promote her concerts there, with tickets priced low so that workers and students could afford them.[131]

Favre, who arrived in Buenos Aires the evening of Parra's first performance, captures the scene in his autobiography: "She was seated unassumingly on a chair with the guitar on her lap leaning against her belly, her head down, her face covered by her long hair, like a curtain that hid part of her face. She sang without exuberance, all you could see was her left hand moving up and down the neck [of her guitar] and her right hand marking the rhythm. . . . The silent concert hall listened and watched this small black dot on a great big stage. It was quite riveting, and clear that she had complete control of her audience."[132] The IFT mounted a temporary exhibit of Parra's tapestries and paintings in its gallery to coincide with her concerts.

Correspondence from this period reveals Parra exploring ways to connect her music and visual art. In a letter to Raúl Aicardi, the director of the Chilean television station Channel 9, she offered to create five-minute segments, each of which would feature an illustration of one of her songs with the song playing in the background. Confident of the nexus that existed between these forms, Parra assured him that "every song can be painted."[133] It was a phrase she would repeat, with variations, moving forward. She would also affirm its inverse: as she once told a colleague, when she composed music, it was as if she were "painting melodies, drawing them."[134]

In her letter, Parra informed Aicardi that she already had one segment prepared: a pairing of her song "The Black Wedding" with a painting on the song's theme. All he needed to do was send her the equipment. She would not even charge him for the television program. Parra helpfully added that Isabel could record the songs to keep things simple. As was so often the case, nothing seems to have come of her proposal.[135]

Parra recorded her sixth LP in Buenos Aires, this one for Odeon Argentina. Upon learning of the Argentine recording decades later, Odeon Chilena producer Rubén Nouzeilles surmised that given Parra's "impulsive and irrepressible character," it was likely that she and she alone had arranged for the recording to be made: "No doubt she asked about the label, spoke with acquaintances or saw the sign from the street, conversed with some executive and they recorded her album." A decades-old invoice, discovered in the salvaged archives of Odeon Argentina and marked "past due," would seem to confirm Nouzeilles's supposition: it states that the cost of the recording was to be paid for in installments by Odeon Chilena and is signed by Violeta Parra, who apparently took it upon herself to represent the Chilean branch of the label for this particular contract. Unlike every other invoice in the substantial dossier, this one was never stamped "Paid."[136]

Parra recorded the LP over several sessions between April 23 and May 4, 1962. Years later, Odeon Argentina's sound engineer José Soler would claim that working with Parra was the high point in a career spanning more than three decades during which he recorded hundreds of musicians, many of them world-renowned.[137] Soler recalled with admiration Parra's professionalism and especially her ability to nail a song in one take: "[She] was very meticulous. . . . She came, sang, and left, and if we had to retake anything it was due to a mistake on our part."[138]

The album contains fourteen songs on voice and guitar, with the technological innovation that Parra overdubbed a second harmony or percussion
part on a few of them. Several are folk songs that she collected. They include
the tonada "Los santos borrachos" (The Drunken Saints); a prime example
of that rich vein of Chilean popular humor that exempts neither God nor other
celestial beings, the song recounts how the saints came down to earth, broke
into a storehouse, and drank all the wine in celebration of Christ's marriage
to the Church. The other songs on the LP are Parra's own compositions, including the festive cueca in praise of *porteños*, as the inhabitants of Buenos
Aires are called, "A cantarle a los porteños" (A Song for the Porteños).

Parra's Argentine LP continued and broadened her repertoire of songs of
social protest. Akin to her manifesto "I Sing the Difference," the political songs
on her Argentine album render first-person testimonials of the social injustices that Parra witnessed in Santiago and her travels. The detailed tableaus
that Parra provides in her songs of the daily struggles of the people in the communities she visited have led scholars to liken her role to that of a "social geographer."[139] "Según el favor del viento" (As the Wind Blows) portrays the
harsh working and living conditions found in the fishing communities on
the Island of Chiloé. The lyrics of "Arriba quemando el sol" (The Sun Burning
Overhead) do the same for the remote mining communities of the Chilean
north, while the song's sparse accompaniment of the pounding of an unchanging guitar chord and *bombo* (an Argentine drum used in folk music) evokes
the searing monotony of the song's title. Parra stands out from the other songwriters who would soon follow her in the Chilean New Song movement for
her attention to women and their work—the woman peeling potatoes in a corner of the woodcutter's boat off the Island of Chiloé, or the women with their
buckets waiting in line at the only water pump in the northern mining town—
in her songs.

The album also includes the song "Levántate, Huenchullán" (Arise, Huenchullán) chronicling the exploitation of Chile's Indigenous people across
"centuries of injustice," from the Spanish conquest to the present day when
"Nowadays it's the Chileans / Taking their bread away from them" (*hoy son
los propios chilenos / los que les quitan su pan*).[140] Parra would soon echo the
song's anticolonial theme in two vast tapestries depicting particularly grue-
some scenes from the Spanish conquest of Chile, *The Conquerors* and *Fresia
and Caupolicán*.

Parra's Argentine LP was released in August 1962 under the title *El folklore de Chile según Violeta Parra* (Chilean Folklore According to Violeta
Parra).[141] It was her first album to feature her own artwork on its cover: an oil
painting of a woman singer with long braids that Parra described as "colored
in, piece by piece" like stained glass in a church.[142] The album was not mar-

keted well, if at all. This was perhaps due to its release date several months after Parra's departure for Europe when she was no longer there to promote it. Or perhaps it was because, as sound engineer Soler suggested in an interview, the record label "couldn't have cared less about her work."[143] Whatever the case, the LP remained largely unknown until noted Argentine singer Mercedes Sosa released her LP *Homenaje a Violeta Parra* (Tribute to Violeta Parra) in 1971. It quickly became one of Sosa's most successful albums, at which point Odeon Argentina rediscovered and reissued Parra's 1962 recording.[144]

The first and seemingly only instance that Parra's songs were published as sheet music during her lifetime was in Buenos Aires in 1962—four in total, arranged for piano, with guitar chords included.[145] It is almost certain that Parra never got to see the sheet music herself. She did attempt, unsuccessfully, to collect an advance on her royalties from the publisher prior to her departure for Europe in late May 1962. Parra then followed up on her failed attempt with an angry and frustrated letter from Europe, yet one more in the long line of angry and frustrated letters that she would write over the course of her lifetime.[146]

Parra received ample recognition for her endeavors in Buenos Aires, including laudatory pieces in the arts and politics newsletter *Revista Vuelo*, the Argentine women's magazine *Claudia*, and the left-leaning newsweekly *Marcha* from neighboring Montevideo, Uruguay.[147] Despite the attention and her notable successes, her daily existence in Buenos Aires was still hand to mouth—as it was and would be in Santiago, Paris, and pretty much everywhere. Her letters are full of complaints about her hardships and details of her various schemes to collect owed funds or raise new ones. At one point, her economic situation got so bad that she moved into a boarding house in the Belgrano neighborhood that, though less centrally located and more run down than the Hotel Fenix, had the advantage of being even cheaper. Parra's new residence was popular among actors, cineastes, painters, and other professionals united by their shared communist leanings and economic penury. Overnight, it became the preferred location for the impromptu fiestas and recitals of the Chilean folklorista and her admiring entourage of young communists.[148]

As regards her love life during this period, Parra sent multiple plaintive letters and at least one telegram to Favre exhorting him to come urgently to join her in Argentina. As much as she missed him, she made clear in her letters that she had no intention of returning to Santiago any time soon, since things were going well for her in Buenos Aires.

On his end, and by his own admission, Favre was a lousy compañero to Parra. He took advantage of her absence from Santiago to go on "a few escapades" that included making the rounds of the city's bars and brothels.

He missed his originally scheduled flight to Buenos Aires due to one such drunken spree, finally showing up at the IFT theater when Parra's concert was already in progress. Far worse, he traveled to Argentina already in treatment for a case of gonorrhea that he had contracted from one of his "escapades," a diagnosis that he shared with Parra the night of his arrival. "Goddam shitty brothel, I'm such an asshole, but no matter, I had to tell her everything," he would write years later in his autobiography.[149]

Parra was devastated by the news. The couple's already tense relationship grew more dysfunctional. According to Favre, Parra became even more possessive and controlling than usual. She was always putting him down and monitoring his breath to ensure he was not smoking (which he was, and which he tried to cover up with mints). "Violeta would hound me and I was helpless against her reproach. The only thing I could do was shut my mouth." If he "continued to live under those hellish conditions," he wrote, "it was only out of remorse."[150]

For her part, Parra would not easily forgive Favre his infidelities and their consequence. She refused to help cover his ocean passage when she departed for Helsinki to attend the World Festival of Youth and Students at the end of May 1962. Favre was broke, as usual, so in essence she abandoned him in Buenos Aires. He would later recall accompanying Parra to the ship "not knowing if we would ever see each other again. I became a little melancholy at that moment."[151] It would take him several months to figure out a way to join Parra in Europe. By then, Parra had forgiven him.

An Interview

As best as I can ascertain, it was during her stay in Buenos Aires that the question of Parra's Indigenous ancestry was first raised in print. The claim was made in an article by journalist Eduardo Guibourg in the Argentine women's magazine *Claudia*. It was made within the larger context of a transnational resurgence in the 1960s of a fascination with Indigenous peoples, whom Westerners perceived, experienced, and in many instances invented as primordial and authentic. In his piece, Guibourg introduces Parra to his Argentine readership as an exalted and exotic being; she was "the high priestess of folklore . . . the oddest, most charming and most famous character in all of Chile" awaiting discovery by Argentina. He goes on to describe her as "a little Indian" (*indiecita*) whose Mapuche great-grandmother had "molded her facial traits, braided her straight black hair, and lit up her eyes with the horizons' waters."[152]

It is important to note here that many Argentines embraced an ideology of Argentine exceptionalism that cast themselves as the "Europeans of South America" well into the twentieth (and most likely the twenty-first) century.[153]

It is entirely possible, therefore, that Guibourg, gazing through a Eurocentric lens, racialized Parra as Indigenous and that she then went along with it.[154] It is equally plausible, however, that Parra informed him of her native roots, which had been previously immaterial or nonexistent. After all, it would not be the first time she reinvented herself. No matter the case, Parra's Indigenous ancestry would become an important, if malleable, element of her foundational narrative of authenticity moving forward.

Beyond establishing her newfound Indigeneity, the article includes one of Parra's clearest and most often-cited declarations of her identification with poor or working-class women. She was already expressing her gender and class solidarity with the wives of woodcutters and miners in her songs. Now she asserted she was one and the same as them; she was everywoman. As she explained, "I am nobody. There are countless women better than me all over Chile! What happened is that they stayed home, cooking and taking care of their children and grandchildren, while I went off to sing with the little that I know. It's as simple as that."[155]

Parra's statement gives a nod to the conventional route that she could have followed as a wife and mother, while downplaying the volcanic initiative and effort demanded by the alternative course that she set for herself. Despite her claim to the contrary, Parra's artistic trajectory was anything but simple. By defining herself as both part Indigenous and everywoman, Parra continued to move away from her role as interpreter of the authentic toward its embodiment. Her claim to authenticity had empowered her to leave behind the customary constraints of her gender to become an artist worthy of discovery. It would soon propel her to new and uncharted pursuits with her return to Europe.

Chapter 7

Europe II

Parra informed the Chilean press of her plans to return to Europe before she had even left Paris in December 1956.[1] She continued to announce any number of upcoming trips to Europe and beyond once she was back in Chile: a tour of Holland, Belgium, and then the Orient; a return to Paris, then on to Japan; a tour of the United States and then France, China, Japan, and India.[2] None of these ambitious itineraries materialized. Parra did not leave Chile again for a full five years, and then it was only for what was meant to be a brief trip to neighboring Argentina for a family emergency.

It is therefore not surprising that when in May 1962 she received an invitation in Buenos Aires from the Chilean Communist Party to join that year's delegation to the World Festival of Youth and Students (WFYS) in Helsinki, Finland, she accepted. After several frustrated attempts and as many or more false announcements, she was finally returning to Europe. As was the case with her first visit, Parra would prolong her stay in Europe well beyond the festival, remaining just over the three years, from June 1962 to August 1965, interrupted by a brief visit to Chile in mid-1964.

When Parra returned to Europe in mid-1962, she encountered a perceptible shift in attitudes toward Latin America, away from the festive escapism of the mid-1950s, toward a more political interest in what was now increasingly being referred to as the "Third World." Some of the impetus for this shift could be traced thousands of miles away to Cuba, with the triumph of its revolution in 1959 and the hopes this inspired the world over. It also reflected the emergence of a new European Left that was committed to standing in solidarity with Third World peoples and their struggles. The sway of more spiritually minded anti-capitalist critiques that held up the Indigenous peoples of Latin America as a symbolic counterforce to the superficiality of rampant consumer society contributed as well. Many of these changes in how Europeans related to Latin America more broadly resonated in the ways they perceived and received Latin American music and art in the 1960s.

Of course, Parra had changed since her first European sojourn as well. When she embarked on her initial transatlantic journey at age thirty-seven, she had never left Chile before. Now forty-four, she was a far more seasoned traveler; she had toured on both sides of the Iron Curtain, had lived in Paris for over a year, and had just wrapped up a successful five-month stint in

Argentina. Back in 1955, she had been carried to Europe on the wave of her success as a folklorista, and she had carted the bronze statuette of the Caupolicán award around with her to prove it. In the volcanic interval between then and her return to Europe seven years later, she had expanded her musical activities to include composing modern guitar instrumentals and film soundtracks, and writing the kind of protest songs that spoke so directly to the hearts and minds of the international Left. She had also taken up the visual and material arts, including ceramics and the painting and tapestry making that would soon earn her the honor of becoming the first Latin American artist to be granted a solo show at the Museum of Decorative Arts, housed in the Louvre Palace.

Parra summarized her transformation in a 1964 interview in the Swiss press. Gesturing toward the floor, she said, "The first time that I came to Europe, I felt myself to be this small." She had returned home to Chile so that she could grow and learn from what she averred was the only school that she had ever known: her people. Now that she was back in Europe, she had complete confidence in her creative potential: "When it comes to art, I am not afraid to try anything: to express myself with a sewing needle, a guitar, a paint brush, or papier-mâché. You have to try everything, to have the courage to explore all the different languages." Europe was an ideal setting for these explorations because "Europe allows us to see our soul as if in a mirror."[3]

As her interview suggests, Parra would continue to extend the range of her artistic expression—"to try everything, . . . to explore all the different languages"—over the course of her time in Europe. As was the case during her first stay, her experiences there would present fecund opportunities for self-discovery and reinvention, which in her case were often the same process.[4] Borrowing her metaphor, Europe would become the mirror in which Parra would simultaneously see herself reflected and project herself in new and empowering ways.

Helsinki

Parra met up with the other Chilean delegates to the 1962 World Festival of Youth and Students at the end of May as they passed through Buenos Aires en route to Helsinki. The delegation included Isabel and Ángel, who were both talented musicians and militants in the CP's youth branch, and Isabel's daughter Tita (then six). Isabel's boyfriend and sometimes musician Enrique Bello Leighton (son of Violeta's friend Enrique Bello) was part of the delegation as well. On May 29, the Chilean delegates together with those from Uruguay and Argentina embarked on the ocean liner that would carry them to Hamburg, Germany, from where they would continue on to Helsinki by train.[5]

The Parras traveled with trunks full of instruments and costumes as well as Violeta's albums to sell. Violeta also brought the paintings and embroidered tapestries that she had made in Argentina, despite their bulk, as she was determined to exhibit them in Europe. She would later depict the scene in her song "Une chilienne à Paris" (A Chilean in Paris):

All of my friends came along
To accompany me to the dock.
Together, everyone brought
All of my things.

Tous mes amis sont venus
au port pour m'accompagner.
Chacun portait dans ses mains
tous mes affaires.[6]

Parra had been a relative newcomer to the interconnected circles of the Chilean folk music scene and the cultural Left on her first transatlantic voyage in 1955. She had found few friends or allies among her shipmates as a result. Seven years later, she was one of the more well-known members of the Chilean delegation and traveled accompanied by family and friends. In keeping with her oversize sense of self, she quickly managed to place herself at the center of the delegates' onboard activities by making the unilateral decision that they would all present a folkloric act as their contribution to the ship-wide traditional celebration marking the vessel's crossing of the equator. Thus began what many of the delegates deemed to be a grueling schedule of rehearsals. As noted, Parra could be a demanding and impatient teacher. "Relentless" was how fellow delegate and communist youth leader Gladys Marín recalled her: "She would assemble us on the ship's deck and everyone had to practice. And she yelled: 'Idiots! Wimps! You look like elephants!'"[7] When not drilling the rest of the Chilean delegation on how to dance the cueca, Parra spent her free time on board embroidering more tapestries.

After two and a half weeks, the ship finally reached Hamburg. From there, the Parras caught a train to East Berlin, in the German Democratic Republic (GDR), where they spent the next week or so. They then traveled to Helsinki, where they arrived after several days of what Violeta described in correspondence as "hustle and bustle—changes of trains, languages, people."[8]

The 1962 World Festival of Youth and Students was organized by the same Soviet communist front organizations and featured similar programming as prior WFSYs—including the festival that Parra attended in Warsaw in 1955. The two festivals that Parra performed at transpired in markedly different contexts and circumstances, however. The Warsaw festival was well funded and had 30,000 participants. It was held in 1955 Soviet-controlled Poland where the entire country, from the state apparatus to its populace, had expressed enthusiasm for the festival, while all dissent had been stifled. The Helsinki festival, in comparison, drew only 13,400 participants, a contrast almost certainly related to the festival's reduced financing.[9] It was also held in neutral territory.[10] This allowed the United States and Britain to mount an elaborate campaign to discredit and disrupt the Soviet-sponsored WFYS, including a competing festival featuring daily jazz concerts, an exhibition of US modern art and architecture, and the publication of the anti-festival newsletter *Helsinki Youth News* in three languages.[11] As a result of the combined efforts of Soviets and Westerners, Helsinki was turned into a veritable battlefield in the ideological Cold War over the ten days in late July and early August that the festival took place. The conflict spilled out onto the streets, with skirmishes between anti-festival and pro-festival youth, and demonstrations that turned into street clashes between police and rioting crowds of 2,000 to 3,000.[12]

The Chilean delegates' participation in the Helsinki WFYS played out against this backdrop. Their delegation of seventy-two was smaller than previous delegations, and the delegates' living conditions, transportation, and other facilities were far less accommodating than those of festivals past.[13] Making matters worse, the delegates found themselves the frequent target of anti-festival sentiment, most dramatically when anticommunist demonstrators shouted "Nyet festival!" ("No festival!" in Russian) and threw rocks and bottles at the buses transporting festival participants between sites.[14] When asked about the hostilities years later, Ángel recounted that the bus they were riding in had been stoned and that tomatoes, but thankfully not rocks, were thrown at them when they marched down the street in the delegates' parade.[15]

Neither the organizational challenges nor the political turmoil that surrounded the 1962 WFYS impeded the Parras from representing their country with distinction. They performed numerous times and were awarded a gold medal in the folkloric dance division, "authentic national amateurs."[16] Violeta won another gold medal for her solo performance and once again served on a panel of judges for the folk songs and dances competition (see figure 7.1). She also exhibited her artwork for the first time in Europe as part of a group show held in the Helsinki Kulttuuritalo (Hall of Culture). Her entry in the catalogue lists eight art objects, eleven paintings, twelve "rugs [her tapestries]," nine records, and seven photos.[17] "I truly do not understand how I could accomplish all this in eight days," she bragged in a letter to her Argentine friend Joaquín Blaya.[18] (Violeta was not the only Parra to be recognized at the Helsinki festival; her daughter Isabel received a medal for "her natural and original way of singing, playing, and dancing"—an honor that Violeta failed to mention in any of her published statements or correspondence.[19])

Figure 7.1 Violeta Parra performing at the World Festival of Youth and Students in Helsinki, August 1, 1962. Photo by Yrjö Lintunen. The People's Archive, Helsinki, Finland.

The Parras' invitation to the festival had been, in Isabel's words, "stingy."[20] The organizers had only guaranteed them passage one way, with the assurance that they would figure out how to get them home from Europe when the time arrived. Instead, the Parras found themselves all but stranded in Helsinki after a promised post-festival concert tour of the Soviet Bloc countries fell through. Fortunately, a sympathetic festival official was able to negotiate a last-minute award from the GDR-based League of Friendship Societies guaranteeing the Chilean performers return tickets to their homeland in exchange for a ten-day performance tour of the German Democratic Republic.[21] The Parras were not only relieved but pleasantly surprised to learn that the tickets were open-ended and did not expire for two years.

Their eventual return to Chile now secured, the Parras next traveled with a small group of Chilean delegates some 2,100 miles to Baku, the capital city of Azerbaijan. Violeta, who had fallen ill during the festival, ended up being admitted to a hospital there while the rest of her party went on to Moscow. Erroneously diagnosed and operated on for appendicitis, she in fact had had a gallbladder attack—one of the recurrent ailments from which she routinely suffered since her liver had been weakened by hepatitis. After ten days of convalescence, she was finally cleared to leave and rejoin her family and the rest of their contingent in Moscow.

The Chilean delegates' tour of the Soviet Union was more tourist- than performance-oriented. This frustrated Parra, as she had hoped that the visit would provide her family ensemble with the opportunity to earn much-needed concert revenue.[22] Though disappointed, Parra had only praise for all that socialist modernity appeared to offer its Soviet citizens, from housing for workers, to higher education, to radio stations that did not transmit "utter nonsense." In her letter to the politically centrist Blaya, Parra reaffirmed her faith in communism, wondered how it was possible that he did not share her confidence, and proclaimed that "this century is ours."[23]

From Moscow, the Parras traveled once again to the GDR. They spent the next ten days performing at festivals, factories, and workers' vacation resorts in and around East Berlin.[24] They also appeared on television and recorded several songs for the GDR state-run record company, V.E.B. Deutsche Schallplatten Berlin.[25] These were released two and a half years later on the 1965 compilation album titled *Süd- und mittelamerikanische Volksmusik* (South and Central American Folk Music), alongside songs performed by folk ensembles from Brazil, Mexico (technically North America), and Central America.[26]

The Parras' contribution to the compilation are the only known recordings of Violeta, Isabel, and Ángel Parra singing together in harmony. They were also the first of Violeta's recordings to incorporate the Andean-associated instruments of quena (played by Ángel) and bombo (played by Isabel) in their musical arrangements. The songs themselves include Violeta's biting critique of the Catholic Church and, more generally, religious hypocrisy, "Por que los pobres no tienen" (Because the Poor Do Not Have), sung in this case by Isabel:

Because the poor do not have
A place to look toward,
They cast their eyes up to heaven
Holding infinite hope
That they'll find what has been taken
Away from them here on earth.

And continuing with the lie,
Their confessor has this to impart:
He says that God doesn't favor
Revolution of any sort,
No grievance or workers' union,
That may offend his heart.

Porque los pobres no tienen
adonde volver la vista,
la vuelven hacia los cielos
con la esperanza infinita
de encontrar lo que a su hermano
en este mundo le quitan.

Y pa' seguir la mentira,
lo llama su confesor.
Le dice que Dios no quiere
ninguna revolución,
ni pliego ni sindicato,
que ofende su corazón.[27]

In addition to the Parras' musical activities, Violeta exhibited her artwork at an East Berlin gallery.[28] The Parras fulfilled their performance obligations in the GDR, then traveled to Genoa, Italy, to meet the ocean liner that was meant to bring Violeta's twelve-year-old daughter Carmen Luisa to join the rest of the family in Europe. Carmen Luisa was supposed to be traveling under the care of Marta Orrego Matte, Ángel's fiancée at the time and the daughter of one of Chile's aristocratic families.

Violeta, who had not seen Carmen Luisa since she left for General Pico at the close of 1961, waited anxiously for her daughter's ship to arrive.[29] When it finally made port, it was carrying Marta Orrego Matte and her friend Frida Sharim, but no Carmen Luisa (for reasons that are unclear). Violeta blamed Orrego for Carmen Luisa's absence and publicly accused her of being a "shitty bourgeois," a pituca (rich snob) who could travel to Europe whenever she wanted while Violeta's daughter was stuck back in Chile.[30] Though Violeta's violent reaction was well within character, one might wonder whether the strength of her emotions was affected by the shadow cast by the loss of her infant daughter Rosa Clara at the onset of her first visit to Europe now that she found herself back in Europe while her youngest living daughter remained in Chile.

The ugly scene led to a rupture in the family. Ángel, Isabel, and Tita departed for Paris with Marta and Frida (but without their traveling companion Enrique Bello, who stayed in Italy).[31] Violeta traveled instead to Geneva, where she believed the Swiss medical system would be able to cure her of her liver problems.

In different contexts and years apart, Isabel and Ángel would each describe the train ride to Paris as the moment when they decided to cut the "umbilical cord" and strike out on their own as a musical duo.[32] Within days of their arrival in Paris, the siblings landed a gig at La Candelaria, a Latin American–themed boîte in the Latin Quarter that was just down the street from L'Escale. They would perform as a duo over the ensuing months and years that they remained in Europe and across their musical careers.

Meanwhile, Violeta's visit to Geneva ended up a mere detour on her way to Paris. She arrived there not far behind Isabel and Ángel, where Carmen Luisa joined her a few weeks later. Violeta would spend the bulk of her second European stay living between Paris and Geneva, the latter city because it was Favre's hometown, to which he eventually returned from Buenos Aires in late 1962.

The 1960s Parisian–Latin American Folk Music Scene

In September 1962, Parra arrived in Paris from her brief stopover in Geneva. At last, she was once again in "the beautiful city of Paris" (*la belle ville de Paris*)—as she lovingly referred to it in "Une chilienne à Paris" (A Chilean in Paris), a song she composed in French and in the style of a French waltz during her second stay there. The Parisian–Latin American folk music scene that she rejoined was as or even more vibrant than it had been when she had lived there in the mid-1950s. Paris (along with other cosmopolitan cultural centers) saw the emergence of two overlapping trends in the 1960s: the increasing popularity of Andean-inspired folk music, and the association of Latin American folk music with protest and revolution. Parra both helped to shape and benefited from these trends over the course of her second European sojourn.

The Andean-inspired folk music that was becoming so popular in the 1960s was, in essence, the transnational invention of urban musicians, many of whom were at first concentrated in Buenos Aires and Paris. By the mid- to late 1960s, they were joined by musicians in Santiago, La Paz, and elsewhere. Together, they drew on traditional Andean musical practices to create a music that was conceived and experienced as Indigenous and therefore primordial in the Western imaginary. Their adoption of some of the instrumentation from the Andean region was central to this process, especially the quena or the *flûte indienne* (Indian flute), as it was known in France: a flute, usually made of bamboo, with a notched mouthpiece. The folk ensemble Los Incas, whose Argentine and Venezuelan members met while performing at L'Escale in the late 1950s, were among the earlier purveyors of Andean-inspired music in Paris. In 1960, they were joined by Los Calchakis, a band founded by Argentine and French musicians that took its name from the Indigenous people of the Argentine Andes.[33] Both Los Incas and Los Calchakis would achieve international stardom by the late 1960s, as the Andean-inspired musical movement that they helped create became a craze in Paris and worldwide.[34]

The other trend gaining momentum in the Parisian-Latin music scene of the early 1960s linked Latin American folk music with political protest. It stemmed from the French Left's perception of Latin America, and by extension its music, as a primary site for anti-imperialist struggles and revolution. This association would be strengthened after the 1973 military coup when Chilean musicians in exile—notably the bands Quilapayún and Inti-Illimani, along with Isabel and Ángel Parra—gave voice to Chilean resistance against the dictatorship. Given that Latin American folk music was becoming synonymous with Andean-inspired music at the same time that it was becoming increasingly associated with leftist politics, the two trends were closely intertwined from the onset.[35]

Parra was an eager protagonist of these interrelated musical trends. As regards the Andean-inspired one, she had arrived in Paris already primed for it. In the late 1950s, she had briefly incorporated Andean-related folk songs—along with French, Italian, and Israeli ones—into her concert repertoire, having brought them back to Chile from her first Parisian stay. More recently, she had spent the first five months of 1962 in Argentina, where Andean influences held notable sway in the country's folk boom.

Her children Isabel and Ángel had a hand in the matter as well. They had both learned how to play mainstay instruments of the Andean-inspired music ensembles before they arrived in Paris: Isabel, the bombo, and Ángel, the quena. In Isabel's case, it had been just barely before their arrival, as she had purchased her bombo on her stopover in Buenos Aires and, very much her mother's daughter, had taught herself how to play it aboard ship. Ángel, for his part, was one of the first Chilean musicians of his generation to learn to play the quena (though he would later abandon it to concentrate solely on the guitar).[36] All these factors would seem to have encouraged Violeta's own embrace of Andean-inspired musical practices. So too, undoubtably, did her Parisian public's fascination with all things Andean.

And embrace these practices she did. Over the course of her second stay in Europe, Parra reincorporated the Andean songs that she had learned during her first visit there into her repertoire and added several others. A quick study when it came to new musical instruments, she soon learned to play the bombo. She encouraged Favre, a classically trained clarinetist, to take up the quena once the couple were reunited in Europe. She composed new, Andean-sounding songs and instrumentals that the two performed together as a duo in France and Switzerland and that they later recorded in Chile. She invented new, "Andean-style" costumes for the Parra family ensemble to complement the innovations to her repertoire: long ponchos and sandals for everyone, man, woman, or child.[37] The way the Parras promoted their group also changed, as they were now announced as performing "music from Chile and the Andes"— which is a strange distinction, geographically speaking, given that the Andes mountain range extends nearly the entire length of Chile.[38] Continuing the trend, Parra's bilingual songbook (French and Spanish), published in 1965 by the Maspero press, is titled *Poésie populaire des Andes* (Folk Poetry from the Andes).[39]

As regards the leftist politics engulfing the Parisian–Latin American folk music scene, Parra was an early and forceful proponent. Granted, the Argentine musician Atahualpa Yupanqui predated her in this regard. But Parra was most certainly the forerunner in her native Chile of the politically engaged songwriting that would come to define Chilean New Song by the close of the 1960s. Continuing on the course she first set with her 1961 LP *All of Violeta Parra*, she wrote many of what would become her most widely recognized protest songs during her second European sojourn. She published their lyrics in her 1965 songbook and recorded them for the French record label Barclay (though the material was only released posthumously). According to Ángel, Violeta even earned the nickname "the Communist" at L'Escale due to the marked political content of her sets.[40]

To be clear: Parra did not write protest songs because they were trending. She wrote them because they expressed her political beliefs. As people who knew her at the time have attested, she did not just sing about leftist causes; she actively supported them.[41] She participated in a three-day Easter March from Lausanne to Geneva calling for nuclear disarmament.[42] She joined in demonstrations protesting the imprisonment of Spanish communist leader Julián Grimau, who despite an international campaign that included pleas for clemency from both Pope John XIII and Soviet leader Nikita Krushchev was executed by the Franco regime on April 30, 1963.[43] More enduring, she wrote the song "¿Que dirá el santo padre?" (What Would the Holy Father [Pope] Say?) in denunciation of his murder:

The more injustice I'm seeing
Mr. Prosecutor,
The stronger becomes my will
To keep on singing.
How high the wheat is growing
In the fields now,

Watered with your blood,
Julián Grimau.

Entre más injusticia,
señor fiscal,
más fuerzas tiene mi alma
para cantar.
Lindo se dará el trigo
en el sembra'o,
regado con tu sangre,
Julián Grimau.[44]

In sum, in her readiness to write her growing repertoire of protest songs, which she then performed for free in solidarity at political events, Parra was not so much responding to the popularity of revolutionary music from Latin America as she was fostering it.

"Mixed-blood Indian" and "Poor among the Poor"

As Parra assumed new creative roles, she found new ways of understanding and explaining who she was and why she did what she did. Back in the early 1950s when she reinvented herself as a folklorista, she had constructed a foundational narrative of authenticity based on her provincial origins, her campesina mother, her musician schoolteacher father, and a childhood spent imbibing the folklore of Chile. Around the time of her second European stay, she revised this narrative in two ways: first, she added the new component of her Indigeneity, and second, she consolidated her identity as a poor person.

These revisions to Parra's narrative both coincided and correlated with the innovations to her repertoire and performance practices favoring Andean-inspired and revolutionary music. Both had a basis in her family history and/or lived experience, and both relied at least in part on exaggeration and even invention. They also frequently went hand in hand, as illustrated by a 1963 piece in the *Tribune de Genève* that described Parra as a "mixed-blood Indian, from the south of Chile, poor among the poor, too ragged to have ever gone to school."[45]

The claim that Parra had Indigenous ancestry was most likely valid, given Chile's history of race relations. It was first made in Buenos Aires, from where Parra carried it to the cultural capitals of Europe. Her Indigenous ancestry was an asset in all of these sites, as it linked Parra to a pristine and noble past in the cosmopolitan imaginary. It was also oddly measurable. Her 1962 interview with Eduardo Guibourg for the Argentine magazine *Claudia* made reference to Parra's great-grandmother. Over the course of her second stay in

Europe, reporters would continue to note her Indigenous ancestry, only now with ascending proximity. The generational distance was first shortened from great-grandmother to grandmother, then to mother.[46] And at least one of Parra's admirers became convinced that Parra herself was Indigenous.[47]

How much of Parra's incremental Indigenous heritage was attributable to how others perceived her and how much of it was an attempt on her part to shape their perception escape precise gauge. What is certain is that Europeans more often than not assumed that Parra had Indigenous ancestry or, in the parlance of the day, "Indian blood." Several reviewers who attended her public appearances made note of her "Indian-ness." One reporter from the literary review *Les Lettres Françaises* wrote of her "strange face of an Indian with strong traits," for example, while a columnist for the *Glasgow Times* described her as "a little, dark, eager woman, very Indian-looking with a mane of black hair streaming down her back to well below the waist."[48] And when Swiss art critic and documentary filmmaker Marie-Magdeleine Brumagne asked Parra point blank whether or not she was Indian, Parra's reply that she had "a little bit of Indian blood" led Brumagne to enthusiastically exclaim, "It shows!"[49]

Without necessarily any effort on her part, then, Parra became a sort of screen upon which her European audience projected their romantic notions of how Indigenous people from South America looked and behaved. Perhaps the most vivid examples of how instantaneously and thoroughly Parra could become Indigenized in the European imagination are found in the writings of two Swiss women who befriended her and supported her artistic endeavors: Brumagne and the artist and theater director Raymonde Gampert. Both shared their impressions of their initial encounter with Parra in their memoirs.

For Brumagne, it occurred in an art gallery in Geneva, most likely in late 1964.[50] Brumagne walked into the room where Parra was showing her tapestries and found herself at a loss for words. Noting how moved Brumagne was by her artwork, Parra offered to tell her all about it through her songs. She took out her guitar, went to the first tapestry, and began to sing. Brumagne recalls, "I could no longer tell where I was on that rainy winter day. As if by magic, the walls had disappeared, leaving in their place vast Andean plateaus, under a clear, high-altitude sun. Indian men and women dressed in ponchos come and go in this setting that Violeta has created for us, at 10:00 o'clock in the morning, in this place beyond history, thousands of kilometers from her native Chile!"[51]

Like Brumagne, Gampert first met Parra at an exhibit in a small gallery in Geneva, probably in early 1963.[52] She spied Parra working on a mask in the corner and struck up a conversation with this "fiery slip of a woman" who was "as strange as her masks." Parra invited Gampert to visit the apartment that she and her children shared with Favre in Geneva. When Gampert arrived, she was met with the "marvelous vision" of Parra and her children, who greeted her with dance and song. Parra then taught her how to make her own masks, all the while talking to her in a rudimentary French that, according to Gampert's transcription, resembled the broken style of "Indians" speaking English in 1950s Hollywood Westerns: "Me, Indian from Chile. Me have five children. Me like to dance and sing. Me have been in Indian desert with very old people. Me learn old songs from Chile."[53]

Brumagne's and Rampert's similarly over-the-top exoticizations provide a sense of the very real cultural prejudices that Parra had to contend with, even or especially in the case of her most ardent fans, as she struggled to define herself as an artist in Europe. At the same time, this kind of stereotyping seemed to work in her favor in terms of inspiring interest in her person and artistry.

For these and other reasons, Parra's response to the generalized propensity of Europeans to cast her in the role of "Indian" was complex. The rising levels of her Indigenous ancestry recorded across this period suggest that she encouraged her European beholders to Indigenize her, or at least did not object when they did. One can also hope, given her ironic sense of humor, that she at times discretely mocked her European admirers, especially when their behaviors became too outlandish. For while I do not for an instant believe that the gallery walls gave way to the Andes mountains at the sound of her singing, I can certainly imagine a scenario where Parra would have deliberately communicated in a "broken" French as a sort of inside-joke rejoinder to Gampert's preconception about her lack of fluency in the language. The very plausibility of Gampert's anecdote indicates that Parra's seeming acquiescence or willingness to play the part of an Indigenous woman from South America in order to fulfill the exoticizing fantasies of her entitled European public may have had a subversive edge to it.

Parra's second revision to her foundational narrative was the consolidation of her identity as a poor person. As with her Indigeneity, her self-portrayal as poor played into European assumptions about Latin America—in this case mostly accurate—as a site of extremes in poverty and wealth. And just as Parra sometimes overstated the degree of her Indigenous lineage, she at times exaggerated the extent of her and her family's poverty.

Parra had been representing herself as poor at least since her autobiography in verse, penned in the late 1950s. Over the course of her second European sojourn, the economic hardship that she and her siblings had known as children became a standard component of her life story. In interviews, she would recount how their mother was left penniless with ten children to raise after the death of their father; how their mother would make the children clothing out of bits of rags; how the children went barefoot in the cold Chilean winters; and how they had turned to singing to put food on their table.[54] At times, Parra would now claim that she had been too poor to ever have attended school. Or she would omit the detail of her more privileged schoolteacher father from the narrative. Typically, she would stress that she was still poor in the here and now.[55] Bridging the past with the present, she had her mother sew her a colorful patchwork dress that she wore to her public appearances in Europe as a symbolic reminder—or performance—of the poverty that she had known as a child.

Moving out from her own experience, and as she had already done in her autobiographical décimas, Parra recast her maternal grandfather as a poor and exploited campesino, in essence superimposing the exploitation of Chilean agricultural workers on her own family history. She now also explicitly linked the hardships that she and her family (and other families) had endured to her current activities as a politically engaged songwriter and visual artist. As she explained in a 1963 interview, "When I recalled the poverty I had known, I realised that I had to place my artistic abilities at the service of my people. My contribution to these struggles are my new songs that stress the present sufferings and future desires of my countrymen."[56] In a similar vein, in her 1965 Swiss documentary Parra recounts the inspiration for her tapestry *The Revolt of the Campesinos*: "I was sad because my grandfather was a campesino . . . and the boss paid him so little, almost nothing. . . . All of the Chilean campesinos are very poor, like my grandfather was. I cannot remain like this [folding her arms across her chest]. I am outraged by the situation. That's why I made this tapestry."[57]

It is beyond question that the two revisions to Parra's foundational narrative responded to European expectations concerning the Indigenous and downtrodden peoples of Latin America. I would caution, however, against dismissing their adoption as mere evidence of Parra's pandering to her European audience. Though they may have served that purpose, they also signaled a transformation in how Parra self-identified. Parra's latest reinvention corresponded to a period in her life when she was transitioning from the more circumscribed role of folklorista to that of a fearless and authentic artist intent on exploring "all the different languages." It transpired within a European context shaped by the particular yearnings and heightened sensitivities of the historic moment, ones that she shared with her European fans. Recalling her midthirties turn to the authentic as a folklorista, Parra's reframing of her foundational narrative as a musician and visual artist in her mid-forties, though doubtlessly influenced by the perspectives of others, also reflected her own changing values, practices, and understanding of her place in the world.

Back in Paris

Parra arrived in Paris in September 1962 and straightaway resumed her gig at L'Escale, where she once bragged she had been pledged "lifelong employment."[58] Shortly after her arrival, she learned that a pair of Chilean musicians were performing at a nearby Latin American folk music club called La Candelaria and went to check them out, only to discover that they were none other than Isabel and Ángel. The two generations of Parras were happy to see each other and mended their rift.[59]

Beyond finding and reconciling with her children, Violeta received the added bonus of landing her own gig at La Candelaria which, along with L'Escale, was one of the Latin Quarter's hottest Latin American–themed venues. Most well-known folk artists on tour from Latin America performed there. The club's Paris-based lineup included the newly formed band and soon-to-be Andean sensation Los Calchakis, along with the Parra musicians in various configurations.

A month or two after Violeta's arrival in Paris, Carmen Luisa finally joined her there after family and friends back in Chile put the money together for her airfare. Her trip had been horrible. Her plane had been diverted to another airport, so no one was there to greet her after her long journey. She was barely twelve and knew no French. She would later recall her mother's dramatic reaction when they were finally reunited; "She hugged me, she asked me a thousand questions, she sobbed, and in the middle of all this she sang me that song." Here, Carmen Luisa was referring to "Paloma ausente" (Absent Dove), the song Violeta had composed to mark the occasion:

> I spend endless nights looking skyward
> In my thoughts one single desire
> That my little dove descend unwounded
> She who comes lofted by the winds . . .
>
> I will don a dress of butterflies
> Tomorrow when my little dove arrives
> In my hands tricolored flags
> A thousand little sparkles in my eyes.

> *Paso lunas enteras mirando al cielo*
> *con un solo deseo en el pensamiento:*
> *que no descienda herida mi palomita*
> *la que viene fundida a los elementos . . .*
>
> *Voy a ponerme un traje de mariposa*
> *mañana cuando llegue mi palomita*

en los dedos banderas de tres colores
y en las pestañas miles de candelillas.[60]

Carmen Luisa continued, "That very night she took me to the place where she worked and introduced me to half the world, she was so pleased. They spoke French to me, and I didn't understand a damn thing. . . . She finished singing at four in the morning and we went to visit some other bars . . . all in the Latin Quarter and with the same vibe."[61] The entire evening left a deep impression on Carmen Luisa. She was used to going to bed early so she could be up and ready for school the next morning and had known little, if anything, up until then of her mother's nocturnal life as a professional musician.

With Carmen Luisa in Paris at last, two generations of working musician mothers now had to resolve the question of caring for their children while earning a living—as the option followed by countless working musician fathers of leaving them in the care of their current or ex-wives was not available to either Violeta or Isabel. The answers that they came up with remain something of a mystery. Where, for instance, was six-year-old Tita while her mother Isabel performed at La Candelaria in those weeks before her young aunt Carmen Luisa joined the Parra clan in Paris? Once Carmen Luisa arrived, it is probable that the two children stayed in whatever room Violeta was renting at the time while their mother and grandmother were out gigging. When the Parra family performed as an ensemble in Paris, Geneva, or elsewhere, the problem resolved on its own, as the children sang and danced in the show—to the great delight of their European audiences, based on the reviews.

As regards the girls' formal education, it is not clear whether either of them attended school while in Paris. A musician colleague who roomed in the same building as Violeta and her youngest daughter recalled Carmen Luisa as something of a rascal; "instead of going to school, she would go here and there, around the streets and plazas, the street was her school."[62] Isabel's daughter Tita, who grew up to be a musician, would later admit that she "didn't go to school much" during the two years that she spent in Paris, "but like all children I absorbed every note, melody, and rhythm that I heard."[63]

Within weeks of Carmen Luisa's arrival, Favre showed up in Paris. He had been stuck in Buenos Aires for months. After multiple failed enterprises, he was finally able to purchase his transatlantic passage when a Geneva theater company where he had once worked as a stagehand rehired him and wired him an advance on his salary. He landed in Genoa in late October or early November 1962 and immediately took an overnight train to Paris to find Parra. In his memoir, he recalls how the Parra family threw a big party to welcome him that was attended by "all of their friends, and their friends' friends and their acquaintances, etc. etc."[64] After a loving but brief reencounter with Parra, Favre departed for Geneva where his job with the theater company awaited.

Parra would spend most of the next two years living between Paris and Geneva. When in Paris, she sustained herself and Carmen Luisa with the steady, if meager, income that she earned at L'Escale and La Candelaria, augmented by the occasional gig at some other Parisian club or restaurant. She was also hired to perform at a folk music festival and other more formal events, where she often appeared as "Violeta Parra and her ensemble" or simply the "Violeta Parra Ensemble." The ensemble could be made up of any combination of Isabel, Ángel, Carmen Luisa, and Tita, along with Favre, once he learned to play the quena.[65]

Parra's work routine in Paris was jam-packed and demanding. On a typical night, she would play a solo set at La Candelaria at 9:00 P.M., followed by a joint set with Isabel and Ángel at 10:15, then go down the block to L'Escale to perform additional sets that lasted well into the early morning. L'Escale was as smoke filled and its audience as inattentive and noisy as it had been when she first played there in the 1950s, and La Candelaria was not any better. Even as she kept up with and arguably helped to shape trends in the Parisian–Latin American folk music scene, Parra was still not a great fit with its boisterous atmosphere. Spanish Republican exile and fellow L'Escale musician Paco Ibáñez noted that people sometimes grumbled, "Here comes that Chilean woman again" when she arrived because of her insistence that they maintain silence throughout her entire set.[66] For his part, Rafael Gayoso, a founding member of the hugely successful Latin American folk music band Los Machucambos, recalled with regret that Parra was "not really a hit! She was ahead of her time. And we, who were singers ourselves, couldn't appreciate the wonderful things that she did. It was only afterward that we realized how extraordinary she was."[67]

As had been the case during her first Parisian sojourn, Parra's living quarters consisted of a succession of single rooms that she rented in bargain hotels and boarding houses located near—or, in the case of La Candelaria, whose owner ran a pension for musicians in the same building, above—the clubs where she performed in the Latin Quarter. No matter how late she went to sleep, Parra would wake early the next morning to work on her tapestries and other artwork. She spent a good portion of her time in bed, in part because of her habit of using her bed as an office and art studio and in part because her bed was inevitably the most prominent piece of furniture in whatever room she was renting.

Parra cultivated a rich social life in Paris. According to Carmen Luisa, "all of the Chileans who passed through [there]" visited her.[68] Violeta made new friends as well. Several of her friends and acquaintances would later comment on her hospitality. Fellow musician Paco Ibáñez recollected how Parra would drop by his room, which was one floor below hers, to share some dish that she had made and the occasional new song "fresh from the oven."[69] Argentine publisher and music producer Javier Álvarez wrote in his memoir of a soup Parra prepared for him upon his arrival in Paris after a grueling trip: "It tasted like heaven. . . . Violeta's warmth . . . restored me to life."[70] Rafael Gayoso of Los Machucambos related with humor the time that Parra was so happy because the by-then chart-topping band had recorded her song "The Black Wedding" that she invited them over for dinner, but instead of the sit-down meal that he expected, they had all sat on her bed and shared wine, bread, and cheese.[71] And a Genevan friend traveling on a shoestring budget related how Parra invited him to stay with her in Paris and how surprised he had been to learn that he would be sharing the same bed with Parra and her daughter and granddaughter.[72]

When not entertaining her guests in whatever one-room flat she was occupying, Parra liked to frequent the Café Danton, a gathering spot for expatriate Chileans. The café became Parra's Parisian version of the Santiago Café Sao Paolo and she often could be found there surrounded by a multinational group of her admirers that Chilean author and diplomat Jorge Edwards characterized as an "exotic and vigorous clan."[73]

Geneva

Sometime in December 1962, Favre received a desperate call from Parra. She was worried that little Tita might have contracted tuberculosis and was herself suffering from liver pains again. Favre drove to Paris that night with his brother and sister-in-law. The scene he discovered upon his arrival alarmed him: the entire Parra family was crammed into a wretched little room, barely four meters by four meters, with just one tiny window overlooking a courtyard that stank of burnt cooking oil. "It was pitiful. Titina [Tita] was lying in bed next to Violeta with a terrifying fever."[74]

Favre wanted to take everyone back to Geneva immediately, but Parra insisted that she needed to first make some arrangements. They ended up leaving Paris two days later. Violeta, Isabel, Ángel, Tita, and Carmen Luisa crammed into the car with Favre and his brother and sister-in-law. According to Favre, "it was like a slapstick comedy. . . . We were all literally piled on top of each other. Eight people in a car that was made for four, traveling 500 kilometers."[75]

Favre drove everyone to his parents' home in Geneva. Thankfully, both Violeta and Tita recovered from their ailments, though in Violeta's case it required another hospital stay.[76] With her daughter Tita out of danger, Isabel returned with Ángel to their musical activities in Paris while Violeta, Carmen Luisa, and Tita remained with Favre in Geneva.

Violeta spent the next six months or so sharing Favre's apartment with him.[77] Carmen Luisa and Tita lived with them much of the time, though at one point Violeta took the girls to the nearby town of Onex to stay for a few weeks with a family that she had met through her Swiss communist connections.[78] Isabel and Ángel traveled to Geneva to perform with the rest of their family as "Violeta Parra and Her Ensemble" whenever a concert opportunity arose, or for a moment of respite from the grueling pace of being a Left Bank Latin American folk musician in the 1960s, or, in Isabel's case, to visit her daughter Tita.

The flat that three generations of Parras shared with Favre consisted of two rooms in an artists' community that occupied much of a dilapidated old house near the city's downtown. The house had a long courtyard running down its center with a willow tree in the middle. Several metal workers had their workshops on one side, while a collection of painters, sculptors, and poets made their homes and studios on the other.[79] At first, the complex did not have electricity, but then Favre remembered how the Parras would siphon power from electric company cables in Santiago and set up a similarly illicit connection in Geneva.[80] On Saturdays, the local Spanish-speaking community would gather in the courtyard for lengthy repasts where Parra made a large pot of beans, the guests brought wine, and the singing started after the meal and continued well into the evening.[81]

To arrive at the unit where Parra and the girls now lived with Favre, one had to climb a steep, narrow set of steps that was more like a ladder than a staircase. The apartment was heated by a coal-burning stove, and most of its furniture was made from wooden crates. Like all of Parra's residences, it also served as her studio. Isabel likened it to an "art factory" because Violeta was always producing some new project or another.[82] The metaphor also seems apt, given Parra's unusual assembly-line technique of painting several canvases at once, one color at a time, because, as she explained in an interview, each color corresponded to a different emotion—and because that way she would not have to be constantly cleaning her paint brushes.[83] In addition to her paintings and tapestries, Parra began to create elaborate masks like the ones that first caught the attention of Geneva theater director and artist Raymonde Gampert (the one who Parra purportedly spoke to in broken French). Parra made them out of papier-mâché, paint, and mosaics of all types of materials; dried beans, rice, pieces of mirror, broom bristles, and, according to Gampert, human hair.[84]

Though nowhere near the level of Paris, Geneva was still a cosmopolitan city, especially since the United Nations made its European headquarters there. Over the next six months, Favre basically assumed the roles of Parra's manager and booking agent, working hard to arrange art shows and concerts for her both in Geneva and in nearby Lausanne.[85] A man of all trades, he oversaw all the logistics of the various events he organized, from building sets, to transporting Parra's work by wheelbarrow, to supplying the alcoholic beverages for the group of friends who spent the day hanging her pieces for an art exhibit.

Within a month of her arrival, the Geneva Galerie Connaitre mounted a weeks-long solo show of Parra's artwork that included paintings, masks, tapestries, and ceramics. Parra also performed at the gallery. In a missive home to the magazine *Ercilla*, she bragged that the venue had been so crowded at the recital she gave there that its owners had to borrow chairs from neighboring establishments. She boasted further that she had sold one of her tapestries for $450, a considerable sum for the time. To Parra, it would have represented a small fortune (though given her propensity to exaggerate, the price she reported may well have been higher than the actual one she received).[86]

In contrast with the Santiago press, which had shown scant appreciation for Parra's work as a visual artist, her first Geneva exhibit earned gushing reviews in the local press. Much as it had been in Chile, Parra's artwork was perceived as intuitive and naïve in Geneva and throughout Europe, but with an additional European twist that linked it to its presumed Indigenous roots. In a piece particularly rich in comparisons, a reporter for the *Tribune de Genève* employed all of the familiar tropes and then some. Parra was "a primitive genius" whose work evoked the painting "of the Australian aborigines, but with the freedom and boldness of lines that recall [Henri] Matisse." It was infused with "spontaneity . . . [and] nourished by Indian traditions . . . total originality."[87]

Geneva may have been home to an active art scene, but it was not known for its nightlife. With no steady gig in sight, Favre and friends took it upon themselves to organize performance opportunities for Parra. Her first Swiss concert was at the Théâtre Cour de Saint-Pierre, a small theater in Geneva's old town. Like many of Parra's European recitals, the show was a family affair. Parra opened with a solo set, then was joined by her three children and granddaughter for the second. Favre read French translations of the songs' lyrics from off stage, and he and his brother ran the curtains and lighting. Parra invented a set of fanciful masks for the performers to wear on their procession-like entrance to the stage.[88] As she now did whenever and wherever she performed, she also mounted a pop-up exhibit of her artwork, in this case in the theater's lobby.

As her first Geneva gallery show and her first Geneva recital demonstrate, Parra managed to turn her art exhibits into concerts and her concerts into art exhibits. She also went out of her way to serve her public traditional Chilean food and beverages. In essence, she relocated her multiplex Chilean independence celebration fonda—music, dancing, decorations, traditional food and drinks, pop-up art gallery, the works—to the theaters, courtyards, galleries, and other public spaces where she performed in Geneva and across Europe.[89] Ramón Huidobro Domínguez, who was the newly appointed Chilean ambassador to the United Nations as well as one of the few members of the Chilean diplomatic corps in Europe to show an interest in Parra, recalled how moved he had been when the curtains were pulled back in the Geneva theater to reveal "a typical fonda with miniature Chilean flags for all to see. We had the sensation of being in the park on September 18th."[90]

The work was exhausting, perhaps even more so than in Chile because Parra had fewer relatives and friends in Europe to assist her. In a letter to a friend back home, she complained about performing at an outdoor workers festival where she was paid a pittance to sing cuecas from noon until midnight in some corner of the event site, while "those who played the twist and everything else" earned good money and performed on the main stage. On a brighter note, she recounts how several festival attendees brought her the finest drinks and food to show their appreciation for her singing. At another performance, this one with her family ensemble, members of the audience had refused to leave the theater after the concert and had instead flooded the stage to congratulate the Parras and shower them with questions. "It makes me proud to tell you of such beautiful occurrences," she wrote her friend. "Everyone in Geneva knows we are here."[91]

Parra's Swiss friends organized at least one house concert for her during this period. Homemade recordings of this and another Geneva house concert in 1965 confirm how adept Parra was at winning over a European audience.[92] She performed a diverse set of songs at both. She explained each song's origins and meaning and encouraged the audience to pose questions. She asked Favre for assistance in translating at the 1963 concert, but by 1965 could speak directly to her public in near-perfect French. Both concert recordings are punctuated by the audiences' warm applause and frequent laughter, as Parra was very funny in a spontaneous and often self-deprecating way. She substituted the Spanish lyrics of some songs with the syllables "la-la-la" so that her audience could sing and clap along. At the end of one particularly boisterous chorus, she exclaimed, "You sing so well I'll have to take you all back to Chile with me!"[93]

On the home front, and in what appears to have been a pattern, Parra and Favre's relationship in Geneva was fraught with tensions that only seemed to get worse the more time that they spent together. Friends from the period describe Parra behaving in ways that were controlling and even abusive. Favre had taken up the quena so that he could join Parra when she performed. Parra, in turn, had appointed herself his drillmaster. She would banish him to a corner to practice while she and their friends socialized and only allow him to rejoin the circle after she deemed enough progress had been made on his end to warrant it.[94] If he tried to come back too soon, she would grab whatever was lying next to her and throw it at his head. In addition to having violent tendencies, Parra was also very possessive. Favre claims that she went to the extreme of not wanting him to perform in public for fear that other women would look at him. The ongoing quarrel this provoked was partially resolved when Favre promised to close his eyes when he played the quena so that he would not see the admiring women in the audience.[95]

One frequent visitor to the artists' colony summed up the couple's relationship: "They were always fighting. It's just that Violeta had a very strong personality."[96] And so things continued until, in June 1963, the couple reached yet another near breaking point in their tumultuous relationship and Parra decided to return to Paris. Reports that Isabel and Ángel's duo was becoming quite the rage on the Parisian–Latin American folk music scene may have also influenced her decision to return there. As Favre points out in his autobiography, if there was one thing that Violeta disliked, it was to "take the back seat."[97]

Recordings and a Festival

That Parisian summer of 1963 was a gloomy one for Parra. She poured out her heart in correspondence. In a letter to Nicanor, she lamented that "Paris offers me not even one kiss, nor even the hint of a smile."[98] In one to her dear friends "Anita" and "Cuto" (Ana Urrutia and Ángel Custodio Oyarzún), "archangels" of Parra's first and now second Parisian sojourn, she complained that her children and granddaughter were away on vacation "like all of Europe" (including, presumably, the letter's addressees) and that Paris in August was an "artists' graveyard." She confided further that she was heartbroken and could not sleep. She signed off, "from a frustrated girlfriend, who cries singing, who embroiders her sorrows, and who paints her missteps."[99]

Things began to pick up for Parra toward the end of the summer. In mid-August, she went into the studio with Isabel and Ángel to work on two recording projects for the French record label Barclay. The LP *Au Chili avec Los Parra de Chillan* [sic] (In Chile with the Parras from Chillán) was released in November 1963.[100] As its liner notes make clear, "the Parras" in this instance refers narrowly to the popular duo formed by Isabel and Ángel Parra. Though intended to showcase the siblings' music, the album was an intergenerational project nonetheless: in addition to Isabel and Ángel's parts, it featured Violeta on vocals, guitar, and percussion on one track, and a duet by Carmen Luisa and Tita on another. Most of the tracks were of folk songs that Violeta collected, while the rest were original songs by Violeta, Ángel, and Roberto Parra.

Beyond contributing to her children's album, Violeta also recorded material for an anticipated solo LP of her own songs with the same label. For reasons unknown, it was not released during her lifetime.[101] In correspondence, Parra described it as "an album of revolutionary songs" that she had composed while in Europe. Effectively, her 1963 recording comprised many of what would eventually become her most well-known politically engaged songs.

To highlight one, "La Carta" (The Letter) is Parra's song that many commentators agree represents the "birth certificate of the Chilean New Song movement."[102] Like most of her songs, it was inspired by events that affected her personally. In November 1962, she received a letter informing her that her brother Roberto had been arrested at a demonstration for higher wages and improved social services. The protest was organized by Chile's most important labor confederation, the Central Union of Chilean Workers (Central Única de Trabajadores de Chile or CUT). It took place in a working-class neighborhood and was violently repressed by the police, resulting in six deaths and dozens of detainees—Roberto among them.

What stands out about the song's lyrics are the immediacy and strength of their emotion. One has the impression that Parra has just read the letter, that she is outraged by its contents, and that she must now share that outrage with us, her listeners:

> They sent me a letter
> In the early mail.
> In this letter they tell me
> They dragged my brother off to jail
> And heartlessly they shackled him
> And threw him in a cell, yes.

> *Me mandaron una carta*
> *por el correo temprano*
> *En esa carta me dicen*
> *que cayó preso mi hermano*
> *y, sin lástima, con grillos,*
> *por la calle lo arrastraron, sí.*

She tells of Roberto's unjust imprisonment:

> The letter states the crime
> That Roberto has committed:
> His support of the strike
> That already had finished.
> If this truly is a crime,
> I should also go to prison, yes.

La carta dice el motivo
que ha cometido Roberto:
haber apoyado el paro
que ya se había resuelto.
Si acaso esto es un motivo,
presa también voy, sargento, sí.

She reports on her own situation:

I am here so very distant
Awaiting information,
The letter comes to tell me
There's no justice in my nation:
Hungry people ask for bread,
Bullets fly in retaliation, yes.

Yo que me encuentro tan lejos,
esperando una noticia,
me viene a decir la carta
que en mi patria no hay justicia:
los hambrientos piden pan,
plomo les da la milicia, sí.

Parra concludes the song:

I'm lucky to have a guitar
So I can cry out my pain;
And I have nine brothers and sisters
Besides the one they took away.
They're Communists, all nine
With the favor of God's grace, yes.

Por suerte tengo guitarra
para llorar mi dolor;
también tengo nueve hermanos
fuera del que se engrilló.
Los nueve son comunistas
con el favor de mi Dios, sí.[103]

The last, and perhaps most controversial line from the song represents both a simplification—not all of Parra's siblings were communists—and an early expression of Liberation Theology, an approach to Christianity where religious faith and communist ideals are not viewed as being at odds with one another, rather part of a same and righteous struggle for social justice.

Parra recorded other memorable politically engaged songs for the first time that August in Paris. "Un río de sangre corre" (A River of Blood Flows) pays homage to Chilean labor leader Luis Emilio Recabarren, Mexican revolutionary Emiliano Zapata, Spanish poet Federico García Lorca, and Congolese independence leader Patrice Lumumba, among others.[104] "Santiago, penando estás" (Santiago, How You Are Suffering) continues Parra's practice as a social geographer by depicting the cruelty that the modernization of Chile's capital city entailed:

The little birds aren't singing,
They don't have anywhere to nest;
The branches where they used to sing
Have already been cut.
Next they'll cut down the trunk
And in its place install
A privy and a bar.

Los pajarillos no cantan,
no tienen dónde anidar;
ya les cortaron las ramas
donde solían cantar.
Después cortarán el tronco
y pondrán en su lugar
una letrina y un bar.[105]

"Ayúdame, Valentina" (Help Me, Valentina) is Parra's tribute to the first woman to go to space, Soviet cosmonaut Valentina Tereshkova. In yet another critique of Church officialdom and religious hypocrisy, Parra asks her,

What will we do with so many
Treatises from High Heaven?
Help me please, Valentina,
You who have flown so far,
Tell me once and for all
That up above there's no mansion
Tomorrow it will be created
By the ingenuity of man.

¿Qué vamos a hacer con tanto
tratado del alto Cielo?
Ayúdame, Valentina,
ya que tú volaste lejos,
dime de una vez por todas

que arriba no hay tal mansión;
mañana la ha de fundar
ya el hombre con su razón.[106]

In contrast with "The Letter," where Parra welds her communist sympathies to her personal relationship with God by thanking them for her nine communist siblings, "Help Me, Valentina" conveys a more traditional leftist denunciation of religion as "the opium of the people."

Barclay never released the material Parra recorded in August 1963 as an album.[107] It was instead released posthumously in 1971 by the Chilean record label DICAP as the LP *Canciones reencontradas en Paris* (Songs Rediscovered in Paris).[108] Parra would record one additional track for Barclay within the year; the original instrumental "Cachimbo," with the participation of Isabel on tambourine and Favre on quena (who thanks to rigorous effort and an even more rigorous taskmaster was by then proficient on the instrument). It appears on the 1965 compilation LP *Toute L'Amerique Latine* (All of Latin America) featuring songs from a variety of Latin American countries and album notes in French, English, German, and Italian. The LP's cover displays the photo of an Indigenous woman wearing a bowler hat that identifies her as from Bolivia, although few, if any of the musicians featured on the compilation were Indigenous and none were from Bolivia.[109] The two Parras plus Favre are billed as "Los Parra de Chillán" (The Parras from Chillán), and Violeta's name is spelled incorrectly as "Violetta."

Parra's friends and fellow musicians Los Calchakis also appear on the *All of Latin America* album. Parra first heard the band perform at its 1962 audition at La Candelaria. Impressed with the band members' musical abilities, she became the Latin American folk ensemble's mentor. She introduced Los Calchakis to the director of Barclay records. The band would end up recording almost all of its albums on the label, including its global hit *La Flûte Indienne*. In an homage written in the early 1970s, founding member Héctor Miranda acknowledged Parra's importance to the band's trajectory and listed the many gifts that she had conferred on its members: "an appreciation for authentic songs, a refusal of shallow concessions or gratuitous influences, the love of simple things, and above all else, the sensation of knowing, through Parra, the soul of the Indo-American lands."[110]

Oddly enough, the only LP by Parra herself to be released during her second stay in Europe ended up being a 1964 compilation of songs drawn from her two 1956 recordings for the label Le Chant du Monde and with the same title of *Songs and Dances of Chile*. In a marketing ploy comparable in its cultural distortion to the conga drum found on the cover of her 1956 album, the artwork for Parra's 1964 Le Chant du Monde LP capitalizes on the era's

Figure 7.2 Isabel Parra, Violeta Parra, and Ángel Parra performing at the 1963 Fête de l'Humanité. Collection L'Humanité 83 Fi 246 31, Archives du Parti Communiste Français, Archives Départementales de la Seine-Saint-Denis.

fascination with Indigenous peoples. How else can one explain its cover photo, which in lieu of Violeta Parra shows a Mapuche woman in traditional dress on horseback, simple rope reins in one hand and a woven basket in the other?[111]

At long last the summer ended, and the Parisians returned from their August vacations. In September, Violeta performed with Isabel and Ángel at that year's Fête de l'Humanité (Festival of Humanity). This was the French Communist Party's annual festival and fundraiser for its daily newspaper, which lent its name to the event. The 1963 festival was held over a weekend in a park on the outskirts of Paris. It featured appearances by many of France's most popular singers as well as bands performing Francophone *rock and roll* and pop.[112] It drew a massive attendance of some 600,000 people across two days.[113]

The Parras performed in the Plaza Julián Grimau, named for the recently martyred Spanish communist. They shared the stage with musical acts from Cuba, Czechoslovakia, Hungary, Senegal, Cameroon, and Bulgaria. An unpublished photo from the *L'Humanité* archive shows Violeta, Isabel, and Ángel dressed in mismatched costumes on stage, the children in their huasa and huaso outfits and their mother in her invented Andean garb (see figure 7.2). The incongruity is intriguing. Did it result from a lack of communication or miscommunication between family members? Was it a manifestation of Parra's aspiration to become the be-all and end-all of cultural emissaries from Chile and Latin America in Europe, in this instance by covering all the bases, costume-wise?

By now, Parra was well known enough for the festival organizers to announce her as a "Chilean star," but not well known enough to have her name spelled correctly in the festival's program, where it appeared alternately as Violetta Parra or Violeta Para.[114] Misspellings aside, performing at the Fête de l'Humanité in front of a crowd of thousands was a high point of both Parra's second European stay and her entire musical career. It inspired her to write an enthusiastic letter to the Chilean CP secretary general Luis Corvalán urging the party to establish a similar festival in Chile. The party took her up on her idea the next year when it held the first of what became annual "festive gatherings of the communist family."[115] The CP continued to hold the event annually until the military dictatorship shut the festival down in 1973.

Chapter 8

Total Artist

Parra returned to Paris from Geneva at the end of June 1963 determined to have her artwork exhibited there. She did not aim low. Her first choice of venues was the French National Museum of Modern Art. Accordingly, she requested the support of Carlos Morla Lynch, Chilean ambassador to France since 1959 and an amateur musician, with whom she had been able to establish a rapport. Ambassador Morla Lynch obligingly penned a letter to the museum's director, Jean Cassou.

Morla Lynch introduced Parra as a Chilean artist and a renowned *folkloriste*. He continued, "Mme. Violeta Parra is additionally the creator of tapestries, paintings, and ceramics of folk inspiration." Noting that she had already exhibited her work in Chile, in a group show at the Museum of Modern Art in Rio de Janeiro, and in solo shows in Geneva and Berlin, he requested that the museum director "grant Mme. Violeta Parra an appointment wherein she would be able to express her desires in person, and to offer her, to the extent possible, whatever is needed for the development and dissemination of her artistic activities in France."[1]

In a characteristic display of both her exaggerated optimism and iron will, Parra announced in a letter dated August 23, 1963, "I have one foot in and one foot out of the Museum of Modern Art in Paris. I will not rest until I exhibit there."[2] She left no record as to why the Museum of Modern Art was her initial choice for her proposed exhibit. Perhaps the museum had appealed to her because her only previous participation in a major art exhibit had been at Rio's Museum of Modern Art in 1961. Or perhaps her interest stemmed from the Parisian Museum of Modern Art's 1962 exhibit of Latin American art featuring works by several Chilean artists of her acquaintance as well as her new friend and fellow La Candelaria musician Héctor Miranda.[3] Or because her friend the artist Nemesio Antúnez was then the director of the Chilean Museum of Contemporary Art in Santiago.

Parra would have had artistic reasons to favor the museum as well. Her cubist-like figures could conceivably be associated with works by Picasso, an artist she aspired to meet some day. Her metal sculptures, in turn, could be viewed as creatively proximate to those of Alexander Calder.[4] Her use of found materials, which in her case was as much out of necessity as an aesthetic choice, would seem to place her in or adjacent to the pop art movement.[5] More generally, the dreamlike quality and folkloric aspects of her artwork would appear to link her to Marc Chagall, who reportedly was her favorite painter along with Jean Miró.[6]

Given her predilection for these last two artists and the influence that they and other modern masters may have had on her own work, there is every reason to believe that Parra first approached the Museum of Modern Art because she considered herself to be a modern artist. The decision as to whether she was a modern artist inspired by the primitive (à la Picasso) or the folk (à la Chagall) or simply a folk artist was not hers to make, however. Museum director Mr. Cassou decided not to act on the Chilean ambassador's recommendation.[7] Instead, he passed Ambassador Morla Lynch's letter down to museum underling Bernard Dorival, who then sent it on to a different institution all together: the Paris Museum of Decorative Arts (Musée des Arts Decoratifs or MAD).

Founded in 1905, MAD occupies a wing of the Louvre Palace known as the Marsan Pavilion. Though it shares the same palatial complex with the Louvre Museum, MAD is nonetheless an independent entity specializing in the decorative arts: furniture, glassware, ceramics, metalwork, jewelry, textiles, fashion, and graphic design. Beginning in the late 1950s, MAD began mounting retrospectives by famous modern artists as well, including Picasso (1955), Chagall (1959), and Henri Matisse (1961).[8] Parra would not be given a solo show at MAD in that capacity, however, but as someone associated with folk and Indigenous cultures. On October 1, 1963, Dorival wrote a short letter of introduction to Monsieur Michel Faré, MAD head curator, that by and large echoed the Chilean ambassador's letter to the director of the Museum of Modern Art—with the exceptions that Dorival added the embellishment that the "folk traditions" that Parra drew from were "Indian" and misspelled Parra's name in two places ("Madame Violetta Para").[9]

Following up on Dorival's letter, Parra made an appointment to meet with Monsieur Faré at his office. The ensuing sequence of events would prove to be an emotional rollercoaster. Monsieur Faré first told her that the museum would exhibit her artwork and that she needed to come up with enough material to fill two of the museum's enormous galleries. Parra went straight to work creating more pieces in anticipation of her show. Then, when she met with Monsieur Faré several weeks later, he delivered the devastating news that the selection committee had overridden his decision and canceled her show. Despairing, Parra burst into tears. Her display of emotion disarmed the museum official. In a letter to Favre, Parra describes how Faré took her hands in his and told her to bring all her artwork to his office that same afternoon. Parra returned a few hours later, weighed down with her tapestries and paintings, and Monsieur Faré assured her that they were marvelous. He promised that he would bring them to the selection committee's next meeting and convince its members to reverse their decision. He begged Parra to be patient, saying that she would soon have her response.[10]

It was presumably during this anxious waiting period that Parra wrote the letter to her friend in which she posed the guiding question of this biography: "How could I have an exhibit at the Louvre, I, who am the ugliest woman on the planet, who come from a tiny country, from Chillán, at the end of the earth?"[11] The following week, to her great joy, she received the news that her exhibit had been restored to the museum's calendar. It would be the first solo show by a Latin American artist in the history of the Museum of Decorative Arts.

The Myths

The above account is pieced together from documents housed in the Museum of Decorative Arts' archives and Parra's press interviews and personal correspondence. Perhaps not surprisingly, given its protagonist, the story of how Violeta Parra came to have a solo show at the Museum of Decorative Arts began to be mythologized almost immediately. The process was fueled by two contradictory anecdotes, each of which contained elements of truth, and neither of which was completely accurate. One suggests that Parra "performed" her authenticity or "otherness" to live up to the exoticizing expectations of a cosmopolitan audience that was incapable of viewing her on an equal footing as one of their own. The other reveals the rebellious nature of her performance. Significantly, both accounts appear to have originated with Parra herself.

The first version of events is related by her friend, the photographer Sergio Larraín:

> [Violeta] had all of this artwork and no idea where to exhibit it. So she went to see some guy and after she explained to him what she wanted, that person gave her a business card with two addresses on it. One of them said street such-and-such, number such-and-such, and she set off to find it. She soon found herself in front of an enormous building so she looked at the paper again to make sure it was the street number that she had been given. They had given her the address of the Louvre! She was standing there—she told me—with her hair in two braids and her rolled-up tapestries in her arms, without even a letter of recommendation, all alone.[12]

The anecdote captures the sense of wonder that Parra must have felt upon arriving for the first time at Monsieur Faré's office, only to realize that it was housed within the Louvre Palace.[13] At the same time, through a series of omissions and embellishments aimed at emphasizing Parra's naiveté, it down-plays the intentionality of her bold pursuit to procure a major venue to exhibit her artwork in the first place. The record shows that, in fact, Parra was sent to the museum not by just "some guy," but by Museum of Modern Art official Bernard Dorival with his written recommendation. And although the detail that she was wearing braids lends a folkloric aura to the tableau, it seems unlikely, as Parra does not appear with that hairstyle in photos from the period.

The second anecdote portrays Parra's solo show in the Louvre Palace as entirely the product of her own volition. As she explained to Chilean reporter Raquel Correa, "I had passed by the Louvre Palace . . . a lovely little house. And I thought to myself: I need to show my things there. Nowhere else but there."[14] Parra's implicit claim that the Louvre was her first and only desired venue for mounting an exhibition of her artwork is contradicted by archival documentation showing that her initial contact was with the Museum of Modern Art. As this is the case, the anecdote is perhaps best understood as evidence of Parra's wholehearted embrace of MAD as the ideal venue for her artwork after the fact. Regardless of its inaccuracies, this particular telling of events underscores Parra's strong sense of self and purpose as an artist, as well as her belief in the value of her work.

Given their divergences, any attempt to reconcile these two anecdotes with each other or the historical record appears futile. Instead, the contrasting accounts may more usefully be interpreted as contributing, each in its own way, to Parra's ongoing self-construction as an authentic artist. In the first, Parra constructs herself as authenticity personified by positioning herself as a naïve woman standing outside (and "other" to) an artworld within which she was operating in all actuality with some success. In the second anecdote, which appears to have been concocted above all to impress her Chilean compatriots, she casts herself as David—she is "a tiny woman"—versus Goliath—the contemporary artworld, as symbolized in this case by what she affectionately refers to as "a lovely little house," the colossal Louvre Palace.

Though lacking in biographical precision, each story offers a partial response to the question: How does an "ugly" woman of undistinguished origins from a country on the cultural periphery become seen and valued at the cultural center? The first anecdote suggests that it involved maintaining the appearance of purity and authenticity in the eyes of others, something that her very success could easily undermine. The second anecdote underscores how thoroughly subversive it was for her to pose the question in the first place, for in asserting that she was the author of her own artistic triumph, Parra successfully destabilized the hierarchies of class, race, and gender that would have barred her entrance to the artworld where she now claimed space.[15]

The Exhibit

Parra's preparations for her MAD exhibit spanned from when she first learned of her initial acceptance sometime in the Parisian fall of 1963 to its opening day in April 1964, when she could be found still putting the final stitches on her newest tapestry. She spent at least part of the time working at Favre's flat in Geneva. At one point she convinced or, better put, connived a Swiss friend who was traveling to Paris to take her back there with him. He agreed, and on the day of their departure learned to his surprise that he would be transporting not only Violeta but also her daughter Carmen Luisa and more tapestries and paintings than he believed could possibly fit in his car, a VW bug.[16]

Somehow they made it to Paris. Favre soon joined them there to assist Parra with the preparations. Violeta turned the small, one-room apartment that she shared with Carmen Luisa and Favre into an all-purpose art studio and framing shop. Carmen Luisa recalls, "The room was sheer bedlam, with my mother putting finishing stiches here and there, and the *gringo* [slang for foreigner] hammering away and framing everything, and the floor covered with every color of yarn and everything hanging all over the place."[17] Violeta continued to entertain visitors in her newest one-room abode just as she had in all her previous ones. A photo from the period captures the scene of Isabel and a friend seated so close to Violeta's bed as to be almost touching it with their feet, while Violeta and Ángel are seated on the bed itself—or, to be more precise, on top of one of Violeta's tapestries, which serves as its bedspread.[18]

Violeta next commandeered the fifth-floor flat above La Calendaria where Ángel was living with his fiancée Marta because it had more space and better lighting than the one she was renting.[19] As the exhibit's opening date neared, Parra convinced the Museum of Decorative Arts staff to let her and Favre work in a designated area in the Louvre Palace's spacious basement.[20]

Parra received what was for her unprecedented support from the Chilean embassy in Paris for her show. This was thanks in part to the lobbying efforts of her friend, the author and then–cultural attaché Jorge Edwards, who convinced the embassy to cover the printing costs for the exhibit's catalog.[21]

The museum took charge of the printed invitations. The text read, "Chilean Tapestries by Violeta Parra."[22] In keeping with Parra's status as an artist from the "developing world," the invitation's wording gave primacy to the artistic objects and their geographic origin rather than to their creator. This together with the number of times Parra's name was misspelled in France corroborate that she remained unable to achieve standing as an individual artist and was instead more akin to the "flavor of the month" in the European mindset. It is easy to imagine, for instance, the invitation for MAD's subsequent exhibit to read something like "Indonesian Puppets by [Artist whose name is ultimately

Figure 8.1
Violeta Parra at the
Museum of Decorative Arts.
Originally published in *Vea*,
February 9, 1967.

not that important and is therefore often misspelled in official correspondence and the media]."

Parra's exhibit opened on April 8, 1964. An assortment of art critics, collectors, reporters, and prominent members of the Parisian and expatriate Latin American artistic community attended the opening. Favre was there, filming everything for a planned-for (but never realized) documentary. So were Isabel, Ángel, Carmen Luisa, Tita, and many of Violeta's friends and acquaintances. French television archival footage shows the museum's spacious galleries filled with people viewing Parra's artwork and milling around. In a photo of the event, Parra can be seen dressed in a stylish jacket and skirt ensemble, her hair long and loose, conversing with visitors (figure 8.1).[23]

The exhibit contained sixty-one pieces in all, making it likely the most extensive showing of Parra's work in her lifetime and perhaps since.[24] They included twenty-two tapestries, twenty-six paintings, and thirteen wire sculptures and masks. Their dimensions ranged from small paintings and wire sculptures that were barely a foot tall to larger tapestries that were up to ten feet wide.[25]

The exhibit's catalog was written by MAD official Yvonne Brunhammer. She refers to Parra as a "total artist, musician, painter, sculptor, ceramicist, poet." She notes that many people in France will already know Parra through her recordings of Chilean folk music and original songs. Brunhammer then explains that "music and color are linked for Violeta Parra, who has moved quite naturally from one to the other."[26] She then cites the phrase that Parra used to convey this phenomenon: "Every song is a canvas ready to be painted."[27]

Parra's words affirmed her understanding of the holistic relationship between her musical and visual work.[28] Indeed, many of the pieces in her MAD exhibit are easily paired with either the songs she collected or her own compositions. Some are explicit illustrations of songs, such as her tapestry *The Betrothed Campesinos*, which according to the show's catalog is a visual representation of the Chilean folk song "Parabienes a los novios" (Congratulations to the Betrothed).[29] Other possible pairings include her works depicting religious imagery—Christ on the cross, his ascension, Saint Peter's disavowal—with poet-songs that cover the same topics; her painting of the wake for the little angel with the songs sung at the same ritual; her tapestry *The Circus* with "La cueca del payaso" (The Clown's Cueca); and her tapestry of a couple dancing a cueca with any of the twenty-four cuecas featured on her LP *La cueca presentada por Violeta Parra* (The Cueca, as Presented by Violeta Parra). More potential pairings cover political themes, such as her painting *The Conquerors Murder the King* and her song "Levántate, Huenchullán" (Arise, Huenchullán), or her painting *The Innocent Prisoner* and her song "La carta" (The Letter) denouncing her brother Roberto's arrest and incarceration for participating in a protest.

Several of Parra's pieces reference Mapuche iconography and Chilean folk art. As Parra explained in a 1963 interview, "I began my research on colour as I had on songs, and I found what I was looking for among the natives, in their fabrics, [and] in the [folk] ceramics of the various regions of Chile."[30] In terms of the influence that Mapuche visual culture had on her artwork, she stated in a later interview, "I use an enormous amount of colors in my tapestries, but at their base are the Araucanian ones of yellow, black, purple, red, green, and pink."[31] Mapuche culture also appears as a theme in her artwork, as when Parra depicted the *machitún* ceremony in her painting by that title—a piece that could later be paired with her song "El Guillatún" about the Mapuche ritual that gives it its name, recorded in 1966.[32]

In terms of the influence of Chilean folk art on Parra's work, the distinctive ceramics made by the women of the towns of Pomaire and Quinchamalí outside her hometown of Chillán appear in a few of her paintings and tapestries.[33] Parra also paid homage to the Quinchamalí potters, who were known for their black ceramics, by naming her tapestry of the figure of Christ embroidered in black yarn *The Christ of Quinchamalí*.

Several of Parra's works in the exhibit were self-referential. *The Bald Singer*, which happened to be the tapestry she was using as a bedspread before the exhibit opened, is one example. It portrays the family scene of Violeta singing and playing her harp, with Isabel seated beside her, a dog sleeping at her feet, and Tita and a second dog off to one side (see figure 6.2).[34] The exhibit also included the paintings *Party at Violeta's Home*, *Violeta and Her Children*, and *Carmen Luisa*, as well as figurative masks of Parra's children and granddaughter.

Parra's show at the Museum of Decorative Arts lasted just under five weeks. She spent every day at the museum for the duration. According to one museum official, she practically lived there.[35] Parra chatted with visitors, demonstrated her embroidery techniques, sang and played the guitar, played recordings of her singing over loudspeakers that the museum installed for that purpose, and served up a sampling of empanadas and traditional drinks from Chile. *Le Monde* art critic P. M. Grand described the scene: "Violeta is present . . . to play the guitar, to sing sad and expressive music, to invent as she embroiders. . . . Petite and brunette . . . simple and complex like a figure from Lorca."[36] His review epitomizes the way many of Parra's European admirers failed to distinguish between the artist and her artwork: under their exoticizing gaze, Violeta Parra embodied authenticity.

P. M. Grand's piece and other reviews of Parra's MAD exhibit and subsequent shows in France and Switzerland confirm that Parra's artwork found a level of appreciation in Europe that it had yet to attain in Chile. The praise it earned from the European press followed an established script that was both gendered and colonialist. Parra's artwork was childlike; it possessed a "true naivete, as authentic as the truth that emanates, vociferous and joyful, from the mouths of children."[37] It was natural; it had "evolved as freely or organically as a flower or plant grows."[38] It was primitive/Indigenous; it had "a certain savagery that brought to mind the art of the Incas."[39]

A few reviewers tied Parra's work specifically to Chile; it was "the lively expression of an entire people, of an entire culture."[40] Others linked it to a more amorphous South America, compressing the diverse continent into a single and stereotypical entity, as European art critics were wont to do. One reviewer, for instance, stated that Parra's work transmitted "messages from South America . . . a country where one lives intensely, always in communion with nature, a simple merging of the human species with the species of plants or animals."[41]

Most reviewers recognized that Parra's artwork was not merely folk art, that the artist's touch was also at play. But they linked Parra's creativity not to an inherent and transcendent artistic genius—à la Picasso or Chagall—but to the unconscious spontaneity of the naïve. Perhaps the words of art critic Madeleine Brumagne best capture the contradictory way that Parra's reviewers simultaneously credited her for the inventiveness of her work while negating her agency as an artist: "Through the stylization of attitudes and the symbolism of colors, the artist has caught life itself on the fly and, without realizing it herself, turned it into art. A brute art [art brut] that is at the same time very refined, authentic."[42] Whether Parra's European reviewers tied her authenticity to a specific, premodern subgroup of humanity (the naïve or the brutes) or cultural region (Chile or the "country" of South America), the result was the same: they denied Parra the authority and presumed universality of the modern artist.

Parra, for her part, reinforced her European audience's perception by claiming that "everything I do emerges naturally . . . in a spontaneous and instinctive way."[43] Parra offered as proof the flower-that-was-a-bottle-that-was-a-woman anecdote of her first attempt at making a tapestry.[44] Along the same lines, Parra would explain that she never traced the image she wanted to create on a new tapestry in advance. Instead, she would embroider one section, then another, no matter the tapestry's dimensions, and only view the piece in its entirety when it was finished and unfolded. Parra repeated the anecdote and the explanation of her approach to embroidering near verbatim until, as with many of her narratives, they acquired an almost scripted quality (which, in this case, was paradoxical, given their shared purpose of highlighting Parra's spontaneity). Together with her lack of formal training in the arts, both anecdote and explanation became standard elements of Parra's biography as a visual artist. Akin to Parra's recently acquired Indigenous ancestry, when it came to Parra's representation as an artist guided solely by intuition it was never that clear who was leading and who was following.

Parra's MAD exhibit was a success by all measures. News of it traveled swiftly to Chile. Ambassador Morla Lynch sent a glowing, if brief, report touting the show's "exceptional success" and the "significant prestige" of its having taken place in the Louvre Palace.[45] The exhibit also inspired one of the few articles about Parra to appear in Chile's conservative daily, El Mercurio, during her lifetime. Reporter Francisco Díaz Roncero noted that Parra's works were being shown in one of the world's most coveted exhibit halls in the world and praised "the great power of their folk expression." In keeping with the template, tried-and-true by now on both sides of the Atlantic, he concluded that they were "[works of] great art, simple, spontaneous, natural made by someone who knows nothing of [art] academies or studies."[46]

Parra was very pleased with the show's reception. In a celebratory letter to her friend Blaya, she crowed, "Everyone was enchanted by the little Chilean woman. Every day the value of my work grows."[47] She reported having sold several of her tapestries, including one for 7,000 new francs to the Baroness Rothschild, and another for US$500 to her "Chilean aristocrat friend" Arturo Pratt, who also bought a mask.[48] In an interview, Parra explained her sliding scale: "The baroness paid like a baroness, the Chileans, like Chileans."[49] Parra also sold several paintings for US$100 each.[50]

The exhibit thus provided Parra with a much-needed economic boost. Over and beyond this and other tangibles, Parra made clear in her correspondence just how much the exhibit meant to her. What comes through in her letter to Blaya is her intense pride at her success:

When I visited your home, only I knew the value of my work. In Chile, even though I had exhibited it, nobody said anything. . . . But here: success with the art critics, the public, sales; and what matters above all else, artistic success, as I am the first South American to have a show in the Marsan Pavilion of the Louvre Museum. It is easy to have one's work included in a group show, but to have a solo exhibit is like catching the moon in one's hands. And I have done it.[51]

In a letter to Favre, who had returned to Geneva, written around ten days before the exhibit closed, Parra confided how sad she was that her exhibit was ending and how certain she was that the day after "will be a horrible day." She shared her emotional state of mind; "I am sort of sad, but not that much. I think it is the worry of not knowing exactly what my fate will be after the museum."[52] Parra's question regarding her fate was a weighty one. Where does one go after having an exhibit of such historic import and in such a majestic setting? What could possibly follow that would not in some way feel like a demotion after having caught the moon in one's hands?

After the Exhibit

Finally, the day that Parra dreaded arrived. Her MAD exhibit closed on May 11, 1964. Even while the show was still running, Parra had been busy laying the groundwork for what she hoped would come next. She wrote letters and sent catalogs to those people she thought could help her. She received promises of assistance. In a letter to Favre, she recounted having gotten offers from museum directors in Italy, the Netherlands, and Belgium. An Italian jeweler had spoken to her about a palace in Florence. The Czech ambassador to France had proposed a trip to Prague. Not wanting to get her hopes up, Parra wrote, "I have to believe in one tenth of this bouquet of flowers."[53]

Parra's skepticism was well placed. Few, if any, of the exhibits that purportedly had been promised to her by interested art curators and collectors materialized. There is no record, for instance, of a second solo show in France during her lifetime. Parra was able to place some pieces at the Galerie Benezit, which specialized in works by so-called naïve painters, and a few others (likely her metal sculptures) at La Porte Ouverte, a gallery on the fashionable Rue Saint Honoré that sold "unique and utilitarian pieces [of furniture], sculptures and lamps out of metal, marionettes, and artisanal jewelry."[54] More impressively, French art critic and collector Anatole Jokavosky chose to include Parra in his encyclopedic tome, *Peintres naïfs* (Naïve Painters), published the year of her death in 1967.[55]

As regards her work as a musician, Parra presumably continued her bread-and-butter gigs at L'Escale and La Candelaria even as she prepared frantically for her MAD exhibit, then spent every day at the museum during its monthlong run. She took on a few additional musical projects over the first half of 1964 as well. In February, she was one of several musicians to provide accompaniment for an evening of contemporary Latin American poetry at the Théâtre de Plaisance. Eve Griliquez, the actress and comedienne who put together the soirée, asked Parra to accompany the show's section devoted to Pablo Neruda at the suggestion of one of the musicians from the Paraguayan band Les Guaranis. "For Chile, Violeta Parra is tops!" he had informed her.[56]

The show featured recitations of French translations of works by poets Pablo Neruda, Nicolás Guillén (Cuba), and César Vallejo (Peru) and the presence of Guatemalan author and soon-to-be Nobel Prize–winner Miguel Ángel Asturias (1967) and Paraguayan writer Helvio Romero, both of whom happened to be in Paris at the time.[57] The small theater was packed and the audience enthusiastic. Parra sang Chilean folk songs, her own compositions, and her setting of a poem by Pablo Neruda. In his review, Polish journalist and poet Charles Dozynski declared that "the revelation of the evening comes to us from Chile with Violeta Parra, with her strange face of an Indian with strong traits that lights up suddenly with a laugh or a cry, and who translates the ancient nobility of a people whose traditions Neruda has illustrated magnificently in his 'Canto General,' with a voice of husky and sweet intonations."[58]

Griliquez's assessment of Parra's performance was equally positive. She next invited Parra to be part of the more elaborate variety show that she was directing called "Vivre" (To Live). Advertised as a "secular oratory," it wove together an eclectic array of acts by artists who were considered the best in their respective fields. In addition to Parra's contribution of several songs (and

Figure 8.2 Alberto Quintanilla, Violeta Parra, and Bachir Touré from the cast of *Vivre*, Paris. *L'Humanité*, May 11, 1964. Collection L'Humanité 2935PER/173, Archives du Parti Communiste Français, Archives Départementales de la Seine-Saint-Denis.

a pop-up exhibit of her artwork in the theater's lobby), it included original music and a performance by composer Jean Wiéner, a set by French chanteuse Christine Sèvres, African poetry recited by Senegalese actor and musician Bachir Touré, songs in Quechua and Spanish performed by Peruvian singer Alberto Quintanilla, a piece performed with marionettes, and Griliquez herself singing "the blues in French" (see figure 8.2).[59] The show opened on May 7 and played four nights a week through June 5, which meant that it had a four-day overlap with the last week of Parra's MAD exhibit.[60] Considering that a show of that breadth does not open without several rehearsals, it is safe to presume that Parra was very busy during the month of May 1964.

Vivre received mixed reviews in the press, as did Parra's performance in it. A piece published in the communist daily *L'Humanité* was overwhelmingly positive, including its appraisal of Parra: "Violetta [*sic*] Parra proposes a stopover in Chile, and what a stopover! . . . She has an incredible presence when it comes to folk music."[61] In contrast, the music critic for the weekly *Arts* praised Christine Sèvres, but panned all of the other acts for being so lousy that the show should have been called not "Vivre" (To Live), but "Survivre" (To Survive). Demonstrating that not all Europeans were admirers of Latin American folk music, he wrote that Sèvres was so good that she could even make you forget "the tedium of Chilean and Peruvian folklore."[62]

Though not a formal review, Peruvian folk singer Quintanilla's commentary provides a rare opportunity to grasp how Parra's assignation or adoption of an Indigenous identity within a European context might clash with the more culturally defined understanding of Indigeneity prevalent in Latin America. As regards his performing alongside Parra in the revue, Quintanilla found the overall experience "unpleasant because she represented herself as an Indian, but did not speak any native language, whereas I did. This resulted in a needless competition [between us]."[63] His criticism suggests that were Parra to have asserted an Indigenous identity in Quintanilla's native Peru or her native Chile, she likely would have been viewed as an imposter.

One notable post-MAD-exhibit event was Parra's purchase of a VW van with money from the sales of her artwork. Ángel described it: "It was a sort of van, with curtains, that she used like a trailer home. She would park it on a street in Paris and sleep there. She kept all her stuff in it, from a portable stove to her tapestries, paintings, and instruments."[64] The VW van, along with Parra's penchant for wearing peasant blouses and long skirts, led more than one of her acquaintances to conclude that she "was a hippie before hippies were cool."[65]

Though potentially a practical solution for someone as nomadic as Parra, the van also created problems. First, Parra did not know how to drive. Second, Favre, who did, had accumulated so many tickets over years of driving other people's cars badly—"without a license, without brakes, against traffic, and beyond the logical world of the Swiss"—that he owed substantial fines that he would need to clear up before he could renew his driver's license.[66] Third, the van had to be moved every three hours when parked in Paris to avoid getting a ticket.[67] Parra took driving lessons to try to resolve the first obstacle, though it is uncertain whether she ever actually learned how to drive.[68] It is also unclear whether Favre ever resolved the problem of his license by paying the fines that he owed. What is certain is that Parra began accumulating her own stash of Parisian parking tickets and the corresponding hassles that resulted from not paying them.[69]

Parking tickets were the least of her worries. Life was never carefree for Parra. She suffered from profound bouts of homesickness for Chile, especially after her children and granddaughter returned there in mid-1964. Her relationship with Favre continued to be strained across this period as well. Parra was possessive to the point of obsession. She sent one friend to spy on him in Geneva and convinced another to drive her there unannounced in the hope (or fear) that she would catch Favre romancing another woman in flagrante—though her suspicion in this instance proved unfounded. Beyond being wracked with jealousy, Parra missed Favre terribly when they were not together. He would sometimes call her at La Candelaria, since she had no phone of her own, and they would catch up that way. Mostly, however, they wrote to each other.

Indeed, Parra was a prodigious letter writer. She wrote numerous love letters to Favre in Geneva and plenty of other letters to family and friends in Santiago and, in Blaya's case, General Pico. Some are in prose, others are lengthy poems, some rhymed, others in free verse. More than a few are painful to read, as through them Parra expresses the depths of her depression, loneliness, emptiness, confusion, anger, and utter exhaustion. In one, Parra writes, "If instead of letters they were thread, I would have enough to bind all the world's wounds." She continues, "and of course I could also stitch shut the traps of those who speak badly of me, and there are more of them out there than I would think possible."[70]

Parra left evidence that she wanted her letters preserved. She wrote as much at one point to Favre, instructing him to "save my letters. . . . They will be helpful later on, when Titiana [Tita] wants to know her grandmother's secrets."[71] Isabel would end up publishing many of them in her book, *El libro mayor de Violeta Parra* (Violeta Parra's Ledger). Some are so hauntingly beautiful that literary critics have made them the object of their inquiry.[72] I offer a fragment of one of her love letters to Favre here as example:

Someone seems to have been here. . . . I don't remember very well, and he left one morning while I was sleeping. I think that he kissed my face or maybe I dreamed all of that. . . .

What other details, what other details? Aha! He washed his feet every night. And he liked salami, wine, and bread.

All of this must be true, because why would I be inventing or dreaming of guitars with salami, or pants with a blond man inside of them who washes his feet. Surely this gentleman must be somewhere. After all, salami can be found anywhere and water to wash one's feet with as well. . . .

Pants, check, guitar, check, salami, check, four strands of hair, check. . . . And a clarinet too. Nobody here plays clarinet. And yet there it is lying peacefully in its case.

I don't understand anything. If you see him around, this gentleman who washes his feet every night, tell him that the pants, the salami and the wine, the guitar and the clarinet.

. . . My name is Violeta Parra, but I am not so sure. Only that the clarinet is here, in front of my eyes. Maybe it plays by itself. I'm going to look at it. Its wood is soft, as soft as the skin of a guy who slept by my side and washed his feet.

Is it possible for a man to change himself into a clarinet? . . .

Here is a bottle of wine, bread, salami, and also a very ugly, very small woman who weeps all the time, who knows nothing of life, who understands nothing.[73]

Wardrobe Dilemma

Sometime in mid-1964, Parra decided to return to Chile for a few months. She wanted to see her family. She also wanted to take advantage of her return ticket before it expired—and, one imagines, avoid the "artists' graveyard" of another summertime in Paris. She made sure to obtain a letter of support prior to her departure from MAD curator Michel Faré addressed to the rector of the University of Chile. In it, Faré attests to the success of Parra's MAD exhibit, notes that proposals to show her work at other museums were already in progress, and encourages the rector to back Parra's future projects in her homeland.[74] Faré also arranged for Parra to leave her van in the museum's parking garage while she was away. As Parra notes in her song "A Chilean in Paris," Monsieur Faré was "so very sweet."

Parra traveled home triumphant from her solo show at MAD and determined to show up dressed in a style commensurate with her European success. The problem was that she had spent much of the money she had made from the exhibit on her van purchase, while the rest had somehow vanished. In two separate letters to Favre, she expressed genuine concern that she would make a bad impression due to the sorry state of her wardrobe, which she described as "ugly and worn." She pleaded with him to either send money or else buy the clothing items on the list she had provided him on credit and send them to her in Paris. "It is not that I have become pretentious, it's just that I look poor," she explained.[75]

Parra's desire not to appear poor highlights the contradictions and complexities that identifying as a poor person could engender. On the one hand, her allegiance to the pueblo and corresponding disdain for the rich were unyielding elements of her identity. On the other hand, Parra wanted to demonstrate to her compatriots that she was becoming a world-class artist, and was determined to dress accordingly.

On a broader scale, Parra's wardrobe dilemma calls into question whether those elements of class and ethnic-racial identity that enhanced her authenticity as an artist in Europe would do the same for her in Chile. In the case of her identity as a poor person—introduced in her autobiography in décimas and consolidated in Europe, where she had come to symbolize the downtrodden masses of the Third World in the eyes of her audience—the answer was a qualified yes. Yes, because Parra's narrative of poverty ultimately prevailed, and qualified because in Chile, where those masses resided, many were substantially poorer than she. People like the maids lined up outside the radio station seeking employment that time Parra was confused for one of them. Or like Luisa, the Mapuche woman who was both Parra's housecleaner and the inspiration for her manifesto, "I Sing of the Difference." Or, for that matter, like most of Parra's folk informants.

Parra's life had been privileged in comparison. Though from rural Malloa, Parra's mother had been raised with a level of comfort unknown to the majority of Chile's agricultural workforce, while Parra's father had been a schoolteacher and classically trained musician who had taught his children arias and encouraged their other artistic pursuits. In adulthood, Parra's overlapping professions of folklorista, musician, and visual artist afforded her opportunities that most Chileans could not even imagine, including her travels to Europe. Scarce as the economic rewards of her diverse professional activities may have been, she nonetheless owned a plot of land in La Reina, purchased with the royalties from her 1954 popular single, "The Gardener," as well as the house that sat on it thanks to her successful lawsuit against US big band leader Les Baxter. Though her rich or pituca/o friends may have found it rustic, her "house of sticks" was a model of comfort when compared with the squalid conditions of those who lived in the burgeoning shantytowns that ringed Santiago. Violeta's tendency to mask these social advantages while highlighting and, in some instances, inflating (or even inventing) the hardships she and her family had endured is what lead her brother Nicanor to humorously accuse her of being a "social descender" or someone who downplays their social status.

Violeta was skilled at constructing and performing identities. Most of her followers in Chile, as in Europe, accepted the poorer version of her and her family's history without question. Many of her Chilean fans had been primed to embrace this version of Parra since her reinvention in the 1950s as a folklorista who performed her authenticity off stage as well as on. Bound together in a representational spiral, Parra and her admirers would accentuate Parra's otherness vis-à-vis the culturally sophisticated milieu that many of them inhabited but that she presumably did not. The thoroughness and speed with which Parra and her Chilean devotees prevailed in imposing her socially descending foundational narrative would be confirmed in early 1967 by the number of obituaries that echoed its components, true or otherwise—her impoverished tenant-farming maternal grandparents, her seamstress mother who toiled through the night to feed ten children—and its omissions—her wealthy-by-provincial-standards paternal grandparents and schoolteacher father.[76]

As to the question of whether Parra's Indigenous identity—first announced in Buenos Aires, then augmented in Europe—was transferrable to Chile, the answer was a categorical no. In Europe and European-identified social circles in Argentina, Parra was perceived as having clear and defining "Indian" features. Her Indian-ness, in turn, added value to her work from the perspective of both artist and audience. In Chile, in contrast, the cultural boundaries that separated native peoples from Chileans during Parra's lifetime made it unlikely that she would either self-identify or be racialized as Indigenous.[77] There, the consensus view—including Parra's—was that the families she visited in the south of Chile who spoke and sang in Mapudungun, dressed in traditional Mapuche attire, and lived in traditional Mapuche *rucas* (huts) in traditional Mapuche communities were Indigenous. Parra was not, and any attempt on her part to claim an Indigenous identity bore the risk of making her appear an imposter or inauthentic—which, in essence, was Quechua-speaking Peruvian musician and *Vivre* cast member Alberto Quintanilla's criticism of her.

Significantly, Parra makes no mention of an Indigenous forebear in her autobiography in verse, despite devoting several of its décimas to her family lineage. Nor can I find an instance of Parra claiming Indigenous ancestry in any of the interviews that she granted in Chile over the years. She must have raised the possibility at some point with her mother Clarisa, however, as Carmen Luisa could still recall the incident years after it occurred. Her grandmother had insisted that Violeta was lying, that there had "never been any Indian in the family." Carmen Luisa had believed Violeta, though, because Clarisa could be a little "mediocre" (read racist) in this regard.[78]

Clarisa's vehement disavowal of an Indigenous relative, no matter how distant, points to the other reason why Violeta was unlikely to have been racialized as Indigenous within a Chilean context: any acknowledgment that her physical traits were likely the result of a mixture of European and Native ancestry would automatically impugn large swaths of the Chilean population that shared those same traits at a time when deep-seated prejudices against native peoples permeated Chilean society.

The fact that Parra was not racialized as Indigenous in Chile did not mean that she was not racialized there. She was, but through the prism of class. In keeping with the confluence of classism and racism in Chilean society, the very traits that led many Europeans to perceive her as "Indian"—her darker skin hue and small stature—led many Chileans to perceive her as a mujer del pueblo (woman of the people) in the class-based meaning of pueblo as the working poor. Take the list of attributes that Pablo Huneeus, an upper-class Chilean who met Parra when he was working as a researcher for the United Nations in Geneva, compiled to explain why the majority of the Chilean diplomatic corps would not give her the time of day: "That *huasa* [country girl] with a *chillanejo* [from Chillán] air, short, *morena* [dark-skinned], and cheeky did not fit the 'image of the country' that the S.O.B.'s in the government ministries peddled."[79] The traits that purportedly earned Parra the rejection of Chile's diplomatic elite included "short" and "dark," not because they identified her as an *india* (Indian), but as a huasa, used derisively in this case to mean something like a "hillbilly" or ignorant peasant woman.

In acutely class-conscious Chilean society, Parra's appearance as a mujer del pueblo could contribute to her exclusion or inclusion, depending on the context. For many members of Chile's more European-looking upper class, her petite stature and darker skin were evidence of her class-racial inferiority. Inversely, members of the pueblo with whom Parra shared what were commonly perceived as the physical markers of their social class might welcome her resemblance to them. When folk informant Rosa Viveros described Parra as morena (dark-skinned), and "about the same height as me," for example, she was interpreting Parra's physical attributes as signs that Parra and she were "the same" or equals.[80]

Santiago Interlude

Parra flew back to Chile in August 1964, presumably dressed in new clothing.[81] She had received some recognition in Chile over the course of her two-and-a-half-year absence. There had been press coverage of her show at the Museum of Decorative Arts—which most everyone including Parra referred to simply as "the Louvre." The Department of Education had approved a new and obligatory national high school curriculum that included some of the traditional songs that she had collected, along with others collected by Margot Loyola and Cuncumén.[82] Two of her paintings had been included in the 1963 group show, Instinctive Painting, organized by the director of the Museum of Folk Art of the Americas Tomás Lago, an old friend of Nicanor and Violeta, in conjunction with the University of Chile's Art Extension Program. In the exhibition pamphlet, Lago praised the works on display for their innocent and childlike qualities.[83] Apparently, *El Mercurio* art critic Antonio R. Romera was not convinced in the case of Parra's paintings. A rare voice for the time, he questioned whether her artwork should be labeled "instinctive," writing, "In Violeta Parra, the naïve is intermingled with deliberate intention. Put another way, it is not so naïve."[84]

Parra had also been twice excluded during her time away in Europe, although the extent to which she was aware of this remains uncertain. The first exclusion was recounted by Leopoldo Castedo, a historian and Spanish Republican exile who made Chile his second home. He and his wife, Carmen Orrego, director of the University of Chile's Musical Education Extension program, had served together on the organizing committee for Image of Chile, a weeklong program of cultural activities held in Washington, D.C., under the auspices of the US State Department in September 1963. When they proposed that Parra be brought to DC to participate in the gala, a high-ranking official from the Chilean embassy in the United States had expressed his outrage at "such a crazy idea." "Why would we bring that penniless slob [rota desgreñada] into the company of such distinguished figures, and to represent Chile no less?"[85] His strenuous objection to their proposal may well have reflected the conservative politics of then-president of Chile Jorge Alessandri, under whom the diplomat served. At the same time, his use of the term rota, employed in this instance as a class insult, stands as yet another example of the pervasive and unabashed classism of Chilean society that Parra had to contend with throughout her life.

The details of Parra's second exclusion are somewhat vague. Apparently, Thiago de Mello, the Brazilian cultural attaché to Chile who had invited Parra to be part of the 1961 group show at the Museum of Modern Art in Rio, later arranged for her artwork to be included in Chile's exhibit at the 1963 São Paulo Art Biennial. Its selection was allegedly controversial, however, as most contemporary Chilean art critics did not consider Parra to be a "real painter." According to one source, her pieces made it all the way to São Paolo, where the Chilean officials who were in charge of mounting the exhibit refused to hang them.[86]

Parra returned to Chile just as the 1964 presidential race was entering its last weeks. She threw herself into the campaign for Salvador Allende, candidate for the leftist coalition, the Popular Action Front (Frente de Acción Popular or FRAP). Parra performed at political rallies alongside Isabel and Ángel and other leftist musicians, many of whom would go on to found the Chilean New Song movement.[87] On the artistic front, she participated in the massive art show Exhibition in Solidarity with the People of Chile. Allende himself had put out the call to artists and intellectuals the world over to show their solidarity with his campaign by contributing a piece to the exhibit, which received over 1,000 submissions, including paintings, sculptures, books, musical scores, and handicrafts. Parra donated her painting The Death of the Little Angel, depicting the ritual of the wake for the little angel (now part of Chile's Museum of Contemporary Art's collection).[88]

Allende's rival in the presidential campaign was Eduardo Frei Montalva, leader of the newly formed Christian Democratic Party, whose reformist political platform coincided with the goals of the US-backed Alliance for Progress, and whose campaign was supported by millions of clandestine dollars furnished by the CIA. On September 4, 1964, Frei won the presidential election handily with 56 percent of the votes versus Allende's 39 percent.[89] Parra was beyond disappointed with the election's outcome. At a postelection meeting called by the Communist Party, she publicly criticized its leadership for what she considered to be its weaknesses. According to Nicanor, who was also in attendance, "She turned into a raving lunatic! And she didn't leave one man standing, and that was at a general meeting of the Central Committee! And the epithets that she used . . . !"[90]

While in Chile, Violeta recorded a single of cuecas with Isabel for the new record label Demon, a subsidiary of RCA. The cuecas were arranged in the style of folkloric sister acts (and música típica artists), with Ángel on guitar and studio musicians on piano, bass, drums, and tambourine.[91] The single's release was timed to coincide with the September Independence Day festivities. Violeta was very happy with it and crowed that it should be featured on every jukebox in Santiago.[92]

Parra also recorded much of the material for the Odeon LP that would be released the following year under the title *Recordando a Chile* (Chile on My Mind) during her 1964 interlude in Santiago.[93] It included the whimsical song that she had composed in French in the style of a French waltz, "Écoute moi, petit" (Take Heed, My Little One). The song's lyrics provide a clue as to why Parra was once again eager to return to Europe. In its chorus, she asks, "How is it that I'm in Paris now?" (*Comm'il est que je suis à Paris?*) In its verse, she answers,

It was my brother who prompted me
To understand music well.
It was my brother who told me:
"You have to work the clay."
"Airplanes," he told me,
"Straight to Paris they go.
Do not fear, your artwork
It is not valued here.
Take heed, my little one."

*C'est mon frère qui m'a fait
bien connaître la musique.
C'est mon frère qui m'a dit:
"Il faut travailler l'argile."*

Il m'a dit: "Les avions
ils vont droit jusqu'à Paris.
N'aies pas peur, tes travau
ils n'ont rien à faire ici."[94]

Parra's Last Year in Europe

Parra went back to Europe in October 1964, where she stayed until her final return to Chile mid-1965. She convinced her friend Adela Gallo to accompany her there. Gallo recalled, "It was after we lost the '64 [presidential] campaign, Violeta told me, we've got nothing going on here, let's go to Europe."[95] The plan was that they would travel across Europe in Parra's van for six months. Parra would perform, Gallo would film her, and then they would send the material to be aired on Chilean television. Parra covered their travel expenses, and the two left for Paris within days of each other, Parra by plane and Gallo by ship because it was cheaper.

Gallo arrived in Paris a few weeks later expecting Parra to be there to greet her, but Parra was nowhere to be found. Gallo fended for herself as best she could alone in a strange city where she had few contacts and could not speak the language. Parra arrived a week later and met up with Gallo at the Café Danton, informal headquarters for Chilean expatriates in Paris.[96]

Gallo would later imply that Parra's delay had been of a romantic nature. Parra's flight to Paris had made a stopover in Madrid, where Parra purportedly had been reminded of the existence of a certain Pepito (most likely her Spanish lover, Paco Rus) to whom she had entrusted her guitar before leaving Paris at the end of her first European stay eight years prior. She got off the plane to go find him and retrieve her guitar. Pepito was very happy to see her again, and the reunited lovebirds left Madrid on an excursion to other parts of Spain for a few days. Parra then managed to talk her way onto another flight and showed up in Paris a week late, her newly recovered guitar in hand.[97]

Gallo's account of Parra's dalliance in Spain, if accurate, suggests that Parra allowed herself the freedom in her relationships with men that was tolerated, if not condoned, for men in Chilean society, but not for women. Parra laid out her unconventional philosophy of love in an interview with the women's magazine *Eva*, granted toward the end of her mid-1964 interval in Santiago: "One of the most beautiful things about love is that a lover can move on, but the sentiment remains. One lover leaves, but another will always come along, without our ever forgetting the former one. On the contrary, [that past lover] helps us to better care for the one who is to come." She concludes, "We women and men are essentially made up of what everyone whom we have ever loved has left in our hearts."[98] Parra's belief in the essential equality of women and men, expressed in this last statement and enacted in her purported affair with Pepito, underpinned her ongoing rebellion against patriarchy's constraints.

Finally back in Paris, Parra went to L'Escale, only to learn that the club no longer had a spot for her in its lineup; when she did not show up at the start of September as promised, the club manager had hired a replacement.[99] Apparently, Parra's boast that the boîte had assured her lifelong employment was yet another of her overstatements. As for La Candelaria, it was no longer an option. The last time Parra had performed there she had thrown a bombo—a large drum, potentially far more injurious than a shoe or maraca—at someone in the audience who was eating and talking while she sang, and the owner had decided he would rather have his customers safely enjoy a meal at the club than have Parra work there.[100]

Parra's hopes of finding steady work in Paris dashed, she convinced Gallo to drive her to Geneva. They picked up Parra's van from the MAD parking lot and arrived unannounced at Favre's doorstep late that night.[101] Gallo went back to Paris the next day. As for Parra's proposal that she and Gallo produce a documentary on Parra's European performances for Chilean television, it never happened. In an interview years later, Gallo declared that it would have been a great project but that it had been doomed from the start. Asked why it failed, she replied it was because Parra "got bored, because she got sick, because she caught a cold . . . because everything and because she didn't feel like it."[102]

The day Gallo returned to Paris was also the day that Parra upped the tally of guitars that she broke on people's heads, only this time she did so with an added twist. Favre recounts the incident in his autobiography. It was Sunday afternoon and the couple were alone at last to enjoy each other's company. They heard a loud knocking at the door. Favre's musician friends had come to pick him up so that they could all go to the airport, as arranged, to serenade another friend who was arriving from Peru. Favre, who had forgotten all about the plan, yelled through the door for them to go without him. They responded that that was fine, but that they needed the guitar that they had left in his flat the previous day. Parra yelled at them to stop fucking around, but they insisted that they needed the guitar. Favre continues, "All of a sudden, I see Violeta get up from the bed, take the guitar, throw the door wide open, and stand in front of my stunned friends, and [she did] all this completely naked. She takes the guitar in her two hands and hits the guy closest to her over the head with it, and she makes him a beautiful poncho [out of the guitar] that goes all the way down to his elbows, and shouts: 'You wanted the guitar? Well, here it is!' Then she shut the door and double-bolted the lock."[103]

Parra lived with Favre in Geneva for most of the remainder of her time in Europe, roughly from November 1964 to August 1965, returning to Paris only for brief periods. She devoted much of her time to creating more tapestries, paintings, masks, and other pieces, which she exhibited on at least three occasions at local galleries. She also continued to write new songs and musical works. She composed several instrumentals with marked Indigenous influences for guitar, quena, and percussion to perform as a duo with Favre. In a sign that her musical nationalism was waning, she learned how to play the Venezuelan cuatro, a small, guitar-like instrument named after its four strings—though Parra insisted on renaming it the "guitarilla" or "little guitar" in a quirky effort to distance it from its country of origin.[104]

Parra also added a new medium to her artistic portfolio around this time: bas reliefs that she made from papier-mâché. In a 1965 interview, she explained, "I did not have money to buy paint, so I thought to myself: I have to invent something that you can't buy in a store, but that you can find lying around. . . . And all of a sudden I remembered having seen toys made out of paper a long time ago. I tried it out and was happy with the results, so I kept on going."[105]

Parra's lack of funds for basic arts supplies confirms what she matter-of-factly declared in a letter to Blaya: "Of course, you cannot make a living with art." With morbid prescience, she further stated that "art only bears its true fruit after the cadaver of its creator is devoured by worms." "That's why my guitar will always be my first line of defense when it comes to economic matters," she affirmed.[106]

Effectively, Parra continued to earn her living through music throughout this period, as she had done most of her life, while Favre worked as a painter-plasterer. Parra never landed a steady gig in Geneva that was comparable to L'Escale. Instead, she performed wherever she could: at small theaters, house concerts, and miscellaneous other venues and events. These days, she was often joined by Favre, who was swiftly becoming a master quena player. With most of the "Violeta Parra Ensemble" now back in Chile, Parra devised an ingenious way to create a fuller sound: she propped her bombo on its side and added a bass pedal to it, like on the bass drum in a drum set. Reminiscent of the one-person bands of the family circuses of her youth—or of Santiago street performers then and now—this allowed her to keep a basic rhythm with her foot as she played the guitar or another instrument with her hands. A photo from this period shows Parra and Favre seated close together on stage. She is strumming her cuatro dressed in the patchwork dress that her mother made her. He is playing the quena dressed in costume—poncho and a knitted cap with ear flaps—as an "Indian" from the Andes.[107]

A Documentary and a Book

In early 1965, Swiss art critic Marie-Magdeleine Brumagne—the same critic who had imagined herself on an Andean plateau when she first met Parra—

visited Parra in the apartment/art studio that she shared with Favre to shoot a documentary for Swiss television. The resulting eighteen-minute film, *Violeta Parra, brodeuse chilienne* (Violeta Parra, Chilean Embroiderer) is the only documentary made about Parra during her lifetime.[108] As such, it provides a unique visual record of the way Parra sang, the artistic techniques she used, her surroundings, and other aspects of her life and work as an artist and musician. At the same time, it constitutes a vivid enactment of what could be referred to as Parra's performance of authenticity.[109] Or, perhaps more accurately, as a duet performance between Parra and her interviewer, for the entire documentary is shaped by Brumagne's and Parra's preconceived notions of the authentic and Parra's status as its representative.

Parra appears in her patchwork dress, her hair loose and unkempt. The documentary shows her sequentially singing her plaintive song "¿Qué he sacado con quererte?" (What Have I Gotten from Loving You?), modeling a figure out of papier-mâché, embroidering on a large piece of burlap, painting on multiple canvases that are hanging on the wall, and dancing the cueca.

Many of the questions that Brumagne poses are meant to probe Parra's creative processes in the realm of the visual arts. "How did you make this mask?" "What are the themes that you represent in your tapestries, and are they different from the ones you cover in your paintings?" "Are you able to make them up in your head, by instinct?" Parra's responses are unassuming and open. She is a simple woman, no different from any other. Her first attempt at embroidery was a failure, and her second started as a flower that turned into a bottle that turned into a woman's head. She may be inventive, but "anyone can invent things. It's not as if it were my specialty alone." When asked if she had any training in embroidery, she answers emphatically, "No, no, no, I know nothing. The stitch I use to embroider is the simplest in the world. [And] I do not know how to draw." In combination, Parra's answers to Brumagne's often leading questions support the notion that her artistry is intuitive, not intentional—a notion that is reinforced by the film's offscreen narration, which is read (and likely written) by Brumagne.

Brumagne also asks Parra a series of questions about personal matters that, one may deduce, were of great interest to Brumagne and, by extension, Parra's European public. They include "Are you Indigenous?," to which Parra replies with what was an exaggeration, if not a boldface lie: "My grandmother was Indian . . . so I believe that I have a little bit of Indian blood"—garnering Brumagne's enthusiastic response, "It shows!" Revealingly, Parra continues, "I am mad at my mother for not having married an Indian. In any case, as you can see, my way of life is almost the same as theirs." When Brumagne complements Parra for her "beautiful dress," Parra explains that her mother made it for her, then links it to her poverty, past and present: "When I was little, my mother saved scraps of material to make my dresses. My mother was very poor, she had ten children to raise and no money. She still doesn't have any money today. . . . I, too, never have any money. I'm just like my mother."

In answer to the arguably bizarre question of which expressive medium Parra would choose, if she had to select just one, from the many that she employed as a poet, musician, tapestry-maker, and painter, Parra replies by declaring her commitment to the Chilean pueblo: "I would choose to remain among my people. . . . They are who motivate me to do all of these things." The film's narration, Brumagne's questions, and Parra's responses thus mutually reinforce each other to construct Parra as the humble yet powerful voice of her people.

Violeta Parra, Chilean Embroiderer debuted on Swiss television in May 1965. Parra would have one more triumph in the final months of her second European sojourn: after years of attempts to see her ethnographic work in print, she finally succeeded when the French editorial Maspero published her book, *Poésie populaire des Andes* (Folk Poetry from the Andes)—with its title's reference to the Andes, instead of Chile, presumably a marketing strategy. The left-leaning press was to book publishing what the communist-affiliated Le Chant du Monde label was to the record industry. It was best known for publishing works that denounced French colonialism, including Frantz Fanon's *The Wretched of the Earth*, first published in France in 1961 (and promptly censored by French authorities). Parra's bilingual (French-Spanish) book was part of the press's literary series *Voix* (Voice[s]), aimed at granting "a 'voice' to those people whose cultures were disappearing or in danger."[110]

Folk Poetry from the Andes includes lyrics of folk songs Parra collected along with brief explanations of their various genres, and translated excerpts from the manuscript that would be published posthumously as *Cantos folklóricos chilenos* (Chilean Folk Songs). Its final section is devoted exclusively to Parra's original songs, the majority of which are *chansons révolutionnaires* (revolutionary songs).[111]

The book received positive notice across a range of publications, from the left-leaning journals *Partisans* (published by Maspero) and *Europe* to the more mainstream daily *Le Monde*.[112] Parra's publishing success in Europe sharply contrasted with her numerous and ultimately failed attempts to get her work published in Chile.

Parra presented her book in May 1965 at an event organized by the Geneva poetry group Poesie Vivante (Living Poetry).[113] All in all, life in Geneva seemed to be going well for her (see figures 8.3 and 8.4). Her creative juices were flowing. In a letter to her friend Amparo Claro, who was then residing in Paris, Parra details her many projects, present and future: She had no more room on her walls to hang her paintings as she had produced ten new ones, all

Figure 8.3
Gilbert Favre in the Geneva apartment he shared with Violeta Parra, n.d. Courtesy of Barbara Erskine and Patrick Favre.

in her latest style of bas reliefs. She and Favre were planning to go on tour across Europe in Parra's van. They would start in Italy, then travel to other countries. She was busy preparing their repertoire and already had twenty songs, seventeen of which were originals as she was composing, on average, one song per day. She had received a windfall check for 700 Swiss francs, and the apartment she shared with Favre, though still in its usual state of disarray, now had cupboards fully stocked with everything from bacon to cream of chestnuts. Favre was "the same good guy as always," and she "as fussy as ever." In a demonstration of her awareness of the threat that her often violent mood swings posed to her current state of contentment, she wrote, "Too bad we cannot cast a personality in plaster." She signed the letter in her signature third person: "A big hug from Violeta Parra."[114]

Having convinced her friend to serve as a sort of agent for her in Paris, Parra also sent Claro a list of potential clients and suggested that Claro try selling her tapestries in front of some of the city's more upscale hotels as well.

Figure 8.4 Violeta Parra in the Geneva apartment she shared with Gilbert Favre, n.d. Courtesy of Barbara Erskine and Patrick Favre.

Parra's other plans were more grandiose. First, she was still determined to have an exhibit at the Museum of Modern Art in Paris, as she initially had proposed two years earlier. Accordingly, she urged Claro to arrange a meeting with the museum's director; "With these new pieces, I am going to enter the Museum of Modern Art like a bullet. I'm sure of it." Second, Parra hoped to meet with Pablo Picasso himself to show him her artwork and solicit his support. "If it goes well," she wrote Claro, "the price of my tapestries will go through the roof."[115] Unfortunately for Parra, Claro lacked experience and, likely, talent as an agent. In the end, she failed to arrange any meetings or sell even one piece.

Then Violeta received a letter from Isabel saying that she was needed in Chile. Although Violeta never specified exactly what the issue was, correspondence from this period makes clear that one or more of her children were in trouble. Violeta immediately put all her plans on hold and began what would end up being a months-long hustle to gather the necessary funds for her and Favre's return to Chile: "I need every penny to see my little ones. . . . I have to get back to them. It all makes me so sad! . . . Everything was going so well and now everything has changed in an instant."[116]

Parra reached out to her friends for support. Gampert organized two benefit house concerts.[117] Brumagne convinced Geneva gallery owner Edwin

Engelberts to mount an exhibit of Parra's work. Parra and Favre drove to Paris to collect several pieces that she had left there the year before to include in the exhibit, and retrieved other pieces from Brumagne's home in Lausanne where they were being stored.

The haphazard way in which Parra left her artwork in the care of friends and acquaintances created logistical challenges. On one occasion, several of her bulkier tapestries that had been strapped down to the roof of her van flew off and onto the roadside while being transported from one place or another, to the great distress of all those involved.[118] Parra's dispersal of her artwork during her lifetime continues to complicate its full accounting and retrieval to this day. Sadly, those pieces such as her ceramics or wire sculptures that could not easily be tied to the top of a vehicle or packed into a trunk have all but vanished.

Franc by franc, Parra and Favre amassed the money that they would need to make the journey back to Chile, Parra through her art sales and music and Favre through his day job as a house painter. Parra's letters reveal that she had at least a rudimentary understanding of the local art market and its price spectrum. In a letter to her children in Santiago, she provides a detailed accounting of her sales. The good news was that the proceeds would now cover not only the cost of her and Favre's travel to Chile but also the presents and *encargos* (requested items) she planned to bring back with her.[119]

Parra and Favre agreed that Favre would travel back to Chile by sea. In addition to being less expensive, this would allow him to transport his film equipment and Parra's instruments and artwork. Parra signed over her van to him, which he was to sell to help pay for his ocean liner ticket. She meant to leave for Chile before he did but got held up in Paris until August 1965. She left most of her tapestries and paintings behind in Geneva, scattered between Favre's apartment and other sites, as she intended to return there in 1966 for what she asserted on more than one occasion was an already-in-the-works show at the city's Museum of Art and History—a venerable institution that, if not quite the Louvre Palace, still had an impressive neoclassical façade and occupied an entire city block of downtown Geneva.[120]

A Farewell Interview

Shortly before leaving Geneva for the last time, Parra was interviewed for the Swiss magazine *Radio-TV Je Vois Tout*, though for reasons unknown the piece was only published in 1970.[121] A more extensive audio version has since been made available.[122] The interview was conducted at Favre's apartment as Parra was getting ready to return to Chile after three years in Europe. In the audio recording, Parra speaks to the reporter and photographer in a relaxed and friendly tone, and in fluent French. The overall impression is that she is taking stock of her situation, as one might do when preparing for a major journey home after being away for so long. She pulls out a box full of reel-to-reel tapes and talks about her work as a folklorista: over 200 folk songs recorded on LPs produced in Chile, the German Democratic Republic, Argentina, France, and England. She explains how she composes music, seeing as she does not know musical theory or notation: she gets a melody in her head and it just comes out ("It's as easy as making soup. . . . I'm sure you could do it too"). She shows the journalists her artwork and vaunts her achievements: past shows at the Louvre and the Museum of Modern Art in Brazil, and one—she is almost certain—coming up within a few months at Geneva's Museum of Art and History. On the topic of abstract art, she notes that all her sculptures are figurative but thinks she might create some abstract pieces in the future as "I like a good abstract." She plugs her recently released book of folk songs and original songs, *Folk Poetry of the Andes*.

When asked if she is popular in Chile, Parra boasts that she is "more well-known than the housefly." To the question of what her relationship with her public is like, she responds, "I do not see a difference between the artist and the public, it's the miracle of contact." In a more intimate passage, she talks about how much she misses her children and explains why she left their father, her first husband (he wanted someone to cook and to clean, and "it just wasn't that interesting" to her). She hints at her struggles with depression (sometimes she does nothing at all, no playing the guitar, no tapestries, nothing at all, not even sweeping the floor). On a more philosophical note, she laments that the modern world is destroying Indigenous and folk cultures, expresses her fears for the future of humanity, and affirms where she stands on all of this: "I am happy to be able to wander back and forth between my very ancient soul and this present-day life."

As they wrap up, the reporter asks Parra if she plans to continue traveling. True Chilean pat'e perro (wanderer) that she was, she responds, "Yes, I will do so all my life because I can't stay in one place. I haven't left for Chile yet and I'm already thinking about what I will do when I return here from Chile."

In August 1965, shortly after the interview was conducted, Parra returned home to Santiago. Eighteen months later, on February 5, 1967, she committed suicide. As the Swiss reporter who interviewed her in mid-1965 would write in the introduction to his article when it finally appeared in 1970, "And what was supposed to be but an *au revoir* [until I see you again] became an *adieu* [farewell]."[123]

Chapter 9

New Songs

Parra's announced arrival from Europe in August 1965 was eventful in that she did not arrive as announced. Favre had returned earlier by ship to Chile, where he had immediately been incorporated into Isabel and Ángel's musical activities. A few weeks after his arrival, he received a letter from Violeta containing the information for her return flight to Chile. He alerted the press, whose interest in Violeta was high due to her European success. Word traveled, and on the day of her expected arrival an "enormous crowd" was at the airport to greet her, with "cameras to film her descent from the airplane, reporters, photographers, plus friends and a multitude of *fans*." One by one, the passengers deplaned, but no Violeta. The angry reporters demanded an explanation, and all Favre could do was show them her letter detailing her travel plans.[1]

The next day, Favre received a telegram from Parra explaining that she had missed her connecting flight in Brazil and would provide him with her new itinerary soon. When she sent him her new flight information, he once again notified the press of Violeta Parra's impending arrival. This time, however, there was less fanfare and fewer people awaited her: just Favre, some family members, two or three colleagues, and one or two reporters.[2] A reporter from the communist daily *El Siglo* later recalled how a few people at the airport had recognized Parra and applauded as she passed by.[3] The miscommunication, frustration, and scattered applause surrounding Parra's return to Chile set the tenor of her final year and a half of life.

A New Folk Music Scene

Parra was returning to a country on a path of accelerated social transformation and increased political polarization, and these trends would only deepen over the remainder of the decade. President Eduardo Frei's Christian Democratic government had come to power in 1964 and embarked on an agrarian reform program that would further the organization and radicalization of rural workers. The following year saw the founding of the Far Left political party, the Revolutionary Left Movement (Movimiento de Izquierda Revolucionaria or MIR) that advocated for revolutionary change through armed struggle. The mobilization of urban workers and students intensified across the period, with frequent strikes and other labor disputes, and with demonstrations of thousands of protesters. Meanwhile, the *pobladores* or poor urban dwellers led several successful land takeovers in the greater Santiago region.

On the cultural front, the expanding educational opportunities and buying power of the children of Chile's growing middle class and a small segment of more privileged working-class families shifted the country's youth culture into high gear. To give just one example of its vertiginous rise, the three Chilean youth-oriented entertainment magazines *El Musiquero*, *Rincón juvenil*, and *Ritmo de la juventud* were all founded between 1964 and 1965. As or more impacting as increased consumerism and youth's cultural influence was the generalized sense among leftists, young and old alike, that "revolution and the second independence of Latin America were . . . just around the corner."[4]

In keeping with the immediacy, reach, and conformity of the global music industry, the musical panorama Parra encountered upon returning to Chile closely resembled the one she had just left behind in France: rock and roll was still king on both sides of the Atlantic and The Beatles were well on their way to becoming the most popular band everywhere and of all time.[5] Isabel, Ángel, and Carmen Luisa had all become instant Beatles fans. Even a determined cultural nationalist like Violeta was not immune to the English band's charms.[6] According to her soon-to-be daughter-in-law Marta Orrego Matte, Violeta was so impressed by the way The Beatles revolutionized music that she declared, "That's what we need to start doing."[7] Her favorite Beatles song was "Yesterday."[8]

In terms of Chilean music, "new" was the operative term in the mid-1960s. The two most popular musical genres literally declared their newness in their respective labels of "nueva ola" (new wave) and "neofolklore," also known as the "new folkloric wave." The young pop stars of the Chilean *nueva ola* sang in English using adopted Anglo names in a style that was a cross between US rock and Italian balladry, though a few of them eventually added Spanish-language songs to their repertoire.[9] The *neofolkloristas* (neo folk singers), who were just behind the "new wavers" in Chilean music rankings, performed folk-derived music in various modernized styles.[10] Music critic and producer Camilo Fernández recorded and promoted both new musical genres on his new record label, Demon. By the end of the decade, a third new musical genre, this one associated with the political Left, would take on the name of *nueva canción* or "new song."

As is often the case with popular musical genres, these new categories were poorly defined. Neofolklore was particularly so. Its versatile roster featured the hit all-male vocal ensemble Los Cuatro Cuartos (The Four Fourths) and their female counterparts, Las Cuatro Brujas (The Four Witches). They performed jingle-esque arrangements of folk songs in elaborate four-part harmony, accompanying themselves on guitars and the Argentine bombo, in a style that was strongly influenced by both the latest trends in Argentine folk-derived music and radio advertising. The end result sounded something like Chilean folk music meets the Argentine folk revival meets doo-wop. But the amorphous label "neofolklore" also encompassed several of the leftist musicians who would become associated with the Chilean New Song, including Patricio Manns, Rolando Alarcón, Isabel and Ángel Parra (both as soloists and as the duo Los Parra), and Víctor Jara.[11] The neofolklore craze would peak in 1966, when both Los Cuatro Cuartos and the duo Los Parra earned top awards from the record industry, then decline as fast as it had risen. Los Cuatro Cuartos would break up within the year, while Los Parra would lose the passing label of neofolkloristas and become known as New Song artists by the end of the decade.

Brief though its moment may have been, neofolklore presented its young adherents with a fresh and appealing folk-derived alternative to both música típica and the more traditionalist songs of the 1950s Chilean folk revival. Neofolklore also had its share of detractors, including many música típica artists and traditionalist folkloristas.[12] They accused the neofolkloristas of producing a music that was neither "new" nor folkloric, rather an imitation of the latest fads in Argentina. They also condemned the neofolkloristas' decision to eschew the huaso and huasa outfits that both música típica artists and traditionalist folkloristas wore with patriotic pride and perform instead in fashionable attire: suits and ties for the men, stylish dresses for the women. In a debate published in *Ecran* between the proponents of the rival folk music styles of música típica and neofolklore, the musical director of Los Cuatro Cuartos explained the neofolkloristas' position: "To us, it seems absurd to have to dress up in a certain way to sing a tonada or cueca. . . . None of us were born in the countryside. . . . We do not dress like huasos when we're on the street, so we do not presume to do so on stage."[13]

Somewhat surprisingly, Parra was not among neofolklore's critics, at least not initially. When asked her opinion on the "so-called new wave of folklore" shortly after her return to Chile, she answered, "I believe that those who oppose the new bands are reading out of the same old playbook." "I support all those who sing, dance, [and] create," she continued, "and I'm on the side of the so-called new wave, even if it brings the wrath of all the by-the-book academics down upon me."[14]

Parra's favorable response to the latest trend in folk-derived music was likely influenced by the fact that her musician children were considered to be among the genre's rising stars. It was almost certainly influenced by the fact that the popular neofolklore band Las Cuatro Brujas recorded two of her songs, one in 1964 and the other in 1965, both of which became instant hits.[15] Parra's approval of neofolklore seems to have weakened with time, however, as when she was asked to offer her opinion on the trend a mere four months after her return interview her response was more critical: "These new folk musicians don't know which way they're going. If they want to tinker with our music, they are tinkering with it. If they want to make money, they are making it. But if they want to be the standard-bearers of our national music, then they will have to live up to those standards."[16]

Neither the música típica artists nor the more traditional folkloristas were able to compete with the trendier neofolkloristas in record sales. Beyond this point in common, the fates of the two "old wave" folk genres diverged in the mid-1960s. Música típica managed to retain its status as the obligatory musical staple of Chilean independence celebrations and similarly patriotic occasions (and continues to do so in the twenty-first century). Performers of more traditional-sounding music did not fare as well. The traditionalists had never commanded more than a niche audience at the peak of the 1950s Chilean folk revival. That audience began to dwindle by the end of the decade, and the process accelerated across the 1960s. By the time Violeta Parra returned to Chile for the last time, the folk revival that she had helped to lead was arguably in its final throes.

The Peña de los Parra

The changing social, political, and musical landscapes would have significant consequences for Parra. She would face the challenge of establishing herself as a 1960s singer-songwriter in an environment where she was best known for being a leader of the 1950s traditional folk revival, now considered passé. Parra would feel the repercussions at an interpersonal level as well. In the same way that she had been a powerful force in the folk movement of the previous decade, her children Isabel and Ángel were now playing a key role in the revitalization and innovation of Chilean folk music of the 1960s. Their growing popularity, coupled with her commensurate sense of irrelevance, strained the relationship between the two generations of Parras.

It was not so much that Violeta struggled to find her bearings in the shifting cultural tides. Still extraordinarily resourceful and productive, she always seemed to know what her next creative project would be. Nor could it be said that she was behind the times. On the contrary, like her children, she was up-to-date with or even a step ahead of many of the newest trends in Latin American folk music. It was that she often failed to receive the recognition that she craved and that she so adamantly believed she deserved for her efforts. Her failing mental health over her final years would only compound the situation.

The younger Parra musicians had made their influence felt from the moment they returned to Santiago in 1964. Enthused by the musical discoveries of their recent encounter with the Parisian–Latin American folk music scene, they helped shape and propagate the hybridized Latin American folk music that would flourish in Chile from the mid-1960s until the 1973 military coup, then be carried throughout the world by exiled Chilean musicians. As Ángel explained, "I always say that I studied for four years in Paris, but at night, in the cabarets . . . I learned Latin American folklore, how to play the cuatro, charango, tiple, quena, zampoña. And when I came back to Chile with my sister, we brought all of those instruments with us."[17] Isabel shared her brother's appreciation: "I began to play with Mexicans, Venezuelans, Paraguayans. . . . Paris opened up the Latin American continent to us . . . and I assimilated that Parisian way of singing Latin American music, which was spectacular, because . . . Paris was teeming with the best singers and songwriters in those years."[18]

Both Violeta and Favre contributed to this process of the Latin Americanization of the Chilean folk music scene as well. Favre, now considered part of the Parras' musical clan, helped to popularize the Andean quena. For her part, and although she had at first needed some persuading, Violeta returned from Paris with a Venezuelan cuatro that she now played regularly. In the year and a half that followed, she would acquire several charangos (small Andean guitars traditionally made with the shell of an armadillo) on her visits to Bolivia. She would keep one for herself and sell the others to Chilean colleagues back in Santiago who were eager to join the growing cohort of transnational Andean-inspired musicians.[19]

The Parras and Favre's introduction of musical elements from the Parisian–Latin American hybridized folk music scene, and particularly those with Andean resonance, would revolutionize the folk music scene in Chile in the mid-1960s.[20] Yet it is worth recalling here that Ángel arrived in Europe in 1962 already a quena player, while Isabel purchased her first bombo in Buenos Aires that same year. Their cases exemplify the cross-pollination that was occurring between Buenos Aires, Paris, Santiago, La Paz, and various other sites where Latin American folk music was in fashion. They serve to confirm that the transformations in question are best understood as moving not unidirectionally but rather within cultural loops.[21]

But by far Isabel and Ángel's greatest impact on the contemporary Chilean folk music scene was their decision to establish their own peña or folk music club, the Peña de los Parra. They hatched this idea while still in Paris. Their goal, in essence, was to create a venue in Santiago that would provide them with steady work akin to what they found at the Left Bank boîtes. They placed the project on hold during their first year back in Chile to dedicate themselves to other tasks such as performing for Salvador Allende's failed presidential campaign, appearing on radio and television, and recording with the new record label Demon.

For lodgings, they moved into a large, run-down colonial-style house in downtown Santiago that belonged to the family of Juan Capra, a young artist and musician who rented out its rooms to other young artists and musicians.[22] At the start of 1965, Capra left Ángel in charge of the house while he went off to study art in Paris. That is when the Parra siblings put their plan into action. They roped their uncles Roberto Parra and Juan Cereceda into building a small wooden stage in one of the house's large rooms along with rustic wooden tables and benches. A friend donated a case of cheap wine, other friends loaned the glasses to serve it in, and the folk music club opened in April 1965.[23]

The Peña de los Parra offered its public the opportunity, novel for its time and place, to experience some of the most influential folk musicians of the era perform in an intimate setting. The club's décor could best be described as homespun bohemian. A succession of audiences graffitied its white wall with their names, romantic declarations, poetry, political slogans, and drawings. Candles were set in empty wine bottles at every table, while fishing nets hung from the ceiling just as they did at L'Escale.

The Peña's original lineup included the Parra siblings and singer-songwriters Ricardo Alarcón and Patricio Manns. Within months they were joined by singer-songwriter Víctor Jara. The Peña musicians performed in casual dress that reflected the global youth fashion trends of the 1960s: turtlenecks, leather jackets, and blue jeans for the men and, for Isabel, short dresses and skirts. They thereby signaled to the members of their audience that they were no different from them. At the same time, the club's reduced space mandated that the musicians sing only a few feet away from their public. By blurring the distinctions and minimizing the physical distance between presenters and spectators, the Peña de los Parra offered its attendees a new way of experiencing the authentic, one that was linked not to an idealized rural past as proposed by the 1950s folkloristas but to an intense and "real" present.

Beyond its intimate ambience and talented lineup, the Peña was defined by its founders' leftist political ideals and commitment to expressing their politics through song. Together with an expanding cohort of songwriters of corresponding militancy, Peña musicians Ángel Parra, Ricardo Alarcón, Patricio Manns, and Víctor Jara wrote and performed songs that addressed the pressing social issues of the day: workers' protests, the fight for land reform, the student movement. They denounced US imperialism and voiced their solidarity with the Cuban Revolution and the people of Vietnam, all through song. Their preferred way to refer to the kind of songs they performed, prior to adopting the moniker of "new song" in 1969, was "committed" or "engaged songs"—as opposed to "protest songs," which they considered to be too confining a label.[24]

The left-leaning Peña de los Parra was a success from the moment it opened its doors. It was frequented by an eclectic mix of university students, political activists, writers, intellectuals, artists, amateur folk singers, and tourists. To be clear, the folk club was not a place where the working class or pueblo gathered. Rather, it was a site where more privileged leftists, both Chilean and foreign, came together to express and celebrate through music their shared political ideals and hopes for a more just society.[25] The club, which was open Thursday through Sunday, was constantly packed. Demand grew so great that the musicians started putting on two shows a night. By the time Parra returned to Chile in August 1965, the line to get into the club routinely stretched around the block.

The Peña provided a space for songwriters to try out new material, exchange ideas, and forge collaborations. In after-hour sessions that often lasted until dawn, the house musicians would swap songs with each other and with other musicians who came to the Peña after finishing their gigs at other clubs. These creative interchanges occurred during the brief span in the mid-1960s when political divisions had yet to harden between the leftist musicians who headlined at the Peña and those musicians who shared the label of "neofolkloristas" with them but whom Ángel would later categorize as "apolitical [and thus] right wing."[26]

This relative peace did not signify the absence of debates about the role that politics should play in music or that music should play in politics, just that the different factions had yet to reach the impasse they would arrive at by the close of the decade concurrent with the growing political polarization of Chilean society. Already in the Peña's first years, a breach opened between the leftist musicians and those from the more jingle-esque branch of neofolklore due to the political content of the Peña musicians' lyrics. As this occurred, the question of whether musicians should use their music to promote social change became a frequent topic of discussion in youth-oriented magazines associated with the music industry, whose reporters usually targeted their criticism at certain songwriters for their leftist tendencies. Of far greater impact, a de facto system of censorship was put into place to pressure radio stations not to air songs that were considered too politically radical—which, as Ángel would later explain, meant songs with any political content at all.

Not one to avoid controversy, Parra was drawn into the polemic. Her contribution was the song "Mazúrquica modérnica" (Modernified Mazurka), which appears on her last LP, *Las últimas composiciones de Violeta Parra* (Violeta Parra's Latest Compositions). Through the clever use of added syllables and other wordplay, Parra delivers a biting denunciation of the hypocrisy of those who would blame socially conscious songwriters for the ills of society:

I have been questionized by some individuals
asking if songs that are agitational
pose dangeration unto the multitudes:
this questionization is simply infantilated!
Such a thing only a dolt would suggestify,
within myself silently I observified.

To this inquisitivity I then respondified
that when the belly demandifies sustenance
good Christians dig in their heels and bellicosify
for the beans and the onions that they can consumify.
There is no regiment able to impedify
the little people once they become hungrified.

Me han preguntádico varias persónicas
si peligrósicas para las másicas
son las canciónicas agitadóricas:
¡ay, qué preguntíca más infantílica!
Solo un piñúflico la formulárica,
pa' mis adéntricos yo comentárica.

Le he contestádico yo al preguntónico:
cuando la guática pide comídica
pone al cristiánico firme y guerrérico
por sus poróticos y sus cebóllicas.
No hay regimiéntico que los deténguica,
si tienen hámbrica los populáricos.[27]

The Peña de los Parra became the model for the proliferation of folk clubs that opened in Santiago, Valparaíso, and other cities and towns within the next few years. In 1966 alone, fifteen to twenty new peñas were established at universities, union halls, neighborhood centers, and commercial establishments the length of Chile.[28]

Like the concurrent folk revivals of the 1950s, the reinvigorated Chilean folk music scene of the 1960s both reflected and shaped transnational trends; folk clubs with characteristics similar to the Peña de los Parra and the numerous Chilean peñas modeled after it were opening and thriving in New York, London, Paris, and other cultural centers throughout the world and across the decade, while singer-songwriters armed with guitars were writing politically engaged songs to perform in them.[29]

The Peña de los Parra would continue to be at the center of the political-cultural movement that would take on the name Chilean New Song in 1969, two years after Violeta's death.[30] New Song musicians would participate in the broader movement for political and social change in Chile and help propel it forward through their cultural activism. Largely shut out of mainstream media by the close of the 1960s, they would create their own record company and means of distribution. They would play a key role in mobilizing support for Salvador Allende's successful 1970 presidential campaign and become the musical voice of the short-lived Popular Unity coalition government that followed, one of whose slogans was "There Can Be No Revolution without Songs."

Though she was no longer alive, Parra would nonetheless have a profound impact on this younger generation of musicians, especially with the 1971 release of her LP *Canciones reencontradas en Paris* (Violeta Parra—Songs Rediscovered in Paris) containing the "revolutionary songs" that she recorded for the Barclay label in Paris in 1963. This was when Parra's politically engaged songs would first become widely known in Chile. In an oft-cited quote from a 1972 interview, Víctor Jara describes Parra's contribution to the Chilean New Song: "In the creation of this type of [politically engaged] songs, the presence of Violeta Parra is like a star that will never go out. . . . [She] showed us the path, and all we are doing is following it."[31]

The US-backed military coup of September 11, 1973, upended all of this. Soldiers ransacked and shuttered the Peña de los Parra—although according to Carmen Luisa they left Violeta's albums unscathed.[32] Víctor Jara was among the thousands of workers, students, and activists taken to a makeshift prison camp in the Chile Stadium, where he was tortured and killed.[33] Ángel Parra was imprisoned, then freed by a successful international campaign, after which he joined Isabel and thousands of other Chileans in exile. The military destroyed the New Song artists' albums, censored their music, and unofficially banned their signature instruments of charango and quena. The overwhelming majority of musicians, artists, writers, media people, filmmakers, and poets who appear in this book suffered the brutality of the dictatorship of General Augusto Pinochet.

Parra's Homecoming

Parra finally arrived back in Chile in mid-August 1965 and went straight from the airport to the Peña de los Parra. She had arranged for her mother to live in her house of sticks during the three years that she was away in Europe.

This is why Favre, upon returning to Chile several weeks before Parra, had moved into one of the rooms in the large house where the Peña was located. Parra now joined him there.

Parra's family and friends threw a welcome back party on her first evening home. At some point in the festivities, Rolando Alarcón, Patricio Manns, and Ángel took turns performing their newest compositions for her.[34] Violeta thus resumed her role as mentor to a younger generation of Chilean folk musicians, now expanded beyond the 1950s revivalist folk ensembles to include some of the most important singer-songwriters of the emerging New Song movement. Manns would later describe the relationship Violeta developed with them: "She guided many of our compositions . . . offered serious critical objections— but also warm praise—discussed with each of us individually the distinctive features of our creative endeavors, gave advice, challenged us, encouraged us." As he saw it, Parra's character represented the synthesis of her profound feminine tenderness and her "willful, aggressive, dominating, and obtrusive" traits. "When Violeta was right, it was better to shut up. And sometimes, also, when she was only half right. Or when she was wrong."[35]

Within days of her return, Parra held a press conference at the Peña where she offered an account—exaggerated, though no more than usual—of her European exploits.[36] The press conference was reasonably well attended. Parra's relations with the media over the remainder of her life would be a mixed bag. On the one hand, she was considered enough of a public figure to warrant the attention of the press—"more well-known than the housefly," as she had put it in her interview in Geneva shortly before her return to Chile.[37] On the other hand, the attention she received often highlighted not her talent or ac-complishments but her eccentricities or, in the case of an attempted suicide in January 1966, far graver concerns. As regards those new entertainment magazines founded in the mid-1960s and aimed at a more youthful audience, Parra was too old to be of much interest to them, except perhaps as the mother of rising folk stars Isabel and Ángel Parra. In Chile's politically polarized en-vironment, furthermore, Violeta, Isabel, and Ángel Parra and their many artist colleagues who were associated with the cultural Left could count on being all but ignored by those media outlets that were associated with the Right. As Violeta commented in that same mid-1965 Swiss interview, "In Chile some newspapers are not very nice to me; the Right's newspapers, the bour-geoisie's. . . . Every time I get involved with politics, these people get mad at me; they want me to just be a singer."[38]

Parra guest-starred at the Peña her first weekend home (see figure 9.1). Favre accompanied her on the quena for several numbers. As she invited him to join her on stage, she enthusiastically announced, "Trips to Europe have consequences. . . . Allow me to present to you my husband!"[39]

Figure 9.1 Violeta Parra performing at the Peña de los Parra. Photograph by Julio Bustamante. Archivo CENFOTO-UDP, Fondo Julio Bustamante, N000004, Violeta Parra en la Peña, 1965.

In fact, the couple never formalized their relationship. According to Favre, Parra would have preferred it if they had done so, but he had resisted; it would have been hellish, in his view, given Parra's possessive nature, and besides, "Why get married, anyway?"[40] Apparently, he was unfamiliar with Parra's October 1964 interview with the Chilean woman's magazine *Eva*, granted just before her return to Europe from her Santiago interlude (and thus just before her purported stopover fling with Pepito in Spain). In the interview, Parra expresses a comparably dismissive opinion to Favre's on the institution of marriage: "Personally, I steer clear of all conventions as best I can. Sometimes I feel bad that people, just because they love each other, have to go and get a marriage license . . . or that they get all dressed up in order to go to Church, whereas I believe that the only thing a true love would want would be to keep her love and her beloved hidden in order to delight in intimate celebrations of the heart."[41]

Although they apparently shared an equally dim view of marriage, Parra and Favre nonetheless referred to each other as husband and wife in public. Perhaps this was because there was no alternative language at the time to describe their relationship. For Favre, their feigned status came with certain benefits, and he made sure to let bartenders and restaurant owners know he was Parra's husband if he thought it might lead to free drinks or food.[42] As for Parra, she clearly enjoyed claiming that Favre was her husband. She even went so far in one interview as to specify the city where the couple had wed (Paris).[43] Her pretense likely reflected her noted possessiveness, as referring to Favre as her husband was a way to mark him as hers. Ever contradictory, she seems to have wanted their relationship to be viewed as conventional in society's eyes even as she both asserted that she was unconventional and acted in ways that supported her assertion. To that last point, in what was a clear and unconventional act of gender subversion, she is reported to have sent Favre letters under the name "Gilbert Parra."[44]

Violeta ran into tensions with the younger musicians of the Peña de los Parra almost immediately. The issue was simple: they operated the club as a collective, and Violeta wanted them to do things her way. Manns recalls, "She wanted to have her hand in everything and when she got to the *peña* she wanted to be in charge, to change things. . . . We put our foot down and told her 'Violeta, you are a guest here. That's all. . . . You can't just waltz in here and begin to change things on a whim.'"[45]

Violeta did not listen. Take, for instance, the time when she proposed to the Peña collective that they make a much-needed expansion of the club by tearing down one of its walls. They considered, but ultimately rejected her idea. She would not be dissuaded, however, and Ángel came home one day to find her, pick hammer in hand, having a go at the wall herself. The structural damage already done, the collective hired an architect to finish the task and Violeta got her way.[46]

Although her proposed remodel was a success in the end, other conflicts would prove more intractable. Her relationship with the founding Peña musicians quickly went from tense to dysfunctional. Things got so bad at one point that the two generations of Parra musicians stopped talking to one another altogether.[47]

According to Carmen Luisa, the underlying problem was Violeta's apprehension that her children were becoming independent: "Violeta wanted her children to sing what she wanted; in other words, to continue her control over them. . . . My mother was very matriarchal, very strong."[48] Favre concurred. He believed, further, that Violeta was to some degree jealous of her children's success: "I think that Violeta had a little bit of a complex vis-à-vis her children. All of a sudden, they were enormously successful, and their popularity bothered her a little bit. I think that she would have liked it better if she had played an important role in their success. The fact that they could manage just fine on their own made her feel as if they were getting away from her."[49]

Favre's supposition that Parra envied her children's success is neither confirmed nor refuted by her posthumously published letters. Her public discourse on the matter was inconsistent. At times she would praise Isabel and Ángel.[50] Other times she would demur that it was not her place to opine on her children's artistic talents for "it would be unseemly for me to do publicity for my own family."[51] This may also have been one of those instances when what Parra did not say was as important as what she did. The case of Ecuadorian poet Jorge Enrique Adoum comes to mind: he claimed in his memoirs both to have been a dear friend of Parra's during her second European stay and to have had no idea that Isabel and Ángel of the popular duo Los Parra were her children.[52]

Whatever their cause, the tensions made Violeta's living situation at the Peña de los Parra unsustainable. She and Favre moved back to her house of sticks in La Reina within a month of her arrival. Favre recounts that the couple felt more free and independent there than they had in downtown Santiago but that "with isolation, the quarrels between us began again."[53] More concerning than their frequent fights was Parra's escalating propensity to violence. Favre recalled one particularly vicious argument when she took a rock and hit him so hard in the back that he could not move.[54] She then spent the next three days nursing him back to health.

In need of a break from their constant fighting, Favre left on a trip to northern Chile at the end of September. Parra wrote to him in Antofagasta a few weeks later asking him to return to Santiago so that he could help her with a major endeavor that she was planning for the month of October together with her friend, the photographer Sergio Larraín: to mount a large fonda or temporary performance venue at the 1965 Santiago International Fair (*Feria Internacional de Santiago* or FISA). In his autobiography, Favre admits that he was relieved to receive her letter, as he had "no fucking idea" what he was doing up north.[55] He returned to Santiago days later.

Parra and Larraín's joint enterprise would prove consequential. It furnished Parra with both the inspiration and actual circus tent that would become her Carpa de La Reina. The Santiago International Fair was a major outdoor exposition of agricultural products and machinery. To attract more visitors, the fair organizers offered folk musicians free plots on the fairgrounds for them to construct fondas to perform in. Seeing an opportunity, Larraín and his business associate, a German woman named Gretel, made

Parra a proposal: their firm would set up the fonda, and Parra and her clan would provide the entertainment as well as traditional food and beverages. This is when Parra and Gretel came up with the idea that the ideal venue would be a circus tent. They had one made especially for the occasion, purchased on credit. The end result was a fonda much like the ones Parra had run with the help of family and friends in the late 1950s and the early 1960s, scaled up to accommodate up to 400 visitors at a time.[56]

When the fair was over, Parra made the solo decision that she would keep the tent for herself and convert it into a folk arts center. The oversize fonda had been successful in every way except financially; its total proceeds proved insufficient to cover the one-time cost of the tent's manufacture in addition to the usual expenses of running the enterprise. But Parra could not be convinced of this. She had faithfully delivered the fonda's daily earnings to Larraín's accountant, and they had seemed to her to more than enough to pay for the tent as well. "Violeta lived day to day and was not really made for bookkeeping and all that" is how Larraín would later explain it.[57]

The Santiago International Fair concluded with the question of the ownership of the tent unresolved. Or at least it was unresolved from Larraín and his partner's point of view. Parra was certain that she had earned the tent and that it was now hers. After much arguing back and forth, Larraín and his partner finally agreed to let Parra keep the tent. Larraín assumed at the time that Parra would also be taking on the debt attached to it. Parra considered the tent—debt free—to be payment for her services, fair and square. This difference of opinion would end the friendship that Parra and Larraín forged over years of collaboration and shared adventures.

The tent now in her possession, Parra's next challenge was to locate a site to raise it on. After much knocking on doors, she found her answer: Fernando Castillo Velasco, district mayor of La Reina and longtime admirer of Parra's work, would cede her the use of a substantial plot of land free of charge for thirty years. La Reina was the same, mostly middle-class community on the outskirts of Santiago where Parra's house of sticks was located. Parts of La Reina were more developed than others. The ten-acre expanse that Parra was granted to set up her Carpa was in a largely undeveloped area that was difficult to reach by public transportation. Favre and others tried to warn Parra that the location was far from ideal for establishing an entertainment venue, but there was no convincing her. As she told Favre in her signature third person, "If they want to see Violeta, they'll just have to walk."[58]

Her decision firm, Parra threw herself heart and soul into the creation of her cultural center. She retained a married couple to live on the grounds and assist with various tasks. The husband worked in construction alongside Favre, while the wife cooked the meals and helped to keep order. When Favre and the husband were unable to raise the tent between the two of them, Parra hired a crew of workers to help. Her brother Roberto would show up now and then to lend a hand as well. All together, they pulled up trees, took them to the sawmill to make planks, and then used the planks to build a wooden structure to support the tent along with a stage for the musicians. They dug two holes, one for a well and the other for a septic tank. They made adobe bricks out of straw mixed with the earth that they had dug up to level the tent's dirt floor. They used the bricks to build two rooms behind the stage, one for Violeta and the other for Carmen Luisa, who had been staying with various relatives since returning to Chile with Isabel in 1964. They built a hut for the groundskeeping-housekeeping couple and an outhouse for everyone.[59] Step by step, they readied the Carpa de La Reina for its opening day in mid-December 1965.

"I Have Not Stopped Working . . ."

The Carpa was hardly the sole undertaking to occupy Parra's time now that she was back in Chile. As she informed a reporter shortly after her arrival from Europe, "I returned home eager to get some rest, but I have not stopped working since the moment my feet touched the ground."[60] In effect, Parra was as active—or volcanic—as ever during her first year back home. People who knew her describe how she woke up every morning at dawn, finished her household chores by 7:00 A.M., then remained busy with other pursuits until late in the evening. The body of work Parra produced during this period provides ample proof of her creative energies. At the same time, her spurts of activity, interspersed as they were with bouts of depression, are consistent with the present-day consensus that she suffered from bipolar disorder (formerly termed manic depression).[61]

Foremost on Parra's full agenda were her live performances. Though no longer a resident, she continued to play regularly at the Peña de los Parra (figure 9.2). She appeared on *Chile ríe y canta* (Chile Laughs and Sings), a weekly folk music radio show, broadcast live from a downtown Santiago theater, that drew a large in-person audience of youth eager to see their favorite neofolklorista recording artists.[62] She was part of the musical lineups at a variety of fundraisers, celebrations, and other events: a benefit concert for people displaced by that winter's adverse weather; the two-year anniversary of *Chile Laughs and Sings*; the festival commemorating twenty-five years of the Communist daily *El Siglo*; the closing ceremony of the Seventeenth Congress of the Chilean Communist Party; the gala send-off concert for the huaso band Los Quincheros before its members embarked on a tour of the Soviet Union.[63] Parra made guest appearances on several other radio shows besides *Chile Laughs and Sings* and on a few television programs as well.

Outside Santiago, Parra spent a week performing at the Peña de Valparaíso, one of the many folk clubs modeled after the Peña de los Parra to open that year.[64] Matriarch and mentor that she was, Parra swept into the Valparaíso peña on the arranged day and proceeded to demand that the entire setup of stage, tables, and chairs be rearranged. It was. As occurred with the Peña de los Parra musicians, the young Valparaíso musicians took turns performing for her. In return, Parra gave them her criticism and praise, along with practical advice on how to improve their vocal technique: "Sing cuecas for at least two hours every day, lying on your back with a guitar on your chest."[65] Gonzalo "Payo" Grondona, an important figure of the Chilean New Song who was present that day, would later provide an inventory of Parra's personality traits: "Very friendly, bad-tempered, professionally demanding, bossy, matriarchal, intuitive, hard-working, pushy, prone to favoritism, opinionated, tribal, daring."[66]

The Peña de Valparaíso organizers went all out to promote Parra's shows. They placed announcements in local newspapers and posted hand-painted signs throughout the city (which were promptly removed by the police). They arranged for Parra to be interviewed on television. Parra arrived at the station and asked her hosts if she would be paid for her appearance, learned that she would not, and decided that in that case, she would not sing. She spent the entire thirty minutes of the show chatting about her trips abroad and her experiences in the Chilean countryside. Every so often, she would pick up one of the many instruments she had brought with her to the studio, explain its origins, and even strum a few bars. But she would not sing. Meanwhile in the control booth, the show's producer was frantically signaling for her to sing, to no avail. The interview ended and, livid, he demanded, "Weren't you supposed to sing?" Feigning innocence, Parra responded, "Oh! But nobody told me." She went on: "As you know, I am a peasant so I don't know anything about these things, and they make me very nervous." After Parra left the building with her entourage, she burst into laughter and exclaimed, "That will teach those shameless bastards a lesson!"[67]

The peña organizers' publicity campaign paid off. The line to get into Parra's opening show at the club stretched around the block. Demand was so great that Parra ended up extending her performances in Valparaíso through the following weekend.

Parra took on several recording projects in that first year back home. In August 1965, she went into the studio to complete the album she had begun working on during her visit to Santiago the previous year, which was released under the title *Recordando a Chile* (Chile on My Mind) shortly after. The LP features Parra's original songs performed with arrangements that, departing from her usual folk singer simplicity of voice and guitar, rely on varied instrumentations—including a horn section on one track. The recording was very much a family project, with Isabel on vocals and percussion, Ángel on guitar and quena, and Hilda on vocals. It also includes a track of Nicanor reading the lengthy poem he wrote for Violeta in 1960, "Defense of Violeta Parra," over Violeta's improvised guitar accompaniment.

Beyond a positive review in *El Siglo* and as was the case with all of Parra's prior recordings, *Chile on My Mind* received little notice in the press.[68] It was selected by the popular radio show *Discomanía* as one of the top five albums of Chilean music produced in 1965, however.[69] The program was hosted by Ricardo García, who had been the announcer for Parra's 1954 debut program on Radio Chilena *Violeta Parra Sings*, and who had remained a steadfast supporter through the years. Parra's recognition from *Discomanía* was one of the rare awards that she received in Chile over the course of a decades-long and prolific career as a musician and an artist.

Also in her first weeks back in Chile, Parra made a studio recording of the first ten décimas from her autobiography interspersed with instrumental fragments on guitar. Like her written autobiography, the recording would only be released posthumously.[70]

Sometime in the second half of 1965 Parra recorded an EP of Indigenous-sounding instrumental pieces, many of them composed while she was in Europe.[71] Released in January 1966, it featured Violeta on guitar, cuatro, and percussion, Favre and Ángel on quenas, and Isabel on bombo. Favre is identified on the album not by name but by Violeta's nickname for him: the "Musician from a Foreign Land."

Violeta also contributed to her brother Roberto's first LP, *Las cuecas de Roberto Parra* (Roberto Parra's Cuecas).[72] Produced in the second half of 1965 but not released until after Violeta's death in 1967, *Roberto Parra's Cuecas* was the second album in Odeon's new Urban Folklore series. In his liner notes for its inaugural volume, artistic director Rubén Nouzeilles explained the series' intention to highlight folk music that was "distinctly urban" and promised that in doing so it would allow listeners to "peer into . . . the city's underworld [*bajos fondos*]."[73] Roberto's LP featured his "cuecas choras" or "gangster cuecas," a subgenre of cuecas, chiefly of his own invention, that told the stories of criminals, prostitutes, and prisoners with a mix of social realism, street humor, and a strong dose of slang.[74] According to the liner notes, the cuecas were "gems of our urban folklore," composed by a "chronicler of Santiago who writes his chronicles with a guitar, kerosene can, tambourine, and a shout."[75]

Almost a decade after Violeta's controversial addition of an empty oil can to the musical instrument collection of the folk art museum in Concepción, a major Chilean record company thus adopted her more expansive definition of folklore as incorporating urban as well as rural manifestations. Fittingly,

Violeta played the *tarro* or large can on two of the cuecas on her brother's album. She also contributed the *animaciones* (animations, literally; cheering)— the shouted *dichos* or rhymed sayings that are traditionally used to "animate" the cueca. The dichos she yells poke fun at widows (one of whom has a second husband hiding under the bed), saints (who are flirting with each other), and even the devil himself (who chokes on a chicken bone while dancing in a cantina).

In addition to her musical work, Parra continued to engage with the visual arts throughout this period. She made a series of small mural paintings in one of the rooms in the Peña de los Parra. Too broke to buy proper art materials, she turned the discarded cardboard box from the refrigerator Nicanor bought for the Carpa into a canvas for one of her paintings.[76] As regards her participation in more formal art events, in December 1965 she once again had a booth at the annual open-air Arts Fair. She is also reported to have had at least two gallery shows during this period, a first (and then a second) for her in Chile; one at the Communist Party–affiliated Galería Vanguardia, and the other at the Galería Merced.[77]

Parra appears on the whole to have been less active in the realm of the visual arts during her final year and a half in Chile than she had been in Europe. This may have reflected a shift in interest on her part, away from painting, embroidery, and sculpture and toward songwriting and her Carpa. It was likely also related to the Chilean art world's near complete lack of interest in, let alone support for, her work. In Paris, Parra had reached the historical pinnacle of being the first Latin American to have a solo show at the Museum of Decorative Arts. Despite the cachet that her unprecedented European success would typically have afforded her in Chile, she would not be given the opportunity to exhibit her work at a Chilean art institution of equivalent national prestige during her lifetime.

In part this resulted from the Chilean art world's promotion of abstract art during this period, a practice that was both encouraged and supported by US cultural Cold War policies.[78] The organizers of the 1965 Arts Fair literally mapped their conceptual hierarchy of art forms onto the fair's physical layout by arranging the booths in an "orderly and progressive manner," from the "simplest" folkloric handicrafts at one end of the fair to the "most revolutionary" abstract works at the other.[79] But Parra's exclusion from the rarified milieu of Chile's fine arts was also assuredly linked to the very biographical components that enhanced her authenticity as a folklorista and an artist. Her relatively modest origins and lack of formal education or artistic training prevented her from receiving official support for her work. The fact that she was a woman in a male-dominated field was undoubtedly another contributing factor, especially since some of her artwork was in the female-defined medium of embroidery and therefore deemed more akin to homecraft than to "serious art."[80] This would seem confirmed by the only notice Parra's artwork received in press coverage of the 1965 Arts Fair; a mention of her "burlap sacks embroidered with yarn" in a short paragraph listing several of the craftswomen with works on display that year.[81]

No one from the fine arts community declared Parra's artwork unworthy of consideration. They simply ignored her. As one source described, "It wasn't as if they cussed at her, no, everyone was perfectly polite. It just didn't go anywhere."[82] In a 1966 interview, Nicanor railed against the collective indifference of his compatriots. Comparing his sister to the Chilean artist Roberto Matta, an abstract painter famous in both Chile and France, Nicanor proclaimed—exaggeratedly—that Matta himself had yet to attain the level of recognition that Violeta had earned as an artist in Europe. "Of course, here in Chile," Nicanor continued, "she is calculatedly ignored. Is it not shameful that the government of this country—not to mention the School of Fine Arts—does not take note of the feats of this extraordinary woman?" "Did you know," he asked the reporter, "that the one hundred or so pieces that were displayed in the Louvre (two gigantic rooms with a view of the Tuileries Garden) remain all but abandoned in Paris because no official institution is interested in repatriating them? For shame!"[83] Artist Mario Carreño would be equally blunt in his criticism, offered at an academic roundtable memorial for Violeta in 1968: "Violeta Parra had to disappear in order for people in Chile to realize that her work was of exceptional quality."[84]

The Carpa de La Reina

After two months of preparations, the Carpa was at last ready to open. The finished structure was some forty yards in diameter, with a dirt floor covered in sawdust, like at the circus.[85] The yellow tent's dome was supported by poles in the middle and wooden walls around its sides that Parra adorned with her paintings, tapestries, and shelves of pottery. It had a large stove in the middle, a wooden stage, wooden chairs and tables, a sound system, kitchen, garden, chickens, and a dog. Parra named the entire complex the "Carpa de La Reina" (Queen's Tent) after its location in the neighborhood La Reina (The Queen), and not, as she liked to joke with reporters, because she was a *reina* or queen.[86]

Parra had big plans for the Carpa. She would host shows there on Friday and Saturday evenings and a children's matinee on Sundays. The audience would enjoy performances by the most talented folk artists of the era, culminating with Parra herself. They would savor an array of Chilean traditional food and drinks prepared especially by her. The Carpa would also serve as an art space where she would exhibit her varied creations, as well as a school for the folk arts. The school's flyer and registration form announced that folk-loristas Margot Loyola, Raquel Barros, Gabriela Pizarro, and Violeta Parra would teach the adult music classes; Silvia Urbina, Rolando Alarcón, and Hilda Parra those for children; and sculptor Teresa Vicuña and painter Margot Guerra the art classes.[87] Parra also planned to develop the grounds around the Carpa into a park that would be a "veritable tourist attraction." It would feature an assortment of animals that were typical to Chile, which would grant it "a characteristic seal of authenticity."[88]

Parra thus envisioned the Carpa as a place where all her endeavors would come together under one roof—or, more exactly, one tent. According to one source, she also hoped it would prove an alternative to her children's Peña de los Parra. The trendy folk club had developed a sizable upper-class following, and Parra proposed to foster an environment that was less pituco (snobby) and more *popular* (read, for the pueblo).[89] Jealousy over her children's success was likely another and interrelated motivating factor.

Beyond its intended functions, the Carpa was Parra's new home. She resided there with Favre, Carmen Luisa, and the groundskeeping couple, having once again left her house of sticks to her mother. Specifically, Parra lived in a room at the back of the tent, with dirt floors and rustic furniture. A young reporter for *El Mercurio* who interviewed Parra at the Carpa was noticeably surprised to learn that she resided there and not, as he had presumed, in a downtown apartment or fancy house like most artists of her international stature. Parra had ushered him into the space by declaring, "Come in. . . . This is my home, this is how I live." She noted that it must have seemed strange to him that she lived this way and explained, "For me, this is comfort, I grew up in the countryside and lived like this for a long time and I have never changed my lifestyle."[90]

Parra thereby asserted—or, more accurately, invented—that living at her Carpa constituted a return to her roots. According to Isabel, her mother's resolution to live there, and not in her simple but comfortable house of sticks located in the same neighborhood, signified a "total rejection of the conventional, a return to the earth." Violeta no longer wanted to have anything to do with "carpets nor houses with shiny floors" and reproached Isabel and Ángel for their "bourgeois lifestyle."[91] Violeta's decision to live in relative isolation at the Carpa, deprived of many of the comforts of modern life, may also have been an indication of her worsening mental state.

The Carpa de La Reina was inaugurated with great fanfare on December 17, 1965. Local authorities, Parra's friends and relatives, and members of the press were all in attendance. Not one to underestimate her import, Parra had sent an invitation to the president of the republic, Eduardo Frei. He was a no-show but purportedly sent a personal note excusing his absence.[92] Violeta performed that day along with Isabel, Ángel, folkloristas Margot Loyola and Gabriela Pizarro, and other invited musicians. At 5:00 P.M., she and the mayor of La Reina cut the tricolor ribbon representing the colors of Chile. The mayor gave a speech, a priest gave a blessing, and a circus band played. The fiesta then started in earnest with the attendees all dancing the cueca. At one point, Violeta released a bunch of helium balloons into the evening sky. In his book about his mother, Ángel describes how she appeared on that day: "Glowing, her eyes are bright as she prepares the delicacies that she will serve to her friends, she sings, smiles, goes back and forth from the kitchen to the stage."[93] Violeta was happy.

The Carpa's inauguration constituted the high point of the venue's brief existence. The day's success would not be replicated, even during the patriotic celebrations of the following September. In life, the grandiose project that Parra dreamed was never realized. Those who loved Violeta would later speak of the Carpa de La Reina with sorrow. They would recall the sense of foreboding that it gave them, coinciding as it had with her deteriorating mental health. "If only she had never taken it on," Ángel would lament.[94] Isabel would characterize the Carpa as "the beginning of the end."[95] For his part, Nicanor would claim to have known from the first time he laid eyes on the circus tent that it would one day be Violeta's "tomb."[96]

Attempted Suicide

Parra's excitement at the Carpa finally being open quickly faded in the face of the challenges of running it. Attendance was spotty at best after its mid-December launch. Favre recalled how Parra's friends and supporters purchased some fifty tickets between them to help out financially, but they did not bother to actually show up at the Carpa. "It was the greatest affront she had suffered in her life as a singer. Her despair was such that she paced in circles without saying a word the whole day long."[97] Juxtaposed, President Frei and the no-show ticket-buyers attested to Parra's standing in Chile roughly a year before her suicide; a valued national figure, she was considered important enough to receive a congratulatory note from the president for opening her cultural center at the Carpa but not interesting enough for people to make the trip out there to hear her perform.

Meanwhile, Parra's plan to operate a school of folk arts at the site never materialized. Despite the school's prestigious roster of would-be instructors, people did not register for its courses. "I never taught one class in that tent," Teresa Vicuña would later recount with regret.[98] As for Parra's proposal of a native zoo, it never advanced beyond her acquisition of a llama of unknown provenance and a small monkey that in the end did not survive Santiago's climate.[99]

Within a month of the Carpa's inauguration, Parra fell into a severe depression. As her mental illness became more pronounced, friends and family noted her increasingly erratic behavior and the mounting violence of her angry outbursts. Parra's declining mental state manifested itself on her body as well. She developed a rash that specialists diagnosed as a "nervous allergy." Carmen Luisa described her mother's symptoms: "Her ailment was driving her crazy, it made her life impossible, she was scratching and scratching all day, she had blisters all over. She couldn't sleep." A doctor prescribed Violeta barbiturates to calm her nerves. Carmen Luisa continued, "Truth be told, she took pills to sleep, to calm herself down, to be able to eat. . . . It was horrible."[100]

On January 12, 1966, Parra arranged to be interviewed at the Carpa de La Reina by a reporter from the magazine *Aquí Está* as part of her largely unsuccessful effort to draw attention to the recently opened venue. When the reporter asked, "What type of rewards has your artistic career bestowed upon you?" her answer was scathing: "Absolutely none. Only sacrifices and continual battles. Everything that you see here is the product of my own financial woes. In Chile, people just don't understand certain things."[101] Two days later when the magazine's photographer went to the Carpa to shoot some pictures to accompany the story, he discovered Parra passed out in her room. She was rushed to a nearby medical center, where she was treated for an overdose of barbiturates.

Members of Parra's family maintained that Parra's overdose had been unintentional, that the whole thing was just a terrible accident, and several media outlets echoed their claim.[102] In a somewhat ghoulish bedside interview at the hospital where she was being treated, Parra suggested otherwise. *Ecran* reporter Nora Ferrada conducted the interview. Parra greeted her by berating her and the media in general for their lack of support: "What's up, my friend? Now you come to see me?! Where were you on the countless occasions that I invited the press and radio to visit my Carpa?!" Parra went on to itemize the substantial sums she had spent on a new sound system, a fully equipped kitchen, and posters and flyers that had yet to be distributed. She complained about how alone she had been in her efforts, as her costs were so great and the return on ticket sales so meager that she was unable to hire help. Instead, she had to cook, serve, wait on tables all on her own, and then sing for her audience. "Doesn't that seem like too much to you?"

Parra next recounted the circumstances of her overdose: she had been in a bad mood because no one had been able to help her remedy an allergy that left her no peace. "I was exhausted. . . . I didn't want to have anything to do with anyone. I had a little container of sleeping pills and I took seventeen of them. . . . I took all of them! . . . I am tired of struggling."[103]

As Parra's opening reprimand suggests, her hospitalization for a drug over-dose received considerably more media attention than the inauguration of her Carpa—or, for that matter, any of her other activities over that last year and a half of her life. Her bedside interview with *Ecran*, for instance, would be the first and last feature story published about Parra in Chile's premier entertainment magazine for the period from her triumphant return from Europe in August 1965 to her death in February 1967. Parra vented her frus-tration at this state of affairs in that interview and on other occasions. It is also entirely possible that no amount of attention or praise would have satis-fied her, given her outsize sense of self-importance—a personality trait that was likely linked to her mental illness.

Parra's suicide attempt would be the breaking point in her relationship with Favre. It was not the act itself that Favre found untenable; it was how she tried to use it to emotionally blackmail him afterward. The couple had had one of their all-too-frequent fights the morning of her overdose, this one over what color to paint the doors leading into the Carpa's tented area. Favre had wan-dered off on the premises to cool down, then ran to Parra's side when he heard the photographer shout for help. He stayed by her bed at the hospital until she finally came to. When Parra awoke, she turned to Favre and told him, "If you do not do what I tell you, I will commit suicide for real." In his autobi-ography, Favre recounts that he felt like he had been gut-punched, but he remained calm. "My way of thinking and seeing things was transformed from one minute to the next. My mind told me: 'You have to get out of here really fast and you have to go really far.'"[104]

And that is what he did. Favre remained at the hospital for another hour or so, then returned to the Carpa where he packed up his reel-to-reel tape re-corder, camera, clarinet, and quena. He went first to the Peruvian embassy, which turned him away, then to the Bolivian one, where he was welcomed and issued a visa. From there, he went to the train station. He sold his clarinet to a music shop keeper for the rock bottom price of exactly the amount of his fare from Santiago to La Paz, and within a few hours was on his way to the Bolivian capital. Parra would later write the song "Run-Run se fue p'al norte" (Run-Run Left to Go Up North)—with Run-Run being one of her several pet names for Favre—about his journey and her experience of their separation.

On a train of forgetting
before the day had dawned
from a station somewhere in time,
determined to depart,
Run-Run left to go up north
don't know when he'll return

he'll return for the birthday
of our solitude . . .

With the movement of the wheels
calendar pages fall
as the numbers of the year
float down upon the rail.
The more the iron wheels turn
the more clouds in the month,
and the longer stretch the rails,
more bitter the aftermath.

Run-Run left to go up north
there's nothing left to say.
And so such is life then
the thorns of Israel,
crown of mortification,
crucifixion of love,
the nails of martyrdom,
vinegar and bile.
Oh, oh, oh, poor me!

En un carro de olvido,
antes del aclarar,
de una estación del tiempo,
decidido a rodar,
Run-Run se fue pa'l norte,
no sé cuándo vendrá;
vendrá para el cumpleaños
de nuestra soledad . . .

El calendario afloja,
por las ruedas del tren,
los números del año
sobre el filo del riel.
Más vueltas dan los fierros,
más nubes en el mes,
más largos son los rieles,
más agrio es el después.

Run-Run se fue pa'l norte,
qué le vamos a hacer.
Así es la vida entonces:

espinas de Israel,
amor crucificado,
corona del desdén,
los clavos del martirio,
el vinagre y la hiel.
¡Ay ay ay de mí![105]

"How Wonderful Is My Carpa Now!"

As she had done times before, Parra dragged herself back from the brink of despair—at least for the space of a year. She had been found soon after ingesting the pills, so her recovery was swift. She regained enough strength while still in the hospital to promote the Carpa. Parra promised *Ecran* reporter Ferrada that she would not rest until it was fully up and running, and she extended an enthusiastic invitation to the magazine's readership to attend a fundraiser there. Parra programmed the event for January 29—a mere two weeks after she had been admitted to the hospital.[106]

Determined as ever, Parra solicited the entire folk music community to come out and support her.[107] Folklorista Héctor Pavez was among the first to answer her call. One of her most loyal colleagues, Pavez had given Parra a hard time when he visited her at the hospital and saw her hooked up to an IV: "What are you doing there looking so ridiculous? Aren't you Violeta Parra? . . . And your work? And the Carpa?" Parra had asked him if he would be willing to work with her there. "With you, Violeta, I will work on anything," he responded. "I am here, at your beck and call."[108]

Pavez made good on his word. He began showing up at the Carpa at dusk to get Parra out of bed—where, as was her custom, she spent a large part of her waking hours. Together, they would prepare that evening's offerings of empanadas, *anticuchos* (meat skewers), and *mistela* (a traditional alcoholic beverage), then Pavez would go on stage and entertain the guests as they began to arrive while Parra finished the preparations. Pavez was joined in his efforts by folkloristas Gabriela Pizarro (then Pavez's wife) and Margot Loyola, both of whom now performed regularly at the Carpa, having realized how much Parra needed their support. Family members rallied as well. Roberto, Lautaro, and Carmen Luisa—who, in true Parra fashion, was coming into her own as a singer—all performed in the Carpa's weekly lineup and helped with the day-to-day tasks of running the place.[109] Isabel and Ángel played there occasionally, as did Violeta's niece Clarita Parra (Eduardo's daughter).[110] Concerned for his mother's well-being, Ángel arranged for many of the musicians who performed at the Peña de los Parra to do a second shift at the Carpa as well.[111] Parra enlisted the Traditional Puppet Theater of Chile to perform Sunday matinees.[112]

Parra hired the Mapuche musical ensembles Los Araucanos and Huenchullán to round off the Carpa's lineup on special occasions. As performers, both groups more closely resembled a modern spectacle than the traditional Mapuche singing that Parra had recorded in the south of Chile in the 1950s.[113] In the case of Huenchullán, Parra helped shape their stage act. One source recounts that the Mapuche trio came to audition at the Carpa accompanied by a young dancer who pranced around as if she were a ballerina. Parra had told them: "What the fuck is this? No, no way. The three of you can play here, but lose the idiot." The source interpreted Parra's conditional offer of employment as evidence that "she liked things to be authentic!"[114] The anecdote establishes both that Parra supported Mapuche musicians and that she contributed to the social construction of Mapuche authenticity in 1960s Chile.

Violeta also took on the project of mentoring the up-and-coming folk ensembles Quelentaro and Grupo Chagual, both of which began appearing regularly at the Carpa. In an interview, members of Chagual explained how Parra became like their musical "godmother." They would go to the Carpa every Tuesday night from seven until midnight, where Parra would make them repeat a certain verse up to thirty times, often until the guitarists' fingers bled, until it finally came out the way she wanted it. "It felt like she would never forgive us our mistakes, but in the end . . . she did it so that we would get better. . . . [It was an] unforgettable time in our lives."[115]

As both her intervention at Huenchullán's audition and her mentoring style indicate—and in sharp contrast to the collectively run Peña de los Parra—Violeta was the supreme boss at the Carpa de La Reina. She oversaw every aspect of every evening's performance: which musicians would be in the lineup, the order of their appearance, and even the songs that they would perform.[116] She also continued to enforce her policy that the audience maintain silence during her act, if not with complete success then at least with more than she had had at clubs on the Left Bank of Paris. The imposed solemnity was broken by the rousing set of cuecas that closed every show.

With the support (and compliance) of friends, colleagues, mentees, and familia, Parra made the venue work, at least for a time. In correspondence, Parra happily related that 150 people had been at the Carpa on Saturday. She had served grilled meats, fried empanadas, sopaipillas, soup, mate, coffee, and mistela. She was contemplating adding Swiss fondue to the menu. "How wonderful is my Carpa now!"[117]

Her hopes and energies on the mend, Parra convinced the Odeon record company to produce the LP *La Carpa de La Reina* (The Carpa de La Reina).[118]

Figure 9.2 Violeta Parra performing at the Peña de los Parra, 1966. Photograph by Raúl Álvarez. Collection Museo Nacional de Bellas Artes, Santiago (note: the Museo Nacional de Bellas Artes has been unable to locate the heirs of Raúl Álvarez).

The collective album featured tracks by Carpa regulars Violeta, Roberto, Lautaro, Héctor Pavez, Grupo Chagual, and Quelentaro. It was recorded over various sessions and released in mid-1966 to scant notice or distribution beyond at the Carpa and the Peña de los Parra.[119] It includes Parra's cueca in support of Latin American unity, "Los pueblos americanos" (The Peoples of America): "When, oh when will it happen . . . That America becomes / A single pillar? . . . And one flag" (*¿Cuándo será ese cuando . . . que la América sea / solo un pilar? . . . y una bandera*).[120] For their contribution, Chagual recorded

"Corazón maldito" (My Cursed Heart), one of several of Parra's original songs that she herself would never record:

Oh my cursed heart
Careless and wanton, yes . . .
Blind, deaf and voiceless
From birth's first moment, yes . . .
You cause me torment.

Corazón maldito
sin miramiento, sí . . .
ciego, sordo y mudo
de nacimiento, sí . . .
Me das tormento.[121]

Rereleased tracks from Parra's earlier recordings—as a solo artist, with Las Hermanas Parra, and in duet with Isabel—appear on several compilation LPs produced around this time as well. They include the Odeon compilation of música típica cuecas, *Cuecas a pata pelá* (Barefoot Cuecas); the Odeon three-disk box set produced for the international market *Imagen Musical de Chile* (Musical Image of Chile); the first compilation LP of neofolklore put out by the label Demon, *Todo el Folklore* (All the Folklore), Vol. 1; and Odeon's *Cantos de Rebeldía* (Songs of Rebellion).[122] This last compilation, the brainchild of Odeon artistic director Rubén Nouzeilles, represented an attempt by the label to capitalize on the rising popularity of protest music. In aggregate, the songs Parra contributed to these compilations could be slotted into all four of the overlapping categories of folk musics from the decade: música típica, traditionalist folk music, neofolklore, and protest songs. Impressive as this was, the very breadth of categories that Parra's singing was associated with may have rendered her less easy to brand, thus less marketable, thus less attractive in the eyes of the music industry.

In a sign that things were going well for her, Parra was invited to appear on the TV program *Negro en el blanco* (In the Hot Seat) in April 1966. The popular show had a provocative "hot seat" format: the guest star—usually a politician or some other important figure—would sit on a high stool in the middle of the set, where they were interrogated by an off-camera panel of reporters and select intellectuals. Parra agreed to go on the show on the condition that no one mention her suicide attempt. She took her seat, dressed in a simple black dress with her long hair loose, the faithful representative not of television stardom but of everywoman—or perhaps Parisian bohemia; it is hard to tell (see figure 9.3). Parra proceeded to take questions from the panel. She defended the validity of all music that had sincere intentions, from a cueca

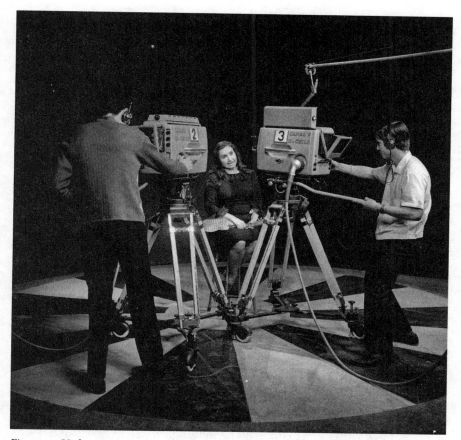

Figure 9.3 Violeta Parra on the set of the TV show *Negro en el blanco*. Photograph by Julio Bustamante. Archivo CENFOTO-UDP, Fondo Julio Bustamante, N000037, Violeta Parra: negro en el blanco, March 30, 1966.

from Chiloé to a Beatles song. At one point, she protested, "Why do you ask me such difficult things? I am just a cook at the Carpa de La Reina, who sings and paints for the fun of it." In their review of the show, an *Ecran* TV reporter praised Parra for "her authenticity and sincerity" and for bringing "a breath of fresh air that was missing to the program, which often suffers from pomposity and solemnity." The reporter closed with a "Well done, Violeta!"[123]

Parra's appearance on *In the Hot Seat* would not be the only time that she identified herself as a cook. On the contrary, with the establishment of the Carpa she appended the culinary arts to her expanding list of creative activities. When asked to list them in a November 1966 interview, she responded, "I have many bad habits. I paint, collect [folklore], compose, interpret folk poetry, I am a sculptor and also a cook. I cook marvelously."[124]

La Paz and Back

Parra visited Favre in Bolivia several times over the last year of her life. Favre had arrived in La Paz and immediately began working toward opening the city's first peña: the Peña Naira. The folk club, which shared its space with the already-established Naira Art Gallery, opened on March 4, 1966. It was an instant success, filling to capacity most nights, with people spilled out into the courtyard and street. Favre lived in a small room off one of the interior patios of the same building that housed the peña and gallery, which is where Parra stayed when she visited him.[125]

In what by now could be considered an established pattern, Parra and Favre got along better when they were apart than when they were together. As Favre narrates in his autobiography, the gut-wrenching strength of his emotions that led him to flee Parra while she was still in the hospital soon dissipated, and he decided to write her a letter detailing his efforts and adventures in La Paz and inviting her to visit him there. She accepted and, within weeks of receiving his invitation, sent a telegram announcing her arrival in La Paz. According to Favre, the couple's subsequent reunion was "warm, as if nothing had happened." Parra asked Favre to return to Santiago. Favre refused, as he did not want to leave the Peña Naira and La Paz to return to a "dead-end situation." Parra understood, and they agreed to take turns visiting each other without abandoning their respective projects.[126]

There are no clear-cut answers as to whether Favre's account accurately captures Parra's sentiments at the time. Her sole published letter to Favre in La Paz is filled with loving concern and longing, as well as boastful news of her Carpa and other activities.[127] Yet the letter also displays Parra's insecurity when, referring to Favre by one of the many pet names that she used for him, she inquired, "Do you love me, Chinito?" The raw vulnerability of her question, asked by a woman who was known to refer to herself in the third person and who could imagine her artwork hanging on the walls of the most prestigious cultural centers of Europe, is grounds for pause.

Although Favre's autobiography records only one of Parra's trips to La Paz, multiple sources indicate that she traveled to and from La Paz two or three times in the last year of her life.[128] The visit that Favre details occurred in May 1966. Parra headlined at the Peña Naira for the two weekends that she was there (see figure 9.4). Most of the other musicians who performed with her were from the club's regular lineup. They included the panpipe ensemble Los Choclos and the house band that Favre had put together. Known at the time simply as the "Peña Naira group," by year's end the band would adopt the name "Los Jairas" or "The Lazy Ones" in the Indigenous language Aymara. In addition to Favre on the quena, the ensemble comprised some of Bolivia's

Figure 9.4 Violeta Parra and Gilbert Favre performing at the Peña Naira, 1966.
Courtesy of Barbara Erskine and Patrick Favre.

most virtuoso folk musicians, master charango player Ernesto Cavour among them. Los Jairas would quickly become Bolivia's preeminent folk ensemble of the twentieth century both nationally and internationally.[129]

Favre took Parra around the city during their downtime. They visited marketplaces and the workshops where artisans made the elaborate masks that are worn during carnival and other festivities. According to Favre, Parra fell in love with La Paz. The sights and sounds inspired her to make her own art, and she devoted several days to painting. By week's end, she had produced enough material to mount an exhibit at the Naira Gallery, where she sold every piece.[130]

Parra's May 1966 visit to La Paz received substantial coverage in the local press, including positive reviews of both her musical performance and artwork. A reporter for the La Paz newspaper *El Diario*, for instance, wrote, "Last night's presentation confirmed all the wonderful things that are said about [Violeta Parra]. Beyond a doubt, she possesses exceptional gifts that justify her prestige and fame."[131]

Parra was greatly impressed by the musicians she met in La Paz. She was particularly taken with Los Choclos, a panpipe ensemble made up of musicians who shined shoes for a living.[132] The sounds they produced were very distinctive, especially those emanating from the largest panpipes with their deep vibrations. According to Favre, the first time Parra heard the group she determined then and there to find a way to bring them to perform in

Santiago.[133] She was perhaps also partial to the panpipe players because they were so clearly pueblo and because her brothers Roberto and Eduardo had both worked as shoe shiners in their youth in Chillán during the lean years after their father's passing. She promised to make all the necessary arrangements to bring Los Choclos to Chile. Favre liked the idea and offered to help raise the money for their train fares and accompany them on their tour.

After two weeks in La Paz, Parra flew back to Santiago. She brought back a charango crafted by a master luthier, a gift from Cavour and the other members of the Peña Naira's house band.[134] She would use the charango to accompany herself on both the collective LP, *La Carpa de La Reina*, and her solo album, *Las últimas composiciones de Violeta Parra* (Violeta Parra's Latest Compositions), including on her most famous song, "Gracias a la vida" (Thanks to Life). On either this trip or a later one to La Paz, Parra bought several additional charangos, which she then sold to her fellow musicians back in Santiago.[135]

Returning to Chile at the end of May 1966, Parra met Ángel Cereceda Orrego, Ángel and Marta Orrego Matte's first child and Violeta's second grandchild. "This is the best album of the year," she happily declared in reference to the newest addition to the Parra clan.[136] Ángel Cereceda Orrego would grow up to become the musician Ángel Parra, whose name is identical to his father's and who has performed as a solo artist, as a member of the popular rock band Los Tres, and in jazz combos.[137]

Back in Santiago, Parra right away began making arrangements for Los Choclos to come and perform. In late June 1966, five members of the panpipe ensemble traveled to Santiago with Favre as their guide.[138] After several days, they arrived at their destination and went straight from the train station to perform at the Carpa.[139]

A reporter from the youth entertainment magazine *Rincón Juvenil* described Parra's presence that evening: "Violeta is the soul of the Peña [Carpa]. She is everywhere. She welcomes those friends who have come to greet her. She waits on her regular customers. She pours wine into glasses, then serves it from trays. . . . She serves as master of ceremonies. . . . She plays the guitar . . . she sings." The reporter noted how the audience applauded after every new composition that she debuted and how they sang along with her on the grand finale, her ever-popular "The Black Wedding." Her set concluded, Parra then introduced "her Bolivian Indians, Los Choclos," who were met with a renewed round of enthusiasm when they performed their traditional music and dance.[140] According to Favre, Los Choclos upstaged Parra, though he reckoned she was not in the least bit bothered by it. On the contrary, she seemed proud to have been the one who delivered the masterstroke by bringing "her Bolivian Indians" to Chile.[141]

On July 1, 1966, after two weeks of nonstop activity performing at various venues and on radio and television, Favre and Los Choclos returned to La Paz. Their tour had gone so well that they could afford to travel back by plane. Parra tried to convince Favre to stay on in Santiago, but he was resolute. In his autobiography, Favre explains that he was sad to leave Parra because he loved her a lot and because their time together had been fantastic, as if they had been granted a fresh start. He determined, nonetheless, that "I could not let myself be caught up in sentimentality and I absolutely needed to get it through my head that, after a few months, things would have gone back to how they had been before. Of that I was certain."[142]

Although Parra and Favre would meet again over the subsequent months in both La Paz and Santiago, Favre made no further reference to her in his autobiography. Notably, he did not write of her suicide, though his friends would later attest that it left him devastated. When a Bolivian newspaper reporter asked for his comments just days after Parra's death, he stated, "Violeta was a very difficult and extremely sensitive person, in other words, too demanding in her relationships. . . . Demanding as a singer and as an artist in general. I can confirm that most people were incapable of understanding her." He noted that Parra loved La Paz and had made plans to visit again in January 1967 but that those plans had not been realized. He shared that "this definitive act of self-elimination" was not her first attempt to take her own life. He concluded, "Her death, in my opinion, was a problem of excessive loneliness."[143]

Chapter 10

Last Songs

The final months of Violeta Parra's life were marked by her declining mental health. Parra remained active despite this. She managed, mostly, to keep her Carpa functioning. She performed regularly at the Peña de Los Parra and on radio and television. She traveled throughout Chile with the folk music touring company Chile Laughs and Sings. She visited Favre in Bolivia. She recorded her undisputed masterpiece *Las últimas composiciones de Violeta Parra* (Violeta Parra's Latest Compositions), chosen by *Rolling Stone* (Chile) as the best Chilean album of all time.[1] Ironically, in this instance, the Spanish word for "latest" (*últimas*), as in "latest compositions," is the same word for "last." On February 5, 1967, two months after the album's release, Violeta Parra took her life with a single gunshot to the temple.

I face writing this final chapter with trepidation, as I fear that as a biographer I will be expected to explain the act—foretold, yet unfathomable—of Parra's suicide. Oftentimes in my life, a specific line from a song will surface, from memory to consciousness, that captures how I am feeling in that moment and guides my steps forward. The lyric that comes to mind when I contemplate the last months of Parra's life is from her experimental piece "The Sparrowhawk": "I have no place to be" (*Yo no tengo donde estar*). Parra sings the phrase three times in a row, like a mantra, slowing down with each repetition. I hold that these few words with their halting cadence express the underlying tensions of Parra's final months far better than any I could produce for that purpose.

Chile Laughs and Sings

In mid-July 1966, not long after Favre and Los Choclos returned to La Paz, Parra embarked on a tour of Chile's southernmost region of Patagonia. It was the first of three tours organized by folk music promoter extraordinaire René Largo Farías that Parra would go on that year. Largo Farías used the umbrella name Chile Laughs and Sings (*Chile ríe y canta*) for the multiple activities he produced to further his "vigorous crusade" to defend Chilean culture from foreign influences.[2] The purpose of the Chile Laughs and Sings tours was to bring nationally renowned musicians from Santiago's versatile folk scene to perform for the rest of Chile. The tours were subsidized in part by the Christian

Democratic government's agrarian reform program. They received sponsorship from Radio Minería and the youth entertainment magazine *El Musiquero* as well. Though Largo Farías himself was a communist supporter, he had a warm and caring demeanor that made it easy for him to recruit artists from across the political spectrum, from the conservative Huasos Quincheros to Communist Party militant Víctor Jara and fellow traveler Violeta Parra. "She adored Largo Farías," a folklorista colleague recalled. "We all adored him."[3]

Parra's involvement with Chile Laughs and Sings dated back to August 1965, when she appeared on its live radio show as one of her first Santiago gigs post-Europe. In the last year of her life, Parra would travel the length of Chile with the organization, from southern Patagonia to Chile's northern border with Peru. The tours themselves were grueling. They relied on a combination of chartered buses, trains, planes, and boats, depending on the route, and almost always involved long treks between the various points on the itinerary. The touring musicians would remain in and around a city or town for several days or sometimes weeks, performing at a variety of venues: stadiums, theaters, parks, union halls, schools, rural settlements, and mining camps. Whatever the setting, they were always joined by the local talent, the most standout of whom Largo Farías would then invite to perform in Santiago on his weekly radio show.

The July 1966 Chile Laughs and Sings tour to Patagonia was both Parra's first tour with the organization and her first visit to the region. The other musicians on tour included representatives of various styles of Chilean folk-derived music and an ensemble of "authentic Easter Islanders."[4] Together, they performed at several venues in Punta Arenas, the capital of the Magallanes province in southern Patagonia, as well as at nearby rural settlements and more distant mining camps that they reached by plane. The musicians were enthusiastically received wherever they performed, so much so that the organizers added a special farewell concert to the tour.

The gala performance was held at an indoor stadium in Punta Arenas in front of a standing-room-only audience of 4,500. When it was Parra's turn to take the stage, she opened with her popular song "La jardinera" (The Gardener), which earned her the loudest and longest ovation of the evening. The following day, a local newspaper published a glowing review of the show: "[It] had allowed the audience to see up close those artists and composers that they had only known through recordings. They could almost reach out and touch the famous Violeta Parra, who described herself as a 'short woman' as her feet do not touch the floor when she is sitting. . . . [She] performed for those in attendance in all her simplicity and at the acme of her artistic career, remaining with the public for more than her allotted time because they would not let her leave the stage."[5]

Parra received two gifts from her fans in Punta Arenas. The first was a thick woolen shawl knitted by the women from a Mothers' Center there. The second was a chair designed especially so that her feet would reach the ground. It was built by a local carpenter, who was likely inspired by Parra's onstage comment regarding her diminutive height.[6] Both Parra's public self-description as a "short woman" and the carpenter's gift of a chair made to her size could be interpreted as coded statements of class allegiance in a society where differences in height were often overlaid with differences of class. Within this context, both the handcrafted gifts and outsize response that Parra received from her Puerto Montt admirers suggest that they were celebrating one of their own.

Parra was moved by the whole experience. In an interview granted on January 1, 1967, she credited her tour to Punta Arenas with sparking her creative reawakening: "I began to feel, my heart and my blood began to vibrate like a person who has been reborn." She explained why touring with Chile Laughs and Sings had such an impact on her: "To feel close up the love that the public has for its artists is something that touches the soul and that is not easily forgotten. . . . And that is how, with my hoarse voice, at forty-nine years of age and with my ordinary physique, I can confirm that the people of Chile are able to appreciate the efforts of someone who has broken her heart and has bled in order to achieve one thing: to fuse her artist's soul with the artist's soul of her public."[7]

Parra composed her contemplative song "Volver a los diecisiete" (To Be Seventeen Again) inspired by an incident that occurred on her first tour with Chile Laughs and Sings. It involved Parra and Pedro Messone, former member of the chart-topping neofolklore band Los Cuatro Cuartos who was then performing as a solo artist. According to Messone, the touring party stopped to stretch their legs at a deserted beach while traveling by bus to their next destination. When the driver signaled it was time to leave, everyone hurried back to the bus. Midway there, Messone noticed that Parra was still a ways down the beach and went back for her. He took her by the hand and the two ran to the waiting bus. As they were running, Messone exclaimed, "Look at us, we're like a pair of seventeen-year-olds." Parra gave him a strange look and asked him to repeat the phrase. They boarded the bus, and she went to sit at the back and wrote the lyrics for what would become one of her most well-known songs:

> To be seventeen again
> After living a hundred years
> Is like deciphering signs
> Without being wise enough.

To become again all at once,
As fragile as a moment,
To feel again so moved
Like a child encountering God,
That is what I am feeling now
In this instant of promise.

Volver a los diecisiete
después de vivir un siglo
es como descifrar signos
sin ser sabio competente.
Volver a ser de repente
tan frágil como un segundo,
volver a sentir profundo
como un niño frente a Dios,
eso es lo que siento yo
en este instante fecundo.[8]

The incident and, more generally, the two musicians' friendship led to speculation that Parra and Messone, who was twenty-one years Parra's junior, had a love affair while on tour.[9] Parra may have started the rumor herself. She certainly encouraged it. As reported in *Ecran*'s weekly gossip column, "Superconfidential," she dedicated a song to Messone at a concert held in Santiago shortly after they returned from Punta Arenas.[10] A few months later, around the time of the release of her new LP *Las últimas composiciones de Violeta Parra* (Violeta Parra's Latest Compositions), she went all out: following the advertising adage that all publicity is good publicity, she confessed on air and in front of a live audience that she and Messone had had a "steaming romance" while on tour together. Parra quickly walked back her claim, stating it had just been a joke for Innocents' Day, the Chilean equivalent of April Fool's Day. But, according to a magazine piece on the alleged "idyll," it was too late; Messone's "panty-throwing fans" had already been driven mad with jealousy.[11]

As for Messone, he consistently denied that there was any truth to the rumor when asked about it over the years. Parra and he had been good friends, nothing more. Yes, she could have violent moods at times, but she was also tender and wise; in short, she possessed those qualities that "a woman in her forties has to offer a man in his twenties."[12]

Zapicán

Parra returned from her first tour with Chile Laughs and Sings in the middle of an unusually inclement winter. Torrential rains kept the public away from the Carpa and turned its dirt floor into a muddy field. Both Carmen Luisa and Héctor Pavez recalled one particularly violent storm when the wind whipped the tent's main pole back and forth, tearing the canvas in its wake. They had stayed up all night, poking at the Carpa's canvas dome with long poles to prevent the water from accumulating and bringing down the entire structure with its weight, soaked to the bone and covered in mud. Violeta had sobbed through it all. When the rains finally ceased in the early morning, Carmen Luisa described her mother as "torn to shreds, just like the tent, she was so terribly sad."[13]

It was around this bleak time that the Uruguayan artisan, musician, and former political prisoner Alberto Zapicán came into Parra's life.[14] He would become her handyman, musical partner, and companion in her last months. He was at the Carpa the day she committed suicide and was most likely the last person to see her alive.

Zapicán was thirty-nine when he met Parra, who was nine years his senior. He had had a hard life by any measure. He was born to a sheepherding family deep in the Uruguayan countryside. His mother had abandoned him and his father when he was seven years old, taking his siblings along with her. In reaction, his father had chained him to a tree to prevent him from leaving as well.[15] Zapicán escaped as soon as he could, which was two years later at age nine. He survived by working odd jobs as an itinerant laborer throughout Uruguay. An autodidact, he had taught himself to read and write at age sixteen. Influenced by the 1950s folk boom in neighboring Argentina, he also learned to play the bombo along the way.[16] His experience working in sugarcane fields led him to become a labor organizer and political activist, and he served two years in jail in the early 1960s for his involvement in the Uruguayan guerrilla organization the National Revolutionary Movement (Tupamaros).

Zapicán snuck into Chile upon his release, as it was the closest country with which Uruguay had no extradition treaty. He made his way to Valparaíso, where he befriended the folk singer Osvaldo "Gitano" Rodríguez. Rodríguez learned that Zapicán was a great admirer of Violeta Parra and offered to take him to Santiago to hear her sing. Rodríguez was also aware of how much Parra was struggling to keep her Carpa from failing and hoped that Zapicán, a man of all trades, might be able to help out.

Zapicán's first encounter with Parra could not be described as warm and friendly. On the contrary, she walked up to him after her performance and asked point blank, "What are you, some kind of a jerk? You just sit there and don't applaud?" A taciturn man, Zapicán was not in the habit of clapping. He responded to Parra's initial hostility with silence and even refused to shake her hand when offered it. Perhaps impressed by how firmly he held his own, Parra invited him and Rodríguez to stay for a late supper. According to Zapicán, Parra stopped acting so aggressively toward him when she grasped that he was "as or more brutish than she was."[17] Besides, she liked the idea of having someone come and work for her and was eager to iron out the details.[18]

Parra had asked Zapicán all sorts of personal questions that evening. One of the things that he shared was that he had been a political prisoner. According to Rodríguez, "It was not easy for him to talk. He seemed aloof, almost timid, like someone who was seeking refuge in a ranch hand's silence."[19] Parra's song "Pupila de águila" (Eye of the Eagle) was almost certainly inspired by Zapicán's story and their ensuing relationship:

> A little bird came by to perch under my little tree.
> Night had fallen, in the dark he was difficult to perceive.
> He was lamenting that he'd been imprisoned in a cage,
> And that his feathers, one at a time, had been plucked away.
> I wanted to cure him with tender care, but the little bird
> Maintained the silence of the tomb until the daytime stirred.
>
> Then came the sunlight and the sky brightened and the wind shook free
> All of the branches of my little tree and anyone could see
> That this little bird was pained in his soul even more than me.

> *Un pajarillo vino a posarse bajo mi arbolito.*
> *Era de noche, yo no podía ver su dibujito.*
> *Se lamentaba de que una jaula lo hizo prisionero,*
> *que las plumillas, una por una, se las arrancaron.*
> *Quise curarlo con mi cariño, mas el pajarillo*
> *guardó silencio como una tumba hasta que amaneció.*
>
> *Llegan los claros de un bello día, el viento sacudió*
> *todo el ramaje de mi arbolito y allí se descubrió*
> *que el pajarillo tenía el alma más herida que yo.*[20]

Zapicán showed up at the Carpa soon after their initial conversation with a bombo hanging over his shoulder, ready to work in exchange for room and board. He did any number of chores: he repaired the holes in the tent, added new supports, and built a bigger and sturdier stage. Parra wanted him to install indoor plumbing as well, although it does not appear that he ever did.

In his free time, when he thought no one else was around, Zapicán would play the bombo and sing or, as he described it, "[make] those loud whoops that are customary for people of the Uruguayan countryside." One day Parra happened to overhear him during one of his more inspired moments. Zapicán recalls, "She told me: 'From now on you have to put down the hammer, pick up your bombo, and play with me.'"[21] The two rehearsed and began performing

Figure 10.1 Violeta Parra with Alberto Zapicán, n.d. Photograph by Javier Pérez Castelblanco. Courtesy of the family of Javier Pérez Castelblanco.

as a duo (figure 10.1). They performed in Santiago and, judging from a photograph of them boarding a plane together, on tour on at least one occasion.[22]

Parra's relationship with Zapicán would prove as turbulent as her relationships with other men. But beyond their musical collaboration, for which there is a record, the nature of their liaison is unclear. Zapicán always insisted that their bond was both loving and platonic; they slept in the same room, but in separate beds. In an interview granted at age ninety, when asked for the umpteenth time whether he had been Parra's last romantic partner, his answer was unambiguous, if somewhat crude: "I was not her partner, if you mean by that that we were lovers. If you need for me to be clearer than that, we did not fuck. . . . We were [partners] in our work, in our life goals as regards cultural matters, or, more precisely, in song."[23]

As for Parra, she seemed to have fallen for Zapicán hard and fast—though this did not necessarily mean that she had given up on her relationship with Favre. According to Carmen Luisa, Zapicán had been working for Violeta for barely a week when Violeta announced that he would be living at the Carpa because "it needed a man and because he was the most marvelous man on earth."[24]

Parra's feelings for Zapicán are revealed in her songs and correspondence. In terms of the songs, in addition to her song "Pupila de águila" (Eye of the Eagle), she wrote the contrastingly lighthearted song "El Albertío" (Little Alberto), whose title is a wordplay on Zapicán's first name, Alberto:

I do not know why God
Would so generously bestow
A hat with so much ribbon
On a person who has no head!

¡Yo no sé por qué mi Dios
le regala con largueza
sombrero con tanta cinta
a quien no tiene cabeza![25]

Parra also expressed her feelings toward Zapicán in a letter to their mutual friend Osvaldo Rodríguez. She wrote it when Zapicán had disappeared from the Carpa after a fight, without notice and without informing Parra where he was going. Her letter inquires as to his whereabouts and describes their budding relationship. Like her love letters to Favre, this one could also be considered a literary work: "While unraveling his sharp-edged silence with great difficulty, I discovered in him incredibly beautiful details. He hammered here, sawed there, worked away and even gave me an autumn leaf as a gift, an act that culminated in the apparently perfect fusion of our souls. I say apparently, because the carpenter giver-of-leaves is not to be found in any corner of the tent."

Parra's letter seems to contradict Zapicán's frequent assertions that their relationship had always been platonic. Or it reaffirms Parra's propensity for inventive thinking. There is no way to know for sure. Parra writes, "In front of almost the whole neighborhood, and in a blue light that was bluer than the color blue, I received a kiss from him. That kiss was not from a man, but from a hungry lion. . . . That kiss hurt me and all of those that I received afterward hurt me, they brought me to the bed three times, to become better acquainted with the lion."

Parra clarifies that although it was true that she had wanted to forget Favre once and for all, Zapicán had been mistaken to think that this was the reason she had latched on to him. She had no reason to do so; "It is well known that Violeta Parra is the most accompanied woman on the planet. Every day at the peña [de los Parra] some adoring man shows up who would like nothing better than to join me in pulling petals off of flowers." At one point in her letter, Parra upends the gender hierarchy by asserting her sexual dominance over Zapicán and linking it to her creative powers as a woman: "I penetrated him, like a needle in a complicated embroidery."[26]

Patuda (Outrageous)

Parra's sexual assertiveness, as expressed in this transgressive sentence as well as in the letter as a whole, constituted an outright rebellion against those gender norms that assigned women the role of passive and submissive partner in their sexual relations. There are reasons to believe that Parra was sexually assertive in life as well as on the page. She had two husbands and numerous lovers over the years. She promoted the unconventional philosophy that past lovers helped one better love one's present lover. Patricio Manns claimed that she flirted with every man who came within arm's length. He elaborated: "Violeta was coquettish to the core and a little 'rumba-esque,' like those Spanish women who dance flamenco and emit a sexual aroma when they pass by."[27] He noted that she had even tried to seduce him, though it did not go anywhere: "She would say, 'Why don't we spend the night here, all cozy and warm. . . . ?' 'No, I have things to do,' I would say, 'and besides, you don't have any wine.' 'Yes, I do. Here is a carafe.' . . . She was *patuda* [outrageous]. Short, round, and she'd grab you in the middle of the street and kiss you on the lips."[28]

Manns used the word *patuda* to describe Parra—Chilean slang for someone who is outrageously scandalous or scandalously outrageous. Patuda is also an apt term to describe a woman who consistently broke with patriarchal conventions and who thereby provoked the moral outrage of the would-be enforcers of said conventions.

And there was plenty of sanctimony to go around. Meting it out was an activity so common in Chile in Parra's time that it was (and is, still to this day, in some circles) referred to by the phrase "the 'What will people say?' [*el ¿'Qué dirán?'*]." It was also applied disproportionately to women. With two former husbands, a third "husband" of undetermined status (Gilbert Favre) in Bolivia, and rumored love affairs with several other men, Parra was an easy target. She lived out her last years under the gendered weight of the disapproval of large swaths of Chilean society, from religious conservatives to Communist Party moralists.

Some people have misogynistically associated Parra's patuda comportment with mental illness, "diagnosing" her as hypersexual or a nymphomaniac.[29] Parra's declining level of care for her appearance and personal hygiene, occurring as her mental health also declined, is sometimes viewed in that same light. Her body odor appears especially to have been an issue. Parra was purported to bathe only rarely, if at all, while on tour with Chile Laughs and Sings. According to one source, the other musicians on the road with her would sarcastically refer to her behind her back as "Dolly Pen," a popular brand of deodorant.[30] Meanwhile, back in Santiago, Parra's wish that Zapicán install indoor plumbing never materialized, and the Carpa remained notably lacking in those conveniences that favored cleanliness in modern life such as an indoor bathroom and a laundry room. In their absence, the residents of the Carpa relied on an outdoor wooden trough to wash their bodies and clothing alike, with results that may have been less than optimal. Parra's eschewal of conventional hygiene in her last months was also inextricably linked to her worsening mental health, one of the physical symptoms of which was a rash that prevented her from bathing.

Yet I would argue that it is too simplistic to assign Parra's lack of personal hygiene in this last stage of her life to her challenging circumstances, failing mental health, or a combination of the two. Allegations that she was dirty or smelled bad date back at least to her residency at the University of Concepción, when she would return to the Fine Arts building after spending long days collecting folklore among women who looked like her and who, one may suppose, also smelled like her. I would venture that Parra's lack of personal hygiene, though unquestionably exacerbated by her mental illness, at the same time contained an element of rebellion against the class prejudices that she had experienced since childhood.

This interpretation is supported by an anecdote from Favre's autobiography. The incident occurred as Parra and Favre were frantically preparing for Parra's solo exhibit at the Paris Museum of Decorative Arts. A party of well-off people had arranged to visit Parra in the one-room flat that doubled as her art studio to see her work. According to Favre, Parra's antipathy toward that class of people was so great that she purposefully refrained from washing for several days in order to force them to face the fact that poverty has a smell. Her preparations evidently succeeded, as the resulting odor was, "in effect, abominable." Parra's bourgeois guests did not let on that they minded, then sent her a thank you gift of a large package of soap. When she and Favre saw its contents, they burst into laughter; "the 'bourgeois' had won."[31]

Parra's anti-bourgeois protest points to the fact that personal hygiene or "cleanliness" is as much a social construct as beauty or authenticity—or, for that matter, sanity.[32] One could argue, further, that modern bourgeois norms of cleanliness are constructed to differentiate social groups from one another in order to reinforce the existing social order. Parra appears to have been both aware of this and inclined to reject it.

That Parra was mentally ill is confirmed by her multiple attempts and final suicide. She also is reported to have sought psychiatric treatment in the last year of her life, though few people knew that at the time.[33] I do not pretend to proffer a diagnosis of her mental state here beyond the consensus opinion that she suffered from depression and probably bipolar disorder. The latter would explain the intensity of her emotional highs and lows and likely some of her personality traits and behaviors as well. I do insist, however, that

Parra's mental illness cannot be understood without an accounting of the social inequities of her era: Parra was a fiercely independent woman who lived and worked in a society where women performers were routinely sexually harassed; politicians and government officials, liberal and conservatives alike, frequented brothels; and respectable men maintained two households and married second and then third wives far younger than themselves. It was a society where some members of the middle and upper classes deemed their perfect grooming and impeccable dress, made possible by their affluence and the labors of their servants, to be a mark of their superiority over those people who lived in homes without running water, who could not afford more than one outfit, and who were considered "dirty" by the former. While not discounting the gravity of her mental illness, I maintain that Parra's anti-conventional conduct that many dismissed as "crazy" in her time might well be assessed as a fitting response to the hypocrisies of bourgeois Chilean society.

Within this larger context of mental and social struggle, Ángel's memory of the last time that he saw his mother takes on added poignancy. Ángel had passed by the Carpa before leaving for his in-laws' beach house for the summer holidays and found Violeta practicing an alternative and rural-based form of self-care. His final image of his mother was of her drying her hair in the sun after washing it "the way campesinos do" with the bark of the *quillay*, a tree native to Chile, also known as the "soap bark tree."[34]

Violeta Parra's Latest (and Last) Compositions

In August 1966, Parra went into the recording studio to begin work on her final LP, *Las últimas composiciones de Violeta Parra* (Violeta Parra's Latest Compositions). She recorded it with the RCA Victor label, the same company that had produced Las Hermanas Parra's singles in the late 1940s and early 1950s, and not with Odeon Chilena.[35]

Her decision to leave Odeon was no small matter. Parra's professional relationship with Odeon and its artistic director Rubén Nouzeilles dated back over a decade to her first solo EP as a folklorista in 1954. Parra had been the inaugural artist for the Folklore of Chile series that Nouzeilles initiated, and she had recorded her first five Chilean LPs with the series. Her most recent collaborations with Nouzeilles had been her 1965 solo album *Recordando a Chile* (Chile on My Mind) and the collective 1966 album *Carpa de La Reina*.

Those would be her final recordings with Odeon—Parra's choice, not Nouzeilles's. Nouzeilles would later recall Parra's last visit to his office. He had been as struck by her pale and gaunt appearance as by the beauty of the new song that she sang for him, "Gracias a la vida" (Thanks to Life). "It was a tremendous shock, it broke me up, I was so moved, not just by the effect of her music, but by her ghostly figure and the quiet way she sang it. I realized that she was at the edge of an abyss . . . and it hurt me greatly to see her in such a lamentably self-destructive state."[36]

Parra had refused to renew her contract that day. In Nouzeilles's reading of the events, this refusal was symptomatic of Parra's declining mental state: "It was a moment in her life when she was letting go of many things and she didn't want to hear another word about contracts."[37] On her end, Parra may have been pursuing a contract with more favorable terms, given the pittance she received from her long-term one with Odeon.

Whatever her reasons, Parra produced her last LP with RCA Victor. According to sound engineer Luis Torrejón, she recorded the album's fourteen songs in seven three-hour sessions over a period of a month and a half. Echoing the experience of the Buenos Aires sound engineer who recorded her 1962 LP, Torrejón recalled Parra as having a clear idea of how to do things, never being out of tune, and able to land a song in two or three takes.[38] The album was Parra's first and only one to use reverb, a more recently developed recording technique that lent a warmer and fuller quality to her voice. She sang four of the songs in duet with Zapicán, who also played bombo on the recording. Isabel and Ángel contributed to the LP as well, Isabel on small percussion and Ángel on guitar. Torrejón relates that the original plan was for Isabel, Ángel, and Zapicán to participate on every song, but Violeta ended up recording the album's last tracks by herself "because everyone was fighting. . . . The others did not want to come [to the studio]. And she came by herself because we had to finish the album."[39]

Violeta Parra's Latest Compositions was released in November 1966. The LP's cover features a black-and-white close-up of Parra, her hair loose, face unadorned, dressed simply, strumming her charango as she looks off in the distance. Taken at the Carpa by the photographer Javier Pérez Castelblanco, the photo emphasizes Parra's identity as an authentic artist, without pretense or artifice. It has since become one of her most iconic images. It is reproduced on this book's cover.[40]

Many people at the time (and since) suspected that Parra chose the album's title, with its double meaning in Spanish, because she knew that the songs on the LP would also be her last. Her choice of the word "compositions" is also telling, as with it she defined herself as a composer at a time when the category was all but restricted to men with formal training in classical music.[41]

In keeping with its title, the songs on the album are all Parra originals. They include "Mazúrquica modérnica" (Modernified Mazurka), her satirical take on those who would criticize politically engaged singers for their songs; the heartbreaking lament "Run-Run se fue al norte" (Run-Run Left to Go Up

North); the philosophical "Volver a los diecisiete" (To Be Seventeen Again); two songs inspired by Zapicán, "Pupila de águila" (Eye of the Eagle) and "El Albertío" (Little Alberto); the cueca "Pastelero a tus pasteles" (Cobbler, Stick to Your Last), whose opening line cheerfully announces "I am going, I am going to Bolivia" (*Ya me voy, ya me voy para Bolivia*); a song about the traditional Mapuche ceremony of prayer and gratitude "The Guillatún"; the "Cueca de los poetas" (The Poets' Cueca), with lyrics by Nicanor Parra; and "Rin del angelito" (Dance of the Little Angel), a song that evokes the campesino ritual of the wake for the little angel:

> That beloved little angel
> Is now going on up to heaven
> To pray for mother and father,
> Brothers, sisters, grandparents.
> When death takes hold of the body,
> The soul goes looking for its place
> Inside of a poppy flower
> Or in a little canary . . .
>
> Seeing the dear little angel
> The butterflies are delighted
> Gathering all round the cradle,
> Slowly they circle so quiet.
> When death takes hold of the body
> The soul then directly takes flight
> To say hello to the moon and
> On the way to greet the starlight.

> *Ya se va para los cielos*
> *ese querido angelito*
> *a rogar por sus abuelos,*
> *por sus padres y hermanitos.*
> *Cuando se muere la carne,*
> *el alma busca su sitio*
> *adentro de una amapola*
> *o dentro de un pajarito . . .*
>
> *Las mariposas alegres,*
> *de ver el bello angelito*
> *alrededor de su cuna,*
> *le caminan despacito.*
> *Cuando se muere la carne,*
> *el alma va derechito*

a saludar a la Luna
y de paso al lucerito.[42]

The LP also includes the song that would eventually become her most well-known one, "Gracias a la vida" (Thanks to Life). Parra sings it solo, accompanying herself on the charango in a style that was new and, according to Bolivian master charango player Ernesto Cavour, "absolutely original."[43] In it, Parra gives thanks for her senses and what they enable her to see and hear, for sounds and the alphabet and what they allow her to express, for her tired feet and the many places they have taken her, for her heart that allows her to discern good from evil, and for laughter and tears that let her distinguish joy from sorrow, the "materials" of her song, which is also your song and everyone's song.

Ironically, the album also includes the song that may be considered the negation of "Gracias a la vida" (Thanks to Life): "Maldigo del alto cielo" (I Curse the Heavens Above). Juxtaposed, the lyrics of the two songs capture the highs and lows of Parra's shifting emotions in the last year of her life.

In the one, Parra gives thanks to life for giving her:	In the other, she curses:
. . . two bright stars that, when I open them, / Perfectly I distinguish what's white from what's black / And in the high heavens the starry backdrop . . . (. . . *dos luceros que, cuando los abro, / perfecto distingo lo negro del blanco / y en el alto cielo y su fondo estrellado* . . .);	. . . what's white, / What's black and what is yellow . . . A star with its luminescence . . . (. . . *lo blanco, / lo negro con lo amarillo* . . . *la estrella con sus reflejos* . . .);
my hearing that, with all of its range, / Registers night and day, crickets and canaries . . . (. . . *el oído que, en todo su ancho, / graba noche y día, grillos y canarios* . . .);	. . . The trilling of the canary / The cosmos and its planets . . . (. . . *el trino de la canaria / el cosmos y sus planetas* . . .);
sounds and the alphabet's letters / And with them the words that I think and proclaim (. . . *el sonido y el abecedario / con él las palabras que pienso y declaro* . . .);	. . . the word "love" / With all of its rubbish . . . (. . . *el vocablo "amor" / con toda su porquería* . . .);
the steps taken by my tired feet / On them I have walked through cities and marshes, / Beaches and deserts, mountains and prairies . . . (. . . *la marcha de mis pies cansados / con ellos anduve ciudades y charcos, / playas y desiertos, montañas y llanos* . . .);	. . . the wide open sea / Its harbors and its inlets . . . moon and landscape, / Valleys and deserts . . . (. . . *del ancho mar / sus puertos y sus caletas* . . . *luna y paisaje, / los valles y los desiertos* . . .);
my heart that drums in its chamber / . . . when I see goodness so far removed from evil (. . . *el corazón que agita su marco / . . . cuando miro el bueno tan lejos del malo* . . .)[44]	everything that's true / And that's false and that's uncertain . . . (. . . *todo lo cierto / y lo falso con lo dudoso* . . .)[45]

These opposite takes on life are encapsulated in the songs' refrains: "Thanks to Life" (*Gracias a la vida*) and "How great is my suffering!" (*¡Cuánto será mi dolor!*). The two songs also contrast musically. "Gracias a la vida" (Thanks to life) is melodic and slow-paced, and Parra performs it as a gentle and intimate solo. "Maldigo del alto cielo" (I Curse the Heavens Above) is a dissonant, angry song that Parra performs as a duet with Zapicán, the two singers alternating between faster verses over a driving guitar and bombo accompaniment, and out-of-time, a cappella musical phrases that augment the song's dramatic effect.

Troubles at the Carpa

The Carpa de La Reina remained open throughout this period. It was not an easy venue to maintain. It had its better moments, like when Parra's friends and colleagues rallied around her in the aftermath of her attempted suicide at the start of 1966 or when Los Choclos headlined there later that year. For the most part, however, attendance was lackluster.

The greatest contributing factor to this state of affairs was precisely what Parra's friends and relatives had tried to warn her about, to no avail: the Carpa's location. The venue was difficult to reach by public transportation during the day, and it was nearly impossible to leave late at night without a private vehicle or taxi. Those who arrived by car still had to hike a good 300 yards up a dirt path from the parking area to get to the tent.

Santiago's climate did not help matters. In winter, the small charcoal heaters that Parra placed throughout the Carpa proved largely ineffective at protecting whatever audience there was from the cold. In summer, the tent became unbearably hot, besides which much of its potential clientele both preferred and had the resources to seek out cooler climes on vacation. Winter or summer, the dirt road that led to the Carpa—along with the tent's dirt floor—turned into a muddy quagmire when it rained, preventing even those people who owned cars from venturing there. The problem of low turnout was magnified by the sheer expanse of the circus tent; with its capacity to seat some 400 to 500 spectators, it could seem empty even with an audience of a hundred or more. Most times attendance was nowhere near that.

Beyond low turnouts, Parra had to deal with her disillusionment that the people who did show up were not the audience she had envisioned when she first decided to build a center for the folk arts. Instead of offering an alternative to the Peña de los Parra's pituco environment, Parra's Carpa drew a similar audience; people from Chile's middle and upper classes (the car-owning classes), along with tourists passing through Santiago and folk-music-loving employees of the many nongovernmental organizations headquartered there at the time.[46] Argentine reporter Alfonso Alcalde, Parra's friend and biographer, described them as "a sophisticated audience" made up of "upper-class snobs and tourists," noting further that this was not what Parra had intended for her Carpa and that the contradiction wounded her.[47]

Parra was also unhappy that the Carpa did not attract more young people. As one newspaper reporter observed, most of the people who attended the Carpa were older and married couples. The reporter relayed further that Parra lamented "the indifference of young people toward these folk music gatherings," a slight she felt the more acutely since she had dedicated a song especially to them, "Me gustan los estudiantes" (I Like Students):

> Long live students
> Garden of joy and delight!
> They're birds that aren't frightened
> by animals or by police,
> and they're not afraid of bullets
> or the pack of howling beasts.
> That's right, I say, that's right,
> long live astronomy.

> ¡Que vivan los estudiantes,
> jardín de las alegrías!
> Son aves que no se asustan
> de animal ni policía,
> y no les asustan las balas
> ni el ladrar de la jauría.
> Caramba y zamba la cosa,
> que viva la astronomía.[48]

Regardless of its makeup, the Carpa's audience was routinely so sparse that Parra could not make ends meet with what she took in at the door. Her sister Hilda remembers Violeta turning in circles inside the huge tent, wringing her hands, sick with worry as whatever money she brought in on performance nights had to cover the expenses for herself, her family, and staff for the entire week. "And it wasn't enough!"[49] A stickler for paying her performers, Violeta would use her own earnings from playing at the trendier and more accessible Peña de los Parra to cover the Carpa musicians' pay along with their taxi fares there and back.[50] She also went into debt in order to keep the place going. Her periodic absences when on tour with Chile Laughs and Sings or visiting Favre in La Paz did not help matters.

Parra also had to contend with the frequent harassment of city bureaucrats. With the exception of the district mayor of La Reina who had ceded her the

Carpa's site, city officials were hostile to the project. They came to shut off her electricity more than once, purportedly because Parra did not have permission to use it at that location because technically it was a park. Each time, Parra would have to wade through days or weeks of red tape to get the electricity turned back on. Sometimes, instead of wading and waiting, she would siphon electricity from a nearby power line as she had done at her house of sticks, but then city officials would come to the Carpa to disconnect it. They also accused Parra of selling liquor without a license. They hassled her about the site's sanitation system (or lack thereof). On more than one occasion, police showed up to search the entire complex, a form of harassment that Zapicán was convinced was politically motivated, since Parra was a known leftist.[51]

There were also the constant quarrels between Parra and some of her neighbors. Arts Fair organizer Lorenzo Berg, who happened to also be the chair of La Reina's neighborhood council, recalled receiving several complaints from Parra's more affluent neighbors: they did not like that "she hung her clothing out to dry in the trees, emptied her trough on the road, and made all sorts of noise with her run-down loudspeaker."[52] Zapicán came to her defense. With the contempt of a poor man, he dismissed the Carpa's faultfinders as being so wealthy that they owned not just one but two or three cars. They were people who had never set foot in the Carpa. How, then, he asked, could they possibly appreciate the value of the cultural work that was being performed there?[53]

In the end, Parra's Carpa de La Reina became a rather desolate place. Even the month of September 1966, the one month in the year when there was guaranteed demand for folk music in Chile, was not the success that Parra had hoped it would be. She made every effort in anticipation of hosting her first (and what would end up being her last) independence celebrations at the Carpa. She decorated the tent with streamers and prepared traditional food and drink especially for the occasion. She programmed an entire day of activities on Chile's Independence Day of September 18th, with potato sack races, kite-flying competitions, and a dance contest.[54] She hired special guest artists for the occasion: the neofolklore group Voces Andinas, folklorista Silvia Urbina, and a trio of Mapuche musicians who traveled all the way from Wallmapu for the occasion.[55] But the people did not come. They opted instead for the traditional fondas in the parks in and around Santiago, or for the trendy peñas in the city's center. Argentine musician José Aravena, who was part of the Carpa's September 18th lineup, noted the expectant musicians' forlorn reactions, especially Parra's: "[It] had been a failure. . . . We sang softly to ourselves. . . . The unease was palpable."[56]

Authenticity and Its Limits

The contrast between the Carpa de La Reina and the Peña de los Parra was striking. The collective of young musicians who ran the popular folk club in downtown Santiago had expanded its capacity—with a little demolition help from Violeta—and doubled the number of shows, and still there were long lines of people waiting to get in on weekends. As Violeta continued to perform there regularly, she was unavoidably aware of how well the folk club that shared her name was doing. According to Ángel, "The thing we had going was popular, really popular, and that was hard on my mother."[57]

Isabel's and Ángel Parra's musical careers, both as a duo and as soloists, were taking off in tandem with the Peña's popularity. The duo appeared regularly on radio and had a steady television presence as well. Their debut LP, *Los Parra de Chile*, won the Demon record label's 1966 award for Gold Album of the Year, and it and their other recordings frequently appeared on top ten radio charts.[58] Both siblings were also doing well as solo artists. Ángel, in particular, was increasingly recognized for his songwriting and composing skills. His 1965 "Oratory of the People," a major work composed in the genre of a folk mass and performed by a folk orchestra and full choir, received overwhelmingly positive reviews, while none other than Pablo Neruda, Chile's most illustrious living bard, chose Ángel to set a series of his poems to music.[59] The press treated both Ángel and Isabel like local pop stars. Chile's premier entertainment weekly *Ecran*, for instance, reported on their respective marriages (both occurring, coincidently, in 1966), summer vacation plans, and, in Ángel's case, the birth of his first child and his astrological sign (Cancer) and forecast.[60]

It was not just that Isabel's and Ángel's stars were rising, it was that they often seemed to eclipse their mother. Their duo was known simply as Los Parra (The Parras), a name that implicitly rendered the rest of the musicians in the Parra clan irrelevant, Violeta included. Founder of the Demon record company Camilo Fernández seemed intent on advancing this process further, from downgrade to erasure. He had successfully recruited both Isabel and Ángel to be among the first artists to sign with Demon, whose principal competitor was the well-established record company Odeon Chilena where Violeta was signed for over a decade. This rivalry, in turn, may explain the distinct spin Fernández gave to his 1966 piece in the youth magazine *Musiquero* announcing Isabel's first LP on the Demon label. Fernández declared Isabel "the most popular and highest quality woman singer of our folklore," then followed with a statement that could be interpreted as implying that Violeta was somehow no longer alive: "The daughter of Violeta Parra, . . .

[Isabel] has become her mother's successor, thanks to the rich legacy bequeathed to her in life."[61]

Though not over yet (as Fernández would seem to suggest), Violeta's musical career was not doing nearly as well as her children's. The popular radio show *Discomanía*, hosted by her longtime supporter Ricardo García, had named her Best Songwriter of the Year for her 1965 LP *Recordando a Chile* (Chile on My Mind), but the award was largely honorific, as it was not linked to sales.[62] More substantially (or insubstantially), the only songs by Parra to make the charts during this period (or, as far as I can ascertain, during her lifetime) were the ones covered by neofolklorista stars Las Cuatro Brujas and by her daughter Isabel, whose version of Violeta's "The Gardener" made the top ten in weekly record sales in February 1966.[63] As an article in the entertainment magazine *Ritmo de la juventud* (The Rhythm of Youth) helpfully pointed out to its youthful readership, the song that Violeta Parra composed and recorded twelve years previously "has recently triumphed after all that time . . . and all thanks to her daughter."[64]

In terms of Violeta's live performances, she was still able to fill the house when she performed at venues like the Peña de Valparaíso that were outside her usual radius. She was not much of a draw in Santiago, however. And while the mainstream media considered Isabel's and Ángel's musical activities and social lives newsworthy, they seemed to be only moderately interested in Violeta (except when she was hospitalized for a drug overdose or claimed to have had an affair with Pedro Messone). Tellingly, the headline of a 1966 piece in *Rincón juvenil* (Young People's Corner) on the Carpa de La Reina is angled from the viewpoint of the younger generation: "Ángel and Isabel Parra: 'Our Mother Is Our Greatest Source of Pride.'"[65]

The growing disparity between the musical careers of the two generations of Parras raises the question, why didn't Violeta Parra enjoy the same popularity as her children? On the surface, she would appear to have been easily incorporated into the reinvigorated folk music scene that Isabel, Ángel, and the other young folk singers in their orbit were building, so similar to the one she had known in Paris yet so grounded in the Chilean Left. Violeta, akin to her children, had already adopted the more intimate performance style of the boîtes of Paris's Latin Quarter. She was also among the first of a wave of Santiago-based musicians to incorporate Andean-inspired instruments like the quena and charango into her music, along with those associated with other Latin American countries such as the Argentine bombo and Venezuelan cuatro. Most importantly, she was one of the earliest and most talented composers of the politically engaged songs that would earn her posthumous recognition as the "mother" of the Chilean New Song.[66]

In some regards, the answer to the question is simple: Violeta was not a good fit. First, there was the issue of her age. Then in her late forties, Violeta was old enough to be—and, in Isabel and Ángel's case, literally was—the younger folk singers' mother. A September 1966 article in *Ecran* covering the various independence celebrations at Santiago's folk clubs underscores this generational gap; it refers to Isabel and Ángel as "young folkloristas," and to Violeta as one of the most "antigua" folkloristas—an adjective whose multiple meanings include "ancient," "elderly," "long-serving," and "old-fashioned."[67]

There was also evidently not much room for women among the ranks of musicians who would forge the Chilean New Song movement in the late 1960s and early 1970s. Women had participated in the 1950s folk music revival at or near numeric parity with men, including as its leaders.[68] Their comparative paucity among the New Song musicians was no doubt related to what Ángel Parra would later acknowledge was the "generalized machismo" of the Chilean Left.[69] The emblematic New Song group Quilapayún, founded in 1966, may serve as example: the group's name means "the three bearded ones" in Mapudungun; its members wore long ponchos associated with male-defined gaucho culture; and, according to one of its members, their voices were "very virile" and their performance style "masculine, but not *machista*."[70] To state the obvious, the attributes of beards, gaucho attire, virile voices, and masculinity exclude most women.

In addition to being too old and a woman, Parra was arguably too associated with the Chilean folk revival of the 1950s. Unlike their predecessors, Isabel and Ángel's cohort of folk singers were no longer confined musically by national borders or temporally to bygone days. Together with their young fans, this new generation sought authenticity not in an idealized rural past but in the unmasking of modern society in the urgent present through the baring of the artist's soul. From their perspective, the "folkloric shows" of the 1950s folkloristas, with their didactic solemnity and huaso and huasa costumes, seemed staged and "corny." The traditional music that the 1950s folkloristas collected and performed, in turn, sounded dull and monotonous.[71] In an interview, Isabel Parra reflected on her generation's shift: "All of a sudden, a magnificent world of [Latin American] music opened up to us, and all of that Chilean folklore became a little passé, we moved on to other things."[72]

This generation gap had political dimensions as well. The 1950s folkloristas' notion that there existed some sort of shared chilenidad or Chilean identity waiting to be discovered became increasingly untenable with the growing political polarization of Chilean society, while their spiritual nationalism clashed with the radical internationalism of a new generation of folk musicians who saw themselves as part of the "Third World" and as standing in solidarity with the anticolonialist struggles of Vietnam and Angola.

It is worth underlining two things here. First, Parra was no longer a practicing folklorista by the time she returned from her second European sojourn in mid-1965, having completed the bulk of her work collecting and recording folk material in the 1950s. As a case in point, the last year she released an LP of traditional material was 1959. With few exceptions, the material on her subsequent solo albums, from the release of her 1961 LP *Toda Violeta Parra* (All of Violeta Parra) onward, consisted of Parra's original compositions. Second, Parra had been composing politically engaged songs at least since the start of the 1960s and had written nearly all of what would become her most well-known ones by mid-decade—including the purported "birth certificate of the Chilean New Song movement," her song "La Carta" (The Letter).[73]

None of this mattered, however. What mattered was the Chilean public's perception of her, and that was overwhelmingly as a leading proponent of the 1950s Chilean folk revival, now waning or already waned. Arts Fair director Lorenzo Berg characterized this lack of recognition for the songs that Parra wrote after her folkloric stage as "deadly": "She knew that she had more talent than a lot of people out there who were strutting their success and receiving support. Today it seems obvious to us that her songs are hits, that international stars record them in various languages, but back then things were different. Eighty percent of the people had no idea they existed."[74] Jorge Coulon and Eduardo Carrasco, respective founding members of the iconic New Song groups Inti-Illimani and Quilapayún, confirmed Berg's assessment that many people—themselves included—were unaware of the breadth of Parra's songwriting talents while she was alive. Coulon recalled being acquainted with Parra's music only through the versions of her songs by neofolklore sensations Las Cuatro Brujas, while Carrasco stated that "most people showed little interest while she was alive in what she was doing."[75] Parra's contribution to the New Song would only be fully realized after her death.[76]

Parra's overriding status as a folklorista appears to have had the same effect of obscuring her creative activities as a visual artist as it did her talents as a songwriter. She had displayed her artwork at the annual Arts Fair four of the seven years since it was founded in 1959, including in 1965. She had spent the bulk of the other three years in Europe, where she had exhibited her artwork in solo and group shows in Helsinki, East Berlin, Geneva, Lausanne, and Paris—including her groundbreaking show at the Museum of Decorative Arts. Yet the only mention of her by a reporter covering the 1965 Arts Fair for the Santiago daily *La Nación* highlights Parra's involvement not in her capacity as a visual artist but as a folklorista: she was "the inevitable Violeta Parra," performing folk songs for all to enjoy.[77]

The irony is pronounced. Parra was becoming passé precisely at the moment when she was creating new and what were arguably her most transcendent musical and visual works. In a sense, she had become a victim of the success of her midlife turn to the authentic. Though it lacks a fixed meaning, authenticity is always constituted as an alternative or "other" to modern society. Reinvented as a folklorista, Parra appealed to her authenticity-seeking fanbase as the representative of pure and unchanging traditions in the face of a superficial and ever-changing world. This made it difficult, if not impossible, for her admirers to conceive of her having a creative trajectory that evolved through different stages, like that of modern artist Pablo Picasso, whose work Parra so admired, or of her own brother, the modern poet Nicanor Parra.

The success of Parra's reinvention as the authentic alternative to modernity's woes was also hard to sustain. For something (or someone) to be experienced as authentic, it must produce a sense of discovery or revelation. Once that sense of revelation wears off, seekers of the authentic tend to move on, propelled by the promise of their next "discovery." This was the case of many of Parra's followers, whose numbers ebbed as they left folklore behind to embrace the latest trend to offer them a renewed sense of meaning and fulfillment to counter the alienation of their modern lives.

The Pueblo and Violeta

Not all of Parra's admirers were authenticity-seekers. Though difficult to quantify, multiple sources indicate that Parra was able to establish and maintain a critical mass of loyal followers whose life circumstances ensured they would not be overly influenced by the latest trends. They were found in the shantytowns and rural hamlets where people gathered around the radio on Sundays to listen to Parra's 1954 surprise hit show, *Violeta Parra Sings*, or any of its later iterations. They resided in the provincial cities, campesino settlements, and mining camps that Parra visited on tour with Chile Laughs and Sings in the last year of her life. They were Parra's beloved pueblo.

Patricio Manns writes of Parra's performance in a theater in Puerto Natales, some 1,880 miles from Santiago in the far south of Chile. Parra had spoken to the audience that evening: "I've never been here before, but perhaps some of you know me." A young woman had stood up and responded, "Everyone knows you here. You sing on the radio and your name is Violeta."[78] In a similar vein, the mother of Chilean playwright Luis Barrales told him that Parra was "super well known" in her childhood town of Laja, some sixty miles south of Concepción. Growing up there, Barrales's mother had innocently believed that Parra lived nearby because of the way everyone talked about her as if they knew her personally.[79]

In Puerto Natales, Laja, and other sites that were *popular* in the class-based sense that they were where the non-elite gathered, people loved and admired

Parra, not because she was perceived to incarnate an authenticity that they longed to know and experience but because they saw and heard themselves represented in her. They inundated the radio station with fan mail thanking Parra for playing "our music." They offered her gifts in accordance with that sense of identification: the thick woolen shawl that was knitted by the women from the Mothers' Center in Punta Arenas and that was just like the shawls that they wore, or the small chair made by a local carpenter to fit Parra's small stature that was similar to the stature of most poor women in Chile. They referred to Parra as the young woman in the Puerto Natales theater had done, and as people across Chile do to this day, on a first-name basis as "Violeta."

Final Months

In October 1966, Violeta left the Carpa in Ángel's care to embark on her second tour with Chile Laughs and Sings. This one took her nearly the length of Chile. Distances between towns, especially in the north, were extremely long, and the pace of travel was demanding as the musicians performed two shows in a town, then moved on. They tried to rest as best they could on the bus between gigs—all of them except for Parra, that is. She suffered from insomnia and insisted on playing her guitar at all hours. Exasperated, her fellow travelers threw things at her to try to get her to stop. Reminiscing years later, one of them commented, "If we had realized [her transcendence], we would have never thrown shoes at her head."[80] The tour had triumphant moments, including when a spontaneous chorus of over 10,000 people joined Parra in singing one of her popular songs at the Arica stadium.[81] It had its unusual moments as well, such as when Parra received the gift of a llama from the inhabitants of the town of Parionacota in the Andean province of Arica (which may or may not have been the llama that ended up at the Carpa).[82]

At some point during the northern part of the tour, Parra made a spur-of-the-moment decision to visit Favre in La Paz. The couple's complicated relationship had grown even more complicated since Parra's previous visit, as she had since become embroiled in her ill-defined relationship with Zapicán. Meanwhile, in La Paz, Favre had earned a reputation as a womanizer, a status that his autobiography confirms. This, in turn, made his friends there apprehensive that one of his love interests might show up at the Peña Naira while Parra was visiting.[83] To further confound matters, Zapicán appears to have traveled to La Paz at some point during this period as well. The record is spotty, but he seems to have gone there on his own impetus, in the hope of interceding with Favre on Parra's behalf, though his efforts proved in vain.[84]

Parra rejoined the Chile Laughs and Sings tour in Arica at the end of October in time to catch the plane home to Santiago, where she resumed her life at the Carpa. Her album *Violeta Parra's Latest Compositions* was released at the end of November. It received little notice in the press, though lyrics of several of its songs would be published in both the communist daily *El Siglo* and the youth entertainment magazine *Rincón Juvenil* in January 1967. Also in November, Parra recorded guitar and xylophone parts on her ten-year-old granddaughter Tita's debut album; a children's-themed single on the Demon label featuring a song by Tita's uncle Ángel on one side and her grandmother Violeta on the other.[85] Released in December 1966, it would be Violeta's last recording.

Parra also traveled with her entourage of Carpa musicians to perform at the Peña del Mar, the new folk club that her friend Osvaldo Rodríguez and others had opened in the resort town of Viña del Mar. Once again, she played several nights to a full house and extended her engagement to accommodate the demand. Rodríguez remembered a lighthearted moment when Parra played soccer with some boys in the public square, then posed for a photograph, her foot on the soccer ball and her arms fisted in a victory gesture, surrounded by the crew from the peña. But he also recounted what Parra shared with him during a more intimate moment: that she felt sick and tired, that she wasn't the person she once had been, that the Carpa caused her too many headaches. "She was weighed down by debt and by the indifference of others; it took a lot out of her to sing."[86]

In early December 1966, Parra went on her last tour with Chile Laughs and Sings. Again, she traveled as far north as Arica, and again she appears to have gone on to La Paz on the spur of the moment to visit Favre.[87] She bought a revolver while she was there. She told her Bolivian friends that it was to scare off wild dogs at the Carpa. Within two months, she would use it to kill herself.[88]

Shortly after Parra's return from her tour of northern Chile and side trip to La Paz, Favre and his band Los Jairas traveled to Santiago to perform at the international "Festival of Festivals" organized by Chile Laughs and Sings producer Largo Farías. In addition to the Bolivian (and Swiss) band Los Jairas, the event featured Uruguayan singer-songwriter Daniel Viglietti and Argentine and Chilean musicians, including invited folk ensembles and soloists from Chile's provinces. Violeta Parra was one of the festival's headliners, though she was assigned the less-than-optimal performance slot of Friday afternoon.[89] Los Jairas closed the three-day folk music extravaganza. According to a review in *El Mercurio*, they "stole the show."[90]

Los Jairas stayed in Santiago for a week or so, performing at the Carpa and other venues, and on radio and television. On the evening that they were booked to play at La Carpa, the lineup also included the up-and-coming folk band Quilapayún as well as an ensemble of Mapuche musicians. Parra was to be the show's final act. In his history of Quilapayún, founder Eduardo Carrasco writes of the "indelible memory" that evening produced. The musicians had gathered around the Carpa's wood stove, drinking wine and waiting for their audience to arrive. They were still waiting two hours later. "And then," Carrasco recalled, "with a mixture of disappointment, sadness, and spite, without having agreed upon anything in advance, we began a strange ritual: we started to play for each other. By the time it was Violeta's turn to perform we had long recovered our usual good spirits. We all sang to the empty tent as if the multitudes were listening. That was the last time we saw Violeta."[91]

"A Sheep in Wolf's Clothing"

Parra's mood was dark as 1966 came to a close. According to Zapicán, "You could predict what was going to happen next . . . [Parra] was very depressed, very angry."[92] He had to monitor her constantly. Then she made another attempt on her life: she locked herself in her room and cut her wrists. Zapicán, suspecting something was amiss, broke down the door before it was too late.[93] He and the couple who worked at the Carpa now hid everything from her: knives, shaving razors, scissors. They confiscated her revolver and hid it as well.

There were plenty of other signs that Parra's mental health was deteriorating. According to Carmen Luisa, Violeta would wake up one morning as happy as a could be, feeling marvelous, and the next morning she would be an ogre who told everybody off, who found everything just horrible. "Out of nowhere she would begin to cry, and I would ask her what's wrong and she would tell me to go to hell."[94]

Parra's distress manifested itself in her body as well. She continued to suffer from the rash that her doctors had diagnosed as a "nervous allergy" and developed sores all over her body from her constant scratching. The itching and wounds gave her no peace during the day and kept her up all night. In her effort to escape her discomfort, she turned to tranquilizers and alcohol. Folklorista Osvaldo Cádiz remembers going with his wife and fellow folklorista Margot Loyola to visit Parra at the Carpa in her last months. They found her drunk and feverish, showing signs that she had not eaten in days.[95]

As Parra's behavior became more and more erratic, her relationships with just about everyone—family, friends, colleagues, music industry and media people, members of the Communist Party—became strained to the breaking point. Carmen Luisa and Zapicán, who were the two people most intimately linked to her at the time, experienced the worst of it. When not in a depressive state that impeded her from caring for Carmen Luisa (or anybody), Violeta zealously tried to control every aspect of her adolescent daughter's life. She violently shut down a performance by Quilapayún at the peña in Valparaíso, for example, after discovering that Carmen Luisa, who was seeing one of the band members, had snuck away to be with him without her mother's permission. According to Eduardo Carrasco, the shouting, recriminations, and hair-pulling were such that Quilapayún had to stop playing midway through the show.[96] In another disturbing incident, Violeta is reported to have cut off Carmen Luisa's hair while she slept, then wept for days, filled with remorse.[97]

Parra's relationship with Zapicán was similarly fraying. Noting that their conflicts often turned physical, Zapicán declared Parra the most violent person he had ever known, then corrected himself, seeing as his father had kept him chained to a tree for two years when he was a child. Zapicán offered as proof of Parra's violent streak the time she had broken his bombo in anger. He had punched Parra's guitar in return because "I spoke the same language that she spoke."[98]

Violeta fought with Isabel and Ángel, too. Her dream had been that they and their families would all come and live with her and Carmen Luisa at the Carpa. She would tell them, "Let's all go to La Reina with spouses, in-laws, grandchildren, and pets. Comforts are crap, and people get consumed by their household affairs."[99] She accused her two eldest children, now successful musicians, of having become bourgeois in their tastes. Ángel would later concede that she had not been wrong.[100] Both he and Isabel had married "up" when they wed their respective spouses; Ángel, to Marta Orrego Matte, from an aristocratic family, and Isabel, to Tito Rojas, a medical doctor and musician.[101] Both siblings now lived in spacious homes in well-off Santiago neighborhoods. Given their success, Violeta's fantasy that Isabel and Ángel and their families would forgo the comforts of modern life to join her at the Carpa was unrealistic; a "demented idea" is how Isabel described it.[102] This did not prevent Violeta from being furious with her children for not taking her up on her proposal.

Parra ended several long-term professional relationships and friendships during this period. She severed her musical collaboration of over a decade with Odeon record producer Rubén Nouzeilles when she broke her contract with the label. Her old friend the photographer Sergio Larraín attempted to trade a tapestry that she had lent him for the considerable sum that was still owed on the circus tent and she became furious and demanded that he return the tapestry immediately, insisting it was hers and so was the tent. When he went to the Carpa with the tapestry, but without its frame, her fury only grew. "Violeta told me 'I never want to see you again, go fuck yourself!' . . . And that's how it was, I never saw her again, she never saw me again. In the end she was so enraged that it was scary to go see her."[103]

Parra's relationship with the Central Committee of the Chilean Communist Party is also alleged to have soured during her final months.[104] A friend who visited her around this time recounts how Parra railed against the party for abandoning her even though she had been a faithful collaborator for years.[105] Other sources recall her expressing similar feelings of betrayal.

Parra also appears to have grown increasingly violent during this period. In addition to her physical altercations with Zapicán and the beatings she gave Carmen Luisa, she is purported to have punched the artist Nemesio Antúnez; a Chilean diplomat based in Argentina on a visit to Santiago; and José Aravena, the Argentine guitarist who performed at the Carpa for several months in 1966, and who quit after she gave him a bloody nose.[106]

Parra spent her last months, then, fighting with pretty much everyone she knew—and, one can only assume, with strangers as well. In an oft-cited passage of his 1960 poem "Defensa de Violeta Parra" (Defense of Violeta Parra), Nicanor famously described his sister as a "sheep in wolf's clothing." As Quilapayún member Eduardo Carrasco points out, this meant that the vast majority of people who crossed paths with Violeta saw only her wolf side.[107] Parra's anger would also surely have been viewed through a gendered lens that made it unacceptable a priori for a woman. Regardless of how her rage was interpreted, the end result was that Parra was not so much ignored as avoided in this last phase of her life.

And yet, the consensus of those who knew and esteemed her was that were it not for her combative spirit, there would not have been a Violeta Parra. The Peruvian writer José María Arguedas believed that Parra had no choice but to be aggressive "up to the last moment of her life. She was a force who bore the burden of her extraordinarily lucid consciousness of her own worth and, through this, of the value and quality of all that she had sought and found in the working classes."[108] Sergio Larraín compared her to a "storm that comes out of nowhere and flattens everything in its wake. And she made herself heard."[109] Perhaps musicologist and colleague Gastón Soublette summed it up best: "[Parra was an] inspired, creative, strong, and brave woman, who faced life without ever compromising her worldview . . . which was that of a marginalized person in relation to what is often called the 'system'; but . . . her courage and rage also carried with them a fair amount of skill and dexterity which allowed her to maneuver her way around the onerous barriers, both societal and institutional, that the world erected."[110]

"I Have No Place to Be"

Parra spent her last Christmas Eve at a family gathering at Ángel's home. Ángel and Isabel had much to celebrate that evening, as their duo had just been chosen as the year's "Best Musical Act on Television" by *Ecran*.[111]

Uruguayan singer-songwriter Daniel Viglietti, who was there too, would later recall the evening: The family and friends had dined at a long table set up outside in the patio, with a waiter in white gloves standing by, ready to serve them. Violeta had sat, not with the adults, but at the "kids'" table. After dinner, the teenagers had brought out their guitars and sung songs by Italian popstar Antoine and US protest singer Bob Dylan. Violeta had listened to them intently. Later, the entire party had begged her to sing, chanting "Sing, Violeta, sing!" She had declined, however, claiming she was too tired.[112]

Parra welcomed in the new year with a radio interview conducted by Chile Laughs and Sings producer René Largo Farías, who may have been the only friend and colleague with whom she was not fighting. Based on the transcript, she sounds as if she were finally at peace . . . or defeated; it is difficult to know without access to the audio. Gone were the exaggerated lists of her accomplishments and announcements of impending tours to Europe, the United States, and Asia. Instead, she elaborated what could be considered her credo at the end of her life: "I am very content to have reached a point in my work when I don't even want to make tapestries, nor paintings, nor the occasional poem anymore. I am happy to have been able to put up my Carpa and to work today with living elements, with my public near me; a public that I can feel, touch, talk to, and incorporate into my soul." Parra wished all her listeners a happy New Year, then closed the interview in her signature third person: "May the dreams of all Chileans come true, and may Violeta Parra have the good fortune to continue singing as she has until now so as to finish the work that she has set out to do."[113]

January 1967 in Santiago was as much of an "artists' graveyard" as that month of August Parra had spent in Paris a few years back.[114] Both Isabel and Ángel were on vacation with their respective in-laws at one of the many beachfront resort towns not far from Santiago. Isabel had invited Violeta to join them, but she had responded that she would have plenty of time to vacation once she was dead and buried.[115] Most of the other people Violeta was (or had once been) friends with were out of town as well. Even the usually packed Peña de los Parra, where Violeta continued to perform regularly while her children were away, was almost empty on those warm Santiago nights.

Sensing that Violeta was near the brink, Nicanor and Zapicán conspired to pull her back from it. They hatched the idea of a trip to lift her spirits. Parra would travel with Zapicán to Argentina and his native Uruguay, then continue on to Europe.[116] Contacts in Montevideo and Buenos Aires were enlisted and train tickets purchased for the second week in February.

Parra had another tour booked with Chile Laughs and Sings before then, however, this one traveling south to Puerto Montt and the Island of Chiloé.

The touring musicians were scheduled to depart on February 2. Largo Farías, who ran his enterprises with a collective spirit, called a meeting of the participants a few days prior.

The musicians gathered at his apartment to go over the details of the tour. Parra arrived late and visibly upset. She announced to her colleagues that the wind had blown down her tent, and that she needed to be paid double and in advance for her participation in the tour so that she could hire laborers to fix it. Patricio Manns, the only musician to have left a detailed record of the meeting, claims to have volunteered to donate half of his earnings from the tour to help Parra with her cause. The other musicians grumbled that this would not be fair, that they had expenses too, and offered to instead organize a fundraiser when they got back from the tour. According to Manns, Parra's proposal was then put to a vote, which she lost hands down. After angrily asserting that, in that case, she would not join the tour, Parra stormed out, pausing as she passed by Manns to take his face in her hands and give him a languorous kiss. "With this, I bid you all farewell," she declared, then left, slamming the door behind her.[117]

With her Carpa literally falling down around her, Parra decided that it was time for her to move back into her house of sticks. She went there days before her suicide to inform her mother that she wanted the house back. Clarisa, whose temper was known to be as explosive as Violeta's, did not come out of the house to talk to her daughter. Carmen Luisa recalled that day: "My grandmother answered her from inside the house with some crazy threats, that she was going to beat her up, and the like. . . . And she would have. Can you imagine? . . . That's the way it was."[118]

Parra was forty-nine years old, with little material comfort to show for all her hard work and the many unsurmountable obstacles that she had somehow surmounted. She now found herself shut out of the first and only home she had built for herself and her family. The lyrics from her experimental piece for voice and guitar, "The Sparrowhawk," rang true as she entered the final days of her life: "I have no place to be" (*Yo no tengo donde estar*).

Parra does not appear to have had a place to be when viewed from a wider angle, either. Europe had seemed promising at one time. Parra had found many of her first and, in some cases, only successes there. She recorded her first two LPs of Chilean folk music for the French label, Chants du Monde; published the only book of her songs in her lifetime with the French press Maspero; and held her unprecedented and unmatched solo exhibit at the Museum of Decorative Arts. But as much as her European public appreciated her, they also exoticized her, thereby reminding her that she did not belong. Besides, as her songs and letters document, Parra felt a deep homesickness for Chile whenever she was in Europe, especially when her immediate family members were not there with her. In the end, Europe could not offer Parra a place to be.

Finding a place for herself in her native Chile proved equally problematic. Parra was largely excluded from its elite educational and cultural institutions. But she was also marginalized by those whom one could assume to be her allies (including those who would claim or reclaim allegiance to her upon her death). She was on the outs with the Communist Party, the only political organization that she had ever supported or that had supported her through its network of connections, both national and international, in better times. And she was dismissed as too folkloric and therefore passé by the younger musicians at the forefront of the new trends in folk and protest music that were taking the country by storm.

Parra also found it hard to find a place for herself as a woman in patriarchal society. Denied the agency and inventiveness of a male artist, she was instead banished to that artistic realm of the instinctive, primitive, and naïve reserved for those categories of people who were less well-suited for modernity—women, along and overlapping with certain ethnic and racialized groups. In Chile, Parra was further the target of disparaging rumors, tainted with misogyny, regarding her creative work: that she must have stolen her popular song "La jardinera" (The Gardener) because there was no way she could have written it herself; that Nicanor was the true author of her songs' lyrics; that she had fabricated the whole story about her Louvre exhibit and even had fake press clippings made for her in Paris to support her pretense that it had occurred.[119] And Parra faced the moral reproach, that ubiquitous "What will people say?," that all patuda or outrageous women faced for challenging the rules that would govern women's comportment.

For all of these reasons—she was too poor, too uneducated, too unrefined, too old, too folkloric, too communist, not communist enough, too woman, not womanly enough—Parra found that there was no place where she belonged. Add to that her sorrow over Favre's absence, jealousy of her children's success, frustration at the failure of the Carpa, and a generalized sense that she had not gotten what she deserved, that she was owed something, and one begins to grasp the accumulating mental health crisis that was the final stage of her life.

"I Bid You Farewell"

After multiple attempts on her life, Parra's suicide appears to have been both predicted and planned. In Chilean folk tradition, the singer will sometimes signal that they are nearing the end of their song with the phrase "Ordeno la despedida" or "I bid you farewell."[120] The phrase's literal translation is "I order the farewell." As in English, the Spanish verb "to order" can mean both "to give an order" or to command, and "to put in order" or to arrange. Parra ordered her farewell according to the two meanings of the phrase.

Parra announced her intention to "order" or command her own death with the same will and focus that she approached most things in life. She broached the topic with diverse people on multiple occasions in the months before she died. Héctor Pavez recounts how she asked him if he ever thought about the fact that he was going to die someday. He answered, "Yes, it's horrible, I just can't believe it," and Parra responded, "You have to decide death. Command it! Not let death come to you."[121] Margot Loyola recalled Parra making a similar claim: "*Comadre* [Dear friend], you have to decide the moment of your death."[122]

Parra also did some ordering or arranging of her affairs in preparation for her farewell. In the days before she committed suicide, she displayed the classic signs of someone who was planning their own death. For one, she began giving away her possessions. Her sister Hilda remembers visiting her at the Carpa, which Violeta had somehow managed to repair, the week that she died. Violeta had insisted on giving her a handwoven blanket, a tape recorder, a typewriter, and a suitcase full of clothing and other miscellaneous items that she had brought back with her from Europe. When Hilda protested that Violeta needed all these things herself, Violeta had told her not to worry; she would buy everything again and brand new on her upcoming trip to Argentina. Violeta also gave Hilda an autographed copy of her newest LP *Violeta Parra's Latest Compositions*, which according to Hilda was something Violeta had never done before.[123]

The day before her suicide, Violeta ate lunch at Nicanor's house. It was a Saturday afternoon. She had arrived late, bearing the unusual gift of three ducks. Nicanor noticed that she was in a strange mood and decided to try to distract her with a new project. He proposed she write a novel, but Violeta scoffed and told him that he would have to write it himself, that she was very tired.[124] At the end of their meal, Violeta asked Nicanor what last song he would like to hear her sing. She wanted it to be "Un domingo en el cielo" (One Sunday in Heaven), a humorous song about the saints all throwing a drunken birthday party in heaven. Nicanor requested his favorite song instead, "Según el favor del viento" (As the Wind Blows). Violeta obliged, then sang "One Sunday in Heaven" as her farewell song, Sunday being the next day. Nicanor would later realize that she had already made her decision, that she had come to say goodbye.[125]

From Nicanor's, Violeta went to the Peña de los Parra, where she performed songs from her latest LP. She also offered it for sale. A young man who worked there recalled the evening: "She stepped gracefully between the wicker stools, making her appeal to the audience: 'Come and buy my new album *Las últimas composiciones de Violeta Parra* [Violeta Parra's Latest Compositions],' repeating the title for emphasis." He continued, drawing on the double meaning of the Spanish word *últimas*: "In effect, in the hours that followed, the album would become a record of her last songs."[126]

Violeta woke early as usual the following morning and yelled for Carmen Luisa or Zapicán to bring her some tea. She next got up and had breakfast, then closed herself in her room. According to Zapicán, she kept on playing the same song over and over again on the record player: Isabel and Ángel's hit cover of the Venezuelan song "Río Manzanares" (Manzanares River):

> Manzanares River, let me cross over
> for my ailing mother has sent for me to come.
>
> My mother is the only star
> that illuminates my fate
> and if she is to die
> I will go to heaven with her

> *Río Manzanares, déjame pasar,*
> *que mi madre enferma me mandó llamar . . .*
>
> *Mi madre es la única estrella*
> *que alumbra mi porvenir*
> *y si se llega a morir*
> *al cielo me voy con ella.*[127]

The summer heat was suffocating that afternoon. Parra came out of her room for lunch but did not say a word during the entire meal, then shut herself in her room again. She drank one glass of wine after another while writing what would end up being an extensive suicide note. She had searched the caretakers' shack when they were out on errands and found the revolver she had brought from Bolivia. According to one out of the many retellings that Zapicán offered of the events of that day, Parra left her room at one point to ask him, "Where will a bullet not fail?" He had pointed to his temple.[128]

At 6:00 P.M., Violeta Parra fired one shot into her right temple. Carmen Luisa ran to her mother's room and discovered her body, slumped over her guitar, the revolver still in her hand.[129] Several sources describe Violeta's room as strewn with sheets of paper. On one of them she had outlined her latest and what would now remain an unfinished project, "Symphony of the Circus."[130]

The letter Violeta wrote that day was addressed to Nicanor. The Carpa's caretaker delivered it to him that evening, along with the news of her death. Nicanor resisted making the letter public for decades, and the original was ostensibly lost. Some fifty years after Violeta wrote it, he shared a handwritten copy he had made of the letter with Chilean journalist Sabine Drysdale, who published excerpts of it in her 2019 biographical essay, "Violeta Parra: La violenta Parra" (The Violent Parra). In it, Violeta rails against seemingly everyone except Nicanor, from her mother and children to then-president Eduardo Frei, to Fidel Castro, Vladimir Lenin, and the Chilean Communist Party. Her words document her profound sense of abandonment and betrayal at the end of her life: "I had nothing. I gave everything. I wanted to give and found no one willing to receive."[131]

Legacies

Word of Parra's suicide quickly spread, and the Carpa de La Reina started to fill with people: family, friends, fellow musicians and artists, well-wishers, the press. A wake was held the next day where hundreds of people filed past Parra's coffin, set on the stage at her Carpa, to pay their respects. The traditional singers from Puente Alto were there. The Circus Artists Union, the Folkloristas Union, Guitarists of Chile, the Actors Union, various Mothers' Centers, the Communist Youth's Central Committee, and *El Siglo* all sent representatives to take turns standing vigil. A reporter from *El Siglo* described the general public as humble; it was made up of "women with a bag of bread or a kilo of sugar in their hands, silent, expectant, incredulous in the face of what had happened."[132]

Crowds of people lined the streets the following day for Parra's funeral procession. Vendors from the flower market blanketed her coffin with rose petals as it passed by. Musicians, artists, radio announcers, reporters, writers, and several senators, Salvador Allende among them, joined Parra's family at the cemetery for her funeral services. Thousands were in attendance, including, reportedly, several of Isabel and Ángel Parra's fans hoping to catch a glimpse of their favorite artists.[133] The Chile Laughs and Sings musicians, who were in Patagonia when they learned of Parra's suicide, canceled the remainder of their tour and returned to Santiago to be there.

Parra received far more attention from the mainstream media in death than she had in life. Radio stations that would never have considered playing her music interrupted their programming to announce her death the night of her passing. News of her suicide made the front page of every major newspaper except the conservative *El Mercurio*.[134]

Obituaries followed. The reporter from the women's magazine *Eva* noted Parra's slight build and campesina features and recounted how her struggles had begun at an early age "as one of ten siblings, children of a poor tenant-farming family" that often had nothing to put on its table.[135] For Tito Mundt, writing for the daily *La Tercera*, Parra was "a typical *mujer del pueblo* [woman of the people]" who represented the "authentic Chile."[136] *El Siglo* reporter Luis Alberto Mansilla (pseud. Pastor Aucapan) likened Parra to "a folkloric version of King Midas": "she had brought the gold that was [the soul of our people] into the light and carried it to the world, to Paris, Berlin, Moscow."[137] A reporter for the youth entertainment magazine *Rincón Juvenil* wrote that "[Violeta] belonged to all of Chile, to Chileans, to its *pueblo*, with her deeply rooted and absolute dedication to something that is absolutely our own: FOLKLORE."[138] Reporting for the weekly *Vea*, Raquel Correa wrote, "Neither [Violeta's] voice nor her face was attractive. But her visage almost appeared beautiful when she smiled sweetly, with those lively eyes and voice of a pure campesina, she had the enchantment of the authentic."[139]

Parra's death was followed by expressions of regret and the search for explanations. Many blamed her suicide on one or another of her former lovers, rumored or real—Alberto Zapicán, Pedro Messone, and, most often, Gilbert Favre. Others focused on her isolation at the Carpa. Almost everyone acknowledged the role that social neglect and even rejection played in her ultimate despair. As the Chilean artist Eduardo Martínez Bonatti bluntly stated at a roundtable organized in her honor, "We failed [her] as human beings."[140]

The musical tributes and other homages began almost immediately and continue to this day. So too does the process of taking stock of Parra's formidable legacy, in the materials she collected as a folklorista, and in her creative activities as a musician, visual artist, and poet. Considerable effort has also been made to conserve and promote Parra's work, a high point of which was the establishment of the Violeta Parra Museum in 2015, currently housed at the Catholic University of Chile in Santiago.

In the ensuing decades, and particularly with the advent of the internet and social media, Parra has increasingly become an international figure. The detailed examination of her impressive afterlife would fill another book. Suffice it to state that Violeta Parra continues to be reinvented. Concerns that she might someday be forgotten have given way to fears that her memory is being distorted under neoliberalism. Many consider this to be the case regarding the tribute performed at the 2017 Viña del Mar Festival to mark the centennial of her birth: an over-the-top—and apparently lip-synched—production of a medley of her songs that could rival any performance at a US Grammy Awards ceremony or Eurovision Song Contest.[141]

Sometimes Parra is reinvented perversely, as when Far Right candidate José Antonio Kast inserted an image of her playing the guitar onto his campaign billboards for the 2021 Chilean presidential election. (It was removed once the Violeta Parra Foundation threatened legal action.)[142] Other times she is reinvented bizarrely, as with a "self-portrait of Violeta Parra" that was put up for auction on eBay. The painting of a woman with long blond hair and blue eyes that was clearly neither painted by Violeta Parra nor a portrait of her listed a starting price of 500 British pounds.[143] (I do not know if it ever sold.)

But Violeta Parra is also being reinvented by successive generations of musicians, artists, and social activists, in Chile and elsewhere, who recognize themselves in her work and who draw inspiration from it. They include the traditional poets who stubbornly insist on keeping their practice alive, just as Parra did, and who have written décimas and other styles of folk poetry dedicated to her across the years. The hundreds of unhoused people who organized a land takeover and, when granted the land by the Popular Unity government in 1972, renamed it the "Violeta Parra Settlement" in her honor.[144] The New Song artists who carried her music with them into exile after the 1973 military coup and introduced it to people standing in solidarity with Chile throughout the world. The thousands of people living under the Pinochet dictatorship who walked out of their workplaces and homes at noon on August 9, 1984, as part of a daylong protest and sang "Gracias a la vida" (Thanks to Life) in one voice.[145] The Ukrainians who adopted the same song in their fight for democracy during the Orange Revolution in 2004 and 2005.[146] The people of the working-class Santiago neighborhood of Yungay who in December 2019 organized a performance of Parra's song "Miren cómo sonríen" (Look How They Smile), an angry screed against the hypocrisy of bad governments. The elaborate production included the participation of a community choir, dance ensemble, brass band, guitarist, charango player, and the rap artist Dkdasez. Recorded by drone, the final scene of the video shows everyone standing together in the barrio's central plaza, fists raised high, in front of a banner that reads "Change Everything."[147]

———

This biography of Violeta Parra is my contribution to the ongoing debate on the meanings of her life and work. It has traced Parra's trajectory, from her semiurban, semirural upbringing in southern Chile, to her years of performing "whatever the public asked for," to her midlife turn to the authentic as a folklorista, to her "volcanic" eruption as an artist. It has explored how she actively participated in the construction of authenticity in Chile, Argentina, and the cultural centers of Europe on both sides of the Iron Curtain. Parra staked her right to do so on her unwavering identification with the Chilean people. An extraordinary artist who proudly declared herself ordinary, she took those social characteristics that should have rendered her invisible and transformed them into assets. They were what made her authentic.

Authenticity would prove an unstable platform for Parra's multifaceted artistic career. The results of her efforts to clear a path where none existed included both the triumph of her exhibit in the Louvre Palace and the loneliness of her last months at the Carpa. Parra's struggles attest to how difficult it was for her to break through the barriers of social exclusion of her era.

How does a woman of undistinguished origins and anticonventional beauty ("the ugliest woman on the planet") from a provincial town ("from Chillán") in southern Chile ("a tiny country . . . at the end of the earth") become a world-renowned artist whose impact continues to reverberate across the decades? My long answer is this biography. If I were to attempt a short answer, it would be this: Violeta Parra drew inspiration from the materials she gathered as a child and unearthed as a folklorista to produce original works that have withstood the test of time. A practiced everything-ist, she reinvented herself as barroom singer, flamenco artist, folklorista, modern composer, painter, sculptor, ceramicist, tapestry-maker, cook, queen of her Carpa, and everywoman. She ignored or rejected social restrictions and gave free and full rein to her creativity. She drew strength from her commitment to the Chilean pueblo and to oppressed peoples the world over. She was patuda or outrageous enough to imagine it possible, and tenacious enough to make it be so. I leave the last words to her:

> Thanks to life for all it has given me.
> It has given me laughter, it has given me tears.
> And so I distinguish joyfulness from sorrow,
> the materials that together make up my song
> and your song, which is the same song,
> and everyone's song, which is my own song.

> *Gracias a la vida que me ha dado tanto.*
> *Me ha dado la risa y me ha dado el llanto.*
> *Así yo distingo dicha de quebranto,*
> *los dos materiales que forman mi canto*
> *y el canto de ustedes que es el mismo canto,*
> *y el canto de todos, que es mi propio canto.*[148]

Acknowledgments

I have experienced writing this book as a collective effort without borders, so great has been the support and generosity that people have shown me over the years. I would like to thank the scholars in Chile, the United States, and other places whose research is foundational to my understanding of Violeta Parra's life and work. I owe special debt to self-declared "fanatic academics" Juan Pablo González, Claudio Rolle, and Oscar Ohlsen, whose *Historia social de la música popular de Chile*, volumes 1 and 2, have proven indispensable to my work. So have studies by musicologists Jorge Aravena Décart, Olivia Concha Molinari, Daniela Fugellie, Jedrek Mularski, Daniel Party, Fernando Ríos, Javier Rodríguez Aedo, Christián Spencer, Rodrigo Torres Alvarado, and Mauricio Valdebenito. My interpretations of Parra's poetry, song lyrics, and letters have been enriched by works in the fields of literature and interdisciplinary studies, especially those by Marjorie Agosín, Inés Dölz-Blackburn, Alejandro Escobar Mundaca, Paula Miranda, and Patricia Vilches. Art historians who have helped me to see Parra's artwork in new ways include Lorna Dillon, Viviana Hormazábal, Isabel Plante, Felipe Quijada, and Serda Yalkin. I have been privileged to have been in dialogue with many of the people listed here over the course of my research and am grateful for their guidance and friendship.

Several people have read and commented on this book in its entirety. I would like to thank my two book reviewers for the University of North Carolina Press, Juan Pablo González and Heidi Tinsman. Every aspect of this work has been enhanced by their comments, suggestions, and expertise. Marjorie Elaine, who read an almost-there draft, offered excellent edits and looked for those passages that gave her "pause"—which was her sisterly way of saying that they still needed work. I wrote the first chapters of this book while in a writing circle with Marisela Chávez and Laura Talamante, whose interest in the project and sound writing advice helped me to find my voice and launch. I would also like to express my appreciation for those colleagues and friends who read and commented on portions of this book along the way, including Angi Neff, Juanita Davis, Mauricio Valdebenito, and Angela Vergara. Special thanks to Angela, who was my go-to person on any number of queries, from the meaning of a certain *chilenismo* or uniquely Chilean saying, to whether my one-paragraph summaries of Chilean history did the job. The effects of her prompt and gracious responses may be seen throughout the book.

I am hard pressed to adequately describe Nancy Morris's contribution to this book. As its unofficial editor, Nancy has read and reread portions of it since June 2018—new chapters, revised sections, paragraphs, sentences, phrases. An obstinate wordsmith, she would often send me texts with the specific word that we were looking for, now found, or addressing some other equally essential matter. Nancy is additionally one of the few people I know with whom I don't feel the need to tone down my admittedly over-the-top enthusiasm for all things Violeta Parra and Chilean New Song, as our personalities and passions are well matched in this regard.

Nancy and Patricia Vilches are responsible for this book's translations of Parra's poetry and lyrics. Although I purposely held myself back from joining in, I was privy to many an intricate discussion involving meaning and meter. I am beyond impressed with the results of their collaboration and cannot thank them enough for their gifts.

I am grateful to my editor Andreína Fernández, for her thoughtful comments and suggestions and above all for believing in me and this book. My thanks also to Elizabeth Orange, Lindsay Starr, and all of the other wonderful people at The University of North Carolina Press, and to Abigail Michaud, production editor at Westchester Publishing Services.

My research took me both physically and virtually to archives in Argentina, Chile, Ecuador, England, Finland, France, the Netherlands, Switzerland, and the United States. Special thanks to the directorship and staff of the Biblioteca Nacional de Chile, including José Manuel Sepúlveda Carvajal, Soledad Abarca de la Fuente, Bernardo Noziglia Reyes, Georgina Serey, and Daniela Tobar. My thanks also to María Eugenia Cisternas Valenzuela at the Fondo Margot Loyola, Francisco Miranda Fuentes at the Mediateca of the Universidad de Chile, Sandra Gutiérrez Alcamán at the Archivo General Histórico of the Ministerio de Relaciones Exteriores de Chile, and Isidora Cruz España at the Santiago Centro de Documentación de las Artes Escénicas in Chile; Guillemette Delaporte at the Bibliothèque des Arts Décoratifs, Maxime Courbin at the Archives Départementales de la Seine-Saint-Denis, and Marc Chabanne with Mémoires d'Humanité in France; Céline Strub at the Bibliothèque de Genève, Andrea Marca from the Roberto Leydi collection, Giuliano Castellani at the Swiss National Library, and Madeleine Leclair at the Musée d'ethnographie de Genève in Switzerland; Julian Carr at the BBC Written Archives Centre and Vedita Ramdoss at the British Library in England; Laura Braga at the Biblioteca Nacional de Argentina; Rafael Montenegro Cárdenas at the Biblioteca de la Casa de la Cultura Ecuatoriana in Ecuador; Harvey Todd at the Lomax Collection and Aaron Bittel at the UCLA Ethnomusicology Archive in the United States; and the staff at the International Institute of Social History (IISG) in Amsterdam, the Kansan Arkisto–People's Archive in Helsinki, and the Biblioteca Utopía—Centro Cultural de la Cooperación Floreal Gorini and Centro de Documentación e Investigación de la Cultura de Izquierdas in Buenos Aires. I am also indebted to the staff at my home library at Cal State LA, especially to Joseph Gerdeman for his consistent help with interlibrary loan services, and prior to that, to the staff at the California State University Dominguez Hills Library. I could not have written this book without the assistance of the archivists and librarians listed here and so many others. Their generous support took on new meaning during the COVID pandemic when it allowed me to continue my research and remain connected during a period of otherwise enforced isolation.

Several colleagues shared the materials they gathered through painstaking research with me. My thanks to Alejandro Escobar Mundaca, whose work motto is "my research findings are your research findings"; María Antonieta Arauco Méndez in La Paz, historian of Los Jairas and La Peña Naira; Fernando Rios, who passed on his press clippings concerning Parra's visits to La Paz; Daniela Alejandra Fugellie Videla, who shared her research on Parra's 1964 exhibit at the Musée des Arts Décoratifs; Carolina Tapia, who granted me full access to her findings on Parra's participation in the annual Feria de Artes Plásticas in Santiago; and Justyna Laskowska-Otwinowska and Javier Foxon Calvo, who helped me gain a fuller understanding of Parra's activities at the 1955 World Festival of Youth and

Students in Warsaw. Special thanks to Hannes Solo, who shared digital copies of his collection of Parra's recordings along with his expertise. My gratitude also to documentary filmmaker Antoine Sextier, historian of the Parisian boîte L'Escale, for his insights and giving spirit. Other colleagues who gave of their time and resources include Carlos Ferrer Peñaranda, Antonio J. González, Pablo Huneeus, Claudio Mercado, Ignacio Ramos Rodilla, Julio Fernando San Martín, and Hannah Snavely. This biography has been greatly enriched by their contributions.

I would like to express appreciation for my fellow historians of Chile, women, and gender Elizabeth Hutchison, Corinne Pernet, Karin Rosemblatt, Heidi Tinsman, and Soledad Zarate. Our friendship reaches back to when some of us were researching out dissertations in Chile in the early 1990s and has only grown richer with time. Other scholars from across the disciplines whose work and conversation have helped shape my own include Rolando Álvarez Vallejos, Laura Briceño Ramírez, Oscar Chamosa, Gisela Cramer, Alvar de la Llosa, Patricia Díaz Inostroza, Ellen Dubois, Chris Ehrick, Christopher Endy, Jane L. Florine, Jesse Freedman, Stefano Gavagnin, Matthieu Gillabert, Manfred Engelbert, Marisol Facuse, Kymm Gauderman, Pia Koivunen, Joni Krekola, Helene Lorenz, Shanna Lorenz, Gisèle-Audrey Mills, Carlos Molinero, José Moya, Micaela Navarrete, Patricia Oliart, Fabiola Orquera, Rosa Maria Pegueros, Cristián Reveco, Jonathan Ritter, Romina Green Rioja, Nick Rutter, Maximiliano Salinas Campos, Juan Enrique Serrano Moreno, David Spener, Dolores Trevizo, Osiel Vega Durán, Pablo Vila, and Eric Villagordo.

I received invaluable research assistance from Carolina Tapia, director of the Archive of Oral Literature and Folk Traditions at the Biblioteca Nacional de Chile. I am grateful for her insights on Parra's visibility in the press and other topics as well. My thanks to Carolina Gonzales and Carolina Watson for additional research assistance in Chile, to Magdalena Szkwarek for research assistance in Warsaw, and to Amalia Rioja for her transcriptions. Cal State LA Latin America Studies alumni Gladys García and Teresa Rodríguez Sotelo helped me in the preparation of my notes and bibliography.

I am fortunate to be able to reproduce several priceless photographs of Parra in this book. My thanks first and foremost to Javiera and Paula Pérez Escalante, Javier Pérez Castelblanco's daughters, for granting me permission to reproduce his photos. I am also grateful to Gilbert Favre's widow Barbara Erskine and brother Patrick Favre, the family of L'Escale musician Romano Zanotti, and Valentina Valenzuela of the Museo in Concepción who went out of her way to make sure I would be able to include photos by Sergio Larraín.

I am grateful to the National Endowment for the Humanities for its funding of this project. I also thank the College of Natural and Social Sciences at Cal State LA and the College of Arts and Letters at California State University Dominguez Hills for supporting my work. My participation in the International Colloquium on Violeta Parra in celebration of the centennial of her birth, held in Santiago in 2017, was a definitive high point in this endeavor. My thanks to the Consejo Nacional de la Cultura y las Artes, the Fundación Violeta Parra, and the Equipo Coordinador Violeta Parra 100 for their generous invitation and warm hospitality.

I am blessed to have wonderful colleagues at Cal State LA, my current academic home, as well as at California State University Dominguez Hills, my former campus. Gabriela Fried Amilivia, Rafael Gómez, Sandy Gutierrez, Enrique Ochoa, Douglas Ramon, and Alex Villalpando have been consistent sources of wisdom and friendship, as have all of my other *colegamigues* in Latin American Studies and across campus. My thanks to Victor Mojica for his photograph of me and to Michele Bury for design advice. All of my gratitude to my students, who never cease to inspire, and who are as much my teachers as I am theirs.

The seeds of this project were planted in 1980 when I wrote my undergraduate honors thesis on Parra's autobiography in décimas, and I would like to recognize the late professors Evelyn Picón Garfield and José Amor y Vásquez for their guidance. This means that this book has been unusually long in the making—or at least I hope it is unusual, for the sake of other book writers. I also hope that this book's prolonged growth period may excuse any unintended omissions from these acknowledgments.

As Parra writes in her décimas, "The last is first" (*El último es el primero*). I wish to thank my mother Cynthia for being my role model as a scholar and feminist, my sisters Margy and Tina, brothers-in-law Jack and Tom, children Gabi and David, son-in-law Josh, niece Mimi, and granddaughters Mikaela and Amaya. You hold me up and fill my life with joy. I have unending gratitude for my *ausentes-presentes*; my father Sidney, who taught me that hard work can be fun if you love what you do, and my late husband César Torres, who is with us always, and especially when we share songs over a bottle of wine. Finally, I would like to acknowledge my community of friends. I could not have written this book without all of your love and support. And so I dedicate this book to you, my *familia*.

Glossary

abajista "social descender"; word invented by Nicanor Parra to denote the opposite of an arribista or social climber

animación shouts and sayings meant to cheer on or "animate" a singer

anticucho meat skewer

arpillera embroidered tapestry, often on burlap; burlap

arribista social climber

boliche working-class bar or "dive"

bombo large drum, originally from Argentina

campesino/a person of rural extraction, peasant, agricultural worker

canto a lo divino canto a lo poeta on a religious theme

canto a lo poeta literally, "songs in the style of the poet"; form of traditional poetry based on the décima or ten-line verse (referred to as poet-song in this book)

casa quinta large "country-style" house

centésima hundred-line verse

charango small Andean guitar, traditionally made with the shell of an armadillo

charrango zither-like instrument made out of a plank of wood and wires pulled taut over two bottles

chicha drink made from fermented maize

chilenidad Chilean identity, "Chilean-ness"

chillanejo/a person from Chillán

china female partner of a huaso, also known as a huasa

choro someone who is clever and daring; vulva or vagina

circo pobre literally "poor circus"; family circus

contrapunto traditional poetic duel or debate

corrido style of ballad, common in Mexico

criollo/a native, from here

cuatro four-string guitar, originally from Venezuela

cueca Chilean song and dance style

cuplé song style, originally from Spain

décima ten-line verse

dicho rhymed saying

empanada meat-filled pastry

familia family, extended family
farruca form of flamenco music
folklorista folklorist, folk singer
fonda temporary, rustic entertainment venue
fundamento canto a lo poeta theme
fundo large agricultural estate

gringo slang for "foreigner"
guaracha song and dance style of Afro-Caribbean origin
guitarrón twenty-five-string guitar unique to the Chilean countryside

habanera Cuban song and dance style
huasa female partner of the huaso; also known as china
huaso skilled horseman
huaso band musical ensemble that performs música típica in huaso attire

indio/a "Indian," an Indigenous person
inquilino tenant farmer, agricultural worker tied to a landed estate through service
   obligations

kultrun Mapuche ceremonial drum

lira popular broadsides of traditional poetry

machi Mapuche spiritual leader and healer
matraca noise-maker
mingaco collective work, celebration of collective work
morena/o dark-skinned person
mujer del pueblo "woman of the people," working-class woman, everywoman
música criolla literally, music that is native or "from here"; repertoire of pan–Latin
   American song styles
milésima thousand-line verse
mistela traditional alcoholic beverage
música típica chilena folk-derived urban music

neofolkore style of folk-derived music, often with elaborate vocal arrangements
neofolklorista someone who performs neofoklore
nueva canción New Song, politically engaged songs
nueva ola new wave; (in Chile) musical style that is a cross between US rock and Italian
   balladry

paso doble traditional Spanish dance
pat'e perro literally, "dog's paw"; Chilean idiom for wanderer
patron landed estate owner
peón day laborer
picardía clever humor, often with sexual innuendo

pifilka Mapuche flute
pituco/a rich person, snob
poblador poor urban dweller
ponche punch
popular of the people, working-class
pueblo the folk, working class, working poor

quena Andean flute with a notched mouthpiece, usually made of bamboo
quenista quena player
quinta de recreo rustic open-air restaurant

ranchera style of song
reina queen
roto/a poor person, tramp, vagabond
ruka traditional Mapuche hut
rumbera woman who dances the rumba

santo/a saint
sevillanas folk music and dance from Sevilla, Spain
sopaipillas traditional fried pastry

tarro large can
típica/o typical, folkloric
tiple small guitar with metal strings, originally from Colombia
tonada lyrical Chilean song style
tony clown
trilla wheat-thrashing, celebration that accompanies wheat-thrashing

vals Peruvian song style in three-four, waltz

zambra flamenco dance
zampoña panpipe

Notes

Abbreviations in the Notes

BNdeCh   Biblioteca Nacional de Chile
FVP   Fundación Violeta Parra
INA   L'Institut national de l'audiovisuel, Paris, France
MAD   Musée des Arts Décoratifs
RFI   Radio France Internationale
RTF   Radiodiffusion-Télévision Française

Introduction

1. "Violeta Parra," La Biennale de Venezia, www.labiennale.org/en/art/2022/milk-dreams/violeta-parra.

2. Parra to Amparo Claro, n.d., in Štambuk and Bravo, *Violeta Parra*, 126. This and all other translations are my own unless otherwise noted, with the notable exception of Parra's poetry and song lyrics, which are translated by Nancy Morris and Patricia Vilches.

3. Peterson, *Creating Country Music*, 3.

4. Bendix, *In Search of Authenticity*, 8.

5. Dillon, "Religion and the Angel's Wake." For an English-language publication on the wake for the little angel, see Orellana, "*Versos por Angelito.*"

6. "Baja de Las Tasas de Mortalidad Infantil," Memoria Chilena, BNdeCh, www.memoria chilena.gob.cl/602/w3-article-93237.html. A project of the Biblioteca Nacional de Chile, Memoria Chilena is a platform of digital resources created by experts in the field based on material found in the library's collections. I rely on Memoria Chilena here and throughout the book for summaries on a variety of topics pertaining to Chilean history and culture.

7. David Grazian makes this point in the context of his study of the Chicago blues scene in *Blue Chicago*, 16–17.

8. Turino, "Are We Global Yet?," 62.

9. I use "protest songs" as shorthand here for songs that denounce social injustice. There has been much discussion, both during Parra's times and among present-day musicologists and historians, on the proper terminology to use to describe this music. See Pablo Vila's "Introduction," in Vila, *Militant Song Movement*, 2–5. The bibliography on Chilean New Song is extensive. For a brief overview, see "La nueva canción chilena," Memoria Chilena, BNdeCh, www.memoriachilena.gob.cl/602/w3-article-702.html. For an excellent historical summary in English, see Nancy Morris, "New Song in Chile: Half a Century of Musical Activism," in Vila, *Militant Song Movement*, 19–44.

10. San Martín, *Lalo Parra*, 15.

11. I refer to Violeta Parra as Parra throughout most of this book and not as Violeta, which is how she is almost always referred to in biographical writings. My decision to do so

is influenced by the fact the Nicanor Parra is almost always referred to as Parra in biographical writings. See, for example, the siblings' contrasting "mini-sites" at Memoria Chilena: "Violeta Parra," Memoria Chilena, BNdeCh, www.memoriachilena.gob.cl/602/w3-article -7683.html; and "Nicanor Parra," Memoria Chilena, BNdeCh, www.memoriachilena.gob .cl/602/w3-article-3629.html.

12. The Museo Violeta Parra's website includes a searchable Centro de Documentación containing links to recordings, photographs, publications, press clippings, interviews, discography, and personal documents; www.museovioletaparra.cl. The Fundación Violeta Parra's website contains a more extensive photograph collection than that of the Museo Violeta Parra; www.fundacionvioletaparra.org/. Its other content largely overlaps with that of the museum. Parra's mini-site at Memoria Chilena provides documents, photographs, audiovisual materials, bibliography, and links to other relevant Memoria Chilena webpages; "Violeta Parra," Memoria Chilena, BNdeCh, www.memoriachilena.gob.cl/602/w3 -article-7683.html.

13. V. Parra, *Décimas*.

14. Parra, Bravo, Larraín, and Soublette, *Cantos folklóricos chilenos*. A few sources report that a first edition of the book was published in 1959, but I have found no evidence to support their claim.

15. I. Parra, *El libro mayor*. I refer to the book's second edition, published in 2009, unless specified otherwise. Isabel Parra has never clarified how she selected letters for publication or if she edited them. It is my hope that the Fundación Violeta Parra will grant researchers access to Violeta Parra's letters in the future.

16. García, *Violeta Parra en sus palabras*.

17. V. Parra, *En el Aula Magna de Concepción*.

18. Diserens and Brumagne, *Violeta Parra*.
The documentary's audio text is transcribed and translated into Spanish in García, *Violeta Parra en sus palabras*, 69–76.

19. Violeta Parra's webpage on the digital daily Cancioneros.com provides an exhaustive list of the songs she composed and collected (including annotated lyrics and samples of their audio recordings) and her most comprehensive discography; www.cancioneros .com/ct/4/0/violeta-parra. Audio for many of Parra's recordings is found at the website Discoteca Nacional Chile, discotecanacionalchile.blogspot.com. The website of the Museo Violeta Parra displays photos of Parra's tapestries, paintings, and works in papier-mâché from the museum's collection; www.museovioletaparra.cl. Paula Miranda, in collaboration with the Fundación Violeta Parra, has compiled the most complete collection of Parra's poems, *Violeta Parra: Poesía*.

20. Štambuk and Bravo, *Violeta Parra*. Osvaldo "Gitano" Rodríguez, Leonidas Morales T., and Juan Armando Epple have all published interviews that have proven indispensable to this project; see bibliography.

21. Á. Parra, *Violeta se fue*; E. Parra, *Mi hermana Violeta Parra*; R. Parra, *Vida, pasión y muerte*.

22. Favre, "Les mémoires"; Bernstein, *Findings*; Ginsberg, *South American Journals*.

23. Parra's classmate is one of many interviewees in the documentary directed by Luis R. Vera, *Viola chilensis*.

24. Herrero, *Después de vivir*; Sáez, *Violeta Parra: La vida intranquila*; Oviedo, *Mentira todo lo cierto*.

25. "Discografía de Violeta Parra," Cancioneros.com, www.cancioneros.com/cc/4/0/discografia-de-violeta-parra.

26. Personal correspondence, July 18, 2023.

27. "Miguel Picker, Director / Producer / Editor," Latinos Beyond Reel, https://latinos beyondreel.com/about/miguel-picker/; Sebastián Picker, Sebastián Picker Retrospective, www.sebastianpicker-retrospective.com/.

28. Verba, "Violeta Parra: Her Life." The conference was held at the University of Southern California, Los Angeles.

29. The concert was supported by an Artists in the Community grant from the Los Angeles Cultural Affairs Department and recorded and released as Desborde, *Tribute Concert to Violeta Parra*.

30. See entries by Verba in the bibliography. Several concepts and events covered in this biography were first explored in the works listed.

31. "Trayectoria," FVP, accessed November 20, 2022, www.fundacionvioletaparra.org/trayectoria.

32. "Biografía de Violeta Parra," Municipalidad de San Carlos.

33. "La ardua disputa entre San Carlos y San Fabián por la cuna de Violeta Parra," *La Discusión* (Chillán), August 6, 2008. Parra biographers Herrero, Oviedo, and Sáez all write that Parra was born in San Carlos and do not raise the issue of her contested birthplace. Herrero, *Después de vivir un siglo*, 19; Oviedo, *Mentira todo lo cierto*, 18; Sáez, *La vida intranquila*, 18.

Chapter 1

1. The magazine's primary function was the promotion of Hollywood stars and other luminaries of the international entertainment industry, with news of Chilean stars and cultural activities relegated to its back pages. See "Ecran (1930–1969)," Memoria Chilena, BNdeCh, www.memoriachilena.gob.cl/602/w3-article-588.html.

2. Marina de Navasal, "Conozca a Violeta Parra," *Ecran*, June 8, 1954, 18.

3. Chile, Dirección General de Estadística, *Censo de población de la República de Chile levantado el 15 de diciembre de 1920* (Santiago: Soc. imp. y litografia Universo, 1925), 167–68.

4. Violeta Parra's mother was known by both the names Clara and Clarisa. I use Clarisa here and throughout the book because it is how Violeta referred to her mother in both her autobiography in décimas and her manuscript that would eventually be published as *Cantos folklóricos chilenos*.

5. Lucía D'Albuquerque, "La Parra madre y los otros Parra," *Revista del Domingo de El Mercurio* (September 24, 1978).

6. Vicuña, "Entrevista," 72.

7. I. Parra, *El libro mayor* (1985), 33.

8. Luis Sánchez Romero, "Doña Clarisa Sandoval habla sobre su hija," *La Tribuna*, February 5, 1990.

9. Macarena Hermosilla, "Canto con historia," *Qué Pasa*, February 12, 2000, 51.

10. Marcela Escobar Quintana, "La infancia de los Parra (según el tío Lalo Parra)," Archivo Chile Centro de Estudios Miguel Enríquez, accessed February 9, 2024, https://www.archivochile.com/Cultura_Arte_Educacion/vp/d/vpde0031.pdf.

11. Vicuña, "Entrevista," 72.

12. Morales T. and Parra, *Conversaciones con Nicanor Parra*, 31.

13. Štambuk and Bravo, *Violeta Parra*, 30.

14. Also known as El Huape or El Guape.

15. Though economic and social inequality prevailed throughout the Central Valley, they were more extreme in the northern region. In the southern region where the Ñuble province is located, the landed estates were not as large or numerous and were surrounded by a significant number of small independent farmers. Though neither as dependent nor as destitute as the inquilinos (tenant farmers) to the north, the farmers of Ñuble were still by and large beholden via commercial and debt ties to the local *patrón* or landed estate owner. For a history of land tenure in Ñuble, see Bengoa, *Haciendas y campesinos*, 143–50.

16. Those readers who are familiar only with mythologized versions of Parra's biography may be surprised by the narrative offered here regarding the relative well-being of both sets of grandparents. Biographer Víctor Herrero does an excellent job, based on painstaking archival research, at debunking this all-too-common portrayal of Parra as campesina and poor; Herrero, *Después de vivir un siglo*, 40–41.

17. "So What Exactly Is 'Blood Quantum'?," 2018 Interview with Elizabeth Rule, doctoral student in Native American Studies, Brown University, accessed January 1, 2024, www.npr .org/sections/codeswitch/2018/02/09/583987261/so-what-exactly-is-blood-quantum.

18. For a history of the "myth of Chilean racial homogeneity," see Walsh, "'One of the Most Uniform Races."

19. Prejudices against Indigenous people in Chile during Parra's time are detailed in Pike's "Aspects of Class Relations in Chile, 1850–1960."

20. Morales T. and Parra, *Conversaciones con Nicanor Parra*, 36 and 54–55.

21. Marina Latorre, "Nicanor Parra en un mar de preguntas," *Portal* 4 (November 1966): 3.

22. I. Parra writes about her first communion in *El libro mayor*, 46; Á. Parra writes about Carmen Luisa's baptism in *Violeta se fue*, 57; Drysdale writes about Rosa Carmen's baptism in the biographical essay "Violeta Parra," 494.

23. D'Albuquerque "La Parra madre y los otros Parra," 6. Although she does not specify the year, Clarisa's recollection that "things got real bad for people from one moment to the next" suggests that Violeta's maternal grandparents' economic downturn was linked to the worldwide economic crisis of 1929 and the 1930s.

24. Ferrero, *Escritores a trasluz*, 88.

25. V. Parra, *Décimas*, 99.

26. "Epidemias," Memoria Chilena, BNdeCh, www.memoriachilena.gob.cl/602/w3-article -93708.html.

27. V. Parra, *Décimas*, 49.

28. The title of the 1999–2001 *telenovela* (soap opera) *Yo soy Betty, la fea* (I Am Betty, the Ugly One) provides a more recent example of this phenomenon; "Yo soy Betty, la fea," IMDb, www.imdb.com/title/tt0233127/?ref_=fn_al_tt_1. The show was adapted in the United States as the 2006–10 television series *Ugly Betty*; "Ugly Betty," IMDb, www.imdb .com/title/tt0805669/?ref_=fn_al_tt_1.

29. R. Parra, "Hablan de ella los que no tienen idea como fue," *Fortín Mapocho* (February 5, 1989).

30. Cámara de Diputados de Chile, "Sesión 48 (February 9, 1967)," *Sesiones de la Cámara de Diputados* (Santiago, Chile: La Cámara, 1967), 4686.

31. García and Osorio, *Ricardo García*, 102.

32. *Censo de población* [. . .] *1920*, 200. *Wallmapu* means "the surrounding land" in Mapudungun, language of the Mapuche.

33. San Martín, *Lalo Parra*, 27.

34. Alfonso Molina Leiva, "Violeta Parra," *Suplemento Dominical de El Mercurio*, October 16, 1966. Reproduced in García, *Violeta Parra en sus palabras*, 103.

35. Quezada, *En la mira de Nicanor Parra*, 99.

36. Miranda, Loncón, and Ramay, *Violeta Parra en el Wallmapu*.

37. For a discussion of how Parra and Víctor Jara helped to make Indigenous cultures visible through their music, see Crow, *Mapuche in Modern Chile*, 130–37.

38. Collier and Sater, *History of Chile*, 214–21. Ibáñez won the presidency with 98 percent of the votes in what historian Brian Loveman termed a "carefully controlled election"; Loveman, *Chile*, 247. In her autobiography in verse, Parra refers to Ibáñez as a "dictator" and holds him responsible for her father's depression and eventual demise following the loss of his teaching position in Lautaro; *Décimas*, 73–76.

39. Regional identifiers like *chillaneja* are not capitalized in Spanish.

40. Morales T. and Parra, *Conversaciones con Nicanor Parra*, 60.

41. Public education at the primary level has been free in Chile since 1860 and obligatory since 1920. See "Inicios de la instrucción primaria en Chile (1840–1920)," Memoria Chilena, BNdeCh, www.memoriachilena.gob.cl/602/w3-article-3565.html.

42. Vera, *Viola chilensis*, 7:50.

43. Sánchez Romero, "Doña Clarisa Sandoval habla sobre su hija."

44. V. Parra, *Décimas*, 68.

45. San Martín, *Lalo Parra*, 23–24.

46. Morales T. and Parra, *Violeta Parra*, 71–72.

47. Parra recounts these and other childhood pastimes in her autobiography in verse.

48. "Violeta Parra: Folklorista tierna y rebelde," *Ercilla* (February 8, 1967), 9.

49. Morales T. and Parra, *Violeta Parra*, 73.

50. González and Rolle, *Historia social*, 371.

51. V. Parra, *Décimas*, 108.

52. Navasal, "Conozca a Violeta Parra," 18.

53. Hernán Valdés, "Violeta Parra da opiniones sobre el folklore nacional," *La Nación*, December 19, 1954.

54. The décima tradition is found throughout Latin America. The canto a lo poeta represents how the poetic form evolved in Chile's Central Valley. See "Canto a lo poeta," Memoria Chilena, BNdeCh, www.memoriachilena.gob.cl/602/w3-article-3320.html.

55. "El diablo en el paraíso," at "Cancionero de Violeta Parra," Cancioneros.com, www.cancioneros.com/nc/485/0/el-diablo-en-el-paraiso-violeta-parra. Note: Parra performs the song as a sirilla (Chilean dance form descendant from the Spanish seguidilla), and not as a poet-song.

56. "Guitarrón," Memoria Chilena, BNdeCh, www.memoriachilena.gob.cl/602/w3-article-93518.html.

57. Nicanor Parra is the author of *La cueca larga*, a book-length poem based on the folk idioms and rhythm associated with the cueca, first published in 1958; N. Parra, *La cueca larga*. Roberto Parra wrote a memoir in décimas about his love affair with a prostitute from the same Valparaíso brothel where he worked as a musician; R. Parra, *Décimas de la*

Negra Ester. It was adapted for the stage by Andrés Pérez in 1987 and has been seen by an estimated 6 million people worldwide; "Roberto Parra (1921–1995)," Memoria Chilena, BNdeCh, www.memoriachilena.gob.cl/602/w3-article-794.html. Both Roberto and Eduardo Parra wrote book-length poetic biographies of Violeta: R. Parra, *Vida, pasión y muerte*; and E. Parra, *Mi hermana Violeta Parra*. Lautaro Parra produced an album of original songs relating the history of the Parra family based on the traditional styles of cantos, tonadas, and *periconas* as well as reams of unpublished autobiographical décimas; Lautaro Parra, accessed February 9, 2024, http://lautaroparra.blogspot.com.

58. González and Rolle, *Historia social*, 26.

59. González and Rolle's tome *Historia social* offers a comprehensive study of popular music in Chile during this period.

60. An early form of record player that played 78 rpm discs and was powered by a hand crank.

61. Morales T. and Parra, *Violeta Parra*, 73.

62. For a discussion of both the usefulness and complexities of engaging with the emic meanings of musical labels, and particularly the label *típica/o* in Latin America, see Hutchinson, "'Típico, folklórico or popular.'"

63. González and Rolle, *Historia social*, 363–70.

64. For more on the "masculinization of the tonada," see González and Rolle, *Historia social*, 389.

65. "Huaso," Memoria Chilena, BNdeCh, www.memoriachilena.gob.cl/602/w3-article -91938.html; González and Rolle, *Historia social*, 375–78.

66. The duration of Parra's field recording of folk informant Gabriel Soto singing the poet-song "Verso por el Rey Asuero" is 6:44 minutes; Mercado, *Chosto Ulloa*, 511.

67. In his analysis of the recordings classified as "Chilean musical folklore" held in the BNdeCh, sociologist Sebastián Gallardo found that only 16 out of 150 contained poet-songs and that only 28 out of the 1800 songs found in the recordings were of poet-songs. Gallardo, "Canto a lo poeta," 1.

68. González and Rolle, *Historia social*, 185–87.

69. Herrero, *Después de vivir un siglo*, 51.

70. Collier and Sater, *History of Chile*, 221–23.

71. Vergara, *Fighting Unemployment*, 53–62.

72. Corvalán, *De lo vivido y lo peleado*, 17.

73. V. Parra, *Décimas*, 97–98.

74. V. Parra, *Décimas*, 53–54.

75. V. Parra, *Décimas*, 96.

76. Escobar Quintana, "La infancia de los Parra."

77. San Martín, *Lalo Parra*, 27.

78. Štambuk and Bravo, *Violeta Parra*, 38.

79. V. Parra, *Décimas*, 119–22.

80. Badal, *Roberto Parra*, 4.

81. V. Parra, *Décimas*, 133.

82. Hermosilla, "Canto con historia," 51.

83. Štambuk and Bravo, *Violeta Parra*, 32.

84. For more on the history of the circus in Chile, see Ducci, *Años de circo*.

85. Štambuk and Bravo, *Violeta Parra*, 34–43.

86. In Spanish, *todista*; Ducci, *Años de circo*, 129.

87. Štambuk and Bravo, *Violeta Parra*, 36.

88. Escobar Quintana, "La infancia de los Parra."

89. Štambuk and Bravo, *Violeta Parra*, 39.

90. Eduardo and Lautaro each served terms as president of the Union of Circus Performers of Chile. Oscar Parra became "Tony Canarito," the "Singing Clown"; Padilla, *Canarito*.

91. Ducci, *Años de circo*, 125. I hypothesize that the circus owner's son was from an earlier union, for, if not, then Hilda married her half sister's son. (Note: the year given for Hilda's marriage is incorrect.)

92. Ducci, *Años de circo*, 126.

93. The circus inspired the creative activities of other Parra siblings as well. Oscar recorded an LP of original songs covering various aspects of life in the circus: *Las Cuecas del Señor Corales*, RCA Victor CML-2517, 1967. Though it was released after her death in 1967, Oscar credited Violeta with both the idea and impetus for the project; Padilla, *Canarito*, 111–13. Although Nicanor never performed in the circus, the circus nonetheless appears as a recurrent theme in his work.

94. Las Hermanas Parra, Los Campesinos, untitled EP; V. Parra, *La cueca*. The song was a traditional circus cueca that Parra collected.

95. V. Parra, *Décimas*, 49–50.

96. Bauer, *Chilean Rural Society*, 163; Bengoa, *El poder y la subordinación*, 22.

97. Gabriel Pardo, "Nicanor Parra cumple 90 años: La antipolítica de Parra," *El Mercurio*, September 5, 2004.

98. Valenzuela Yuraidini, "El cuerpo chileno dividido sociogenéticamente," and Rojas Flores, "Los rasgos físicos de los chilenos," in Góngora Escobedo and Sagredo B., *Fragmentos para una historia*, 23–40 and 41–117.

99. There is some discrepancy regarding Violeta's age when she moved to Santiago. Given that Nicanor was already enrolled in the Instituto Pedagógico when she got there, she most likely arrived in the capital sometime after the new academic year started in March 1933 and before her October birthday when she turned sixteen.

100. "Yo canto la diferencia," at "Cancionero de Violeta Parra," Cancioneros.com, www.cancioneros.com/nc/1594/0/yo-canto-la-diferencia-violeta-parra.

Chapter 2

1. N. Parra, *Poemas y antipoemas*.

2. For a photo of Parra taken around this time, see photo captioned "Llegando del sur, Quinta Normal, Santiago. Entre 1932–1934," "Fotografías," FVP, www.fundacionvioletaparra.org/fotografias.

3. Badal, *Roberto Parra*, 9.

4. Eduardo "Lalo" Parra, "Mi hermano Nicanor," *The Clinic*, October 21, 2004, 70.

5. Morales T. and Parra, *Violeta Parra*, 69; Štambuk and Bravo, *Violeta Parra*, 47.

6. "Reseña Histórica, Internado Nacional Barros Arana," Ministerio de Educación, accessed May 27, 2024, https://cdnsae.mineduc.cl/documentos/8499/ProyectoEducativo8499.pdf. A postcard of the INBA from the Archivo Fotográfico Dirección de Arquitectura is viewable online; "Internado Barros Arana," Archivo Fotográfico Dirección de Arquitectura,

accessed November 20, 2022, www.afda.cl/detalle_imagen.php?i=PL-000018%7C0%7C1 %7C0. The INBA's bleakest hour occurred after the military coup of September 11, 1973, when it was occupied by a military regiment and transformed into a transit center for prisoners. Hundreds of political prisoners were tortured there. Some were murdered. "Internado Nacional Barros Arana," Memoria Viva, https://memoriaviva.com/nuevaweb/centros -de-detencion/metropolitana/internado-nacional-barros-arana/.

7. Patricio Aylwin, president from 1990 to 1994.

8. Morales T. and Parra, *Conversaciones con Nicanor Parra*, 79.

9. N. Parra, *Así habló Parra en El Mercurio*, 50.

10. Luis Oyarzún, "Crónica de una generación," 181. One of the INBA "mythical ones," Oyarzún traced the spiritual and metaphysical roots of Nicanor's antipoetry back to those heady times and, more concretely, to the view from Violeta's room in the house where she was staying, which looked out over an underground construction project, thus allowing the budding poets to "peer into the depths" of the torn-up street to "catch a glimpse of the antipodes." "Crónica de una generación," 188.

11. "Internado Nacional Barros Arana," Internado Nacional Barros Arana, accessed November 4, 2022, www.inba.cl.

12. Morales T. and Parra, *Violeta Parra*, 69–71.

13. Parra attended the Escuela Normal de Niñas No. 1, as did the Nobel Prize–winning poet Gabriela Mistral. "Recordando la escuela celebramos 76 años de vida," Museo de la Educación Gabriela Mistral, accessed July 14, 2023, www.museodelaeducacion.gob.cl /noticias/recordando-la-escuela-celebramos-76-anos-de-vida.

14. Núñez Prieto, "Las escuelas normales," 37. For a brief overview of the normal schools, see "Escuelas normales en Chile (1872–1974)," Memoria Chilena, BNdeCh, www.memo riachilena.gob.cl/602/w3-article-100627.html.

15. Štambuk and Bravo, *Violeta Parra*, 50.

16. Collier and Sater, *History of Chile*, 291.

17. Collier and Sater, *History of Chile*, 232–33.

18. Eduardo would later claim that Violeta confided as much to him at the time; Marcela Escobar Quintana, "La Infancia de Los Parra (según el tio Lalo Parra,)" Archivo Chile CEME, accessed November 20, 2022, https://www.archivochile.com/Cultura_Arte _Educacion/vp/d/vpde0031.pdf.

19. E. Parra, "Mi hermano Nicanor."

20. Štambuk and Bravo, *Violeta Parra*, 51.

21. González and Rolle, *Historia social*, 329–30.

22. Macarena Hermosilla, "Canto con historia," *Qué Pasa*, February 12, 2000, 51.

23. González and Rolle, *Historia social*, 220.

24. Salazar, "Apuntes sobre la Edad Dorada."

25. When a reporter asked Roberto Parra in a 1993 interview how many years he had been performing in brothels, he responded, "Almost all my life, up to just recently." Ivan Badilla, "Roberto Parra—Atorrante, poeta y canto," *Análisis*, January 7, 1993, 27. For Eduardo Parra, see E. Parra, *Eduardo "Lalo" Parra*, 69–74.

26. See Héctor Pavez's recollection in Štambuk and Bravo, *Violeta Parra*, 60.

27. I deduce Violeta and Hilda Parra's nonfolkloric stage outfits from Isabel Parra's testimony, as I have yet to locate photographs of the sisters performing as a duo in evening attire. I. Parra, *El libro mayor*, 52.

28. González and Rolle, *Historia social*, 226–56; and Rinke, Perl, and Palma, *Encuentros con el Yanqui*.

29. Štambuk and Bravo, *Violeta Parra*, 51.

30. Parra wrote the only boleros, valses, and corridos that appear on a composite list of 121 songs she composed over her lifetime during this earlier period in her career as a songwriter; I. Parra, *El libro mayor*, 238–42.

31. Marina de Navasal, "Conozca a Violeta Parra," *Ecran*, June 8, 1954, 18.

32. I. Parra, *El libro mayor*, 48–49.

33. Navasal, "Conozca a Violeta Parra," 18.

34. E. Parra, *Mi hermana Violeta Parra*, 67–69.

35. In his qualitative analysis of the lyrics of Chilean cuecas, musicologist Felipe Solís Poblete found references to only three types of women workers: singers, bartenders, and prostitutes, which, as he points out, are all professions linked to service and entertainment. "La reproducción de valores patriarcales," 148–49.

36. V. Parra, *Décimas*, 149–56. For a broader discussion of the representation of urban violence in Parra's *Décimas*, see Vilches, "El cuerpo femenino." Folk singer Margot Loyola recounted an incident when a drunk man tried to force his way into the hotel room that she shared with her sister one evening after they had performed at a rodeo. Her sister managed to fend him off and kick him out of the room. Loyola described it as "just part of the job [*gajes del oficio*]." Arenas, *Margot Loyola*, 27.

37. Štambuk and Bravo, *Violeta Parra*, 52.

38. Claudia Guzmán, "Así eran los tiempos de La Carlina," *El Mercurio*, September 19, 2004.

39. See Spencer, "El maricón del piano," 627–38. For more on brothel matron "La Carlina" and the cuecas she inspired, see Rojas, *El que sae, sae*, 56–58.

40. Along similar lines, in a 1993 piece published in the weekly *Análisis*, Roberto Parra and his interviewer shared concern for Roberto's reputation based not on the fact that he had worked in brothels most of his life but that his manliness might be called into question because of the common practice on the part of brothel owners of hiring openly gay men or trans people. Badilla, "Roberto Parra," 27–28.

41. "Habla el personaje desconocido de la familia Parra," *Onda*, 5, November 5, 1971, 12.

42. V. Parra, *Décimas*, 147.

43. Teitelboim, *La vida*, 200–201.

44. I. Parra, *El libro mayor*, 44–45. Luis Jaime Cereceda caused a controversy in 2000 when he filed an unsuccessful lawsuit claiming hereditary rights to a share of Violeta Parra's estate. Cristóbal Peña F., "El hijo desconocido de Violeta Parra," *La Tercera*, August 27, 2000.

45. Štambuk and Bravo, *Violeta Parra*, 54.

46. I. Parra, *El libro mayor*, 44.

47. Štambuk and Bravo, *Violeta Parra*, 56. To see a family photo from this period, visit "Especial—Isabel Parra: 'la Violeta está aquí para recordarnos quiénes somos,'" Revista Universitaria, https://revistauniversitaria.uc.cl/especial/isabel-parra-la-violeta-esta-aqui-para-recordarnos-quienes-somos/16143/.

48. Á. Parra, *Violeta se fue*, 33. For more on Spanish music in Chile, see González and Rolle, *Historia social*, 348–56; Chamorro and Perret, *Memoria del flamenco en Chile*.

49. Navasal, "Conozca a Violeta Parra," 18.

50. Oviedo, *Mentira todo lo cierto*, 33.

51. I. Parra, *El libro mayor*, 52.

52. Štambuk and Bravo, *Violeta Parra*, 55.

53. "Mosaico Radial," *Ecran*, February 11, 1947, 30.

54. I. Parra, *El libro mayor*, 52; González and Rolle, *Historia social*, 353–54; Štambuk and Bravo, *Violeta Parra*, 56.

55. Luz María Astorga, "Retrato hablado de Violeta Parra," *Revista del Domingo de El Mercurio*, October 31, 1982, 11.

56. Nora Ferrada, "Entrevistas al revés: Isabel y Ángel Parra," TV Supplement, *Ecran*, June 17, 1966, 29; Mario Cruz, "La cueca triste de los Parra," *Flash*, September 2, 1966, 38; and "Ángel e Isabel recuerdan a Violeta," *Suplemento de El Mercurio*, May 2, 1993.

57. I am assuming here that Parra was making a wordplay on her name, which is also the name of the violet flower. None of the sources available provide an explanation as to Parra's choice of stage name.

58. Alcalde, *Toda Violeta Parra*, 32–33.

59. Photo 5, captioned "Baile español ('Violeta de Mayo' y 'Chabelita [nickname for Isabel]'), "Iconografía"; I. Parra, *El libro mayor*, n.p.

60. Ducci González, *Años de circo*, 126.

61. Á. Parra, *Violeta se fue*, 43.

62. "Artes y emoción de España: Carmen Amaya," *La Hora*, February 23, 1950. For more on Carmen Amaya's South American tour, see Goldberg, "A 'Heart of Darkness.'" A series of photos of Carmen Amaya shot in Santiago at Javier Pérez Castleblanco's Rays Studios in 1946 appear in Pérez Castleblanco, *La fotografía de Javier Pérez Castelblanco*, 259–73. Pérez Castleblanco also shot the photos of Parra that appear as this book's cover and as figure 6.4.

63. Carmen Amaya herself emphasized this through songs like "Gypsy Inheritance," in which she proudly proclaimed, "I am of the Gypsy race . . . I am the daughter of Gypsy parents / And I have the blood of kings / In the palm of my hand (*Soy de la raza Cale* [sic] . . . *Hija de padres Gitanos / y tengo sangre de reyes / en la palma de la mano*)." Goldberg, "'Heart of Darkness,'" 101–2.

64. Navasal, "Conozca a Violeta Parra," 18.

65. "Habla el personaje desconocido," 13.

66. Fuenzalida, "Nicanor Parra, collage con artefacto," 63.

67. Fuenzalida, "Nicanor Parra, collage con artefacto," 62–63.

68. Á. Parra, *Violeta se fue*, 32–34.

69. According to Ángel, Cereceda's Communist Party militancy was "almost a virtue," as far as his mother was concerned; Á. Parra, *Violeta se fue*, 38.

70. Štambuk and Bravo, *Violeta Parra*, 54.

71. In September 1948, Videla's government passed the "Law for the Permanent Defense of Democracy," also known as the *ley maldita* or "cursed law." It declared the Communist Party illegal, erased thousands of its members from the electoral rolls, and sent its leaders into concentration camps or exile. See Huneeus, *La guerra fría chilena*.

72. I. Parra, *El libro mayor*, 45; Štambuk and Bravo, *Violeta Parra*, 57.

73. Communist Party official Eduardo Contreras claimed Parra was active in the Frente Nacional de Mujeres (Women's National Front), and his claim has been repeated by others. Contreras, *Violeta Parra, el origen del canto*, 13. Contreras did not provide a source for his

assertion, and I am unable to find information about an organization by that name functioning in Chile in the 1940s. I also have not uncovered evidence that Parra participated in the women's suffrage movement. She must have been aware of the CP-affiliated Movimiento Pro-Emancipación de las Mujeres de Chile (Movement for the Emancipation of Chilean Women) or MEMCH, however, because a representative of the pro-suffrage organization spoke directly after Parra at the 1947 May 1st rally commemorating International Workers' Day in Santiago; "Todos los sectores del pueblo rindieron homenaje a los mártires," *El Siglo*, May 2, 1947. For a brief summary of the women's suffrage movement in Chile, see "Voto Femenino," Memoria Chilena, BNdeCh, www.memoriachilena.cl/602/w3-article-93508 .html. For a brief history of MEMCH, see " El Movimiento Pro-Emancipación de las Mujeres de Chile MEMCH (1935–1953)," Memoria Chilena, BNdeCh, www.memoriachilena .gob.cl/602/w3-article-3611.html.

74. "Agradecen padres de Ramona Parra," *El Siglo*, February 15, 1946, quoted in Salgado, "La familia de Ramona Parra," 142.

75. "Todos los sectores del pueblo." I located this article thanks to a citation in Bravo Vargas, "¡Ni fiesta ni congoja!," 162.

76. The photo can be viewed at "Violeta Parra en acto politico," CEDOC, Museo Violeta Parra, www.museovioletaparra.cl/cedoc/violeta-parra/. The photo may have been taken at the May 1, 1947, rally, which *El Siglo* toted as one of the largest workers' gatherings in Chilean history. It must have been taken before *El Siglo* was shut down under the "Law for the Permanent Defense of Democracy" in September 1948.

77. I. Parra, *El libro mayor*, 46.

78. "Mamá Violeta," interview with Ángel Parra by Catalina Mena, *Paula*, June 17, 2006, 48.

79. Štambuk and Bravo, *Violeta Parra*, 59.

80. Astorga, "Retrato hablado de Violeta Parra," 11; and Hubert Joanneton, "Violeta Parra: Une Grande Artiste Chilienne," *Radio-TV Je Vois Tout*, 38, September 17, 1970, 24, reproduced and translated in García, *Violeta Parra en sus palabras*, 109.

81. Maitencillo is a beach town near Valparaíso.

82. V. Parra, *Décimas*, 148.

83. Štambuk and Bravo, *Violeta Parra*, 59–60.

84. Štambuk and Bravo, *Violeta Parra*, 53; Merino, *Horas perdidas en las calles*, 215.

85. Štambuk and Bravo, *Violeta Parra*, 61.

86. R. Merino, *Horas perdidas en las calles*, 209; Padilla, *Canarito*, 57–58.

87. Á. Parra, *Violeta se fue*, 81.

88. Chile's marriage code, originally written in the 1880s, did not allow for divorce until it was amended in 2004, making Chile the last nation in the Western Hemisphere to grant the legal right to divorce. Though it cost them, Chileans routinely managed to find ways around the situation by convincing the local authorities that they had committed an error in their original application for a marriage license. See Cox, "Divorcio en Chile."

89. Although Luis Cereceda was not Carmen Luisa's biological father, he is named as such on her birth certificate. According to Carmen Luisa, this was an act of kindness on his part as Violeta was not legally separated from him at the time of Carmen Luisa's birth and, even if she were, she would have been unable to marry Arce because he was still a

minor and his parents would not have granted him permission; Rodríguez, *Cantores que reflexionan*, 164.

90. Á. Parra, *Violeta se fue*, 47.

91. Á. Parra, *Violeta se fue*, 83–84.

92. I. Parra, *El libro mayor*, 52.

93. Macarena Gallo, "Amparo Claro recuerda a su amiga Violeta Parra en su centenario: 'Violeta siempre tuvo el germen del suicidio,'" *The Clinic*, September 23, 2017.

94. Štambuk and Bravo, *Violeta Parra*, 62–64.

95. Roberto and Eduardo Parra formed the parallel duo, Los Hermanos Parra, which recorded a few singles for RCA Victor around roughly the same time as their sisters did. Scant information exists on the Parra brothers' duo. See "Lalo Parra," MusicaPopular.cl, www.musicapopular.cl/artista/lalo-parra/.

96. The folkloric sister acts traced their roots to the family-owned, after-hour entertainment establishments known as *casas de canto* (music houses) featuring the singing of duos and trios of women, usually sisters, that flourished in Santiago and other Chilean cities in the late nineteenth and early twentieth century. In the late 1920s and early 1930s, a few of their more celebrated sister acts were picked up by the Chilean music industry. See González and Rolle, *Historia social*, 313–16 and 371–74; and Spencer, "Finas, arrogantes y dicharacheras."

97. González and Rolle, *Historia social*, 330–31.

98. González and Rolle, *Historia social*, 338–39 and 512.

99. González and Rolle, *Historia social*, 334–35. I put "music hall" in italics to denote that it is an English loanword to Spanish.

100. Štambuk and Bravo, *Violeta Parra*, 60.

101. González and Rolle, *Historia social*, 435. For more on the popularity of Mexican music in Chile, see Mularski, "Mexican or Chilean."

102. Navasal, "Conozca a Violeta Parra," 18; Štambuk and Bravo, *Violeta Parra*, 61; González and Rolle, *Historia social*, 218.

103. Las Hermanas Parra's discography is included in Violeta Parra's discography; "Discografía de Violeta Parra," Cancioneros.com, www.cancioneros.com/cc/4/0/discografia -de-violeta-parra. According to Hilda, the duo's first single was a cover of the popular vals "Mujer ingrata," the next Violeta's vals "Judas," followed by others that Hilda could not remember "because we made the records and then we never bothered with them again"; Štambuk and Bravo, *Violeta Parra*, 61.

104. I put "sketch" in italics to denote that it is an English loanword to Spanish.

105. The sole exception was the Peruvian vals by Nicanor Casas Aguayo that appears on Las Hermanas Parra's single as "Ven." Its actual title is "Ven, Adorada Mujer."

106. Royalties for composer rights were low to begin with. In Parra's case, she was only able to begin collecting hers after 1953, when her folklorista colleague Margot Loyola transcribed her songs for her—a legal requirement of the copyright procedure that Parra was unable to fulfill on her own, as she did not know how to read and write music. Herrero, *Después de vivir un siglo*, 95.

107. Marina de Narvasal, "Conozca a Ester Soré," *Ecran*, March 23, 1954, 18. The Spanish word *negra* is used as a term of endearment in Chile and other South American countries. Although *negra* could also be translated as "black" or, less commonly, "dark," Chilean

ethnomusicologist Juan Pablo González assures me that in the case of Ester Soré it was used solely as a term of endearment; personal correspondence, December 21, 2023.

108. González and Rolle describe Ester Soré as the "faithful representative of the beauty canons of criollo-urban culture of the Chilean middle class in full economic and political ascent"; *Historia social*, 384.

109. Štambuk and Bravo, *Violeta Parra*, 52 and 58.

110. V. Parra, *Décimas*, 157–58.

111. Štambuk and Bravo, *Violeta Parra*, 65.

112. Štambuk and Bravo, *Violeta Parra*, 64.

113. Á. Parra, *Violeta se fue*, 66.

114. Vicuña, "Entrevista," 73.

Chapter 3

1. Jorge Edwards, "Vida y andanzas por el mundo de Violeta Parra," *Eva*, March 1, 1957, 26–27.

2. Herrero titles the section of his biography that covers Parra's life until her emergence as a folklorista "Violeta antes de Violeta" (Violeta before She Was Violeta). For other examples, see Alcalde, *Toda Violeta Parra*, 10; and Lihn, "A la manera del señor Corrales," n.p.

3. As scholars of folk "revivals" make clear, the term itself is misleading, as "these movements transform rather than revive traditions"; Austerlitz, "Birch-Bark Horns and Jazz," 194.

4. Quote is from the transcribed excerpt of a 1958 program on Radio Chilena, available at "Entrevista a doña Flora: Anticueca (Violeta Parra—Florencia Durán de Leyton)," "Cancionero de Violeta Parra," Cancioneros.com, accessed November 20, 2022, www.cancioneros.com/nc/12852/0/entrevista-a-dona-flora-anticueca-violeta-parra-florencia-duran-de-leyton. Audio of the interview is available on V. Parra, *Cantos chilenos*.

5. On the history of folklore studies in Chile, see Dannemann, "Los estudios folklóricos," and Donoso Fritz, "La batalla del folklore."

6. Barr-Melej, *Reforming Chile*.

7. "Reglamento de transmisiones de radiodifusión: 1944; Art. 15," quoted in González and Rolle, *Historia social*, 220.

8. González and Rolle, *Historia social*, 414–17; and Subercaseaux, *Historia de las ideas*, 3:113–14.

9. Collier and Sater, *History of Chile*, 291.

10. Stéphany, "Notes sur la poésie chilienne," 54.

11. Rios, "La Flûte Indienne," 147.

12. Hagedorn, *Divine Utterances*, 9–12.

13. "Nueva folklorista: Gabriela Pizarro," *Ecran*, October 23, 1956, 21.

14. Klimpel lists sixteen women (including Margot Loyola and Violeta Parra) under the category "Música folklórica" (Investigadores, Recopiladores y Compositoras) in her book, *La mujer chilena*, 202–3.

15. González, Ohlsen, and Rolle, *Historia social*, 324.

16. Navasal, "Conozca a Margot Loyola," *Ecran*, September 15, 1953, 18; Sergio Sauvalle, "In Memorium: Gabriela Elena Pizarro Soto (1932–1999)," *Revista musical chilena* 54, no. 193 (January 2000), 120.

17. This was made clear in a party-sanctioned thought piece on the "revolutionary importance of folklore," published in 1956 in the communist review *Principios*. It noted folklore's growing popularity among the "progressive sectors" of Chile, and advocated for its further dissemination as a means to counter "the horrendous influence of the penetration of North American cultural imperialism" and toward "our national liberation." Reyes, "Importancia del folklore nacional," *Principios* no. 37 (1956), 31–32. Gómez Gálvez and Rodríguez Aedo analyze the article in "'Entre la hoz y el martillo,'" which is how I learned of its existence.

18. Huneeus, *La guerra fría chilena*; and Ulianova, "Algunas reflexiones sobre la Guerra Fría."

19. "Folk Singers, Social Reform, and the Red Scare," Library of Congress, www.loc.gov /item/ihas.200197399/.

20. Fernández Larraín, *Informe sobre el comunismo*; "Radio Noticias," *Ecran*, November 2, 1954, 18. Radio Agricultura was run by the conservative National Agricultural Society (Sociedad Nacional de Agricultura or SNA).

21. Austerlitz, "Birch-Bark Horns and Jazz"; Brocken, *British Folk Revival*; Cantwell, *When We Were Good*; Chamosa, *Breve historia del folklore*; Cohen, *Rainbow Quest*; Marchini, *No toquen*; Mitchell, "Visions of Diversity"; Reuss, "American Folksongs"; and Rosenberg, *Transforming Tradition*.

22. Livingston, "Music Revivals."

23. S. H. C., "Nos invadió la música extranjera," *El Siglo*, September 19, 1961; reproduced in García, *Violeta Parra en sus palabras*, 52. Canadian-US pop singer Paul Anka was consistently in the top rankings of the Chilean music industry at the time; González, Ohlsen, and Rolle, *Historia social*, 502.

24. González, Ohlsen, and Rolle, *Historia social*, 605–31.

25. Marina de Navasal, "Conozca a Violeta Parra," *Ecran*, June 8, 1954, 20.

26. Mularski, "Singing Huasos." Anthropologist Raúl Hernán Contreras Román characterized música típica chilena as Chile's quintessential "invented tradition"; "El pueblo creador," 201.

27. For a discussion of the origins of the woman folklorista's costume, see González, Ohlsen, and Rolle, *Historia Social*, 326.

28. Navasal, "Conozca a Violeta Parra," 20. The named musicians were the Dúo Rey-Silva, Dúo Bascuñán-Del Campo, and Margarita Alarcón.

29. S. H. C., "Nos invadió la música extranjera," in García, *Violeta Parra en sus palabras*, 51.

30. Štambuk and Bravo, *Violeta Parra*, 82.

31. "Raul Gardy: Gran señor de la canción chilena," *Ecran*, December 28, 1954, 18.

32. Morales T. and Parra, *Violeta Parra*, 74.

33. For more on the *lira popular*, see "Lira Popular (1866–1930)," Memoria Chilena, BNdeCh, www.memoriachilena.gob.cl/602/w3-article-723.html. For an English-language article on the lira popular, see Verba, "Las Hojas Sueltas [Broadsides]."

34. Facuse and Olea, "Poesía y resistencia," 104–5. The party also organized the First National Conference of Popular Poets and Singers (Primer Congreso Nacional de Payadores y Cantores Populares) in April 1954, with the participation of seventy-two popular poets as well as Nicanor Parra, Pablo Neruda, Tomás Lago, and Margot Loyola. Facuse and Olea, "Poesía y resistencia," 106–8. I have been unable to ascertain if Violeta Parra was present at the conference.

35. Morales T. and Parra, *Violeta Parra*, 74–77. New Song musician Patricio Manns insisted that Violeta told him that she was familiar with the lira popular from her childhood days; in Epple, *Entre mar y cordillera*, 112. Nicanor Parra refutes Manns's claim in his interview with Morales, asserting that the broadsides of poetry barely circulated when he and Violeta were children and, furthermore, that he never saw Violeta with one of them. Morales T. and Parra, *Violeta Parra*, 84–85.

36. Morales T. and Parra, *Violeta Parra*, 68.

37. Lenz, *Sobre la poesía popular*, 515.

38. Liner notes, V. Parra, *Violeta Parra* (1955). My gratitude to Hannes Salo for generously sharing digital images and sound from this and several other of Parra's recordings with me.

39. Navasal, "Conozca a Violeta Parra," 18.

40. Vicuña, "Entrevista," 73.

41. For more on Margot Loyola, see "Margot Loyola (1918–2015)," Memoria Chilena, BNdeCh, www.memoriachilena.gob.cl/602/w3-article-3596.html. For work in English on Loyola, see Snavely, "Ramifying Folklore."

42. "Caupolicán presidió la fiesta en el Municipal, e hizo llorar, reír, tiritar a los laureados," *El Clarín*, June 30, 1955, 15, quoted in Venegas, *Violeta Parra en Concepción*, 29–30n43; Hernán Millas, "Guitarra 'convirtió' a Violeta Parra," *Ercilla*, March 15, 1955, 1.

43. The Mediateca of the Universidad de Chile in Santiago houses several of Parra's collecting recordings. Others are held at Musée d'ethnographie de Genève.

44. According to the 1952 Chilean census, the population of the Comuna de Barrancas grew from 9,264 in 1940 to 31,669 in 1952. INE, *XII Censo general de población y I de vivienda levantado el 24 de abril de 1952: Tomo III, Nucleo Central*, xviii.

45. For an English-language publication on the wake for the little angel, see Orellana, "Versos por Angelito."

46. V. Parra, "Comentario," track B1, *La cueca presentada por Violeta Parra*.

47. Pinkerton, "Chilean Guitarrón," 212–13.

48. Academic folklorists Raquel Barros and Manuel Dannemann worked with the same group of folk informants in the late 1950s; "El Guitarrón en el Departamento de Puente Alto."

49. For a photo of Parra holding a guitarrón, see photo captioned "En la Universidad de Chile, con el guitarrón. Santiago, 1957," "Fotografías," FVP, www.fundacionvioletaparra .org/fotografias. There are no known recordings of Parra playing the guitarrón, which has led to some debate as to whether she actually knew how to play the complex instrument. Chilean musician and musicologist Mauricio Valdebenito hypothesizes that Parra learned to play it at a rudimentary level but not with sufficient mastery to want to make a recording of her efforts; personal correspondence, November 12, 2023.

50. Parra, Bravo, Larraín, and Soublette, *Cantos folklóricos chileno*, 1st (1979) and 2nd (2013) editions.

51. Á. Parra, *Violeta se fue*, 58.

52. V. Parra, *Décimas*, 25.

53. Interview with Alfonso Letelier's son, Miguel Letelier. M. Letelier, interviewer unknown, *Violeta Parra: Grandes chilenos*, Televisión Nacional de Chile, 2008, 5:35–6:20.

54. Rodríguez, *Cantores que reflexionan*, 167; Ángel Parra, quoted in Herrero, *Después de vivir un siglo*, 163.

55. Štambuk and Bravo, *Violeta Parra*, 75.

56. Quoted in Patricia Chavarría Z., "Gracias a Violeta," *Quinchamalí: Artes, letras y sociedad* 17 (1st semester, 2017): 131.

57. Quoted in Herrero, *Después de vivir un siglo*, 123.

58. Quoted in Venegas, *Violeta Parra en Concepción*, 201.

59. Štambuk and Bravo, *Violeta Parra*, 76.

60. Vicuña, "Entrevista," 71.

61. Raúl Frocari Rinaldi and Norberto Folino, "Una tarde con Violeta Parra," *Vuelo*, May 1962. My thanks to Antonio J. González, author and former member of the editorial board for the Argentina magazine *Vuelo*, for generously sharing this article with me.

62. Reproduced in Parra, Bravo, Larraín, and Soublette, *Cantos folklóricos chilenos* (2013).

63. Vicuña, "Entrevista," 71.

64. See, for example, the song Parra collected that is included in academic folklorists' Raquel Barros and Manuel Danneman's songbook, *El romancero chileno*, 68. Whereas the songbook's other entries provide detailed information (name and occupation of the folk informant, place and year that the song was collected, name of the collector) Parra's states, "Collected by Violeta Parra, in Chiloé, and donated to the Institute, without further data." In their article, "Sonidos de un Chile profundo,"Chilean researchers Mariana León Villagra and Ignacio Ramos Rodillo discuss the contrast in styles between "academic collectors" and "collaborators with the archives" like Violeta Parra who collected their own material and then donated it to the University of Chile's archive of traditional music; 29–30.

65. The quote is from an interview with Mario Céspedes, conducted January 5, 1960, at the Universidad de Concepción, transcribed and published in García, *Violeta Parra en sus palabras*, 44. Audio of the interview is available on V. Parra, *En el Aula Magna de Concepción*.

66. Quoted in Lavín, "Margot Loyola y Osvaldo Cadiz," 176.

67. Štambuk and Bravo, *Violeta Parra*, 85.

68. Chilean sociologist Pablo Huneeus, quoted in Štambuk and Bravo, *Violeta Parra*, 123.

69. Štambuk and Bravo, *Violeta Parra*, 84–85.

70. Štambuk and Bravo, *Violeta Parra*, 84.

71. I. Parra, *El libro mayor*, 46.

72. Catalina Mena, "Mamá Violeta," *Paula*, June 17, 2006, 48–49.

73. Á. Parra, *Violeta se fue*, 85–86.

74. Isabel Parra, interview by Cristian Warnken, *Desde el Jardín*, 2018; 29:01

75. "Ángel e Isabel recuerdan a Violeta," *Suplemento de El Mercurio*, May 2, 1993.

76. Á. Parra, *Violeta se fue*, 113.

77. Štambuk and Bravo, *Violeta Parra*, 120.

78. "Estos discos podrían ser un diario de vida," *Emol* (*El Mercurio On-line*), June 14, 2010, www.emol.com/noticias/magazine/2010/06/14/418547/estos-discos-podrian-ser-un -diario-de-vida.html.

79. As performers, both Isabel and Ángel adopted their mother's last name, and not their father's or their father's followed by their mother's (Cereceda Parra), as is customary. This no doubt is a reflection of the way that their musical pathways were so linked to hers.

80. "Isabel Parra: La firme y dulce voz de Isabel," in Pancani and Canales, *Los necios*, 38.

81. "Por estas y otras razones—Imágenes de Violeta Parra," *Música* (Havana, Cuba) 32 (1973): n.p.

82. Štambuk and Bravo, *Violeta Parra*, 104.

83. Rodríguez, *Cantores que reflexionan*, 167.

84. Ruy-Pérez Benítez, *Cuarenta años de "Mañanitas Campesinas,"* 78; and Sáez, *La vida intranquila*, 62.

85. Varas, *Tal vez nunca*, 223.

86. González and Rolle, *Historia social*, 370.

87. Štambuk and Bravo, *Violeta Parra*, 82.

88. Varas and González, *En busca de la música chilena*, 53.

89. Edwards, "Vida y andanzas," 26.

90. Alfredo Lefebvre, "Un excepcional concierto fue ofrecido por Violeta Parra," *El Sur* (Concepción), May 12, 1957, quoted in Venegas, *Violeta Parra en Concepción*, 94.

91. Enrique Bello, "El sábado ofrecerá un concierto la conocida folklorista Violeta Parra," *El Sur*, August 22, 1957, quoted in Venegas, *Violeta Parra en Concepción*, 103.

92. I. Parra, *El libro mayor*, 64.

93. Museo de Arte Popular Americano/Facultad de Bellas Artes, Universidad de Chile. *Museo de Arte Popular Americano*.

94. Pablo Garrido, "Folklore de Ñuble," *La Nación*, July 7, 1960.

95. "¿Surge nuevo valor folklórico?," *Ecran*, November 3, 1953, 19.

96. Accounts differ regarding both who first brought Parra to the radio station and whom she was introduced to there. According to Margot Loyola, she first brought Parra to the station, where she introduced her to José María Palacios; Bello et al., "Análisis de un genio popular," 72. According to Raúl Velasco's daughter Gloria Velasco, her father, who was then the managing director of the station, was the one who first brought Parra to its offices; Rengifo Lira and Rengifo Grau, *Los Cuatro Huasos*, 62. According to Gastón Soublette, Parra brought herself to the radio station and introduced herself to Soublette; Soublette, "Prólogo," in Parra, Bravo, Larraín, and Soublette, *Cantos folklóricos*, 10. For an in-depth discussion of Parra's radio show, see Verba, "Violeta Parra, Radio Chilena." Since publication, I have learned that Radio Chilena, though initially an independent station, was acquired by the Fundación Cardenal Caro in January 1954; "Balance Radial de 1954," *Ecran*, February 15, 1954, 18–19. The new information does not fundamentally alter the substance of my analysis.

97. I. Parra, *El libro mayor*, 58. Rubén Nouzeilles, artistic director for the record company Odeon Chilena, used almost identical language to describe his first encounter with Parra: "I realized that I had come face to face with someone who was extremely special; she did not come from the countryside, but from another planet." "Violeta no venía del campo, sino de otra planeta," *La Época*, February 9, 1990, 24.

98. Celedón, *Memorias que olvidé*, 44–45.

99. Bañados, *Confidencias de un locutor*, loc. 466.

100. Ecran, "Gran programa de chilenidad," *Ecran*, April 6, 1954, 19; Isidoro Bassis Lawner, "'Caupolicanes' entregaron periodistas especializados," *Ecran*, July 2, 1957, 13.

101. According to the owner of La Popular, the bar where Parra performed música criolla in her twenties and early thirties, Parra was "always dressed badly, the same way as she was in her final days." Štambuk and Bravo, *Violeta Parra*, 52.

102. "Violeta Parra y el folklore," *Ecran*, December 22, 1953, 35 and 41.

103. Ecran, "Alcance de una labor folklórica: Violeta Parra," *Ecran*, October 19, 1954, 18.

104. Štambuk and Bravo, *Violeta Parra*, 96–97.

105. Štambuk and Bravo, *Violeta Parra*, 95.

106. Parra claimed to be receiving fifty letters a day in her 1954 interview with Hernán Valdés, "Violeta Parra da opinions sobre el folklore nacional," *La Nación*, December 19, 1954. Isabel and Ángel Parra remembered the sacks of letters their mother brought home from the station that they then used to stoke their stove during the winter months; I. Parra, *El libro mayor*, 62; Štambuk and Bravo, *Violeta Parra*, 95.

107. Štambuk and Bravo, *Violeta Parra*, 82. For a discussion of Parra's role in the guitar-rón's revival, see Pinkerton, "Chilean Guitarrón."

108. In a verse from his autobiography in décimas, for example, Eduardo "Lalo" Parra recounts how Violeta joined his band after her separation from her first husband but that he wasn't sure how long it would last because "Her temperament is a two-edged sword. / A singer, a very good sister / super-loving during the week / but also very bossy" (*su genio es una espada / de dos filos afiliada. / Cantora, muy buena hermana, / querendona en la semana / pero siempre muy mandona*). E. Parra, *Autobiografía en décimas*, 99.

109. Quoted in "Violeta Parra: Quien nace flor y árbol al mismo tiempo, no muere nunca," *Vistazos* 4, November 1997, 5.

110. I. Parra, *El libro mayor*, 78.

111. Rodríguez, *Cantores que reflexionan*, 190. Adela Gallo was a photographer when Parra met her. Gallo had worked as a truck driver in her twenties, making her one of the first and few women to enter the profession. Irene Domínguez and Cristian Vila Riquelme, "Despedida a Adela Gallo," *Araucaria de Chile* 26 (1984): 219.

112. There is no consensus as to why the show ended. Ricardo García stated it was for "internal problems," quoted in I. Parra, *El libro mayor*, 61. Others have surmised it was because of financial difficulties.

113. Morales T. and Parra, *Violeta Parra*, 78.

114. Bello et al., "Análisis de un genio popular," 75.

115. For a full list of attendees, see Fernández Larraín, *Informe sobre el comunismo*, 129–30.

116. Herrero, *Después de vivir un siglo*, 165.

117. Las Hermanas Parra, untitled single, Odeon 89–952.

118. Á. Parra, *Violeta se fue*, 93–95; I. Parra, *El libro mayor*, 54.

119. The notice did not specify which radio station, just that it was in Santiago; "Alcance de una labor folklórica."

120. "Radio Noticias," *Ecran*, November 2, 1954, 18.

121. Rengifo Lira and Rengifo Grau, *Los Cuatro Huasos*, 62.

122. V. Parra, *Violeta Parra* (1955). Las Hermanas Parra's singles were packaged in generic sleeves featuring the RCA Victor logo.

123. Nouzeilles, liner notes, V. Parra, *Violeta Parra* (1955). The notes' obvious exaggeration of the longevity of Parra's career as a folklorista—at best three years at the time of the album's release—may have been a ploy by Odeon Chilena to rebrand its newly contracted recording artist, as all of Parra's prior recordings were with Las Hermanas Parra for rival record company RCA Victor.

124. In 1944, Las Hermanas Loyola (The Loyola Sisters), the duo that Margot Loyola formed with her sister Estela, recorded a *canto a lo divino* (song to the divine; poet-song on a religious theme), included on a single with RCA Victor; Ruiz Zamora, "Discografía de Margot Loyola," 44.

125. This may explain why the recording has yet to be rereleased, despite the spate of reeditions of Parra's albums that have appeared in the twenty-first century.

126. This was the case for *Violeta Parra con su guitarra* (Violeta Parra and her guitar), Parra's second EP on the Odeon label, which was released within months of her first and which, like the first, included two poet-songs.

127. The first stanza is adapted from the poem "Boda de negros" by Francisco de Quevedo (1580–1645). Continuing a racist practice dating back to the Renaissance, if not earlier, Parra's lyrics exoticize Black people. For a history of the song, see Osiel Vega Durán, "Casamiento de negros de Violeta Parra: Lo moderno y modernizante en la aparición de un texto que cruza siglos de literatura, música y política," *Tema Musical* (online), 1, no. 1 (September 2023), https://osielvega.wixsite.com/temamusical/post/casamiento-de-negros, 2023.

128. *New Capitol Albums for May & June, 1956*. Parra's recordings of "Qué pena siente el alma" and "Casamiento de negros" also appear on the 1956 Capitol Records release *Santiago!*, a compilation of Chilean música típica, primarily produced for the US and Canadian market; V. Parra et al., *Santiago!*

129. Baxter,' *Round the World with Les Baxter*. The liner notes for "Melodia Loca" describe the song as "a Chilean theme, also called the 'Drive-You-Crazy-Song' because its monotonous melody and odd chord progressions are said to have driven many Chileans to suicide."

130. Parra's name appears in the copyright registry for the song "Melodia Loca," Ardmore Music Corporation, May 19, 1959. Copyright Office, Library of Congress, *Catalog of copyright entries—Music*, ser. 3, pt. 5, vol. 13, no. 1, January–June 1959, 332.

131. According to Sáez, the invitation came days before being awarded the Caupolicán; *La vida intranquila*, 77. Margot Loyola recalled it arriving a month after the ceremony; Štambuk and Bravo, *Violeta Parra*, 104. Her claim does not seem plausible, however, given Parra's departure for Europe in early July 1955.

132. Ecran, "La entrega de los premios 'Caupolicán' 1954," *Ecran*, July 5, 1955, 3.

133. "Entretelones de la noche del 28," *Vea*, July 6, 1955, 18. For a photo of Parra receiving the prize, see I. Parra, *El libro mayor*, 61.

134. Herrero, *Después de vivir un siglo*, 178.

135. "Caupolicán presidió la fiesta." Parra declared in the same interview that she was leaving the next day for Milan, Italy, by invitation of the city's folklorists. As this was clearly not the case, her claim may constitute an early example of the numerous exaggerated and/or simply false statements Parra made to the Chilean press about impending trips to Europe and other destinations over the remainder of her life. In this instance, her claim may have been prompted by her desire to avoid mentioning that her final destination was Warsaw, where she would participate in the World Festival of Youth and Students, as festival delegates had been instructed to be discrete given that the Chilean Communist Party remained technically illegal at the time. See "Leonidas Zapata recrea gira a Varsovia con Violeta Parra y explica el origen [*sic*] de una de sus décimas," *Alerce* 5, no. 46 (June 2018): n.p.

Chapter 4

1. Javier Rodríguez Aedo's article "Violeta Parra a través de sus viajes por Europa (1955 y 1962)" offers an excellent complement to both this chapter and chapters 7 and 8.

2. Marina de Navasal, "Volvió Violeta Parra," *Ecran*, January 1, 1957, 23. Parra recorded the song for the Le Chant du Monde label in March 1956. It was first released on the 1975 LP *Violeta Parra, cantos de Chile*.

3. According to the World Festival of Youth and Students' Facebook page, the most recent festival was the Nineteenth, held in Sochi, Russia, in 2017. World Festival of Youth and Students, Facebook, accessed June 9, 2024, www.facebook.com/19WFYSWorldFestivalof YouthandStudents/?ref=page_internal.

4. Koivunen, "The World Youth Festival," 125.

5. Rupprecht, *Soviet Internationalism after Stalin*, 56–57 and 67–68.

6. In addition to Violeta Parra, the roster of Chilean folk musicians who participated in the festival over the years includes Isabel and Ángel Parra, Conjunto Cuncumén (with Rolando Alarcón and Víctor Jara), Inti-Illimani, Nano Acevedo, and Luis Advis. Mularski, *Music, Politics, and Nationalism*, 37.

7. Brazil's delegation was second at 107, and Argentina's third at 49. Krzywicki, *Post-stalinowski karnawał radości*, 304–5. My thanks to María Laszczok for her translation.

8. Sáez, *La vida intranquila*, 77–78.

9. "Con 'Fiesta de la Chilenidad' se despidió a los delegados de Chile al Festival de Varsovia," *El Siglo*, June 30, 1955.

10. A Chilean visitor to the World Festival of Youth and Students held in Moscow in 1957 noted that the cost of just the airfare from Santiago to Moscow was as much as a Chilean craftsman made in a year. Quoted in Rupprecht, *Soviet Internationalism after Stalin*, 53.

11. V. Parra, *Décimas*, 161–64.

12. Luz María Astorga, "Retrato hablado de Violeta Parra," *Revista del Domingo, El Mercurio*, October 31, 1982, 9.

13. Štambuk and Bravo, *Violeta Parra*, 106.

14. V. Parra, *Décimas*, 165–67.

15. Quoted in Herrero, *Después de vivir un siglo*, 212.

16. V. Parra, *Décimas*, 167.

17. Figures are from table 3.1 in Koivunen, "The 1957 Moscow Youth Festival," 49.

18. Gillabert, "Varsovie 1955 et la Guerre froide globale," 56. Footage of the WFYS in Warsaw is available for view at "Międzynarodowa Warszawa Zwiastuje Koniec Stalinizmu," *E-Kartka z Warszawy*, http://ekartkazwarszawy.pl/kartka/miedzynarodowa-warszawa -zwiastuje-koniec-stalinizmu/.

19. "Hoy comienza Festival de la Juventud en Varsovia," *El Siglo*, July 7, 1955.

20. Sáez, *La vida intranquila*, 80–81.

21. These included Conjunto Cuncumén and the University of Chile's choir and theater company. Herrero, *Después de vivir un siglo*, 192.

22. Štambuk and Bravo, *Violeta Parra*, 107.

23. Herrero, *Después de vivir un siglo*, 192–93; Rodríguez Aedo, "Violeta Parra a través de sus viajes," 33–36. My thanks to Javier Foxon Calvo and Magdalena Szkwarek in Warsaw for their generous research assistance.

24. "Violeta Parra descubre el telón de nuestro folklore," *Crónica* (Concepción), May 13, 1957, quoted in Venegas, *Violeta Parra en Concepción*, 87.

25. Štambuk and Bravo, *Violeta Parra*, 107.

26. V. Parra, *Décimas*, 167–72.

27. For a study of Soviet revived and expanded interactions with Latin America in the post-Stalinist period of the Cold War, see Rupprecht, *Soviet Internationalism after Stalin*.

28. Rupprecht, *Soviet Internationalism after Stalin*, 87–93.

29. Quoted in Herrero, *Después de vivir un siglo*, 194–95.

30. Oscar Vega, "Con la folklorista Violeta Parra," *La Discusión*, December 23, 1957, quoted in Venegas, *Violeta Parra en Concepción*, 89.

31. V. Parra, no title, Leningradsky Zavod.

32. Parra learned "Meriana" from Margot Loyola, who, in turn, learned it from Rapa Nui traditional singer Felipe Riroroco; Miranda, "Violeta Parra, Creative Researcher," 87n11. On the Soviet single, the song is titled "Девушка," which in Russian means "lass."

33. Jorge Edwards, "Vida y andanzas por el mundo de Violeta Parra," *Eva* 15, no. 624 (March 1, 1957): 28; "Leonidas Zapata recrea gira a Varsovia con Violeta Parra y explica el origen [*sic*] de una de sus décimas," *Alerce* 5, no. 46 (June 2018): n.p.

34. The available sources are unable to confirm how Parra received word of her daughter's death.

35. Navasal, "Volvió Violeta Parra."

36. V. Parra, *Décimas*, 160.

37. See "Rosita se fue a los cielos" and "Verso por confesión" (first line, "Cuando salí de aquí"), V. Parra, *Décimas*, 185–88. Parra set "Verso por confesión" to music, titled the resulting song "Verso por la niña muerta," and recorded it on *Violeta Parra: El folklore de Chile*, vol. 1.

38. Štambuk and Bravo, *Violeta Parra*, 110.

39. Rodríguez, *Cantores que reflexionan*, 164.

40. Zig-Zag, "Folklore," *Zig-Zag*, September 17, 1955, 30.

41. "Violeta Parra canta en Paris," *Ecran*, October 25, 1955, 19.

42. Argentine journalist Julio Huasi, for example, recounts that a colleague warned him not to think so highly of Parra. When Huasi asked the colleague why, the colleague responded, "Listen, when she went to the Festival of Youth in Warsaw, she gave up everything to travel, including her newborn daughter." Julio Huasi, "Los siete golgotas de Violeta Parra," *El Porteño*, June 1986, 71.

43. V. Parra, *Décimas*, 187–88.

44. Here, I borrow Daniel J. Sherman's wording from his study of French primitivism during this period, convinced that it applies equally to exoticism. Sherman, *French Primitivism*, 3.

45. Looseley, *Popular Music*, 11.

46. For a discussion of the Anglophile rock invasion of France, see Looseley, *Popular Music*, 21–35. Elvis Presley topped the charts in both France and Chile in 1956.

47. French music critic and author Jacques Vassal noted that a few French musicians from this period tried to popularize French folk songs but concluded that their efforts remained "courageous and isolated attempts." Vassal, *Français, si vous chantiez*, 42.

48. All of three women appear in the six-page index of the otherwise encyclopedic publication *Les Amériques latines en France* (published in 1992). Violeta Parra is not one of them. Leenhardt, Kalfon, Mattelart, and Mattelart, *Les Amériques latines en France*.

49. Nazem Ghemraoui, "Entretien avec Romano Zanotti, un des fondateurs des Machucambos," Maison Orange—Salsa et danses du monde, January 30, 2006, http://maisonorange.fr/entretien-romzan.html.

50. Leenhardt, Kalfon, Mattelart, and Mattelart, *Les Amériques latines en France*, 41–48.

51. Yupanqui's reputation continued to rise even after his mid-1950 return to Argentina, most notably when his Le Chant du Monde album *Minero soy* won the prestigious Grand Prize of the Charles Cros Academy for Best Foreign Album of the year in 1952. Pujol, *En nombre del folclore*; Orquera, "From the Andes to Paris"; and Rios, "La Flûte Indienne," 155.

52. Massuh, *Nací para ser breve*, 155. For an article in English on María Elena Walsh, see Bach, "A Child's Wisdom in a Poet's Heart."

53. Edwards, "Vida y andanzas," 28.

54. V. Parra, *Décimas*, 181.

55. Sextier, *L'Escale*; Rios, "La Flûte Indienne," 150–51.

56. Plisson, "Les musiques d'Amérique latine," quoted in Aravena-Decart, "Représentations et fonctions sociales," 235. Literary critic and translator Jason Weiss makes a similar point about Latin American writers in the era, who due to Latin America's history of colonial dependence had little knowledge of each other until they met in Paris, quoted in Mularski, *Music, Politics, and Nationalism*, 37.

57. "Don Quijote de la guitarra," *Revista Ñ/Clarín*, November 14, 2012, www.clarin.com/musica/paco-ibanez-canta-poetas-latinoamericanos_0_HyroTpjwQg.html. The club continued to be a showcase for Latin American music in Paris well into the twenty-first century.

58. The song was set to the music of "El condor pasa." For a history of "El condor pasa," see Rios, "La Flûte Indienne," 159–62.

59. Nazem Ghemraoui, "Entretien avec Rafaêl Gayoso—Un des fondateurs des Machucambos," *Maison Orange—Salsa et danses du monde*, January 5, 2006, http://maisonorange.fr/ent-gayoso.html.

60. Ghemraoui, "Entretien avec Romano Zanotti."

61. According to Antoine Sextier, director of the documentary *L'Escale*, only two other women performed at L'Escale during the same period as Parra: Julia "Julita" Cortés and the Spanish singer Carmela "Carmen" Requeta; personal correspondence, February 1, 2024.

62. See, for example, Benjamin Goldstein, liner notes for Los Machucambos, *Vuelve junto a mi—Los Machucambos*, Frémeaux & Associés FA511, 2009.

63. When founding member of Los Machucambos Rafael Gayoso was asked about Parra in a 2015 radio interview, for example, he commented, "At first we didn't take her very seriously. She was not an attractive woman." "París, 1960: Escuchar 'Los Machucambos' y bailar en el Escale," interview by Asbel López, *París América*, RFI, April 24, 2015, 18:28–18:48.

64. Luis Alberto Mansilla, "Interview with Margot Loyola," *Revista Ahora*, September 28, 1971.

65. Loyola was visiting Paris as part of a prolonged European tour that also included an extensive visit to the Soviet Bloc nations. "Entrevista: Margot Loyola, intérprete de la danza y la canción de Chile," *Revista Musical Chilena* 12, no. 59 (January 1, 1958): 24–28.

66. Quoted in Arenas, *Margot Loyola*, 39.

67. Navasal, "Volvió Violeta Parra."

68. Štambuk and Bravo, *Violeta Parra*, 113–14.

69. Štambuk and Bravo, *Violeta Parra*, 108.

70. "Violeta Parra descubre el telón de nuestro folklore," quoted in Venegas, *Violeta Parra in Concepción*, 88.

71. Sáez, *La vida intranquila*, 84–85.

72. Edwards, "Vida y andanzas," 44.

73. V. Parra, *Décimas*, 181.

74. For more on Rivet, see Laurière, *Paul Rivet*; and "Paul Rivet (1876–1958)," Musée de l'Homme, accessed November 9, 2022, www.museedelhomme.fr/en/paul-rivet-1876-1958. I have thus far been unable to locate the recordings.

75. Letter from Serge Flateau, Artistic Director of Programming, Radiodiffusión Télévision Françiase (RTF), to Miss Violeta Parra, December 29, 1955, Paris; in the Archives of Paul Rivet, Muséum national d'Histoire naturelle, http://bibliotheques.mnhn.fr.

76. Jodorowsky, *Spiritual Journey*, xiv–xv.

77. "Canciones Folklóricas de Chile," 1956, digital file code A03146, audio recording number 4010, UNESCO Digital Archives. Parra also claimed to have made recordings for the French National Sound Archives, then housed at the Sorbonne. See Edwards, "Vida y andanzas," 45. I have thus far been unable to locate them.

78. Alten, "Le Chant du monde," par. 2.

79. Casanova, "Jalons pour une histoire."

80. V. Parra, *Chants et danses du Chili*, vols. 1 and 2.

81. Gérard Imbert, liner notes to Violeta Parra, *Cantos de Chile*.

82. The songs are "Paimiti" and "Meriana," with the latter also appearing on Parra's Soviet-produced single.

83. See, for example, G. Ribemont-Dessaignes, "Chronique des Disques—Folklore," *Gazette de Lausanne*, February 8, 1958, 13; J. B., "Chili: Chants et Danses (No. 1) par Violeta Parra, guitare et chant," *Disques* 83–84 (December 1956): 891; and C. S. "Folklore: Amérique du Sud," *Disques* 99 (May–June 1958): 519.

84. J. B., "Chili: Chants et Danses."

85. V. Parra, *Décimas*, 182.

86. Andréa Cohen, "Violeta Parra et ses enfants," *L'Atelier de la création*, RadioFrance, December 21, 2007, 45:29–45:39, www.radiofrance.fr/franceculture/podcasts/l-atelier-de-la-creation-14-15/violeta-parra-et-ses-enfants-rediffusion-5388758.

87. Parra and Sandoval, *Violeta más viva que nunca*.

88. Vega, "Con la folklorista Violeta Parra," quoted in Venegas, *Violeta Parra en Concepción*, 90.

89. "París, 1960: Escuchar 'Los Machucambos' y bailar en el Escale," 18:55–19:00.

90. V. Parra, *Décimas*, 182.

91. Štambuk and Bravo, *Violeta Parra*, 114. A photo of Parra and Rus captioned "in an existentialist bar in Paris" is found in Edwards, "Vida y andanzas," 26.

92. V. Parra, *Décimas*, 182.

93. Pujol, *Como la cigarra*, 97. Parra made a lasting impression that day: in Walsh's poetic memoir, written years after the incident, she depicts Parra as a "crazy witch" flying through the Parisian skies on her guitar-case-broomstick. Walsh, *Diario brujo, 1995–1999*, 169.

94. Cohen, "Violeta Parra et ses enfants," 45:04–45:08.

95. Navasal, "Violeta Parra hizo llorar a los franceses," *Ecran*, December 11, 1956, 19. The article consists of excerpts from a letter to Odeon Chilena's lead sound engineer, Luis Marcos Stuven.

96. "Television Programme as Broadcast Tuesday 15th May 1956," BBC Written Archives Centre.

97. She was paid £30 for recording twenty songs, which is roughly the equivalent of US $875 in 2022; contract between Parra and the BBC, May 10, 1956, BBC Written Archives Centre.

98. The master tape of the recording eventually made its way to Chile, as songs from it appear on the following releases: V. Parra, *Violeta Parra*, vol. 6 (1984); and *Violeta Parra: El folklore y la pasión*.

99. Letter from Arístides Aguilera to the Music Bookings Manager [no name given], January 18, 1956, "Violeta Parra," BBC Archive.

100. Brocken, *British Folk Revival*.

101. The council was founded in London in 1947. Karpeles, "International Folk Music Council."

102. Brumfield, "Jean Ritchie's Field Trip—Scotland," 50. For more on Kingsley, see Wilfrid M. Appleby, "Contemporary Guitarist," *Guitar News*, no. 13 (June–July 1953), 1–3.

103. Memo to Mr. Ian Grimble, April 27, 1956, "Violeta Parra," BBC Written Archives Centre.

104. Violeta Parra, recorded by Alan Lomax, 1955, London, T171R01, Lomax Digital Archive, https://archive.culturalequity.org/. Lomax does not appear to have ever used the recordings in his broadcasts. On Lomax's career at the BBC, see Gregory, "Lomax in London."

105. Pujol, *Como la cigarra*, 104–5.

106. "Rhythmes du Chili," *Rhythmes et images d'Amérique Latine*, Paris Inter, Paris, August 28, 1956, PHD89003668, INA. Parra's show was the fifth installment in a six-part series featuring music from Brazil, Ecuador, Mexico, Colombia, and Chile.

107. Navasal, "Violeta Parra hizo llorar."

108. Schlesser, *Le cabaret "rive gauche,"* 643–44.

109. Vicuña, "Entrevista," 74. I am assuming here that the folk festival Parra refers to in her interview with Vicuña was the Hommage de Paris au Folklore International, held June 2 and 3, 1956.

110. The second volume was most likely released soon after Parra's departure to Chile as it was reviewed in the "Chronique des Disques," *Gazette de Lausanne*, February 8, 1958.

111. Sáez, *La vida intranquila*, 87.

112. Produced by Radio France, the show was still in existence in 2024, albeit as a podcast, making it one of the longest-running shows in the history of French media; www.radiofrance.fr/franceinter/podcasts/le-masque-et-la-plume.

113. "*Le masque et la plume*," recorded November 26, aired December 2, 1956, RTF, PHD88020896, INA. Parra's performance is from 19:40–26:18.

114. Edwards, "Vida y andanzas," 45.

115. Navasal, "Violeta Parra hizo llorar."

116. Edwards, "Vida y andanzas," 27.

117. Edwards, "Vida y andanzas," 26.

118. Nazem Ghemraoui, "Entretien avec Romano Zanotti."

Chapter 5

1. "Reencuentro con Violeta Parra," *El Mercurio*, December 26, 1999. Although Letelier did not specify the year of his encounter with Parra at the annual Arts Fair, held in Decem-

ber, I deduce it was 1959 based on the fact that Parra performed fragments of "El Gavilán" on the radio in January 1960; Céspedes, "En la radio," in García, *Violeta Parra en sus palabras.*

2. The poem is available at "Nicanor Parra," Universidad de Chile, accessed February 14, 2024, www.nicanorparra.uchile.cl/antologia/otros/defensavioleta.html.

3. I. Parra, *El libro mayor*, 85.

4. Á. Parra, *Violeta se fue*, 134.

5. Isabel Parra was sixteen when she had Tita. Tita carries her mother's name Parra and her maternal grandfather's name Cereceda. None of Tita Parra's online biographies provide information regarding the identity of her father.

6. V. Parra, *Décimas*, 183–84.

7. Herrero, *Después de vivir*, 285.

8. Štambuk and Bravo, *Violeta Parra*, 114; Sáez, *La vida intranquila*, 107.

9. "El refugio que permanece," *Revista universitaria* 142 (2017), Especial Violeta Volcánica, https://revistauniversitaria.uc.cl/especial/violeta-parra-el-refugio-que-permanece/16297/.

10. McClennen, "Chilex," 5.

11. The conceptual cousin to the practice of advertising Parra's European success was to lament that Europeans were better able to appreciate Chilean artists than Chileans themselves. See, for example, the piece penned by an *Ecran* columnist writing under the pseudonym "Hablador" decrying the lack of interest in Chile for Parra's recordings of folk music: "Los profetas fuera de casa . . . y otros detalles . . . ," *Ecran*, May 22, 1956, 20–21.

12. V. Parra, *Violeta Parra, el folkore de Chile*, vol. 1. All of Parra's previous recordings had been either EPs or singles. The original LP does not include the name of the author of the liner notes. They have since been identified as Raúl Aicardi; "Discografía de Violeta Parra," Cancioneros.com, www.cancioneros.com/nd/2673/4/el-folklore-de-chile-violeta-parra.

13. Camilo Fernández, "Album de Discos," *Ecran*, January 8, 1957, 31.

14. "En diciembre debuta Violeta Parra en Radio Chilena," *Ecran*, November 6, 1956, 21.

15. "Violeta Parra en Radio Chilena," *Ecran*, September 3, 1957, 21.

16. V. Parra, untitled single, Odeon 87–045, 1957, 78 rpm, released February 1957. The recording has not been rereleased at time of writing, most likely because it has yet to be located.

17. Camilo Fernández, "Album de Discos," *Ecran*, January 22, 1957, 30–31.

18. Interview with Rubén Nouzeilles, "'Violeta no venía del campo, sino de otro planeta,'" *La Época*, February 9, 1990.

19. Jorge Edwards, "Vida y andanzas por el mundo de Violeta Parra," *Eva*, March 1, 1957, 45.

20. Alfonso Letelier, "Violeta Parra," *Revista Musical Chilena* 21, no. 100 (April–June, 1967): 110.

21. Spencer, " Folklore e idiomaticidad," 8–10.

22. Eduardo Bello describes Parra's anticuecas as "work that deserves to figure among the greatest compositions of classical music for the instrument in any part of the world"; "Análisis de un genio popular," 69. Chilean composer and musicologist Fernando García states, "In my opinion perhaps the greatest Chilean composer would be Violeta Parra. Her 'Anticuecas' are concert music for guitar. . . . Esthetically speaking, the result of her work is perhaps the most important ever created in Chile." "Entrevista a Fernando García," *Pluma y Pincel*, no. 179 (1998): 47.

23. Odeon MSOD/E-51020, 1957, 45 rpm.

24. See, for example, Camilo Hernández, "Album," *Ecran*, December 31, 1957, 30.

25. Liner notes, *Violeta Parra—Composiciones para guitarra*. In addition to writing the liner notes, Soublette played classical flute on two of the EP's tracks. Magdalena Vicuña copied Soublette's liner notes almost verbatim in her piece on Violeta Parra; Vicuña "Entrevista." The album can be heard in its entirety at *Discoteca Nacional Chile*, https://discotecanacio nalchile.blogspot.com/2017/05/violeta-parra-composiciones-para.html. For a discussion of how contemporary reviews and more recent scholarly works on Parra's "modern" compositions reinforce the academic and Eurocentric hierarchy of classical music over "popular" or "folk" music, see Aravena-Décart, "Música popular y discurso académico"; and Uribe, "Violeta Parra en la frontera del arte musical chileno.

26. "Album," *Ecran*, December 31, 1957, 30.

27. Compare, for example, the contemporary discussion regarding Violeta Parra's modern compositions with journalist Marina Latorre's assessment of her brother Nicanor Parra's creative abilities, originally published in the 1966 art review *Portal*: "Nothing that comes out of his pen or his typewriter for publication is the fruit of improvisation. His poetry . . . is the result of the lucid reflections of a mathematician, of a modern man facing his era and the new phenomena that it has engendered with a level-headed and fresh consciousness." Latorre, "Nicanor Parra en un mar de preguntas," *Portal* 4 (November 1966): 2.

28. Marina de Navasal, "Museo de música popular creó Violeta Parra," *Ecran*, March 18, 1958, 14. Parra's dismissal of any need for formal musical training did not prevent her from bragging that she had received pointers from Spanish master guitarist Andrés Segovia, whom she claimed to have met during the classical guitarist's tour of Chile in August 1957.

29. See, for example, the concert program published in "Violeta Parra actuará hoy en Salón de Honor," *Crónica*, May 11, 1957, quoted in Venegas, *Violeta Parra en Concepción*, 92. The program's French songs all appear on the prize-winning album of French folk revivalist Jacques Douai, *Chansons poétiques anciennes et modern*, BAM LD-306, 1955. The Israeli song is most likely "Ehrets Zavat Chalav" (Land of Milk and Honey), recorded by 1950s Israeli folk-singing sensation Yaffa Yarkoni. Parra probably learned the Italian song, whose correct title is "Quel Mazzoline de Fiori," from the singing of Les Compagnons de la Chanson. The Andean song, with the correct spelling of Jujuy (Argentine province), was first recorded in Argentina in the 1940s by the folk group Los Hermanos Abalos, then made its way to Paris, where it was recorded by Les Quatre Guaranis on their 1953 album, *Les Quatre Guaranis: Musique folklorique de l'Amérique latine* (BAM EX-221), and by Los Incas on their 1956 album, *Chants et danses de l'Amérique Latine* (Philips N 77.306); Aravena-Decart, "Représentations et fonctions sociales," 182n1, 189–90. I have been unable to identify the song in Quechua.

30. Epple, *Entre mar y cordillera*, 36.

31. "La desconocida amistad del fotógrafo Sergio Larraín y Violeta Parra," *La Tercera*, July 15, 2012.

32. Parra, Bravo, Larraín, and Soublette, *Cantos folklóricos chilenos* (1979). There is considerable variance among Parra's biographers regarding the chronology of her collecting excursions. In the case of her trip to document the Fiesta de la Tirana, I base my chronology on Sergio Larraín's photo-essay "La Tirana," published in *O Cruzeiro Internacional* 1, no. 15 (November 11, 1957), 28–33. Referenced in Miguel Del Castillo, "Sergio Larraín na revista *O Cruzeiro Internacional*," IMS (Instituto Moreira Salles), n.d., https://ims.com.br/2016/05/04

/sergio-larrain-na-revista-o-cruzeiro-internacional/. Soublette summarized his collecting trips with Parra in a 2005 interview; Canales, "De los cantos folklóricos chilenos," 21.

33. Drysdale, "Violeta Parra," 502.

34. Both pieces appear on her 1957 EP, *Violeta Parra—Composiciones para guitarra.*

35. Navasal, "Violeta Parra hizo llorar a los franceses," *Ecran*, December 11, 1956, 19.

36. González, "Estilo y función social," 84.

37. The songs of the Mapuche also inspired a genre of songs popular in 1940s known as *canción mapuchina*; González and Rolle, *Historia social*, 404–8; González, "Estilo y función social."

38. Štambuk and Bravo, *Violeta Parra*, 112–13.

39. Miranda, Loncón, and Ramay's book *Violeta Parra en el Wallmapu* offers a detailed account of Parra's experience in Wallmapu along with analyses of the material she collected. I base the chronology of Parra's collecting expeditions to Wallmapu on their work, on Gastón Soublette's testimony in Štambuk and Bravo, *Violeta Parra*, 83, and on the newspaper article "Violeta Parra descubre el telón de nuestro folklore," *Crónica*, May 13, 1957, quoted in Venegas, *Violeta Parra en Concepción*, 91.

40. INE (Chile), *XII Censo general de población y I de vivienda levantado el 24 de abril de 1952: Tomo I, Resumen del país* (Santiago: El Servicio), 46.

41. Miranda, Loncón, and Ramay, *Violeta Parra en el Wallmapu*, 68.

42. Miranda, Loncón, and Ramay, *Violeta Parra en el Wallmapu*, 32; Ernesto González Bermejo, "Isabel Parra, enemiga del olvido y la desesperanza," *Crisis*, August 1975, 48.

43. Miranda, Loncón, and Ramay, *Violeta Parra en el Wallmapu*, 21. Coauthors Miranda, Loncón, and Ramay characterize Parra's collecting practice as "dialogical ethnology" in that her role as an investigator was "not to organize or edit, but to create an atmosphere in which the sung and spoken words can flow reciprocally without any type of restrictions." They conclude that Parra's work among the Mapuche contributed to the "decolonization of knowledge and of research on indigenous peoples." *Violeta Parra en el Wallmapu*, 57.

44. "Violeta Parra de nuevo en Radio Chilena," *Ecran*, June 11, 1957, 21; "Violeta Parra en Radio Chilena," *Ecran*, September 3, 1957, 21; "Crónica," *Revista Musical Chilena* 11, no. 53 (June–July 1957): 55.

45. Štambuk and Bravo, *Violeta Parra*, 83.

46. Stéphany, "Notes sur la poésie chilienne," 54. Writer and translator Fanchita Gonzalez-Batlle made a similar claim in her explanation as to why Parra's bilingual book, *Poésie populaire des Andes*, did not contain any songs that are "purely Indian," stating that "apparently [the songs] have not evolved." Fanchita Gonzalez-Batlle in V. Parra, *Poésie populaire des Andes*, 8.

47. Miranda, Loncón, and Ramay, *Violeta Parra en el Wallmapu*, 35.

48. See Elisa Loncón, "Violeta Parra: Los vínculos de su obra con la cultura Mapuche y originaria," in Consejo Nacional, *Después de vivir un siglo*, 165–95.

49. V. Parra, *Violeta Parra: El folklore de Chile*, vol. 1.

50. The other three albums are *Violeta Parra: El folklore de Chile*, vol. 2; *La cueca presentada por Violeta Parra*; and *La tonada presentada por Violeta Parra*.

51. Aicardi, liner notes for V. Parra, *Violeta Parra: El folklore de Chile*, vol. 1.

52. "Album de discos," *Ecran*, September 17, 1957, 30–31. As far as I can ascertain, none of the other three volumes were reviewed in *Ecran*.

53. Hablador, "No queremos música nuestra y otras detalles . . . ," *Ecran*, October 1, 1957, 29.

54. See Guerrero and Vuskovic, *La música del nuevo cine chileno*; Mouesca, *El documental chileno* and *Plano secuencia de la memoria*; Salinas, Stange, and Salinas Roco, *Historia del cine experimental*. *Mimbre* is available for viewing on YouTube.

55. Sergio Bravo, quoted in Jacqueline Mouesca, "Sergio Bravo: Pionero del cine documental chileno," *Araucaria de Chile* 37 (1987): 105.

56. For more on Parra and Bravo's collaboration, see Guerrero and Vuskovic, *La música del nuevo cine*, 33–61.

57. Navasal, "Isabel, ¿Heredera del cetro folklórico de Violeta Parra?," *Ecran*, May 14, 1957, 21.

58. Isabel Parra, no title, Odeon 87–056.

59. "Album de discos," *Ecran*, October 8, 1957, 30.

60. I. Parra, *El libro mayor*, 108. The untitled EPs are Odeon DSOD-E 50176, 1958, 45 rpm; and Odeon DSOD-E 50182, 1958, 45 rpm.

61. Population figure of 130,000 is from Herrero, *Después de vivir*, 251.

62. Fernando Venegas's in-depth investigation of Parra's residency in Concepción has proven invaluable for this section.

63. Venegas, *Violeta Parra en Concepción*, 69–86.

64. Herrero, *Después de vivir un siglo*, 250.

65. The theater company was the Teatro de la Universidad de Concepción or TUC.

66. "Alumnos del Curso Folklórico de Violeta Parra realizarán presentación pública," *La Patria*, January 10, 1958, cited in Venegas, *Violeta Parra en Concepción*, 164; "En breve Universidad . . . ," *El Sur* (Concepción), December 8, 1957, quoted in Venegas, *Violeta Parra en Concepción*, 158.

67. Marina de Navasal, "Museo de música popular creó Violeta Parra," *Ecran*, March 18, 1958, 14. The photographs that Parra took of her informants in Concepción have yet to be located; Venegas, *Violeta Parra en Concepción*, 271n153.

68. Gastón Soublette, liner notes, V. Parra, *La cueca presentada por Violeta Parra*.

69. Venegas, *Violeta Parra en Concepción*, 149.

70. Valladares and Vilches, *Rolando Alarcón*, 43.

71. Venegas, *Violeta Parra en Concepción*, 123.

72. Olga Muñoz, Parra's friend in Concepción, quoted in Venegas, *Violeta Parra en Concepción*, 136.

73. Venegas, *Violeta Parra en Concepción*, 131–35. Parra's attempts to collect traditional campesino clothing beyond the wooden shoes were largely unsuccessful. As she lamented in a 1960 performance, "the Chilean *campesina* [today] has no other outfit than that which the Arabs [*los turcos*] sell at the market in Chillán," quoted in Pablo Garrido, "Folklore de Ñuble," *La Nación*, July 7, 1960.

74. Venegas, *Violeta Parra en Concepción*, 136.

75. Cáceres, *La Universidad de Chile*, 44–47.

76. Folklorista Gabriela Pizarro's list of musicians who emerged from the "seasonal school" folk courses includes Víctor Jara, Rolando Alarcón, Silvia Urbina, Patricio Manns, Alejandro Reyes, and herself. "Gabriela Pizarro en la Historia de Nuestro Canto I," in *Chile Ríe y Canta*, no. 2 (March–April 1992): 20. For rare, if fleeting, footage of Parra performing

with Cuncumén at the International Summer School of the University of Chile in 1959, see "Escuelas Internacionales de Verano (1959)," Cinechile, https://cinechile.cl/pelicula/escuelas-internacionales-de-verano/, 20:22–20:54.

77. Venegas, *Violeta Parra en Concepción*, 85.

78. Venegas, *Violeta Parra en Concepción*, 244.

79. Interview with former pupil Mireya Mora, in Rodríguez and Lavín Infante, *Hijos del Bío Bío*, 293.

80. "Violeta Parra y Chiloé—La recopilación del '59," proalarte.com, September 22, 2016; www.proalartelcom/2016/09/violeta-parra-y-chiloe.html, accessed June 24, 2019 (site discontinued).

81. Mireya Mora, quoted in Venegas, *Violeta Parra en Concepción*, 251.

82. "Violeta Parra y Chiloé."

83. Venegas, *Violeta Parra en Concepción*, 245–51. The song "Yo soy la recién casada" is also called "¿Para qué me casaría?" Dölz and Agosín discuss Parra's repertoire of traditional songs about marriage in their book *Violeta Parra, o La expresión inefable*, 19–27. They note how the songs in question are "coated with irony, sarcasm, mockery and rejection" and conclude that "they seem to summarize Parra's position on marriage and her identification with the satirical tone that pervades songs of this type"; 21.

84. "Toda Violeta Parra," *La Bicicleta*, special issue, vol. 1 (1982): 29. "El sacristán" appears on Parra's 1957 LP, *El folklore de Chile*, vol. 1.

85. Mireya Mora, quoted in Venegas, *Violeta Parra en Concepción*, 51.

86. Kerschen, *Violeta Parra*, 104–5, 261. Based in part on original research, Kerschen's biography narrates Parra's life story as if seen through her own eyes. For a discussion of the role played by brothels in the bohemian nightlife of Concepción, see López Fonseca and Moreno Betancur, "Luces y sombras en la Bohemia."

87. Venegas, *Violeta Parra en Concepción*, 251.

88. Tomás Eloy Martínez, quoted in Figueroa, "Gonzalo Rojas y los encuentros de escritores," 71.

89. José Ricardo Morales, "Violeta Parra," 113–14.

90. Teitelboim, *Un hombre de edad media*, 479–80.

91. Figueroa, "Gonzalo Rojas y los encuentros," 84.

92. Á. Parra, *Violeta se fue*, 140; Venegas, *Violeta Parra en Concepción*, 161–62.

93. Parra jokingly named the piece she composed in Antúnez's honor "Los manteles de Nemesio" (Nemesio's Table Linens) because "when Nemesio paints, his paintings come out looking like tablecloths." As recalled by Olga Muñoz, quoted in Venegas, *Violeta Parra en Concepción*, 162.

94. For a list of folk and original songs that appear on the soundtrack of *Trilla*, see Venegas, *Violeta Parra in Concepción*, 172. Violeta Parra and her musical contribution to the film are mentioned in the film review "4 valiosos documentales realizadas por el Centro de Cine Experimental," *Ecran*, August 18, 1959. The reels for *Casamiento de Negros* have not been located.

95. Sanjinés, *Teoría y práctica*, 133–34.

96. Consuelo Saavedra Quiroga, "Violeta Parra en Concepción," *Quinchamalí: Artes—Letras—Sociedad* 17 (1st semester, 2017): 119–20.

97. Ángel Parra, quoted in I. Parra, *El libro mayor* (1985), 57.

The epopee (epic poem) is available at "Epopeya de las bebidas y comidas de Chile," Memoria Chilena, BNdeCh, www.memoriachilena.gob.cl/602/w3-article-93714.html.

98. Alcalde, *Toda Violeta Parra*, 20–21.

99. Á. Parra, *Violeta se fue*, 141.

100. Venegas, *Violeta Parra en Concepción*, 289; Saavedra, "Violeta Parra en Concepción," 121.

101. Consuelo Saavedra, quoted in Venegas, *Violeta Parra en Concepción*, 130.

102. Venegas, *Violeta Parra en Concepción*, 129–30. Mireya Mora, a former theater student who was a daily visitor to the School of Fine Arts when Parra lived there, explained in an interview with historian Fernando Venegas what might be considered by twenty-first-century standards her and others' excessive sense of social decorum: "We're talking about the year of '58"; Venegas, *Violeta Parra en Concepción*, 130.

103. Personal correspondence with Venegas, October 27, 2023.

104. Venegas, *Violeta Parra en Concepción*, 287.

105. Carolina Marcos, "Los tormentosos amores de Violeta Parra y su vínculo con Escámez," *La Discusión*, February 2, 2016.

106. Osvaldo Cáceres González, "Amores de Violeta en Concepción," *Quinchamalí: Artes—Letras—Sociedad* 17 (1st semester, 2017): 124.

107. Macarena Gallo, "'Violeta Parra no podía vivir sin un hombre haciéndole el amor,'" *The Clinic*, September 26, 2010.

108. Saavedra, "Violeta Parra en Concepción," 120–21.

109. Marcos, "Los tormentosos amores"; Luz María Astorga, "Retrato hablado de Violeta Parra," *Revista del Domingo de El Mercurio*, October 31, 1982.

110. V. Parra, *Violeta Parra—El folklore de Chile*, vol. 2.

111. Vega, "Con la folklorista Violeta Parra," *La Discusión*, December 23, 1957.

112. Venegas, *Violeta Parra en Concepción*, 279.

113. Á. Parra, *Violeta se fue*, 144.

114. Á. Parra, *Violeta se fue*, 139.

115. Á. Parra in I. Parra, *El libro mayor* (1985), 57.

116. Herrero, *Después de vivir*, 277.

117. V. Parra, *Décimas*, 195.

118. Interview with Adela Gallo, in Rodríguez, *Cantores que reflexionan*, 189. Gallo implies that Parra's despair was caused by a falling out she had with film director and photographer Sergio Bravo.

119. Mario Céspedes, "En la radio," in García, *Violeta Parra en sus palabras*. Audio available on V. Parra, *En el Aula Magna de Concepción*.

120. Céspedes, "En la radio," 43. In the interview, Parra names dancers Jaime Yori and Max Somoza from the Modern Dance Ballet, founded in 1959, as potential candidates for roles in the ballet.

121. Oviedo, *Mentira todo lo cierto*, 76.

122. It has been staged several times since, including by the Ballet Folklórico de Chile (Bafochi).

123. The version recorded by Letelier appears on *Violeta Parra—Canciones reencontradas en París*, Alerce CDAL 0353, 1999, compact disc. The version recorded by Miranda appears on *Violeta Parra, cantos de Chile*.

124. Miguel Letelier Valdés, "Reencuentro con Violeta Parra," *El Mercurio*, December 28, 1999; Daniel Navarrete Alvear, "Desnudaron secretos de la obra de Violeta Parra," *El Diario Austral* (Valdivia), November 20, 2009.

125. Quoted in Oporto, *El diablo en la música*, 19.

126. From a letter to Isabel Parra, published in V. Parra, *Cancionero: Virtud de los elementos*, 2.

127. See Miranda, Loncón, and Ramay, *Violeta Parra en el Wallmapu*, 70–72; and Oporto, *El diablo en la música*, 177–85.

128. Oporto, *El diablo en la música*, 17.

129. Manns, *Violeta Parra*, 47.

130. The three untitled Las Hermanas Parra EPs released in the late 1950s are Odeon DSOD/E-50097, 45 rpm; 1957; Odeon DSOD/E-50169, 1958, 45 rpm; and Odeon DSOD/E-50137, 1958, 45 rpm. Based on the sound quality, it would appear that the tracks on the 1957 release were actually recorded in the early 1950s; "Discografía de Violeta Parra," Cancioneros.com, www.cancioneros.com/nd/2724/4/odeon-dsode-50097-ep-hermanas-parra-los-campesinos. Odeon paired the sisters' duo with an all-male folk trio (either Los Campesinos or Los Hermanos Lagos) on all three EPs. Odeon also produced a series of compilation LPs titled *Fiesta chilena* during this period that included rereleased tracks by Parra, both as a solo artist and with Las Hermanas Parra. Parra's appearance alongside Los Huasos Quincheros and other música típica artists is evidence of the porousness of the categories employed by the Chilean music industry in the 1950s and 1960s. The *Fiesta chilena* LPs are listed at "Discografía de Violeta Parra," Cancioneros.com, www.cancioneros.com/cc/4/o/discografia-de-violeta-parra. Odeon would continue to release compilations that included tracks by Violeta Parra from its back catalog for decades.

131. For more on Campos and other studio musicians specialized in the guitar during this era, see Valdebenito, *Con guitarra es otra cosa*.

132. Nicanor mentioned a potential recording with Campos in Morales T. and Parra, *Violeta Parra*, 80. The entry for the CD *Su majestad la cueca, vol. 3—La cueca de los Parra* in the discography at Cancioneros.com lists Campos among the musicians who accompanied Las Hermanas Parra; "Discografía," Cancioneros.com, www.cancioneros.com/nd/2700/4/su-majestad-la-cueca-vol-3-obra-colectiva.

133. Personal conversation with Mauricio Valdebenito, December 2022. The incident is recounted in Rojas, *El que sae, sae*, 99. Rojas dates the incident to early 1950s. Based on the chronology of Parra's other love interests, I surmise that it is likely to have taken place sometime after her return from Europe in December 1956.

134. N. Parra, *La cueca larga*, 1958, illustrated by Nemesio Antúnez.

135. I. Parra, *El libro mayor*, 84.

136. Quote is from the transcribed extract of a Radio Chilena program from 1958, available at "Entrevista a doña Flora: Anticueca (Violeta Parra—Florencia Durán de Leyton)," "Cancionero de Violeta Parra," Cancioneros.com, accessed November 20, 2022, www.cancioneros.com/nc/12852/0/entrevista-a-dona-flora-anticueca-violeta-parra-florencia-duran-de-leyton. Audio is available at V. Parra and Durán de Leyton, "Violeta entrevista."

137. Parra's mood would veer from disappointment to exhilaration seconds later in the same interview as she detailed her vision for her experimental ballet, "The Sparrowhawk"; V. Parra, *En el Aula Magna*.

138. Lavín Almazán, *Vuelan las plumas*, 175.

139. In my research, I have found evidence of her teaching courses in Santiago, Concepción, Valparaíso, Chillán, Castro, Arica, and Antofagasta.

140. Sáez, *La vida intranquila*, 108–9; Jara, *Unfinished Song*, 48–49; Herrero, *Después de vivir*, 311, 343. There is discrepancy as to whether she mounted her first fonda in 1958 or 1959.

141. For more on the fondas, also called *ramadas*, see "Las ramadas," Memoria Chilena, BNdeCh, www.memoriachilena.gob.cl/602/w3-article-3545.html.

142. Sáez, *La vida intranquila*, 108. For a photo of what Parra's fonda looked like when it was vacant, see photo captioned "Ramada de Violeta," "Fotografías," FVP, www.fundacion violetaparra.org/fotografias.

143. I. Parra, *El libro mayor*, 110.

144. Herrero, *Después de vivir*, 311.

145. Letter by the poet Francisca Ossandón to fellow poet Humberto Díaz-Casanova, Santiago, September 20, 1960. Biblioteca Nacional Digital: Archivo del Escritor, www .bibliotecanacionaldigital.gob.cl/bnd/623/w3-article-317710.html.

146. Ángel discovered the manuscript's pages arranged in no particular order in a clay pot in Violeta's room after her death. He put them in order and sent the manuscript to Editorial Nascimiento in June 1973. The manuscript was not published as a book until 1979, with the six-year lapse most likely attributable to the military coup and subsequent dictatorship. Rodríguez Musso, "Más sobre los Parra," *Araucaria de Chile* 16 (1981): 176.

147. Navasal, "Museo de música popular creó Violeta Parra"; Vicuña, "Entrevista," 75–76.

148. Drysdale, "Violeta Parra," 487.

149. Céspedes, "En la radio de la Universidad de Concepción," in García, *Violeta Parra en sus palabras*, 32.

150. V. Parra, *Décimas*, 27.

151. Favre, "Les mémoires du Gringo," 50.

152. V. Parra, *Décimas*, 29–30.

153. Cited in Ferrero, *Escritores a trasluz*, 88. In his discussion of Parra's family origins, Herrero states that "both the wealth of the Parras [paternal grandparents] and the poverty of the Sandovals [maternal grandparents] seem to have become distorted with time"; Herrero, *Después de vivir*, 40–41. I concur with Herrero in the case of Parra's maternal grandparents. In the case of her paternal grandparents, I have not found it the case that their wealth is distorted so much as that they themselves are omitted from the narrative.

154. V. Parra, *Décimas*, 31.

155. Morales T. and Parra, *Conversaciones con Nicanor Parra*, 31.

156. See, for example, Roberto Careaga, "Nicanor Parra: 'La Violeta siempre fue abajista, yo siempre fui arribista,'" *La Tercera*, September 5, 2019.

157. The presentation must have taken place after the death of former president Carlos Ibáñez del Campo on April 28, 1960, as Parra makes reference to his death in her décimas; V. Parra, *Décimas*, 103–4.

158. Virginia Vidal, "Violeta Parra ya tiene museo," *Punto Final*, December 17, 2015– January 6, 2016, 21.

159. Parra's autobiography in verse was first published in Chile by Editorial Pomaire in 1970; Leonidas Morales T., "El retorno de las décimas de Violeta Parra," *Suplemento de La*

Época, May 28, 1989. It has seen several editions since in Chile as well as Cuba and Venezuela.

160. Violeta Parra, "Velorios de Angelitos."

161. Céspedes, "En la radio de la Universidad de Concepción," in García, *Violeta Parra en sus palabras*, 40; V. Parra, *En el Aula Magna de Concepción*. Parra's centésimas are published in V. Parra, *Centésimas del Alma*. The CD *Décimas y centésimas* consists of recordings of Parra reading her décimas and centésimas.

Chapter 6

1. Marcela Escobar, "Hechicera de gran poder," *Suplemento de El Mercurio*, March 10, 2001.

2. Vicuña, "Canto alegre al dolor," *Solidaridad*, March 2–15, 1985, 18.

3. Sáez, *La vida intranquila*, 106.

4. There is some confusion as to whether Parra contracted hepatitis in 1959 or 1960.

5. Varas and González, *En busca de la música chilena*, 60.

6. Diserens and Brumagne, *Violeta Parra, brodeuse chilienne*, 10:30–11:49.

7. Juan Ehrmann, "La que cantó en París," *Ercilla*, August 26, 1964; reproduced in García, *Violeta Parra en sus palabras*, 64.

8. Yalkin, "Violeta Parra at the Louvre," 140.

9. Tita Parra, "Tradición y rupture en la canción chilena," *Mundo, problemas y confrontaciones* 2 (1987–88), 81.

10. I. Parra, *El libro mayor*, 111.

11. Interview with Ivonne Brunhammer [*sic*] by Carlos Vergara, "Iré a Chile cuando se abran las prisiones y haya terminado la dictadura militar," *Fortín Diario*, March 18, 1989.

12. Carolina Tapia Valenzuela provides a comprehensive history of the fair in her thesis, "La Feria de Artes Plásticas."

13. Multiple sources claim that works that Parra displayed at her 1964 solo exhibit at the Museum of Decorative Arts were initially rejected by the Chilean Arts Fair's selection committee. This does not appear to have been the case, however; personal correspondence with Chilean art historian Carolina Tapia Valenzuela, February 20, 2020. If the charge is so frequently made, it is because of its plausibility.

14. "Píldoras de la Exposición," *El Siglo*, December 7, 1959. As far as I can ascertain, there is no visual record of Parra's "Pablo pitchers." Much gratitude to Carolina Tapia Valenzuela for generously sharing with me excerpts from press reviews that she gathered regarding Parra's participation in the Arts Fairs.

15. Tapia, "La Feria de Artes Plásticas," Anexo 4, n.p.

16. Camilo Taufic, "Arco Iris en el Forestal," *Ercilla*, December 9, 1959, 17.

17. "Cuadros, música y buen humor en la Feria de Artes Plásticas," *La Nación*, December 8, 1959.

18. Víctor Carvacho, "Tercera Feria de Arte en el Forestal," *La Nación*, December 10, 1961.

19. Palacios, "Segunda Feria de Artes Plásticas," *El Diario Ilustrado*, December 7, 1960. Translation is by Yalkin, "Folk, the Naïve and Indigeneity," 18–19.

20. Orlando Cabrera, "Los artistas chilenos ya ganaron la calle," *La Nación*, December 10, 1959.

21. Tapia, "La Feria de Artes Plásticas," 71.

22. The film is accessible at " Los artistas plásticos de Chile," Centro Cultural La Moneda, www.cclm.cl/cineteca-online/los-artistas-plasticos-de-chile/. Parra appears from 14:34 to 14:45.

23. "Arte chilena contemporanea," *O Jornal* (Rio de Janeiro), October 13, 1961. Other artists in the group show included Nemesio Antúnez, Fernando Krahn, and Lorenzo Berg.

24. Quoted in Bello et al., "Análisis de un genio popular," 74.

25. Morales T. and Parra, *Violeta Parra*, 71 and 82; I. Parra, *El libro mayor*, 52.

26. The resulting songs are "Cueca larga de los Meneses," recorded on *Violeta Parra: El folklore de Chile*, Vol. 2; "Cueca larga de los Meneses," pt. 2, recorded on *La cueca presentada por Violeta Parra*; "El Chuico y la Damajuana" and "El hijo arrepentido," recorded on *Toda Violeta Parra*; and "La cueca de los poetas," recorded on *Las últimas canciones*.

27. Santiago: Editorial Universitaria—La Voz de la Poesía, 1960, EP, 33⅓ rpm.

28. V. Parra, *Recordando a Chile*. According to a piece published in *Ercilla*, Nicanor Parra wrote the poem in an effort to win Violeta the Arts Fair organizers' forgiveness for her disruptive behavior at the inaugural fair of 1959 so that they would allow her to participate in the second one in 1960; "Con Cuecas y Arpilleras por Europa," *Ercilla*, April 24, 1963, 5.

29. For Claribel, see Ferrero, *Escritores a trasluz*, 86. For Ginsberg, see Vadim Vidal, "Allen Ginsberg trepa por Chile," in Zona de Contacto de *El Mercurio*, June 13, 2003.

30. Ginsberg's entry for March 3, 1960, written under the influence of morphine, offers a strange mixture of cozy domesticity and the grotesque: "Violetta [*sic*] Parra is touching the guitar & singing ... the kitten stretching under her foot, Violetta's nose is eaten by worms and wrinkled, singing." Ginsberg, *South American Journals*, 70.

31. Marina de Navasal, "'Descubriendo' nuestro Chile musical," *Ecran*, October 14, 1958, 23. To see a photo of Parra with Claudia Arrau and others, visit "De izquierda a derecha, María Concha Subercaseaux, Benjamín Subercaseaux, Claudio Arrau y Violeta Parra," Memoria Chilena, BNdeCh, www.memoriachilena.gob.cl/602/w3-article-69871.html.

32. The symphony performed eighteen concerts on the tour, which was sponsored by President Eisenhower's special program for cultural presentations. See "Philharmonic Wins Praise in Santiago," *New York Times*, May 22, 1958; and "Philharmonic in Chile," *New York Times*, May 25, 1958.

33. Bernstein, *Findings*, 221. For more on "Image of Chile," see "Chile Introduces Its Arts to U.S.," *New York Times*, September 23, 1963.

34. The song, "Versos por la sagrada escritura," appears on V. Parra, *Folklore de Chile*, vol. 1 (1957); Alvaro Gallegos, "Violeta Parra's Centennial and Bernstein's Love for the Nueva Canción Movement," *Prelude, Fugue & Riffs* (Fall/Winter 2017/2017), 5. In an unpublished interview with musicologist Paul Laird, Bernstein states, "[The song] is based, almost stolen, from the Chilean folk music by Violeta Parra. It's an album of Violeta Parra. ... I could play you part of it and you'd be astonished at the similarity. You'd say, 'but that's a direct steal,' and you'd be right." Quoted in Wright, "Confronting the Celebrant," 29. Wright dismisses the claim that is sometimes made that "'The Word of the Lord'" bears any specific relation to the song "Casamiento de negros"; see chapter 2, "*Gracias a* Violeta Parra: 'The Word of the Lord,'" in Wright's dissertation, 27–37.

35. Karlanga (pseud.), "Radio Cooperativa ... Conocemos Chile," Radiomaniacos—El Foro de la Radio en Chile, accessed July 24, 2019, www.radiomaniacos.cl/foros/index.php ?showtopic=930&page=11.

36. Herrero, *Después de vivir*, 299–300.

37. Julio Huasi, "Violeta de América," *Casa de las Americas* 11, no. 65–66 (March–June 1971): 97.

38. Á. Parra, *Violeta se fue*, 151.

39. Interview with Urbina, *Acordes Mayores*, Radio Cooperativa, first aired September 20, 2012, accessed June 16, 2024, www.youtube.com/watch?v=rNzgbgGz-8w, 17:37-19:21.

40. For cultural histories of Chilean humor, see Salinas Campos, *En el chileno el humor vive* and *La risa de Gabriela Mistral*.

41. Valladares and Vilches, *Rolando Alarcón*, 50.

42. Lyrics reproduced at "Cancionero de Violeta Parra," Cancionero.com, www.cancioneros.com/nc/1248/0/puerto-montt-esta-temblando-violeta-parra.

43. See Salinas Campos and Irarrázaval, *Hacia una teología*.

44. Pablo de Rokha, quoted in I. Parra, *El libro mayor*, 104.

45. Sáez, *La vida intranquila*, 105.

46. Parra to Bunster, December 16, 1960, Biblioteca Digital de la Universidad de Chile, https://bibliotecadigital.uchile.cl/discovery/delivery/56UDC_INST:56UDC_INST/12202299230003936.

47. "Cueca corta de Violeta Parra," *Ercilla*, November 25, 1959, 2.

48. Štambuk and Bravo, *Violeta Parra*, 65.

49. Hurtado, Edwards, and Guilisasti, *Historia de la televisión chilena*.

50. For a photo of Violeta and Ángel Parra assembling a Christmas crèche at the television station, see the photo captioned "Televisión Canal 9. Santiago. Diciembre 1960," "Fotografías," FVP, www.fundacionvioletaparra.org/fotografias.

51. I. Parra, *El libro mayor*, 116.

52. Vera-Meiggs, "El eslabón encontrado," 26–27.

53. Herrero, *Después de vivir*, 174–75.

54. I. Parra, *El libro mayor*, 108.

55. Sáez, *La vida intranquila*, 106–7.

56. Huasi, "Violeta de América," 96. The record executive Isabel referred to was named Enrique Epple.

57. Huasi, "Violeta de América," 96.

58. "Chile debiera llamarse Violeta, si no, que se llame chuchunco," *El Mercurio*, February 5, 1984.

59. I. Parra, *El libro mayor*, 73.

60. It is also fair to assume that Parra received very little in royalties from her and Las Hermanas Parra's rereleased tracks on Odeon's 1958–61 compilation series, *Fiesta Chilena*, listed at "Discografía de Violeta Parra," Cancioneros.com, www.cancioneros.com/cc/4/0/discografia-de-violeta-parra.

61. The contest ran from August 12 through December 13, 1960. Parra was eliminated by August 30; "Los lectores seleccionan a sus favoritos," *Ecran*, August 30, 1960, 24.

62. Alcalde, *Toda Violeta Parra*, 19.

63. I. Parra, *El libro mayor*, 108.

64. Quoted in Jorge Teillier, "Sobre el mundo donde verdaderamente habito o la experiencia poética," "Jorge Teillier—poéticas," Retablo de literature chilena, Universidad de Chile, accessed June 10, 2024, https://uchile.cl/cultura/teillier/poeticas/1.html.

65. Herrero, *Después de vivir*, 238.

66. Vidal, *Hormiga pinta caballos*, 155.

67. Á. Parra, *Violeta se fue*, 135.

68. Vidal, *Hormiga pinta caballos*, 155.

69. J. Jara, *Unfinished Song*, 45.

70. "Gabriela Pizarro en la Historia de Nuestro Canto I," in *Chile Ríe y Canta*, no. 2 (March–April 1992): 18–19.

71. For more on Conjunto Cuncumén, see "Cuncumén," Memoria Chilena, BNdeCh, www .memoriachilena.gob.cl/602/w3-article-95907.html. For more on Millaray, see "Grupo Millaray," Memoria Chilena, BNdeCh, www.memoriachilena.gob.cl/602/w3-article-94359 .html.

72. "Gabriela Pizarro en la Historia de Nuestro Canto II," in *Chile Ríe y Canta*, no. 3 (Mayo 1992): 20.

73. Gioconda Espina, "Adicea pública y privada," *Revista venezolana de estudios de la mujer* 22, no. 48 (January–June 2017): 169.

74. Iván Ljubetic Vargas, "Mario Zamorano Donoso, un héroe del siglo veinte," Centro de Extensión de Investigación Luis Emilio Recabarren, posted May 5, 2020, accessed June 16, 2024, www.facebook.com/permalink.php?id=140379633188261&story_fbid=670759143483638.

75. Contreras, *Violeta Parra, el origen del canto*, 13.

76. Corvalán, *De lo vivido y lo peleado*, 90.

77. I. Parra, *El libro mayor*, 133; J. Jara, *Habla y canta Víctor Jara*, 23.

78. Álvarez Vallejos, *Arriba los pobres del mundo*, 29–77. Former CP militant and Parra contemporary Aída Figueroa wrote in her memoir that the party could be "very strict in the control of the private life of its militants," although she herself had never felt the "weight of its discipline." She noted the two exceptions whom the party "did not touch": Pablo Neruda and the photographer Antonio Quintana. Figueroa Yávar, *Después de mucho vivir*, 71–72. The photo of Parra modeling clay at the Arts Fair (figure 6.1) is by Quintana.

79. Aída Figueroa, for example, recalled Parra as being very "full of herself" and "self-absorbed," quoted in Drysdale, "Violeta Parra," 490.

80. Morales T. and Parra, *Violeta Parra*, 79.

81. I. Parra, *El libro mayor*, 198.

82. I. Parra, *El libro mayor*, 112.

83. I. Parra, *El libro mayor*, 111.

84. Anecdote recounted by Chilean author José Ángel Cuevas, quoted in Cuevas Estivil, "Imagens poéticas e decolonização," 335. For a photo of Parra sitting in her bed at the house of sticks, see photo captioned "En su casa, Segovia 7366. La Reina, Santiago. 1960," "Fotografías," FVP, www.fundacionvioletaparra.org/fotografias.

85. Rodríguez, *Cantores que reflexionan*, 172.

86. José Ángel Cuevas, quoted in Cuevas Estivil, "Imagens poéticas e decolonização," 335.

87. For Nicanor, see Luz María Astorga, "Retrato hablado de Violeta Parra," *Revista del Domingo de El Mercurio*, October 31, 1982; for Ángel, see "Ángel e Isabel recuerdan a Violeta," *Suplemento de El Mercurio*, May 2, 1993.

88. Sáez, *La vida intranquila*, 107.

89. Favre is credited with developing his own vibrato-style of playing that was later imitated by other musicians, from Bolivia to Switzerland. Céspedes, "New Currents in 'Música Folklórica,'" 226; Rios, "La Flûte Indienne," 153.

90. Rodríguez, *Cantores que reflexionan*, 241.

91. Favre, "Les mémoires du Gringo," 38–41.

92. Á. Parra, *Violeta se fue*, 19.

93. Favre, "Les mémoires du Gringo," 50–51.

94. Favre, "Les mémoires du Gringo," 55–56.

95. Favre, "Les mémoires du Gringo," 62.

96. The letters are published in I. Parra, *El libro mayor*. Favre's autobiography is "Les mémoires du Gringo."

97. V. Parra, *Toda Violeta Parra*. The album is both Parra's fifth LP and volume 8 in the series. The interceding volumes 5, 6, and 7 feature the folk ensemble Cuncumén.

98. See "Fernando Krahn" Artistas Visuales Chilenos—Museo Nacional de Bellas Artes, accessed November 13, 2022, www.artistasvisualeschilenos.cl/658/w3-article-40376.html.

99. Liner notes, *Toda Violeta Parra*.

100. Liner notes, *Toda Violeta Parra*. I put "Happy Birthday" in italics to denote that it appears in English in the liner notes.

101. The lyrics come from Del canto XI, "Las flores de Punitaqui," de "Canto General" (1950). The guitar piece is "Tres palabras." The resulting song is titled "El Pueblo" (also called "Paseaba el pueblo sus banderas rojas"); "Cancionero de Violeta Parra," Cancioneros.com, www.cancioneros.com/nc/539/0/el-pueblo-o-paseaba-el-pueblo-sus-banderas-rojas-pablo-neruda-violeta-parra.

102. "El chuico y la damajuena" and "El hijo arrepentido."

103. Parra is likely to have recorded the song "Arriba quemando el sol" at the same time. The recording was not included on the LP, however, and was only first released on the 1990 compilation cassette, *Testimonio*. See "Discografía de Violeta Parra," Cancionero.com, www.cancioneros.com/nd/2895/4/testimonio-obra-colectiva.

104. Ángel Parra and Atahualpa Yupanqui were lifelong friends. In 1969, Ángel Parra recorded an entire LP of Yupanqui's songs, *Canciones funcionales—Ángel Parra interpreta a Atahualpa Yupanqui* (Peña de los Parra, DCP-3). The two musicians performed together at Yupanqui's last recorded live performance, held February 8, 1992, at the Volkshaus Theater in Zurich (available on YouTube). According to Ángel, Favre arrived at his mother's house with tapes of George Brassens and listened to them all the time. Alex Décotte, "El Gringo Bandalero/1," *Zig Zag Café*, Radio Televisión Suisse, 2001, 31:52–32:14; www.youtube.com/watch?v=OBq3wqWkUhw.

105. Lyrics accessible at "Cancionero de Violeta Parra," Cancioneros.com, www.cancioneros.com/nc/697/0/hace-falta-un-guerrillero-violeta-parra.

106. Herrero discusses Parra's support for the Cuban Revolution in *Después de vivir*, 325–26.

107. Favre, "Les mémoires du Gringo," 62–64.

108. Lyrics accessible at "Cancionero de Violeta Parra," Cancionero.com, www.cancioneros.com/nc/1594/0/yo-canto-la-diferencia-violeta-parra.

109. Liner notes, *Toda Violeta Parra*.

110. The photo in figure 6.4 and others taken at the same photo shoot are published for the first time in Pérez Castelblanco, *La fotografía de Javier Pérez Castelblanco*, 207–25. The book assembles a first selection of the photographer's work, from the late 1930s to his death in 2006. Its intent is to "begin to settle the debt with one of the most important twentieth-century Chilean photographers whose work up until now has not received the

attention and recognition that it deserves"; Ignacio Aguirre, "Archivo de Javier Pérez Castelblanco," Pérez Castelblanco, 15.

111. Hugo Arévalo, *Violeta Parra, flor de Chile*, Chile, 1994, 114 min.

112. Pérez Castelblanco, *La fotografía de Javier*, 207–25. Although the book dates the photo shoot as occurring in 1962, it must have been 1961, as Parra was in Argentina and then Europe in 1962.

113. Parra Moreno, *El hombre del terno blanco*, 79–84; Héctor Pérez Farías, "Violeta Parra en General Pico," Junta de Historia Regional General Pico, accessed February 16, 2020, www.generalpicohistoria.com.ar/ver_barrioytema.php?id=141 (site discontinued).

114. Parra Moreno, *El hombre del terno blanco*, 85–86.

115. For a photo of Parra performing at the peña El Alero, see photo captioned "Recital en la Pampa argentina. 1961," "Fotografías," FVP, www.fundacionvioletaparra.org/fotografias. (The caption has the wrong year, as Parra resided in General Pico in 1962.)

116. Luciérnaga Curiosa (pseud. Miguel Machesich), "Cuando Violeta Parra fue pampeana: Testimonios de sus olvidados días en General Pico," originally published in *La Galera*, supplement of *La Reforma* (General Pico), August 15, 2010; reproduced at mmachesich.wordpress.com (blog), accessed October 20, 2014 (site discontinued).

117. Luciérnaga Curiosa (pseud. Miguel Machesich), "Cuando Violeta Parra fue pampeana"; Pérez Farías, "Violeta Parra en General Pico"; Herrero, *Después de vivir*, 346–49. For a photo of Parra with Cristián in the Blaya home, see photo captioned "Con el hijo de Joaquín Blaya. Pampa argentina. 1961," "Fotografías," FVP, www.fundacionvioletaparra.org/fotografias. (The caption has the wrong year, as Parra resided in General Pico in 1962.)

118. Elvira Eiras de Arias, quoted in Pilar Alvarez Masi, "Violeta Parra Sandoval: Retratos pampeanos de una vida inabarcable," "Voy a contarte una historia" (blog), accessed February 1, 2020, https://cronicasylibros.wordpress.com/?s=violeta+parra.

119. I. Parra, *El libro mayor*, 172.

120. Argentina Dirección nacional de estadística y censos, *Censo Nacional De Población De La República Argentina 1960. T.1., Total Del País* (1965), Cuadro no. 1, 2. The population of Greater Santiago was approximately 1.9 million in 1960; *Población Del País; Características Básicas De La Población, Censo 1960* (1964), Cuadro no. 5, 6. The population of General Pico in 1960 was 18,133; Instituto Nacional de Estadística y Censos (Argentina), *Censo Nacional De Poblacion, Familias Y Viviendas, 1970; Resultados Provisionales* (1971), Cuadro 12.4, 118.

121. Letter to Gilbert Favre, Buenos Aires, in I. Parra, *El libro mayor*, 123 (the letter is dated 1961, but this must be an error, as Parra only arrived in Buenos Aires sometime in early 1962); letter to Joaquín Blaya, August 21, 1962, in I. Parra, *El libro mayor*, 137.

122. I. Parra, *El libro mayor*, 117.

123. Aravena-Decart, "Représentations et fonctions sociales," 250n2.

124. Chamosa, *Breve historia del folclore Argentino*; Molinero, *Militancia de la canción*. The peña El Alero was founded on April 21, 1961, and remains open in 2024; www.facebook.com/cc.elalero/.

125. Letter to Raúl Aicardi, I. Parra, *El libro mayor*, 117.

126. I. Parra, *El libro mayor*, 131.

127. Back cover of Parra's 1959 LP, *La tonada presentada por Violeta Parra*.

128. Álvarez, *Memorias*, 47–48.

129. I. Parra, *El libro mayor*, 117.

130. "Renovando la tradicion," *La Prensa*, June 26, 2011. The theater was closed under the military dictatorship of Juan Carlos Onganía but later reopened in response to popular protest.

131. Plante, "Buenos Aires en la producción"; Castedo, *Contramemorias de un transterrado*, 319.

132. Favre, "Les mémoires du Gringo," 77–78.

133. I. Parra, *El libro mayor*, 117.

134. Rigoberto Carvajal and Marco Antonio Moreno, "Violeta Parra, genial hasta en los insultos," *Fortín Mapocho*, February 12, 1989.

135. I. Parra, *El libro mayor*, 117.

136. Luque, "El disco ausente," 60.

137. Sergio Pujol, "El arte de grabar discos," Sergiopujol.com, accessed April 28, 1920, http://sergiopujol.com.ar/2018/07/04/el-arte-de-grabar-discos/ (site discontinued).

138. Luque, "El disco ausente," 60.

139. González, Ohlsen, and Rolle, *Historia social*, 387.

140. Also known as "Arauco tiene una pena." The song may have been inspired by Neruda's epic poem, "Canto General," as the names of the Araucanian warriors at the end of each verse are the same as those that appear in the poem. Musicologists have detected the presence of Mapuche musical elements in the song's composition; J. P. González, "Estilo y función social," 103–5.

141. V. Parra, *El folklore de Chile según Violeta Parra*.

142. Parra's letter to Favre from Buenos Aires suggests that the painting was of Isabel Parra. I. Parra, *El libro mayor*, 129. In contrast with the original painting on the LP's cover, the text on its back cover is recycled from Parra's earlier releases on Odeon Chilena.

143. Luque, "El disco ausente," 56.

144. Sosa, *Homenaje a Violeta Parra*. For a discussion of Mercedes Sosa's relationship to Parra's music, see Karush, *Musicians in Transit*, 168–69. In addition to Parra's 1962 Odeon Argentina release, Argentine musician, writer, and cultural promoter Norberto Folino recorded Parra singing four songs on a portable tape recorder that he set up in her Buenos Aires hotel room and later released as the EP, V. Parra, *Temas inéditos—Homenaje documental*.

145. The National Library of Argentina has the sheet music of all four songs. Only one is a first edition, published June 15, 1962. The other three are later editions of sheet music that was first copyrighted in 1962.

146. Alcalde, *Toda Violeta Parra*, 49–50.

147. Raúl Frocari Rinaldi and Norberto Folino, "Una tarde con Violeta Parra," *Vuelo*, May 1962; Guibourg, "Violeta Parra: Una voz sobre los andes," *Claudia*, July 1962, 21–25; Alberto Ciria, "Casi retrato para Violeta Parra," *Marcha* (Montevideo), March 30, 1962, 23.

148. Favre, "Les mémoires du Gringo," 78; Herrero, *Después de vivir*, 358–59.

149. Favre, "Les mémoires du Gringo," 76–78.

150. Favre, "Les mémoires du Gringo," 79.

151. Favre, "Les mémoires du Gringo," 80.

152. Guibourg, "Violeta Parra," 22.

153. Elena, "Argentina in Black and White."

154. Guibourg was not the only Southern Cone writer at the time to experience Parra as Indigenous. Uruguayan writer Emir Rodríguez Monegal, who saw Violeta perform at

Nicanor's home in La Reina in the early 1960s, described her physical appearance as follows: "Dark [*oscura*], dressed in black, straight long black hair combed simply, accentuated Indian traits"; "Encuentros con Parra," *Número* (Montevideo), 2nd epoch, 1, no. 1 (April–June 1963): 60.

155. Guibourg, "Violeta Parra," 22. Alcalde appears to have referenced and embellished this interview in his book *Toda Violeta Parra*, 41.

Chapter 7

1. Navasal, "Violeta Parra hizo llorar a los franceses," *Ecran*, December 11, 1956, 19.

2. Navasal, "Volvió Violeta Parra," *Ecran*, January 1, 1957, 23; Jorge Edwards, "Vida y andanzas por el mundo de Violeta Parra," *Eva*, March 1, 1957, 45; "Ciclo de recitales inicia mañana en Lota folklorista Violeta Parra," *La Patria*, Concepción, May 14, 1958, quoted in Venegas, *Violeta Parra en Concepción*, 265–66.

3. J. Lz., "Violeta Parra: 'Chaque personne est une fleur dans mon travaille,'" *24 Heures*, November 21, 1964; translated into Spanish in García, *Violeta Parra en sus palabras*, 79–80.

4. Agosín and Dölz Blackburn identify Parra's "constant desire to construct herself [*autoconstrucción*], together with her creative activity, as the loci of her formidable strength." *Violeta Parra, santa de pura greda*, 19.

5. For a photo of Parra waving goodbye from the ocean liner, see the photo captioned "A Europa junto a sus hijos y nieta. 1962," "Fotografías," FVP, www.fundacionvioletaparra.org/fotografias.

6. Violeta Parra, "Une Chilienne à Paris" (1964), in "Cancionero de Violeta Parra," Cancioneros.com, www.cancioneros.com/nc/1522/0/une-chilienne-a-paris-violeta-parra.

7. I. Parra, *El libro mayor*, 133.

8. I. Parra, *El libro mayor*, 135.

9. Figures are from table 3.1 in Koivunen, "The 1957 Moscow Youth Festival," 49.

10. The 1962 Helsinki festival was only the second WFYS to be held in a neutral country, the first having been in Vienna, Austria, in 1959.

11. Then anti-communist CIA operative and future leader of the women's movement, Gloria Steinem, edited the newsletter and was part of the US delegation to the festival. Communist-leaning young activist and future Black Panther Angela Davis was also a delegate. Krekola and Mikkonen, "Backlash of the Free World," 240–41.

12. Krekola and Mikkonen, "Backlash of the Free World," 244.

13. R. Cornell, *Youth and Communism*, 150.

14. Paul E. Sigmund, "Helsinki—The Last Youth Festival?," *Problems of Communism* 11, no. 5 (1962): 58.

15. Herrero, *Después de vivir*, 374.

16. "Les lauréats des concours artistiques," n.p., Festivaali 1962 arkisto Hd, Kansan Arkisto.

17. Dillon, *Violeta Parra's Visual Art*, 32. A copy of the exhibition's program is provided in Appendix 1-B.

18. I. Parra, *El libro mayor*, 135.

19. Hans Otten,"Isabell [*sic*] Parra: Unser Titelbild," *Neue Berliner Illustrierte*, 43, October 1962, 3, cited in Rodríguez Aedo, "Violeta Parra," 44.

20. "Estos discos podrían ser un diario de vida," *Emol* (*El Mercurio On-line*, website), June 14, 2010, www.emol.com/noticias/magazine/2010/06/14/418547/estos-discos-podrian -ser-un-diario-de-vida.html.

21. Document from the president of the Liga Für Völkerfreundschaft Der Deurschen Demokratischen Republik regarding honorary award donated to the festival, July 2, 1962, Festivaali 1962 arkisto Hd, Kansan Arkisto.

22. The Soviet Union encouraged tourism at the time, under the same reigning doctrine of peaceful coexistence that fostered the biennial WFYS. See Gorsuch, *All This Is Your World*.

23. I. Parra, *El libro mayor*, 137.

24. "Violeta Parra Sandoval," *Neues Deutschland*, September 6, 1962.

25. Aucapan (pseud. Luis Alberto Mansilla), "Violeta Parra," *El Siglo*, February 7, 1967.

26. Süd—und mittekamerikanische Volksmusik, Eterna 8 30 014—Lieder de Volker N7, LP, 33⅓ rpm; "Discografía de Violeta Parra," Cancionero.com, www.cancioneros.com /nd/1763/4/sud-und-mittelamerikanische-volksmusik-obra-colectiva. My thanks to Selke Mattheis for translation assistance.

27. "Toda Violeta Parra," *La Bicicleta*, special series, vol. 2 (1983): 30.

28. "Besuch aus Chile," *Berliner Zeitung*, September 1, 1962, 8; "Violeta Parra Sandoval," *Neues Deutschland*, September 6, 1962; Karl Schönewolf, "Weitere Musikberichte aus: Berlin," *Musik und Gesellschaft*, October 1962, 614; Vicentini, "Violeta Parra: Rhythms, Songs and Colours," *Women of the Whole World* 1, 1963, 23–26.

29. Sáez, *La vida intranquila*, 128.

30. Herrero, *Después de vivir*, 378.

31. Enrique Bello Leighton stayed on in Italy, where he joined a theater company; "Con cuecas y arpilleras por Europa," *Ercilla*, April 24, 1963, 5.

32. Ernesto González Bermejo, "Isabel Parra, enemiga del olvido y la desesperanza," *Crisis* (August 1975): 48; Á. Parra, *Mi nueva canción chilena*, 82.

33. The band's name comes from Calchaquí, Indigenous people of the Argentine Northwest.

34. Rios, "La Flûte Indienne."

35. Rios, "Andean music, the Left."

36. Ángel plays the quena on the LP *Süd- und mittelamerikanische Volksmusik*.

37. Rodríguez Musso, *La nueva canción chilena*, 73. For a photograph of the Parra ensemble performing in the costumes, see photo 16, "Violeta, Gilbert, Isabel, Ángel, Carmen Luisa y Tita en concierto, Ginebra, Suiza," in I. Parra, *El libro mayor*, n.p.

38. For a discussion of why Chile is considered an "Andean" country geographically, but not culturally or economically, see González, "The Chilean Way to the Andes," 1. To view a poster announcing the ensemble in this way, see the photo captioned "Afiche de recital. 1963," "Fotografías," FVP, www.fundacionvioletaparra.org/fotografias.

39. V. Parra, *Poésie populaire des Andes*.

40. Rios, "La Flûte Indienne," 153.

41. Interview with Paco Ibáñez, in Á. Parra and Sandoval, *Violeta más viva que nunca*.

42. Vera, *Viola chilensis*, 42:50–43:30. Herrero dates Parra's participation in the annual Easter march as occurring March 27 to 29, 1964; *Después de vivir*, 404. Favre places it in 1963, shortly after Parra's concert at the Théâtre Cour de Saint-Pierre in Geneva; "Les mémoires du Gringo," 93–94. I assess Favre to be correct in this instance, as the later date would have

been during Parra's show at the Musée des Arts Décoratifs and, by all accounts, Parra was in Paris at the time.

43. The song is also known as "Julián Grimau." Grimau, like Parra, attended the 1962 World Festival of Youth and Students in Helsinki, only in his case under a false name and in disguise. There is no indication that Grimau and Parra met there.

44. "Toda Violeta Parra," *La Bicicleta*, special issue, vol. 2 (1983): 25.

45. A.A.K., "A la Galerie Connaitre, Violeta Parra ou l'art spontané," *Tribune de Genève*, February 5, 1963.

46. J. Lz., "Violeta Parra," in García, *Violeta Parra en sus palabras*, 79.

47. Gampert, *A la découverte du théâtre*, 79.

48. Charles Dobzynski, "Poésie d'Amérique Latine," *Les Letters Françaises*, February 27–March 4, 1964, 9; Phyllis Jenkins, "Paris Letter," *Glasgow Herald*, April 24, 1964, quoted in Fugellie, "Les tapisseries chiliennes." My heartfelt thanks to Chilean musicologist Daniela Fugellie for generously sharing this and other reviews found in the MAD archives with me.

49. Diserens and Brumagne, *Violeta Parra, brodeuse chilienne*, 4:35–4:51.

50. The art gallery was most likely the Galerie d'Arts des Nouveaux Grands Magasins, where Parra was part of a joint show in November 1964; M. M. Brumagne, "Cronique Artistique—Violeta Parra—Colette Rodde," *Tribune de Lausanne*, n.p., November 5, 1964.

51. Brumagne, *Qui se souvient de sa vie?*, 135.

52. Gampert, *A la découverte du théâtre*, 77. Although Gampert does not name the gallery, the location she gives in her memoir identifies it as the Galerie Connaitre, where Parra exhibited her masks, tapestries, and ceramics in late January and early February 1963.

53. Gampert, *A la découverte du théâtre*, 77–79.

54. Vicentini, "Violeta Parra," 25; J. Lz., "Violeta Parra," in García, *Violeta Parra en sus palabras*, 79.

55. See, for example, Diserens and Brumagne, *Violeta Parra, brodeuse chilienne*, 3:47–4:03.

56. Vicentini, "Violeta Parra," 25. The article is written in English with British spelling.

57. *Violeta Parra, brodeuse chilienne*, 7:58–8:58.

58. Juan Ehrmann, "La que cantó en París," *Ercilla*, August 26, 1964; reproduced in García, *Violeta Parra en sus palabras*, 64.

59. There are varied accounts in the sources available regarding how long it took for the two generations of Parras to find each other and who did the finding.

60. "Toda Violeta Parra," *La Bicicleta*, special series, vol. 2 (1983): 25.

61. Štambuk and Bravo, *Violeta Parra*, 120.

62. Rodríguez, *Cantores que reflexionan*, 117.

63. "Tita Parra," MusicaPopular.cl, www.musicapopular.cl/artista/tita-parra/.

64. Favre, "Les mémoires du Gringo," 87.

65. Favre filmed a home movie of the Parra family performing a cueca together during this period. The movie, with an unrelated song for its soundtrack, is available for viewing on Isabel Parra's Facebook page, www.facebook.com/41701312361/videos/3596990 98272678.

66. Vera, *Viola chilensis*, 25:39–26:00.

67. Nazem Ghemraoui, "Entretien avec Rafaêl Gayoso—Un des fondateurs des Machucambos," *Maison Orange—Salsa et Danses Du Monde*, January 5, 2006, http://maisonorange .fr/ent-gayoso.html.

68. Štambuk and Bravo, *Violeta Parra*, 120.

69. Karina Micheletto, "Entrevista al músico español Paco Ibáñez: 'Me siento catalán, vasco, andaluz y un poco argentino,'" *Página 12*, November 11, 2012; and Micheletto, "Paco Ibáñez, antes de su quinta visita a la Argentina: 'Mis padres son Yupanqui y Brassens, yo estoy en el medio,'" *Página 12*, September 3, 2010, www.pagina12.com.ar.

70. Álvarez, *Memorias*, 47.

71. Interview with Rafael Gayoso, in Andréa Cohen, "Violeta Parra et ses enfants," *L'Atelier de la création*, RadioFrance, December 21, 2007, 32:41–33:25, www.radiofrance.fr /franceculture/podcasts/l-atelier-de-la-creation-14-15/violeta-parra-et-ses-enfants -rediffusion-5388758.

72. Vera, *Viola chilensis*, 40:03–40:45.

73. Sáez, *La vida intranquila*, 131; Edwards, *Persona non grata*, 49.

74. Favre, "Les mémoires du Gringo," 89.

75. Favre, "Les mémoires du Gringo," 90.

76. Sáez, *La vida intranquila*, 130.

77. For photos of Parra and Favre in their Geneva apartment, see figures 8.3 and 8.4 in this book, and the photo captioned "En su taller en Ginebra, junto a Gilbert Favre. 1964." "Fotografías," FVP, www.fundacionvioletaparra.org/fotografias.

78. Pascal Holenweg, "Gracias a la Violeta," Lecourier.ch, October 31, 2017, https:// lecourrier.ch/2017/10/31/gracias-a-la-violeta/.

79. Štambuk and Bravo, *Violeta Parra*, 123.

80. Claudio Venturelli, interviewed in Vera, *Viola chilensis*, 38:18–38:20.

81. Herrero, *Después de vivir*, 390–91.

82. I. Parra and Agüero, *Violeta Parra, pintora chilena*.

83. *Violeta Parra, brodeuse chilienne*, 16:05–17:18.

84. Gampert, *A la découverte du théâtre*, 77.

85. Štambuk and Bravo, *Violeta Parra*, 123.

86. "Con cuecas y arpilleras."

87. A.A.K., "A la Galerie Connaitre."

88. For a photo of the ensemble performing in their masks, see Vera, *Viola chilensis*, 42:04.

89. For a photo of Violeta performing with Carmen Luisa at a fonda-like setting in Geneva, 1963, see the photo captioned "Con su hija Carmen Luisa en una fonda en Ginebra. 1963," "Fotografías," FVP, www.fundacionvioletaparra.org/fotografias.

90. I. Parra, *El libro mayor*, 148.

91. Letter to Adriana [Borghero], Geneva, 1962, reproduced in I. Parra, *El libro mayor*, 140.

92. The 1963 concert is V. Parra, Recording of a concert in the home of Walther Grandjean. Part of the 1965 concert was released as V. Parra, *Violeta Parra en Ginebra*, and another part, with some overlap, as V. Parra, *En vivo en Ginebra*.

93. V. Parra, *En vivo en Ginebra*, track 24.

94. Herrero, *Después de vivir*, 395–96.

95. Favre, "Les mémoires du Gringo," 102.

96. Claudio Venturelli, quoted in Herrero, *Después de vivir*, 395.

97. Favre, "Les mémoires du Gringo," 95.

98. I. Parra, *El libro mayor*, 157.

99. I. Parra, *El libro mayor*, 150–51.

100. Á. Parra and I. Parra, *Au Chili avec Los Parra*.

101. The songs Parra recorded that summer were released posthumously in different combinations and formats over the years, beginning with *Canciones reencontradas en París*.

102. Barraza, *La nueva canción chilena*, 37; González, Ohlsen, and Rolle, *Historia social*, 389.

103. "Toda Violeta Parra," *La Bicicleta*, special series, vol. 2 (1983): 24. This version substitutes "revolutionaries" for "communists," most likely in an anti-sectarian gesture.

104. For information on the six revolutionaries that the song honors, see Engelbert, *Lieder aus Chile*, 254–55.

105. "Toda Violeta Parra," *La Bicicleta*, special series, vol. 2 (1983): 25.

106. "Toda Violeta Parra," *La Bicicleta*, 24. I have changed the punctuation in the cited lyrics to reflect that the song's opening lines are a question.

107. Barclay director Ariana Ségal claimed that it was not released because the nine songs Parra recorded were not sufficient for an LP, but this does not explain why Parra did not record one or two more songs to complete the project; Ségal, liner notes, *Un río de sangre*, Arion ARN 34222, 1974.

108. The record label DICAP (Discoteca del cantar popular) was founded in 1967 by the youth branch of the Chilean Communist Party to record and promote the work of independent artists on the Left.

109. Bolivia and Peru are represented on the album by Los Calchakis, a group made up of Argentine and Chilean musicians.

110. Héctor G. Miranda, liner notes, *Canciones reencontradas en París*.

111. *Chants et danses du Chili* (1964). To view the cover, visit "Discografía de Violeta Parra," Cancioneros.com, www.cancioneros.com/nd/2732/4/chants-et-danses-du-chili-violeta-parra.

112. Drott, "Music, the Fête de L'Humanité," 234. I put "rock and roll" in italics to denote that it is an English loanword to French.

113. "Succès sans precedent de la fête de notre journal 600,000 a la Courneuve," *L'Humanité*, September 9, 1963.

114. "Et pendant 2 jours sur la scène internationale," *L'Humanité*, September 7, 1963, 10; "Dimanche 8 septembre," *L'Humanité Dimanche*, September 8, 1963, 14.

115. Corvalán, *De lo vivido y lo peleado*, 90.

Chapter 8

1. Letter from Morla Lynch to Cassou, n.d., Violeta Parra dossier, MAD Archives.

2. I. Parra, *El libro mayor*, 172.

3. The Chilean artists were Roberto Matta and Delia de Carril. Musée d'art moderne de la ville de Paris, *Exposition L'art Latino-Américain a Paris: 2 Août–4 Octobre 1962* (Paris: Musée d'Art Moderne), 1962.

4. J. R. Morales, "Violeta Parra," 119.

5. Dillon, *Violeta Parra's Visual Art*, 100–107.

6. Isabel Cruz Amenábar, "Violeta Parra artista visual," in Fundación Violeta Parra, *Violeta Parra, obra visual*, 31; Á. Parra, in Epple, *Entre mar y cordillera*, 51.

7. For a discussion of the factors that may have influenced Cassou's response, see Plante, "Las 'tapisseries chiliennes,'" par. 8–10.

8. Brunhammer, *Le Beau dans l'utile*.

9. Letter from Dorival to Faré, October 1, 1963, Violeta Parra dossier, MAD Archives.

10. I. Parra, *El libro mayor*, 175–76. The letter is addressed to "Chinito," which was one of Parra's many pet names for Favre. Although the book identifies the letter as having been written in 1963, I assess it was written in 1964, most likely in February, based on the letter's reference to a performance at the Théatre Plaisance that took place on February 20, 1964.

11. Letter to Amparo Claro, cited in Štambuk and Bravo, *Violeta Parra*, 126.

12. Štambuk and Bravo, *Violeta Parra*, 125–26.

13. This same image, by and large, is recreated cinematographically in Andre Wood's biopic, *Violeta se fue a los cielos*, except that Wood relocates it to the interior of the museum; *Violeta se fue a los cielos*, Wood Productions, Maiz Productions, and Bossa Nova Films, 2011.

14. Quoted in Raquel Correa, "Las guitarras lloran a Violeta Parra," *Vea*, February 9, 1967, 17. Alejandro Jodorowsky offers a more elaborate telling of this anecdote in the preface to his memoir, *The Spiritual Journey*, xv–xvi.

15. Parra proffers what is essentially a third telling how of how she came to have her solo show at MAD in her waltz, "Une chilienne à Paris" (A Chilean in Paris). In its last verse, Parra humorously celebrates the success of her efforts:

> And it makes me weary to say
> That through the window I jumped.
> That is not true my dear friends,
> It was the door.

> *Et je m'embête en disant*
> *que j'ai sauté la fenêtre.*
> *Ça c'est pas vrai, mes amis,*
> *c'etait la porte.*

The verses call to mind the jovial warning that ends the serenade Parra collected, "Señores y señoritas" (Ladies and Gentlemen): "If they don't open the door for me, / I will enter through the window" (*Que si no me abren la puerta, / me dentro por la ventana*). In "A Chilean in Paris," Parra reverses the means of entry; no need to climb through the window—she walked in the door. Lyrics for "Una chilena a Paris" (Une chilienne à Paris) and "Señores y señoritas" (2nd version with Violeta Parra), available at "Cancionero de Violeta Parra," Cancionero.com, www.cancioneros.com/ca/4/0/cancionero-de-violeta-parra.

16. Herrero, *Después de vivir*, 406–7.

17. Štambuk and Bravo, *Violeta Parra*, 127.

18. The photo appears in FVP, *Violeta Parra: Obra Visual*, 23.

19. Daniel Hopenhayn, "Ángel Parra, músico: 'Si nos repartíamos su obra entre los familiares, mi mamá habría vuelto a sacarnos la cresta,'" *The Clinic*, October 29, 2015.

20. Vergara, "Iré a Chile cuando se abran las prisiones y haya terminado la dictadura militar," *Fortín Diario*, March 18, 1989.

21. Juan Ehrmann, "La que cantó en París," *Ercilla*, August 26, 1964; reproduced in García, *Violeta Parra en sus palabras*, 65.

22. The invitation announced both Parra's show and the concurrent exhibit of musical sculptures by the Baschet Brothers. Violeta Parra dossier, MAD Archives.

23. "Exposition de tapisseries chiliennes," *Journal de Paris*, April 8, 1964, RTF, Paris, 1:05, INA. Unfortunately, the video no longer has audio. Footage from the *Journal de Paris* program can be seen in the video by Alejandro Mundaca, *Violeta Parra Louvre: Paris, 1964*, 5:56, posted on YouTube, October 15, 2015, www.youtube.com/watch?v=bLm2a_PlWGw.

24. The Museo Violeta Parra had forty-two pieces of Parra's works when it opened in 2017 and is unlikely to have acquired twenty additional pieces since then; Ministerio de Educacion, "Decreto 274 l Declara Monumento Nacional en la categoria de monumento histórico a 42 obras artisticas de Violeta Parra, ubicadas en el museo de Violeta Parra, comuna y provincial de Santiago, region Metropolitana," Biblioteca del Congreso Nacional de Chile, November 4, 2017, www.bcn.cl/leychile/navegar?idNorma=1110181.

25. Yalkin, "Violeta Parra at the Louvre," 148.

26. MAD, *Violeta Parra: Musée des arts décoratifs*, n.p.

27. Parra uses virtually the same phrase in her 1962 interview (published in 1963) with Vicentini, "Violeta Parra: Rhythms, Songs, and Colours," *Women of the Whole World* 1, 1963, 26.

28. For studies that focus on the integrative nature of Parra's work, see Dölz Blackburn and Agosín, *Violeta Parra, o La expresión inefable*; and Mundaca, "Translating Poetics."

29. "Parabienes a los novios" appears on *Violeta Parra, Chants et danses du Chili II*; lyrics available at "Cancionero de Violeta Parra," Cancioneros.com, www.cancioneros.com/nc/1563/0/viva-dios-viva-la-virgen-o-parabienes-a-los-novios-popular-chilena. Though not part of the MAD exhibit, another example of a literal pairing is Parra's elaborate painting *Casamiento de negros* and her hit song by the same title. FVP, *Obra Visual*, 33.

30. Vicentini, "Violeta Parra: Rhythms, songs and colours," 26. The article is written in English with British spelling.

31. Francisco Díaz Roncero, "'Tapices de Violeta Parra' es La Exposición que se inaugura hoy en el Palacio del Louvre," *El Mercurio*, April 8, 1964.

32. For more on the links between Mapuche culture and Parra's visual works, see Dillon, *Violeta Parra's Visual Art*, 47–80; Hormazábal, "La obra visual de Violeta Parra," 140–69; and Miranda, Loncón, and Ramay, *Violeta en el Wallmapu*, 69.

33. Viviana Hormazábal González, "Quinchamalí y Violeta Parra," *Quinchamalí: Artes, letras y sociedad* 17 (1st semester, 2017), 114–17.

34. Nicanor Parra gave the tapestry the name *The Bald Singer* after the play *The Bald Soprano* by Eugène Ionesco; Yalkin, "Folk, the Naïve and Indigeneity," 18.

35. Vergara, "Iré a Chile cuando se abran."

36. "Trois variations sur thèmes populaires," *Le Monde*, April 17, 1964.

37. J. Lz., "Violeta Parra: 'Chaque personne est une fleur,'" in García, *Violeta Parra en sus palabras*, 80.

38. A. K., "St-Prex: Poète, folkloriste, peintre et chanteuse Violetta [sic] Parra présente ses oeuvres récentes," *Gazette de Lausanne*, August 6, 1965.

39. D. B., "Colette Rodde, Saint-Maur, Violeta Parra," *Nouvelle Revue de Lausanne*, November 10, 1964, 2.

40. A. K., "St-Prex: Poète, folklorist."

41. M. H., "Vernissages—Galerie des Nouveaux Magasins," *Le Peuple*, November 13, 1964.

42. M. M. Brumagne, "Cronique Artistique—Violeta Parra—Colette Rodde," *Tribune de Lausanne*, n.p., November 5, 1964.

43. Augustín Oyarzún L., "Nací con una guitarra bajo el brazo," *Aquí Está*, January 20, 1966, 7; reproduced in García, *Violeta Parra en sus palabras*, 91.

44. See, for example, Diserens and Brumagne, *Violeta Parra, brodeuse chilienne*, 10:30–11:49.

45. Carlos Morla Lynch, "Exposión en el Louvre de Violeta Parra," Embajada de Chile en Francia, Oficios ordinarios enviados al Ministerio de RR.EE. de Chile, November 1–December 31, 1964, Francia, Fondos Paises, Archivo General Histórico, Ministerio de Relaciones Exteriores, República de Chile.

46. Díaz Roncero, "'Tapices de Violeta Parra,'" *El Mecurio*, April 8, 1964. The article quotes Parra recounting both her spontaneous approach to embroidering and the flower-bottle-woman anecdote. The communist daily *El Siglo* also published a piece on the exhibit, "Los tapices de Violeta en Museo del Louvre," April 14, 1964. Note the headline refers to Parra on a first-name basis, reflecting her then-warm relationship with the Chilean Communist Party.

47. Letter dated June 19, 1964, in I. Parra, *El libro mayor*, 185.

48. Letter from Violeta Parra to Favre, April 1964; cited in I. Parra, *El libro mayor*, 180. For more on the Baroness Rothschild's purchase, see Štambuk and Bravo, *Violeta Parra*, 125; and Favre, "Les mémoires du Gringo," 98–99.

49. Ehrmann, "La que cantó en París," in García, *Violeta Parra en sus palabras*, 65.

50. Letter to Joaquín Blaya, June 19, 1964, in I. Parra, *El libro mayor*, 185.

51. June 19, 1964, in I. Parra, *El libro mayor*, 184–85.

52. May 1, 1964, in I. Parra, *El libro mayor*, 182–83.

53. I. Parra, *El libro mayor*, 182.

54. "Galerie Benezit," Marie Amalia, www.marieamalia.com/galerie-benezit/; "La Porte Ouverte (advertisement)," *L'Oeil*, no. 109–114 (January–June, 1964), n.p.

55. Jakovsky, *Peintres Naïfs*, 295.

56. Griliquez and Tenaille, *Le libre parcours*, 31.

57. C. C., "M. G. Asturias et Elvio Romero au Théâtre Plaisance," *Les Lettres Françaises*, February 20–26, 1964, 9.

58. Charles Dobzynski, "Poésie d'Amérique Latine," *Les Lettres Françaises*, February 27–March 4, 1964, 9.

59. Charles Dozynski, "Poésie et Chanson," *Les Lettres Françaises*, May 14–20, 1964, 11. To see a photo of Parra and other performers in the show, visit "Violeta Parra y amigos en el Théâtre de Plaisance," Museo Violeta Parra, www.museovioletaparra.cl/cedoc/violeta-parra-y-amigos/.

60. The show's poster is reproduced in I. Parra, *El libro mayor*, 187.

61. Georges Léon, "Au Théatre de Plaisance: Vivre," *L'Humanité*, May 11, 1964. For other positive reviews of the show, see Dozynski, "Poésie et Chanson" and "Les dessous de l'Affiche," *La Defense*, June 1, 1964, 2.

62. Jean Monteaux, "15 minutes de Christine Sevres [sic] rachètent un spectacle," *Arts*, May 13–19, 1964, 7.

63. Jorge Paredes Laos, "[Entrevista] Alberto Quintanilla: 'Nos falta interesarnos más por el Perú,'" *El Comercio/El Dominical*, December 26, 2017, https://elcomercio.pe/eldominical /emtrevista-alberto-quintanilla-falta-interesarnos-peru-noticia-484382-noticia/. Biographer Karen Kerschen writes that Parra enjoyed imitating the musicality of the Indigenous language even though she could not speak it, which Kerschen likely learned from her interviews with Gilbert Favre; Kerschen, *Violeta Parra*, 185.

64. Štambuk and Bravo, *Violeta Parra*, 124.

65. Interview with Rafael Gayoso, "Paris, 1960: Escuchar 'Los Machucambos' y bailar en el Escale," *Paris America*, RFI, April 24, 2015, www.rfi.fr/es/francia/20150424-paris-1960 -escuchar-los-machucambos-y-bailar-en-la-escale, 18:49–18:54. Chilean writer Virginia Vidal, who was Parra's contemporary, described her along similar lines as a "precursor to the hippies"; Vidal, *Hormiga pinta caballos*, 155.

66. Letter from Parra to Amparo Claro, January 1965, in Štambuk and Bravo, *Violeta Parra*, 124.

67. Ehrmann, "La que canto en Paris," in García, *Violeta Parra en sus palabras*, 67.

68. Letter to Favre, August 1964, in I. Parra, *El libro mayor*, 193.

69. Andréa Cohen, "Violeta Parra et ses enfants," *L'Atelier de la création*, RadioFrance, December 21, 2007, 39:30–39:50, www.radiofrance.fr/franceculture/podcasts/l-atelier-de -la-creation-14-15/violeta-parra-et-ses-enfants-rediffusion-5388758.

70. Paris, 1962, in I. Parra, *El libro mayor*, 147.

71. Letter to Favre, Paris, 1962, in I. Parra, *El libro mayor*, 147.

72. See Agosín and Dölz Blackburn, "Las Cartas: *El libro mayor de Violeta Parra*," in *Violeta Parra o La expresión inefable*, 91–102; J. R. Morales, "Violeta Parra," 115–16; and Morales T., "Violeta Parra."

73. I. Parra, *El libro mayor* (1985), 128–29. The 2nd edition of *El libro mayor* leaves off the words "muy fea" (very ugly); I. Parra, *El libro mayor* (2009), 190.

74. Michel Faré to Eugenio González, May 15, 1964, Violeta Parra dossier, MAD Archives.

75. I. Parra, *El libro mayor* (1985), 190–94.

76. See, for example, Lidia Baltra, "Violeta Parra—Todavía se muere de amor," *Eva*, February 17, 1967, 74; and "¡Que se apaguen las guitarras!: Trágica muerte de Violeta Parra," *Clarín*, February 6, 1967, 16.

77. This situation has changed in recent decades in tandem with changing racial attitudes that make it more likely for Parra to be identified as having Indigenous ancestry.

78. Rodríguez, *Cantores que reflexionan*, 166.

79. Štambuk and Bravo, *Violeta Parra*, 122.

80. Venegas, *Violeta Parra en Concepción*, 201.

81. The photo that accompanies an article about Parra's European adventures, as recounted at a press conference held at the downtown Santiago Crillón Hotel in August 1964 and published soon after, shows Parra, dressed in a stylish dress and black heels, sitting on a cushion on the floor of what may or may not be an area of the hotel. Unfortunately,

there is no way to know for sure. Juan Ehrmann, "La que cantó en París," *Ercilla,* August 26, 1964, 30. For more on the press conference, see "Violeta ahora canta con guitarra, pinceles, y aguja," *Ecran,* August 25, 1964, 28–29.

82. Herrero, *Después de vivir,* 399.

83. Universidad de Chile and Museo de Arte Popular Americano, *Exposición,* n.p. The exhibit was held from June 18 to July 6 in the Hall [*Sala*] of the University of Chile.

84. Romera, "Pintura instintiva," *El Mercurio,* June 30, 1963, 11.

85. Leopoldo Castedo, *Contramemorias,* 321.

86. Julio Huasi, "Violeta de América," *Casa de las Americas* 11, no. 65–66 (March–June 1971): 97. Herrero writes that Parra participated in the 1962 São Paulo Art Biennial (*Después de vivir,* 434), but this cannot be the case, as the art show was not held that year. I surmise that the incident was most likely to have occurred (if at all) at the 1963 Biennial. A preliminary search by the organization's staff found no mention of Parra in the São Paulo Art Biennial archives; personal correspondence with archivist Marcele Souto Yakabi, March 9, 2020.

87. Ángel claimed that the younger musicians' participation in the 1964 presidential campaign was the turning point when it came to welding their musicianship to their political activism: "Overnight, at the same time, everyone discovered political music." Á. Parra, *Mi nueva canción,* 89.

88. The exhibit was held from June 30 to October 8 on the third floor of the Edificio España, Santiago. Gonzalo Arqueros, "Violeta Parra."

89. Table 11.1, Collier and Sater, *History of Chile,* 309.

90. Morales T. and Parra, *Violeta Parra,* 95–96.

91. I. Parra, "Ven acá, regalo mio / En los altos de Colombia."

92. Letter to Carmen Luisa, I. Parra, *El libro mayor,* 196.

93. V. Parra, *Recordando a Chile.*

94. V. Parra, "Écoute moi, petit," "Cancionero de Violeta Parra," Cancioneros.com, www.cancioneros.com/nc/438/0/ecoute-moi-petit-violeta-parra.

95. Rodríguez, *Cantores que reflexionan,* 190.

96. Rodríguez, *Cantores que reflexionan,* 190–91.

97. Rodríguez, *Cantores que reflexionan,* 191.

98. Graciela Romero, "Violeta partió de nuevo," *Eva,* November 27, 1964, 34.

99. Rodríguez, *Cantores que reflexionan,* 188–89.

100. Recounted by Daniel Davinsky, "Violeta Parra, La guitarra indócil," Fogón Latinoamericano, May 7, 2017, accessed June 16, 2024, http://fogonlatinoamericano.blogspot.com/2017/05/violeta-parra-la-guitarra-indocil.html.

101. Favre, "Les mémoires du Gringo," 101.

102. Rodríguez, *Cantores que reflexionan,* 188. Gallo would end up staying on in Paris for years, where she became the housekeeper and personal secretary for the Afro-Cuban artist Wilfredo Lam; Irene Domínguez and Cristian Vila Riquelme, "Despedida a Adela Gallo," *Araucaria de Chile* 26 (1984): 20.

103. Favre, "Les mémoires du Gringo," 102.

104. Morales T. and Parra, *Violeta Parra,* 81. Parra would similarly Chileanize the spelling of *charango* to *charrango.*

105. Hubert Joanneton, "Violeta Parra: Une Grande Artiste Chilienne," *Radio-TV Je Vois Tout,* 38, September 17, 1970, 24. The interview is translated and reproduced in García, *Violeta Parra en sus palabras,* 105–9.

106. Letter to Blaya, June 19, 1964, Paris, in I. Parra, *El libro mayor*, 185.

107. Photos 18/19, captioned "Concierto con Gilbert en Ginebra," I. Parra, *El libro mayor*, n.p.

108. Diserens and Brumagne, *Violeta Parra, brodeuse chilienne*.

109. For a discussion of Parra's performance of authenticity, see Verba, "To Paris and Back."

110. Joseph, "François Maspero et la typographie," par. 5.

111. V. Parra, *Poésie populaire des Andes*, 8.

112. Raymond Jean, "Chants de la terre kabyle et des Andes," *Le Monde*, September 11, 1965; Juan Marey, "Violeta Parra: *Poésie populaire des Andes*," *Europe* 43, nos. 435–36 (July–August 1965): 323–24; Robert Paris, "Poesie populaire des Andes par Violeta Parra," *Partisans*, 22 (October 1965): 74–76.

113. "Les activités du groupe 'Poésie Vivant," *Poésie vivante*, no. 12 (June–July 1965): n.p. A few of Parra's songs in translation appear in the poetry club's newsletter, "Anthologie permanente Poésie Vivante: Une chanson de Violeta Parra (Chili)," *Poésie vivante*, no. 10 (March 1965): 16.

114. Macarena Gallo, "Las cartas desconocidas de Violeta Parra," *The Clinic*, September 18, 2017.

115. Gallo, "Las cartas desconocidas de Violeta Parra."

116. Gallo, "Las cartas desconocidas de Violeta Parra."

117. I. Parra, *El libro mayor*, 201. Parra misspells her name as Grampert in her letter.

118. Letter to Amparo Claro, January 1965, published in Štambuk and Bravo, *Violeta Parra*, 124–25.

119. Letter to Chabelita (Isabel), Ángel, Carmen Luisa, and Titina, Paris, June 1965, I. Parra, *El libro mayor*, 201–2. For additional evidence of Parra's understanding of the art market, see her letter to Marie-Magdeleine Brumagne, transcribed in Brumagne, *Qui se souvient de sa vie?*, 140.

120. A. K., "St-Prex: Poète, folklorist, peintre." A photo of the Geneva Museum of Art and History is available at www.mahmah.ch/visite/horaires-acces.

121. Joanneton, "Violeta Parra," 19–24.

122. "Entrevista en francés a Violeta Parra," on V. Parra, *En vivo en Ginebra*, track 1.

123. Joanneton, "Violeta Parra," 19.

Chapter 9

1. Favre, "Les mémoires du Gringo," 109. I put "fans" in italics to denote that it is an English loanword to French.

2. Favre, "Les mémoires du Gringo," 108–9. There are a few discrepancies between how Favre relates the events in his autobiography and the series of articles concerning Parra's August 1965 arrival to Chile published in *El Siglo*. *El Siglo* reports at least four false anticipated arrival announcements; "Llega Violeta Parra," *El Siglo*, August 18, 1965. Favre, for his part, claims that weeks passed between Parra's thwarted and final arrivals; Favre, "Les mémoires du Gringo," 110. Favre's depiction of Parra's actual arrival (108–10) is also more dismal than the one offered in *El Siglo* ("Ayer llegó Violeta Parra: Éxito en Europa," August 19, 1965).

3. S. H. C., "La folklorista que conoció todo el mundo," *El Siglo*, February 7, 1967.

4. Bernardo Subercaseaux, "Violeta Parra: Una vida y una trayectoria (1917–1967)," in Consejo Nacional de la Cultura y las Artes, *Después de vivir un siglo*, 33.

5. Charles Stockdale, "The 100 Most Popular Rock Bands of All Time," Business Insider, October 1, 2018, www.businessinsider.com/the-100-most-popular-rock-bands-of-all-time-2018-9#1-the-beatles-100.

6. I. Parra, *El libro mayor*, 209; Á. Parra, in Epple, *Entre mar y cordillera*, 51.

7. Coriún Aharonián, "Retrato de Violeta por Ángel Parra," *Marcha*, July 23, 1971, 27.

8. Á. Parra, *Violeta se fue*, 25.

9. For more on *nueva ola*, see González, Ohlsen, and Rolle, *Historia social*, 631–87. Despite similarly sounding names, there is no relationship between the Chilean *nueva ola* and the nouvelle vague film movement in the late 1950s and 1960s in France or new wave music in the United States in the late 1970s and 1980s.

10. For more on neofolklore, see González, Ohlsen, and Rolle, *Historia social*, 337–56.

11. Valladares and Vilches, *Rolando Alarcón*, 70–71.

12. See, for example, interview with Raúl de Ramón, "Folklore," *El Musiquero* 3, no. 38 (February 1967), 17.

13. "Dice Urquidi: El folklore no puede ser solo tonadas y cuecas . . ." *Ecran*, April 6, 1965, 41.

14. "El regreso de Violeta Parra," *Vistazo*, September 7, 1965, 10; reprinted in García, *Violeta Parra en sus palabras*, 84. For another example of Parra's positive appraisal of neofolklore from around the same time, see Sergio H. Carrasco, "Violeta Parra: El tercer regreso," *El Siglo*, August 29, 1965.

15. Ruy-Pérez Benítez, *Cuarenta años*, 85–86; "Las Cuatro Brujas," MusicaPopular.cl (blog), www.musicapopular.cl/grupo/las-cuatro-brujas/.

16. Agustín Oyarzún L., "Nací con una guitarra bajo el brazo," *Aquí Está*, January 20, 1966, 7; published in García, *Violeta Parra en sus palabras*, 90.

17. Daniel Hopenhayn, "Ángel Parra, músico: 'Si nos repartíamos su obra entre los familiares, mi mamá habría vuelto a sacarnos la cresta,'" *The Clinic*, October 29, 2015.

18. "Isabel Parra: La firme y dulce voz de Isabel," in Pancani and Canales, *Los necios*, 39.

19. "Violeta Parra, La guitarra indócil," Fogón Latinoamericano (blog), May 7, 2017, accessed January 22, 2024, http://fogonlatinoamericano.blogspot.com/2017/05/violeta-parra-la-guitarra-indocil.html.

20. Andean-inspired music was particularly popular in Chile in the 1960s. In his history of Quilapayún, founding member Eduardo Carrasco explained both Andean-inspired music's appeal and the vital role that the Parras played in promoting it: "We turned toward the autochthonous, toward the strictly Indigenous, which up until that moment was practically unknown in Chile. Only the Parras had discovered this type of music, but there was no band dedicated to disseminating these songs. We felt the enormous necessity to seek out our roots, to know our origins, to understand who we were and who we had been." Carrasco, *Quilapayún*, 21. For further discussion of the Andean-inspired music scene in Chile, see González, "Música chilena andina 1970–1975," and "Chilean Way to the Andes." For more on the Parras' contribution, see Rios, "La Flûte Indienne," 153–57.

21. See Turino, "Are We Global Yet?"

22. Other persons of note who passed through the house include Chilean sculptor Sergio Castillo, French revolutionary theorist Regis Debray, and Venezuelan writer Elisabeth Burgos-Debray. Castillo, "Castillo, escultor," 28; and Debray, *Hija de revolucionarios*, 25–26.

23. Montealegre and Chavarria, "Presencia de Violeta Parra."

24. *Canción comprometida* in Spanish.

25. Joan Jara, Víctor Jara's widow, described it as having "a small, rather elite audience"; Jara, *Unfinished Song*, 104.

26. Cited in Valladares and Vilches, *Rolando Alarcón*, 80. Ángel was not entirely off base. Luis Enrique "Chino" Urquidi, member and producer of Los Cuatro Cuartos and producer of Las Cuatro Brujas, became a member of the rightist National Party. After the coup, he cowrote the march "Alborada" in support of the military. Herrero, *Después de vivir*, 448.

27. "Toda Violeta Parra," *La Bicicleta*, special series, vol. 2 (1983): 27.

28. González, Ohlsen, and Rolle, *Historia social*, 231.

29. In his article, Rossen Djagalov dubs the singer-songwriters the "guitar poets" and lists thirteen of them, including French musician Georges Brassens, Chilean musician Víctor Jara, and US musicians Pete Seeger, Phil Ochs, and a pre-electric Bob Dylan. Djagalov, "Guitar Poetry," 148. Significantly, Djagalov includes no women on his roster. If one assumes, contrary to Djagalov's practice, that Parra was a "guitar poet" as well, she stood out from the other guitar poets of her era precisely because she was a woman.

30. Although the Chilean New Song movement emerged in the mid-1960s, it did not get its name until the first Festival de la Nueva Canción in 1969.

31. "Entrevista a Víctor Jara," *El Caimán Barbudo* 54 (March 1972): 3.

32. Carmen Luisa, cited in Rodríguez, *Cantores que reflexionan*, 173.

33. The stadium was renamed the Víctor Jara Stadium in 2003.

34. Patricio Manns, "Las últimas visiones de Violeta Parra," *The Clinic*, September 18, 2017; Herrero, *Después de vivir*, 439.

35. Manns, *Violeta Parra*, 63–64. Manns's accounts of his relationship with Parra ran both hot and cold. His 1977 book *Violeta Parra: La guitarra indócil* (since rereleased in multiple editions) celebrated their close personal relationship, which Manns would continue to describe as "a solid and creative friendship" forty years later; Manns, "Las últimas visiones de Violeta Parra." In contrast, and in the context of refuting the claim that Parra was somehow the "mother" of the Chilean New Song, Manns claimed, "I don't have anything to do with Violeta. I knew Violeta . . . how long? . . . less than a year, and in that year I would have seen her three times, once on a tour of the North, and another on a tour of the South, and we were not always talking to each other," quoted in Pancani and Canales, *Los necios*, 65.

36. For examples, Parra claims that her autobiography in décimas was published in France ("Ayer llegó Violeta Parra," *El Siglo*), and she adds Greece to the list of countries she visited ("El regreso de Violeta Parra," in García, *Violeta Parra en sus palabras*, 83).

37. Hubert Joanneton, "Violeta Parra: Une Grande Artiste Chilienne," *Radio-TV Je Vois Tout*, 38, September 17, 1970, 24.

38. Joanneton, "Violeta Parra," 24.

39. Lidia Baltra, "Violeta Parra—Todavía se muere de amor," *Eva*, February 17, 1967, 74.

40. Favre, "Les mémoires du Gringo," 60.

41. Graciela Romero, "Violeta partió de nuevo," *Eva*, November 27, 1964, 33–34.

42. Favre, "Les mémoires du Gringo," 69 and 133–34.

43. "El regreso de Violeta Parra," in García, *Violeta Parra en sus palabras*, 85.

44. Julio Huasi, "Los siete golgotas de Violeta Parra," *El Porteño*, June 1986, 73.

45. Quoted in Herrero, *Después de vivir*, 442–43.

46. Alvaro Godoy, "La Peña de los Parra," *La Bicicleta* 7, no. 62 (August 20, 1985): n.p.

47. Rodríguez, *Cantores que reflexionan*, 169.

48. Rodríguez, *Cantores que reflexionan*, 165.

49. Favre, "Les mémoires du Gringo," 111.

50. See, for example, Fernando Reyes Matta, "El mundo personal de Violeta Parra," *7 Días*, September 24, 1965, 24.

51. Oyarzún L., "Nací con una guitarra bajo el brazo," in García, *Violeta Parra en sus palabras*, 92.

52. Adoum, *De cerca y de memoria*, 460.

53. Favre, "Les mémoires du Gringo," 112.

54. Favre, "Les mémoires du Gringo," 114.

55. Favre, "Les mémoires du Gringo," 119.

56. Štambuk and Bravo, *Violeta Parra*, 135–36. There is disagreement over the Carpa's capacity, with estimates ranging from 200 to 1,000. Most accounts fall somewhere around 400.

57. Štambuk and Bravo, *Violeta Parra*, 136.

58. Favre, "Les mémoires du Gringo," 122.

59. Aravena Llanca, *Lo visible indecible en Violeta Parra*, 59 and 63.

60. "El regreso de Violeta Parra," in García, *Violeta Parra en sus palabras*, 83.

61. Dr. Raúl Vicencio, who treated Parra in her last years, would later make the claim that she suffered from bipolar disorder; Herrero, *Después de vivir*, 454; Drysdale, "Violeta Parra," 515.

62. González, Ohlsen, and Rolle, *Historia social*, 350.

63. "Festival folklórico en el Silvia Piñeiro," *El Siglo*, August 25, 1965; "En Festival de 'El Siglo,'" *El Siglo*, August 25, 1965; Sáez, *La vida intranquila*, 146. Los Quincheros' tour was part of a cultural exchange marking the resumption of diplomatic relations between Chile and Russia. The band's gala send-off was held in August 1966 in a downtown Santiago theater with a capacity for over 1,000. It featured a lineup of musicians whose political affiliations ranged from the conservative Los Quincheros to known communist supporter Violeta Parra. Mackenna Besa and Los Huasos Quincheros, *Quincheros*, 125–26. Both the concert and Los Quincheros' USSR tour highlight the nuanced nature of Cold War cultural politics in Chile in the early 1960s, particularly when compared with the political polarization of the Popular Unity years or the repression and violence of the military dictatorship that followed.

64. Its full name was the Peña de la Escuela de Arquitectura de la Universidad de Chile de Valparaíso but it was known as the Peña de Valparaíso; González, Ohlsen, and Rolle, *Historia social*, 231.

65. Rodríguez, *Cantores que reflexionan*, 44.

66. Sáez, *La vida intranquila*, 149.

67. Rodríguez, *Cantores que reflexionan*, 43–44; and Héctor Alfonso Souza Valencia, "La contribución de la Peña Folclórica de la Universidad de Chile sede Valparaíso para el

desarrollo y conservación de la musica y danzas folclóricas de Chile," MA thesis, Universidad de Playa Ancha, June 2020, accessed February 24, 2024, https://issuu.com/gatobizarro/docs/estudio_pe_a.docx.

68. "Folklore," *El Siglo*, October 24, 1965.

69. "Lo mejor del año en opinion de Discomanía," *Musiquero*, no. 25 (December 1965): 22–23. The other four LPs were *Imagen de Chile* by Los de Ramón, *Misa a la chilena* by Vicente Bianchi, *Oratorio para el pueblo* by Ángel Parra, and *Los Fabulosos Cuatro Cuartos* by Los Cuatro Cuartos.

70. V. Parra, *Décimas* (LP). The LP was released in 1976 by Alerce, the record company that Ricardo García and others founded in 1975 for the dual purpose of supporting emerging folk artists and, whenever possible, rereleasing albums that were banned by the military dictatorship then in power. In the LP's liner notes, García writes that the recording was the last one Parra made. This appears to be an error, however, as Parra mentioned the recordings in an interview granted soon after her return from Europe and published in September 1965 ("El regreso de Violeta Parra," in García, *Violeta Parra en sus palabras*, 85).

71. V. Parra and Favre, *Violeta Parra y Gilbert Favre*.

72. R. Parra, *Las cuecas de Roberto Parra*. The other Parra musicians who participated, alongside well-known studio musicians, were Hilda Parra's son Nano Parra on "animation" and guitar, her daughter María Elena Báez on "animation," and Lautaro Parra on percussion. The LP was recorded in the second half of 1965 but only released after Violeta's death in 1967. "Discografía de Violeta Parra," Cancioneros.com, www.cancioneros.com/nd/2684/4/las-cuecas-de-roberto-parra-roberto-parra.

73. Nouzeilles, liner notes, Trio Los Parra, *20 cuecas con salsa verde*. The series' inaugural volume features the Trio Los Parra, formed by Hilda Parra and her children Nano Parra and María Elena Báez. The entire series consists of seven LPs produced between 1967 and 1973.

74. Roberto Parra, or "Tío Roberto," as he was known, became recognized for his *cuecas choras* during the Pinochet dictatorship, when they were performed by the popular rock trio Los Tres, of which his grandnephew Ángel Parra (né Ángel Cereceda Orrego) was a founding member. In Chilean slang, the word *choro* means someone who is "daring, admirable, brave, clever, and also vulva or vagina"; Carreño Bolívar, "Libercueca," 161.

75. Bello, liner notes, R. Parra, *Las cuecas de Roberto Parra*.

76. Pedro Bahamondes, "Los retazos perdidos de Violeta Parra que retornan a Chile," *La Tercera*, February 25, 2018.

77. "Violeta Parra y Gilbert Favre," *El Siglo*, November 28, 1965; I. Parra, *El libro mayor*, 253.

78. The array of institutions working in concert to promote abstract art at the time included the International Council of the Museum of Modern Art in New York (MoMa), the Pan American Union, the Central American Agency (CIA), and multinational companies. Dillon, "Violeta Parra's Contribution," 157–58.

79. "La VII Feria de Artes Plásticas fue inaugurada oficialmente ayer," *La Nación*, December 5, 1965.

80. Yalkin, "Violeta Parra at the Louvre," 147n34.

81. Anita Hurtado, "La mujer en la Feria del Mapocho," *Suplemento Mujeres de La Nación*, December 12, 1965. Although I am unable to ascertain where Parra's booth was placed along the 1965 arts fair's continuum from folk to abstract art, I deem it highly likely,

based on Hurtado's piece, that it would have been at the end where the folkloric handi-crafts were located.

82. Ester Matte, quoted in Luz María Astorga, "Retrato hablado de Violeta Parra," *Revista del Domingo de El Mercurio*, October 31, 1982.

83. Marina Latorre, "Nicanor Parra en un mar de preguntas," *Portal* 4 (November 1966): 3.

84. Bello et al., "Análisis de un genio," 70.

85. Alegría et al., "Violeta Parra," 110.

86. Oyarzún L., "Nací con una guitarra bajo el brazo," in García, *Violeta Parra en sus palabras*, 89. The neighborhood of La Reina in fact derives its name from the surname Larraín, though this may not be widely known. See Wikipedia, "La Reina," https://es .wikipedia.org/wiki/La_Reina. My thanks to Juan Pablo González for pointing this out.

87. The flyer and registration form are reproduced in I. Parra, *El libro mayor*, 205.

88. Photo caption, "Violeta Parra no trató de suicidarse," *Aquí Está*, January 20, 1966, 6.

89. María Cristina Jurado and Sergio Caro, "El último amor de Violeta," *El Mercurio*, February 21, 2017.

90. Alfonso Molina Leiva, "Violeta Parra," *El Mercurio*, October 16, 1966; reproduced in García, *Violeta Parra en sus palabras*, 102.

91. I. Parra, *El libro mayor*, 209.

92. Rigoberto Carvajal, "Violeta Parra, genial hasta en los insultos," *Fortín Mapocho*, February 12, 1989.

93. Á. Parra, *Violeta se fue*, 29. The program for the Carpa's inauguration is reproduced in I. Parra, *El libro mayor*, 205. For press coverage of the inauguration, see "¡Vamos donde Violeta!" *Radiomania*, January 1966, 22.

94. Drysdale, "Violeta Parra," 510.

95. I. Parra and Leyla Ramírez, "Viola artesana," 9.

96. Drysdale, "Violeta Parra," 487.

97. Favre, "Les mémoires du Gringo," 126.

98. Quoted in Jurado and Caro, "El último amor de Violeta."

99. I. Parra, *El libro mayor*, 207.

100. Štambuk and Bravo, *Violeta Parra*, 155–56.

101. Oyarzún L., "Nací con una guitarra bajo el brazo," in García, *Violeta Parra en sus palabras*, 90.

102. "Violeta Para no trató de suicidarse," *Aquí Está*, January 20, 1966, 6; "Un error casi le cuesta la vida a Violeta Parra," *La Tercera de la hora*, January 15, 1966; "Ingirió por error barbitúricos. Violeta Parra en franca mejoría," *El Siglo*, January 15, 1966.

103. Nora Ferrada, "Violeta Parra y su drama," *Ecran*, January 25, 1966, 37, reprinted in García, *Violeta en sus palabras*, 95–97.

104. Favre, "Les mémoires du Gringo," 127.

105. "Las últimas composiciones de Violeta Parra," *El Musiquero* 37 (January 1967): 36.

106. Ferrada, "Violeta Parra y su drama," in García, *Violeta en sus palabras*, 97.

107. "Aun que se muera la madre tienen que cantar," *El Siglo*, February 6, 1968, 10.

108. Štambuk and Bravo, *Violeta Parra*, 142.

109. Then fifteen, Carmen Luisa performed at the Carpa and occasionally at the Peña de los Parra as well. Later, in 1972, she recorded a single with the record company DICAP; DICAP/Peña de los Parra JJS-125. She was apparently preparing to record her first LP with the

label in 1973, but the project was cut short by the military coup; Javiera Parra, Flor de Parra (blog), posted December 8, 2011, accessed February 24, 2024, https://issuu.com/orange242 424/docs/flor_de_parra.

110. Roker, "Lo vi y lo cuento," *Rincón Juvenil*, June 8, 1966.

111. Valladares, *La cueca larga del Indio Pavez*, 79.

112. The Compañía Tradicional de Títeres de Chile was formed by artistic collaborators and husband-and-wife team Jaime Morán and Luisa María Morales; "Jaime Morán y Luisa María Morales," *Revista 795*, no. 6 (December 2021): 105.

113. Miranda, Loncón, and Ramay, *Violeta Parra en el Wallmapu*, 68.

114. Štambuk and Bravo, *Violeta Parra*, 151. For more on Parra's friendship and musical collaboration with Mapuche musicians Lautaro Manquilef (né José de Calasanz Manquilef) and Juan Lemuñir, see Miranda, Loncón, and Ramay, *Violeta Parra en el Wallmapu*, 29–30 and 68–69.

115. "Aunque se muera la madre tienen que cantar," *El Siglo*, February 6, 1968.

116. Valladares, *La cueca larga del Indio Pavez*, 86.

117. Letter to Favre, Santiago, 1966, in I. Parra, *El libro mayor*, 208.

118. V. Parra et al., *La Carpa de la Reina*.

119. Herrero, *Después de vivir*, 463.

120. "Toda Violeta Parra," *La Bicicleta*, special series, vol. 2 (1983), 26.

121. Violeta Parra, "Corazón maldito," "Cancionero de Violeta Parra," Cancionero.com, www.cancioneros.com/nc/302/0/corazon-maldito-violeta-parra.

122. Parra et al., *Cuecas a pata pelá; Imagen musical de Chile; Todo el folklore, Vol. 1; Cantos de rebeldía*.

123. "Violeta Parra en TV," *Ecran TV*, April 12–18, 1966, 7, inserted in *Ecran*, April 12, 1966; Sáez, *La vida intranquila*, 153.

124. "Habla folklorista chilena: Corazón del pueblo nada tiene que ver con errores politicos," *El Diario* (La Paz), May 22, 1966. My thanks to Fernando Rios for generously sharing this and other articles in the Bolivian press with me.

125. The Peña Naira remained a popular venue until it was closed in 1971 under the Banzer dictatorship. Its owner Pepe Ballón was tortured and imprisoned, then exiled. Rodrigo Olavarría, "Gilbert Favre: Un afuerino no tan afuerino," posted June 1, 2008, www.cancioneros .com/co/131/2/gilbert-favre-un-afuerino-no-tan-afuerino-por-rodrigo-olavarria. The folk club eventually reopened under different ownership. It is closed as of this writing.

126. Favre, "Les mémoires du Gringo," 165.

127. I. Parra, *El libro mayor*, 207–8.

128. "Habla folklorista chilena," *El Diario*, May 22, 1966; "Pesar por la muerte de la folklorista Violeta Parra," *El Diario*, February 10, 1967; María de los Angeles Baudoin, "Una copa, una quena y el recuerdo de Peña Nayra [sic]," *Puntos Suspendidos*, December–January 1995–1996, 22–23; and interviews with Ernesto Cavour and Leni Ballón, daughter of Peña Naira's founder Pepe Ballón, in Ramiro Quiroga, "Testimonios de Violeta Parra en la Paz."

129. Rios, *Panpipes* and *Ponchos*, 192–242. In what could be considered the inverse of Europeans' exoticization of Indigenous peoples, though based on the same Eurocentric hierarchy, Los Jairas' popularity within Bolivia was enhanced by the band's Swiss quena player. As Ballón would later explain, "The fact that a foreigner played the quena was the

reason that our folklore began to be accepted. People would stop and say, 'Ah! How beauti-fully he plays!' And as people from France and Spain frequented the peña, soon those people from our high society, the '*hamburguesía*' [play on the word 'hamburger' and the Spanish word for 'bourgeoisie'] of our country began to draw near." Germán Arauz Crespo, "Galería Naira: Un espacio que revolucionó la música nacional," *La Razon/Ventana*, May 16, 1993, 13.

130. Favre, "Les mémoires du Gringo," 165.

131. "Actuó con éxito en 'Naira' famosa folklorista chilena," *El Diario*, May 20, 1966.

132. Rios, *Panpipes and Ponchos*, 144.

133. Favre, "Les mémoires du Gringo," 165.

134. Cavour, "Quién inventó el charango?" in Cavour, *El charango*, 270; Arauco, *Los Jairas y El Trío Domínguez*, 82.

135. "Violeta Parra, La guitarra indócil," *Fogón Latinoamericano* (blog).

136. Sáez, *La vida intranquila*, 154.

137. "Ángel Parra Orrego," MusicaPopular.cl (blog), www.musicapopular.cl/artista/angel-parra-orrego/.

138. Favre mentions ten musicians in his autobiography. Los Choclos member Jorge Miranda, who also went on the trip, remembers them only being five, which photos of their tour appear to confirm.

139. Ian Thomson, transport economist based in Santiago, calculates that the journey took upward of six days; personal correspondence, February 22, 2022.

140. Ellipses in the original text. Osmur (pseud.), "Ángel e Isabel Parra: 'Nuestro mayor orgullo es nuestra madre,'" *Rincón Juvenil* 81 (July 6, 1966): 7. For a photo of Los Choclos performing at the Carpa with Favre and Parra, see the photo captioned "En la Carpa de la Reina," "Fotografías," FVP, www.fundacionvioletaparra.org/fotografias.

141. Favre, "Les mémoires du Gringo," 180.

142. Favre, "Les mémoires du Gringo," 183.

143. "Pesar por la muerte de la folklorista Violeta Parra," *El Diario* (La Paz), February 10, 1967, 5.

Chapter 10

1. Pablo Márquez Farfán, "Violeta Parra presente," Revista Universitaria N°142: Especial Violeta Parra, January 1, 2017, https://revistauniversitaria.uc.cl/especial/violeta-parra-presente/16477/.

2. Largo Farías, *Fue hermoso vivir contigo*, 32.

3. Nano Acevedo, quoted in Soto and Navarrete, "Chile rió, canto y luchó," 20.

4. "El programa 'Chile ríe y canta' llegará a Punta Arenas para ser presentado en el teatro Municipal," *La Prensa Austral*, July 14, 1966. The article does not name Parra, most likely because her participation had yet to be confirmed.

5. "Chile ríe y canta se despidió de Punta Arenas con gimnasio lleno," *El Magallanes*, July 21, 1966.

6. Alexander Santander Olate, "Violeta Parra: Chile ríe y canta, Magallanes—julio de 1966," *El Fortín del Estrecho*, 20:194 (September 4, 2000): 8, https://issuu.com/fortinestrecho/docs/el_fortin_194.

7. Interview on Radio Magallanes, Santiago, January 1, 1967. Transcribed and published in René Largo Farías, "Un testimonio desconocido de la Violeta Parra," *Chile ríe y canta* 1 (December 1999): 11, republished in García, *Violeta Parra en sus palabras*, 113–14.

8. "Toda Violeta Parra," *La Bicicleta*, special series, vol. 2 (1983): 26.

9. In a 2016 interview with Víctor Herrero, Patricio Manns insisted that this was the case: "[Messone] was one of those guys that only went out with pretty girls from rich neighborhoods, but [he and Parra] went for a walk together, they had a few drinks, they got turned on, they went to a hotel and they got it on." In Herrero, *Después de vivir*, 473.

10. Mercedes Silva, "Superconfidencial," *Ecran TV* (September 27–October 3), 24, inserted in *Ecran*, September 23, 1966.

11. Hernán Norambuena, "Viví un idilio con Messone," *Flash*, January 13, 1967, 22–23.

12. Carmen Barros and Miguel Davagnino, "Pedro Messone," *Acordes Mayor*, CooperativaFM, Santiago, October 4, 2012, https://cooperativa.cl/noticias/entretencion/musica/musica-chilena/acordes-mayores-pedro-messone/2012-10-04/225943.html, 9:42–10:50.

13. Štambuk and Bravo, *Violeta Parra*, 145–46.

14. Zapicán's birthname was Alberto Giménez Andrade. He named himself Zapicán after the Uruguayan hamlet where he was from; "El último compañero de Violeta Parra: Alberto Zapicán, discrete, fino y sencillo," elciudadano.com, July 10, 2017, www.elciudadano.com/entrevistas/el-ultimo-companero-de-violeta-parra-alberto-zapican-discreto-fino-y-sencillo/07/10/; Fernando Figueroa, "'El Albertío' rompe el silencio: Habla el inspirador de Violeta Parra," *Revista de arte* 3 (January–February 1989): 10.

15. Figueroa, "'El Albertío' rompe el silencio."

16. Guillermo Pellegrino, "El grito de la tierra," *El País Cultural* (Montevideo) 13, no. 627 (November 9, 2001): 7.

17. Luz María Astorga, "Retrato hablado de Violeta Parra," *Revista del Domingo de El Mercurio*, October 31, 1982, 10.

18. Pellegrino, *Las cuerdas vivas*, 160–61.

19. Rodríguez, *Cantores que reflexionan*, 107.

20. "Las últimas composiciones de Violeta Parra," *El Musiquero* 37 (January 1967): 37.

21. Štambuk and Bravo, *Violeta Parra*, 147.

22. The photo appears (among other places) in Pellegrino, "El grito de la tierra."

23. Drysdale, "Violeta Parra," 512–13.

24. Rodríguez, *Cantores que reflexionan*, 170.

25. "Toda Violeta Parra," *La Bicicleta*, special series, vol. 2 (1983): 29. The wordplay is that Parra combines Zapicán's first name of Alberto with the word "advertido [shrewd]" (which is sometimes pronounced "alvertío"); "El Albertío," "Cancionero de Violeta Parra," Cancionero.com, www.cancioneros.com/nc/442/0/el-albertio-violeta-parra.

26. I. Parra, *El libro mayor*, 211–14.

27. Macarena Gallo, "Patricio Manns y la muerte de Ángel Parra: 'Soy el sobreviviente de esa generación que echó a patadas la vieja cancion,'" *The Clinic*, March 15, 2017, www.theclinic.cl/2017/03/15/patricio-manns-la-muerte-angel-parra-sobreviviente-esa-generacion-echo-patadas-la-vieja-cancion/.

28. Marisol García, "Patricio Manns, cantautor y escritor," De Gira (blog), August 20, 2009, https://solgarcia.wordpress.com/2009/08/20/entrevista-patricio-manns/ (since discontinued).

29. Aravena Llanca, *Lo visible indecible*, 159–61; Carolina Rojas, "Mónica Echeverría: 'Violeta Parra no fue una virgen,'" *Revista Ñ, Clarín*, November 3, 2010. Mónica Echeverría, who knew Parra when she was alive, is also the author of the novel *Yo, Violeta*, which portends to tell Parra's life story in first person, based in part on Echeverría's original research (Santiago: Plaza Janés, 2010). Apparently, some of its passages are quite steamy.

30. Aravena Llanca, *Lo visible indecible*, 127. Aravena claims to have heard this from Patricio Manns.

31. Favre, "Les mémoires du Gringo," 97.

32. Jacqueline Dussaillant Christie includes a discussion of the "battle against human odors" in twentieth-century Chilean society in her article "Consumo y belleza: Los cuidados del cuerpo femenino, siglos XVIII–XX," in Góngora and Sagredo, *Fragmentos para una historia*, 489–91.

33. Drysdale, "Violeta Parra," 515; Herrero, *Después de vivir*, 454; Sáez, *La vida intranquila*, 161.

34. Drysdale, "Violeta Parra," 514–15.

35. The rights to this album, which is undeniably Parra's most important recording, have been under legal dispute for decades. See, for example, "Violeta Parra: La extensa batalla legal que impide publicar 'Las últimas composiciones' y que podría llegar a su fin," *The Clinic*, November 25, 2023.

36. Štambuk and Bravo, *Violeta Parra*, 156.

37. "'Violeta no venía del campo, sino de otro planeta,'" *La Época*, February 9, 1990, 24.

38. Rodrigo Alarcón, "Luis Torrejón, el hombre que grabó *Las últimas composiciones de Violeta Parra*," diarioUchile-Cultura, October 3, 2017, https://radio.uchile.cl/2017/10/03/luis-torrejon-el-hombre-que-grabo-las-ultimas-composiciones-de-violeta-parra/.

39. Sergio Araya Alfaro, "Entrevista con Luis Torrejón, técnico de grabación: 'El ingeniero de grabación que inicia y termina una grabación,'" *Cuadernos de etnomusicología* 10 (Fall 2017), 35.

40. Other photos from the same shoot are reproduced in Pérez Castleblanco, *La fotografía de Javier Pérez Castelblanco*, 227–57. Akin to the iconic photo of Che Guevara that was taken by Alberto Korda but rarely attributed to him, this photo of Violeta Parra had been reproduced countless times but is rarely attributed to Javier Pérez Castelblanco and is even at times erroneously attributed to other photographers.

41. José Manuel Izquierdo, "Definir al compositor en Chile," *Enfoque Simuc*, November 15, 2018, www.simuc.org/sections/columns/enfoque/2018.6-15.11.2018.php.

42. "Rin del angelito," "Cancionero de Violeta Parra," Cancionero.com, www.cancioneros.com/nc/1336/0/rin-del-angelito-violeta-parra.

43. Quoted in Herrero, *Después de vivir*, 477.

44. "Las últimas composiciones de Violeta Parra," *El Musiquero*, 36.

45. "Toda Violeta Parra," *La Bicicleta*, special series, vol. 1 (1982): 26.

46. Valladares, *La cueca larga*, 85.

47. Alcalde, *Toda Violeta Parra*, 48.

48. "Toda Violeta Parra," *La Bicicleta*, special series, vol. 3 (1984): 20.

49. Štambuk and Bravo, *Violeta Parra*, 141.

50. Epple, *Entre mar y cordillera*, 113.

51. Štambuk and Bravo, *Violeta Parra*, 148–49.

52. Quoted in Astorga, "Retrato hablado de Violeta Parra."

53. Štambuk and Bravo, *Violeta Parra*, 148.

54. Sáez, *La vida intranquila*, 156.

55. "Las peñas: Un nuevo rostro para el '18," *Ecran TV* (September 20–26, 1966), 23, inserted in *Ecran*, September 16, 1966.

56. Aravena Llanca, *Lo visible indecible*, 153.

57. Drysdale, "Violeta Parra," 514.

58. González, Ohlsen, and Rolle, *Historia social*, 351; "Los discos de la semana," *Ecran TV* (March 8–14, 1966), 10, inserted in *Ecran*, March 8, 1966; "Lista de éxitos de Radio Santiago," *Ecran*, October 19, 1965, 45; "Los 10 favoritos de la Discomanía," *Ecran*, January 11, 1966, 44–45.

59. The project was released as the album *Arte de pájaros*, Demon LPD-031, 1966. It was also produced as a television program; "'Voz para el camino,' Canal 9," *Ecran*, January 17, 1967, 12.

60. See, for example, Nancy Grünberg, "Ola de matrimonios," *Ecran TV* (week of November 30–December 6), 9, inserted in *Ecran*, November 26, 1965; "Las estrellas le hablan," *Ecran*, October 19, 1965, 42.

61. "Isabel Parra," *Musiquero*, no. 35 (November 1966), 12.

62. "Medallas de oro Discomanía," *Ecran TV* (February 1–7, 1966), 36, inserted in *Ecran*, February 1, 1966.

63. "Los superventas," *Ecran TV* (week of February 15–21), 12, inserted in *Ecran*, February 15, 1966.

64. Alfredo Barra, "Isabel y Ángel Parra son los herederos de la canción chilena," *Ritmo de la Juventud*, April 12, 1966, 19. My thanks to Alejandro Mundaca for sharing with me this and numerous other articles that he uncovered through painstaking research.

65. Osmur (pseud.), "Ángel e Isabel Parra: 'Nuestro mayor orgullo es nuestra madre,'" *Rincón Juvenil* 81 (July 6, 1966): 6–7.

66. Patricio Manns adamantly objected to this honorific on more than one occasion; see, for example, Pancani and Canales, *Los necios*, 65, and "Recuento," in Lawner, Soto, and Schatan, *Salvador Allende*, 367. He seemingly stands alone in this regard, however.

67. "Las peñas: Un nuevo rostro para el '18."

68. Fernando Barraza, chronicler of the Chilean New Song, lists only three women performers—Charo Cofré, Isabel Parra, and Silvia Urbina—on his roster of New Song artists, compiled in 1972. Barraza, *La nueva canción chilena*, 86–93. Their reduced number stands in contrast to the sixteen women folkloristas listed in Klimpel's *La mujer chilena*.

69. Á. Parra, *Mi nueva canción*, 48.

70. E. Carrasco, *Quilapayún*, 83; and as quoted in J. Jara, *Unfinished Song*, 107 (italics used in the original).

71. In a 1971 interview, Isabel Parra stated, "[Chilean] folklore is monotonous, bland, monochrome, and saccharine in its content. Personally, we know folklore but we only sing it rarely because it in no way fulfills us." Pedro Simón, "Dále palo a los momios: Entrevista a Isabel Parra," *Música* 10 (September 16, 1971): n.p.

72. Quoted in Ernesto González Bermejo, "Isabel Parra, enemiga del olvido y la desesperanza," *Crisis* (August 1975): 48.

73. Barraza, *La nueva canción chilena*, 37.

74. Quoted in Astorga, "Retrato hablado de Violeta Parra," n.p.

75. Coulon is interviewed in Cifuentes, *Fragmentos de un sueño*, 7; Carrasco is interviewed in Televisión Nacional de Chile, *Violeta Parra*, 46:40–46:47.

76. Parra's songs would later feature prominently in both Inti-Illimani and Quilapayún's repertoires.

77. "En la Feria de Artes Plásticas palpita el alma y la forma de la tierra chilena," *La Nación*, December 8, 1965. Apparently, the only other notice that Parra received in the press for her participation in the 1965 Arts Fair was the mention of her "burlap sacks embroidered with yarn" in Anita Hurtado's piece, "La mujer en la Feria del Mapocho," *Suplemento Mujeres de La Nación*, December 12, 1965.

78. Manns, *Violeta Parra*, 96.

79. Luis Barrales, "La vecina Violeta Parra," *Qué Pasa*, September 29, 2017, 45.

80. Carolina Marcos, "Los dolores de la folclorista más grande," *La Discusión*, August 28, 2011, 37, www.bibliotecanacionaldigital.gob.cl/colecciones/BND/oo/RC/RC0261435 .pdf.

81. René Largo Farías, "La Viola Volcánica," originally written in 1977, reprinted in *Chile Ríe y Canta* 3 (May–June 1992).

82. Manns, "Recuento," in Lawner, Soto, and Schatan, *Salvador Allende*, 369.

83. Ramiro Quiroga, "El cuarteto andino: Peña Naira, Pepe Ballón, Gilbert Favre, y Violeta Parra," in "Testimonios de Violeta Parra en La Paz."

84. Drysdale, "Violeta Parra," 513; Germán Aruaz Crespo, "Galería Naira: Un espacio que revolucionó la música nacional," *Ventana/La Razón*, May 16, 1993, 13; María de los Angeles Baudoin, "Una copa, una quena y el recuerdo de Peña Nayra [*sic*]," *Puntos Suspendidos*, December–January 1995–1996, 23; Lupe Cajías, "Los últimos días de Violeta Parra y su visita a 'Peña Naira,'" in Cajías, *Antes de que me anochezca*, 52; Pellegrino, "El grito de la tierra," 7.

85. Demon SD-0164 (1966). Tita Parra appears simply as "Titina" on the disc.

86. Rodríguez, *Cantores que reflexionan*, 105–7.

87. Parra could have gone to La Paz on her own accord, unrelated to the Chile Laughs and Sings tour, but that seems unlikely.

88. Interview with Ernesto Cavour, "De cómo Violeta Parra se trajo a Chile un charango de Bolivia y también un revolver," in Ramiro Quiroga, "Testimonios de Violeta Parra en La Paz."

89. Sáez, *La vida intranquila*, 160; "Festival folklórico internacional se inicia hoy," *El Mercurio*, December 16, 1966, reproduced in Arauco, *Los Jairas*, 136.

90. "Conjuntos extranjeros," *El Mercurio*, December 19, 1966, reproduced in Arauco, *Los Jairas*, 137.

91. Carrasco, *Quilapayún*, 67. Carrasco recalled the evening as occurring at the end of winter, but Los Jairas performed at the Carpa in December 1966, which is the end of spring in Chile.

92. Drysdale, "Violeta Parra," 513.

93. Štambuk and Bravo, *Violeta Parra*, 157–58.

94. Štambuk and Bravo, *Violeta Parra*, 154–55. Unlike Isabel and Ángel, who rarely criticized their mother in public forums, Carmen Luisa candidly discussed the challenges she faced in her relationship with her mother: "We had wonderful times together and others that were terrifying. . . . In truth it was difficult to live with someone who could be

so different from one day to the next, who you never knew what she was about to do. I can tell you this, because I was the only one who was with her until the end"; Štambuk and Bravo, *Violeta Parra*, 154–55.

95. Drysdale, "Violeta Parra," 518.

96. Carrasco, *Quilapayún*, 66–67.

97. Julio Huasi, "Los siete golgotas de Violeta Parra," *El Porteño*, June 1986, 71–72.

98. Astorga, "Retrato hablado de Violeta Parra."

99. I. Parra, *El libro mayor*, 209.

100. Quoted in Herrero, *Después de vivir*, 448.

101. Nancy Grunberg, "Isabel Parra encontró la formula de la felicidad," *Rincón Juvenil* 102 (November 30, 1966): 16–17.

102. María Cristina Jurado, "Isabel Parra: 'Esa carta me dió pena," *Revista Ya de El Mercurio*, August 17, 2019, 24.

103. Štambuk and Bravo, *Violeta Parra*, 139.

104. Violeta was not the only Parra to at times have a problematic relationship with the Chilean Communist Party. Nicanor was "excommunicated" for a lengthy period following a 1970 incident when he was photographed drinking tea with US first lady Patricia Nixon while on a tour of the White House as part of a PEN delegation from Latin America. In contrast with her brother's public falling out with the CP, Violeta's relations with the party were never the subject of official pronouncements. Whatever rumors or rejections she may have incurred remained below the surface of in-party or public debate.

105. Amalia Chaigneau, quoted in Drysdale, "Violeta Parra," 514.

106. Matías Correa D., "Gastón Soublette: 'Violeta no era capaz de controlar su ira,'" *Afiche en la pared*, March 26, 2007, http://afichenlapared.blogspot.com/2007/03/gastn -soublette-violeta-no-era-capaz-de.html; Zapicán, quoted in Astorga, "Retrato hablado de Violeta Parra"; Aravena Llanca, *Lo visible indecible*, 241–43.

107. Eduardo Carrasco, "Violeta Parra y los mitos," Opinión Cultura (blog), Cooperativa 93.3, February 17, 2012, http://blogs.cooperativa.cl/opinion/cultura/20120217114935/violeta -parra-y-los-mitos/.

108. Bello et al., "Análisis de un genio popular," 72.

109. Štambuk and Bravo, *Violeta Parra*, 95.

110. I. Parra, *El libro mayor*, 78.

111. "Los triunfadores de 1966," *Ecran TV* (December 27, 1966–January 2, 1967), 3, inserted in *Ecran*, December 27, 1966.

112. Daniel Viglietti, "Violeta Parra en el silencio," *Marcha*, February 17, 1967; and "Cuatro artes de luna," *Brecha* 9, no. 431 (March 4, 1994), 23.

113. "Un testimonio desconocido de la Violeta Parra," in García, *Violeta Parra en sus palabras*, 114.

114. I. Parra, *El libro mayor*, 151.

115. I. Parra, *El libro mayor*, 215.

116. Štambuk and Bravo, *Violeta Parra*, 158.

117. Herrero, *Después de vivir*, 489–91; M. Gallo, "Patricio Manns y la muerte de Ángel Parra"; Patricio Manns, "Las últimas visiones de Violeta Parra," *The Clinic*, September 18, 2017.

118. Rodríguez, *Cantores que reflexionan*, 165.

119. I. Parra, *El libro mayor*, 64; Rodríguez, *Cantores que reflexionan*, 172 and 190.

120. Parra uses the phrase in her décima, "No tengo la culpa, ingrato," in *Décimas*, 206; and in a poem published in I. Parra, *El libro mayor*, 215.

121. Štambuk and Bravo, *Violeta Parra*, 155.

122. Arenas, *Margot Loyola*, 75.

123. Štambuk and Bravo, *Violeta Parra*, 159–60.

124. Štambuk and Bravo, *Violeta Parra*, 160.

125. Quezada, *En la mira de Nicanor Parra*, 51.

126. Carlos Necochea, quoted in I. Parra, *El libro mayor*, 204.

127. By Venezuelan composer José Antonio López, written in the style of the Venezuelan folk song genre of *joropo*. Lyrics available at Cancionero.com, www.cancioneros.com/nc /5683/0/rio-manzanares-jose-antonio-lopez.

128. From an interview with Zapicán in *Violeta Parra, flor de Chile*. This detail is omitted from Zapicán's numerous other accounts of the day of Parra's suicide.

129. Štambuk and Bravo, *Violeta Parra*, 162. There is a discrepancy in the sources as to whether Carmen Luisa or the Carpa's caretaker found Violeta's body.

130. "Se suicidó Violeta Parra," *La Nación*, February 6, 1967; "¡Que se apaguen las guitarras! Trágica muerte de Violeta Parra," *Clarín*, February 6, 1967; "Con un disparo Violeta Parra puso fin a su dolor," *Flash*, February 10, 1967, 2–3.

131. Drysdale, "Violeta Parra," 520.

132. S. H. C., "La folklorista que conoció todo el mundo," *El Siglo*, February 7, 1967.

133. "El pueblo sepultó a su folklorista," *La Tercera*, February 8, 1967.

134. Felipe Retamal and Pablo Retamal N. "¿Cómo se contó la muerte de Violeta Parra en la prensa?," *La Tercera*, February 5, 2020.

135. Lidia Baltra, "Violeta Parra—Todavía se muere de amor," *Eva*, February 17, 1967, 40.

136. Tito Mundt, "Lo que se llevó Violeta Parra," *La Tercera*, February 8, 1967.

137. Aucapan (pseud. Luis Alberto Mansilla), "Violeta Parra," *El Siglo*, February 7, 1967.

138. Nancy Grünberg, "Violeta Parra . . . Run Run . . . Se fue para siempre . . . ," *Rincón Juvenil*, February 15, 1967.

139. Raquel Correa, "Las guitarras lloran a Violeta Parra," *Vea*, February 9, 1967, 16.

140. Bello et al., "Análisis de un genio popular," 74. Interestingly, Martínez Bonatti's contribution to the 1968 roundtable organized in Parra's eulogy was to make the case that she was a modern artist.

141. Alejandra Jara, "¿Hubo playback en el homenaje a Violeta Parra? La polémica que marcó la obertura de Viña 2017," *La Tercera*, February 20, 2017.

142. "Rechazan uso de imagen de Violeta Parra en campaña chilena," *Prensa Latina*, December 11, 2021, www.prensa-latina.cu/2021/12/11/rechazan-uso-de-imagen-de-violeta -parra-en-campana-chilena.

143. Posting on eBay, March 6, 2013, since removed.

144. Subercaseaux and Londoño, *Gracias a la vida*, 131.

145. Stern, *Battling for Hearts and Minds*, 281.

146. Elena De Costa, "A Political Voice & Activist: Mercedes Sosa and the Silent Majority in Latin America—From Poetic Song to Political Act," *International Communication Research Journal* 54, no. 2 (2019): n.p.

147. Josi Villanueva, "Violeta Parra—Miren como sonríen—Barrio Yungay," recorded December 8, 2019, www.youtube.com/watch?v=N_jod-stP6k.

148. "Las últimas composiciones de Violeta Parra," *El Musiquero* 37 (January 1967): 36.

Bibliography

Primary Sources

Archives

Argentina
  Biblioteca Nacional de Argentina, Buenos Aires
  Biblioteca Utopía, Centro Cultural de la Cooperación Floreal Gorini, Buenos Aires
  Centro de Documentación e Investigación de la Cultura de Izquierdas, Buenos Aires
Chile
  Archivo de Música Popular Chilena, Instituto de Música, Pontífica Universidad
    Católica de Chile, Santiago (online consultation)
  Archivo General Historico, Ministerio de Relaciones Exteriores de Chile, Santiago
  Archivo Mujeres y Géneros, Catálogo Fondo Audiovisual, Archivo Nacional Histórico,
    Santiago
  Archivo Sonoro, Mediateca, Universidad de Chile, Santiago
  Biblioteca Nacional de Chile
  Fondo Documental Margot Loyola, Pontífica Universidad Católica de Valparaíso
    (correspondence)
Ecuador
  Biblioteca de la Casa de la Cultura Ecuatoriana (correspondence)
England
  BBC Written Archives Centre (correspondence)
  British Library (correspondence)
Finland
  Kansan Arkisto / The People's Archive, Helsinki (correspondence)
France
  Bibliotheque National de France, Paris
  L'Institut national de l'audiovisuel (INA), Paris
  Musée des Arts Décoratifs Archives, Paris (correspondence)
  Paul Rivet Collection, Muséum national d'Histoire naturelle, Paris (correspondence)
  Photographs of L'Humanité, Archives Départementales de la Seine-Saint-Denis
  UNESCO Archives (correspondence)
Netherlands
  World Festival of Youth and Students Collection, IISG (International Institute of
    Social History), Amsterdam
Switzerland
  Bibliothèque de Genève, Geneva
  Fondo Roberto Leydi, Centro di dialettologia e di etnografia, Bellinzona, Switzerland
    (correspondence)
  Musée d'ethnographie de Genève (correspondence)

United States
  Alan Lomax Collection, Library of Congress (correspondence)
  Allen Ginsberg Archive, Special Collections, Stanford University, Palo Alto
    (correspondence)
  Enrique Lihn Papers, Research Collections, Getty Museum, Los Angeles
  Fernando Alegría papers, Special Collections, Stanford University Library,
    Palo Alto
  History of Aviation Archives, University of Texas at Dallas (correspondence)
  Jorge Edwards Collection, Rare Books and Special Collections, Princeton University
    Library, Princeton (correspondence)
  Library of Congress, Washington, DC
  UCLA Ethnomusicology Archive, Los Angeles

Journals, Magazines, and Newspapers

ARGENTINA
Claudia
La Prensa
Revista Vuelo

BOLIVIA
El Diario (La Paz)

BRAZIL
Correia da Manha (Rio
  de Janeiro)
O Jornal (Rio de Janeiro)

CHILE
*Anales de la Universidad
  de Chile*
Aquí Está
Araucaria de Chile
*Atenea: Revista trimestral
  de Ciencias, Letras y
  Artes*
La Bicicleta
*Boletín de la Universidad
  de Chile*
*Boletín del Instituto de
  Literatura Chilena*
*Boletín informative de la
  Universidad de
  Concepción*
Clarín
The Clinic

El Diario Ilustrado
La Discusión
  (Concepción)
Ecran
La Época
Ercilla
Eva
Finis Terrae
Fortín Mapocho
La Hora
El Magallanes
El Mercurio
El Musiquero
La Nación
*Plan (Política
  latinoamericana
  nueva)*
Pomaire
La Prensa Austral
Punto Final
Revista Análisis
Revista de Arte
Revista Hoy
Revista Musical Chilena
Rincón juvenil
Ritmo de la juventud
El Siglo
La Tercera
Vea
En Viaje
Zig-Zag

FRANCE
Les Arts
Europe
Le Figaro
France Dimanche
L'Humanité
Le Jardin des arts
Les Lettres Françaises
Le Monde
Paris Théatre
Partisans
La Revue de Paris
Revue des Deux Mondes

GERMAN DEMOCRATIC
REPUBLIC
Berliner Zeitung
Musik und Gesellschaft
Neues Deutschland
*Women of the Whole
  World*

SCOTLAND
Glasgow Times

SWITZERLAND
Feuille d'Avis de Lausanne
Gazette de Lausanne
Journal de Genève
Journal de Montreaux
La Liberté

Le Matin—Tribune de
　Lausanne
Nouvelle Revue de
　Lausanne
Le Peuple
Poésie vivante

Radio-TV Je Vois Tout
Tribune de Genève
24 Heures

UNITED STATES
New York Times

URUGUAY
Brecha
Marcha
El País Cultural

Documentary Films

Agüero, Ignacio. *Violeta Parra, pintora chilena.* Fundación Violeta Parra, 2010.

Arévalo, Hugo. *Violeta Parra, flor de Chile,* 1994. 114 min.

Arrieta, Ximena, and Hermann Mondaca, dirs. *Prontuario de Roberto Parra.* Grupo Proceso, 1996. 47 min.

Diserens, Jean Claude, and Madeleine Brumagne. *Violeta Parra, brodeuse chilienne.* RTS—Radio Televisión Suisse, 1965. 18:38 min.

Fundación Violeta Parra. *Violeta Parra—Bordadora chilena.* Fundación Violeta Parra, 2010.

Lauro, Jorge di. *Los artistas plásticas de Chile.* Cineam, 1960. 16 min.

Marras, Sergio. *Materiales de demolición.* Canal 1, 2012. 29 min.

Moreno, Sebastián. *Sergio Larraín, el instante eterno.* Las Películas del Pez, 2021. 84 min.

Orellana, Gastón. *La Carpa, un sueño Violeta.* Natalia Contesse and the Escuela de Folclor y Oficios, Chile, 2013. 12 min.

Parra, Ángel, and Daniel Sandoval. *Violeta más viva que nunca.* Santiago: Evolución Producciones, 2017. 32 min.

Sextier, Antoine. *L'Escale.* Franchute Production, 2022. 45 min.

Televisión Nacional de Chile. *Violeta Parra: Grandes chilenos.* 2008.

Vera, Luis R. *Viola chilensis: Violeta Parra vida y obra.* Luis R. Vera Producciones, Alerce La Otra Música, 2003. 85 min.

Websites

Archivo Chile. Centro de Estudios "Miguel Enríquez" (CEME). www.archivochile.com.

Archivo de Referencias Críticas, Biblioteca Nacional de Chile. www .bibliotecanacionaldigital.gob.cl/bnd/628/w3-propertyvalue-966899.html.

"Biografía de Violeta Parra." Municipalidad de San Carlos. https://munisancarlos.cl/web /index.php/antecedentes/biografia-de-violeta-parra.

Cancionero discográfico de cuecas chilenas. Fonoteca Nacional de Chile. http://dev .cancionerodecuecas.cl/#!/home.

Cancioneros.com. Diario Digital de Música de Autor. www.cancioneros.com/.

Centro de Documentación/CEDOC. Museo Violeta Parra. www.museovioletaparra.cl /cedoc/.

Discoteca Nacional Chile. https://discotecanacionalchile.blogspot.com.

Favre, Gilbert. "Les mémoires du Gringo." Le Gringo Favre. https://gringobandolero.ch /autobiography/.

Fundación Violeta Parra. www.fundacionvioletaparra.org/.

Lautaro Parra. http://lautaroparra.blogspot.com.

Memoria Chilena. Biblioteca Nacional de Chile. www.memoriachilena.gob.cl/.

Museo Violeta Parra. www.museovioletaparra.cl.

MúsicaPopular.cl. La enciclopedia de la música popular chilena. www.musicapopular.cl.

Música Tradicional Chilena. https://musicatradicional.cl.

PERRERAC. Enciclopedia del cantar popular. https://perrerac.org.

UNESCO Digital Archives. https://unesdoc.unesco.org/archives.

"Violeta Parra." Archivo de Autores. Proyecto Patrimonio. www.letras.mysite.com /archivovioleta.htm.

"Violeta Parra." La Biennale de Venezia. www.labiennale.org/en/art/2022/milk-dreams /violeta-parra.

Published Works by Violeta Parra

TEXTS

Fundación Violeta Parra (FVP). *Violeta Parra: Obra visual.* 2. ed. Santiago: Fundación Violeta Parra, Ocho Libros, 2007.

Museo Violeta Parra (Santiago), Consejo Nacional de la Cultura y las Artes (Chile), and Fundación Violeta Parra (Chile). *Museo Violeta Parra: Catálogo exposición permanente: Violeta, humana y divina.* Octubre, 2015. [Santiago]: Museo Violeta Parra, 2015.

Parra, Violeta. *Cancionero: Virtud de los elementos.* Santiago: Fundación Violeta Parra, 1993.

———. *Cancionero: Virtud de los elementos.* 2. ed. Santiago: Fundación Violeta Parra, 2005.

———. *Centésimas del Alma.* Santiago: Ediciones Biblioteca Nacional de Chile, 2019.

———. *Décimas: Autobiografía en verso.* Buenos Aires: Editorial Sudamericana, 1988.

———. *Poésie populaire des Andes.* Paris: F. Maspero, 1965.

———. *21 son los dolores: Antología amorosa.* Santiago: Ediciones Aconcagua, 1976.

———. "Velorios de Angelitos," *Pomaire,* 3:16 (December 1958–February 1959), 1.

———. *Violeta del pueblo.* Madrid: A. Corazón, 1976.

———. *Violeta Parra.* Paris, N.F.C Editeur, n.d.

———. *Violeta Parra: Poesía.* Edited by Paula Miranda Herrera. Valparaíso: Fundación Violeta Parra, Editorial de la Universidad de Valparaíso, 2016.

Parra, Violeta, Sergio Bravo, Sergio Larraín, and Luis Gastón Soublette. *Cantos folklóricos chilenos.* Santiago: Ed. Nascimento, 1979.

———. *Cantos folklóricos chilenos.* 2. ed. Fundación Violeta Parra. Santiago: Ceibo Ediciones, 2013.

Parra, Violeta, Olivia Concha, Rodolfo Norambuena, Rodrigo Torres Alvarado, and Mauricio Valdebenito. *Composiciones para guitarra: Transcripciones.* Santiago: Sociedad Chilena de Derecho de Autor, Fundación Violeta Parra, 1993.

Parra, Violeta, and Juan Andrés Piña. *Volver a los 17.* Santiago: Editorial Los Andes, 1995.

Discography

VIOLETA PARRA

Antología Violeta Parra—Grabaciones originales en EMI Odeon 1954–1966. EMI Odeon 914974–2, 2012, compact disc.

Canciones reencontradas en París. DICAP/La Peña de los Parra DCP-22, 1971, 33⅓ rpm.

Cantos Chilenos. Oveja Negra 590253, 2010, compact disc.

Cantos de Chile. Le Chant du Monde LDX 74572/73, 1975, 33⅓ rpm.

Chants et danses du Chili: Violeta Parra, chant et guitare. Vol. 1, Le Chant du Monde LDY-4060, 1956, 33⅓ rpm.

Chants et danses du Chili: Violeta Parra, chant et guitare. Vol. 2, Le Chant du Monde LDY-4071, 1956, 33⅓ rpm.

Chants et danses du Chili: Violeta Parra, guitare et chant. Le Chant du Monde, LD-S-4271, 1964, 33⅓ rpm.

Décimas. ALP-204 CD0005, Alarce, 1976, 33⅓ rpm.

Décimas y centésimas. Alerce ALCL-784, 1993, compact disc.

El folklore de Chile según Violeta Parra. Odeon LDI-503, 1962, 33⅓ rpm.

En el Aula Magna de Concepción. Interview with Mario Céspedes, Radio Universidad de Concepción, January 1960. Oveja Negra 590260, 2010, compact disc. 58:21.

En vivo en Ginebra (Violeta Parra). Oveja Negra 590262, 2010, compact disc.

La cueca presentada por Violeta Parra: El folklore de Chile. Vol. 3, Odeon Chilena LDC-36038, 1959, 33⅓ rpm.

La tonada presentada por Violeta Parra: El folklore de Chile. Vol. 4, Odeon Chilena LDC-36054, 1959, 33⅓ rpm.

Las últimas composiciones de Violeta Parra. RCA Victor CML-2456, 1966, 33⅓ rpm.

Recordando a Chile. EMI-Odeon LDC-36533, 1965, 33⅓ rpm.

Temas inéditos—Homenaje documental. Mandioca MSD-016, 1987, EP.

Toda Violeta Parra. Odeon LDC-36344, 1961, 33⅓ rpm.

Untitled single. Leningradsky Zavod 25501/25502, 1955, 78 rpm.

Violeta Parra. Odeon Chilena DSOD/E-50040, 1955, 45 rpm.

Violeta Parra. Vol. 6, EMI-Odeon 44-0586-4, 1984, cassette.

Violeta Parra, acompañada de guitarra: El folklore de Chile. Vol. 2, Odeon Chilena LDC 36025, 1958, 33⅓ rpm.

Violeta Parra, cantos de Chile. Le Chant du Monde LDX 74572/73, 1975, 33⅓ rpm.

Violeta Parra, composiciones para guitarra. Odeon MSOD/E-51020, 1957, 45 rpm.

Violeta Parra con su guitarra. Odeon DSOD/E-50059, 1955, 45 rpm.

Violeta Parra: El folklore de Chile. Vol. 1, Odeon LDC-36019, 1957, 33⅓ rpm.

Violeta Parra: El folklore de Chile. Vol. 2, Odeon LDC-36025, 1958, 33⅓ rpm.

Violeta Parra: El folklore y la pasión. EMI-Odeon 8-30971-2, 1994, compact disc.

Violeta Parra en Ginebra. Warner Music Chile 857380702-2, 1999, double compact disc.

Violeta Parra y Gilbert Favre: El Moscardon. EMI-Odeon MSOD/E-51029, 1966, 45 rpm.

COLLECTIVE ALBUMS AND COMPILATIONS

Parra, Violeta, et al. *Santiago!* Capitol T 10020, 1956, 33⅓ rpm.

———. *Cantos de rebeldía*. Odeon LDC-36559, 1966, 33⅓ rpm.

———. *Cuecas a pata pelá*. Odeon LDC-36998, 1966, 33⅓ rpm.

————. *Imagen musical de Chile*. Odeon O-2001, 1964, 33⅓ rpm.

————. *La Carpa de La Reina*. EMI-Odeon LDC-36581, 1966, 33⅓ rpm.

————. *Süd- und mittelamerikanische Volksmusik*. Eterna 8 30 014—Lieder der Völker N° 7, 1965, 33⅓ rpm.

————. *Testimonio*. EMI 104975, 1990, cassette.

————. *Todo el folklore. Vol. 1*. Demon LPD-017-X, 1965, 33⅓ rpm.

OTHER ARTISTS

Baxter, Les. *'Round the World with Les Baxter, His Orchestra and Chorus*. Capitol Records, 1956, T-780, 33⅓ rpm.

Desborde. *Tribute Concert to Violeta Parra/Peña homenaje a Violeta Parra*. Desalambrar Recordings, 1996, compact disc.

Las Hermanas Parra. Untitled single. Odeon 89–952, 1954, 78 rpm.

Las Hermanas Parra, Los Campesinos. Untitled EP, Odeon DSOD/E-50097, 1957, 45 rpm.

Mercado, Claudio. *Chosto Ulloa, Santos Rubio: Dos cantores nombrados*. Chimuchina Records, 2014, compact disc.

New Capitol Albums for May and June, 1956: For Radio-TV Program Use. Capitol Records, 1955, PRO 261-PRO 264, 33⅓ rpm.

Parra, Ángel. *Angel Parra y su guitarra*. Demon, 1965, 33⅓ rpm.

Parra, Ángel, and Isabel Parra. *Au Chili avec Los Parra de Chillan*. Barclay 86078, 1963, 33⅓ rpm.

Parra, Isabel. "Ven aca, regalo mio / En los altos de Colombia." Demon SD-055, 1964, 45 rpm.

Parra, Roberto. *Las cuecas de Roberto Parra*. EMI-Odeon LDC-36259, 1967, 33⅓ rpm.

Los Parra de Chillán et al. *Toute L'Amerique Latine*. Barclay, 1965, 33⅓ rpm.

Sosa, Mercedes. *Homenaje a Violeta Parra*. Philips 6347035, Argentina, 1971, 33⅓ rpm.

Trio Los Parra. *20 cuecas con salsa verde*. EMI-Odeon/LDC-36266, 1967, 33⅓ rpm.

Interviews, Memoirs, Testimonies, and Other Published Primary Sources

Acevedo, Nano. *Los ojos de la memoria*. Santiago: Cantoral Ediciones, 1995.

Adoum, Jorge Enrique. *De cerca y de memoria: Lecturas, autores, lugares*. Quito, Ecuador: Ediciones Archipiélago, 2003.

Adriasola, Claudia. *Así lo vió Zig Zag*. Santiago: Empresa Editora Zig-Zag, 1980.

Álvarez, Jorge. *Memorias—Jorge Álvarez*. Buenos Aires: Queleer S.A., 2014.

Astudillo Rojas, Cecilia. *Extracto de artículos y entrevistas realizadas a Margot Loyola entre 1957 y 2007*. Article. Fondo de Investigación y Documentación de Música Tradicional Chilena Margot Loyola Palacios, Pontificia Universidad Católica de Valparaíso, Chile. n.d.

Baeza Gajardo, Mario, ed. *Cantares de Pascua: Antología de villancicos que se cantan en Chile*. Santiago: Del Pacífico, 1961.

Baltra Montaner, Lidia. *De la farándula a la trinchera: Memorias de la última periodista de Ecran, la legendaria revista de cine*. Santiago: Ediciones Radio Universidad de Chile, 2018.

Bañados, Patricio. *Confidencias de un locutor*. Santiago: Editorial Cuarto Propio, 2013.

Barros, Raquel, and Manuel Dannemann. "El Guitarrón en el Departamento de Puente Alto." *Revista musical chilena* 14, no. 74 (1960): 7–45.

———. "Guía metodológica de la investigación folklórica." *Mapocho* 2, no. 1 (1964): 168–78.

———. "Los problemas de la investigación del folklore musical chileno." *Revista musical chilena* 14, no. 71 (1960): 82–100.

Bello, Enrique. "Homenaje a Violeta Parra." *Boletín de La Universidad de Chile*, no. 74 (May 1967): 60–61.

Bello, Enrique, José María Arguedas, Raquel Barros, Mario Carreño, Manuel Dannemann, Margot Loyola, Eduardo Martínez Bonatti, José Ricardo Morales, José M. Palacios, and Teresa Vicuña. "Análisis de un genio popular hacen artistas y escritores: Violeta Parra." *Revista de educación*, no. 13 (1968): 66–76.

Bernstein, Leonard. *Findings*. New York: Simon and Schuster, 1982.

Brumagne, Marie Magdeleine. *Qui se souvient de sa vie?* Lausanne, Switzerland: L'Age d'Homme, 1992.

Bustos Mandiola, Jaime. *Crónicas de un ex locutor de radio*. Santiago: Bravo y Allende Editores, 1996.

Cajías, Lupe. *Antes de que me anochezca: 40 años contando historias*. La Paz, Bolivia: Lupe Cajías, 2018.

Campa, Colette, and Patricio Manns. "Entretien avec Patricio Manns." *Cahiers du monde hispanique et luso-brésilien*, no. 29 (1977): 205–11.

Castedo, Leopoldo. *Contramemorias de un transterrado*. Santiago: Fondo de Cultura Económica, 1997.

Celedón, Jaime. *Memorias que olvidé en alguna parte*. Santiago: Aguilar, 2001.

Cifuentes Seves, Luis. *Fragmentos de un sueño: Inti-Illimani y la generación de los 60*. Santiago: Ediciones Logos, 1989.

Corvalán, Luis. *De lo vivido y lo peleado: Memorias*. Santiago: LOM Ediciones, 1997.

Dannemann, Manuel. "Los estudios folklóricos en nuestros ciento cincuenta años de vida independiente." *Anales de la Universidad de Chile* 128, no. 120 (1960): 203–17.

———. "Variedades formales de la poesía popular chilena." *Atenea* 33, no. 372 (1956): 45–71.

Debray, Laurence. *Hija de revolucionarios*. Translated by Cristina Zelich. Barcelona: Editorial Anagrama, 2018.

Edwards, Jorge. *Persona non grata*. 2. ed. Barcelona: Barral Editores, 1973.

Epple, Juan Armando. *Entre mar y cordillera: Conversaciones sobre poesía, Violeta Parra y la nueva canción chilena*. Concepción: Ediciones LAR, 2012.

———. "Entretien avec Angel Parra: Preguntas por Violeta Parra." *Cahiers du monde hispanique et luso-brésilien* 48 (1987): 121–26.

Epple, Juan Armando, and Patricio Manns. *Patricio Manns: Actas del cazador en movimiento*. Colección Testimonio. Santiago: Mosquito Editores, 1991.

Fernández Larraín, Sergio. *Informe sobre el comunismo rendido a la convención general del Partido Conservador Unido, el 12 de octubre*. Santiago: Zig-Zag, 1954.

Ferrero, Mario. *Escritores a trasluz*. Testimonios. Santiago: Editorial Universitaria, 1971.

Figueroa Yávar, Aída. *Después de mucho vivir: Memorias*. Santiago: RIL Editores, 2016.

Gampert, Raymonde. *A la découverte du théâtre*. Genève: Le Petit Crève—Coeur de René Gampert, 1979.

García, Marisol, ed. *Violeta Parra en sus palabras: Entrevistas (1954–1967)*. Santiago: Catalonia Escuela de Periodismo UDP, 2016.

García, Ricardo, and José Osorio. *Ricardo García: Un hombre trascendente*. Santiago: Pluma y Pincel, 1996.

Ginsberg, Allen. *South American Journals: January–July 1960*. Edited by Michael Schumacher. Minneapolis: University of Minnesota Press, 2019.

Griliquez, Eve, and Frank Tenaille. *Le libre parcours d'Eve Griliquez*. Paris: Layeur, 2005.

Grouès, Delphine, and Angel Parra. "Si alguien quiere entender a La Violeta (Entrevista)." *Ixquic (Revista: Australia)*, no. 9 (December 2008): 1–4.

Guarany, Horacio. *Memorias del cantor: Casi una biografía*. Buenos Aires: Editorial Sudamericana, 2002.

Hernández Ojeda, Jaime. *1960: Memorias de un desastre*. Valdivia: Arte Sonoro Austral Ediciones, 2011.

"The International Folk Music Council: Its Formation and Progress." *Journal of the International Folk Music Council* 1 (1949): 3–4.

Jakovsky, Anatole. *Peintres Naïfs: A Dictionary of Primitive Painters*. New York: Universe Books, 1967.

Jara, Joan. *An Unfinished Song: The Life of Victor Jara*. New York: Ticknor & Fields, 1984.

Jara, Víctor. *Habla y canta Víctor Jara*. La Habana: Casa de las Américas, 1978.

Jara, Víctor, Raúl Encina T., and Rodrigo Fuenzalida H. *Víctor Jara: Testimonio de un artista*. Santiago: CERET—Centro de Recopilaciones y Testimonio, 1988.

Jodorowsky, Alejandro. *The Spiritual Journey of Alejandro Jodorowsky: The Creator of El Topo*. Rochester, Vt.: Park Street, 2008.

Lago, Tomás. *Remembranza de Violeta Parra*. Santiago: Museo de Arte Popular, 1968.

Lambert, Jean-Clarence. *L'Art latino-américain à Paris: Exposition, 2 août—4 octobre 1962, Musée d'art moderne de la ville de Paris*. Paris: Musée d'Art Moderne de la Ville de Paris, 1962.

Largo Farías, René. *Fue hermoso vivir contigo compañera*. Mexico: Samo, 1975.

Lavín Almazán, Vivian. "Margot Loyola y Osvaldo Cadiz." In *Vuelan las plumas: Conversaciones con escritores y artistas en el Metro de Santiago*, 2. ed., 163–81. Santiago: Ediciones Radio Universidad de Chile, 2009.

Lenz, Rodolfo. *Programa de la Sociedad de Folklore Chileno, fundada en Santiago el 18 de julio de 1909*. Santiago: Imprenta y Encuadernacion Lourdes, 1909.

———. *Sobre la poesía popular impresa de Santiago: Contribución al folklore chileno*. Santiago: Soc. Imprenta I Litografía Universo, 1919.

Letelier, Alfonso. "In memoriam Violeta Parra." *Revista musical chilena* 21 (1967): 109–11.

Letelier Llona, Marta. *Aculeo, tierra de recuerdos*. Santiago: Editorial Andrés Bello, 1991.

Lihn, Enrique, and Daniel Fuenzalida. *Enrique Lihn entrevistas*. Santiago: J. C. Sáez Editores, 2005.

"List of Authoritative French Folk Music, Records, Released 1945–1959." *Ethnomusicology* 6, no. 1 (1962): 39–41.

Loyola, Margot. *La tonada: Testimonios para el futuro*. Valparaíso: Pontifica Universidad Católica de Valparaíso, 2006.

———. *Por el mundo: Memorias de viaje*. Santiago: Sello Raíces, 1989.

Mackenna Besa, Benjamín, and Los Huasos Quincheros. *Quincheros: Andanzas de cuatro guitarras*. Santiago: Edebé, 2003.

Manns, Patricio. *Hemos hecho lo querido y hemos querido lo hecho*. Santiago: Editorial Hueders, 2017.

———. "Recuento." In *Salvador Allende: Presencia en la ausencia*, edited by Miguel Lawner, Hernán Soto, and Jacobo Schatan, 363–77. Santiago: LOM Ediciones, 2008.

————. *Violeta Parra: La guitarra indócil.* Colección Los Juglares. Madrid: Ediciones Júcar, 1977.

————. "Violeta Parra: Hojas Nuevas." *Araucaria de Chile,* no. 38 (1987): 112–22.

Marín, Gladys. *Gladys Marín.* 2. ed. Santiago: América Libre, 2004.

Mello, Thiago de. *O povo sabe o que diz.* 2. ed., rev. E aum. Rio de Janeiro, RJ: Civilização Brasileira, 1992.

Merino, Roberto. *Horas perdidas en las calles de Santiago.* Santiago: Editorial Sudamericana, 2000.

Miranda, Hector. *Los Calchakis: La mémoire en chantant.* Paris: F. X. de Guibert, 2004.

Morales T., Leonidas, and Nicanor Parra. *Conversaciones con Nicanor Parra.* Santiago: Editorial Universitaria, 1990.

Mouesca, Jacqueline. "Sergio Bravo: Pionero del cine documental chileno." *Araucaria de Chile,* no. 37 (1987): 102–10.

Mundt, Tito. *Memorias de un reporter.* Santiago: Editorial Orbe, 1965.

Musée des Arts Décoratifs. *Violeta Parra: Musée des Arts Décoratifs . . . Paris . . . 8 Avril–11 Mai 1964.* Paris: Musée des Arts Décoratifs, 1964.

Museo de Arte Popular Americano/Facultad de Bellas Artes, Universidad de Chile. *Museo de Arte Popular Americano.* Santiago: Editorial Universitaria, 1954. www.memoria chilena.gob.cl/602/w3-article-126732.html.

Museo de Arte Popular Americano/Instituto de Extensión de Artes Plásticas, Universidad de Chile. *Exposición de pintura instintiva.* Santiago: Museo de Arte Popular Americano, 1963.

Neruda, Pablo. *Confieso que he vivido: Memorias.* Barcelona: Editorial Seix Barral, 1974.

"Número extraordinario dedicado a los encuentros de escritores chilenos." *Atenea* 35, no. 380–81 (April–September 1958).

Oyarzún, Luis. "Crónica de una generacion." *Atenea* 35, no. 380–81 (April–September 1958): 180–89.

————. *Diario.* Colección memoria y testimonio. Concepción, Chile: Literatura Americana Reunida, 1990.

Palacios, Jorge. *Retrato hablado.* Santiago: Dolmen Ediciones, 1997.

Pancani, Dino, and Reiner Canales. *Los necios: Conversaciones con cantautores hispanoamericanos.* Santiago: LOM Ediciones, 1999.

Parra, Ángel. *Mi nueva canción chilena: Al pueblo lo que es del pueblo.* Santiago: Catalonia, 2016.

————. *Violeta se fue a los cielos.* Santiago: Catalonia, 2006.

Parra, Isabel. *El libro mayor de Violeta Parra.* Madrid, España: Ediciones Michay, 1985.

————. *El libro mayor de Violeta Parra: Un relato biográfico y testimonial.* 2. ed. Santiago: Editorial Cuarto Propio, 2009.

Parra, Nicanor. *Así habló Parra en El Mercurio.* Edited by María Teresa Cárdenas. Santiago: Aguilar Chilena de Ediciones, 2012.

————. *La cueca larga.* Editorial Universitaria, 1958.

————. *Poemas y antipoemas.* Santiago: Editorial Nascimiento, 1954.

————. "Poetas de la claridad por Nicanor Parra." *Atenea (Concepción),* no. 500 (Semester 2009): 179–83. (Speech originally delivered in 1958 at the Primer Encuentro de Escritores Chilenos, Universidad de Concepción, 1958.)

Parra, Nicanor, Niall Binns, and Ignacio Echevarría. *Obras completas & algo +*. Barcelona: Circulo de Lectores, Galaxia Gutenberg, 2006.

Parra, Roberto. *Décimas de la Negra Ester y otras yerbas*. Santiago: Editorial Fertíl Provincia, n.d.

———. *Las cuecas del tío Roberto—Memoria chilena*. Santiago: Autoediciones Populares/ Taller Lican Rumi, 1989.

———. *Roberto Parra: La vida que yo he pasado*. Edited by Ana María Moraga and Manuela Rojas C. Santiago: Pehuén Editores, 2012.

———. *Soy zurdo de nacimiento: Las cuecas de Roberto Parra*. Santiago: LOM Ediciones, 2011.

———. *Vida, pasión y muerte de Violeta Parra*. Edited by Miguel Naranjo Ríos. Santiago: Ediciones Tácitas, 2013.

Parra, Violeta. Recording of concert in home of Walther Grandjean, Geneva, Switzerland, 1963/1964, by F. J. Selleger. Mastered by Yves Cerf, 2006. www.youtube .com/watch?v=wVNhBPqPAds.

Parra Sandoval, Eduardo. *Eduardo "Lalo" Parra: Autobiografía en décimas*. Santiago: Sociedad Chilena del Derecho de Autor, 2001.

———. *Mi hermana Violeta Parra: Su vida y obra en décimas*. Santiago: LOM Ediciones, 1998.

Pereira Salas, Eugenio. "Los estudios folklóricos y el folklore musical de Chile." *Revista musical chilena* 1, no. 1 (May 1945): 4–12.

———. "Nota sobre los orígenes del Canto a lo Divino en Chile." *Revista musical chilena* 16, no. 79 (1962): 41–48.

Pérez Castelblanco, Javier. *La fotografía de Javier Pérez Castelblanco*. Santiago: Liquen, 2021.

Petreman, David A. "Entrevista con Francisco Coloane." *Hispania (USA)* 72, no. 3 (1989): 607–9.

Pizarro, Palmenia. "Alma en los labios, poesía en la canción." In *Wurlitzer: Cantantes en la memoria de la poesia chilena*, edited by Jorge Montealegre, 322–24. Santiago: Editorial Asterion, 2018.

Pizarro S., Gabriela. *Cuaderno de terreno: Apuntes sobre el romance en Chile*. Santiago: Autoediciones Populares, 1987.

Plath, Oreste. *Folklore religioso chileno*. Santiago: PlaTur, 1966.

Ramiro Quiroga, Juan Carlos. "Testimonios de Violeta Parra en La Paz." *Mar con Soroche*, no. 7 (March 2009): 5–16.

Rengifo Lira, Eugenio, and Catalina Rengifo Grau. *Los Cuatro Huasos: Alma de la tradición y del tiempo*. Santiago: Sociedad Chilena del Derecho de Autor, 2008.

Revista musical chilena. "Entrevista: Margot Loyola, intérprete de la danza y la canción de Chile." *Revista musical chilena* 12, no. 59 (January 1, 1958): 24–28.

Rodríguez, Osvaldo. *Cantores que reflexionan: Notas para una historia personal de la nueva cancion chilena*. Madrid: Literatura americana reunida, 1984.

Rodríguez Monegal, Emir. "Encuentros con Parra." *Números (2nd Epoch)* 1, no. 1 (June 1963): 57–74.

Rojas, Mario. *El que sae, sae: Crónica personal de la Cueca Brava*. Santiago: Ocho Libros, 2012.

Rokha, Pablo de, and Carlos Hermosilla. *Mundo a mundo: Epopeya popular realista; Estadio primero, Francia: Multitud*. Santiago: Multitud, 1966.

Ruiz Zamora, Agustín. "Conversando con Margot Loyola." *Revista musical chilena* 49, no. 183 (January–June 1995): 11–41.

———. "Discografía de Margot Loyola." *Revista musical chilena* 49, no. 183 (January–June 1995): 42–58.

Ruy-Pérez Benítez, Ofelia. *Cuarenta años de "Mañanitas campesinas."* Santiago: Ediciones Rumbos, 1991.

Salinas, Horacio. *La canción en el sombrero: Historia de la música de inti-illimani.* Santiago: Catalonia, 2013.

Sanhueza Herbage, Fernando, and Juan Orellana Peralta. *La juventud y la estrategia del comunismo internacional.* Santiago: Ed. Universidad Católica, 1962.

Sanjinés, Jorge. *Teoría y práctica de un cine junto al pueblo.* 2. ed. Artes. México: Siglo Veintiuno Editores, 1980.

Santa Cruz, Domingo. "Música Chilena en la Radio." *Revista musical chilena* 3, no. 19 (January 1, 1947): 3–10.

Štambuk, Patricia, and Patricia Bravo. *Violeta Parra: El canto de todos.* Santiago: Pehuén, 2011.

Stéphany, Pierre. "Notes sur la poésie chilienne." *Partisans*, no. 16 (August 1964): 53–58.

Stitchkin Branover, David. *Primer encuentro de escritores chilenos: Del 20 al 25 de enero de 1958.* Concepción: Impr. Lito Concepción, 1958.

Subercaseaux, Bernardo, and Jaime Londoño. *Gracias a la vida: Violeta Parra, testimonio.* Buenos Aires: Galerna, 1976.

Teitelboim, Volodia. *La vida. Una suma de historias.* Random House Mondadori S. A., 2003.

———. *Un hombre de edad media.* Santiago: Editorial Sudamericana, 1999.

Universidad de Chile, UNESCO. *Arte popular chileno: Definiciones, problemas, realidad actual.* Santiago: Universidad de Chile, 1959.

Universidad de Concepción. *VI Escuela Internacional de Verano: 1960.* Concepción: Universidad de Concepción, 1960.

Vega, Carlos. "La forma de la cueca chilena." *Revista musical chilena* 3, no. 20–21 (June 1947): 7–21.

Vera-Meiggs, David. "El eslabón encontrado (Entrevista a Nieves Yankovic y Jorge Di Lauro)." In *Nuestro cine: Colección Yankovic—Di Lauro*, 20–40. Cineteca Nacional de Chile, 2018.

Vial Lecaros, Ximena. *Cuando conocí a Nemesio . . . biografía oral sobre la vida de Nemesio Antúnez.* Santiago: Ediciones Taller 99, Diciembre 2019.

Vicuña, Magdalena. "Entrevista: Violeta Parra, hermana mayor de los cantores populares." *Revista musical chilena* 12, no. 60 (1958): 71–77.

Walsh, María Elena. *Diario brujo, 1995–1999.* Buenos Aires: Espasa, 1999.

———. *Fantasmas en el parque.* Buenos Aires: Alfaguara: Aguilar, Altea, Taurus, 2008.

———. *Viajes y homenajes.* Buenos Aires: Suma de Letras Argentina, 2004.

Warnken, Cristián. *La otra fiesta: Conversaciones con Cristián Warnken.* Santiago: BHP Billiton, 2011.

Weiss, Jason. "An Interview with Alejandro Jodorowsky." *Taxi Rain* (online edition), Winter 1999. https://raintaxi.com/an-interview-with-alejandro-jodorowsky/.

Wiéner, Jean. *Allegro appassionato.* Paris: P. Belfond, 1978.

Zaldívar, Mario. "Julita Cortés." In *Costarricenses en la música: Conversaciones con protagonistas de la música popular 1939–1959*, 155–61. San José, Costa Rica: Editorial de la Universidad de Costa Rica, 2006.

Secondary Sources

Acevedo, Nano. *Folkloristas chilenos: Retratos verídicos 1900–1950*. Santiago: Cantoral Ediciones, 2004.

Adlington, Robert, ed. *Red Strains: Music and Communism Outside the Communist Bloc*. Proceedings of the British Academy. Oxford: Published for the British Academy by Oxford University Press, 2013.

Advis, Luis, and Juan Pablo González Rodríguez. *Clásicos de la música popular chilena*. Vol. 1, *1900–1960*. Santiago: Sociedad Chilena del Derecho de Autor; Ediciones Universidad Católica de Chile, 1994.

———. *Clásicos de la música popular chilena*. Vol. 2, *1960–1973*. Santiago: Sociedad Chilena del Derecho de Autor; Ediciones Universidad Católica de Chile, 1998.

Agosín, Marjorie. "Bibliografía de Violeta Parra." *Revista interamericana de bibliografía* 32, no. 2 (1982): 179–90.

———. *A Dream of Light and Shadow: Portraits of Latin American Women Writers*. Albuquerque: University of New Mexico Press, 1995.

———. "Violeta Parra, pintora: Su talento desconocido." *Plural*, December 1989.

Agosín, Marjorie, and Inés Dölz Blackburn. *Violeta Parra, santa de pura greda: Un estudio de su obra poética*. Santiago: Planeta Biblioteca del sur, 1988.

Aguirre, Lautaro, and Victoria Castillo. "Gabriela Pizarro: La lucha por una cultura popular." *Araucaria de Chile*, no. 38 (1987): 77–82.

Alburquerque Fuschini, Germán. "La red de escritores latinoamericanos en los años sesenta." *Revista Universum Universidad de Talca*, no. 15 (2000): 337–50.

Alcalde, Alfonso. *Toda Violeta Parra: Antología de canciones y poemas*. 5. ed. Buenos Aires: Ed. de la Flor, 1981.

Alegría, Fernando. "Nicanor Parra, el anti-poeta." *Cuadernos Americanos* 110, no. 3 (June 1956): 209–20.

———. *Poesía chilena en el siglo XX*. Santiago: Ediciones Literatura Americana Reunida, 2007.

———. "Violeta Parra." In *Creadores en el mundo Hispánico*. Santiago: Editorial Andrés Bello, 1990.

Alegría, Fernando, Patricio Manns, and Osvaldo Rodríguez. "Violeta Parra: Veinte años de ausencia." *Araucaria de Chile*, no. 38 (1987): 101–11.

Alfaro M., Elena, ed. *44 Muestra internacional de Artesanía UC, Violeta artesana, año 2017*. Published in conjunction with an exhibition of the same title, organized by and presented at the Parque Bustamante de Providencia in Santiago, 2017. https://issuu.com/artesaniauc/docs/catalogo_artesaniauc_violeta_artesa.

Alten, Michèle. "Le Chant du Monde: Une firme discographique au service du progressisme (1945–1980)." *Les cahiers de l'ILCEA*, no. 16 (2012). https://doi.org/10.4000/ilcea.1411.

———. *Musiciens français dans la guerre froide, 1945–1956: L'indépendance artistique face au politique*. Logiques sociales, Musiques et champ social. Paris: L'Harmattan, 2001.

Álvarez Vallejos, Rolando. "Ser comunista en Chile: Identidad y cultura política en tiempos de pasión revolucionaria (1965–1973)." In *Arriba los pobres del mundo: Cultura e identidad politica del partido communista de Chile entre democracia y dictadura, 1965–1990.* Santiago: LOM Ediciones, 2011.

Álvarez Vallejos, Rolando, Manuel Loyola, and Olga Ulianova, eds. *1912–2012 El siglo de los comunistas chilenos.* Ariadna Ediciones, Instituto de Estudios Avanzados de la Universidad de Santiago, 2012.

Antezana-Pernet, Corinne. "Peace in the World and Democracy at Home: The Chilean Women's Movement in the 1940s." In *Latin America in the 1940s: War and Postwar Transitions,* edited by David Rock, 166–86. Berkeley: University of California Press, 1994.

Antúnez, Nemesio, ed. *Pintura instintiva chilena: Museo Nacional de Bellas Artes.* Santiago: n.p., 1972.

Antúnez, Nemesio, and Hernán Garfias. *Carta aérea.* Santiago: Editorial Los Andes, 1988.

Aparicio, Frances R., and Cándida Frances Jáquez. *Musical Migrations: Transnationalism and Cultural Hybridity in Latin/o America.* New York: Palgrave Macmillan, 2003.

Arauco, María Antonieta. *Los Jairas y El Trío Domínguez, Favre, Cavour: Creadores del neo-folklore en Bolivia (1966–1973).* La Paz, Bolivia: All Press Labores Gráficos, 2011.

Aravena-Décart, Jorge. "Música popular y discurso académico: A propósito de la legitimación culta de las 'anticuecas' de Violeta Parra." *Revista musical chilena* 58, no. 202 (December 2004): 9–25.

———. "Opciones armónicas, estilo musical y construcción identitaria: Una aproximación al aporte de Violeta Parra en relación con la música típica." *Revista musical chilena* 55, no. 196 (2001): 33–58.

———. "Représentations et fonctions sociales des musiques d'inspiration andine en France (1951–1973)." PhD diss., Université de Franche-Comté, 2011.

Aravena Llanca, Jorge. *Lo visible indecible en Violeta Parra: Un mito de iniciación obsesiva.* Santiago: Palabra e Imagen, 2017.

Araya, Juan Gabriel. *Nicanor en Chillán.* Concepción, Chile: Ediciones Universidad del Bio-Bio, 2000.

Arenas, Desiderio. *Margot Loyola.* Santiago: Sociedad Chilena del Derecho de Autor, 1998.

Arenas Codou, Mario. *Geografía humana de la provincia de Ñuble.* Concepción, Chile: Universidad de Concepción, 1963.

Ariz Castillo, Yenny. "La ciudad de Concepción en la vida y en la obra de Violeta Parra." In *Diálogos para el Bicentenario: Concepción-Alicante,* edited by María Nieves Alonso and Carmen Alemany Bay, 67–80. Concepción, Chile: Editorial Universidad de Concepción, 2011.

Arqueros, Gonzalo. "Violeta Parra: La muerte del Angelito." In MAC (Museo de Art Contemporánea), Facultad de Artes, Universidad de Chile. *Catálogo razonado: Colección MAC,* 459–62. Santiago: Museo de Arte Contemporánea, 2017.

Arriagada Veyl, Patricio, Víctor Ibarra B, and Javiera Müller Blanco, eds. *El Semanario Pro Arte: Difusión y crítica cultural (1948–1956).* Santiago: RIL editores, 2013.

Artières, Philippe, and Michelle Zancarini-Fournel, eds. *68: Une histoire collective, 1962–1981.* Paris: La Découverte, 2008.

Arzola S., Benicio. *San Carlos, Ñuble: Su tierra, sus hombres, su historia.* Santiago: n.p., 1989.

Ascher, Carol, Louise A. DeSalvo, and Sara Ruddick, eds. *Between Women: Biographers, Novelists, Critics, Teachers, and Artists Write about Their Work on Women.* Boston, Mass.: Beacon, 1984.

Astorga Arredondo, Francisco. "El canto a lo poeta." *Revista musical chilena* 54, no. 194 (2000): 56–64.

———. "El universo del guitarrón chileno." *Aisthesis* 33 (2000): 219–25.

Atkinson, David. "The English Revival Canon: Child Ballads and the Invention of Tradition." *Journal of American Folklore* 114, no. 453 (2001): 370–80.

Austerlitz, Paul. "Birch-Bark Horns and Jazz in the National Imagination: The Finnish Folk Music Vogue in Historical Perspective." *Ethnomusicology* 44, no. 2 (2000): 183–213.

Bach, Caleb. "A Child's Wisdom in a Poet's Heart." *Americas* 47, no. 3 (May/June 1995): 12–17.

Badal, Gonzalo. *Roberto Parra.* Santiago: Ocho Libros Editores, 1996.

Bareiro Saguier, Ruben. "La literatura latinoamericana en Francia." *Mundo Nuevo,* no. 30 (December 1968): 52–66.

Barraza, Fernando. *La nueva canción chilena.* Santiago: Editora Nacional Quimantú, 1972.

Barr-Melej, Patrick. "Imaginando el campo: Nacionalismo cultural, política y la búsqueda de la chilenidad, 1891–1941." In *Nacionalismos e identidad nacional en Chile, siglo XX,* edited by Gabriel Cid and Alejandro San Francisco, 93–130. East Santiago: Ediciones Centro de Estudios Bicentenario, 2010.

———. *Psychedelic Chile.* Chapel Hill: University of North Carolina Press, 2017.

———. *Reforming Chile: Cultural Politics, Nationalism, and the Rise of the Middle Class.* Chapel Hill: University of North Carolina Press, 2001.

Barros, Raquel, and Manuel Dannemann. *El romancero chileno.* Santiago: Universidad de Chile, 1970.

Bartley, Russell H. "The Piper Played to Us All: Orchestrating the Cultural Cold War in the USA, Europe, and Latin America." *International Journal of Politics, Culture, and Society* 14, no. 3 (2001): 571–619.

Bauer, Arnold J. *Chilean Rural Society from the Spanish Conquest to 1930.* New York: Cambridge University Press, 1975.

Bayly, C. A., et al. "AHR Conversation: On Transnational History." *American Historical Review* 111, no. 5 (2006): 1441–64.

Bello Gómez, Giovanni Enrique, and Tomás Augosto Fernández Tejerina. "Peña Naira: ¿Ruptura o continuidad en el folklore boliviano?" In *Anales de la Reunión Anual de Etnología,* edited by Museo Nacional de Etnografía y Folklore (MUSEF), 329–40. La Paz, Bolivia: MUSEF, 2012.

Bendix, Regina. *In Search of Authenticity: The Formation of Folklore Studies.* Madison: University of Wisconsin Press, 1997.

Benedetti, Mario. *Daniel Viglietti, Desalambrando.* Buenos Aires: Seix Barral, 2007.

Bengoa, José. *La comunidad perdida: Ensayos sobre identidad y cultura; Los desafíos de la modernización en Chile.* Santiago: Ediciones SUR, 1996.

———. *Haciendas y campesinos.* Vol. 2 of *Historia social de la agricultura chilena.* Santiago: Ediciones SUR, 1988.

———. *El poder y la subordinación: Acerca del origen rural del poder y la subordinación en Chile.* Vol. 6 of *Historia social de la agricultura chilena.* Santiago: Ediciones SUR, 1988.

Berman, Marshall. *The Politics of Authenticity: Radical Individualism and the Emergence of Modern Society*. New York: Verso, 2009.

Bernard, Andrew. "Chile." In *Latin America between the Second World War and the Cold War, 1944–1948*, edited by Leslie Bethell and Ian Roxborough, 66–91. New York: Cambridge University Press, 1992.

Bernard, Jean-Pierre A. *Paris rouge: 1944–1964; Les communistes français dans la capitale, Epoques*. Seyssel: Champ Vallon, 1991.

Berthet, Dominique. *Le P.C.F., la culture et l'art, 1947–1954*. Paris: Table Ronde, 1990.

Bethell, Leslie. *Chile since Independence*. New York: Cambridge University Press, 1993.

Bethell, Leslie, and Ian Roxborough. *Latin America between the Second World War and the Cold War, 1944–1948*. Cambridge: Cambridge University Press, 1997.

Bigenho, Michelle. *Sounding Indigenous: Authenticity in Bolivian Music Performance*. New York: Palgrave, 2002.

Birchall, Ian. "Third World and After." *New Left Review* 80 (March–April 2013): 151–60.

Bisama, Álvaro. "Daniel Divinsky: 'Yo Pensaba Que Estaba Contribuyendo a La Revolución'—Revista Dossier." *Dossier*, no. 22 (November 2013): 18–23.

———. *Mala lengua: Un retrato de Pablo de Rokha*. Madrid: Alfaguara, 2020.

Bithell, Caroline, and Juniper Hill, eds. *The Oxford Handbook of Music Revival*. New York: Oxford University Press, 2014.

Boyle, Catherine. "'Gracias a La Vida': Violeta Parra and the Creation of a Public Poetics of Introspective Reflection." *Hispanic Research Journal* 10, no. 1 (2009): 70–85.

Boynik, Sezgin, and Taneli Viitahuhta, eds. *Free Jazz Communism: Archie Shepp-Bill Dixon Quartet at the 8th World Festival of Youth and Students in Helsinki 1962*. Helsinki: Rab-Rab Press, 2019.

Bradu, Fabienne. *El volcán y el sosiego: Una biografía de Gonzalo Rojas*. Ciudad de México: Fondo de Cultura Económica, 2016.

Briggs, Jonathyne. *Sounds French: Globalization, Cultural Communities, and Pop Music, 1958–1980*. New York: Oxford University Press, 2015.

Brizuela, Leopoldo. "Leda Valladares." In *Cantar la vida: Reportajes a cinco cantantes Argentina*, 39–70. Buenos Aires: Libreria "El Ateneo" Editorial, 1992.

Brocken, Michael. *The British Folk Revival*. Aldershot: Ashgate, 2003.

Brumfield, Susan Hendrix. "Jean Ritchie's Field Trip—Scotland: An Examination of Unpublished Field Recordings Collected in Scotland, 1952–53." PhD diss., University of Oklahoma, 2000.

Brunhammer, Yvonne. *Le Beau dans l'utile: Un musée pour les arts décoratifs*. Paris: Découvertes Gallimard, Mémoire des lieux, 1992.

Bucci Abalos, Ennio. "Las galerías de arte en Chile." *Alas y Raices* no. 1 (1999): 56–59.

Burton, Antoinette, and Marilyn Booth, eds. "Critical Feminist Biography II." *Journal of Women's History* 21, no. 3 (2009): 7–12.

Cáceres, Alicia, and Juan Reyes. *Artesanía urbana en Chile*. Santiago: Ministerio de las Culturas, las Artes y el Patrimonio, 2019.

———. *Historia hecha con las manos: Nosotros los artesanos y las ferias de artesanía del siglo XX*. Santiago: Consejo Nacional de la Cultura y las Artes, 2008.

Cáceres Valencia, Jorge. *La Universidad de Chile y su aporte a la cultura tradicional chilena, 1933–1953*. La Florida, Chile: Impr. Esparza, Santiago, 1998.

Cajías, Lupe. *Antes de que me anochezca: 40 años contando historias*. La Paz, Bolivia: Grupo Impresor, 2018.

———. "Los últimos días de Violeta Parra y su visita a Peña Naira." In *Antes de que me anochezca: 40 años contando historias*, 50–52. La Paz, Bolivia: Grupo Impresor, 2018.

———. "'Peña Naira: Veinte años de música y compromiso." In *Antes de que me anochezca: 40 años contando historias*, 47–48. La Paz, Bolivia: Grupo Impresor, 2018.

Canales Cabezas, Reiner. "De los cantos folklóricos chilenos a las décimas: Trayectoria de una utopía en Violeta Parra." MA thesis, Universidad de Chile, 2005.

Cánepa, Gina. "Violeta Parra's Arpilleras: Vernacular Culture as a Pathway to Aesthetic Self-Determination." In *Stitching Resistance: Women, Creativity, and Fiber Arts*, edited by Marjorie Agosín, 181–99. Kent: Solis, 2014.

———. "Violeta Parra y la cultura popular chilena." In *Homenaje a Alejandro Losada*, edited by José Morales Saravia, 113. Lima, Perú: Latinoamericana Editores, 1987.

Cánepa-Hurtado, Gina. "La cancion de lucha en Violeta Parra y su ubicacion en el complejo cultural chileno entre los años 1960 a 1973." *Revista de crítica literaria latinoamericana* 9, no. 17 (1983): 147–70.

Cantwell, Robert. *When We Were Good: Class and Culture in the Folk Revival*. Cambridge, Mass.: Harvard University Press, 1996.

Carol, Alberto Jorge. "Violeta en sus tapices." *Casa de Las Américas* 12, no. 70 (February 1972): 143–48.

Carrasco, Eduardo. *Quilapayún: La revolución y las estrellas*. Santiago: Las Ediciones del Ornitorrinco, 1988.

Carrasco, Lorena Valdebenito. "La vida y la muerte: Intertextualidad y representación de lo femenino en dos mujeres homenajeadas por Violeta Parra." *Artelogie*, no. 13 (January 30, 2019). http://journals.openedition.org/artelogie/2898.

Carreño Bolívar, Rubí. *Av. Independencia: Literatura, música e ideas de Chile disidente*. Santiago: Editorial Cuarto Propio, 2013.

———. "Libercueca: Biopoéticas del sexo y la fusión en la cueca urbana chilena." *Revista de crítica literaria latinoamericana* 36, no. 71 (2010): 151–67.

Casa de las Américas. "Violeta Parra [special issue]." *Música*, no. 32 (1973).

Casanova, Vincent. "Jalons pour une histoire du Chant Du Monde à l'heure de la guerre froide (1945–1953)." *Bulletin de l"institut Pierre Renouvin*, no. 18 (Spring 2004): 141–62.

Castillo, Sergio. "Castillo, Escultor." In *Sergio Castillo Catálogo Obra entre los años 60s al 90s*, edited by Silvia Westermann, 7–61. Santiago: Silvia Westermann, 1997.

Cavour Aramayo, Ernesto. *El charango: Su vida, costumbres y desventuras*. 3rd ed. La Paz, Bolivia: Producciones CIMA, 2003.

Céspedes, Gilka Wara. "New Currents in 'Música Folklórica' in La Paz, Bolivia." *Latin American Music Review* 5, no. 2 (1984): 217–42.

Chamorro Ríos, Catalina, and Vania Perret Neilson. *Memoria del flamenco en Chile: Relatos y fotografías de una historia vivida*. Valparaíso: RIL Editores, 2020.

Chamosa, Oscar. *Breve historia del folclore argentino 1920–1970: Identidad, política y nación*. Buenos Aires: EDHASA Argentina, 2012.

Chauveau, Philippe. 1999. *Les Théâtres Parisiens Disparus: 1402–1986*. Paris: Amandier.

Christiansen, Samantha, and Zachary A. Scarlett, eds. *The Third World in the Global 1960s*. New York: Berghahn Books, 2013.

Cid, Gabriel, ed. *Nacionalismos e identidad nacional en Chile: Siglo XX*. Santiago: Ediciones Centro de Estudios Bicentenario, 2010.

Cineteca Nacional de Chile. *Nuestro cine: Colección Yankovic–Di Lauro*. Santiago: Cineteca Nacional de Chile, 2018. www.cclm.cl/wp-content/uploads/2020/06/1800207_librillo _NUESTRO_CINE_YANKOVIC-DI_LAURO2.pdf.

Clifford, James. *The Predicament of Culture: Twentieth-Century Ethnography, Literature, and Art*. Cambridge, Mass.: Harvard University Press, 1988.

Cohen, Robert D. *Rainbow Quest: The Folk Music Revival and American Society, 1940–1970*. Amherst: University of Massachusetts Press, 2002.

Collectif. *Les musiques du monde en question*. Internationale de l'imaginaire 11. Paris: Actes Sud, 1999.

Collier, Simon, and William F. Sater. *A History of Chile, 1808–2002*. 2nd ed. Cambridge: Cambridge University Press, 2004.

Concha Molinari, Olivia. "Violeta Parra, compositora." *Revista musical chilena* 49, no. 183 (June 1995): 71–106.

Consejo Nacional de la Cultura y las Artes. *Después de vivir un siglo*. Santiago: Consejo Nacional de la Cultura y las Artes, 2017.

Contreras, Eduardo. *Violeta Parra, el origen del canto*. Cuadernos Casa de Chile 27. México, D.F.: Casa de Chile en México, 1979.

Contreras Román, Raúl H. "El pueblo creador representado: Margot Loyola y Violeta Parra en el encuentro de la izquierda y la música folclórica en Chile." *Cuicuilco revista de ciencias antropológicas* 23, no. 66 (August 2016): 197–221.

Contreras Uribe, Simón. "Encuentros de escritores en Concepción: Relaciones sociales, políticas e intelectuales." *Revista de humanidades*, no. 43 (June 2021): 325–47.

Cornell, Diane E. "The Performance of Gender: Five Comparative Biographies of Women Performers in Música Popular Chilena." PhD diss., University of Illinois at Urbana-Champaign, 2001.

Cornell, Richard. *Youth and Communism: An Historical Analysis of International Communist Youth Movements*. New York: Walker, 1965.

Costa, René de. *Conversaciones con Parra: Chicago, 1987*. Santiago: Banco Estado, 2016.

Costa Garcia, Tânia da. "Canción popular, nacionalismo, consumo y política en Chile entre los años 40 y 60." *Revista musical chilena* 63, no. 212 (2009): 11–28.

———. "Reconfigurando la canción, reinventando la nación: La folclorización de la música popular en Brasil y en Chile en los años cuarenta y cincuenta." *Historia (Chile)* 45, no. 1 (2012): 49–68.

Cox, Loreto. "Divorcio en Chile: Un análisis preliminar tras la nueva Ley de matrimonio civil." *Estudios públicos*, no. 123 (Winter 2011): 97–101.

Cross Gantes, Amalia. "Pintura instintiva: Sobre la invención de un concepto y su definición histórica." *Revista 180*, no. 37 (2016): 1–6.

Crow, Joanna. *The Mapuche in Modern Chile: A Cultural History*. Gainesville: University Press of Florida, 2013.

Cuevas Estivil, Patricia Virginia. "Imagens poéticas e decolonização na obra de Violeta Parra." PhD diss., Universidade Estadual do Oeste do Paraná, 2018.

Dannemann, Manuel. "Aportes de la sociedad chilena de historia y geografía al estudio de la cultura folclórica." *Revista chilena de historia y geografía*, no. 171 (2011): 179–96.

Dannemann, Manuel, and Eduardo Castro Le-Fort. *Enciclopedia del folclore de Chile*. Santiago: Editorial Universitaria, 1998.

Davenport, Lisa E. *Jazz Diplomacy: Promoting America in the Cold War Era*. Jackson: University Press of Mississippi, 2009.

Díaz-Inostroza, Patricia. Violeta y Gilbert: Una historia de amor, locura y música. Patricia Díaz-Inostroza, 2023.

Dillon, Lorna. "Defiant Art: The Feminist Dialectic in Violeta Parra's Arpilleras." In *Identity, Nation, Discourse: Latin American Women Writers and Artists*, edited by Claire Taylor, 53–66. Newcastle upon Tyne, UK: Cambridge Scholars Publishing, 2009.

———. "Religion and the Angel's Wake Tradition in Violeta Parra's Art and Lyrics." *Taller de Letras*, no. 59 (2020): 91–109.

———. "Repositioning the Popular: The Hybrid Aesthetics of Violeta Parra's Paintings Machitún, Las Tres Pascualas, and Casamiento de Negros." *Studies in Latin American Popular Culture* 36 (2018): 145–60.

———. "The Representation of History and Politics in Violeta Parra's Art: The Political Dialectic of Violeta Parra's Art." In *Seeing in Spanish: From Don Quixote to Daddy Yankee—22 Essays on Hispanic Visual Cultures*, edited by Ryan Prout and Tilmann Altenberg, 252–65. Newcastle upon Tyne, UK: Cambridge Scholars Publishing, 2011.

———, ed. *Violeta Parra: Life and Work*. Woodbridge, Suffolk: Tamesis, 2017.

———. *Violeta Parra's Visual Art: Painted Songs*. Cham, Switzerland: Palgrave Macmillan, 2020.

Djagalov, Rossen. "Guitar Poetry, Democratic Socialism, and the Limits of 1960s Internationalism." In *The Socialist Sixties: Crossing Borders in the Second World*, edited by Anne E. Gorsuch and Diane P. Koenker, 148–66. Bloomington: Indiana University Press, 2013.

Dölz Blackburn, Inés. *Origen y desarrollo de la poesía tradicional y popular chilena desde la conquista hasta el presente*. Santiago: Editorial Nascimento, 1984.

———. "Valorización y perfil de Violeta Parra a través de la prensa chilena, 1967–1990: Una evaluación cronológica." *Revista interamericana de bibliografía* 41, no. 3 (1991): 436–69.

Dölz Blackburn, Inés, and Marjorie Agosín. *Violeta Parra, o La expresión inefable: Un análisis crítico de su poesía, prosa, y pintura*. Santiago: Editorial Planeta Chilena, 1992.

Domínguez, Delia. "Nicanor Parra: La vida sin santos tapados." *Paula* (October 23, 1979): 64–71.

Domínguez, Irene, and Cristián Vila Riquelme. "Despedida a Adela Gallo." *Araucaria de Chile*, no. 26 (1984): 219.

Donoso Fritz, Karen. "La batalla del folklore: Los conflictos de la representación de la cultura popular chilena en el siglo XX." BA thesis, Universidad de Santiago, 2006.

Drott, Eric. "Music, the Fête de l'Humanité, and Demographic Change in Post-War France." In *Red Strains: Music and Communism Outside the Communist Bloc*, edited by Robert Adlington, 105–18. Proceedings of the British Academy. Oxford: Published for the British Academy by Oxford University Press, 2013.

Drysdale, Sabine. "Violeta Parra: La violenta Parra." In *Extremas*, edited by Leila Guerriero, 479–520. Santiago: Ediciones Universidad Diego Portales, 2019.

Drysdale, Sabine, and Marcela Escobar. *Nicanor Parra: La vida de un poeta*. Santiago: Ediciones B, 2018.

Ducci González, Pilar. *Años de circo: Historia de la actividad circense en Chile.* Barcelona, Spain: Circus Arts Foundation, 2012.

Dujovne Ortiz, Alicia. *María Elena Walsh.* Madrid: Ediciones Júcar, Los Juglares, 1982.

Echeverría, Mónica. *Yo, Violeta.* Santiago: Plaza Janés, 2010.

Edwards, Jorge. *Diálogos en un tejado.* Barcelona: Tusquets Editores, 2003.

Egaña Baraona, María Loreto, Iván Núñez P., and Cecilia Salinas. *La educación primaria en Chile, 1860–1930: Una aventura de niñas y maestras.* Santiago: LOM Ediciones: PIIE, 2003.

Elena, Eduardo. "Argentina in Black and White: Race, Peronism, and the Color of Politics, 1940s to the Present." In *Rethinking Race in Modern Argentina*, edited by Paulina L. Alberto and Eduardo Elena, 184–209. New York: Cambridge University Press, 2016.

Engelbert, Manfred. *Lieder aus Chile: Zweisprachige Anthologie = Canciones de Chile: antología bilingüe.* Ediciones de Iberoamericana. Frankfurt am Main: Vervuert, 2017.

———. "Poesia y pintura en la vida de Violeta Parra." Paper presented at First International Literature & Critical Latin American, Berlín, 1989, 91–110.

Epple, Juan Armando. "Notas sobre la cueca larga de Violeta Parra." *Cuadernos americanos* 224, no. 3 (1979): 232–48.

———. "Violeta Parra: Una memoria poético-musical." *Revista de música y literatura* 1, no. 1 (April 1994): 79–95.

———. "Violeta Parra y la cultura popular chilena." *Revista literatura chilena en el exilio*, no. 2 (1977): 4–11.

Eyerman, Ron, and Scott Barretta. "From the 30s to the 60s: The Folk Music Revival in the United States." *Theory and Society* 25, no. 4 (1996): 501–43.

Facuse, Marisol, and Humberto Olea. "Poesía y resistencia en el Canto a lo poeta en Chile." In *Poésie et praxis*, edited by Jean Pierre Faye and Nina Zivancevic, 95–110. Paris: Editions L'Harmattan, 2013.

Facuse, Marisol, Eric Villagordo, and Juan Enrique Serrano Moreno, eds. "Violeta Parra: Autenticidad, primitivismo y procesos de exotización en los artistas latinoamericanos." Special issue. *Artelogie*, no. 13 (2019). https://journals.openedition.org/artelogie/1704.

Fairley, Jan. "La Nueva Canción Latinoamericana." *Bulletin of Latin American Research* 3, no. 2 (1984): 107–15.

Fernández, Marcos, ed. *Arriba quemando el sol: Estudios de historia social chilena; Experiencias populares de trabajo, revuelta y autonomía, 1830–1940.* Santiago: LOM Ediciones, 2004.

Ferrer, Cecilia. "Alberto Quintanilla: Un andino universal." *Voces: Revista cultural de Lima*, December 2001.

Fields, Marek. *Defending Democracy in Cold War Finland: British and American Propaganda and Cultural Diplomacy in Finland, 1944–1970.* Vol. 7 of *New Perspectives on the Cold War.* Boston: Brill, 2019.

Figueroa, Ana. "Gonzalo Rojas y los encuentros de escritores de la Universidad de Concepción." *Mapocho*, no. 55 (First Semester 2004): 71–85.

Fosler-Lussier, Danielle. *Music in America's Cold War Diplomacy.* Oakland: University of California Press, 2015.

Franco, Jean. *The Decline and Fall of the Lettered City: Latin America in the Cold War.* Cambridge, Mass.: Harvard University Press, 2002.

Friedl Zapata, José Antonio. *Tania la guerrillera: La enigmática espía a la sombra del Che.* Bogotá, Colombia: Planeta, 1999.

Fuenzalida, Héctor. "Nicanor Parra, collage con artefacto." *Boletín de la Universidad de Chile* 102–3 (June–July 1970): 62–73.

Fugellie, Daniela. "'Les tapisseries chiliennes de Violeta Parra': Perspectivas sobre una exposición realizada en el Museo de Artes Decorativas del Palacio del Louvre en 1964." *Artelogie*, no. 13 (January 30, 2019). http://journals.openedition.org/artelogie/3153.

Gallardo, Sebastián. "Canto a Lo Poeta e industria discográfica: Problemáticas de una exclusión." *Revista chilena de literatura*, no. 78 (January 1, 2011).

García, Marisol. *Canción valiente.* Santiago: Penguin Random House Grupo Editorial Chile, 2013.

———. "Violeta Parra en plural." *Estudios públicos*, no. 146 (July 14, 2017).

García Canclini, Néstor. *Hybrid Cultures: Strategies for Entering and Leaving Modernity.* Minneapolis: University of Minnesota Press, 1995.

———. *Transforming Modernity: Popular Culture in Mexico.* Translations from Latin America Series. Austin: University of Texas Press, 1993.

Garcin, Jérôme, Daniel Garcia, and Lionel Leforestier. *Le masque et la plume.* Paris: 10/18 France-Inter, 2005.

Gavagnin, Stefano. "Violet(t)a Parra, presente-ausente: Trayectoria de su recepción italiana entre 1964 y 2000." *Artelogie*, no. 13 (January 30, 2019). http://journals .openedition.org/artelogie/3045.

Gavagnin, Stefano, Laura Jordán González, and Javier Rodríguez Aedo. "Fronteras porosas, sonidos conectados: Transnacionalidad de la Nueva Canción a través de sus escritos." *Cuadernos de música iberoamericana*, no. 35 (September 8, 2022): 39–71.

Gérôme, Noëlle, and Danielle Tartakovsky. *La Fête de l'Humanité: Culture communiste, culture populaire.* Paris: Messidor/Editions Sociales, 1988.

Giddens, Anthony. *Modernity and Self-Identity: Self and Society in the Late Modern Age.* Stanford, Calif.: Stanford University Press, 1991.

Gildea, Robert. *France since 1945.* 2nd ed. New York: Oxford University Press, 2002.

Gillabert, Matthieu. "Varsovie 1955 et la Guerre froide globale: L'internationalisation de l'Europe centrale au prisme du 5e Festival mondial de la jeunesse et des étudiants." *Monde(s)*, no. 18 (November 2020): 51–72.

Glants, Musya, and Pamela Kachurin. "Special Issue: Culture, the Soviet Union, and the Cold War." *Journal of Cold War Studies* 4, no. 1 (2002): 3–5.

Glenn, Matthias. "Coco & rock à La Fête de l'Humanité. Usage politique de la musique rock et pop." In *Musique, Pouvoirs, Politiques,* edited by Philippe Gonin and Philippe Poirrier, n.p. *Territoires contemporains* (online), no. 6 (February 5, 2016). http://tristan .u-bourgogne.fr/CGC/prodscientifique/TC.html.

Goldberg, K. *Border Trespasses: The Gypsy Mask and Carmen Amaya's Flamenco Dance.* PhD diss., Temple University, 1995.

———. "A 'Heart of Darkness' in the New World: Carmen Amaya's Flamenco Dance in South American Vaudeville." *Choreography and Dance* 3, no. 4 (1994): 95–108.

Gómez A., Exequiel, and Elda Sepúlveda V. *Gabriela Pizarro Soto y su andar en el folklore chileno.* Santiago: Fondart, 2002.

Gómez Gálvez, Mauricio, and Javier Rodríguez Aedo. "'Entre la hoz y el martillo': Vínculos entre música culta, folklore y política en Chile durante la Guerra Fría (1947–1973)." *Amérique latine histoire et mémoire, les cahiers ALHIM*, no. 35 (June 21, 2018).

Góngora Díaz, María Eugenia. "La poesía popular chilena del siglo XIX." *Revista chilena de literatura*, no. 51 (1997): 5–27.

Góngora Escobedo, Álvaro, and Rafael Sagredo B. *Fragmentos para una historia del cuerpo en Chile*. Santiago: Aguilar Chilena de Ediciones, 2010.

González, Yanko. "Primeras culturas juveniles en Chile: Pánico, Malones, Pololeo y Matiné." *Atenea (Concepción)*, no. 503 (2011): 11–38.

González Rodríguez, Juan Pablo. "The Chilean Way to the Andes: Music, Politics and Otherness." *Diagonal: Journal of the Center for Iberian and Latin American Music* 2 (2009): 1–7.

———. "Chile y los festivales de la canción comprometida." *Boletín música, casa de las Américas*, no. 45 (Junio 2017): 5–23.

———. "Colonialidad y poscolonialidad en la escucha: América latina en el cuarto centenario." In *Música, musicología y colonialismo*, edited by C. Aharonián, 81–100. Montevideo: Centro Nacional de Documentación Musical Lauro Ayestarán, 2011.

———. "Cristalización genérica en la música popular chilena de los años sesenta." *TRANS—Revista transcultural de música*, no. 3 (1997). www.sibetrans.com/trans /articulo/264/cristalizacion-generica-en-la-musica-popular-chilena-de-los-anos-sesenta.

———. "El canto mediatizado: Breve historia de la llegada del cantante a nuestra casa." *Revista musical chilena* 54, no. 194 (2000): 26–40.

———. "Estilo y función social de la música chilena de Raíz Mapuche." *Revista musical chilena* 47, no. 179 (1993): 78–113.

———. "Evocación, modernización y reivindicación del folclore en la música popular chilena: El papel de la 'performance.'" *Revista musical chilena* 50, no. 185 (1996): 25–37.

———. "La mujer sube a la escena: Estrellas de la canción en el Chile del sesquicentenario." *Neuma (Talca)*, no.1 (December 1, 2010): 10–33.

———. "Llamando al Otro: Construcción de la alteridad en la música popular chilena." *Resonancias: Revista de investigación musical* 1, no. 1 (November 1997): 60–68.

———. "Música chilena andina 1970–1975: Construcción de una identidad doblemente desplazada." *Cuadernos de música iberoamericana* 24 (2012): 175–86.

———, ed. *Música y mujer en Iberoamérica: Haciendo música desde la condición de género*, Actas del III Coloquio de Ibermúsicas sobre investigación musical. Santiago: Ibermúsicas, August 2017.

———. "Tradición, identidad y vanguardia en la música chilena de la década de 1960." *Aisthesis* 38 (2005): 193–212.

———. "Violeta Parra y la nueva canción chilena." *Revista todavía*, no. 14 (August 2006): 48–51.

González Rodríguez, Juan Pablo, Fernando Carrasco, and Juan Antonio Sánchez. *Violeta Parra: Tres discos autorales*. Santiago: Ediciones Universidad Alberto Hurtado, 2018.

González Rodríguez, Juan Pablo, Oscar Ohlsen, and Claudio Rolle. *Historia social de la música popular en Chile, 1950–1970*. Santiago: Ediciones Universidad Católica de Chile, 2009.

González Rodríguez, Juan Pablo, and Claudio Rolle. *Historia social de la música popular en Chile, 1890–1950*. Santiago: Ediciones Universidad Católica de Chile, 2005.

Gorsuch, Anne E. *All This Is Your World: Soviet Tourism at Home and Abroad after Stalin*. New York: Oxford University Press, 2011.

Gorsuch, Anne E., and Diane Koenker, eds. *The Socialist Sixties: Crossing Borders in the Second World*. Bloomington: Indiana University Press, 2013.

Grandela del Rio, Julia. "Miguel Letelier Valdés: Premio Nacional de Arte en Música 2008 [Miguel Letelier Valdés National Arts Prize in Music 2008]." *Revista musical chilena* 63, no. 211 (2009): 7–20.

Grazian, David. *Blue Chicago: The Search for Authenticity in Urban Blues Clubs*. Chicago: University of Chicago Press, 2003.

Gregory, E. David. "Lomax in London: Alan Lomax, the BBC and the Folk-Song Revival in England, 1950–1958." *Folk Music Journal* 8, no. 2 (2002): 136–69.

Gros, Dominique. *Dissidents Du Quotidien: La Scène Alternative Genevoise, 1968–1987*. Lausanne, Suisse: Editions d'En bas, 1987.

Guerra, Cristián. *Los Quincheros: Tradición que perdura*. Santiago: Sociedad Chilena del Derecho de Autor, 1999.

Guerrero, Claudio, and Alekos Vuskovic. *La música del nuevo cine chileno*. Santiago: Editorial Cuarto Propio, 2018.

Guichard, Bruno, Julien Hage, Alain Léger, and Nils Andersson. *François Maspero et les paysages humains*. Lyon: La fosse aux ours, 2009.

Guilbault, Jocelyne. "Interpreting World Music: A Challenge in Theory and Practice." *Popular Music* 16, no. 1 (1997): 31–44.

Gumucio, Rafael. *Nicanor Parra: Poeta imaginario = Imaginary Poet*. Santiago: Ocho Libros Editores, 2006.

———. *Nicanor Parra, rey y mendigo*. Barcelona: Literatura Random House, 2020.

Hage, Julien. "Sur les chemins du tiers monde en lutte: Partisans, Révolution, Tricontinental (1961–1973)." In *68: Une histoire collective, 1962–1981*, edited by Philippe Artières and Michelle Zancarini-Fournel, 87–93. Paris: La Découverte, 2008.

Hagedorn, Katherine J. *Divine Utterances: The Performance of Afro-Cuban Santería*. Washington, D.C.: Smithsonian Institution Press, 2001.

Hale, Charles R. "Cultural Politics of Identity in Latin America." *Annual Review of Anthropology* 26, no. 1 (1997): 567–90.

Hamilton, Nigel. *How to Do Biography: A Primer*. Cambridge, Mass.: Harvard University Press, 2008.

Harmer, Tanya. *Beatriz Allende: A Revolutionary Life in Cold War Latin America*. Chapel Hill: University of North Carolina Press, 2020.

Hayward, Philip, ed. *Widening the Horizon: Exoticism in Post-War Popular Music*. Sydney: John Libbey, 1999.

Hellier, Ruth. *Women Singers in Global Contexts: Music, Biography, Identity*. Urbana: University of Illinois Press, 2013.

Hernandez, Deborah Pacini. "Dancing with the Enemy: Cuban Popular Music, Race, Authenticity, and the World-Music Landscape." *Latin American Perspectives* 25, no. 3 (1998): 110–25.

Hernandez R., Baltazar. *Arte y artistas de Ñuble*. Chillán, Chile: El Autor, 1989.

———. *Las artes populares de Ñuble*. Chillán, Chile: Universidad de Chile, Sede Chillán, 1970.

———. *Notas folklóricas de Ñuble 1990*. Chillán, Chile: Impr. La Discusión, 1990.

Herrero A., Víctor. *Después de vivir un siglo: Una biografía de Violeta Parra*. Barcelona: Lumen, 2017.

Hixson, Walter L. *Parting the Curtain: Propaganda, Culture, and the Cold War, 1945–1961*. New York: St. Martin's, 1997.

Hormazábal González, Viviana. "La obra visual de Violeta Parra: Un acercamiento a sus innovaciones conceptuales y visuales a través del análisis iconográfico de arpilleras y óleos." BA thesis, Universidad de Chile—Facultad de Artes, 2013.

Huasi, Julio. "Violeta de América." *Casa de las Américas* 11, no. 65 (1971): 91–104.

Huerta, Martín. *Yo, Carlina X: La verdadera historia de la prostituta más famosa de Chile como nunca se había contado antes*. Santiago: Ediciones Caballo Desbocados, 2013.

Huneeus, Carlos. *La guerra fría chilena: Gabriel González Videla y la Ley Maldita*. Santiago: Random House Mondadori S.A., 2009.

Hurtado, María de la Luz, Paula Edwards R., and Rafael Guilisasti. *Historia de la televisión chilena entre 1959 y 1973*. Santiago: Ediciones Documentas: Ceneca, 1989.

Hutchinson, Sydney. "'Típico, folklórico or popular'? Musical Categories, Place, and Identity in a Transnational Listening Community." *Popular Music* 30, no. 2 (May 2011): 245–62.

IASPM-AL. "Enfoques interdisciplinarios sobre las músicas populares en América Latina: Retrospectivas, perspectivas, críticas y propuestas." *IASPM-AL*, March 2, 2016. https://iaspmal.com/index.php/2016/03/02/actas-x-congreso/?lang=pt.

Iber, Patrick. *Neither Peace nor Freedom: The Cultural Cold War in Latin America*. Cambridge, Mass.: Harvard University Press, 2015.

Illanes O., María Angélica. *Nuestra historia Violeta: Feminismo social y vidas de mujeres en el siglo XX: Una revolución permanente*. Santiago: LOM Ediciones, 2012.

Instituto Moreira Salles. "Sergio Larraín na revista O Cruzeiro Internacional." May 4, 2016. https://ims.com.br/2016/05/04/sergio-larrain-na-revista-o-cruzeiro-internacional/.

James, Daniel, and Juan Suriano. *Violencia, proscripción y autoritarismo (1955–1976)*. Vol. 9 of *Nueva historia argentina*. Buenos Aires: Editorial Sudamericana, 2003.

Jara, Víctor. *Deja su huella en el viento*. Santiago: LOM Ediciones, 2012.

Jara, Víctor, Claudio Acevedo, and Rodrigo Torres. *Víctor Jara: Obra musical completa*. Santiago: Fundación Víctor Jara, 1996.

Johnston, Gordon. "Revisiting the Cultural Cold War." *Social History (London)* 35, no. 3 (2010): 290–307.

Joseph, Camille. "François Maspero et la typographie de l'édition politique." *Mémoires du livre / Studies in Book Culture*, 3, no. 1 (2011). https://doi.org/10.7202/1007572ar.

Joseph, Gilbert M., and Daniela Spenser, eds. *In from the Cold: Latin America's New Encounter with the Cold War*. Durham, N.C.: Duke University Press, 2008.

Jurado, Omar, and Juan Miguel Morales. *El Chile de Víctor Jara*. Santiago: LOM Ediciones, 2003.

———. *Víctor Jara: Te recuerda Chile*. 3. ed. Ravel 14. Santiago: Txalaparta S.L., 2013.

Kalter, Christoph. *The Discovery of the Third World: Decolonization and the Rise of the New Left in France c. 1950–1976*. New York: Cambridge University Press, 2016.

Karmy, Eileen, and Martín Farías Zúñiga, eds. *Palimpsestos sonoros: Reflexiones sobre la Nueva Canción Chilena*. Santiago: Ceibo Ediciones, 2014.

Karpeles, Maud. "The International Folk Music Council." *Journal of the Folklore Institute* 2, no. 3 (December 1965): 308–13.

Karush, Matthew B. *Musicians in Transit: Argentina and the Globalization of Popular Music*. Durham, N.C.: Duke University Press, 2017.

Kerschen, Karen. *Violeta Parra: By the Whim of the Wind*. Albuquerque, N.Mex.: ABQ Press, 2010.

Kessler-Harris, Alice. *A Difficult Woman: The Challenging Life and Times of Lillian Hellman*. New York: Bloomsbury, 2012.

Kivy, Peter. *Authenticities: Philosophical reflections on musical performance*. Ithaca, N.Y.: Cornell University Press, 1997.

Klimpel Alvarado, Felícitas. *La mujer chilena: El aporte femenino al progreso de Chile, 1910–1960*. Santiago: Editorial Andrés Bello, 1962.

Koivunen, Pia. "Friends, 'Potential Friends,' and Enemies: Reimagining Soviet Relations to the First, Second, and Third Worlds at the Moscow 1957 Youth Festival." In *Socialist Internationalism in the Cold War*, edited by Patryk Babiracki and Austin Jersild, 219–46. Switzerland: Springer International Publishing AG, 2016.

———. "The 1957 Moscow Youth Festival: Propagating a New, Peaceful Image of the Soviet Union." In *Soviet State and Society under Nikita Khrushchev*, edited by Melanie Ilič and Jeremy Smith, 46–65. New York: Routledge, 2009.

———. "The World Youth Festival as an Arena of the 'Cultural Olympics': Meaning of Competition in Soviet Culture in the 1940s and 1950s." In *Competition in Socialist Society*, edited by Katalin Miklóssy and Melanie Ilič, 125–41. New York: Routledge, 2014.

Kosichev, Leonard. *La guitarra y el poncho de Víctor Jara: Siglos y hombres*. Moscow: Editorial Progreso, 1990.

———. "Violeta Parra y La Nueva Canción Chilena." *América Latina (USSR)*, no. 2 (1985): 80–89.

Kotek, Joël. *Students and the Cold War*. Translated by Ralph Blumenau. New York: St. Martin's, 1996.

———. "Youth Organizations as a Battlefield in the Cold War." In *The Cultural Cold War in Western Europe, 1945–1960*, edited by Giles Scott-Smith and Hans Krabbendam, 138–58. London: F. Cass, 2003.

Krekola, Joni, and Simo Mikkonen. "Backlash of the Free World: The US Presence at the World Youth Festival in Helsinki, 1962." *Scandinavian Journal of History* 36, no. 2 (May 2011): 230–55.

Krzywicki, Andrzej. *Poststalinowski karnawał radości: V Światowy Festiwal Młodzieży i Studentów o Pokój i Przyjaźń, Warszawa 1955*. Warsaw: TRIO, 2009.

Kurapel, Alberto. *Margot Loyola: La escena infinita del folklore*. Santiago: Editorial Cuarto Propio, 2018.

Laborde, Miguel. *Santiago, región capital de Chile: Una invitación al conocimiento del espacio propio*. Santiago: Gobierno Regional Metropolitano de Santiago; Publicaciones Bicentenario Presidencia de la República, 2004.

Lafuente, Silvia. "Folclore y literatura en las Décimas de Violeta Parra." *Cuadernos Hispanoamericanos*, no. 5 (1990): 57–74.

Lago, Tomás, and Alejandro Witker, *Tomás Lago: Memorial cultural de Ñuble*. Chillán: Universidad del Bío-Bío, 2006.

Lamadrid Álvarez, Silvia, and Andrea Baeza Reyes. "La recepción de la música juvenil en Chile en los años 60: ¿Americanización de la juventud?" *Revista musical chilena* 71, no. 228 (July 2017): 69–94.

Langenkamp, Harm. "(Dis)Connecting Cultures, Creating Dreamworlds: Musical 'East-West' Diplomacy in the Cold War and the War on Terror." In *Divided Dreamworlds?: The Cultural Cold War in East and West*, edited by Peter Romijn, Giles Scott Smith, and Joes Segal, 217–34. Amsterdam: University Press, 2018.

Largo Farías, René. *La nueva canción chilena*. Cuadernos Casa de Chile. México, D.F.: Casa de Chile, 1977.

Larraín, Jorge. *Identidad chilena*. Colección Escafandra. Santiago: LOM Ediciones, 2001.

Larraín, Sergio, and Gonzalo Leiva Quijada. *Sergio Larrain*. Edited by Agnès Sire. New York: Aperture, 2013.

Larrea, Antonio, and Jorge Montealegre. *Rostros y rastros de un canto*. Santiago: Nunatak y Fondart, 1997.

Lasagni, María Cristina, Paula Edwards, and Josiane Bonnefoy. *La radio en Chile: Historias, modelos, perspectivas*. Santiago: CENECA, 1985.

Laurière, Christine. *Paul Rivet: Le Savant et Le Politique*. Paris: Publications scientifiques du Muséum national d'histoire naturelle, 2008.

Lawner, Miguel, Hernán Soto, and Jacobo Schatan. *Salvador Allende: Presencia en la ausencia*. Santiago: LOM Ediciones, 2008.

Leenhardt, Jacques, Pierre Kalfon, Armand Mattelart, and Michèle Mattelart. *Les Amériques latines en France*. Paris: Découvertes Gallimard, 1992.

Le Foulón, Sofía, ed. *Parra a la vista*. AIFOS Ediciones. Santiago: Ograma Impresores, 2014.

Leiva Quijada, Gonzalo. *Sergio Larrain: Biografía, estética, fotografía*. Fotografía. Santiago: Ediciones Metales Pesados, 2012.

León Villagra, Mariana, and Ignacio Ramos Rodillo. "Sonidos de un Chile profundo: Hacia un análisis crítico del archivo sonoro de música tradicional chilena en relación a la conformación del folclore en Chile." *Revista musical chilena* 65, no. 215 (2011): 23–39.

Lepore, Jill. "Historians Who Love Too Much: Reflections on Microhistory and Biography." *Journal of American History* 88, no. 1 (2001): 129–44.

Leydon, Rebecca. "Utopias of the Tropics: The Exotic Music of Les Baxter and Yma Sumac." In *Widening the Horizon: Exoticism in Post-War Popular Music*, edited by Philip Hayward, 47–71. Bloomington, IN: John Libbey Publishing, 1999.

Liauzu, Claude. "Intellectuels du Tiers Monde et intellectuels français: Les années algériennes des Éditions Maspero." *Bulletins de l'Institut d'Histoire du Temps Présent* 10, no. 1 (1988): 105–18.

Liencura Melillán, Jaime Rodrigo. "El canal de la Chile: Historia y desarrollo de la corporación de televisión de la Universidad de Chile entre los años 1960–1993." BA thesis, Universidad de Chile, 2012.

Lihn, Enrique. "A la manera del señor Corrales." In Nicanor Parra, *Chistes paRRa desorientar a la ~~policía~~ /poesía*. Santiago: Galería Época, 1983.

———. *El circo en llamas: Una crítica de la vida*. Santiago: LOM Ediciones, 1997.

"Literatura Chilena, Número Doble Especial—Nueva Canción / Canto Nuevo Julio / Diciembre de 1985." *Literatura chilena* 9, no. 3–4 (December 1985).

Livingston, Tamara E. "Music Revivals: Towards a General Theory." *Ethnomusicology* 43 (Winter 1999): 66–85.

Looseley, David. *Edith Piaf: A Cultural History*. Liverpool: Liverpool University Press, 2015.

———. *Popular Music in Contemporary France: Authenticity, Politics, Debate*. New York: Berg, 2003.

López, Iraida H. "Al filo de la modernidad: Las décimas autobiográficas de Violeta Parra como literatura." *Anales de literatura chilena* 11, no. 13 (2010): 131–49.

López Fonseca, Luis, and Pablo Moreno Betancur. "Luces y sombras en la Bohemia Penquista de 1957–1960: Producción cultural de Violeta Parra y el aporte del personal de Huachipato." BA thesis, Universidad Católica de la Santísima Concepción, 2018.

Loveman, Brian. *Chile: The Legacy of Hispanic Capitalism*. New York: Oxford University Press, 1979.

Loyola T., Manuel, ed. *Por un Rojo Amanecer: Hacia una historia de los comunistas chilenos*. Santiago: Impresora Valus, 2000.

Luque, Francisco. "El disco ausente." *Revista musical chilena* 65, no. 215 (June 2011): 54–61.

Luraschi, Ilse Adriana, and Kay Sibbald. *María Elena Walsh, o, "el desafío de la limitación."* Buenos Aires: Editorial Sudamericana, 1993.

Mamani, Ariel. "Para la reina . . . apenas una carpa: Innovación y primitivismo en Violeta Parra y su experiencia en La Carpa de La Reina." *Artelogie*, no. 13 (January 30, 2019). http://journals.openedition.org/artelogie/2906.

Marchant, Alfredo Aburto, and Jorge Benítez González. *Voces del barrio Yungay: Primer Concurso de Historias del Barrio Yungay*. Memorias Sociales. Santiago: Escuela de Historia y Ciencias Sociales. Santiago: Editorial ARCIS, 2009.

Marchini, M. Darío. *No toquen: Músicos populares, gobierno y sociedad; De la utopía a la persecución y las listas negras en la Argentina 1960–1983*. Buenos Aires, Argentina: Catálogos, 2008.

Margadant, Jo Burr, ed. *The New Biography: Performing Femininity in Nineteenth-Century France*. Studies on the History of Society and Culture. Berkeley: University of California Press, 2000.

Marques Brum, Maurício, and Camila Marchesan Cargnelutti. "A religiosidade popular e a igreja na canção latino-americana: Uma análise da contribuição de Violeta Parra." *Revista escrita* 2014, no. 19 (December 10, 2014): 352–66.

Marras, Sergio. "Entrevista a Allen Ginsberg." *APSI*, June 1987. www.ornitorrinco.eu /sergio-marras/periodismo/apsi-28.

Martí Fuentes, Adolfo. "La poesía popular de Violeta Parra." *Casa de las Américas* 12, no. 69 (December 1971): 203–6.

Martin, Gerald. *Gabriel García Márquez: A Life*. New York: Bloomsbury, 2008.

Martínez Elissetche, Pacián. *Daniel Belmar: Rescate y memoria*. Hualpén: Trama Impresores, 2009.

Martínez Sanz, María Ester. "Las décimas de Violeta Parra, del yo individual a lo universal." *Taller de letras*, no. 25 (1997): 119–25.

Martínez Ulloa, Jorge. "Anticuecas y antipoesías, un itinerario común e inverso para dos hermanos." *Anales del Instituto de Chile* 32 (2013): 253–73.

Massuh, Gabriela. *Nací para ser breve: María Elena Walsh; La vida, la pasión, la historia, el amor.* Buenos Aires: Sudamericana, 2017.

Mattelart, Armand. "La dependencia de los medios de comunicación de masas en Chile." *Estudios Internacionales* 4, no. 13 (1970): 124–54.

McClennen, Sophia A. "Chilex: The Economy of Transnational Media Culture." *Cultural Logic: An Electronic Journal of Marxist Thought and Practice* 6 (2000). https://doi.org /10.14288/clogic.v6i0.

McSherry, J. Patrice. *Chilean New Song: The Political Power of Music, 1960s–1973.* Philadelphia: Temple University Press, 2015.

Mena, Rosario. "Violeta y los Letelier." *Patrimonio cultural de Chile* (blog). https:// patrimonio.cl/archivo/violeta-y-los-letelier/.

Mendoza, Marcelo. "Gonzalo Rojas." In *Todos confesos: Diálogo con sobrevivientes notables del siglo XX*, 169–96. Santiago: Mandrágora, 2011.

Merino, Luis. "Magdalena Vicuña y la Revista Musical Chilena." *Revista musical chilena* 47, no. 180 (1993): 8–14.

———. "Music and Globalization: The Chilean Case." In *Musical Cultures of Latin America: Global Effects, Past and Present; Proceedings of an International Conference, University of California, Los Angeles, May 28–30, 1999*, edited by Steven Joseph Loza and Jack Bishop, 251–70. Selected Reports in Ethnomusicology. Vol. 11. Los Angeles: Dept. of Ethnomusicology and Systematic Musicology, University of California, Los Angeles, 2003.

Merino, Montero. "Fluír y refluír de la poesía en la música chilena (homenaje a Pablo Neruda)." *Revista musical chilena* 27, no. 123–24 (December 1973): 55–62.

Ministerio de las Culturas, las Artes y el Patrimonio. *Observatorio Cultural: Especial Centenario de Nemesio Antúnez*, 2019.

———. *Observatorio Cultural: Especial Centenario Margot Loyola Palacios*, 2019.

Miranda Herrera, Paula. "Décimas autobiográficas de Violeta Parra: Tejiendo diferencias." In *Actas VI Seminario Interdisciplinario de Estudios de Género en las Universidades Chilenas: Homenaje a Ivette Malverde*, edited by Ivette Malverde, Olga Grau, Margarita Iglesias, and Kemy Oyarzún, 259–84. Santiago: Facultad de Filosofía y Humanidades, Universidad de Chile, Centro de Estudios de Género y Cultura en América Latina, 2000.

———. "Interculturalidad y proyectos alternativos en Violeta Parra: Su encuentro con el canto Mapuche." *Artelogie*, no. 13 (2019). https://journals.openedition.org/artelogie/2794.

———. *La poesía de Violeta Parra.* Santiago: Editorial Cuarto Propio, 2013.

———. "Violeta Parra, Creative Researcher." In *Violeta Parra, Life and Work*, edited by Lorna Dillon, 83–104. Woodbridge, Suffolk: Tamesis, 2017.

Miranda Herrera, Paula, Elisa Loncón, and Allison Ramay. *Violeta Parra en el Wallmapu: Su encuentro con el canto Mapuche.* Santiago: Pehuén Editores S. A., 2017.

Mitchell, Gillian A. M. "Visions of Diversity: Cultural Pluralism and the Nation in the Folk Music Revival Movement of the United States and Canada, 1958–65." *Journal of American Studies* 40, no. 3 (2006): 593–614.

Molina Fuenzalida, Héctor. "Violeta Chilensis." *Filosofía, educación y cultura (Revista: Chile)*, no. 10 (2009): 205–38.

Molinero, Carlos D. *Militancia de la canción: Política en el canto folklórico de la Argentina: 1944–1975.* Buenos Aires: De Aquí a la Vuelta, 2011.

Montealegre Iturra, Jorge. "Humor y sátira visual en Violeta Parra." In *Dibujos que hablan textos 2017–2018: Encuentro de crítica, historia y estética de las narrativas dibujadas, Junio 2019*, 13–24. Santiago: Corporación Cultural Universidad de Santiago, 2019.

———. *Violeta Parra: Instantes fecundos, visiones, retazos de memoria.* Santiago: Editorial de la Universidad de Santiago, 2011.

Montealegre Iturra, Jorge, and Rafael Chavarría Contreras. "Presencia de Violeta Parra en la construcción del imaginario popular de la vía chilena al socialism: La Peña de los Parra y la Carpa de La Reina; La reconstrucción de una memoria testimonial." *Kamchatka: Revista de análisis cultural*, no. 17 (July 30, 2021): 135–54.

Montecino Aguirre, Sonia, ed. *Revisitando Chile: Identidades, mitos e historias.* Santiago: Cuadernos Bicentenario, Presidencia de la República, 2003.

Montero, Gonzalo. "'Entre campo y grabación': Violeta Parra y las tecnologías migrantes." *Studies in Latin American Popular Culture* 36 (2018): 128–44.

———. "Folklore as the Avant-Garde? Experimental Images of 'the Popular' in Mid-Century Chile." *Transmodernity* 9, no. 5 (2020). https://doi.org/10.5070/T495051212.

Morales, José Ricardo. "Violeta Parra: El hilo de su arte." In *Ensayos en suma: Del escritor, el intelectual y sus mundos*, 109–33. Ensayos (Biblioteca Nueva [Firm]). Madrid: Biblioteca Nueva, 2000.

Morales T., Leonidas. "Violeta Parra: Del frío y del calor." In *Carta de amor y sujeto femenino en Chile: Siglos XIX y XX*, 57–72. Santiago: Editorial Cuarto Propio, 2003.

Morales T., Leonidas, and Nicanor Parra. *Violeta Parra: La última canción.* Santiago: Editorial Cuarto Propio, 2003.

Morel, Consuelo, Isabel Zegers, and Ignacio Vicuña. *Historia de la radio en Chile.* Universidad Católica de Chile. Santiago: Centro de Comunicaciones Sociales, EAC, UC, 1974.

Moreno, Albrecht. "Violeta Parra and 'La Nueva Canción Chilena.'" *Studies in Latin American Popular Culture* 5 (1986): 108–26.

Mouesca, Jacqueline. *El documental chileno.* Santiago: LOM Ediciones, 2005.

———. *Plano secuencia de la memoria de Chile: Veinticinco años de cine chileno (1960–1985).* Santiago: Ediciones del Litoral, 1988.

Mularski, Jedrek Putta. "Mexican or Chilean: Mexican Ranchera Music and Nationalism in Chile." *Studies in Latin American Popular Culture* 30 (2012): 54–75.

———. *Music, Politics, and Nationalism in Latin America: Chile during the Cold War Era.* Amherst, N.Y.: Cambria, 2014.

———. "Singing Huasos: Politics, Chilenidad, and Music from 1910–1950." *A Contracorriente* 12, no. 2 (2015): 178–211.

Müller-Bergh, Klaus. "Fulgor y muerte de Violeta Parra." *Revista interamericana de bibliografía* 28, no. 1 (1978): 47–55.

Mundaca, Alejandro E. "Hacia una concepción intersemiótica de la traducción artística de Violeta Parra." *Arboles y rizomas* 11, no. 1 (June 2020): 33–49.

———. "Translating Poetics: Analysing the Connections between Violeta Parra's Music, Poetry and Art." PhD diss., University of Sussex, 2019.

———. "Violeta Parra, una aproximación a la creación interdisciplinaria." MA thesis, Universitat de Barcelona, 2012.

Münnich, Susana. *Casa de Hacienda / Carpa de Circo: María Luisa Bombal, Violeta Parra.* Santiago: LOM Ediciones, 2006.

Muñoz, Diego, ed. *Poesía popular chilena*. Santiago: Quimantú, 1972.

Muñoz de Ebensperger, Gertrudis. *El desarrollo de las escuelas normales en Chile*. Santiago: Prensas de la Universidad de Chile, 1943.

Muñoz Hidalgo, Mariano. *El cuerpo en-cantado: De la antigua canción occidental al canto popular en Cuba y Chile*. Santiago: Universidad de Santiago, 2003.

Muñoz Olave, Reinaldo. *Historia de Chillán*. 2. ed. Santiago: Editorial Andújar, 1997.

Nandorfy, Martha. "'I Sing of Difference': Violeta Parra's Testimonial Songs for Justice." In Vol. 2 of *Rebel Musics*, edited by Daniel Fischlin and Ajay Heble, 148–86. Chicago: Black Rose Books, 2020.

———. "The Right to Live in Peace: Freedom and Social Justice in the Songs of Violeta Parra and Víctor Jara." In *Rebel Musics: Human Rights, Resistant Sounds, and the Politics of Music Making*, edited by Daniel Fischlin and Ajay Heble, 172–209. Montréal: Black Rose Books, 2003.

Naranjo Ríos, Miguel. "Discografía de Violeta Parra." *Estudios públicos*, no. 146 (Fall 2017): 233–62.

Nasaw, David. "AHR Roundtable: Historians and Biography." *American Historical Review* 114, no. 3 (June 1, 2009): 573–78.

Navarrete Araya, Micaela, and Karen Donoso F., eds. *Y se va La Primera—!!! Conversaciones sobre la cueca: Las cuecas de la lira popular, transcripción completa*. Santiago: LOM Ediciones, 2010.

Nieves Alonso, María. "En esto ando por aquí: Violeta Parra." In *Diálogos para el Bicentenario: Concepción-Alicante*, edited by María Nieves Alonso and Carmen Alemany Bay, 51–66. Concepción: Editorial Universidad de Concepción, 2011.

———. "La soberanía sobre la muerte: El caso de Violeta Parra." *Atenea*, no. 504 (2011): 11–39.

———. "Violeta Parra de Chile." In *La rueda mágica: Ensayos de música y literature; Manual para (in)disciplinados*, edited by Rubí Carreño Bolívar, 52–66. Santiago: Ediciones Universidad Alberto Hurtado, 2017.

Noack, Christian. "Songs from the Wood, Love from the Fields: The Soviet Tourist Song Movement." In *The Socialist Sixties: Crossing Borders in the Second World*, edited by Anne E. Gorsuch and Diane Koenker, 167–212. Bloomington: Indiana University Press, 2013.

Nuñez Oyarce, Hernán, and Rodrigo Torres Alvarado. *Mi gran cueca: Crónicas de la cueca brava*. Santiago: Consejo Nacional de la Cultura y Las Artes, Fondart, 2005.

Núñez Prieto, Iván. "Escuelas normales: Una historia larga y sorprendente; Chile (1842–1973)." *Pensamiento educativo, revista de investigación latinoamericana (PEL)* 46, no. 1 (April 30, 2010): 133–50.

———. "Las escuelas normales: Una historia de fortalezas y debilidades, 1842–1973." *Docencia* 15, no. 40 (December 2010): 33–39.

Olate y Herrera, Gustavo. *Mapocho abajo*. Santiago: Neupert, 1970.

Olavarrîa, Rodrigo. "Violeta Parra: 'Elegería quedarme con la gente.'" *Cuaderno (Fundación Pablo Neruda)*, no. 67 (Summer 2011): 13–17.

Olcott, Jocelyn. "'Take Off That Streetwalker's Dress': Concha Michel and the Cultural Politics of Gender in Postrevolutionary Mexico." *Journal of Women's History* 21, no. 3 (September 1, 2009): 36–59.

Olea Montero, Humberto. "El Canto a lo poeta, una genealogía incompleta." *Revista chilena de literatura*, no. 78 (January 1, 2011). https://revistaliteratura.uchile.cl/index .php/RCL/article/view/17905.

Olmedo-Carrasco, Carolina. "El joven envejecido: Arte en Chile de 1988 a 1968." *Izquierdas (Santiago, Chile)*, no. 44 (2018): 3–30.

Oporto Valencia, Lucy. *El diablo en la música: La muerte del amor en El gavilán, de Violeta Parra*. Santiago: Editorial Universidad de Santiago, 2013.

Orellana, Marcela. "Versos por Angelito: Poetry and Its Function at the Wake of a Peasant Child in Chile." *Journal of Folklore Research* 27, no. 3 (1990): 191–203.

Orellana Rivera, María Isabel, and Museo de la Educación Gabriela Mistral. *Educación: Improntas de mujer*. Santiago: Dirección de Bibliotecas Archivos y Museos-Museo de la Educación Gabriela Mistral, 2007.

Orquera, Fabiola. "El proyecto musical de Leda Valladares: Del sustrato romántico a una concepción ancestral-vanguardista de la argentinidad." *Corpus (Buenos Aires, Argentina)* 5, no. 2 (December 2015). http://journals.openedition.org/corpusarchivos/1479.

———. "From the Andes to Paris: Atahualpa Yupanqui, the Communist Party, and the Latin American Folksong Movement." In *Red Strains: Music and Communism outside the Communist Bloc*, edited by Robert Adlington, 105–18. Proceedings of the British Academy. Oxford: Published for the British Academy by Oxford University Press, 2013.

Osgood, Kenneth A. "Hearts and Minds: The Unconventional Cold War." *Journal of Cold War Studies* 4, no. 2 (2002): 85–107.

Osorio Fernández, Javier. "Autonomía, institucionalidad y disputas por la hegemonía: La modernización del campo musical chileno a través de Pro Arte." In *El semanario Pro Arte: Difusión y crítica cultural (1948–1956)*, 145–88. Santiago: RIL Editores, 2013.

———. "Modernización y representación en la canción chilena: Algunas aproximaciones a Violeta Parra y la música popular." In *Espacios de transculturación en América Latina*, edited by Roberto Aedo, 141–59. Centro de Estudios Culturales Latinoamericanos, Facultad de Filosofía y Humanidades, Universidad de Chile, 2005.

———. "Música popular y postcolonialidad: Violeta Parra y los usos de lo popular en la Nueva Canción Chilena." Accessed March 4, 2023. www.academia.edu/4809461 /M%C3%BAsica_popular_y_postcolonialidad_Violeta_Parra_y_los_usos_de_lo _popular_en_la_Nueva_Canci%C3%B3n_Chilena.

Oviedo, Carmen. *Mentira todo lo cierto: Tras la huella de Violeta Parra*. Santiago: Editorial Universitaria, 1990.

Oyarzún, Luis, Tomás Harris, Daniela Schütte G., and Pedro Pablo Zegers B. *Taken for a Ride: Escritura de Paso*. Santiago: RIL Editores, 2005.

Pacheco, Cristián. "Violeta Parra en la ciudad brumosa: Entrevista a Fernando Venegas— La Raza Cómica." *La Raza Cómica*, May 18, 2018.

Padilla, Pablo. *Canarito: El Parra que faltaba; Vida y obra de Oscar Parra Sandoval*. Santiago: RIL Editores, 2008.

Palomino, Pablo. *The Invention of Latin American Music: A Transnational History*. New York: Oxford University Press, 2020.

Palominos Mandiola, Simón, Ignacio Ramos Rodillo, and Karen Donoso, eds. *Vientos del pueblo: Representaciones, recepciones e interpretaciones sobre la Nueva Cancion Chilena*. Santiago: LOM Ediciones, 2018.

Parada-Lillo, Rodolfo. "L'articulation entre tradition et modernité dans la culture: La nouvelle chanson chilienne, 1960–1975." Université Panthéon-Sorbonne, 1992.

Parra, Nicanor, and Iván Carrasco M. *Nicanor Parra: Documentos y ensayos antipoéticos.* Colección Humanidades. Santiago: Editorial Universidad de Santiago, 2007.

Parra, Tita. "Tradición y ruptura en la canción chilena." *Mundo, problemas y confrontaciones* 2 (1988 1987): 79–86.

Parra Moreno, Clara. *El hombre del terno blanco: Mi padre, el tio Lalo Parra.* Providencia, Santiago: RIL Editores, 2013.

Party, Daniel. "Homofobia y la Nueva Canción Chilena." *El oído pensante* 7, no. 2 (2019): 42–63.

Peacock, Margaret. "The Perils of Building Cold War Consensus at the 1957 Moscow World Festival of Youth and Students." *Cold War History* 12, no. 3 (2012): 515–35.

Pedemonte, Rafael. *Guerra por las ideas en América Latina, 1959–1973: Presencia soviética en Cuba y Chile.* Santiago: UAH/Ediciones, Universidad Alberto Hurtado, 2020.

———. "La guerre froide culturelle en Amérique latine: Les espaces d'amitié et d'échange avec l'Union soviétique." *Dialogues* 2 (2012): 137–52.

Pellegrino, Guillermo. *Las cuerdas vivas de América: [Chabuca Granda, Víctor Jara, Violeta Parra, Daniel Viglietti, Atahualpa Yupanqui].* Buenos Aires: Editorial Sudamericana, 2002.

Peña Muñoz, Manuel Peña. *Los cafés literarios en Chile.* Archivo del Escritor, 2001.

Pérez-Laborde, Elga. "Los códigos de la modernidad en los textos poético-musicales de Violeta Parra y Chico Buarque." *Contextos: Revista de humanidades y ciencias sociales,* no. 20 (2008): 139–46.

Pernet, Corinne A. "'For the Genuine Culture of the Americas': Musical Folklore, Popular Arts, and the Cultural Politics of Pan Americanism, 1933–50." In *Decentering America,* edited by Jessica C. E. Gienow-Hecht, 132–68. New York: Berghahn Books, 2007.

———. "The Popular Fronts and Folklore: Chilean Cultural Institutions, Nationalism and Pan-Americanism, 1936–1948." In *North Americanization of Latin America? Culture, Gender, and Nation in the Americas,* edited by Hans-Joachim König and Stefan Rinke, 254–76. Stuttgart, Germany: Verlag Hans-Dieter Heinz Akademischer, 2004.

Peterson, Richard A. *Creating Country Music: Fabricating Authenticity.* Chicago: University of Chicago Press, 1997.

Pick, Zuzana M. "Mimbre (Sergio Bravo. Chile, 1957)." In *Cine documental en América Latina,* edited by Paulo Antonio Paranaguá and José Carlos Avellar, 287–88. Madrid: Cátedra, 2003.

Pike, Frederick B. "Aspects of Class Relations in Chile, 1850–1960." *Hispanic American Historical Review* 43, no. 1 (1963): 14–33.

Pinkerton, Emily Jean. "The Chilean Guitarrón: The Social, Political and Gendered Life of a Folk Instrument." PhD diss., University of Texas, 2007.

Pinochet Cobos, Carla. *Violeta Parra: Hacia un imaginario del mundo subalterno.* Santiago: Univesidad de Chile, 2007.

———. "Violeta Parra: Tensiones y transgresiones de una mujer popular de mediados del siglo XX." *Revista musical chilena* 64, no. 213 (2010): 77–89.

Pino-Ojeda, Walescka. "Autenticidad y alienación: Disonancias ideológico-culturales entre la 'nueva canción' chilena y el rock anglosajón." *Studies in Latin American Popular Culture* 33 (2015): 108–27.

Pintura ingenua en Chile: El patrimonio plástico chileno. Santiago: Ministerio de Educación, Departamento de Extensión Cultural, 1986.

Pizarro S., Gabriela, and Guillermo Ríos. "Gabriela Pizarro en la historia de nuestro canto (Part 1)." Artículo. *Chile ríe y canta*, no. 2 (April 1992): 16–23; "Gabriela Pizarro en la historia de nuestro canto (Part 2)." *Chile ríe y canta*, no. 3 (June 1992): 20–25; "Gabriela Pizarro en la historia de nuestro canto (Part 3)." *Chile ríe y canta*, no. 4 (August 1992).

Plante, Isabel. "Buenos Aires en la producción y circulación de las arpilleras y pinturas de Violeta Parra." In *Intercambios trasandinos: Historias del arte entre Argentina y Chile (siglos XIX–XX)*, edited by Silvia Dolinko, Ana María Risco, and Sebastián Vidal Valenzuela, 155–84. Santiago: Universidad Alberto Hurtado, 2022.

———. "Las 'tapisseries chiliennes' de Violeta Parra entre lo vernáculo y lo internacional." *Artelogie*, no. 13 (January 30, 2019). http://journals.openedition.org /artelogie/2923.

———. "*Les Sud-américains de Paris*: Latin American Artists and Cultural Resistance in *Robho* Magazine." *Third Text* 24, no. 4 (July 2010): 445–55.

Plisson, M. "Les musiques d'Amérique latine et leurs réseaux communitaires." In *Les musiques du monde en question*, 123–34. Internationale de l'imaginaire 11. Paris: Maison des cultures du monde, 1999.

Poiger, Uta G. *Jazz, Rock, and Rebels: Cold War Politics and American Culture in a Divided Germany.* Berkeley: University of California Press, 2000.

Ponce, David. *Silvia Infantas: Voz y melodía de Chile.* Santiago: Editorial Hueders, 2018.

Pontifica Universidad Católica de Chile. "Especial Violeta Volcánica." *Revista universitaria*, no. 142 (2017). Special issue.

Portis, Larry. "Musique populaire dans le monde capitaliste: Vers une sociologie de l'authenticité." *L'Homme et la société* 126, no. 4 (1997): 69–86.

Pozo, José del, ed. *Exiliados, emigrados y retornados: Chilenos en América y Europa, 1973–2004.* Santiago: RIL Editores, 2006.

Presa Casanueva, Rafael de la. *Venida y aporte de los españoles a Chile independiente.* Santiago: Tall. Ed. Lautaro, 1978.

Prevots, Naima. *Dance for Export: Cultural Diplomacy and the Cold War.* Middletown, Conn.: Wesleyan University Press, 2001.

Pring-Mill, R. D. F. *Gracias a La Vida: The Power and Poetry of Song.* Kate Elder Lecture. London: University of London, Department of Hispanic Studies, 1990.

Pujol, Sergio Alejandro. *Como la cigarra: Biografía de María Elena Walsh.* 2. ed. Buenos Aires: Beas Ediciones, 1993.

———. *En nombre del folclore: Biografia de Atahualpa Yupanqui.* Buenos Aires: Emece Editores, 2008.

Purcell Torretti, Fernando, and Alfredo Riquelme, eds. *Ampliando miradas: Chile y su historia en un tiempo global.* Santiago: RIL Editores, Instituto de Historia, Pontificia Universidad Católica de Chile, 2009.

Quezada, Jaime. *En la mira de Nicanor Parra: (Aproximaciones a la vida y obra del antipoeta).* Santiago: Editorial MAGO, 2014.

———. *Nicanor Parra de cuerpo entero: Vida y obra del antipoeta*. Santiago: Editorial Andrés Bello, 2007.

Ramón, Armando de. "La población informal: Poblamiento de la periferia de Santiago; 1920–1970." *EURE* 16, no. 50 (1990): 5–17.

Ramos, Juan G. *Sensing Decolonial Aesthetics in Latin American Arts*. Gainesville: University of Florida Press, 2018.

Ramos Rodillo, Ignacio. "El 'gavilán' de Violeta Parra: Deconstrucción y reconocimiento monstruoso del folklore chileno." In *Pensando el Bicentenario: Doscientos años de resistencia y poder en América Latina*, edited by Simón Palominos Mandiola, Lorena Ubilla, and Alejandro Viveros, 337–51. Santiago: Universidad de Chile, 2012.

———. "Música típica, folklore de proyección y nueva canción chilena: Versiones de la identidad bajo el desarrollismo en Chile, décadas de 1920 a 1973." *Revista NEUMA* 4, no. 2 (n.d.): 108–33.

———. "Políticas del folklore: Representaciones de la tradición y lo popular; Militancia y política cultural en Violeta Parra y Atahualpa Yupanqui." MA thesis, Universidad de Chile, 2012.

Reuss, Richard A. "American Folksongs and Left-Wing Politics, 1935–1956." *Journal of the Folklore Institute* 12, no. 2/3 (1975), 89–111.

Reveco Chilla, Cristián. "Yo canto a la diferencia: La existencia de Violeta Parra como arena de lucha; Persecución, memoria y escritura masculina." *Argonautas: Revista de educación y ciencias sociales* 7, no. 8 (August 30, 2017): 17–35.

Reyes C., Marco Aurelio. *Iconografía de Chillán, 1835–1939*. Chillán: Universidad del Bío-Bío, 1989.

Ribke, Nahuel. "Introduccion: Música popular en el Cono Sur durante el periodo de la Guerra Fria." *Estudios interdisciplinarios de América Latina y el Caribe* 27, no. 1 (2016): 7–12.

Richmond, Yale. *Cultural Exchange and the Cold War: Raising the Iron Curtain*. University Park: Pennsylvania State University Press, 2003.

Rickey, George. "The New Tendency (Nouvelle Tendance-Recherche Continuelle)." *Art Journal* (New York, 1960) 23, no. 4 (1964): 272–79.

Rimbot, Emmanuelle. "Luchas interpretativas en torno a la definición de *lo nacional*: La canción urbana de raíz folklórica en Chile." *Voz y escritura: Revista de estudios literarios*, no. 16 (December 2008): 59–89.

Rinke, Stefan H., Mónica Perl, and Marisol Palma. *Encuentros con el Yanqui: Norteamericanización y cambio sociocultural en Chile, 1898–1990*. Santiago: Centro de Investigaciones Diego Barro Arana, 2013.

Rios, Fernando. "La Flûte Indienne: The Early History of Andean Folkloric-Popular Music in France and Its Impact on Nueva Canción." *Latin American Music Review/ Revista de Música Latinoamericana* 29, no. 2 (Fall–Winter 2008): 145–89.

———. *Panpipes and Ponchos: Musical Folklorization and the Rise of the Andean Conjunto Tradition in La Paz, Bolivia*. New York: Oxford University Press, 2020.

Ríos, Héctor, and José Román. "Nieves Yankovic y Jorge Di Lauro." In *Hablando de cine*, 47–58. Santiago: Ocho Libros, 2012.

Ríos, Miguel. "Discografía de Violeta Parra." *Estudios públicos*, no. 146 (July 14, 2017).

Riquelme, Alfredo. *La guerra fria y la lucha contra el marcathismo chileno*. Santiago: Centro de Investigaciones Diego Barros Arana, 2009.

———. *Rojo atardecer: El comunismo chileno entre dictadura y democracia*. Santiago: Centro de Investigaciones Diego Barros Arana, 2009.

Riquelme, Natalia T. "Marco histórico del desenvolvimiento de Violeta Parra como sujeta subalterna en el escenario socio-cultural chileno en el período 1932–1967." *Cisma: Revista del Centro Telúrico de Investigaciones Teóricas*, no. 3 (2nd semester, 2012): 1–13.

Rivera, Ignacio. "Roles y estructuras de género en la práctica del canto popular femenino." *Revista chilena de literatura*, no. 78 (January 1, 2011).

Rodríguez Aedo, Javier. "Recepción y apropiación estética de la obra musical de Violeta Parra en Europa (1954–1990)." *Nuevo mundo, mundos nuevos* (2018): n.p. http://journals.openedition.org/nuevomundo/72183.

———. "Représentations de l'américanité en contexte global: Le cas de la musique populaire chilienne en Europe." *Travaux et documents hispaniques*, no. 9 (2018): 1–24. http://publis-shs.univ-rouen.fr/eriac/index.php?id=223.

———. "Violeta Parra a través de sus viajes por Europa (1955 y 1962)." *Revista musical chilena* 77, no. 239 (June 2023): 31–60.

Rodríguez Musso, Osvaldo. *La nueva canción chilena: Continuidad y reflejo*. Ciudad de La Habana, Cuba: Casa de las Américas, 1988.

———. "Más sobre los Parra." *Araucaria de Chile*, no. 16 (1981): 175–78.

Rodríguez Pérez, Osvaldo. "Las décimas autobiográficas de Violeta Parra." *Anales (Instituto Iberamericano)*, no. 5–6 (1993–1994): 39–56.

———. "Violeta Parra: Dos poemas de amor destinados al canto." *Anales de literatura hispanoamericana* 28, no. 2 (1999): 1141–50.

Rodríguez Serra, Margarita, and María del Carmen Lavín Infante, eds. *Hijos del Bío Bío: Perfiles humanos*. Concepción, Chile: Editorial de la Universidad Católica de la Santísima Concepción, 2010.

Rolland, Denis, and Marie-Hélène Touzalin. "Un miroir déformant? Les Latino-Américains à Paris depuis 1945." In *Le Paris des étrangers depuis 1945*, edited by Antoine Marès and Pierre Milza, 263–91. Paris: Publications de la Sorbonne, 2014. https://doi.org/10.4000/books.psorbonne.981.

Rolle, Claudio. "La geografía de la música popular tradicional en el Chile a mediados del siglo XX." Rio de Janeiro: Anais do V Congresso Latinoamericano da Associação Internacional para o Estudo da Música Popular, 2004. https://iaspmal.com/index.php/2016/03/02/actas-v-congreso/.

Rosemblatt, Karin Alejandra. *Gendered Compromises: Political Cultures and the State in Chile, 1920–1950*. Chapel Hill: University of North Carolina Press, 2000.

Rosenberg, Neil V., ed. *Transforming Tradition: Folk Music Revivals Examined*. Urbana: University of Illinois Press, 1993.

Rouvière, Valérie. "Le mouvement folk en France (1964–1981)." Document de travail FAMDT/MODAL, 2002.

Ruiz, Agustín. "Mediatización del cancionero tradicional chileno: ¿Folklore musical o música popular?" *Resonancias* 9, no. 17 (November 2005): 57–68.

Ruiz Zamora, Agustín. "Discografía de Margot Loyola." *Revista musical chilena* 49, no. 183 (1995): 42–58.

———. "Margot Loyola y Violeta Parra: Convergencias y divergencias en el paradigma interpretativo de la Nueva Canción Chilena." *Cátedra de artes*, no. 3 (2006): 41–58.

Rupprecht, Tobias. *Soviet Internationalism after Stalin: Interaction and Exchange between the USSR and Latin America during the Cold War.* Cambridge: Cambridge University Press, 2015.

Rutter, Nick. "Enacting Communism: The World Youth Festival, 1945–1975." PhD diss., Yale University, 2013.

———. "Look Left, Drive Right: Internationalisms at the 1968 World Youth Festival." In *The Socialist Sixties: Crossing Borders in the Second World*, edited by Anne E. Gorsuch and Diane Koenker, 193–212. Bloomington, Indiana: Indiana University Press, 2013.

Sáez, Fernando. "La hormiga de Neruda." *Estudios públicos*, no. 94 (Fall 2004): 237–56.

———. *La vida intranquila: Violeta Parra, biografía esencial.* 3. ed. Santiago: Editorial Sudamericana, 1999.

———. *Todo debe ser demasiado: Biografía de Delia del Carril; La hormiga.* Santiago: Editorial Sudaméricana, 1997.

Salas, Ricardo. "El sentido religioso en la poesía popular de Violeta Parra." In *Lo sagrado y lo humano: Para una hermenéutica de los símbolos religiosos; Estudios de filosofía de la religión*, 82–92. Santiago: San Pablo, 1996.

Salas Fernández, Sergio. "La elección presidencial de 1946: El calor de la guerra fría." In *Camino a La Moneda: Las elecciones presidenciales en la historia de Chile, 1920–2000*, edited by Alejandro San Francisco, Ángel Soto, and René. Millar Carvacho, 207–42. Santiago: Centro de Estudios Bicentenario, 2005.

Salas Zúñiga, Fabio. *La primavera terrestre: Cartografías del rock chileno y la nueva canción chilena.* Santiago: Ed. Cuarto Propio, 2003.

Salazar, Gabriel. *Historia contemporánea de Chile: Niñez y juventud.* Vol. 5. Santiago: LOM Ediciones, 2002.

Salazar Naudón, Cristián. "Apuntes sobre la Edad dorada vs la Edad oscura de las clásicas 'Casa de Remolienda' de Santiago." Artículos Para El Bicentenario. Memoria Chilena, 2010.

———. *La vida en las riberas: Crónoica de las especias extintas del Barrio Mapocho.* Vol. 2. Santiago: Ediciones Urbatorium, 2011.

Salazar Rebolledo, Juan Alberto. "La rosa y la espina: Expresiones musicales de solidaridad antiimperialista en Latinoamérica; El Primer Encuentro de la Canción Protesta en La Habana, Cuba, 1967." *Secuencia (Mexico City, Mexico)*, no. 108 (2020). Secuencia (108), e1809. doi: https://doi.org/10.18234/secuencia.voi108.1809.

Salgado, Alfonso. "La familia de Ramona Parra en la Plaza Bulnes: Una aproximación de género a la militancia política, la protesta social y la violencia estatal en el Chile del siglo veinte." *Izquierdas* 18 (April 1, 2014): 128–45.

Salinas, Claudio R., Hans Stange, and Sergio Salinas Roco. *Historia del cine experimental en la Universidad de Chile 1957–1973.* Santiago: Uqbar Editores, 2008.

Salinas Campos, Maximiliano A. *Canto a lo divino y religión popular en Chile hacia 1900.* 2. ed. Santiago: LOM Ediciones, 2005.

———. *En el chileno el humor vive con uno: El lenguaje festivo y el sentido del humor en la cultura oral popular de Chile.* Santiago: LOM Ediciones, 1998.

———. *La risa de Gabriela Mistral: Una historia cultural del humor en Chile e Iberoamérica.* Historia. Santiago: LOM Ediciones, 2010.

————. "Toquen flautas y tambores! Una historia social de la música desde las culturas populares en Chile, siglos XVI–XX." *Revista musical chilena* 54, no. 193 (2000): 47–82.

Salinas Campos, Maximiliano A., and Diego Irarrázaval. *Hacia una teología de los pobres.* Lima: Centro de Estudios y Publicaciones, 1980.

Salvador Jofre, Alvaro Luis. *Para una lectura de Nicanor Parra: (El proyecto ideológico y el inconsciente).* Sevilla: Secretariado de Publicaciones de la Universidad de Sevilla, 1975.

Salvatore, Nick. "Biography and Social History: An Intimate Relationship." *Labour History (Canberra)* 87, no. 87 (2004): 187–92.

Sanfuentes, Olaya. "Latin American Popular Art in a Museum: How Things Become Art." *Artium Quaestiones,* no. 29 (May 7, 2019): 63–89.

San Martín, Julio Fernando. *Lalo Parra: El tío de Chile.* Santiago: Trébol Ediciones, 2021.

————. *Las Comadres: Margot Loyola recuerda a Violeta.* Valparaíso, Chile: Ediciones Universitarias de Valparaíso, 2020.

Santander, Ignacio Q. *Quilapayún.* Madrid: Júcar, 1984.

Saunders, Frances Stonor. *The Cultural Cold War: The CIA and the World of Arts and Letters.* New York: New Press, 2000.

Sauvalle, Sergio. "In Memoriam: Gabriela Eliana Pizarro Soto (1932–1999)." *Revista musical chilena* 54 (2000): 120–22.

Scharfenberg, Ewald. "Elizabeth Burgos: La novia de la revolución." In *Mujeres de exceso.* Caracas, Venezuela: Alfadil Ediciones, Editorial Exceso, 1992.

Schidlowsky, David. *Neruda y su tiempo: Las furias y las penas.* Santiago: RIL Editores, 2008.

Schildt, Axel, and Detlef Siegfried. *Between Marx and Coca-Cola: Youth Cultures in Changing European Societies, 1960–1980.* New York: Berghahn Books, 2006.

Schlesser, Gilles. *Le cabaret "rive gauche": 1946–1974.* Paris: Archipel, 2006.

Schmiedecke, Natália Ayo. "Entre chamantos, smokings e ponchos: Representações identitárias na música popular chilena (1950–1973)." *Anais Do XXI Encontro Estadual de História–ANPUH-SP, Campinas,* September 2012.

Scott, Joan W. "The Evidence of Experience." *Critical Inquiry* 17, no. 4 (1991): 773–97.

Scott-Smith, Giles, and Hans Krabbendam. *The Cultural Cold War in Western Europe, 1945–1960.* New York: Frank Cass, 2005.

Sepúlveda Lafuente, Candelario. *Chillán, capital de provincia: Contribución a su conocimiento y progreso.* Santiago: Imprenta Linares, 1962.

Sepúlveda Llanos, Fidel. *El canto a lo poeta a lo divino y a lo humano: Estudio estético antropológico y antología fundamental.* Santiago: Centro de Investigaciones Diego Barros Arana, 2009.

————. "Nicanor, Violeta, Roberto Parra, encuentro de tradición y vanguardia." *Aisthesis* 24 (December): 29–42.

Serrano, Sol, Macarena Ponce de León Atria, and Francisca Rengifo, eds. *Historia de la educación en Chile, 1810–2010.* Santiago: Taurus, 2012.

Shaw, Lauren. *Song and Social Change in Latin America.* Lanham, Md.: Lexington Books, 2013.

Sherman, Daniel J. *French Primitivism and the Ends of Empire, 1945–1975.* Chicago: University of Chicago Press, 2011.

Snavely, Hannah. "Ramifying Folklore: Margot Loyola and the Transformation of Traditional Music in Chile." PhD diss., University of California Riverside, forthcoming.

Solis Poblete, Felipe. "La reproducción de valores patriarcales a través de los textos de cuecas chilenas." *Resonancias* 17, no. 32 (June 2013): 135–54.

Soto López, Sarai, and Myriam Navarrete Martínez. "Chile rió, canto y luchó: Vida y muerte de René Largo Farías." BA thesis, Universidad de Chile, Santiago, October 2017.

Souza Valencia, Héctor Alfonso. "La contribución de La Peña Folklórica de La Universidad de Chile Sede Valparaíso para el desarrollo y conservación de la música y danzas folklóricas de Chile." Valparaíso, Chile, June 2020.

Spencer, Christian. "El maricón del piano: Presencia de músicos homosexuales en burdeles cuequeros de Santiago y Valparaíso (1950–1970)." In *Enfoques interdisciplinarios sobre músicas populares en Latinoamérica: Retrospectivas, perspectivas, críticas y propuestas; Actas del X Congreso de la IASPM-AL*, edited by V Herom Vargas et al., 627–38. Montevideo: IASPM-AL/CIAMEN, 2013.

———."Finas, arrogantes y dicharacheras: Representaciones de género en la performance de los grupos femeninos de cueca urbana en Santiago (2000–2010)." *TRANS—Revista transcultural de música—Transcultural Music Review* 15 (2011). https://www.sibetrans .com/trans/articulo/371/finas-arrogantes-y-dicharacheras-representaciones-de-genero -en-la-performance-de-los-grupos-femeninos-de-cueca-urbana-en-santiago-de-chile -2000-2010.

———. "Folklore e idiomaticidad: Violeta Parra y su doble pertenencia a la industria cultural." In *Actas del III Congreso Latinoamericano de la Asociación Internacional para el Estudio de la Música Popular IASPM-AL. Bogotá, Colombia, 2000*, 2016. https://iaspmal.com/index.php/2016/03/02/actas-iii-congreso-bogota-colombia-2000/.

Spencer, James. *The Les Baxter Companion*. James Spencer, 2018. Spencer Artist Development. jamesrspencer.com.

Stagkouraki, Eleni. "El empoderamiento de Violeta Parra y sus versos como espacio de enunciación múltiple y afirmación del sujeto femenino." *Artelogie*, no. 13 (January 30, 2019). http://journals.openedition.org/artelogie/3218.

Staraselski, Valère. *La fête de l'Humanité: 80 ans de solidarité*. Paris: Cherche midi, 2010.

Stedile Luna, Verónica. "He encontrado una nueva forma de ser humano: La escritura del cuerpo como intervención política y cultural en la poética de Violeta Parra." BA thesis, Universidad Nacional de La Plata, 2014.

Stern, Steve J. *Battling for Hearts and Minds: Memory Struggles in Pinochet's Chile, 1973–1988*. Durham, N.C.: Duke University Press, 2006.

Subercaseaux, Bernardo. *Historia de las ideas de la cultura en Chile*. Vols. 1, 2, and 3. Santiago: Editorial Universitaria, 2011.

———. "Notes on Violeta Parra (from Folklore to Chilean-Lore)." *Papers in Romance* 2, no. 1 (Autumn 1979): 76–78.

Szmulewicz, Efraín. *Nicanor Parra: Biografía emotiva*. Santiago: Ed. Rumbos, 1988.

Sznajder, Mario. "Who Is a Chilean? The Mapuche, the Huaso and the Roto." In *Constructing Collective Identities and Shaping Public Spheres: Latin American Paths*, edited by Luis Roniger and Mario Sznajder, 199–216. Brighton, UK: Sussex Academic Press, 1998.

Szwed, John F. *Alan Lomax: The Man Who Recorded the World*. New York: Viking Penguin, 2010.

Taffet, Jeffrey F. "'My Guitar Is Not for the Rich': The New Chilean Song Movement and the Politics of Culture." *Journal of American Culture* 20, no. 2 (June 1997): 91–103.

Tamayo Jaramillo, Jairo, and Félix Marín Mejía. *Sentir gitano: 500 años de música española en América*. Medellín. Colombia: Ediciones Gráficas, 1991.

Tapia Valenzuela, M. Carolina. "La Feria de Artes Plásticas en Santiago: Estudio histórico social de un evento incómodo, 1959–1971." MA thesis, Universidad Adolfo Ibáñez, Santiago, 2022.

Teatro IFT: XXX aniversario; Octubre 1962, Buenos Aires. Buenos Aires: Teatro IFT, 1962.

Teitelboim, Volodia. *Neruda: An Intimate Biography*. Texas Pan American Series. Austin: University of Texas Press, 1991.

Tinker, Chris. *Georges Brassens and Jacques Brel: Personal and Social Narratives in Post-War Chanson*. Liverpool: Liverpool University Press, 2005.

Tinsman, Heidi. *Partners in Conflict:The Politics of Gender, Sexuality, and Labor in the Chilean Agrarian Reform, 1950–1973*. Durham, N.C.: Duke University Press, 2002.

Torres Alvarado, Rodrigo. "Cantar la diferencia: Violeta Parra y la canción chilena." *Revista musical chilena* 58, no. 201 (2004): 53–73.

———. "La urbanización de la canción folklórica." *Literatura chilena, creación y crítica* 9, no. 3–4 (December 1985): 25–29.

———. "Músicas populares, memoria y nación (o El caso de la invención musical de Chile)." *Memoria para un nuevo siglo: Chile, miradas a la segunda mitad del siglo XX*, n.d., 357–68. Santiago: LOM Ediciones, 2000.

———. *Perfil de la creación musical en la nueva canción chilena desde sus origenes hasta 1973*. Santiago: CENECA, 1980.

Tsipursky, Gleb. "Domestic Cultural Diplomacy and Soviet State-Sponsored Popular Culture in the Cold War, 1953–1962." *Diplomatic History* 41, no. 5 (2017): 985–1009.

Turino, Thomas. "Are We Global Yet? Globalist Discourse, Cultural Formations and the Study of Zimbabwean Popular Music." *British Journal of Ethnomusicology* 12, no. 2 (2003): 51–79.

———. "Nationalism and Latin American Music: Selected Case Studies and Theoretical Considerations." *Latin American Music Review* 24, no. 2 (2003): 169–209.

Uhlíková, Lucie. "Recollecting versus Remembering: On the Era of the New Folk Songs in Czechoslovakia during the Totalitarian Regime." *From Folklore to World Music: On Memory*, January 1, 2018.

Ulianova, Olga. "Algunas reflexiones sobre la Guerra Fría desde el fin del mundo." In *Ampliando miradas: Chile y su historia en un tiempo global*, edited by Fernando Purcell Torretti and Alfredo Riquelme, 235–60. Santiago: RIL Editores, 2009.

Urbina B., Rodolfo. *Castro, castreños y chilotes: 1960–1990*. Valparaíso: Ediciones Universitarias de Valparaíso de la Universidad Católica de Valparaíso, 1996.

Uribe-Echevarría, Juan. *Flor de canto a lo humano*. Santiago: Gabriela Mistral, 1974.

———. *Tipos y cuadros de costumbres en la poesía popular del siglo XIX*. 2. ed. Santiago: Pineda Libros, 1973.

Uribe Valladares, Cristhian. "Violeta Parra: En la frontera del arte musical chileno." *Intramuros* 3, no. 9 (2002): 8–14.

Urrea Carvallo, María Alicia, and Consuelo Walker Guzmán. "El galerismo y su relación con el mercado del arte en Chile." MA thesis, Universidad de Chile, 2012.

Valdebenito, Lorena. "La luz y la sombra en la cueca larga de Violeta Parra: Una práctica hipertextual." *Revista NEUMA* 11, no. 2 (n.d.): 44–73.

Valdebenito Cifuentes, Mauricio. *Con guitarra es otra cosa: Humberto Campos, Angelito Silva y Fernando Rossi: Guitarristas chilenos.* Santiago: La Pollera Ediciones, SCD, 2019.

———. "Guitarra popular, urbana y chilena." *Resonancias* 16, no. 30 (May 2012): 49–71.

———. "Una poética de la luz, el sonido y el lugar en el documental Mimbre de Sergio Bravo con música de Violeta Parra." *Punto sur*, no. 6 (June 2022): 69–84.

Valdovinos, Mario. "Retrato de la artista atormentada: Décimas de Violeta Parra." *Cuaderno (Fundación Pablo Neruda)*, no. 61 (2008): 4–9.

Valladares Mejías, Carlos. *La cueca larga del Indio Pavez: Nacido en Santiago, inmortalizado en Chiloé.* Santiago: Editorial Puerto de Palos, 2007.

Valladares Mejías, Carlos, and Manuel Vilches P. *Rolando Alarcón: La canción en la noche.* Santiago: Quimantú, 2009.

Varas, José Miguel. *Nerudario.* Santiago: Planeta, 1999.

———. *Los suenos del pintor: Sobre la base de conversaciones con Julio Escámez.* Santiago: Alfaguara, 2005.

———. "Recuerdos de Thiago de Melo." *Araucaria de Chile* 32 (Quarter 1985): 205–7.

———. *Tal vez nunca: Crónicas Nerudianas.* Santiago: Editorial Universitaria, 2007.

Varas, José Miguel, and Juan Pablo González Rodríguez. *En busca de la música chilena: Crónica y antología de una historia sonora.* Santiago: Comisión Bicentenario, Presidencia de la República, 2005.

Vargas, Viviana Bravo, "¡Ni fiesta ni congoja! El 10 de Mayo en tiempos de la Ley Maldita, Santiago, 1948–1958." In *La izquierda en movimiento: Clase trabajadora y luchas populares en América latina (siglos XX y XXI)*, edited by Mariana Mastrángelo and Viviana Bravo Vargas, 151–88. Buenos Aires: CLACSO, 2022.

Vassal, Jacques. *Français, si vous chantiez: À la patrie, la chanson reconnaissante.* Paris: A. Michel, 1976.

Venegas Espinoza, Fernando. *Violeta Parra en Concepción y la frontera del Biobío, 1957–1960: Recopilación, difusión del folklore y desborde creativo.* Concepción: Universidad de Concepción, 2017.

———. "Violeta Parra y su conexión con la cultura popular de la frontera del Biobío (1917–1934)." *Revista de historia* 1, no. 21 (2014): 105–39.

Vera-Meiggs, David. "La obra de Sergio Bravo, protocineasta." *Críticas y estudios*, July 27, 2010.

Verba, Ericka. "Back in the Days When She Sang Mexican Songs on the Radio . . . Before Violeta Parra Was Violeta Parra." In *Violeta Parra: Life and Work*, edited by Lorna Dillon, 63–82. Woodbridge, Suffolk: Tamesis, 2017.

———. "Las Hojas Sueltas [Broadsides]: Nineteenth-Century Chilean Popular Poetry as a Source for the Historian" *Studies in Latin American Popular Culture* 12 (1993): 141–58.

———. "To Paris and Back: Violeta Parra's Transnational Performance of Authenticity." *The Americas* 70, no. 2 (October 2013): 269–302.

———. "'Une Chilienne à Paris': Violeta Parra, auténtica cosmopolita del siglo veinte." *Artelogie*, no. 13 (January 30, 2019). http://journals.openedition.org/artelogie/2963.

———. "Violeta Parra and the Chilean Folk Revival of the 1950s." In *Mapping Violeta Parra's Cultural Landscapes*, edited by Patricia Vilches, 13–26. Cham: Springer International Publishing, 2018.

———. "Violeta Parra: Her Life and Her Poetry." Honors thesis, Brown University, 1980.

———. "Violeta Parra, Radio Chilena, and the 'Battle in Defense of the Authentic' during the 1950s in Chile." *Studies in Latin American Popular Culture* 26, no. 1 (2007): 151–65.

Vergara, Angela. *Fighting Unemployment in Twentieth-Century Chile*. Pittsburgh: University of Pittsburgh Press, 2021.

Vial Correa, Gonzalo. *Historia de Chile, 1891–1973*. Santiago: Editorial Santillana del Pacífico, 1981.

Vicuña, Ignacio. *Historia de los Quincheros, 1937–1977*. Santiago: Ediciones Ayer, 1977.

Vidal, Virginia. *Hormiga pinta caballos: Delia del Carril y su mundo (1885–1989)*. Santiago: RIL editores, 2006.

Vila, Pablo, ed. *The Militant Song Movement in Latin America: Chile, Uruguay, and Argentina*. Lanham, Md.: Lexington Books, 2014.

Vilches, Patricia. "El cuerpo femenino: Efectos estéticos de la politica liberal y la violencia urbana en las Décimas de Violeta Parra." *Ixquic: Revista hispánica internacional de análisis literario y cultural* 9 (December 2008): 61–83.

———. "Geografías humanas y espacios del Chile moderno en las 'Décimas' de Violeta Parra." *Artelogie*, no. 13 (January 30, 2019). http://journals.openedition.org/artelogie/3098.

———, ed. *Mapping Violeta Parra's Cultural Landscapes*. Palgrave Pivot. Cham, Switzerland: Palgrave Macmillan, 2018.

———. "Violeta se fue a los cielos de Andrés Wood: El naufragio de La Carpa de La Reina." *Revista internacional d'humanitats* 29 (September–December, 2013): 63–80.

Von Eschen, Penny M. *Satchmo Blows up the World: Jazz Ambassadors Play the Cold War*. Cambridge, Mass.: Harvard University Press, 2004.

Wade, Peter. "Globalization and Appropriation in Latin American Popular Music." *Latin American Research Review* 39, no. 1 (2004): 273–84.

———. *Music, Race and Nation: Música Tropical in Colombia*. Chicago: University of Chicago Press, 2000.

Walsh, Sarah. "'One of the Most Uniform Races of the Entire World': Creole Eugenics and the Myth of Chilean Racial Homogeneity." *Journal of the History of Biology* 48, no. 4 (2015): 613–39.

Warne, Chris. "The Impact of World Music in France." In *Post-Colonial Cultures in France*, edited by Mark McKinney and Alec Hargreaves, 133–49. London: Routledge, 1997.

Weitzel, Ruby. *Chillán, entrecruces*. Santiago: Fundación Arte y Autores Contemporáneos, 2003.

Westad, Odd Arne. *The Global Cold War: Third World Interventions and the Making of Our Times*. Cambridge: Cambridge University Press, 2005.

Winn, Peter, Elizabeth Q. Hutchison, Thomas Miller Klubock, and Nara B. Milanich. *The Chile Reader: History, Culture, Politics*. Durham, N.C.: Duke University Press, 2013.

Wright, John W. "Confronting the Celebrant of Bernstein's Mass: A Study of Musical Borrowing." PhD diss., University of Cincinnati, 2014.

Yalkin, Serda. "Folk, the Naïve and Indigeneity: Defining Strategies in Violeta Parra's Visual Art." MA thesis, University of New Mexico, 2017.

——. "Violeta Parra at the Louvre: The 'Naïve' as a Strategy of the Authentic." In *Violeta Parra: Life and Work*, edited by Lorna Dillon, 139–56. Woodbridge, Suffolk: Tamesis, 2017.

Zolov, Eric. *Refried Elvis: The Rise of the Mexican Counterculture.* Berkeley: University of California Press, 1999.

Zourek, Michal. *Checoslovaquia y el Cono Sur 1945–1989: Relaciones politicas, económicas y culturales durante la Guerra Fria.* Ibero-Americana Pragensia. Prague [Czech Republic]: Charles University in Prague, 2014.

Zúñiga, Pamela. *El mundo de Nicanor Parra: Antibiografía.* Santiago: Zig-Zag, 2001.

Zuñiga Pérez, Victor, Jorge Meza Recabarren, and Sebastián Köning Besa, eds. *Pudahuel: En el camino de la memoria: De las Barrancas a Pudahuel, 450 años de historia.* Santiago: Ilustre Municipalidad de Pudahuel, 2007.

Index

Loyola, Margot: birthday celebration for, 116; Communist Party affiliation, 65; music of, 71, 88, 129, 170–71, 343n124; on Parra, 79, 107, 112, 148; Parra and, 64, 82–83, 89, 129, 271, 304, 310, 336n106, 341n96; photographs of, *72*; on women performers, 107, 333n36

MAD (Musée des Arts Decoratifs), 1, 2–3, 219–27, 369n15
"Maldigo del alto cielo" (I Curse the Heavens Above; song by Parra), 293–94
Manns, Patricio, 146, 252, 256, 288, 301, 308, 339n35, 376n35, 382n9
Manzano, Alfredo "Manzanito," 132–33, 156, 159
Mapuche people: machitún ceremony, 224; music of, 129–30, 146, 272, 351n43, 363n140; Parra family and, 17–18
marriage, 50, 140, 256–58, 335n88, 353n83
mask making, 208
Maspero press, 199, 242
"Mass: A Theater Piece for Singers, Players, and Dancers" (Bernstein), 161, 358n34
"Mazúrquica modérnica" (Modernified Mazurka; song by Parra), 253–54, 291
"Melodia Loca" (Baxter), 90, 343n129
mentorship, 170–71, 256, 262, 272
"Meriana" (folk song), 98, 345n32
Messone, Pedro, 282–83, 382n9
Meza, Fernán, 95, 97, 107–8
Millaray, 64, 170–71
Mimbre (Wicker; film), 132–33
Miranda, Héctor, 146, 215, 218
"Miren cómo sonríen" (Look How They Smile; song by Parra), 314
Mistral, Gabriela, 125
modern art, 219
Morla Lynch, Carlos, 218, 226
motherhood, 79–80, 89, 95, 99, 144–45, 205
mujer del pueblo (everywoman), 32, 84–85, 151, 189, 234–35, 242, 274, 312–13
Musée de l'Homme, 108–9, 129
Musée des Arts Décoratifs. *See* Paris Museum of Decorative Arts.
Museum of Modern Art in Paris, 218, 244

música criolla, 23, 28, 41–42, 55–56, 59, 66
musical training, 74, 126–27, 336n106, 350n28
musical transcription, 74, 82–83, 128, 187, 336n106
music and visual art, 185, 208–9, 224; 155–56, 208, 218–19, 264
música típica, 23–24, 41, 54, 66, 250, 338n26

National Museum of Folk Art, 136–37
neofolklore, 248–50, 253, 274
Neruda, Pablo: "Canto general," 177, 228, 363n140; Communist Party and, 360n78; events hosted by, 80–81, 88, 152, 160, 172–73; friendship with Violeta, 48; "Pablo pitchers," 156; poem about Parra, 184; poems set to music, 177, 228, 297
New Cinema, 132–34
New Song movement: "La Carta" (The Letter; song by Parra), 212–13; musicians of, 170, 249, 256, 299, 300; neofolklore and, 248–50; Parra's influence on, 170, 255, 256, 314, 376n35
Nicanor senior. *See* Parra Parra, Nicanor (father of Violeta Parra)
Nouzeilles, Rubén, 130, 171, 185, 263, 274, 290–91, 305, 342n123
"nueva ola" (new wave), 248

Odeon Argentina, 185–87
Odeon Chilena: contract with, 168, 290–91, 305, 342n123; Folklore of Chile series, 130–32, *131*, 144, 147; Las Hermanas Parra and, 58, 88, 355n130; recordings with, 89–90, 125, 130–32, 175, 272–74; Urban Folklore record series, 263
oil cans, 136–37, 141, 263–64
oral traditions, 25, 29, 59, 63–64, 68–69
Orrego Matte, Marta, 196, 248, 278
Otero, Renato, 103–4

Painen Cotaro, María, 129, 130
painting, 154–55, 158, 224–25, 236, 264
Palacios, José María, 87, 158–59, 341n96
"Paloma ausente" (Absent Dove; song by Parra), 204–5